HUMBE

ALS No. H1142229

This item should be returned on or before the last date stamped above. If not in demand it may be renewed for a further period by personal application, by telephone, or in writing. The author, title, above number and date due back should be quoted. LS/3

REVIEWS OF UNITED KINGDOM
STATISTICAL SOURCES

VOLUME XII

CONSTRUCTION

AND

THE RELATED PROFESSIONS

REVIEWS OF UNITED KINGDOM STATISTICAL SOURCES

Editor: W. F. Maunder

Volume I	1. *Personal Social Services*, B. P. Davies
	2. *Voluntary Organizations in the Personal Social Service Field*, G. J. Murray
Volume II	3. *Central Government Routine Health Statistics*, Michael Alderson
	4. *Social Security Statistics*, Frank Whitehead
Volume III	5. *Housing in Great Britain*, Stuart Farthing
	6. *Housing in Northern Ireland*, Michael Fleming
Volume IV	7. *Leisure*, F. M. M. Lewes and S. R. Parker
	8. *Tourism*, L. J. Lickorish
Volume V	9. *General Sources of Statistics*, G. F. Lock
Volume VI	10. *Wealth*, A. B. Atkinson and A. J. Harrison
	11. *Personal Incomes*, T. Stark
Volume VII	12. *Road Passenger Transport*, D. Munby
	13. *Road Goods Transport*, A. H. Watson
Volume VIII	14. *Land Use*, J. T. Coppock
	15. *Town and Country Planning*, L. F. Gebbett
Volume IX	16. *Health Surveys and Related Studies*, Michael Alderson and Robin Dowie
Volume X	17. *Ports and Inland Waterways*, R. E. Baxter
	18. *Civil Aviation*, Celia M. Phillips
Volume XI	19. *Coal*, D. J. Harris
	20. *Gas*, H. Nabb
	21. *Electricity*, D. Nuttall

REVIEWS OF UNITED KINGDOM STATISTICAL SOURCES
Edited by W. F. MAUNDER
Professor of Economic and Social Statistics
University of Exeter
VOLUME XII

CONSTRUCTION AND THE RELATED PROFESSIONS

by

M. C. FLEMING
Senior Lecturer in Economics
University of Loughborough

Published for
The Royal Statistical Society and
the Social Science Research Council

by

PERGAMON PRESS
OXFORD · NEW YORK · TORONTO · SYDNEY
PARIS · FRANKFURT

UK	Pergamon Press Ltd., Headington Hill Hall, Oxford OX3 0BW, England
USA	Pergamon Press Inc., Maxwell House, Fairview Park, Elmsford, New York 10523, USA
CANADA	Pergamon of Canada, Suite 104, 150 Consumers Road, Willowdale, Ontario, Canada M2J, 1P9
AUSTRALIA	Pergamon Press (Aust.) Pty. Ltd., P.O. Box 544, Potts Point, NSW 2011, Australia
FRANCE	Pergamon Press SARL, 24 rue des Ecoles, 75240 Paris, Cedex 05, France
FEDERAL REPUBLIC OF GERMANY	Pergamon Press GmbH, 6242 Kronberg/Taunus, Pferdstrasse 1, Federal Republic of Germany

Copyright © 1980 Royal Statistical Society and Social Science Research Council

All Rights Reserved. No part of this publication may be reproduced, stored in a retrieval system or transmitted in any form or by any means: electronic, electrostatic, magnetic tape, mechanical, photocopying, recording or otherwise, without permission in writing from the copyright holders.

First Edition 1980

British Library Cataloguing in Publication Data
Reviews of United Kingdom statistical sources.
Vol. 12: Construction and the related professions
1. Great Britain—Statistical services
I. Title   II. Maunder, Wynne Frederick
III. Fleming, Michael Carl
IV. Royal Statistical Society
V. Social Science Research Council (Great Britain)
314.1   HA37.G7   79–40070

ISBN 0–08–024034–8

For bibliographical purposes this volume should be cited as:
Fleming, M. C., *Construction and the Related Professions*, Pergamon Press Ltd. on behalf of the Royal Statistical Society and the Social Science Research Council, 1980

Set, printed and bound in Great Britain by
Fakenham Press Limited, Fakenham, Norfolk

VOLUME CONTENTS

Foreword   vii

Introduction to Volume XII   ix

Review No. 22: Construction and the Related Professions   xiii

Subject Index to Construction   635

FOREWORD

The Sources and Nature of the Statistics of the United Kingdom, produced under the auspices of the Royal Statistical Society and edited by Maurice Kendall, filled a notable gap on the library shelves when it made its appearance in the early post-war years. Through a series of critical reviews by many of the foremost national experts, it constituted a valuable contemporary guide to statisticians working in many fields as well as a benchmark to which historians of the development of Statistics in this country are likely to return again and again. The Social Science Research Council and the Society were both delighted when Professor Maunder came forward with the proposal that a revised version should be produced, indicating as well his willingness to take on the onerous task of editor. The two bodies were more than happy to act as co-sponsors of the project and to help in its planning through a joint steering committee. The result, we are confident, will be adjudged a worthy successor to the previous volumes by the very much larger 'statistics public' that has come into being in the intervening years.

Dr C. S. SMITH
Secretary
Social Science Research Council
March 1979

Dr I. D. HILL
Honorary Secretary
Royal Statistical Society
March 1979

MEMBERSHIP OF THE JOINT STEERING COMMITTEE
(March 1979)

Chairman: Miss S. V. Cunliffe

Representing the Royal Statistical Society:
Dr W. R. Buckland
Mr M. C. Fessey
Dr S. Rosenbaum

Representing the Social Science Research Council:
Mr A. S. Noble
Mrs J. Peretz
Dr W. Taylor

Secretary: Mr D. E. Allen

INTRODUCTION

In introducing this volume it is tempting to remark upon the various ways in which it sets a record for the series to date. In terms of any physical measure I am sure that it exceeds all previous volumes and the development of this position has been a matter of some editorial concern. The general aim has been to keep each within defined limits in order to constitute a manageable contribution in both output and user terms. However, there are some topics which form such a closely integrated whole that subdivision would bring its own penalties. This is clearly the case with Construction Statistics and the benefits of unified treatment emerge very clearly. A single example may be sufficient for comment: the construction industry produces long-lived assets and it is a natural consequence that much longer historical series are still of current interest than in the case of many other topics. Mr Fleming, with undivided responsibilities, was naturally led to investigate collection procedures during the last war and, as it turned out in the event, this was a task which could scarcely have been accomplished if delayed any longer. It seems right, therefore, that it should be clearly stated here that Mr Fleming has made a valuable contribution to preserving knowledge of collection methods in early series which might otherwise have been lost.

Writing with regard to the series generally, the primary aim is to act as a work of reference to the sources of statistical material of all kinds, both official and unofficial. It seeks to enable the user to discover what data are available on the subject in which he is interested, from where they may be obtained, and what the limitations are to their use. Data are regarded as available not only if published in the normal printed format but also if they are likely to be released to a *bona fide* enquirer in any other form, such as duplicated documents, computer print-out or even magnetic tape. On the other hand, no reference is made to material which, even if it is known to exist, is not accessible to the general run of potential users. The distinction, of course, is not clear-cut and mention of a source is not to be regarded as a guarantee that data will be released; in particular cases it may very well be a matter for negotiation. The latter caution applies with particular force to the question of obtaining computer print-outs of custom specified tabulations. Where original records are held on magnetic tape it might appear that there should be no insuperable problem, apart from confidentiality, in obtaining any feasible analysis at a cost; in practice, it may well turn out that there are capacity restraints which override any simple cost calculation. Thus, what is requested might make demands on computer and programming resources to the extent that the routine work of the agency concerned would be intolerably affected.

The intention is that the sources for each topic should be reviewed in detail, and the brief supplied to authors has called for comprehensive coverage at the level of 'national interest'. This term does not denote any necessary restriction to statistics collected on a national basis (still less, of course, to national aggregates) but it means that sources of a purely local character, without wider interest in either content or methodology, are excluded. Indeed, the mere task of identifying all material of this latter kind is an impossibility. The interpretation of the brief has obviously involved discretion and it is up to the users of these reviews to say what unreasonable gaps become apparent to them. They are cordially invited to do so by communicating with me.

To facilitate the use of the series as a work of reference, certain features have been incorporated which are worth a word or two of explanation.

First, the text of each review is designed, in so far as varying subject-matter permits, to follow a standard form of arrangement so that users may expect a similar pattern to be followed throughout the series. The starting point is a brief summary of the activity concerned and its organization, in order to give a clear background understanding of how data are collected, what is being measured, the stage at which measurements are made, what the reporting units are, the channels through which returns are routed and where they are processed. As a further part of this introductory material, there is a discussion of the specific problems of definition and measurement to which the topic gives rise. The core sections on available sources which follow are arranged at the author's discretion—by origin, by subject sub-division, or by type of data; there is too much heterogeneity between topics to permit any imposition of complete uniformity on all authors. The final section is devoted to a discussion of general shortcomings and possibly desirable improvements. In case a contrary expectation should be aroused, it should be said that authors have not been asked to produce a comprehensive plan for the reform of statistical reporting in the whole of their field. However, a review of existing sources is a natural opportunity to make some suggestions for future policy on the collection and publication of statistics within the scope concerned.

Secondly, detailed factual information about statistical series and other data is given in a Quick Reference List (QRL). The exact nature of the entries is best seen by glancing at the list and accordingly they are not described here. Again, the ordering is not prescribed except that entries are not classified by publication source since it is presumed that it is this which is unknown to the reader. In general, the routine type of information which is given in the QRL is not repeated verbally in the text; the former, however, serves as a search route to the latter in that a reference (by section number) is shown against a QRL entry when there is a related discussion in the text.

Third, a subject index to each review acts as a more or less conventional line of enquiry on textual references; however, it is a computerized system and, for an individual review, the only peculiarity which it introduces is the possibility of easily permuting entries. Thus an entry in the index may appear as

> Building Apprenticeship and Training Council

and also be shown as:

> Apprenticeship and Training Council, Building

as well as:

> Training Council, Building Apprenticeship and

The object at this level is merely to facilitate search by giving as many variants as possible. In addition, individual review subject indexes are merged into a cumulative index which is held on magnetic tape and may possibly be used to produce a printed version from time to time if that seems desirable. Computer print-outs of the cumulative index to date are available on application to me at the Department of Economics, University of Exeter. In addition, selective searches of this index may be made by the input of key-words; the result is a print-out of all entries in which the key-word appears in the initial position in the subject index of any review. Like the cumulative index itself, this is a facility which may be of increasing help as the number of reviews in print grows.

Fourth, each review contains two listings of publications. The QRL Key gives full details of the publications shown as sources and text references to them are made in the form [QRL serial number]; this list is confined essentially to data publications. The other listing is a general bibliography of works discussing wider aspects; text references in this case are made in the form [B serial number].

Finally, an attempt is made to reproduce the more important returns or forms used in data collection so that it may be seen what tabulations it is possible to make as well as helping to clarify the basis of those actually available. Unfortunately, there are severe practical limitations on the number of such forms that it is possible to append to a review and authors perforce have to be highly selective. In the present instance the author has been able to gather a rather rich collection of forms, some of which are virtually unique specimens.

If all or any of these features succeed in their intention of increasing the value of the series in its basic function as a work of reference it will be gratifying; the extent to which the purpose is achieved, however, will be difficult to assess without 'feedback' from the readership. Users, therefore, will be rendering an essential service if they will send me a note of specific instances where, in consulting a review, they have failed to find the information sought.

As editor, I must express my very grateful thanks to all the members of the Joint Steering Committee of the Royal Statistical Society and the Social Science Research Council. It would be unfair to saddle them with any responsibility for shortcomings in execution but they have directed the overall strategy with as admirable a mixture of guidance and forbearance as any editor of such a series could desire. Especial thanks are due to the Secretary of the Committee who is an unfailing source of help even when sorely pressed by the more urgent demands of his other offices.

The author joins me in thanking all those who gave up their time to attend the seminar held to discuss the first draft of his review and which contributed materially to improving the final version. We are most grateful to the staff of Pergamon Press Ltd for all their help, particularly during the vital production stages. The subject index entries for this volume were compiled by Mrs Juliet Horwood who has also been responsible for many other aspects of the work. Our thanks go also to Mrs Gill Skinner, of the Social Studies Data Processing Unit at the University of Exeter, who has written the computer programs for the production of the subject indexes.

Finally, we also wish to record our appreciation for permission granted to produce certain copyright material by the Controller of Her Majesty's Stationery Office.

University of Exeter   W. F. MAUNDER
March 1979

22: CONSTRUCTION AND THE RELATED PROFESSIONS

M. C. FLEMING
University of Loughborough

To Ruth, Anne, Stephen and Rachel
for their patience and understanding

We must carefully distinguish between what we think we know and what we really do and can know.

> Oskar Morgenstern
> *On The Accuracy of Economic Observations*
> (Preface to the second edition, 1963)

A good many would like to do (research) the short way by taking the figures and working on the figures, but most of the time you have to devote to studying whether the figures mean what they seem to mean ...

> Professor A. K. Cairncross, then Director of the Economic Section of the Treasury, in evidence to the Sub-Committee on Economic Affairs, 1966. Printed in *Government Statistical Services, Fourth Report from the Estimates Committee, Session 1966–67*, House of Commons Paper 246, p. 42.

It is difficult to set any limit to the list of statistics which might conceivably be useful to someone somewhere.

> *Report of the (Verdon Smith) Committee on the Censuses of Production and Distribution*, Cmd. 9276 (1954). Para. 6.

PREFACE

The construction industry occupies a position of central importance in the economy because of its pre-eminence in the provision and maintenance of a diverse range of capital goods in virtually every field of economic and social activity. The statistical information available about construction is correspondingly large and diverse and, in many ways, the size and character of this volume are a reflection of this fact. Precise details of the scope and content of the volume are given in the introduction. Here I should like to make some general observations about the character of the work.

I have attempted, generally speaking, to place equal emphasis upon the twin purposes that each Review in the series is meant to serve: those of providing a definitive guide to sources and a critical appraisal of their nature and limitations. Close acquaintance with the construction industry cannot fail to leave one impressed by the difficulties that must unavoidably confront the collection of accurate and comprehensive statistics. In many places I lay stress—as I am bound to do—upon the limitations or potential limitations of particular series or categories of data. It is important that this should not be misinterpreted. It is too readily forgotten that there are few economic statistics which are not subject to margins of error. By drawing attention to the shortcomings of certain statistics for construction does not mean that this sector suffers more than others. At the same time, however, it must be recognized that the collection of data for construction is confronted by problems which are different in degree and, to some extent, in kind from those which confront the collection of data for most manufacturing industries. Naturally it will be appreciated that it does not follow from the identification of actual or potential weaknesses that the data are of no use, for the usefulness of any set of statistics depends upon the purposes for which they are required.

The criticisms which are made in this volume, therefore, are meant to be constructive. They are made in the belief that the critical evaluation of economic statistics is an essential pre-requisite to their use. This volume will have served its purpose if it makes the available data more widely known and if it leads to a qualitative improvement in their use and interpretation.

ACKNOWLEDGEMENTS

Work on the preparation of this Review has extended over many years and it is a pleasure to be able to record my thanks at long last to the large number of people from whom I have received help during this time. To do so, of course, is not meant to shift the burden of responsibility in any way. That remains mine and mine alone. My thanks are due particularly to the officials of government departments, many of whom—particularly those in the Department of the Environment—have had to withstand a veritable bombardment of questions. This being so, I am glad that it is no longer considered improper to refer to civil servants by name.

I should like to express special thanks to Harold Stott, Chief Statistician for Construction during the later stages of the work, who not only found the answers to many questions but read the first complete draft, and the subsequent revised draft relating to MOW–DOE statistics, very closely and commented in great detail. His help extended beyond what one could reasonably be entitled to expect and I am extremely grateful to him. Henry Palca—Harold Stott's predecessor as Chief Statistician—was also kind enough to comment on an early draft dealing with the MOW–DOE statistics and provided special help at a stage when it looked as if many questions would have to remain unanswered. I have also had the great good fortune of being able to call upon the unrivalled knowledge of Mr F. W. Salmon who has been concerned with the collection of construction statistics by the Department of the Environment for very many years. His help at all stages of the project has been quite invaluable. I have also received help from many other officials in the Department of the Environment at different times; my thanks are not lessened by the fact that it is not possible to name them all.

The officials of various other government departments have also answered questions, discussed various matters with me and commented on parts of the draft. Again it is not possible to name them all but I am very grateful, particularly to officials in the Department of Employment and the Department of Industry. I owe a special word of thanks to Mr T. F. Stainer of the Northern Ireland Department of Finance for the trouble he took in relation to the section on Northern Ireland. The staff of various other bodies have also earned my thanks, in particular the Royal Institute of British Architects, the Building Cost Information Service, the Construction Industry Training Board and the Manpower Services Commission.

I have also had the benefit of correspondence with Lady Lea, one-time Chief Statistician at the former Ministry of Works, Ian Bowen—Chief Statistical Officer of the Ministry of Works during the Second World War—and Mr A. W. T. Ellis, an official of the Ministry during the war and for many years afterwards, all of whom allowed me to call upon their memories.

I am also extremely grateful to the large number of people who were good enough to devote their time to reading the first complete draft of the Review and attending a day-long seminar organized by the SSRC in London in May 1977 to discuss it. The support and encouragement received on that occasion provided the stimulus without which the final draft may never have been completed. The numerous detailed comments and suggestions received then and subsequently in writing have led to many improvements. In this respect I owe a particular word of thanks to Margaret Bloom and to Dr Patricia Hillebrandt. I should also like to record here a debt to Dr Peter Stone whose original tutelage on matters relating to the construction industry whilst a member of his staff at the Building Research Station initiated my interest in this field.

My thanks are also due to Professor W. F. Maunder, the editor of the series, for his encouragement during the early stages of the work and for his forbearance as the book seemed to grow beyond all bounds and its completion seemed to remain, year after year, only a distant objective.

Many of the most tedious tasks have been undertaken by research assistants. I have been fortunate in having the services of Kem Jin Teh and Beth Borchardt, both of whom carried out these tasks with great diligence. I should also like to thank the staff of the library of the University of Loughborough, particularly Eric Davies, who has been a constant source of willing help, and those responsible for the inter-library loan service.

Not unusually perhaps, the greatest burden of all has fallen upon the author's wife and children. I am deeply grateful to my wife for her constant support throughout the elephantine gestation period of this work, to my children for their patience and to them all for their active help in its closing stages. To them is owed a debt which can never be repaid, for the time devoted to this book has been time taken from them.

REFERENCE DATE OF SOURCES REVIEWED

This Review is believed to represent the position, broadly speaking, as it obtained at the end of December 1977, although in some cases revisions and additional references have been noted up to the early months of 1978. The most important subsequent changes up to the proof-reading stage (July 1979) are noted in the Addenda on Recent Developments (see pages 23–31).

CONTENTS OF REVIEW 22

List of Tables	13
List of Appendices	15
List of Abbreviations	17
Addenda on Recent Developments	23
Introduction	33

PART I
THE CONSTRUCTION INDUSTRY

1 **The Scope and Arrangement of Part I** — 39

2 **Principles and Problems of Definition, Collection and Measurement** — 42
   2.1 *Principles and Problems of Definition: Construction Activity and the Construction Industry* — 42
   2.2 *Principles and Problems of Collection* — 43
      2.2.1 Methods of Collection — 43
      2.2.2 Registers of Producing Units — 44
   2.3 *Principles and Problems of Measurement* — 45
      2.3.1 Output Measurement Principles — 45
      2.3.2 Output Measurement and Valuation Practices — 47
      2.3.3 Other Measurement Problems — 50

3 **Statistics Collected by the Ministry of Works 1941–54** — 52
   3.1 *Introduction* — 52
   3.2 *The Building Controls 1940–54* — 52
      3.2.1 The Control of Building Operations 1940–54 — 52
      3.2.2 The Control of Building and Civil Engineering Contracting Undertakings 1941–53 — 53

3.3	*Censuses of Contractors in Great Britain 1941–4*		55
	3.3.1	Introduction	55
	3.3.2	The 'Main Trades' and 'Specialist Trades' Contractors	56
	3.3.3	Censuses of the Main Trades and Their Interpretation	57
	3.3.4	Censuses of the Specialist Trades	60
	3.3.5	Special Censuses of Labour Resources, 1944 and 1945	61
3.4	*Censuses of Direct Labour Organizations in Great Britain 1941–4*		61
3.5	*Censuses of Contractors in Great Britain 1945–54*		62
	3.5.1	Introduction	62
	3.5.2	Interpretation	62
	3.5.3	Availability of Census Results 1945–54	63
	3.5.4	The Available Analyses and Their Interpretation	64
3.6	*Censuses of Direct Labour Organizations in Great Britain 1944–54*		70
	3.6.1	Introduction	70
	3.6.2	Local Authorities and Public Utilities	70
	3.6.3	Direct Labour of Government Departments	75
3.7	*Building Control Statistics 1940–54*		76
	3.7.1	Background	76
	3.7.2	Statistics of Work Licensed or Approved in the Period 1941–5	78
	3.7.3	Statistics of Work Licensed or Authorized in the Period 1945–54	78
	3.7.4	Labour Employed, Labour Ceilings and the Value of Work Done on Licensed, Authorized and Direct Government Projects	79
	3.7.5	The Register of Contractors—Registration Statistics	81
3.8	*Output Time Series Compiled by the Ministry of Works before 1955*		81
	3.8.1	Introduction	81
	3.8.2	Gross Output Estimates 1932–45	81
	3.8.3	MOW Output Time Series 1946–55	84
3.9	*Employment Time Series Compiled by the Ministry of Works 1941–55*		90
	3.9.1	Introduction	90
	3.9.2	MOW Employment Time Series 1941–5: The Series Available and Their Interpretation	90
	3.9.3	MOW Employment Time Series 1945–55	92

3.10 *Miscellaneous Labour Statistics Collected by the Ministry of Works 1941–55*   94

    3.10.1 Employment in the Mobile Labour Force and the Special Repair Service   94

    3.10.2 Employment of Prisoners of War on Construction Work 1946–8   95

    3.10.3 Employment on Opencast Coal Production from 1942   95

    3.10.4 The Housing Labour Force and Employment on Air-raid Damage Repairs to Houses in London 1944–5   95

    3.10.5 Statistics Relating to the Payment-by-results Scheme 1941–7   95

    3.10.6 Surveys of Incentive Schemes 1951–5   96

4 **Statistics Collected by the Department of the Environment and Its Predecessor Departments since 1954**   97

  4.1 *Introduction*   97

    4.1.1 The Changes Introduced in 1955   97

    4.1.2 Construction in the Standard Industrial Classification   98

    4.1.3 The Register of Contractors since 1954   99

    4.1.4 General Review of the Enquiries Undertaken since 1954   101

  4.2 *MOW–DOE Censuses of Contractors in Great Britain since 1954*   101

    4.2.1 Introduction   101

    4.2.2 Nature and Coverage of the Censuses   102

    4.2.3 The Available Analyses and Their Interpretation   103

  4.3 *MOW–DOE Censuses of Direct Labour Organizations in Great Britain since 1954*   117

    4.3.1 Introduction   117

    4.3.2 Local Authorities' Direct Labour   118

    4.3.3 Government Departments' and Public Utilities' Direct Labour   122

  4.4 *MOW–DOE Output and Employment Time Series for Great Britain since 1954*   123

    4.4.1 Introduction   123

    4.4.2 Interpretation   124

    4.4.3 Monthly Total Employment Series   125

    4.4.4 Employment Series by Type of Work   126

    4.4.5 Output Series   127

4.5	_Contractors' New Orders Statistics and EEC State of Trade Enquiry for Great Britain_		133
	4.5.1	Introduction	133
	4.5.2	The Nature of the New Orders Inquiry	133
	4.5.3	The New Orders Series and Their Interpretation	136
	4.5.4	EEC State of Trade Enquiry for Contractors in Great Britain	143
4.6	*British Construction Work Overseas*		144
4.7	*Local Authority Design Work in Great Britain*		144
	4.7.1	Introduction	144
	4.7.2	The Statistics Collected and Their Interpretation	145
4.8	*Building Control Statistics 1966–8*		148
4.9	*Miscellaneous Inquiries*		149
	4.9.1	Site Lighting and Winter Building Precautions	149
	4.9.2	Industrialized Building	149

5 Production Statistics Other than Those Collected by the Department of the Environment and Its Predecessor Departments — 150

5.1	*Introduction*		150
5.2	*Construction in the Index of Industrial Production*		150
	5.2.1	The Available Series	150
	5.2.2	Interpretation	153
5.3	*Construction in the Censuses of Production*		155
	5.3.1	Introduction	155
	5.3.2	The Censuses Taken and Subjects Covered	156
	5.3.3	Interpretation	159
	5.3.4	Input–Output Tables	163
	5.3.5	Official Uses of the COP Data for Construction—Summary	164
5.4	*Statistics of Expenditure on Construction Work*		164
	5.4.1	Introduction	164
	5.4.2	Capital Formation Statistics—Official Series, 1938 and 1946 to Date	165
	5.4.3	Comparison of Official Expenditure and Output Statistics	168
	5.4.4	Capital Formation Statistics—Unofficial Historical and Regional Series	173
	5.4.5	Capital Expenditure—Supplementary Sources and Analyses	173
	5.4.6	Current Expenditure on Construction Work	178

5.5	*Production Data for Specific Types of Building*		179
	5.5.1	Introduction	179
	5.5.2	Educational Building in Great Britain	179
	5.5.3	Industrial Building—Industrial Development Certificates	180
	5.5.4	Office Development Statistics	180
	5.5.5	Road Building	180
	5.5.6	Health Service Buildings	181
	5.5.7	Surveys on the Methods Used for Placing Contracts	181
5.6	*Current and Forward Indicators and Forecasts of Construction Activity*		181
	5.6.1	Introduction	181
	5.6.2	Forward-looking Statistical Series and Investment Intentions Surveys	182
	5.6.3	State of Trade Enquiries	184
	5.6.4	Unofficial Surveys of Construction Contracts	187
	5.6.5	Forecasts of Construction Output for Great Britain	187
	5.6.6	The Time Scale of Construction Projects	190
6	**Labour Statistics for Great Britain Other than Those Collected in MOW–DOE Enquiries and in Censuses of Production**		193
	6.1	*Introduction*	193
	6.2	*Employment Statistics Collected by the Department of Employment and Its Predecessor Departments*	193
		6.2.1 Introduction	193
		6.2.2 Methodology	194
		6.2.3 The Published Series and Their Interpretation	194
		6.2.4 Comparison of MOL–DE and Other Employment Series	201
	6.3	*Construction in the Censuses of Population in Great Britain*	204
		6.3.1 Introduction	204
		6.3.2 The Available Data	204
		6.3.3 Interpretation	205
		6.3.4 Comparison of the Census of Population and Other Employment Data	206
	6.4	*Construction Industry Training Board (CITB) Statistics— Great Britain*	208
		6.4.1 CITB Levy Return—Employment Statistics	208
		6.4.2 The CITB Register	209
		6.4.3 CITB Training Statistics	210

	6.4.4	Ad hoc Surveys	210
	6.4.5	Grant and Levy Payments	211
6.5	*Labour Training and Education Statistics for Great Britain*		211
	6.5.1	Background	211
	6.5.2	Apprentice Registration Statistics	211
	6.5.3	Employment of Apprentices/Trainees	212
	6.5.4	Government Training Statistics	212
	6.5.5	Education Statistics	213
6.6	*Qualified Manpower in the Construction Industry in Great Britain*		214
	6.6.1	Introduction	214
	6.6.2	Institute of Building Statistics	215
	6.6.3	General Statistics Relating to the Employment and Supply of Qualified Manpower in the Construction Industry	215
	6.6.4	Earnings of Qualified Manpower in the Construction Industry	219
6.7	*Ad hoc Labour Enquiries*		220
	6.7.1	Background	220
	6.7.2	BRS Survey of Building Operatives' Work 1963–4	220
	6.7.3	GSS Survey of Building Operatives 1965	221
	6.7.4	Surveys for the Phelps-Brown Committee 1967	221
	6.7.5	PEP Survey of Building Operatives 1967	222
	6.7.6	The National Training Survey 1975	222
	6.7.7	GLC Surveys of Labour Availability and Requirements on London Local Authority Construction Sites 1973 and 1974	222
6.8	*Unemployment, Vacancies and Labour Mobility—Great Britain*		223
	6.8.1	Unemployment Statistics	223
	6.8.2	Statistics of Vacancies and Placings	226
	6.8.3	Labour Mobility	227
6.9	*Wage Rates, Earnings, Hours and Labour Costs*		227
	6.9.1	Introduction	227
	6.9.2	Wage Rates and Normal Hours of Work	228
	6.9.3	Actual Earnings and Hours of Work (MOL–DE Enquiries)	230
	6.9.4	Supplementary Sources of Income and Hours of Work	233
	6.9.5	Total Labour Costs	235
6.10	*Accident Statistics for Great Britain*		237
	6.10.1	The HM Factory Inspectorate (HMFI) Statistics	237
	6.10.2	The DHSS Accident Statistics	238
	6.10.3	Interpretation	239

	6.11 *Strike Statistics—United Kingdom*	240
	6.12 *Trade Union Statistics—United Kingdom*	242
	6.12.1 Membership and Industrial Relations	242
	6.12.2 Finance	243
7	**Financial Statistics**	244
	7.1 *Construction in the National Income and Expenditure Accounts*	244
	7.1.1 Accounts for the UK	244
	7.1.2 Regional Accounts	246
	7.2 *Statistics of Company Income and Finance*	247
	7.2.1 Statistics from Company Accounts	248
	7.2.2 Turnover and Profit Margins of Large Companies—Price Commission Returns, 1973 to Date	251
	7.2.3 Bank Advances	251
	7.2.4 Statistics Relating to Quoted Securities	252
	7.2.5 Small Firms in the Construction Industry—Financial and Other Data	252
	7.2.6 Overseas Investment, Earnings and Assets	253
	7.3 *R & D Expenditure Surveys*	253
	7.4 *Company Acquisitions and Mergers*	254
	7.5 *Bankruptcy and Company Liquidation (Insolvency) Statistics*	255
	7.5.1 Introduction	255
	7.5.2 Bankruptcy	256
	7.5.3 Company Liquidations—England and Wales and Scotland	256
	7.5.4 Interpretation	256
	7.6 *Taxation Statistics*	257
	7.6.1 Introduction	257
	7.6.2 Personal and Corporate Income Tax	258
	7.6.3 Selective Employment Tax (SET)	259
	7.6.4 Value Added Tax (VAT)	259
8	**Construction Costs, Prices and Productivity**	261
	8.1 *Indices of Construction Costs and Prices*	261
	8.1.1 Problems and Methods of Measurement	261
	8.1.2 Currently Compiled General Indices of Construction Costs and Prices	266

	8.1.3	Price Adjustment Formulae Indices	275
	8.1.4	Historical Indices of Construction Costs and Prices	277
	8.1.5	Use and Interpretation of the Indices	278
8.2	*Productivity*		280
	8.2.1	General Measurement Problems and Interpretation	280
	8.2.2	*Ad hoc* Sectoral Studies of Productivity	281

9 Construction Industry Statistics for Northern Ireland — 282

9.1	*Introduction*		282
9.2	*Production Statistics for Northern Ireland*		283
	9.2.1	Quarterly Surveys of Output and New Orders	283
	9.2.2	Censuses of Production and Input–Output Analyses	287
	9.2.3	Statistics of Expenditure on Construction Work	290
	9.2.4	Construction in the Northern Ireland Index of Industrial Production	293
	9.2.5	Production Data for Specific Types of Building	294
9.3	*Construction Employment Statistics for Northern Ireland*		295
	9.3.1	Introduction	295
	9.3.2	Department of Manpower Services Employment Statistics	296
	9.3.3	Quarterly Construction Employment Surveys from 1966	297
	9.3.4	Employment Data from the Censuses of Production	299
	9.3.5	Censuses of Population Data for Construction	299
	9.3.6	CITB (NI) Manpower Surveys	300
	9.3.7	Comparison of the Construction Employment Series	301
	9.3.8	*Ad hoc* Construction Manpower Surveys	304
9.4	*Labour Statistics for Northern Ireland other than Employment*		304
	9.4.1	Labour Training and Education Statistics	304
	9.4.2	Unemployment, Vacancies and Labour Mobility	305
	9.4.3	Wage Rates, Earnings, Hours and Labour Costs	306
	9.4.4	Construction Accident Statistics	308
	9.4.5	Strike Statistics	309
	9.4.6	Trade Union Statistics	309
9.5	*Structure of the Construction Industry in Northern Ireland*		309
9.6	*Financial Statistics for Northern Ireland*		310
	9.6.1	Construction in Regional Accounts	310
	9.6.2	Miscellaneous Financial Statistics for Construction	311

PART II
CONSTRUCTION MATERIALS AND PLANT

10 Statistics Relating to Production, Consumption and Foreign Trade   315
   10.1 *Introduction*   315
   10.2 *Construction Materials*   316
      10.2.1 Consumption Statistics   316
      10.2.2 Production and Related Statistics   317
      10.2.3 Overseas Trade in Construction Materials   321
   10.3 *Construction Plant and Equipment*   322
      10.3.1 The Use of Plant in the Construction Industry   322
      10.3.2 Production and Overseas Trade Statistics for Construction Plant   322

11 Construction Materials and Plant Prices   323
   11.1 *Construction Materials Prices*   323
      11.1.1 Department of Industry (and Former Board of Trade) Indices   324
      11.1.2 Ministry of Works' Series 1939–51   326
      11.1.3 Unofficial Historical Series 1845–1939   327
      11.1.4 Actual Price Data   327
   11.2 *Construction Plant Prices*   328

PART III
THE CONSTRUCTION STOCK

12 Statistics of the Construction Stock   331
   12.1 *Introduction*   331
   12.2 *Size, Composition and Characteristics of the Construction Stock*   332
      12.2.1 The Total Stock of Buildings and Works   332
      12.2.2 Stock Statistics for Particular Types of Buildings   337
   12.3 *Changes to the Construction Stock*   340
   12.4 *The Construction Stock and Land*   341
      12.4.1 Land-use Statistics   341
      12.4.2 Development Control Statistics   341
   12.5 *Construction Stock Transactions and Costs*   342
      12.5.1 Sales and Purchases of Existing Buildings   342
      12.5.2 Building Rents and Occupancy Costs   343

PART IV
THE CONSTRUCTION PROFESSIONS

13 Statistics of the Construction Professions — 349
- 13.1 *Introduction* — 349
- 13.2 *Numbers, Characteristics and Employment of the Construction Professions* — 350
  - 13.2.1 General Sources — 350
  - 13.2.2 The Architectural Profession — 350
  - 13.2.3 The Surveying Professions — 353
  - 13.2.4 The Engineering Professions — 354
  - 13.2.5 New Entrants to the Construction Professions and Education Statistics — 356
- 13.3 *Organization and Structure of Professional Practice* — 357
  - 13.3.1 Architectural Practice — 357
  - 13.3.2 Quantity Surveying Practices — 359
  - 13.3.3 Engineering Practices — 359
- 13.4 *Financial Statistics for the Construction Professions—Earnings and Professional Practice Costs and Incomes* — 359
- 13.5 *Statistics of Work Undertaken by the Construction Professions* — 361
  - 13.5.1 Private Architects' Design Work Statistics — 361
  - 13.5.2 Work Undertaken by Private Chartered Quantity Surveyors — 372
  - 13.5.3 Work Undertaken by Consulting Engineers — 373

PART V
CONCLUSION

14 Desirable Improvements and Future Developments — 377
- 14.1 Introduction — 377
- 14.2 The Construction Industry in Great Britain — 377
- 14.3 The Construction Industry in Northern Ireland — 382
- 14.4 Construction Materials and Input–Output Analyses — 383
- 14.5 The Construction Stock — 384
- 14.6 Construction Professions — 385
- 14.7 A Proposal for a Comprehensive and Detailed Official Index of Sources — 385

CONTENTS 11

Quick Reference List 387
   Notes 389
   Table of Contents 391
   Quick Reference List 394
   Quick Reference List Key to Publications 462

Bibliography 496

Appendices 509

Subject Index 635

LIST OF TABLES

(*Note:* A comprehensive guide in tabular form to the statistics available is provided in the *Quick Reference List*. The tables listed here are those incorporated in the main text providing more detailed analyses in amplification or support of the descriptions and commentary given there. The table numbers are decimalized, the first number referring to the chapter in which it appears.)

Table No.	Title	Page
3.1	MOW Construction Census Analyses 1941–4. Contractors—Main Trades Only (Great Britain)	Between 56/57
3.2	MOW Construction Census Analyses 1945–54. Contractors—Main Trades Only (Great Britain)	Between 62/63
3.3	MOW Construction Census Analyses 1945–54. Contractors—Specialist Trades (Great Britain)	64–65
3.4	MOW Construction Census Analyses 1944–54. Direct Labour (Great Britain)	72–73
3.5	Licensed Work—Expenditure Permitted in a Period of 12 Months Without Licence	77
3.6	Gross Output Series 1932–45	83
3.7	MOW Output Time Series 1946–55 (Great Britain)	88–89
3.8	Employment Time Series 1941–5	91
3.9	MOW Employment Time Series 1945–55	93
4.1	MOW–DOE Construction Census Analyses 1957 to Date—Contractors Only (Great Britain)	104–5
4.2	MOW–DOE Construction Census Analyses 1961 to Date—Local Authorities' Direct Labour (Great Britain)	120–1
4.3	MOW–DOE Output Time Series from 1955 (Great Britain)	128–9
4.4	Contractors' New Orders Statistics (Great Britain)	138–9
4.5	Local Authority Design Work (Great Britain)	146
5.1	Subject Guide to Censuses of Production for Larger Firms in Construction 1946–69	Between 156/157
5.2	Guide to the Coverage of Public Authorities' Direct Labour in Censuses of Production 1946 to Date	Between 158/159
6.1	Construction Employment Statistics for Great Britain—Comparison of Sources	203

Table No.	Title	Page
8.1	Currently Compiled General Indices of Construction Costs and Prices	Between 266/267
9.1	Construction Employment Statistics for Northern Ireland—Comparison of Sources	303
10.1	Current Building Materials Statistics—Summary Guide	Between 316/317
10.2	Sources of Current Regional Building Materials Statistics	318
13.1	Construction Professions—Surveys of Earnings and Professional Practice Costs and Incomes	362–7

LIST OF APPENDICES

I.	The Construction Industry as Defined in the Standard Industrial Classification and Analyses of the Scope and Coverage of the Definitions	512
II.	Regional Classification Used for Official Construction Statistics	516
III.	Guide to the Classification of Firms by Trade since 1954	517
IV.	Censuses of Contractors in Great Britain 1941 to date—History of Enquiries made by the Ministry of Works and its Successor Departments (currently Department of the Environment) and Selected Specimen Forms	521
V.	Censuses of Direct Labour Organizations in Great Britain 1943 to date—History of Enquiries made by the Ministry of Works and its Successor Departments (currently Department of the Environment) and Selected Specimen Forms	559
VI.	Site Returns 1941–54—History of Enquiries made by the Ministry of Works and Selected Specimen Forms	583
VII.	Sample Returns of Output and Employment 1945–77—History of Enquiries made by the Ministry of Works and its Successor Departments (currently Department of the Environment) and Selected Specimen Forms	589
VIII.	New Orders Enquiry 1956 to date—History of Enquiries and Selected Specimen Form	601
IX.	EEC State of Trade Enquiry into Construction in Great Britain 1977 to date—History and Selected Specimen Form	607
X.	Return of Overseas Contracts and Sub-contracts 1955 to date—History of Enquiries and Selected Specimen Form	613
XI.	Local Authority Design Work Enquiry 1965 to date—History of Enquiries and Selected Specimen Form	617
XII.	Quarterly Returns of Construction Work in Northern Ireland 1966 to date	623
XIII.	Construction as Defined in the Industrial Classification for the European Communities (NACE)	633

LIST OF ABBREVIATIONS

(Abbreviations used to refer to publications are shown in italics)

A	Annually
AAS	*Annual Abstract of Statistics*
ABCS	*Annual Bulletin of Construction Statistics*
ACAS	Advisory, Conciliation and Arbitration Service
ACE	Association of Consulting Engineers
AJ	*Architects' Journal*
App.	Appendix
APTC	Administrative, Professional, Technical and Clerical
ARCUK	Architects' Registration Council of the United Kingdom
ARP	Air Raid Precaution
ATC	Administrative, Technical and Clerical
AUBTW	Amalgamated Union of Building Trade Workers
B & CE	Building and Civil Engineering
BAA	British Airports Authority
BATC	Building Apprenticeship and Training Council
BBC	British Broadcasting Corporation
BCIS	Building Cost Information Service (RICS)
BCS Supp.	*Bulletin of Construction Statistics Supplement*
BIM	Building Industries and Materials
BMCIS	Building Maintenance Cost Information Service (RICS)
BMP	Building Material Producers (Common alternative to NCBMP—*q.v.*)
BOT	Board of Trade
BOTJ	*Board of Trade Journal*
BRE	Building Research Establishment
BRS	Building Research Station
BSC	British Steel Corporation
BSO	Business Statistics Office
Bus. Mon.	*Business Monitor*
C. Eng.	Civil Engineering
CASEC	Committee of Associations of Specialist Engineering Contractors
CBI	Confederation of British Industry
CCA	Current Cost Accounting
CEGB	Central Electricity Generating Board
CEI	Council of Engineering Institutions
CIRET	Centre for International Research on Economic Tendency Surveys

CITB	Construction Industry Training Board
CL	Civil Licence
CNAA	Council for National Academic Awards
CNC	Cost of New Construction (index)
COD	Census of Distribution
CODOT	Classification of Occupations and Directory of Occupational Titles
COP	Census of Production
CPS	Central Programmes and Statistics
CSO	Central Statistical Office
Ctg	Contracting
Ctrs	Contractors
DAA	Direct, Authorized and Assisted
DE	Department of Employment
DEG	*Department of Employment Gazette*
DES	Department of Education and Science
DHSS	Department of Health and Social Security
DHSS (NI)	Department of Health and Social Services (Northern Ireland)
DIY	Do-it-Yourself
DL	Direct Labour
DMS	Department of Manpower Services (Northern Ireland)
DOE	Department of the Environment
DOI	Department of Industry
DQSD	Directorate of Quantity Surveying Development
DQSS	Directorate of Quantity Surveying Services (formerly DQSD—*q.v.*)
DR	Defence Regulation
DSS	*Digest of Scottish Statistics*
DTI	Department of Trade and Industry
DWS	*Digest of Welsh Statistics*
E & W	England and Wales
EDC	Economic Development Committee (NEDC)
EEC	European Economic Community
EETPU	Electrical, Electronic, Telecommunications and Plumbing Union
EIU	Economist Intelligence Unit
ESA	Employment Services Agency
ET	*Economic Trends*
ETAS	*Economic Trends Annual Supplement*
FAS	Faculty of Architects and Surveyors
FASS	Federation of Associations of Specialists and Sub-contractors
FBI	Federation of British Industry
FCEC	Federation of Civil Engineering Contractors
Fin. Stats.	*Financial Statistics*
FT	*Financial Times*
FTATU	Furniture, Timber and Allied Trades Union
GB	Great Britain
GCE	General Certificate of Education
GDP	Gross Domestic Product
GLC	Greater London Council

GMWU	General and Municipal Workers' Union
GSS	Government Social Survey
GTC	Government Training Centre
HBF	House-Builders Federation
HCS	*Housing and Construction Statistics*
HMFI	Her (His) Majesty's Factory Inspectorate
HMSO	Her (His) Majesty's Stationery Office
HNC	Higher National Certificate
HND	Higher National Diploma
HVCA	Heating and Ventilating Contractors' Association
HWP	Holidays-with-Pay
IAAS	Incorporated Association of Architects and Surveyors
ICE	Institution of Civil Engineers
IDC	Industrial Development Certificate
IEE	Institution of Electrical Engineers
IHVE	Institution of Heating and Ventilating Engineers
ILEA	Inner London Education Authority
IME	Institution of Mechanical Engineers
IOB	Institute of Building
IQS	Institute of Quantity Surveyors
IR Stats.	*Inland Revenue Statistics*
ISE	Institution of Structural Engineers
ISIC	International Standard Industrial Classification
KOS	Key Occupations for Statistical Purposes
LA	Local Authority
LACSAB	Local Authorities' Conditions of Service Advisory Board
LOSC	Labour-only Sub-contract(or)
M	Monthly
M & E	Mechanical and Electrical
MAP	Ministry of Aircraft Production
MBCS	*Monthly Bulletin of Construction Statistics*
MDS	*Monthly Digest of Statistics*
MLH	Minimum List Heading (of the SIC)
MMC	Monopolies and Mergers Commission
MOHLG	Ministry of Housing and Local Government
MOL	Ministry of Labour
MOLG	*Ministry of Labour Gazette*
MOLNI	Ministry of Labour and National Insurance (Northern Ireland)
MOLNS	Ministry of Labour and National Service
MOW	Ministry of Works
MOWB	Ministry of Works and Building
MOWP	Ministry of Works and Planning
MOWT	Ministry of War Transport
MPBW	Ministry of Public Building and Works
MS	Ministry of Supply
MSC	Manpower Services Commission
n/a	Not applicable

NACE	Nomenclature Générale des Activités dans les Communautés Européennes
NBPI	National Board for Prices and Incomes
NCB	National Coal Board
NCBMP	National Council of Building Material Producers
NEDC	National Economic Development Council
NEDO	National Economic Development Office
NES	New Earnings Survey
NFBPM	National Federation of Builders' and Plumbers' Merchants
NFBTE	National Federation of Building Trades Employers
NFBTO	National Federation of Building Trade Operatives
NFCU	National Federation of Construction Unions
NI	Northern Ireland
NID	*Northern Ireland Digest* (of Statistics)
NIER	*National Institute Economic Review*
NIESR	National Institute of Economic and Social Research
NJCBI	National Joint Council for the Building Industry
Nyp	Not yet published
ODP	Office Development Permit
OECD	Organization for Economic Co-operation and Development
ONC	Ordinary National Certificate
OPCS	Office of Population Censuses and Surveys
p.a.	per annum
PAYE	Pay-as-you-earn
PBR	Payment by Results
PC	Private Contractor
PEP	Political and Economic Planning
PER	Professional and Executive Recruitment
PILAH	Price Index of Local Authority Housebuilding
PINCCA	*Price Index Numbers for Current Cost Accounting*
PSA	Property Services Agency (DOE)
Pte	Private
Pub.	Public
Q	Quarterly
QR	Quarterly Return
QRL	Quick Reference List
QS	Quantity Surveyor
QSEs	Qualified Scientists and Engineers
Qtr	Quarter
R & D	Research and Development
R & M	Repairs and Maintenance
RIAS	Royal Incorporation of Architects in Scotland
RIBA	Royal Institute of British Architects
RIBAJ	*RIBA Journal*
RICS	Royal Institution of Chartered Surveyors
RSUA	Royal Society of Ulster Architects
s.a.	Seasonally adjusted

SAAT	Society of Architectural and Associated Technicians
SAS	*Scottish Abstract of Statistics*
SCALA	Society of Chief Architects of Local Authorities
SCE	Scottish Certificate of Education
SEB	*Scottish Economic Bulletin*
SET	Selective Employment Tax
SI	Statutory Instrument
SIC	Standard Industrial Classification
SIPEP	*Statistics on Incomes, Prices, Employment and Production*
SOEC	Statistical Office of the European Communities
SR & O	Statutory Rules and Orders
SSHA	Scottish Special Housing Association
SSRC	Social Science Research Council
T & I	*Trade and Industry*
TGWU	Transport and General Workers' Union
TOPS	Training Opportunities Scheme
TSA	Training Services Agency
TUC	Trades Union Congress
UCATT	Union of Construction, Allied Trades and Technicians
UGC	University Grants Committee
UK	United Kingdom
VAT	Value Added Tax
VOP	Variation of Price
WB	Works and Buildings
WDR	War Damage Repairs
WET	*Welsh Economic Trends*
WO	War Office
WP	Working Principal or Working Proprietor

ADDENDA ON RECENT DEVELOPMENTS

The purpose of these addenda is to take note of the *most important* developments that have occurred in the period between the reference date of the main text (December 1977) and the proof-reading stage (July 1979). Additional publication references are also included here in a separate list under the heading 'Additional References' below. This list includes references to publications which had been announced but for which full particulars were not available at the time the main text was written, but does not include further particulars of publications originally noted as 'forthcoming' or 'not yet published'. The additional publications are numbered serially and prefaced with the letter 'A' to distinguish them from the publications listed in the QRL Key and Bibliography. Reference here to publications in any of these lists is made by means of the appropriate serial reference only, placed within square brackets.

One development of outstanding importance that has occurred has been the introduction of new price indices for construction output and the consequential revision of several constant-price series which involve their use. We consider these changes first. Other developments are then considered in the order in which the relevant subjects are treated in the main text.

New Official Construction Output Price Indices (Section 8.1.2.1)

The new price indices were brought into use by the DOE in the early months of 1978. Up to this time the index used for the deflation of values from current to constant prices was the 'CNC' index. A critical appraisal of this index is provided in Section 8.1.2.1 and the need for a better index is emphasized in Section 14.2 in the discussion of desirable improvements. An official description of the new indices has been published in [A 1]; our discussion here is, therefore, brief and confined largely to comment on their virtues and limitations.

The CNC index was meant to reflect prices for all *new* construction work. However, its method of compilation (it was not based on actual price data but was built up on the basis of changes in the unit costs of factors of production), and the available data combined to produce potentially serious errors—for a full discussion see Section 8.1.2.1.

Unlike the CNC index, the new price indices are based on actual price data and are compiled separately for different types of work. In brief, the method combines information about the value of contracts awarded which is collected in the new orders enquiry (Section 4.5 refers) with estimates of contract duration and the phasing of work to give an estimate of the contribution made to current output by orders placed in preceding periods. These estimates are made first at current prices and then at constant prices by using indices of tender prices for deflation purposes (see Section 4.5.3.3). Dividing the estimate of output at current prices by the estimate at constant prices produces an output price index for the current period. In practice orders are sub-divided into three groups according to expected duration (short, medium or long) and the contribution of each to output in the current period is calculated separately using different time-profiles. A distinction is also made by type of work and between fixed and variable price (VOP) contracts. Since the value of the contribution to output made by VOP contracts is affected after the contract is awarded by changes in the costs of labour and/or materials for which the contractor may be reimbursed, these contracts are revalued on the basis of estimates of the proportions of labour and materials adjustable for cost changes and indices of labour and materials costs.

The new 'output price indices' (also called 'outturn tender price indices') are produced for five types of work: public housing, private housing, public non-housing, private industrial and private commercial. Quarterly series for the period 1970–7 were published for the first time in [A 1]; they are now incorporated in *Housing and Construction Statistics* [QRL 168] from issue No. 25 (Supplementary Table I). The latter also gives an index for 'all new construction', representing a base-weighted average of the five separate indices.

Undoubtedly the new indices do possess virtues, in principle, over the CNC index inasmuch as they are based on actual price data and they do attempt to take account of the mix of output by type of work and the combined effects of the type of price quotation and variations in contract duration on current output price levels. They do face, therefore, the criticisms expressed in the main text and certainly the movement of the new indices during the period of high inflation and high pressure of construction demand in the early 1970s is much more in line with contemporary observation than is the movement of the CNC index. Whether the new indices will live up to expectation in the future, of course, remains to be seen. It will be appreciated that much depends on the reliability of the methodology and the data used in practice for converting new orders into estimates of output and on the reliability of the prior measurement of tender price changes. The methodology requires information about the proportion of contracts on fixed and VOP bases, on their duration and on their phasing over time. But in each of these areas little information has been available in the past and some of the calculations are based, *faute de mieux*, on stability assumptions which may or may not be reasonable. Information in each of these areas, however, is now being improved—details are given in [A 1] p. 101. The tender price indices themselves are considered elsewhere in this Review—see Section 4.5.3.3 (note that the road construction price index referred to as being unpublished in that section is now published—see below) and Section 8.1.

Before turning to examine the effect on the series revised using the new output deflators, two further points are worthy of note. First, although the CNC index has been replaced as an output deflator by the DOE, it is planned to continue the compilation and publication of it for some time since it is used by other organizations. Secondly, it should be appreciated that the new deflators apply to *new* work carried out by *contractors*. Repairs and maintenance work and new work carried out by direct labour organizations are still deflated using a CNC-type index since the new methodology cannot be applied to these sectors—for further details see [A 1] p. 99.

Revised Constant-price Series

Following the preparation of the new price deflators referred to above, various statistical series in which the CNC index had been previously used for deflation purposes were retrospectively revised back to 1970. Four series were affected and we deal with each of these in turn.

Section 4.4.5. Revised DOE Series of Construction Output for Great Britain

The revised output series were first published in a DOE Press Notice on 8 March 1978; they are reproduced in [A 1] Table 3 and in *Housing and Construction Statistics* [QRL 168] No. 26. A comparison of the new and old series is given in [A 1] Table 4. The effect of the revision is varied and in some cases substantial: the effect on the *level* of the series for *new work* (the series principally affected) is to reduce the level in all years except two over the period 1970–7 by amounts ranging from 2.3 per cent to 10.2 per cent: the effect on the annual rate of change was to reverse the direction of change on one occasion (1971–2), to reduce the degree of change at the beginning and end of the period but to intensify the degree of change in the middle of the period.

Section 5.2. Revised Index of Industrial Production

Revisions to the UK index of industrial production which covers both new work and repairs and maintenance work were made in *Trade and Industry* [QRL 352] on 24 March 1978 (p. 670) and *Economic Trends* [QRL 147] No. 293, March 1978 (p. 26). The effect of the changes was to alter the level of the index and the size (but not the direction) of annual rates of change in both the construction index itself and the index for all industries.

Section 5.4.2. Revised Capital Formation Statistics

Since these series refer to expenditure rather than output, there is a difference in timing which is met by applying the price deflator with a lag of one quarter. Revised series were introduced in an article on 'National income and expenditure in the fourth quarter of 1977' in *Economic Trends* [QRL 147] No. 294, April 1978. The revisions affected not only the series for expenditure on buildings and other construction work but also the constant-price series for expenditure on all fixed assets (construction being a major constituent of the total). Analyses of the effects will be found in the article referred to above and in [A 1].

Section 7.1. Revised National Income and Expenditure Accounts

The revised price deflator for construction affected not only the capital formation statistics which are referred to above and which form part of the national income and expenditure accounts, but also had a noticeable effect on the estimates of Gross Domestic Product on both output and expenditure bases. The effects here were summarized in the article in *Economic Trends* [QRL 147] No. 294, April 1978 (p. 74) referred to above.

Other Developments

Section 4.2 and Appendix IV. DOE Censuses of Contractors in Great Britain

Since the completion of the main text a further census has been taken in the normal annual sequence in October 1978. A summary of the results is planned for publication in *Housing and Construction Statistics* [QRL 168] No. 30 with full results following in the usual annual publication [QRL 240]. Two changes were made compared with the return for 1977 (see Appendix IV): the question about the amount of VAT chargeable on construction work was dropped from the 1978 return but a question was added asking for information about all VAT registration numbers held (of relevance in the maintenance of the register of businesses).

Section 4.4. DOE Output and Employment Time Series for Great Britain

A new project-based system for collecting output and employment data from construction firms was introduced in July 1978 with respect to the second quarter of 1978—a pilot test having been run from April 1971 (first quarter) until April 1978 (first quarter). It is intended that this enquiry will replace the returns of the type considered in Section 4.4 but the two types of enquiry are to be run in parallel for a period in order to 'prove' the new enquiry. At the time of writing, no results from it had been published. For further details and discussion of the new enquiry see the sub-section on 'Output and Employment' in Section 14.2.

Section 4.4.3. and Appendix VII. DOE Monthly Employment Returns

The monthly employment return for the months between the quarterly output and employment return has now been dropped—it was last despatched in December 1977.

Section 4.5.3. DOE Contractors' New Orders Statistics

The new orders series were revised retrospectively back to 1964 in *Housing and Construction Statistics* [QRL 168] No. 27, 1978 'to overcome discontinuities caused by changes, particularly the expansion of the statistical register in 1974 and the revision of estimation methods in 1976'. Seasonal adjustments were also recalculated.

Section 5.6.3. State of Trade Enquiries

Electrical Contractors' Association. This Association has conducted a quarterly state of trade enquiry amongst a sample of its members in the UK since the end of 1977. Questions are asked about the size of firm (no. of operatives employed); the percentage distribution of installation work by type of work or client; trading results ('very profitable', 'profitable', etc.); volume of enquiries received (more, same, less, etc.); orders received; operating capacity; labour availability. The results are made available in a quarterly statement [A 11] which is circulated to the press. In the context of this Review it should be appreciated that the activities of members of the Association are not confined to electrical contracting work within the construction industry.

Section 6.2.3. DE Monthly Employment Series

As a consequence of the ending of monthly employment surveys by the DOE at the end of 1977 the DE monthly employment series from February 1978 has had to be estimated. This is done by interpolating the figures obtained from the DOE's quarterly enquiries (Section 4.4.4 refers) when these become available and in the interim using information about the relationship between construction employment and construction output for past quarters—see *DEG* [QRL 135] Vol. 86, 1978, p. 511.

Section 6.6.2. Institute of Building Statistics

IOB Members' Employment. The results of a further survey of the fields of employment of members living in the UK and the Republic of Ireland, carried out in 1976, were published in the Institute's Journal [QRL 69] Vol. 17, January 1979, p. xv.

Sections 6.6.4 and 6.9.4. 1971 Census Income Follow-up Survey

A report of this survey has now been published [A 6]. It does not include statistical data but gives a list of tables which are available on request.

Section 6.8.3. Labour Mobility

A construction industry mobility enquiry, announced in *Statistical News* [B 333] No. 42, was carried out by the OPCS over the period 1978–9 on the basis of interviews with workers in a household survey. It is anticipated that a report will be published in 1980.

Section 6.9.4. Supplementary Sources of Income Data—Salary Surveys

A survey on the income and fringe benefits of construction managers was carried out for the journal *Building* in 1979. A summary of the results, which covered 'more than 2,000 managers' in 'over 120 companies', was published in *Building* [QRL 60], 6 April 1979, pp. 60–66. A full report was published in [A 13]. Comparisons are also made with data drawn from an annual salaries survey conducted by the British Institute of Management. For further details of salary surveys and a general discussion reference should be made to the companion volume in this series by Dean [B 44].

Section 7.2.2. Price Commission Returns

It was announced after the return of the Conservative Government in May 1979 that the Price Commission would be abolished.

Section 7.6.4. Value Added Tax Statistics—Register of Businesses

The registration limit for VAT—of relevance in interpreting the register of businesses statistics—was raised to £10,000 with effect from 12 April 1978 and the de-registration limit was raised to £8,500 from 1 July 1978.

Section 8.1. Construction Costs and Prices

The unpublished historical study of the basis on which published unit rates for construction work were compiled [B 59], referred to in Section 8.1.1.3, has now been published in a shortened form in [A 3].

Road Construction Price Index. The official index of road construction tender prices—referred to in Section 8.1.2 and Section 4.5.3.3 but unpublished at the time the main text was written—is now regularly published. Quarterly figures from 1970 (Q_1) to

1977 (Q_3) were published in [A 1] and these are continued in *Housing and Construction Statistics* [QRL 168] from issue No. 25. An official account of the method of calculation is given in *Housing and Construction Statistics, Notes and Definitions Supplement 1978* [B 250]. The methodology is the same as that used for the DQSS index (Section 8.1.2.6 refers) and reference should be made to that section for further comment.

Section 8.2.2. *Ad hoc* **Sectoral Studies of Productivity**

A further study of the labour requirements of house building—relating to schemes completed in the periods 1967–9 and 1972–5—has been published by the Building Research Establishment in [A 4].

Section 9.3. Construction Employment Statistics for Northern Ireland

The Northern Ireland Department of Manpower Services has commenced the publication of a *Gazette* [A 10] containing statistical series and explanatory articles. At the time of writing (July 1979) two issues have been published. The first issue contained articles on the 'continuous series' of 'employees in employment' and of 'unemployment' and on the New Earnings Survey. The second issue contained articles on the basis of quarterly employment statistics and on industrial analyses and seasonal adjustment of unemployment statistics. Statistical series covering construction (and other industries) have been included as follows:

Employees in Employment, Quarterly, June 1959–June 1971	Issue No. 1
Employees in Employment, Annually, June 1971–June 1977	
Employees in Employment, Quarterly, June 1977–March 1978	Issue No. 2
Unemployment, Monthly, January 1976–August 1978	

Section 9.4.5. Strike Statistics for Northern Ireland

Further analyses of statistical data were included in the *Report of the Review Body on Industrial Relations in Northern Ireland* [A 12]. Those relevant to construction provide annual series for the period 1966–72 of the number of stoppages beginning in each year, the number of workers directly and indirectly involved, the number of working days lost and analyses by cause of stoppage.

Section 12.2.2. Stock Statistics for Particular Types of Building—School Buildings

Two surveys of school buildings in England and Wales were held in 1975 and 1976 in connection with *A Study of School Building* [QRL 334] referred to in Section 12.2.2.2. Some of the results from these surveys have now been published in a separate volume

[A 14]. The aim of the first survey was to establish the sizes and ages of the schools and to compare their capacities with the actual numbers of pupils on roll. The second survey covered a proportion of the schools from the first survey and collected data on particular aspects of the schools such as site area, playing fields, number of storeys, outside W.C.s, etc.

Section 12.5. Construction Stock Transactions and Costs

Surveys of conveyancing (Section 12.5.1.1). A further survey was carried out in November 1977, the results of which have now been reported in [A 2]. These continue the series last published in [QRL 11]. The latest report provides estimates of the sales of land and buildings in England and Wales in November 1977 and comprehensive quarterly figures for all sales over £100,000 in England and Wales; monthly and quarterly estimates of sales based upon stamp duty data and separate estimates from the fourth quarter of 1976 of the total value of residential and non-residential sales. It also provides some new information on leasehold property transactions—by length of tenure and range of rent—and new estimates of the incidence of stamp duty by price range, by type of property and by sector of purchaser.

Commercial and Industrial Property Statistics. A publication under this title was introduced in 1978 [A 7] as a successor to [QRL 122]. Its main purpose is to bring together data relating to commercial and industrial property otherwise available in diverse sources, although it also includes some data not published elsewhere. The first issue contains several of the series on the construction stock (considered in this Review in Chapter 12), on new construction (output, new orders and capital formation—considered in Sections 4.4, 4.5 and 5.4.2 respectively), development control statistics (Section 12.4.2), construction costs (Section 8.1), rents (Section 12.5.2) and miscellaneous financial data (Chapter 7) some of which, relating to property companies and ground rents, etc. is not considered in this Review. Indices of rents for offices, shops and factories (referred to in Section 12.5.2) hitherto only available from 1964 are carried back to 1962 in this publication.

Section 13.2.2. Architectural Profession—Numbers, Characteristics and Employment

RIBA Student Employment Survey 1978. This survey covered students who passed the Part 2 examination in architecture in 1977. Its aim was to discover the extent to which students were entering fields of employment other than architecture and the level of unemployment, to obtain information on the level of RIBA student membership in the post-Part 2 group and to obtain information about the earnings of post-Part 2 practical trainees. A report on the survey was published in [A 15].

Section 13.4. Financial Statistics for the Construction Professions—Earnings and Professional Practice Costs and Incomes

Architects' earnings. A report on the RIBA annual enquiry for 1977 was published in the same series as [QRL 42]. The report for 1978 was published under a different title: *Architects' Employment and Earnings 1978* [A 5]. This updates the information collected in earlier surveys and provides additional data on conditions of service and the incidence of union membership

Costs and Profitability of Private Architectural Practice 1971–1977. The results of the RIBA survey of office costs referred to in Table 13.1—item 2(iv)—as being in progress in 1977 have now been published as [A 8]. The aim of the survey was to collect information on the income, expenditure and profits of private architectural practices and data on individual items of expenditure over the period from 1971 to 1977.

Design costs in the public and private sectors for civil engineering work. A study to evaluate the performance of design offices in the public and private sectors was published by the Economic Development Committee for Civil Engineering in 1978 [A 9]. This includes the results of a survey to obtain comparative design costs data for the two sectors over the period 1971–6. Attention is focused in this survey on the design costs of roads and water projects.

Additional References

(This list is arranged in the same way as the QRL Key and Bibliography—i.e. publications with a named author are listed alphabetically by author first; other publications follow and are arranged alphabetically by title.)

[A 1] Butler, A. D. 'New price indices for construction output statistics', *Economic Trends*, No. 297, July 1978, pp. 97–110.

[A 2] Dunn, A. T. and White, G. C. 'Trends in sales of land and buildings 1973–7', *Economic Trends*, No. 305, March 1979, pp. 100–14.

[A 3] Fleming, M. C. 'Pricing in construction – the relationship of constants to productivity', *Building Technology and Management*, **16** (11), 1978, pp. 5–10.

[A 4] Lemessany, J. and Clapp, M. A. 'Resource inputs to construction: the labour requirements of house building', *Building Research Establishment Current Paper CP 76/78*, Building Research Establishment, Garston, Herts, 1978.

[A 5] Royal Institute of British Architects. *Architects' Employment and Earnings 1978*. RIBA, London, 1978.

[A 6] Office of Population Censuses and Surveys. *1971 Census, Income Follow-up Survey*. Studies on Medical and Population Subjects No. 38. HMSO, London, 1978.

[A 7] Department of the Environment. *Commercial and Industrial Property Statistics ... [year]*. HMSO, London, annually from 1978 (issue for 1977).

[A 8] Royal Institute of British Architects. *Costs and Profitability of Private Architectural Practice 1971–1977*. RIBA Statistics Section, London, 1978.

[A 9] Economic Development Committee for Civil Engineering. *Design and Export*. HMSO, London, 1978.

[A 10] Department of Manpower Services, Northern Ireland. *DMS Gazette*. The Department, Belfast. Planned as a bi-annual publication. Two issues have been published to date: No.1 Spring 1978 and No. 2 1979.

[A 11] Electrical Contractors' Association. *Electrical Contractors' Association State of Trade Enquiry ... [date]*. The Association, London, Quarterly from 1978.

[A 12] Department of Manpower Services, Northern Ireland. *Industrial Relations in Northern Ireland, Report of the Review Body 1971–74*. HMSO, Belfast, 1974.

[A 13] Building Business Unit. *Salaries and Benefits in Building Contracting.* Building Business Unit, London, 1979.
[A 14] Department of Education and Science. *Statistics of Education SS5 School Building Surveys 1975 and 1976.* HMSO, London, 1978.
[A 15] Royal Institute of British Architects. *Student Employment Survey.* RIBA, London, 1978.

INTRODUCTION

The potential scope of statistical information about construction is very wide. Construction work itself is extremely varied since the needs for such work arise in virtually every field of economic and social activity. These needs are widely dispersed geographically and are satisfied by a variety of different production enterprises, not all of which are readily classifiable as part of the construction 'industry', but which are important from the point of view of construction activity as such. The construction process itself is often a long one, proceeding through several distinct stages from the conception of a project to its physical completion on site, and makes large demands for labour with a wide variety of skills, both professional and other, and requires a highly varied input of materials drawn from many different industries. Thus a diverse range of subjects relating to the construction industry, construction activity or the construction process can be defined, all of which may require expression in numerical terms. Further, construction statistics may properly embrace information relating to the existing stock of buildings and works and the land on which they are located. At any one time most of the demand for construction facilities of one kind or another is satisfied by this stock, rather than current output. Indeed, a substantial part of current activity itself is commonly devoted to the repair, maintenance and improvement of the stock already in existence.

The scope of this Review, therefore, is not confined to the construction industry in a narrow sense but embraces all aspects of construction activity and the products which result from it with the exception of housing, which forms the subject of two separate *Reviews* covering Great Britain [B 52] and Northern Ireland [B 57] respectively, and road construction which is also to be covered in a separate *Review* [B 136]. Inevitably, however, there are certain areas of overlap between this Review and those; in the main these occur where housing and roads are integral parts of statistical series covering construction work more generally and cannot be separately distinguished, or where to exclude a reference to the housing and roads constituents would serve no useful purpose. All such references in this study may be traced through the detailed subject index.

Construction was not covered in the earlier series of reviews edited by Professor M. G. Kendall, *The Sources and Nature of the Statistics of the United Kingdom* [B 86], and has never been the subject of any other comprehensive study. In this Review, therefore, not only have the boundaries of the subject area been widely drawn, the objective has been to provide as comprehensive a guide as possible to all the statistical information that is available—but paying particularly close attention to the period since the Second World War and to data that are currently collected or compiled (only brief references are included to statistical sources for pre-war periods). This is coupled of course with the detailed appraisal of the nature and limitations of the data which represents one of the essential purposes of all the reviews in this series.

The coverage of the work extends to the United Kingdom and to information collected by both public and private agencies. Much of the statistical information about Northern Ireland is collected separately, and is dealt with separately wherever appropriate. Attention is also devoted to the statistical information available for Scotland, Wales and regions of England. Although, as indicated above, no comprehensive study of construction statistics has been made before, notice should be taken of a study sponsored by the Ministry of Public Building and Works in 1966 which resulted in the publication of an *Inventory* [B 262] and a *Directory* [B 213] of construction statistics. These were based on direct enquiries made of a large number of potential collecting agencies, both public and private, in Great Britain. The former describes the questionnaires which were in use by these agencies as at 30 June 1966, the ways in which the data obtained were collated, their availability and the place of publication, if any. The *Inventory* itself was not published for general circulation but was deposited in certain selected libraries (see the Bibliography for details). The *Directory* lists each collecting agency alphabetically, the type of information collected by each at the time of the survey and the source of publication; it also includes a subject index. These two works provide a useful source of reference but are limited inasmuch as they cover only such statistics as were being collected at that time and provide little or no evaluation of their nature and limitations. Further, information which was not the subject of an established collection process or which arose incidentally as part of some other activity or which was the result of calculation rather than collection (price indices, for example) was not covered.

The arrangement of material in this volume has been determined as far as possible by the general principle of considering the data available according to subject rather than source or collecting agency. Thus broad subject areas have been defined and each is considered in a separate chapter as far as possible. To have adhered to this arrangement in all cases, however, would have introduced the need for considerable repetition, for some of the principal statistical series are collected by the same agency as part of a single process so that the problems of collection and interpretation are essentially the same in each case. This is particularly true in the case of much of the information about the output, labour employed and structure of the industry collected, currently, by the Department of the Environment (DOE). These three subjects, consideration of which represents a major part of the whole work, are therefore treated together wherever necessary; otherwise they are sub-divided as much as possible so as to deal separately with series which relate solely to some aspect of labour or work done. To some extent, therefore, the arrangement of material is dictated by the nature of the data available. The work as a whole has been divided into four parts in order to achieve an orderly and comprehensible presentation of a very substantial body of detailed material. These are as follows:

    Part I   The Construction Industry
    Part II   Construction Materials, Plant and Equipment
    Part III The Construction Stock
    Part IV The Construction Professions.

A fifth part is devoted to desirable improvements and future developments.

A *Quick Reference List* (QRL) is included at the end of the main text to serve as a means of establishing quickly whether or not a particular category of data is available and where it is published. Each entry in the list is cross-referenced to the place in the main text where it is discussed. The detailed subject index also assists of course in tracing specific subjects.

The statistics discussed in this study are to be found scattered throughout a diversity of publications many of which are not readily accessible. Perhaps at this stage therefore a suitable reference may be made to three general collections of some of the data. Since much of the data collected by the Ministry of Works in the period before the mid-1950s remained unpublished or inaccessible a collection was compiled under the author's direction with the assistance of the DOE concurrently with the preparation of this Review and is now available under the title *Statistics Collected by the Ministry of Works 1941–56* [QRL 321]. In addition, the Building Research Station has published a *Collection of Construction Statistics* on two occasions: in 1968 [QRL 120] and in 1971 [QRL 121]. These brought together data available from a variety of other sources, often providing long runs of figures, and thus provided a convenient source of reference.

PART I

THE CONSTRUCTION INDUSTRY

CHAPTER 1

THE SCOPE AND ARRANGEMENT OF PART I

As we have explained in the Introduction, one of the general rules followed in this study is to consider the statistical information available according to subject rather than source. In principle, statistics relating to the production, labour and structure of the construction industry could be regarded as three separate subjects, but in fact the principal statistics on these subjects are so interconnected, since they have been and are still collected as part of the same collection process, that it is convenient and desirable to consider them together rather than separately. As a consequence some explanation about the arrangement of material is called for.

The statistical information on these subjects which has been collected in the past is extremely varied. The need to consider all of this information fully including all the changes made to it over the years and its limitations has necessitated the extended treatment to which the whole of Part I of this study is given over. The purpose of this introductory section is twofold. The first is to outline the scope of this part of the work and to explain the way in which all the material it contains has been arranged. The second is to provide an overall view of all the information later considered in detail.

The word 'production' is used to refer not only to statistics of the actual output of construction work both in monetary and physical terms, but also to statistics about work at earlier stages of the construction process from the letting of contracts onwards. Statistics about work at earlier, design, stages is considered separately (with one exception) in Part IV. The word 'labour' is also used in a wide sense to cover not only employment and various characteristics of the labour force but also related statistics about unemployment, vacancies, accidents, hours of work, wage rates, earnings, etc. Statistics about the professions related to construction, however, are considered separately in Part IV.

The term 'structure of the construction industry' is used to refer to the various constituent parts of the industry. It covers, therefore, all statistics which provide analyses of the composition of the industry in terms of the numbers, sizes and types of firms (and other organizations which carry out construction work—e.g. direct labour undertakings), and their relative importance in terms of output and employment. Much of the information about the structure of the industry is a by-product of surveys of output and employment and it is for this reason that the information on these matters is so interconnected as to make joint, rather than separate, treatment preferable.

Before the Second World War the only information about these matters collected as part of the same collection process was that obtained in periodic censuses of production taken by the Board of Trade which covered construction along with other industries. These censuses have continued to be taken right up to the present day. But during the

Second World War the Ministry of Works[1] (MOW) obtained powers to collect statistics about construction as part of its responsibilities for the control of construction work in connection with the prosecution of the war effort, powers which were used extensively both during and after the war.[2] Since the war the Ministry of Works and its successor Departments—the Ministry of Public Building and Works (MPBW) from July 1962 and the Department of the Environment (DOE) from November 1970—have continued, as the 'sponsoring' Department for the industry, to conduct regular statistical enquiries up to the present day.[3]

These enquiries provide the principal source of statistics about the construction industry in Great Britain and, when they were initiated, provided the first detailed statistics ever collected on a comprehensive basis. But though the Ministry of Works assumed *primary* responsibility for the collection of statistics about the construction industry and its activities, a responsibility which its successor Departments have retained, it did not assume *sole* responsibility. Other government departments retained responsibilities which were of long standing for the collection of labour and production statistics covering construction along with other industries. Thus for some subjects there is more than one source of information, whilst for others, although there may be only one source, the responsibility may or may not be that of the Ministry of Works and its successors.

This division of responsibilities raises some difficult problems in the reconciliation of differences between the ensuing statistical series; it also poses problems regarding the arrangement of this study in a way best fitted to meet the needs and convenience of its users. The solution adopted is to consider first all statistics collected by the MOW and its successors as a whole quite independently of those emanating from other sources. This method of treatment has the disadvantage that statistics on a specific subject may be examined at more than one place in the text. On the other hand it has the overriding advantage of permitting all the statistics collected by the MOW and its successors to be considered in a coherent context. It would seem advantageous in any case that the principal construction statistics—those collected by the MOW and its successors—should be considered as a whole rather than in piecemeal fashion.

A number of devices are adopted to overcome the disadvantage referred to above. the *Quick Reference List*, which is arranged strictly by subject, and the detailed *Subject Index* are the most important but these are supplemented by numerous cross-references in the text wherever appropriate.

The statistics collected by the MOW and its successors now comprise a very large volume of diverse and complex statistical information extending over a period of nearly forty years, much of which, especially that collected prior to 1955, had never been fully documented before. The analysis of this body of material has required lengthy investigation and demands a correspondingly lengthy examination here. The statistics themselves have not remained comparable over time but fall into two fairly distinct periods

---

[1] We refer to the Ministry as the 'Ministry of Works' throughout although prior to February 1943 its full title differed: from its establishment in October 1940 until June 1942 it was the Ministry of Works and Buildings and then, until February 1943, Ministry of Works and Planning.

[2] Interesting accounts of the control of building during and after the war are to be found in [B 19], [B 90] and [B 135].

[3] It is proposed that the functions of the Department of the Environment in this field will eventually pass to the Business Statistics Office (BSO).

with a break around 1954/5. Accordingly we consider the statistics available for these two periods separately.

The arrangement of this part of the work is therefore as follows. Two chapters, Chapters 3 and 4, are devoted to the statistics collected by the MOW and its successors. Two further chapters are then devoted to all other sources of production and labour statistics respectively for Great Britain. These are followed by two chapters on financial statistics and building costs, prices and productivity. Finally, a separate chapter is devoted to all statistical information about the production, labour and structure of the construction industry in Northern Ireland, most of which is collected separately by Departments of the Northern Ireland Administration. Most of the statistical information comes from official sources but our attention is not confined to official sources alone. Unofficial sources are also considered at appropriate places in the text according to the subjects covered—the main subject areas are *ad hoc* labour surveys, state of trade enquiries conducted by trade associations and price index numbers. As a preliminary to considering the statistics available certain more general problems of definition, collection and measurement are examined separately in Chapter 2.

CHAPTER 2

PRINCIPLES AND PROBLEMS OF DEFINITION, COLLECTION AND MEASUREMENT

This chapter is meant to provide a general background to all the other chapters in Part I of this Review which deal more specifically with the sources and nature of the statistics available about construction activity and the construction industry. The collection and interpretation of statistics in this field raises problems in a particularly acute form compared with most other fields of economic activity and an appreciation of these is necessary for an appreciation of much of the statistical data available. In essence these problems stem from the characteristics of construction work itself—both the process and the product—and of the production units by which it is carried out.

2.1 Principles and Problems of Definition: Construction Activity and the Construction Industry

The scope of construction activity is very wide. This is perhaps best conveyed by the definition employed in the International Standard Industrial Classification (ISIC) [B 261] which refers to the work of construction contractors as follows:

> '... General contractors may be engaged in constructing, altering, repairing and demolitioning (*sic*) buildings; constructing, altering and repairing highways and streets and bridges; viaducts, culverts, sewers, and water, gas and electricity mains; railway road-beds, subways, harbours and waterways; piers, airports and parking areas; dams, drainage, irrigation, flood-control and water-power projects and hydroelectric plants; pipelines; water-wells; athletic fields, golf courses, swimming pools and tennis courts; communication systems such as telephone and telegraph lines; marine construction, such as dredging and under-water rock removal; pile driving, land draining and reclamation; and other types of heavy construction. Businesses primarily engaged in performing mining services such as preparing and constructing mining sites and drilling crude oil and natural gas wells, on a contract or fee basis, are classified in this group.
>
> 'Special trade contractors are engaged in only part of the work of a construction project. Special trade contractors may work on sub-contract from the general contractor or directly for the owner. They may engage in such activities as plumbing, heating and air-conditioning installation; brick-laying, stone setting, tile setting, marble and stonework; carpentry; floor-laying; plastering and lathing; roofing; concrete work; painting and decorating; sheet metal and electrical work; water-well drilling; structural steel erection; excavating and foundation work; wrecking and demolition work; and repair and maintenance work on buildings ...
>
> 'The assembly and installation on the site of pre-fabricated, integral parts into bridges, water tanks, storage and warehouse facilities, railroad and elevated right-of-way, lift and escalator, plumbing, sprinkler, central heating, ventilating and air conditioning, lighting and electrical wiring, etc. systems of buildings and all kinds of structures, is a construction activity. Departments or other units of the manufacturers of the pre-fabricated parts and equipment which specialise in this work and which it is feasible to treat as separate establishments, as well as independent businesses primarily engaged in the activity, are classified in this group.'

The collection of statistics about such activities presents a major difficulty for, unlike most manufacturing activities, where the work is carried out by well-defined and recognizable production units, construction work is carried out by a variety of bodies including not only construction enterprises as such, but also industrial enterprises and other bodies whose main activity is not construction, by public bodies such as local authorities, and by building workers and other individuals acting in a private capacity as well as by individuals on their own account. Enterprises whose main activity is not construction, it may be noted, may carry out work not only on their own account but also under contract for other enterprises or persons. For these reasons a distinction has to be drawn between construction 'activity' and the construction 'industry'. The collection of statistics about the former is naturally a much more difficult task than the collection of data from organizations whose industrial classification can be predetermined on the basis of a well-defined set of principles. Unless the definition of the industry is drawn so wide as to embrace all construction activities, and the collection procedures so reliable as to ensure complete and accurate coverage, the two will not coincide.

Following international recommendations [B 260] the construction 'industry' will normally be narrower in scope than all construction activity. The international standard industrial classification, referred to above, is couched in terms of producing units and the Standard Industrial Classification (SIC) for the United Kingdom follows the principles, though not necessarily the details, of the international recommendation—a full analysis of the UK SIC is provided in Section 4.1.2 and Appendix I which reproduces the definitions employed in successive versions of the classification. Not all statistical enquiries, however, need be carried out on an industrial basis—'production' statistics, in particular, need not be so based (see Section 2.2). Furthermore it is important to appreciate with regard to construction in Great Britain that, despite the introduction of a standard industrial classification in 1948, the principal statistics—those collected by the then MOW—were *not* collected in accordance with it until the mid-1950s, unlike those for construction collected by other agencies. Until that time the MOW data were more comprehensive in terms of construction activity than the data collected from producers classified in accordance with the SIC—full particulars are given in Chapter 3.

2.2. Principles and Problems of Collection

2.2.1. *Methods of Collection*

As with other industrial statistics, statistics of 'production' may be collected either from the clients' or the producers' side of the transaction. The use of these methods should produce identical answers after due allowance is made for time lags between production and 'consumption' (i.e. in the case of construction, expenditure by building owners or occupiers)—including an allowance for stocks and 'work in progress'—and the incidence of taxes, such as VAT, on output or expenditure. Stocks are only of relevance to construction in the case of speculative development by builders—private housing in the main, but also possibly shop, office and warehouse development. Work in progress, on the other hand, is especially important in construction because of the length of time involved in many construction contracts.

Both types of collection method are used in the UK but no attempt is made to cover total construction activity comprehensively by collecting data from all building owners and occupiers. The principal production statistics are collected from the production side.

Labour statistics, by contrast, provide no such choice of collection method (if one disregards the possibility of regular censuses of population including questions on industry of employment, hours of work and earnings, etc.) and must needs be collected from producing units. The collection of data on this basis naturally requires the compilation and maintenance of a comprehensive register of such units.

2.2.2. *Registers of Producing Units*

The compilation of a register of construction enterprises poses two questions: how should its scope be defined and how can such a register be compiled and maintained?

2.2.2.1. *The scope of the register.* Enterprises whose primary activity is construction—the 'general' and 'special' trade contractors referred to in the ISIC quoted above—generally present no problem in terms of definition, although almost inevitably there are cases in practice where the precise position of the boundary between construction and non-construction trades is open to dispute. Shopfitting and roof thatching, both of which are examples of specialist activities currently excluded from the scope of the current UK SIC for construction, would be cases in point.

The inclusion or exclusion of off-site fabrication activities also gives rise to difficult demarcation decisions. The major problem, however, concerns the inclusion of all other, what may be termed by contrast, 'secondary' producers. The practices adopted in the UK at different times, and by different collecting agencies at the same time, have differed. The principles adopted in the SIC, first introduced in the UK in 1948, provide for the construction activities of firms whose primary activity is not construction to be classified to construction if such activities are carried on in units which can be regarded as separate 'establishments' (i.e. the smallest units able to provide the information normally required—e.g. output, employment, etc.). Conversely, non-construction activities carried on by firms whose primary activity is construction may, in principle, be classified separately under their appropriate industrial headings. Much depends, therefore, on the organizational arrangements made by firms for the conduct of such secondary activities and their ability to provide separate information in respect of them. Much depends too on the way the principles are applied in practice by the collecting agencies. The activity of private individuals working in their spare time, either on their own account or perhaps for others in a private capacity, is not within the scope of the SIC. We consider the details of the UK SIC more fully later in Section 4.1.2 and Appendix I.

2.2.2.2. *Register compilation and maintenance.* The compilation and maintenance of a comprehensive register of enterprises for construction itself presents severe difficulties because of the nature of the industry. The number of organizations involved is very large, most of them are very small and the population of firms is continually changing because of the ease with which it is possible to enter (and leave) the industry. It is insufficiently appreciated that simply in terms of numbers the scale of the registration problem for construction (and the consequential effort required in conducting enquiries) is comparable to that for the whole of manufacturing industry.[1] But the problem is intensified further in construction by the fact that the work is undertaken at particular sites and not at a fixed location, as in a factory, which means that there is not necessarily an identifiable 'establishment' from which to collect information: many builders do not operate from a recognizable business address and construction sites are necessarily temporary places of work.

The large number of small firms in the industry is partly due to the widespread practice of sub-contracting parts of the work both on normal 'supply-and-fix' and 'labour-only' bases, and this in itself adds to the difficulties of reliable data collection both on account of compiling a comprehensive register and in actually obtaining reliable returns (this point is discussed further below in the context of measurement). In recent years in Britain (since the 1960s at least) this aspect of the problem has itself been intensified because of the growth in the practice of sub-contracting on a labour-only basis to 'self-employed' gangs or individuals—colloquially referred to as the 'Lump' or, in some areas of the country, the 'Grip'. It is virtually impossible to ensure that such men are all covered on the register. This particular problem is also discussed in more detail later.

In interpreting the statistical information available, therefore, certain general questions need to be considered. These are first, whether it is construction 'activity' which is covered or the construction 'industry'; secondly, what limitations of coverage are imposed by the definitions of these terms, and thirdly what deficiencies, if any, arise in the coverage obtained *within* these definitions on account of an incomplete register or non-response, etc. Finally one needs to consider the nature and 'quality' of the data in terms of the questions asked on the questionnaires and the likely reliability of the returns obtained. The measurement of construction output, in particular, poses certain conceptual and practical problems and it is to these that we now turn our attention.

2.3. Principles and Problems of Measurement

2.3.1. *Output Measurement Principles*

The first question that arises is whether production or output (we use the terms synonymously) should be defined as contracts completed, i.e. structures ready for use or occupation, etc. (in which case some of the work would not be recorded for some considerable time after it was done because of the length of time that construction projects normally take) or as work actually carried out in a period (i.e. work put in place) regardless of whether the project is complete or not. The former is an easier figure to obtain inasmuch as it does not require partial valuations of jobs still under construction and might be considered more useful in the sense that the buildings, or other structures represented, would then be likely to be in 'productive' use as part of the nation's capital stock. On the other hand, such data would give rise to problems of

---

[1] The number of establishments in manufacturing industry in the UK reported in the BSO census of production results for 1972 (the latest summary results available at the time of writing—*Business Monitor PA 1002* [QRL 81] published in 1977) amounted to 87,000. The DOE register for construction in Great Britain recorded 71,000 firms at this time but was expanded to 97,000 firms in 1973 when 25,000 previously unrecorded firms were added to the register [QRL 240].

interpretation since the values recorded for each contract completed would be on varying time bases. Wider economic interest in the contribution made by the activity of the industry to total national output strengthens the claims of a definition based on work done during a specific period of time rather than contracts completed and such a definition is, in fact, the one adopted in UK construction output statistics.

The second question that has to be settled is how to treat the considerable volume of work that is done under sub-contract, for unless steps are taken to differentiate work done under main contract and work done under sub-contract then the aggregation of all returns will lead to an element of double-counting (or even multiple-counting—for work obtained under sub-contract may itself be further sub-contracted).

There are three possible ways of dealing with this difficulty. One is to require contractors to provide returns only of the value of work for which they have been physically responsible, i.e. the value of sub-contract work is returned only by the sub-contractor involved. This is the method used in Great Britain by the DOE and its predecessors. It naturally depends on a fully comprehensive register of contractors and sub-contractors.[2] A second solution, adopted by the Business Statistics Office (BSO) and its predecessors in census of production enquiries, is to require contractors to provide a return of all work done—both by them and for them (thus counting sub-contract work more than once)—but coupled with a separate return of the amounts paid to sub-contractors for work done. A third solution would be to require contractors to provide returns of the value of work done on contracts for which they are directly responsible to clients as principal contractors; these returns would cover their own work and work done for them by sub-contractors but not work done by them under sub-contract since this would be returned by the relevant main contractor in each case. This procedure, therefore, would provide statistics free of duplication directly but it has not been used in UK enquiries.

Regardless of the method adopted to avoid the multiple-counting of sub-contract work, the adoption of a definition which requires the return of the value of work done during a particular period itself raises a number of important considerations for the quality and interpretation of the data, for the returns may have to be made, to a greater or lesser extent, on the basis of estimates of the amount of work actually carried out on particular contracts during the relevant period. Much then depends on the methods used by contractors to make such estimates and on the nature of the guidance on the matter, if any, given in the questionnaires. We consider the details of the relevant output enquiries later: Chapters 3 and 4 and Section 5.3 for Great Britain or the UK and Section 9.2 for Northern Ireland. At this stage we merely note that the returns have left the method of estimation to the discretion of the contractor.[3] This being so, it is important to consider the methods that may be used and their reliability.

---

[2] Since mid-1974 the DOE have asked supplementary questions about the work done *for* them by sub-contractors and the work done *by* them as a sub-contractor—information which is used to estimate unrecorded output due to incomplete coverage of firms and a procedure which should also help to reduce the danger of mis-reporting.

[3] The phraseology used in the questions has not remained unchanged over time but, currently, returns obtained by the DOE require 'estimates of the amounts chargeable to your customers for ... work done' and returns obtained by the BSO in censuses of production for construction refer to: 'an appropriate proportion of the net contract price representing the value of work done ...'.

2.3.2. *Output Measurement and Valuation Practices*

In most cases in the UK (certainly for most new work other than private speculative building—mainly private housing) the builder receives regular (generally monthly) progress payments during the course of a contract based on valuation certificates. Valuations are based on measuring the work completed to date and a certificate is issued showing the amount due when agreement is reached between the client's consulting architect or engineer and the contractor. Actual payments to the builder are based on the valuation less a retention which does not become payable until after the contract has been completed. If these valuation certificates are used as the basis for making the return of output, they provide a firm basis for it albeit one which does not *necessarily* ensure accuracy (we return to this question below). If they are not used, then of course, the builder may use a variety of methods ranging from accurate assessment based on administrative records to those requiring no arithmetic of any kind, mental or otherwise!

The information available about contractors' practices in this respect is very scanty; as far as is known it is confined to that obtained in two investigations made by the MPBW in the late 1960s—one in 1968 when information was obtained from fifty firms and later when firms were interviewed in connection with an enquiry by Lady Lea into the relationship between the statistics of expenditure and output [B 92] (considered in Section 5.4.3). No official report of these investigations has been published but a summary of the findings has been provided by John Sugden, writing as an associate of Professor W. B. Reddaway in his Report on the *Effects of Selective Employment Tax* [B 127] pp. 263–6, in the course of a searching critique of the MPBW statistics at that time, and the account which follows is based on the account given there and in Lady Lea's unpublished report [B 92] which was made available to the author.

Briefly, about half of the firms based their estimates of the value of work done on valuation certificates issued for progress payments purposes. These are likely to be, as Sugden observes, the larger firms. Two-fifths of the firms in these enquiries based their estimates on costing systems and the final one-tenth used a variety of methods. Included amongst the latter were multiplication of the number of operatives employed by a typical output per head (the most common) and the reporting of some fraction of turnover for the last accounting year.

It is clear then, on the basis of these—somewhat limited—enquiries that valuation certificates provide the most common basis of estimation for *main* contractors. Although there appears to be no evidence available for earlier, or later, periods of time there would seem to be no reason to believe that this is not true for the whole of the period with which we are concerned in this Review—the period since the Second World War.

However, it does not follow that returns so based provide an accurate assessment of the work actually done during the period covered by the return. Evidence was collected in the enquiries that some firms based their returns not on the value certified but on the cash payments received (i.e. after the deduction of retention monies). In any one period, part of the cash payments received will, of course, represent the release of retention monies relating to work completed some considerable time in the past. Such monies are normally released in the period of six months following the end of a contract, but the period may be much longer particularly on civil engineering contracts, and, of course, the work on the contract itself, to which the value of the retentions are related, will have extended over a very much longer period. Similarly, part of the cash payments received in any period may relate to variations to the design or specification of work ordered after the letting of the contract: these may not be settled at the time the work is done but left until the contract is complete. On both these counts, therefore, returns based on cash payments received may introduce a timing error.

The significance of such a timing error will depend on the degree of stability in prices, the work-load and the time-lag itself: given stability the timing errors would tend to balance out in the aggregate but, given stability only in the time-lag before retentions and variations are paid, then in times of price inflation and/or rising work-loads, output would tend to be under-stated and vice versa. Shorter or longer time-lags, of course, would respectively reduce or increase the understatement.

Even if the return is based on the amounts certified, error is introduced in DOE-type returns if the contractor fails to deduct the value of work done by sub-contractors (this is included on the certificate *but not separately specified*).[4] Moreover it is common practice to include the value of materials delivered to site in valuation certificates even though they have not actually been used in the work at the time and strictly, therefore, adjustment is required on account of this factor as well if the certificates are to be used as measures of the work actually done. It may be noted too that a lack of coincidence in timing between the returns and the availability of certificates (due to delay in issue, etc.) may also demand that estimates should be made for at least part of the period covered.

Further, it is worth noting that the valuation of work done on contracts in a particular period may itself be affected by a number of other factors which are such that it is possible for widely varying valuations to be placed on comparable work. Valuations are based upon prices for the various elements of the work included in Bills of Quantities. For purposes of valuation, these prices may or may not be adjusted for changes in the costs of labour and/or materials that have occurred since the bill of quantities was prepared, depending on whether or not the contract includes appropriate fluctuation clauses. Contractors quoting at a fixed price, of course, will fix their rates in the light of their future price expectations and these will naturally vary from one contractor to another. Quite apart from this fact, the rates included in a Bill for particular parts of the work may bear little or no relation to the actual costs: they may be completely arbitrary, some rates being pitched at a high level for early parts of the work in order to inflate income during the early part of a contract and vice versa; the rates may or may not include appropriate allowances for overheads and profits; and finally the cost of 'preliminaries',[5] which may amount to as much as 15 per cent of total contract value, may not be recouped *pro rata* over all operations but left as a lump sum. In effect, these factors introduce further timing errors between the work done and the valuations made over the course of a contract.

As in the case of retentions and work variations, discussed above, these timing errors would tend to balance out over all contracts at any one time given stability in prices and the volume of work. But, as before, practices involving delays in payment naturally lead

[4] The fact should be recalled, however, that DOE returns have required separate information about sub-contract work since mid-1974.

[5] 'Preliminaries' are essentially expenses which are incidental to the execution of particular contracts—e.g. insurances, fencing, the provision of temporary roadways, site sheds, offices, canteen facilities, water supply, etc.

to an understatement of output values at times of rising volumes and prices and vice versa. On the other hand, pricing practices of the kind mentioned above, which involve accelerated payments, naturally tend, in the same circumstances, towards overstatement.

Thus, for the various reasons discussed in the preceding paragraphs, the use of valuation certificates as the basis for returns of work done does not necessarily produce a faultless way of obtaining a true valuation of the work actually done, in the sense of costing the resources actually used, during a particular period, especially when construction prices and the workload on the industry are subject to change.

Given the convenience of valuation certificates as a source of reference, it is not surprising that the investigations, referred to earlier, showed this to be the most common method used by the firms who were approached. Depending on the management and accounting systems used by firms, the use of costing records will normally be a much less convenient way of obtaining the necessary information. Arguably, however, it offers a more reliable method for it will more accurately reflect the actual value of work done during the appropriate period. It will not necessarily be exact because costing systems will rarely be precisely up-to-date for one thing and appropriate allowances may not always be made for office overheads (site overheads, of course, are more likely to be covered) and profits. Care is also still required in DOE-type returns (as with valuation certificates), to take out the value of payments to sub-contractors (although again in this connection it should be recalled that the DOE now require a separate return of sub-contract work). The investigations showed, however, that subcontract payments were not always excluded whilst, in the case of overheads and profit, some firms made no allowance and others added a standard percentage.

Over the whole construction period of any one contract the sum of the returns under either system—i.e. valuation certificates or costing records—should produce the same answer as long as a final adjustment is made to the sum of the costing returns to allow for any difference between the *actual* level of profits earned and the levels actually allowed in the earlier returns. It is only the inclusion of profits at an appropriate level (positive or negative) that ensures that the two series will be equated. The returns for any single period of time covering only part of a contract period, however, are almost certainly bound to differ. Quite apart from the profit element and slight differences in timing, the amounts are bound to differ because of the very nature of the tendering system which requires a price to be determined in advance of the execution of the work. For the reasons discussed earlier, the rates for particular operations inserted in the bill of quantities may differ quite markedly from the actual costs of performing the operations. Evidence collected by Lady Lea [B 92] (admittedly, on a limited number of cases) showed that, although the total costs for each project examined and the total of the valuations were the same, the average (weighted) quarterly difference between the valuation for monthly progress payments and the cost of the work (including a profit element) was nearly 50 per cent. In the early stages of contracts, valuations tend to exceed the value of work done.

Thus from the point of view of the aggregate statistics of output, even assuming no change in the use of one system as against the other by contractors in making their returns, this fact may mean that movements in the total values recorded for the economy as a whole may be biased at times of cyclical fluctuations in the level of demand. A downturn in activity, for instance, will not be faithfully reflected in the output figures: *other things being equal* a decline will be under-stated at first and over-stated later.

The other methods, used apparently by 10 per cent of the firms from whom enquiries were made, are much less accurate. The most popular method—multiplication of the number of employees by an output per man factor—can be applied at varying levels of sophistication but can at the best provide only approximate answers. The recording of a fraction of turnover in a previous period can naturally provide an accurate answer only by chance.

The discussion above has been couched very much in terms of main contractors and contracts for which regular stage payments are made. Sub-contractors may likewise use similar methods in making their returns. They, of course, rely on payments from the main contractor and in this case there is generally a longer time delay between the execution of the work and payment for it than in the case of main contractors' work, for the main contractor will generally await payment from the client before paying the sub-contractors. For contracts where progress payments are not made output must be returned on the basis of one of the other methods or not returned at all until the end of the contract.

Questions of valuation also arise in connection with the nature of the work and the enterprise carrying it out. Some work is carried out on a speculative basis, particularly in the private housing sector, for which there will be no contract price and for which the market price may not be known when the return is made. The value of such work must either be estimated on the basis of anticipated market value or returned at cost. In this case there is also the added danger that since the land on which the house stands is often sold together with the house, the value return may include the cost of land as well as the costs of construction. The valuation of work carried out by the building departments of public authorities and the works departments of firms whose main activity is not construction will generally not be on a comparable basis to that of contractors' since it will be valued on the basis of costs, not market prices; it is possible too, that it will not always reflect, in full, administrative overheads.

2.3.3. *Other Measurement Problems*

In comparison with the basic problems that have to be faced in the compilation and maintenance of a comprehensive register of construction enterprises, and the conceptual and practical difficulties that arise in the measurement and interpretation of output values, other problems appear of less significance. Perhaps of equal importance to output statistics are statistics of employment. But here the difficulties are mainly those of collection rather than of concept—the major problem is in ensuring comprehensive coverage, due especially over the last decade or two to the growth in the numbers of men working ostensibly as 'self-employed' under labour-only sub-contract; this, however, is only another aspect of the register problem to which we have already referred.

Another difficulty is in obtaining employment data on a comparable base to output data: the latter necessarily relate to work done over a period of time whilst, by contrast, employment data will normally represent a snap-shot at a point of time. There are good practical reasons for this given the nature of the industry and it may be of little moment in the aggregate at times of relatively stable levels of activity. But disaggregated analyses by type of work, trade of firm, etc. may conceivably be affected and, more important, at times of cyclical variation in activity the two series may move out of phase. And intra-year comparisons of output and employment may be affected by the uneven incidence of seasonal factors on the two sets of data.

Another general problem that afflicts construction in particular is the compilation of accurate regional statistics of construction activity given the fact that construction sites are necessarily temporary places of work: some series attempt to record actual work locations, some do not. The measurement of changes in the volume of output over time (the value of output at constant prices) also presents difficulties that are peculiarly severe in the case of construction because of the difficulties of devising satisfactory price deflators for construction work. These problems are more appropriately considered later in the context of particular enquiries and statistical sources and we devote no further attention to them here.

To conclude this introductory discussion of principles and problems of definition, collection and measurement, it may be said that there is no doubt that the problems which have to be faced in the collection of statistics for construction are in many ways more severe and intractable than those which have to be faced in most of manufacturing industry. As a consequence, construction is often an exception either in being excluded from the scope of general industrial enquiries and statistical series altogether, or in being excluded from the range of analyses made, or in presenting particular problems with regard to the interpretation of results. Thus general statements that are sometimes made about the availability and nature of industrial statistics in Great Britain or the United Kingdom often do not apply to the construction industry. These facts, of course, provide an additional reason to those given earlier for the lengthy examination devoted to the industry in this Review. We naturally consider these problems further as appropriate when examining the nature and limitations of particular sources. We would emphasize, at this stage, however, that the discussion of problems presented here is not meant to detract from the value of the statistics which have been collected. Its purpose is solely to provide a broad backcloth against which the large volume of data about the construction industry and construction activity, considered in detail in the rest of Part I of this Review, may be examined.

CHAPTER 3

STATISTICS COLLECTED BY THE MINISTRY OF WORKS 1941–54

3.1. Introduction

The regular collection of statistical data about the labour, output and organization of the industry began in the early years of the Second World War under powers given to the Ministry of Works in General Defence Regulations and was continued after the war under the same regulations until their revocation in the years 1953 and 1954. Subsequently enquiries were made under the legal authority of the *Statistics of Trade Act 1947*. A more substantive change, however, followed from a change in definitions resulting from the adoption by the Ministry of the definition of the industry ('Building and Contracting') laid down in the Standard Industrial Classification 1948 [B 329]—see Appendix I for details—which did not correspond with the definition used in the Defence Regulations. It is important to note, therefore, that although a Standard Industrial Classification was introduced in 1948, covering construction along with other industries, it did not apply to the principal construction statistics—those collected by the Ministry of Works—until the end of 1954.

The regulations for the control of building provided, in the first place, for the licensing of civil (i.e. private) building 'operations' and for the prior authorization of work for local authorities and public utility undertakings by the appropriate government department; work carried out directly on behalf of the Crown or a government department was also controlled, but by other machinery. In the second place, the regulations provided for the registration of contractors and other employers of building labour who could be, and were, compelled to make statistical returns to the Ministry. Consequently the statistical series available are broadly of two types, first those relating to the operation of controls over building work as such (work licensed or approved and also employment on contracts), and secondly those relating to registered employers and their activities (output and employment). As a preliminary to considering the available data, therefore, it is necessary to consider the nature of the building controls themselves.

3.2. The Building Controls 1940–54—Defence Regulations 56A and 56AB[1]

3.2.1. *The Control of Building Operations 1940–54*

The basis for the control of building work was Regulation 56A which was added to the General Defence Regulations in 1940[2] and came into force on 7 October. This

---
[1] A good deal of the background information in this section is drawn from Kohan [B 90].
[2] By SR & O 1940, No. 1678.

prohibited the carrying out of 'building or constructional operations' in the United Kingdom at a cost exceeding certain prescribed limits (originally £500, the limit was reduced to £100 from 14 April 1941) unless authorized by a specified government department or licensed by the Minister of Works. A 'building or constructional operation' was defined as:

> '... the construction, reconstruction or structural alteration of a building, of works of a kind required for the purpose of a public utility undertaking, or of any other fixed works of construction or civil engineering, including a road'.

The control was flexible inasmuch as financial limits could be altered (they were originally fixed in the regulation but later made variable by the Minister by Order) but it was too narrow for the purpose of controlling all inessential works since it did not cover work on demolition, repair, decoration or the protection of premises against hostile attack. Such work was brought under control by a new regulation, in substitution of the original 56A, which came into force on 1 January 1942.[3] Work required for 'the purpose of providing water, light, heating or other services for a building' was also added to the definition above. The new regulation ensured not only that no single *operation* of more than £100 was carried out without licence, but also limited to an expenditure of £100 the amount of building work of all kinds that might be done on a single *property* (initially defined as a Schedule A unit or a rating valuation unit but later extended to *all* property)[4] in any period of twelve months. This distinction between specific operations and work on a 'property' was retained until 1 July 1945[5] when a general prohibition on the carrying out of building and civil engineering work without a licence or authorization was substituted.

The position of maintenance under the new Regulation, as Kohan [B 90] notes, was a source of difficulty. It was not defined as an operation for which a licence was required in the Regulation but since it was important to ensure that no work was carried out under cover of maintenance which should properly be licensed, the practice was adopted of granting annual maintenance licences, as distinct from 'operational' licences for specific jobs, which merely imposed a limit on the amount which could be spent during a period of twelve months. There was no definition of maintenance in the regulation, and for administrative purposes the Ministry drew up its own working definition (see Kohan [B 90] Appendix IX). Decoration, it should be noted, was not interpreted as maintenance, except when it was incidental to an item of maintenance work, but was classed as an operation for which a separate licence was required.

Regulation 56A remained in force until 10 November 1954. Details of the changes made from time to time in the financial exemption limits, important for interpreting the licensing statistics, are given in Section 3.7.

3.2.2. *The Control of Building and Civil Engineering Contracting Undertakings 1941–53*

Provision for the control of building and civil engineering contracting undertakings was made by Regulation 56AB, which was added to the General Defence Regulations in

---

[3] SR & O 1941, No. 1596.
[4] Extended with effect from 1 August 1945 by SR & O 1945, No. 802 and subsequent Orders.
[5] SR & O 1945, No. 502.

July 1941.[6] It applied to the whole of the United Kingdom but was administered separately in Northern Ireland. The Regulation did two things of importance from the point of view of this study. First it provided that no person could carry out any work in the course of such undertakings after a certain date[7] unless holding a certificate of registration issued by the Minister of Works; it thus led to the compilation for the first time of a comprehensive register of firms doing building and civil engineering work. Secondly it empowered the Minister of Works to make Orders requiring persons employing labour in any of the *activities* covered by the Regulation (see below) to keep such records, to make such returns and to produce such documents and furnish such information in regard to these activities as he may direct.

Building and civil engineering contracting undertakings were defined as undertakings 'consisting wholly or mainly in the carrying on of any of the following activities' together with the carrying out, in conjunction with these activities, 'of any processes, operations or manufactures' incidental to the carrying on of any of the said activities:

(1) 'the construction, alteration, repair, decoration or demolition of buildings';
(2) 'the construction, alteration, repair or demolition of docks, harbours, bridges, roads, viaducts, aqueducts, canals, inland navigations, pipe lines, plant foundations, cooling towers and ponds, cable trenches, cableducts, railways, aerodromes, sea defences, river works, piers, quays, wharves, reservoirs, filter beds, sewage works, sewers, tunnels and gasholders, the erection of overhead line supports, and any works of a similar nature'.

An amendment made in 1944[8] expressly added the provision of water, lighting, heating and other services in connection with building or civil engineering works to the definition above, although as regards practice it would seem that this was more by way of clarification than a substantive change in the scope of the definition.

It should also be noted that a direct labour department of a local authority or public utility undertaking was counted as a building and civil engineering contracting undertaking. But in the case of other organizations (e.g. in manufacturing or distribution) a direct labour department did not need to be registered unless it carried out work under contract for persons outside the organization; originally registration was required if it was 'wholly or mainly' so engaged but in the amended Regulation the scope was widened to 'any' such work.

All building and civil engineering contracting undertakings were required to register in accordance with the Regulation by 1 September 1941. Announcements about the requirement were made in the Press and, it is believed, were broadcast by the BBC.[9]

Some firms registered, it is thought, in order to register their trade name although they were not in business at the time. The Regulation itself was not designed to act as an instrument of control over entry to the industry and it did not provide for the registration of new firms set up after 1 October 1941, but in practice, until the Regulation was amended on 29 June 1944, registration was only granted to applicants who had previously been in business in the industry. Under the amended Regulation, a certificate of registration was granted as a right to any person who had carried on a building or civil engineering business at any time between 1 May 1939 and 1 October 1941, or who had

---

[6] SR & O 1941, No. 1038.
[7] Fixed as 1 October 1941 by SR & O 1941, No. 1162.
[8] SR & O 1944, No. 745 made on 29 June 1944.
[9] Applicants for registration had to obtain the necessary forms (BCE2 and BCE3) from a local office of the MOLNS. Form BCE3 (a specimen copy of which is reproduced in Appendix IV) required a return of employment and output in July and constituted the first census return—see Section 3.3.

acquired or revived a business that at any time had been registered. In addition, the Minister was empowered to issue a certificate of registration if it appeared to him expedient and in the public interest. Control over entry ceased from 21 March 1946: an undertaking had been given to the House of Commons on 6 July 1944 by the Parliamentary Secretary to the Minister of Works that there would be no restriction on the number of firms entering the industry once the labour force had reached 75 per cent of its pre-war size but, in fact, the actual date of decontrol was brought forward after a review of the regulations carried out at the end of 1945.

Apart from securing the registration of contractors and compelling the provision of information, the Regulation was also aimed at preventing excessive overtime and securing the observation of terms and conditions of employment neither more nor less favourable than those fixed by joint agreement in the industry. But with effect from 26 July 1947 these provisions were cancelled so that after this date the regulation remained solely as the basis for registration and the collection of statistical information until it was revoked on 22 November 1953.

The powers conferred by the Regulation were used to take six censuses of registered undertakings at irregular intervals in the period 1941–4, and some twenty-two censuses at regular intervals, at first quarterly and then annually, in the period 1945–53. A further census was taken in May 1954 on the basis of what may be called the '56AB Register' but using the legal powers conferred by the *Statistics of Trade Act 1947*. We consider the information collected in these censuses in Sections 3.3–3.6 below and provide a summary history and specimen questionnaires in Appendices IV and V. Apart from census returns the register was also used, though in a limited way, as the base for sample enquiries from late 1945—these are considered in Sections 3.8 and 3.9 and in Appendix VII. Details of the statistics available about registration itself are contained in Section 3.7 (Sub-section 3.7.5) along with information about the statistics relating to the operation of the other building controls.

3.3. Censuses of Contractors in Great Britain 1941–4

3.3.1. *Introduction*

The first census was taken, as we described earlier (Section 3.2.2), at the same time as compulsory registration when firms were also required to make a return of employment and output in the previous July.[10] Further censuses were taken at intervals throughout the war, not with any regular frequency but apparently as the need for up-to-date census information arose. The data available are considered below and a summary history of the enquiries, together with selected specimen questionnaires, is included in Appendix IV.

At this stage two matters must be emphasized. The first is that very little of the data collected has in fact been published and the following paragraphs provide a guide to the

---

[10] An earlier attempt had been made, in February 1941, to obtain returns from contractors on a voluntary basis giving information regarding operatives directly and indirectly employed by each firm, classified into twenty-two different occupations, and the number of clerical and administrative workers employed, together with particulars of any government or civil contracts on which they were engaged at the time. The detailed results do not appear to be available now, but total employment figures for contractors and for direct labour (separately) are given in Kohan [B 90], p. 95.

statistics known to be available either in a published or otherwise accessible source. A collection of these statistics together with some from MOW files (now held by the DOE) was compiled by the author, with the assistance of the DOE, concurrently with the preparation of this text under the title *Statistics Collected by the Ministry of Works 1941–56* [QRL 321] and is available from the DOE. It remains possible, however, that other analyses may survive undetected in Ministry files. The other matter is that virtually all of the data that appear to be available represent only part of the data known to have been collected. Virtually no data are available for direct labour organizations (see Section 3.4) and little for certain specialist trades of building and civil engineering contractors (see Section 3.3.4) even though they were included in the censuses. Most of the information now available relates to contractors in so-called 'main trades' only. The reason for restricting the analysis of the census data in this way would appear to be that the coverage this gave was one which most closely corresponded to the definition of the industry ('Building and Public Works Contracting') employed by the Ministry of Labour (MOL) in their statistics (for details of these at this period see the official *Guide* [B 241] and, for data, the *British Labour Statistics. Historical Abstract* [QRL 58]—we consider MOL data in this Review only for the post-war period.

3.3.2. *The 'Main Trades' and 'Specialist Trades' Contractors*

Originally the 'main trades' group consisted of twelve 'trades', one of which was a miscellaneous group, and were commonly referred to as the '12 Trades'. Later (after the war) an additional trade, shopfitters, was distinguished, making thirteen trades in all (the '13 Trades'). The composition of this group is set out below. The firms not included in the main trades were the so-called '7 Trades' or 'Specialist Trades' also shown below.

The 'Main Trades' ('13 Trades')
(1) General Builders
(2) Building and Civil Engineering Contractors
(3) Civil Engineering Contractors
(4) Plumbing Contractors
(5) Joinery and Carpentry firms
(6) Painting Contractors
(7) Roofing Contractors
(8) Plastering Contractors
(9) Glazing Contractors
(10) Demolition Contractors
(11) Scaffolding Specialists
(12) Shopfitters
(13) Miscellaneous

The 'Specialist Trades' ('7 Trades')
(1) Constructional Engineers
(2) Reinforced Concrete Specialists
(3) Heating and Ventilating Engineers
(4) Electrical Contractors

Table 3.1
MOW Construction Census Analyses 1941–4. Contractors—Main Trades Only[a] (Great Britain)
(A cross (×) signifies the availability of data)

CENSUS		NUMBER OF FIRMS			EMPLOYMENT										CLERICAL AND ADMINISTRATIVE[b]			OUTPUT (VALUE)		
					OPERATIVES															
								Totals	By Occupation			By Type of Work								
Date	Form Reference	By Trade of Firm	By Size of Firm	By Region	By Trade[c] of Firm	By Size[c] of Firm	By Region	Totals	By Trade of Firm	By Size of Firm	By Region	By Trade of Firm	By Size of Firm	By Region	By Trade of Firm	By Size of Firm	By Region	By Trade of Firm	By Size of Firm	By Region
1941 July	BCE 3		×		×(f)	×(f)						Data not requested				×		Data was requested		
1942 Jan	BCE 3A	×	×		×(f)	×(f)		×(f)				Data not requested				×		Data not requested		
May	BCE 3B	×	×		×(f)	×(f)		×(f)	×	×		×	×			Data not requested		Data not requested		
Nov	BCE 3C[e]	×(f)	×(f)		×(f)	×(f)		×(f)	×	×		×	×		×(f)	×(f)		×(f)	×(f)	
1943 Oct	BCE 3D[e]	×(f)	×(f)	×	×(f)	×(f)	×	×(f)				×	×	×	×(f)	×(f)		×(f)	×(f)	
1944 Jun[d]	—[e]	×	×	×	×	×		×	×	×	×	×	×	×	×(f)	×(f)	×	×(f)	×(f)	×
Nov	BCE 3E[e]	×	×	×	×	×	×	×	×	×	×	×	×	×	×	×	×	×	×	×

PUBLICATION SOURCES. A collection of the analyses indicated in this table has been compiled under the author's direction with the assistance of the DOE under the title *Statistics Collected by the Ministry of Works 1941–56* [QRL 321]. None of the census results appear to have been published at the time: some were included in a *Statistical Bulletin* [QRL 318] which was prepared for use within the MOW during the war, some were published after the war in [QRL 320]—see footnote (f) below. The *Collection* [QRL 321] referred to above includes these and other, unpublished, tables except those for the special voluntary census in June 1944, for which see Section 3.3.5.

(a) The 'specialist' trades and direct labour organizations are considered in Sections 3.3.4 and 3.4 respectively.
(b) Males and females in July 1941 and January 1942, subsequently males only (referred to as 'male clericals').
(c) Divided between 'craftsmen' and 'labourers' (or 'other operatives') only in the censuses from January 1942 to October 1943—see Section 3.3.3 below regarding definitions.
(d) Special voluntary census (see Section 3.3.5 below). Special London censuses were taken in October 1944 and January 1945 (see Section 3.3.5).
(e) Questionnaires not examined for the purposes of this study since no surviving copies have been traced.
(f) Published in *Statistical Tables Relating to the Building and Civil Engineering Industries in War-time* [QRL 320].

(5) Asphalt and Tar-sprayers
(6) Plant Hiring
(7) Flooring Contractors

The use of the term 'specialist trades' is a potential source of confusion. At times, particularly after the war, the term was used to refer to the 'seven trades'. But at other times the term 'specialists' was used to refer to those firms in the main trades group other than the general builders and contractors which comprise items 1–3.

The terminology used in referring to the 'Industry', as such, also serves as a source of confusion since it was not used consistently. The expression 'Building and Civil Engineering Industry' was generally meant to refer to the main trades, and the expression 'Building and Civil Engineering Industries' to embrace the 'seven trades' in addition. However, in a booklet of war-time statistics published after the war [QRL 320] the Ministry uses the expression 'Building and Civil Engineering Industries' in the title but in fact covers the main trades only. These expressions therefore cannot be taken at their face value and particular care needs to be taken to verify the scope of any particular set of data. Where there is any doubt, however, the likelihood is that the data refer to the main trades alone.

3.3.3. *Censuses of the Main Trades and Their Interpretation*

Details of the principal statistics available from the war-time censuses of the 'main trades' are set out in Table 3.1 Details of the statistics available for the 'specialist trades' are given in Section 3.3.4 below and for certain additional enquiries in Section 3.3.5. Since most of the statistics for this period remained unpublished a collection has been compiled by the author, under the title *Collection of Ministry of Works' Statistics 1941–56* [QRL 321] and is available from the Department of the Environment.

There are difficulties confronting the use and interpretation of the available data. Very little information now appears to be available about the reliability of the censuses, so that comment at this distance of time regarding the interpretation of the data must be based to some extent on conjecture. Certain inferences, however, may be drawn through an examination of the questionnaires used and the nature of the guidance given to those completing them; the guidance given is in fact very limited—we note the main definitions or instructions below in discussing the available analyses (see also Appendix IV). Further information may be gleaned by examining the available tabulations of the data themselves. One general matter affecting all enquiries of course is the problem of non-response. It is clear from an examination of the tabulations produced that no adjustments were normally made to allow for non-response—the analyses often refer to 'the number of firms making returns'—so that this needs to be borne in mind in comparing and interpreting most or all of the census analyses.

3.3.3.1. *The labour returns—Operatives.* The censuses were mainly concerned with the collection of information about labour, particularly operatives. The first census asked for the number of 'males over 16 years of age employed ... on building and/or civil engineering work' whereas subsequent censuses asked for those 'on the pay-roll'. The latter is more all-embracing; the former is open to different interpretations, in particular it could well exclude operatives employed in stores or canteens, in the fabrication of components off-site in a builder's yard or work-shop, transport workers, etc. The intended treatment of those away from work sick or on holiday, etc. is not clear but one would presume that they were meant to be included. The reason for restricting the age to 'over 16 years', given that the school-leaving age at this time was 14 years, is also not clear. The most likely explanation would seem to be that it was intended to ensure comparability with the Ministry of Labour's statistics of insured employees on the basis of which a time series with a coverage of 'persons aged 16–64' was available, even though the scope of the unemployment insurance legislation had been lowered to cover persons under the age of 16 many years previously and statistics of insured persons under the age of 16 were also available. Even so, however, there remains a discrepancy between the MOL data and the MOW data in that no upper age limit was specified in the MOW's coverage of operatives. The MOW's lower age limit remained unchanged until November 1954 (Section 4.2.3.3 refers).

The returns of labour obtained in the first census are particularly open to doubt; it is thought that some of those returned as administrative and clerical workers in the second census were returned as operatives in the first since the number of operatives fell between the two censuses but the number of administrative and clerical workers rose (it is suggested that some of the smaller firms may have classed sons or other working partners of the firms as operatives originally but non-operatives subsequently).

Operatives by occupation. The occupations of operatives for which information was generally obtained were as follows:

(1) Carpenters and Joiners
(2) Bricklayers
(3) Slaters and Tilers
(4) Plasterers
(5) Painters
(6) Plumbers and Glaziers
(7) Electricians
(8) Fitters (Heating, Ventilating and Domestic Engineering)
(9) Builders' Labourers
(10) Navvies
(11) All other occupations (except Administrative and Clerical)

The first six and the first eight of these occupations were sometimes referred to as the 'six crafts' or the 'eight crafts' respectively. Some tabulations provided total figures of 'craftsmen' and 'labourers', although the latter was a misnomer inasmuch as it generally covered 'all other occupations' as well as labourers and navvies. In the first census, however, a distinction was made between only two occupational categories, namely 'craftsmen and foremen' and 'others'. In the second census (January 1942) the number of operative categories was expanded to the eleven shown above. (Contractors were also asked to distinguish between operatives aged under 41 and those 41 years of age and over in this census but separate statistics are not included in the sources to which we refer.)

Clerical and administrative staff. The statistics for clerical and administrative staff refer to those insurable against unemployment; at this time non-manual workers earning more than £420 a year were not covered by the national insurance scheme and neither were women aged 60–64. It is not clear whether professional and technical workers were meant to be included in this category nor whether a proprietor or partner who also engaged in manual work (a working principal) was expected to classify himself as an operative or clerical and administrative worker or neither. Tabulations of the results often covered males only and referred to them as 'male clericals' though both administrative and clerical workers were covered (a distinction was made between male and female staff, but not between administrative and clerical workers in the census questionnaires).

3.3.3.2. *Output.* The analyses of output provide a figure of the value of work done in one month. Each contractor was required to return the estimated total value of building and/or civil engineering work done in a particular month including repair and maintenance work. Main contractors were instructed not to include the value of work done for them by sub-contractors in order to avoid double counting such work. It will be appreciated that apart from the problem of non-response there are two potential sources of error in the statistics, one arising from the need to make estimates of the value of work actually done in the month in question and the other arising from the fact that some contractors may not exclude the value of all sub-contracted work—see the discussion in Section 2.3.

3.3.3.3. *Classification by trade and size of firm and region.* It was common to tabulate the results according to trade, size and regional location of firms (location of head office) but it is not clear whether this was regularly done. Certainly practice was not consistent with regard to the tabulations included in the *Statistical Bulletin* [QRL 318]. The results for any one census tended to be reproduced piecemeal over time in different *Bulletins* and some appeared in a published source without appearing in a *Bulletin* at all. Table 3.1, therefore, represents a guide to the analyses *known to be available.*

Analyses by trade of firm. The trades actually distinguished in the analyses by trade of firm were those numbered 1–6 in the 'thirteen trades' group together with a miscellaneous category consisting of all others in the group. Trade classifications were not obtained in each census. The analyses of returns by trade of firm, therefore, are based on the trade description provided by the firm upon initial registration. It was left to each firm to classify itself; no guidance appears to have been given about the way in which firms engaged in more than one kind of trade activity should classify themselves. The intention seems to have been, however, that such firms should classify themselves according to their main activity as indicated by the major part of their turnover. It is perhaps relevant to point out at this stage that a large number of clerks were employed by the Ministry, both at its headquarters in London and in regional offices, dealing with queries both by letter and telephone. At the same time it is well to bear in mind that the scale of the census was very large, involving over 80,000 firms.

Analyses by size of firm. Size of firm was defined according to the number of operatives employed. Firms employing no operatives, however, that is to say firms which consisted of the proprietor only at the time of the census, were excluded from the analyses. The number of such firms is generally recorded, but not the value of work done (when asked for) nor the number of clerical and administrative staff employed. It will be appreciated that these firms could be responsible for work done not only by the proprietor himself working alone but also by operatives who were employed at some time during the month but not on the pay-day to which the return related.

Analyses by region. Regional analyses were based upon the regional location of the firm's head office (or the location of the 'reporting unit' if a firm did not submit a single return through its head office). It will be appreciated that regional classifications on this basis do not necessarily coincide with the regional locations of a firm's labour force and output. In contrast the censuses taken in the early post-war years (1945–54) required firms to indicate the regional locations of their labour force (see Section 3.5). Definitions of the regions used for classifying the data, 'Civil Defence Regions', are given in Appendix II.

3.3.3.4. *Miscellaneous analyses of the censuses of the main trades.* In addition to the general analyses of the war-time censuses two specific *ad hoc* analyses are worthy of note:

(1) *Comparison of returns from an identical group of firms* (*Statistical Bulletin* [QRL 318] No. 27): a comparison of the returns made, in each census from July 1941 to October 1943, by that group of firms (976 in number) which in July 1941 employed 100 or more operatives. The total operatives employed are shown according to each of the twelve trades together with changes in the average size of firms in each group.
(2) *Firms registered in Scotland* (*Statistical Bulletin* [QRL 318] No. 31): a comparison for all censuses, except January 1942, of the number of firms in the main trades registered in Scotland and the number of operatives employed by them (not necessarily in Scotland) together with an analysis of operatives employed in November 1944 according to type of work.

3.3.4. *Censuses of the Specialist Trades*

Although the specialist trades (as defined in Section 3.3.2 above) were covered in the censuses, no statistics were included in the *Statistical Bulletin* [QRL 318] and none appear to have been published. The only data it has been possible to trace were included by the Ministry of Works in unpublished *Evidence* which it presented to the official 'Building Industry Working Party' in 1948 [B 226]. These are included in the *Collection of MOW Statistics* [QRL 321] compiled by the author as follows:

Analysis	*Censuses*
Number of firms analysed by trade	Nov. 1942, Oct. 1943, Nov. 1944
Operatives employed by occupation	Nov. 1942, Nov. 1944

3.3.5. *Special Censuses of Labour Resources, 1944 and 1945*

Three special labour censuses were taken in 1944 and 1945. In June 1944 all firms were asked to make returns on a voluntary basis of the number of operatives employed. The return was incomplete, coverage in the twelve main trades falling short, it is estimated, by 16.5 per cent of operatives employed. Tabulations (as indicated in Table 3.1)—for the twelve main trades only—were included in *Statistical Bulletin* [QRL 318] Nos. 22 and 24. The other two censuses were confined to London. In October 1944 and again in January 1945, a census was taken of labour employed in London by firms registered in the London area (as defined). Analyses of employment by type of work, and estimates of the total building and civil engineering labour force (both contractors and direct labour) by type or work and type of employer at both census dates are to be found in the *Statistical Bulletin* [QRL 318] Nos. 24 and 28.

3.4. Censuses of Direct Labour Organizations in Great Britain 1941–4

The term 'direct labour' is generally applied to the building and civil engineering operatives employed directly on building and civil engineering work by government departments, local authorities and other public authorities including in particular, public utility undertakings. Very little information of any kind, however, is now available about the enquiries relating to direct labour made during the war-time period and the only statistical data available come from censuses of local authorities taken in September 1943 (apparently the first enquiry—[QRL 132] refers) and November 1944. The data for September 1943 provide an analysis of the number of operatives employed by occupation of operative by five types of work; the number of registered local authorities making returns, sub-divided between those with and without operatives, and the total number of operatives, together with some later comparative figures, were also reported in [QRL 132]. The analysis for November 1944 is considered in Section 3.6 along with the data collected in the early post-war censuses since the tabulations available (see Table 3.4 for details) follow the pattern set then.

Direct labour of non-construction firms. Some private firms in industries other than building and civil engineering also employ their own direct labour force. The registration requirement only extended to the building departments of such firms if they carried out work under contract for persons outside the organization of which it formed part (see Section 3.2.2), and in these cases such departments were treated as contractors. But although firms employing direct labour on their own premises alone were not required to register, the Ministry did have power to 'require returns to be made' by Order and such an Order was made in October 1941 requiring persons employing labour in building and civil engineering activities, *other than those required to register*, to make a return of employment and output.[11] Since there was no register of such firms the onus was placed on the firms themselves to obtain a copy of the return (Form BCE4)

---

[11] SR & O 1941, No. 1642. Particulars were required by 22 November 1941 of: 'Number of males over 16 employed on building or civil engineering work (including repairs, maintenance and jobbing) on the last pay day in October 1941'; 'Approximate value of b. or c.e. work done by building departments or repair staffs in October 1941'; and 'Trade description of main business.' The submission date was extended to 2 December by SR & O 1941, No. 1848.

from a local office of the MOLNS. Returns were made by some 8,000 undertakings, but it is thought that many firms failed to respond and, so far as can be ascertained, the data were not published. Data were included by the MOW, however, in its unpublished evidence submitted to the Building Industry Working Party in 1948 showing the number of returns and operatives employed by industry and these have now been reproduced in the *Collection of MOW Statistics 1941–56* [QRL 321]. After the war, it may be noted, estimates of the value of work for which private direct labour forces were responsible were given for a short while in output time series published in the *MDS* [QRL 195]—see Table 3.7.

3.5. Censuses of Contractors in Great Britain 1945–54

3.5.1. *Introduction*

In the post-war period up to 1954 censuses of contractors' output and employment were taken on a regular quarterly basis between May 1945 and August 1949, each February, May, August and November, and then annually in May each year from 1950 to 1954—twenty-three censuses in all. These censuses provided the basis for analyses of the industry according to a number of structural characteristics. In this section we review only the nature of these enquiries and the available analyses of them; the data on output and employment in the industry which are published as time series are only partly based on these enquiries and we consider those series separately below in Sections 3.8 and 3.9.

3.5.2. *Interpretation*

The purpose of this section is to sound a note of caution for it would be unwise to accept the census statistics uncritically at their face value. The central problem of interpretation, as with all enquiries of this kind (whether sample or census based), concerns the accuracy of the data collected. It is not suggested that these statistics are necessarily less reliable than other economic statistics of the time, although it is well to bear in mind the nature of the problems involved in collecting accurate and comprehensive data for construction which were considered at length in Chapter 2.

Inaccuracy may arise in different enquiries for a variety of reasons ranging from non-response, failure by respondents to complete the return accurately and differences in the interpretation of questions and instructions. In addition detailed revisions to the questionnaires themselves from one census to the next may have produced discontinuities for particular categories of data. Any appraisal of these matters must necessarily be based to a large degree on judgement and is certainly best made by those concerned with the collection and contemporary use of the data. The outsider speculating some twenty to thirty years later is inevitably at a disadvantage, although hindsight is sometimes beneficial. Unfortunately there is little or no contemporary evaluation of this kind available. In this connection it is important to remember that the censuses were conducted to collect statistics for administrative purposes and little or none of the data were published. As a consequence information of relevance for the interpretation of each census was perhaps less likely to be recorded systematically and is certainly

Table 3.2
MOW Construction Census Analyses 1945–54. Contractors—Main Trades Only(a) (Great Britain)
(The analyses available are signified by a cross (×) or by a publication reference—all have now been collected together in [QRL 321]—see below under 'Publication Sources')

CENSUS		NUMBER OF FIRMS					NUMBER OF OPERATIVES EMPLOYED(b)											
										By Occupation (Craft)						By Type of Work		
Date	Form Reference	By Size of Firm	By Size of Firm and Region	By Trade of Firm	By Trade of Firm and Region	By Region	By Size of Firm	By Trade of Firm	By Region	Totals	Apprentices	By Type of Work	By Size of Firm	By Trade of Firm	By Region	Totals	By Size of Firm	By Trade of Firm	By Region
1945 May	BCE3/QR1	[QRL 335] [B 314]		[B 314] [B 349]		×	[QRL 335] [B 314]	[B 314]		×		×(d)		×	×(d)				×(d)
Aug	BCE3/QR2	×		×			×	×		×		×(d)		×	×(d)		×	×	×(d)
Nov	BCE3/QR3(c)	[QRL 335]		×		×	[QRL 335]	×	×	×		×(d)	×	×	×(d)		×	×	×(d)
1946 Feb	BCE3/QR4	×		×		×	×	×	×	×			×	×	×(d)		×	×	×(d)
May	BCE3/QR5	[QRL 335]		×			[QRL 335]	×	×	×			×	×	n.r.		×	×	×
Aug	BCE3/QR6	×		×			×	×		×			×	×	×		×	×	n.r.
Nov	BCE3/QR7	[QRL 335]		×			[QRL 335]	×		×		↑	×	×	↑	×	×	×	×
1947 Feb	BCE3/QR8(c)									×									
May	BCE3/QR9	[QRL 336]		[B 349]			[QRL 336]	×	×	×		Data not requested in questionnaires examined	×	×	Data not requested in questionnaires examined		×	×	×
Aug	BCE3/QR10(c)			×				×		×			×	×			×	×	×
Nov	BCE3/QR11	[QRL 336]		×			[QRL 336]			×			×	×			×	×	×
1948 Feb	BCE3/QR12	[B 314]		[B 314]			[B 314]	[B 314]	×	×			×	×			×	×	×
May	BCE3/QR13(c)	[QRL 337]					[QRL 337]			×			×	×			×	×	×
Aug	BCE3/QR14(c)									×									
Nov	BCE3/QR15	[QRL 337]					[QRL 337]			×			×	×			×	×	×
1949 Feb	BCE3/QR16(c)									×			×	×			×	×	×
May	BCE3/QR17(c)	[QRL 37]		[B 349]			[QRL 37]			×			×	×			×	×	×
Aug	BCE3/QR18	[QRL 37]			[QRL 37]		[QRL 37]			[QRL 37]	[QRL 37]		×	×			×	×	×
1950 May	BCE3/QR19	[QRL 38]			[QRL 38]		[QRL 38]			[QRL 38]	[QRL 38]		×	×			×	×	×
1951 May	BCE3/AR1	×	×			×	×			×			×	×			×	×	×
1952 May	BCE3/AR2									×			×	×			×	×	×
1953 May	BCE3/AR3	[B 314]		[B 314]			[B 314]	[B 314]		×		↓	×	×	↓		×	×	×
1954 May	BCE3/AR4	×(e)	×	×(e)		×	×(e)	×(e)	×(f)	×			×	×	×		×	×	×

PUBLICATION SOURCES. All of the analyses referred to in this table have been brought together in *Statistics Collected by the MOW 1941–56* [QRL 321]—a collection compiled under the author's direction with the assistance of the DOE—since much of the data had remained unpublished. Many of the analyses were included in a *Monthly Bulletin of Statistics* [QRL 194] which was prepared for use within the MOW, others were published only on an irregular and *ad hoc* basis—the relevant references are shown in the table. All of these together with other unpublished data are included in the compilation referred to above [QRL 321].

(a) Details of the analyses available for the seven 'Specialist' trades of Contractors and for Direct Labour organizations are provided in Tables 3.3 and 3.4 respectively.
(b) Additional employment statistics are also available as follows:
   (i) *Male Clerical and Administrative Staff* analysed by size of firm, trade of firm and region—November 1945 census only—included in [QRL 321].
   (ii) *Working Principals* analysed by craft—November 1945 and February 1946 censuses only—included in [QRL 321].
   (iii) *Operatives Employed On-site and Off-site* analysed by region and by type of work—February 1948 census—included in [QRL 321].
   (iv) For main trades and specialist trades *combined*:
      Operatives by craft ⎫ Aug. 1949–May 1954 in the September issues of [QRL 71] from 1963. (*N.B.* This source incorrectly attributes the Aug.
      Apprentices by craft ⎭ 1949 census results to May 1949.)
      Apprentices by type of agreement: Aug. 1949–May 1954 (plus Sept. 1955) in [QRL 64]—see Section 3.5.4.4.
      Working Principals: May 1950–May 1954 in *MDS* [QRL 195] as a footnote to the contractors' employment tables (Section 3.9.3 refers).
(c) Questionnaires not inspected for the purpose of this study since no surviving copies have been traced.
(d) Operatives working inside and outside the London Civil Defence Region according to Region of employing firm.
(e) Cross-classification by size and by trade of firm.
(f) Cross-classification by size of firm by region of registration.
n.r.=Data not requested.

difficult or impossible to trace now; indeed it appears that many of the records themselves have been destroyed.

As regards non-response it is most important to note that it appears that no attempt was made to allow for deficiencies in this respect: the reported analyses only represent the data provided by firms making returns. It would have been valuable if at the least some information had been provided about the particular categories of firm (trade and size group) failing to make returns. In this respect it is interesting and useful to compare the statistics of firms registered (see Section 3.7.5) with the census analyses of the number of firms responding, bearing in mind that some firms may be inactive at the time of the census. With regard to other problems, examination of the questionnaires used and the notes and guidance given to those completing them is of course an invaluable aid to the interpretation of the data collected, although by itself of course it can never be sufficient, and every effort has been made to trace copies of as many of the questionnaires as possible. Specimens of some of the questionnaires used and a brief history of some of the detailed changes made are set out in Appendix IV and comment relating to particular categories of data is made below (Section 3.5.4).

3.5.3. *Availability of Census Results 1945–54*

With regard to the availability of the data collected in the censuses from 1945 to 1954, the same general remarks apply as were made about the war-time censuses in Section 3.3.1. That is to say, a great deal of the information collected was not formally published and the guide provided here should be taken as referring to analyses which are known to be available; it is possible that other tabulations may have been made which may still survive on Departmental files but which there is no ready means of discovering.

Many of the tabulations which were prepared were brought together in a *Monthly Bulletin of Statistics* [QRL 194] which succeeded the war-time *Statistical Bulletin* [QRL 318]. Both of these were prepared at the time for departmental use but the post-war *Bulletins* are now available for consultation in the Property Services Agency library in Croydon. All the tabulations that now appear to be available including all those contained in the *Monthly Bulletin of Statistics* [QRL 194], those available from published sources and others which remained unpublished have been brought together in the *Collection of Ministry of Works' Statistics* [QRL 321] referred to earlier. This collection is the only source of results for the May 1954 census—the final census before the reforms of 1955 (Section 4.1.1 refers)—all of which had previously remained unpublished.

Table 3.2 provides a guide to the analyses available and includes references to the relevant published sources.

We would repeat that some of the statistics collected in the censuses about employment or output that were used in the compilation of time series are not covered in the table but are considered in Sections 3.8 and 3.9 below. In these cases the concern is with aggregate data whereas Table 3.2 represents a guide in effect to disaggregates and cross-classifications of the data providing information about the structure of the industry. The most notable gap in this context is the lack of any breakdowns of output (value of work done) to parallel those made for employment and the number of firms, although

Table 3.3
MOW Construction Census Analyses 1945–54. Contractors—Seven Specialist Trades (Great Britain)
(A collection of the analyses available has been compiled under the author's direction in [QRL 321]—see foot of Table 3.2—those available are indicated in this table by a cross (×) or by an alternative publication reference.)

Date of Census	NUMBER OF FIRMS						
	By Size of Firm	By Size of Firm and Region	By Size of Firm and Trade of Firm	By Trade of Firm	By Trade of Firm and Region	By Size of Firm	By Trade of Firm
1945 May				[B 349]			
Nov				×			×
1946 May							
Nov				×			×
1947 May				[B 349]			
Nov				×			×
1948 Feb			×	×			×
1949 May	[QRL 37]			[B 349]		[QRL 37]	
Aug	[QRL 37]				[QRL 37]	[QRL 37]	
1950 May	[QRL 38]				[QRL 38]	[QRL 38]	
1951 May		×					
1952 May							
1953 May							
1954 May(c)	×	×	×	×		×	×

(a) Employment statistics are also available as indicated in footnotes (b) (iii) and (b) (iv) to Table
(b) Figures of the total number of operatives (no breakdown) were included in *MDS* [QRL 195].

the data were collected in most of the censuses (see Section 3.5.4 below). In cases where no analyses are shown to be available and it is also known (through an examination of the relevant questionnaires) that the relevant data were not collected we indicate this fact also in Table 3.2. In many ways the table may be regarded as a jigsaw—the pieces of which indicate either that data are available or that they were or were not collected—but a jigsaw which is incomplete.

As was the case with the war-time censuses, many of the available analyses for contractors are confined to those in the so-called 'main trades' (see Section 3.3.2 above regarding the scope of this term). Such analyses as are known to be available for contractors in the seven 'specialist trades' (see Section 3.3.2 above) are indicated in Table 3.3.

3.5.4. *The Available Analyses and Their Interpretation*

3.5.4.1. *Analyses of the number of firms.* There are two sources of data: the registration statistics discussed in Section 3.7.5 and the census analyses. One deficiency in the census

By Region	NUMBER OF OPERATIVES EMPLOYED(a)						
	By Occupation (Craft)				By Type of Work		By Region
	Totals	Apprentices	By Size of Firm	By Trade of Firm	By Size of Firm	By Trade of Firm	
	×	Data not requested					
×	×						
×	×						
×	×			×		×	
	[QRL 37]	[QRL 37]					
{	[QRL 38]	[QRL 38]					
	(b)						
	(b)		×	×	×	×	×
	(b)		×	×	×	×	×
	(b)		×	×	×	×	×
×	(b)		×	×	×	×	×

In addition to the analyses indicated, analyses are also available of operatives employed cross-classified by size and trade of firm, by size of firm and region of registration and by craft and region of registration.

statistics is one to which we have already referred, namely that the data relate only to firms making returns. In principle, of course, the registration statistics should be complete. But it must be a possibility that some unregistered 'firms' managed to operate and did so by evading the controls over building and the allocation of materials; this possibility perhaps growing stronger with the gradual relaxation of controls over the period.

Another difficulty of interpretation is one relating to definitions. The available census tabulations refer to the number of 'firms' and this has remained true up to the present day. Currently, however, a firm which makes multiple returns (e.g. through regional offices) will be counted more than once—strictly the statistics refer to the number of reporting units rather than the number of firms. It is not thought that there has been any change of practice in this respect so that the same was probably true for the early post-war censuses too. In principle this distinction could be an important one but the author understands that currently, at least, few firms make multiple returns. One final aspect concerns firms which may be in common ownership but which trade separately under separate names. In such cases separate returns may be obtained and again each would be recorded as a separate unit.

3.5.4.2. *The labour returns.* We consider the labour statistics under four separate headings: operatives, apprentices, Working Principals and administrative and clerical staff.

3.5.4.3. *Operatives.* All the censuses required a return of the number of operatives employed according to occupation. The categories distinguished were as follows:

(1) Carpenters and Joiners
(2) Bricklayers
(3) Slaters and Tilers
(4) Plasterers
(5) Painters
(6) Plumbers and Glaziers
(7) Masons
(8) 'Other building craftsmen' (so described before the census for Nov. 1946) then 'Other B & CE craftsmen'
(9) Electricians
(10) 'Other B & CE operatives including steel erectors,[12] labourers and navvies' (so described before the census for May 1946) then 'Other occupations'

The accuracy and reliability of the returns may have been affected by a number of factors. Main contractors were instructed not to include the employees of sub-contractors (and this has been the normal practice in all of the MOW–DOE censuses in this period and subsequently up to the present day) since sub-contractors made separate returns. Clearly there was an opportunity for double counting here if the instruction was not obeyed. Potential difficulties are also present concerning the classification of labour by occupation. Little guidance was given, for instance, as to which operatives should be classified as craftsmen although it may be argued that it would be determined quite clearly in practice by whether or not the man was paid at the craftsmen's rate. More important perhaps is the question of whether or not those making the returns would have regarded the terms 'other building craftsmen' (item 8 in the list above) and 'other B & CE operatives' (item 10 above) as synonymous.

Similarly the interpretation of the term 'operative' itself might be a source of inconsistent practice. It is possible that persons occupied as timekeepers, storemen, nightwatchmen, canteen workers, drivers and plant maintenance mechanics, etc. may or may not be included in one or other of the residual categories. Indeed it is simply not clear from the questionnaires whether or not these types of labour were meant to be included.

Another potential source of error and one related to the last point is a distinction between on-site and off-site labour. Both were presumably meant to be included but no mention is made of it (with the exception noted below) and it introduces a particular problem with respect to the classification of operatives by type of work. For example, operatives employed on plant maintenance cannot be classified by type of building and, if included at all, must be presumed to have been included in the 'other work' category (see below). Even operatives employed on building work proper may not be readily classifiable by type of work if they are employed off-site—for instance, on the particular

[12] Specified from August 1945.

pay-day to which a return relates a joiner working off-site may make several window frames destined for use on jobs falling within different work categories. Thus it would seem reasonable to believe that the failure to define the coverage of the word 'operative' may have led to differences in practice and, in general perhaps, to under-recording of employment (assuming, that is, that all categories of manual labour were meant to be included). It is also reasonable to express reservations about the classification by type of work bearing in mind the kind of problem that arises in connection with off-site labour. The only census questionnaire which referred specifically to off-site labour was that for February 1948, which required the number of operatives employed off-site to be shown separately. No analyses of this information were published at the time but analyses of it by type of work and region have now been included in the *Collection of MOW Statistics* [QRL 321] referred to earlier.

A few further points are relevant regarding the interpretation of the data on operative employment. Foremen it should be noted are covered by the term: each questionnaire indicated that they should be included under their appropriate trade classification. It is possible, therefore, that 'General' foremen, who do not do manual work, may have been returned as operatives as well as 'Working' foremen (a distinction was not drawn between these categories until 1967). It may also be taken that apprentices were included although they were specifically mentioned only on the occasions when a separate return of apprentices was called for (see below). A final point regarding the coverage of the operative employment data is that Working Principals are not covered although they do by definition carry out manual work (separate data were collected but not always published—see below).

3.5.4.4. *Apprentices.* Information about apprentices employed was obtained for the first time in the census in August 1949 at the request of the Building Apprenticeship and Training Council and then in each May census thereafter. Separate data were obtained for apprentices having written indentures and apprentices having verbal agreements each broken down according to occupation (the same occupation as for operatives (see above) with the exception of the last 'other occupations' category).[13] Separate information was also requested about the date of first employment to provide the basis for analysing the intake of apprentices over a period of time.

The tabulations referred to in Tables 3.2–3.4 for the main trades, specialist trades and direct labour forces respectively cover the August 1949 and May 1950 censuses only and, further, do not differentiate between written indentures and verbal agreements. Statistics which were differentiated in this way for each of the censuses taken in August 1949, May 1950, 1951, 1953, 1954 and September 1955 were subsequently published in [QRL 64] Appendix 6, together with total craft labour force data, but broken down by craft only in respect of the May 1954 and September 1955 censuses. It is important to note, however, first that the figures cover contractors only (main and specialist trades combined), secondly that electrical apprentices are excluded and thirdly, that the census for September 1955 is on a different base (see Section 4.1). Occupational data for each census (except September 1955) were subsequently included in the later issues of [QRL 71] covering contractors only (main and specialist trades combined) and again not differentiating between written indentures and verbal

[13] 'Boy labourers' were specifically excluded as were 'Category III boys' in the case of electricians.

agreements. It should be noted that this source incorrectly attributes the first census of apprentices to May 1949, and also claims that no data are available for 1955 although, as we have indicated, such data were published in [QRL 64].

3.5.4.5. *Working Principals.* Separate statistics for Working Principals were collected in all the censuses including a breakdown by occupational category in all the censuses for which questionnaires have been examined up to May 1951 but the only data available appear to be those indicated in the footnotes to Table 3.2.

3.5.4.6. *Administrative and clerical staff.* It would appear that information about this category of labour was dropped from the post-war censuses 1945–54; certainly no tabulations of data appear to be available and it was not included on any of the questionnaires it has been possible to examine.

3.5.4.7. *Output.* A return of the value of work done 'during the three months ended ...' was required in each census, as far as can be ascertained from either the third census (questionnaire not available) or the fourth (February 1946) census. Each required merely a single figure for the value of work done in the quarter with the sole exception of the census for May 1946 which required a breakdown by type of work (see below). The actual wording of the instruction on the questionnaires varied somewhat in the early censuses. The intention would seem reasonably clear, however, namely that the amount that was meant to be returned was an amount representing the value of the work actually done during the period ('i.e. the amount which would be charged to customers for B & CE work actually done') including an estimate for work not completed. For a general discussion of valuation practices see Section 2.3. The data obtained were used in the compilation of time series of output (see Section 3.8) but were not included in any of the census tabulations referred to in Tables 3.2 and 3.3. Reference should be made to Appendix IV for further details.

3.5.4.8. *Analyses by type of work.* A return of operatives broken down by type of work was required in all the censuses. The types of work for which separate data were collected were changed twice during the period. Initially the categories were as follows:

(1) Houses and Flats (including new work, adaptations and conversions, temporary houses, roads and sewers for housing sites but excluding war damage repairs and repairs and maintenance).
(2) Other New Construction (i.e. factories, schools, offices, etc. excluding repairs and maintenance).
(3) War Damage Repairs to:
 (a) Houses and Flats
 (b) Other Buildings.
(4) All Other Work including repairs and maintenance, demolition and debris clearance.

The tabulations available provide analyses for each of these categories. In the census for May 1946 new categories were defined in the questionnaires but with one exception (noted below) the available tabulations of the information continued to distinguish the same categories as before.[14] In 1949 (August or possibly earlier) the classification was revised again in the way shown below; the available tabulations for this and the subsequent censuses follow the classification faithfully:

Houses and Flats
    (1) Site preparation and erection of permanent houses and flats.
    (2) Other housing work.

Non-Housing Work
    (3) New work (including new civil engineering work).
    (4) Other non-housing work.

For guidance given to those making returns under these categories see the notes on the specimen copy of one of the questionnaires used (BCE 3/AR1) reproduced in Appendix IV.

3.5.4.9. *Analyses by trade and size of firm and region—Analyses by trade of firm.* The only change from the practice described earlier was the distinction of the additional trade of shopfitters in the main trades group with effect from May 1950. It would appear that the classification of a firm to a particular trade was made on the basis of information originally supplied at the time of registration (or possibly subsequent amendments): none of the census questionnaires themselves requested information about trade. The same comments would seem to apply as were made earlier (Section 3.3.3).

Analyses by size of firm. The basis for classifying a firm by size remained, as in the analyses of the earlier censuses, the number of operatives employed; it is thus affected by any changes affecting the recording of the number of operatives employed for which see above.

Analyses by region. The most important point about the regional analyses is the change of practice made with effect from the census for May 1946 (BCE 3/QR5). Prior to this date regional data had not been requested on the census forms, except for data about the London Civil Defence Region, and the regional analyses that were made were based upon the location of the head office of the firm making the return (as far as is known the data from firms making more than one return, if any, were classified according to the location of the reporting unit). As a guide to regional activity this was, of course, quite unsatisfactory since at any one time a firm may be working on several sites located in different regions. After this date contractors were asked to provide analyses of the number of operatives employed according to the region in which they were working. This remained true for the rest of the period up to 1954; unfortunately the Ministry was later to revert to its original practice (see Section 4.2). Whilst regional data were

---

[14] For details of the new categories see Appendix IV; they are interesting particularly in that the attempt was made to collect separate data for civil engineering work as distinct from building work.

obtained in this way for employment, it would appear that they were never obtained in respect of output. The definitions of the regions used by the Ministry remained the same over this period as in the war-time statistics based on Civil Defence regions (see Appendix II), thus it is important to note that they did not coincide with the official 'standard regions for statistical purposes' introduced by the Central Statistical Office after the war.

3.6. Censuses of Direct Labour Organizations in Great Britain 1944–54

3.6.1. *Introduction*

As we indicated earlier four categories of direct labour can be distinguished: that employed by local authorities, public utilities, government departments and finally that employed by private firms classified to other industries. The latter, if registered, is treated as part of the contractors' sector (see Section 3.6.4). Direct labour constitutes a significant part of the total labour force employed in construction and likewise its output constitutes a significant part of total construction output, especially in the field of repair and maintenance on which most of the labour tends to be employed. Direct labour forces also represent an important structural feature of the British industry. It is important, therefore, that they should not be neglected, although it is often the case in practice that attention is confined to contractors alone, and often indeed, as we indicate above, only to contractors in the 'main trades'.

Once again we would emphasize that the account we are able to give here is necessarily incomplete and parts of it must be tentative for it has been necessary, as in the case of the censuses of contractors, to try to build up piece by piece a coherent picture of the various censuses taken, the types and nature of the data collected and the analyses available. This has been done, as before, by examining all tabulations of the data which it has been possible to trace (virtually all of the data has remained unpublished), by examining all surviving copies of the questionnaires used and by putting questions to the staff currently concerned with these matters in the Department of the Environment.

Similarly in the account which follows a guide is provided to the analyses which are *known* to be available. But since it is always possible that other analyses survive undetected in Departmental files an account is also given of information which, from an examination of the surviving questionnaires, is known to have been collected. Most of the information available is for local authorities and public utilities. Thus this section is almost wholly concerned with them rather than other employers of direct labour. No information seems to be available for private firms (other than that included in time series—see Table 3.7) and virtually no information for government departments—for what there is see Section 3.6.3 below.

3.6.2. *Local Authorities and Public Utilities*

3.6.2.1. *Coverage and scope of the enquiries.* It should be appreciated that the scale of the enquiries in terms of the number of undertakings involved was quite large although they were, of course, much smaller than for contractors. Regular information about the numbers involved is not available but in 1948 there were about 1,300 local authorities employing direct labour and around 800 public utility undertakings providing separate returns (the number of separate undertakings was subsequently reduced by nationalization), whereas the number of contractors was of the order of 130,000. The scope of the public sector was enlarged during this period by the nationalization of certain industries and services but it would appear that the dates of nationalization did not necessarily coincide with the dates at which they were incorporated in the censuses of direct labour organizations. The services covered around 1948 were electricity, gas, water, transport (road, rail and canal), sewerage, catchment and drainage, docks and a small number of miscellaneous services. It would appear that the direct labour of the coal industry, nationalized in 1947, and that ot the steel industry, nationalized in 1951,[15] were not covered until 1967. As far as can be ascertained the direct labour of regional hospital authorities were not covered.

With regard to the number and frequency of the censuses taken there is some uncertainty. It is reasonably clear that from May 1946 the same timing and frequency were adhered to as for contractors—i.e. quarterly until August 1949 and then annually from May 1950 to May 1954. Prior to May 1946 it would seem that, unlike contractors, only annual enquiries were made.[16]

3.6.2.2. *The statistics collected and their availability.* A brief history of the enquiries together with selected specimen questionnaires is contained in Appendix V. Our attention here is largely confined to the data that are known to be available. As in the contractors' censuses the data collected were largely concerned with the number of operatives employed (information about non-operative labour was not collected), the types of work on which they were employed and their occupations. A guide to the tabulations of these statistics known to be available is set out in Table 3.4. As for contractors, most of the analyses available are located in the Ministry's *Monthly Bulletin of Statistics* [QRL 194] which was prepared at the time for internal use within the Ministry, but is now available for consultation in the library of the Property Services Agency in Croydon. A collection of the data from this and other published and unpublished sources is now available in *Collection of Ministry of Works' Statistics 1941–56* [QRL 321]. Information on the value of output was also collected in many of the censuses; this was not incorporated in the analyses referred to above but is available in separate output time series (see Table 3.7).

3.6.2.3. *The available analyses and their interpretation—Labour.* Statistics were collected for operatives only—clerical and administrative labour was not covered. It must be recognized that local authorities could experience difficulty in providing accurate returns. The questionnaires asked for a return of the number of building and civil

---

[15] It was subsequently denationalized and the assets returned to private ownership over a period of time; in 1967 part of the industry was renationalized (see Section 4.4.5 below regarding the subsequent treatment of the direct labour of the steel industry).

[16] The serial numbering of the questionnaires—see Table 3.4 below—is no guide for it seems merely to have been brought into line with that for the contractors' censuses and does not indicate the number of censuses taken.

Table 3.4
MOW Construction Census Analyses 1944–54. Direct Labour (Great Britain)

(A collection of the analyses available has been compiled under the author's direction in [QRL 321]—see foot of Table 3.2—those available are indicated in this table by a cross (×) or by an alternative publication reference.)

Date of Census	Questionnaire Reference	LOCAL AUTHORITIES — Number of Operatives					
		By Occupation (Craft)		By Type of Work[b]			
		Totals	Apprentices	By Craft	By Region	By Type of Authority	By Size of Direct Labour Force
1944 Nov	BCE3E/LA[a]	×		×			
1945 Nov	BCE3F/LA	×		×			
1946 May	BCE3/QR5/LA	×	Data not requested in questionnaires examined	Data not requested in questionnaires examined	×	×	
Aug	BCE3/QR6/LA	×			×	×	
Nov	BCE3/QR7/LA	×			×	×	
1947 Feb	BCE3/QR8/LA	×			×	×	
May	BCE3/QR9/LA	×			×	×	
Aug	BCE3/QR10/LA	×			×	×	
Nov	BCE3/QR11/LA	×			×	×	
1948 Feb	BCE3/QR12/LA	×			×	×	×[c]
May	BCE3/QR13/LA	×			×	[QRL 132]	[QRL 132][c]
Aug	BCE3/QR14/LA[a]	×					
Nov	BCE3/QR15/LA	×			×	×	
1949 Feb	BCE3/QR16/LA	×			×	×	
May	BCE3/QR17/LA	×			×	×	
Aug	BCE3/QR18/LA[a]	[QRL 37]	[QRL 37]		×	×	
1950 May	BCE3/QR19/LA	[QRL 38][d]	[QRL 38]		×	×	
1951 May	BCE3/AR1 1951/LA	×[d]			×	×	
1952 May	BCE3/AR2 1952/LA	×[d]			×	×	
1953 May	BCE3/AR3 1953/LA	×[d]			×	×	
1954 May[e]	BCE3/AR4 1954/LA	×[e][d]			×	×	×[c]

(a) Questionnaires not inspected for the purposes of this study since no surviving copies have been traced.
(b) An annual time series of operatives employed for the period 1948–58 (not specifying dates of census) by four types of work (New: Housing/Other, R & M: Housing/Other) was published in [B 91].
(c) Feb. 1948: percentage distribution only; May 1948 and May 1954: not cross-classified by type of work.
(d) Figures of the *total* number of operatives (no breakdown) in *MDS* [QRL 195].

3.6.2.2 STATISTICS COLLECTED BY THE MINISTRY OF WORKS 1941–54

Questionnaire Reference	PUBLIC UTILITIES					Date of Census
	Number of Operatives					
	By Occupation (Craft)		By Type of Work			
	Totals	Apprentices	By Craft	By Region	By Type of Authority	
(a)	×		×			1944 Nov
(a)	×		×			1945 Nov
BCE3/QR5/PU	×	Data not requested in questionnaires examined	Data not requested in questionnaires examined	×	×	1946 May
BCE3/QR6/PU	×			n.r.	×	Aug
BCE3/QR7/PU	×			×	×	Nov
BCE3/QR8/PU	×			×	×	1947 Feb
BCE3/QR9/PU	×			×	×	May
BCE3/QR10/PU	×			×	×	Aug
BCE3/QR11/PU	×			×	×	Nov
BCE3/QR12/PU	×			×	×	1948 Feb
BCE3/QR13/PU(a)	×					May
BCE3/QR14/PU(a)	×					Aug
BCE3/QR15/PU	×				×	Nov
BCE3/QR16/PU	×				×	1949 Feb
BCE3/QR17/PU	×			Data not requested in questionnaires examined	×	May
BCE3/QR18/PU	[QRL 37]	[QRL 37]			×	Aug
BCE3/QR19/PU	[QRL 38](d)	[QRL 38]			×	1950 May
(a)	(d)				×	1951 May
BCE3/AR2 … /PU	(d)				×	1952 May
BCE3/AR3 … /PU	(d)				×	1953 May
BCE3/AR4 … /PU	(d) ×(e)			×(e)	×	1954 May(e)

(e) Analyses of operatives employed by craft are cross-classified by size of labour force, type of local authority or public utility and by region. The regional analysis for public utilities, unlike earlier censuses, is based on region of registration.

n.r. = not requested.

engineering operatives ('males, 16 years of age and over on pay-roll on pay-day in ...') who were 'direct employees (permanent and temporary) engaged ... on building and civil engineering work'. Specific instructions were given to exclude contractors' labour. There are two potential sources of error in completing the return. One is the failure to define what was meant by 'building and civil engineering operative' and 'building and civil engineering work' although the breakdowns by occupation and by type of work that were required (see below for details) did provide some additional guidance by virtue of the categories distinguished. The only other guidance given was that men engaged on the 'cleansing or scavenging' of roads were not to be included. More precise guidance was given later, in the period after 1954, which it is useful to compare as a guide to some of the problems likely to have affected these returns—see Appendix V. The other potential source of error is that all building and civil engineering workers employed by the authority in all departments—not just the authority's building and civil engineering department—were meant to be included although it would seem that this was not stressed on the questionnaires until 1951. It is almost certainly true to say, therefore, that there must have been differences in practice in the completion of the returns. The same general reservations apply to the data collected from public utilities for which similarly worded questionnaires were used.

Occupational analyses. The occupational categories distinguished in the available tabulations, as distinct from those specified in the questionnaires (see Appendix V for details), are as follows:

Carpenters and Joiners
Bricklayers
Slaters and Tilers
Plasterers (from May 1946 only in the case of public utilities)
Painters
Plumbers and Glaziers
Electricians
All other building craftsmen ⎫ grouped as 'other operatives' from
Other B & CE operatives including ⎬ May 1946
   labourers and navvies ⎭

Apprentices. Information for apprentices was collected separately from August 1949 as for Contractors (see Section 3.5.4.4).

Output. Statistics of the value of work done seem to have been collected in most of the censuses from 1946 (see Appendix V for details); no detailed analyses appear to be available, but aggregate data were published in conjunction with time series for contractors' output from 1946 (see Table 3.7).

Analyses by type of work. Details of the types of work distinguished in the returns and the changes made during the period are also set out in Appendix V. Prior to May 1946 the classification differed from that used for contractors; from May 1946, however, the two classifications were made identical, although in the case of contractors the revised classification was not used for the purpose of published data—see Section 3.5.4.8.

Analyses by type of authority. In the case of local authorities, analyses were provided for each type of authority in England and Wales and in Scotland separately. In Scotland, it should be noted, the Scottish Special Housing Association (SSHA) also employed a substantial direct labour force, which supplemented the work of those employed directly by local authorities, but it was classified with contractors in MOW statistics. Some separate particulars are available, however, in the SSHA *Annual Report* [B 178].

In the case of public utilities the following types of service undertaking were distinguished:

(1) Electricity
(2) Gas
(3) Water
(4) Transport
(5) Sewerage
(6) Catchment and Drainage
(7) Docks
(8) Miscellaneous

Analyses by size of direct labour force. It is not known whether regular analyses of the size distribution of direct labour forces were made; certainly very little information now appears to be available (see Table 3.4). An unofficial survey of local authority direct labour organizations was made by the Amalgamated Union of Building Trade Workers in 1953/4, the results of which were analysed in [B 76] to show the number of departments and the operatives employed according to size of department, but it should be noted that the number of operatives recorded appears to be little more than half those recorded by the Ministry of Works.

Analysis by region. The regions are as defined in Appendix II. In the case of local authorities it is reasonable to assume that their direct labour forces operated only within the boundaries of the authority. Regional analyses therefore only require that the returns be sorted according to the region in which each local authority is situated; none of the questionnaires actually required a return to be made by region. But in the case of public utilities a return of operatives employed by region ('region in which operatives are working') was called for on all the questionnaires it has been possible to examine in all censuses up to and including February 1948. These always required a breakdown by type of work and region except in the census for August 1946 which required a return by occupation and region instead (no analysis of the latter, however, appears to be available).

3.6.3. *Direct Labour of Government Departments*

Little of the information collected from Government Departments about their direct labour forces was made available. The only employment data available would seem to be annual figures for May each year from 1950 to 1954 included as a footnote to tables on contractors' labour published in the *MDS* [QRL 195]—see Section 3.9.3. Estimates of the value of work done were included as part of general output time series for the period 1946–55 (but not separately distinguished after 1952)—see Table 3.7. A major employer of labour amongst the Departments was, of course, the Ministry of Works itself. In addition, the Ministry was responsible for the 'Mobile Labour Force' formed in June 1946 (see Section 3.10.1).

3.7. Building Control Statistics 1940–54

3.7.1. *Background*

The nature and scope of the building controls were outlined in Section 3.2 above. As indicated there, control was exercised over building operations in accordance with Regulation 56A and over contracting organizations in accordance with Regulation 56AB. Broadly speaking, therefore, there are two consequential sets of statistics relating *directly* to the operation of these controls and it is these with which we are concerned in this section. It will be appreciated, of course, that indirectly virtually all of the statistical data compiled by the MOW in the period 1940–54, other than that relating to building materials and contractors' plant, and to which the whole of Chapter 3 of this work is devoted, arose out of the operation of these controls. The statistics relating to the control of contracting organizations, in particular their registration, are considered in Section 3.7.5 below. The rest of this Section is concerned with the operation of the control over building operations.

The administration of the controls over building operations. The scope of the control is outlined in Section 3.2.1 above. In interpreting the statistical series which resulted from its administration the major factor to take into account is its scope including, in particular, the effects of changes in the financial exemption limits. Another factor, of course, is the importance of evasion of the control although this is something it is not possible to quantify.[17]

It is possible to distinguish three broad categories of work, although each of them is not separately distinguished in the statistics:

(1) 'Direct'—work for a government department.
(2) 'Authorized'—work for other public bodies (local authorities and public utilities) authorized by a government department.
(3) 'Licensed'—work for a private body or individual ('civil building').

In addition a category of 'Assisted' work may be distinguished which was private work for which the government granted financial assistance in aid of specific projects. 'Direct' and 'Assisted' work covered new work and repair jobs of all values. 'Authorized' work, however, excluded repair and maintenance work and new work below the exemption limits prescribed from time to time (see below). Licensing applied to all civil building other than that below the prescribed exemption limits but work covered in annual maintenance licences (see Section 3.2.1) was not generally covered in the statistics of licensing as such.

The financial exemption limits. The financial limit applied to the complete cost of a proposed building operation including the cost of all labour and materials (regardless of whether they were already the property of the building owner or contractor or not, new or second hand, already existing on the site or not), builders' overheads and profit, hire of plant, fees charged for professional and technical services and any other charges paid by the party for whom the work was being done. It was not permissible to avoid the

---

[17] Kohan reports a good deal of evasion [B 90] p. 143; see also [QRL 335–7, 37, 38] for details of prosecutions for contravening the regulations.

obligation to obtain a building licence by splitting an operation into separate stages each of which cost less than the prescribed amount. In calculating the amount spent on any property within the preceding prescribed period of time, the cost of all work had to be included whether it took the form of a single building operation or a series of building operations or maintenance work, whether it was licensed or unlicensed and whether it was carried out by or on behalf of the owner or occupier. The cost of all work carried out on the property by a local authority, including first-aid repairs after damage by enemy action, had also to be included.

Changes in the financial limits were made from time to time by statutory 'Control of Building Operations' Orders. For convenience these changes are summarized here. The limit of £100 set in 1941 (see Section 3.2.1) was reduced to £10 in London in October 1944 and then throughout the Home Counties also, in February 1945. On 1 August 1945 the £10 limit was extended throughout Great Britain and was now applied to work done in a specified period of six months; in addition, however, it was permitted to spend up to £2 per month (non-cumulative) on a single property without a licence. The limit of £10 expenditure in a six months period remained until 30 June 1948 when the limit was raised again to £100 in a period of twelve months. Subsequent changes affected 'licensed' and 'authorized' work differently. In the case of licensed work the changes were as set out in Table 3.5.

Table 3.5
Licensed Work—Expenditure Permitted in a Period of 12 Months* Without Licence

Dates from which Limits Shown Operated	Industrial and Agricultural Buildings†	Warehouses and Storage Buildings, Educational Buildings and Certain Office Buildings‡	All Other Properties Including Houses
	£	£	£
1 July 1948	100	100	100
1 Nov. 1948	1,000	1,000	100
1 Feb. 1950	500	100	100
1 July 1952	500	200	200
1 Jan. 1953	2,000	500	500
1 Jan. 1954	25,000	1,000	1,000

* From 1 January 1953 the permitted expenditure related to the year ended 31 December; previously it related to a period of twelve months ended 30 June.
† Excluding farmhouses.
‡ These categories were classed as 'designated buildings' only between 1 November 1948 and 31 January 1950; for office buildings the limit applied only to those with a floor space of 10,000 sq. ft. or more and, from 1 July 1949, only to those warehouse and storage buildings with a floor space of 5,000 sq. ft. or more.

In the case of 'authorized' work (excluding 'direct' and 'assisted' work) the limit for each job was fixed at £1,000 from 1 November 1948 to 31 January 1950; from 1 February 1950 it was reduced to £500 and then raised again to £1,000 from 1 January 1954.

Licensing by local authorities. With the reduction of the exemption limit to the low level of £10 in 1945, local authorities were empowered to issue licences on behalf of the Minister for all work costing less than £100 and all work in excess of £100 concerned with the provision of additional dwelling accommodation, e.g. the construction of new houses, the rebuilding of houses destroyed by war damage, the conversion of houses into flats, etc. The issue of licences for values exceeding £100 for the repair and maintenance of occupied houses remained the responsibility of the Ministry, but each applicant had to obtain from the local authority concerned a certificate of essentiality. From 1 February 1947 this arrangement was extended to cover all work to dwellings including war-damage repairs to occupied houses and ordinary repairs and alterations (not leading to increased dwelling accommodation) to occupied dwellings. When the general licensing limit of £10 reverted to £100 on 1 July 1948, the effect was to limit the licensing responsibilities of local authorities to housing work only.

The available statistics need to be interpreted in the light of the coverage and changes defined above. We consider the war-time and post-war statistics separately.

3.7.2. *Statistics of Work Licensed or Approved in the Period 1941–5*

For the war-time period, statistics were not published but were regularly incorporated in the *Statistical Bulletin* [QRL 318] which was prepared for departmental use (a set of these is now held by the Statistics Construction Division of the Department of the Environment). The geographical coverage of statistics in the bulletin related to Great Britain. Two monthly series were included relating to projects approved or licensed: one showing the value of government building work approved and the other showing the number and value of civil licences issued. The former was analysed by department and covered all works in 'W.B.A.' lists of approvals[18] over the period October 1941–August 1945. The figures exclude most works under £5,000 and all extensions of existing contracts not requiring approval.[19] Statistics for the period 1942–3 were reproduced in Kohan [B 90] p. 352. The analysis of civil licences issued provides figures of the total number issued and an analysis of value by region monthly for the period December 1941–July 1945 and, from August 1943, an analysis of value by type of work [QRL 318] No. 24 *et seq*. The basis of the value statistics is estimates of the cost made by the applicant.

3.7.3. *Statistics of Work Licensed or Authorized in the Period 1945–54*

After the war, statistics relating to the control of building were published in the *Monthly Digest of Statistics (MDS)* [QRL 195] No. 23 *et seq*. These provide separate analyses (quarterly from the beginning of 1945 and monthly from 1947) of the value of licences issued by the Ministry of Works according to type of work and of the value of those issued by local authorities split into housing and non-housing categories. A series for 'authorized' work was published for the first time in the *MDS* [QRL 195] No. 36,

---

[18] The symbol 'W.B.A.' was a relic of a priority system of building control used in the early years of the war; it was retained to denote approved projects after the priority system was abolished—see Kohan [B 90] pp. 124 and 131 and Bowen [B 19] p. 125.

[19] From the second quarter of 1943 the figures exclude the value of approvals made through a regional procedure for small works (under £5,000 for Service and Supply Departments and under £2,000 for Civil Departments); separate statistics for this are to be found in [QRL 318] No. 21. A separate series for 'small works' (under £5,000) approved by Service and Supply Departments was included in [QRL 318] No. 9 *et seq*. for the period from January 1943.

commencing in August 1947, but not analysed by type of work. Notes on definitions and coverage were published in an annual *MDS Supplement* [B 273]. There are three matters particularly worthy of note in addition to the general points made earlier (Section 3.7.1). First it is important to note that for the purpose of the tables 'direct' and 'assisted' work were regarded as 'authorized' work although technically, of course, such work did not need authorization.[20] Secondly, none of the figures was adjusted for tenders notified as having been withdrawn or for licences notified as having lapsed. Thirdly the *Supplement* [B 273] for 1948 indicates that licences for new house erection were not included at that time.

The *Annual Reports* of the Ministry published for the period from 1945 to 1950, [QRL 335-7, 37, 38], are also a useful published source of information for, in addition to statistics about the value of licences issued by type of work, data are included about the number of applications for annual maintenance licences and the value of those issued—this would appear to be the only source for these data.

Information in somewhat more detail about all these matters (except annual maintenance licences) was included by the Ministry in its internal *Monthly Bulletin of Statistics* [QRL 194] (now available in the PSA library) providing in particular more detailed analyses by type of work (including a distinction between new work and repair and maintenance), regional analyses of the value of operational licences issued from 1949 (*Bulletin* [QRL 194] No. 92 *et seq.*) and more information about local authority licences.

3.7.4. *Labour Employed, Labour Ceilings and the Value of Work Done on Licensed, Authorized and Direct Government Projects*

3.7.4.1. *The war-time period—The statistical returns.* During the war the progress of work on each job was regularly monitored by the MOW by means of a return submitted to it monthly by the Government Department concerned whether as a direct, authorizing or sponsoring agent. These returns were made in respect of each site on Form WB1 or, for civil licence work, on Form WB1/C.L. (see specimen copies reproduced in Appendix VI). A WB1 form was completed usually for every job over £5,000 in value and a WB1/C.L. for each job over £1,000 in value initially (see Appendix VI for further details).[21] In addition most Departments made a monthly summary return of the value of work done and labour employed on jobs both *under and over* £5,000 in value on Form WBS. These included any estimates necessary for jobs not returned as well as those returned on WB1 forms.

The data available. The data obtained in the war-time returns were tabulated in some detail and abridged statements of them were regularly included in the Ministry's

---

[20] A list of the principal Government Departments concerned with building and civil engineering work showing the types of construction carried out, authorized or sponsored by them is to be found in [QRL 335], Appendix I.

[21] It will be seen that WB1 was more detailed than WB1/C.L.: both required a return of the value of work done in the month and the number of employees on the last pay day of the month (both main and sub-contractors' labour combined) but the WB1 form required in addition a breakdown of labour by occupation and a return of certain materials 'received' and 'used'.

Statistical Bulletin [QRL 318] providing monthly labour and value series for 'Government' building as follows:

(1) Number of operatives on Government new building work classified by Departments, by type of work, and by regions.[22]
(2) Value of new work done by type of work.

All of these have now been reproduced in the *Collection of MOW Statistics* [QRL 321]. The only published source of these data hitherto was a summary of the monthly series of operatives employed by Department on both new and other work for the whole period July 1941–July 1945 published in [QRL 319] Table 34 and [B 90] pp. 424–5 (this is also included in the *Collection* [QRL 321]). No occupational analyses of the labour employed were included in these sources although this information was obtained on Form WB1.

Two general points about these data are worth emphasis. One is that although the data are referred to as 'Government' building they covered in fact all work that fell within the scheme for the licensing and authorization of work (apart from certain small projects), not merely 'direct' work for the government. The other is that since the data are based on returns for individual sites it was a simple matter to make regional analyses according to the actual location of the work.

Labour ceilings. As part of the system for controlling the size and composition of demand for building resources, labour in particular, labour 'ceilings' were allocated to Departments. For the post-war period such figures were regularly incorporated in tabulations of labour employed. For the war-time period, however, the only figures readily accessible are for the period Jan.–Sept. 1943 (monthly) included in [QRL 318] No. 8.

3.7.4.2. *The post-war period*. After the war the system of site returns in respect of work that fell within the scope of the scheme for the control of building work, now referred to as the 'National Building Programme' rather than the 'Government Building Programme', was continued—see Appendix VI for details. Both labour and value statistics continued to be obtained in these returns but only the labour statistics are available separately: the value statistics were used in the compilation of the output time series considered in Section 3.8.3 below.

The labour series were included in the *Bulletin of Statistics* [QRL 194] providing data for both labour employed and labour 'ceilings' (later called 'quotas'), divided for each between DAA (direct, authorized and assisted) work (later called 'Government work') and civil licence work (later called 'private work'), all classified by Department (and in some cases sub-classified under Departments), together with separate data for Housing. The labour employed series run monthly for the period January 1946–March 1950 (last appearing in *Bulletin* [QRL 194] No. 53) and the labour ceilings series for the period March 1946–June 1949 (last appearing in *Bulletin* No. 46). Early issues of the post-war *Bulletin* [QRL 194] also included a breakdown by type of work which overlapped with the war-time series.

---

[22] The scope of this analysis widened after September 1943 to include maintenance and salvage (not covered previously) and works costing less than £5,000 (only partially covered previously).

3.7.5. *The Register of Contractors—Registration Statistics*

The scope of the register of building and civil engineering undertakings compiled in accordance with Regulation 56AB is outlined in Section 3.2.2. The Regulation came into force in 1941 but, as far as can be ascertained, statistics relating to the register are available only for the post-war period. Monthly series are available for the period from July 1948 to November 1953 in the internal *Monthly Bulletin* [QRL 194] Nos. 32–96 showing:

(1) Total registrations active at the end of the month and an analysis of changes during the month (new registrations and revivals, cancellations and untraceables, etc.) covering firms in both the main and specialist trades together with local authority and public utility undertakings.
(2) An analysis of the composition of the active registrations according to trade of firm (main and specialist trades), local authority or public utility, each by region.

Statistics for the post-war period prior to July 1948 (summary statistics only of new registrations and revivals, cancellations and the total number of firms active at the end of December in 1946 and 1947) are to be found in [QRL 336] p. 4. A selection of these statistics for the whole period from 1948 to 1953 has been included in the recently compiled volume of *Statistics Collected by the Ministry of Works 1941–56* [QRL 321].

3.8. Output Time Series Compiled by the Ministry of Works before 1955

3.8.1. *Introduction*

The principal sources of data about output (value of work done) available to the Ministry in the period prior to 1955 were the periodic censuses of contractors and direct labour organizations, sample returns from contractors, and returns obtained in respect of individual sites. These are considered in detail in Appendices IV–VII; they have also been considered in previous sections (Sections 3.3–3.7) except the post-war sample and site returns (for which see Section 3.8.3 below). Many of the output data obtained in these returns were not separately published but on the basis of this and other information, the Ministry compiled composite time series of the value of work done. It is these series with which we are concerned in this section. A distinction has to be drawn between the post-war series for the period 1946–55 and those for the period prior to 1946. For the years prior to 1946 a time series of the value of gross output was devised for the period back as far as 1932 although, as we have described, the Ministry did not begin to collect statistics until 1941. Reference should also be made to the official and unofficial historical series of estimates of gross fixed capital formation in buildings and works that are available—see Section 5.4.

3.8.2. *Gross Output Estimates 1932–45*

Three sets of estimates were prepared covering all or part of the period one of which was much more comprehensive in its coverage of work done than the others. Some of these estimates have appeared in several published sources, which we indicate below, others

82 CONSTRUCTION AND THE RELATED PROFESSIONS

are only to be found in the Ministry's war-time *Statistical Bulletin* [QRL 318]. At this stage we would emphasize that caution is required in the use of the published series for the publications in which they appear generally fail to define the coverage of the data adequately. In fact the series generally published were those which were the more limited in scope. Moreover the notes included in the published sources can be misconstrued. Particulars of the series available are given below in Table 3.6.

As we have already stressed, particular care is required in the interpretation of the available series because of limitations in the coverage of output which are not generally made clear in the sources themselves. With one exception, the series appear to be confined to estimates of the work done by contractors in the main trades alone. The exception is series (3) in Table 3.6 which explicitly covers 'all other employers of building labour' as well (but in total only—i.e. not broken down by type of work). The difference in magnitude this makes is substantial, amounting to an increase of some 30–40 per cent on top of the contractors' series (referred to as 'output of the building and contracting trades'). As regards reliability, the series before 1941/2 are certainly likely to be less reliable because of the absence of any regular output returns until 1941.

3.8.2.1. *The estimates for pre-war years.* Series (1) in Table 3.6 was included in the Ministry's *Statistical Bulletin* [QRL 318] during the war in a table entitled 'Activity and Capacity of the Building and Civil Engineering Industry in Great Britain', which brought together statistics about employment and unemployment (Ministry of Labour), the output of cement and bricks, wage rates and earnings. A copy of this table, for the period 1932–45 (output estimates to 1944), is reproduced in Kohan [B 90] Appendix I. The basis of the estimates is stated to be a 'wide variety of sources'; no further explanation is provided but a useful appreciation of the sources available for the pre-war years is to be found in articles by Bowen and Ellis [B 23] and by Bowen [B 18].[23] Indeed the article by Bowen and Ellis [B 23] was directly concerned with the basis of the estimates for 1935 and 1938 included in series (3) (Table 3.6) and since the authors of this article were officials in the Ministry of Works during the war (Bowen was Chief Statistical Officer) the description may be taken as authoritative.[24]

3.8.2.2. *The estimates for the war-time years.* The war-time series, particularly those from mid-1941, may certainly be regarded as more reliable than the pre-war series because of the better sources of information available. Series (2) in Table 3.6, which provides a breakdown of type of work for this period, is based on the returns made in connection with the Government Building Programme (see Section 3.7.4) for the period from mid-1941; for 1940 and the first half of 1941, only rough estimates were possible, based on value figures returned to the Works and Buildings Priority Sub-Committee.[25] The fullest and clearest statement about coverage is provided in [QRL 319], p. 213 where it is made quite explicit that work carried out by firms in the seven

[23] Reference should also be made to [QRL 12] for alternative estimates and commentary on the nature of the statistical sources available, and to [B 169] regarding the nature of one of the sources—series of building plans approved by local authorities—and its use for estimating the value of industrial building.

[24] It may be noted, incidentally, that the figures were subsequently used in the construction of the interim index of industrial production after the war, see [B 259] p. 44.

[25] For details of this committee see [B 90].

3.8.2.2   STATISTICS COLLECTED BY THE MINISTRY OF WORKS 1941–54

Table 3.6
Gross Output Series 1932–45*

Descriptive Title	Breakdown	Coverage	Period Covered	Frequency	Sources Primary	Sources Secondary (Published)
(1) Value of gross output (a)	—	GB	1932–45	Annual	[QRL 318]	[B 90] Appendix I
(1) Value of gross output (b)	—	UK	1932–9	Annual	[QRL 318]	—
(2) Value of work done	By type of work	GB	1940–5	Annual	[QRL 318]	[B 90] p. 426; [QRL 319] Table 54; [QRL 321]; [QRL 320] 1940–3 series
(3) Value of gross output	By type of work	UK	1932–8	Annual	[QRL 318]	[B 23]—1935 and 1938 only

* See Section 5.4.4 regarding gross fixed capital formation series for this period and earlier.
Note: The breakdown by type of work in series (3) is made for the output of the 'Building and Contracting trades' only and is in effect a breakdown of series (1b). Series (2) provides in effect a breakdown of series (1a) for the war-time period.

specialist trades, all direct labour organizations including private firms outside the building and civil engineering industries, and by prisoner-of-war labour is excluded as well as that done by those firms in the main trades themselves which consist solely of Working Principals.[26] Thus coverage extends only to contractors in the main trades (as defined in Section 3.3.2) employing operatives at the time of the census. It is estimated in [QRL 319] that in 1946 the work done by the agencies excluded amounted to about 40 per cent of the total output of building and civil engineering work.

The actual returns in which output statistics were obtained during the war were the censuses (see Appendix IV) and the site returns (see Appendix VI). The censuses provided limited information for an output return was not required in every census and then only provided a figure of the work done in one month alone. The site returns were obtained regularly every month and provide fuller information than the censuses about types of work, but such returns were not obtained from every site and they introduce a special difficulty of interpretation, for whereas the available series purport to cover the main trades alone the site returns covered both the main and specialist trades on a site without distinction (a single return being obtained for a site).

It would appear that in practice the assumption was made that the work of the specialist trades included in the site returns would be balanced by the work done by operatives in the main trades *off-site* (and thus missed from the site return). The validity of this assumption is questionable but there would seem to be no evidence on which to judge for the war-time period; it may be noted, however, that data collected about off-site labour in the census for February 1948 showed that such an assumption was not valid at that time (see Section 3.9.3 below). These factors are perhaps more likely to have affected the estimated breakdown by type of work, rather than the totals, but because of the lapse of time and the absence of detailed information about the method of estimation it is difficult now to be certain. It may be noted, incidentally, that a statement of the likely margin of error of the totals was included in [QRL 320] p. 6, but again its reliability is impossible to assess.

The use to which the census information was put raises a problem inasmuch as it covered only one month of the year; the most likely possibility would seem to be that the data were used to derive output-per-man factors which were then applied to employment series available from the census and/or the MOLNS (see [B 241] and the *Historical Abstract of Labour Statistics* [QRL 58]) to produce annual series.

3.8.3. *MOW Output Time Series 1946–55*

The output time series produced for the period 1946–55 were not restricted in scope to the main trades as were most of the pre-1946 series. Like them, however, they were not the product of a discrete collection process but were based on several types of return from contractors, government departments and other public authorities and also on estimates for categories of work not covered by returns. One of these returns was new and one of the others was utilized to provide more regular information about output

---

[26] The output for which such firms are responsible would be partly that done by Working Principals themselves and partly that done by operatives in employment with these firms at some time during the period to which the output return relates but not on the specified date of the labour return. It is only possible to differentiate such firms after the initiation of the MOW censuses in 1941.

than hitherto. To gain an appreciation of the nature of the series, therefore, especially the breakdowns by type of work, requires that the statistical returns themselves should be considered first.

3.8.3.1. *The statistical returns.* There were four main sources of information for the output series produced from 1946 to 1955, only one of which we have considered previously. The four sources were as follows:

(1) The censuses of contractors and direct labour considered earlier—Sections 3.5 and 3.6 respectively.
(2) Monthly 'sample censuses' of contractors.
(3) Site returns from contractors.
(4) Departmental returns.

The censuses, as we explained earlier, were taken quarterly from May 1945 to August 1949 and then annually in May and were mainly concerned with the collection of employment statistics. Information was requested, however, about the value of work done in the three full months preceding the date of the census, in contrast to the one month once a year in the war-time censuses. Normally a total figure only was asked for (see Sections 3.5.4 and 3.6.2 for comment on the nature of the data collected). The change in the frequency of the census from quarterly to annual, however, after August 1949 meant that value figures were available for only one quarter each year from 1950 from this source. For the other three quarters of the year, therefore, a question was inserted on the monthly 'sample census' of employment which had been instituted in late 1945, albeit with a more limited coverage (main trades only).

The 'sample census'. Details of this enquiry are given in Appendix VII together with specimen forms. The so-called sample census commenced on a monthly basis in September/October 1945 and was originally concerned with employment only. Unlike the full censuses, it should be noted, coverage extended to the main trades only in the period up to 1954. Information was sought about the total value of work done (during the preceding three months) in the enquiries made in January, July and October each year from January 1950 onwards. Breakdowns by type of work were not required until October 1954 (see Appendix VII for further details).

Site returns. Details of these returns are given in Appendix VI. Until the system for the authorization and licensing of building work came to an end in November 1954, contractors were required to make separate monthly returns for individual sites on which authorized or licensed work was in progress in respect of all larger non-housing jobs and all new housing jobs (see Appendix VI for fuller details of coverage). These returns provided data about labour employed and the value of work done in the month. Each region of the MOW summarized the returns for its region and included estimates for returns not received.[27]

Departmental returns. Generally speaking data in respect of the smaller non-housing jobs not covered on site returns were obtained in summary form (as distinct from data for individual sites) directly from the Government Departments involved. In some

---

[27] In all cases the estimate was based on the figure on the last return received.

cases, however, all jobs, large and small, were in fact covered by individual site returns; and in the case of unsponsored civil licence work (i.e. work licensed by the MOW but not sponsored by a Department)[28] estimates were made by the MOW based on licences issued in the previous month.

3.8.3.2. *The published output series, 1946–55.* A summary guide to the series available is provided in Table 3.7, together with brief remarks regarding their bases. The main base of the series was the quarterly information about the total value of work done obtained in the censuses of contractors and direct labour organizations. This had to be supplemented by estimates for the work not covered in the censuses, namely that carried out by the direct labour of government departments and private firms, and, for part of the period, the work done by prisoners-of-war and the costs of components for houses in the pre-fabricated housing programme. With effect from August 1949 the censuses of contractors in the specialist trades and the censuses of the direct labour of local authorities and public utilities provided information about the value of work done in one quarter each year only: thus here too estimates had to be made to complete the series for the other three quarters of the year. Thus from August 1949 the fullest information related to contractors in the main trades alone.

The site and departmental returns were used as the basis for making breakdowns of the work carried out by contractors in the *main trades* according to type of work. These returns lent themselves to classification by type of work in considerable detail, of course, and it is understood that this was done initially for some thirty categories. The breakdowns published represent summary versions of these classifications. It will be appreciated, however, that the coverage of these returns was determined by the scope of the authorization and licensing scheme and thus, as the financial exemption limits were progressively raised their coverage fell.[29] This fact is of crucial importance from the point of view of interpretation of the analyses by type of work for it breaks the continuity of these series and seriously impairs their usefulness for this reason (see Appendix VI for fuller details regarding coverage). Indeed it will be observed from Table 3.7 that after the third quarter of 1952 it was decided to stop publishing the breakdown, although the MOW did in fact continue to make it right up to the third quarter of 1954: it is to be found in the Ministry's *Monthly Bulletin of Statistics* [QRL 194]. The series as a whole were continued up to the first quarter of 1955.

The difference between the value of work obtained from the site and departmental returns and the value obtained in the census represented a residual category covering work of all kinds, both new work and repairs and maintenance, etc. on buildings of *all* types—i.e. not only those which were *not* separately categorized but also those which *were*. The description of this category may be misleading since it was shown simply as 'other work' or even as 'repairs and maintenance'. Apart from work below the exemption limits for authorization or licensing, the work not covered by the site returns was work done under annual maintenance licences and work of conversions, adaptations, repair and maintenance of houses (separately estimated).

---

[28] For details of Departmental responsibilities see [QRL 335] Appendix I.
[29] See Section 3.7.1. In fact the limits were raised and then lowered before being progressively raised in the run-up to abolition in November 1954.

It must be stressed that the detailed breakdown by type of work relates only to the work of the 'main' trades. This in itself introduces a further problem of interpretation because of the difficulty of reconciling the coverage of the site returns with the coverage of the quarterly census and sample returns for, as we warned earlier (Section 3.8.2.2), the site returns were not confined to the work done by contractors in the main trades alone but covered the specialist trades too. There was, therefore, the problem of a mismatch in the coverage of the two types of return, quite apart from the fact that not all of the work undertaken by contractors was covered on a site return in any case. As we explained earlier (Section 3.8.2.2), it seems to have been assumed for practical purposes that the site returns could be regarded as covering the main trades alone on the grounds that the on-site labour of the specialist trades covered on the return could be regarded as equivalent to the off-site labour of the main trades not covered on the return. This, however, was a questionable assumption for two reasons. First, as far as labour was concerned, statistics collected in the census for February 1948 showed the assumption to be invalid and that labour was likely to be overstated (see Section 3.9.3 for further details). Secondly because, as far as the value of work done was concerned, the site return would, presumably, include the value of components, etc. prepared off-site, as well as the work done on site by the specialist trades, and thus the assumption here would necessarily produce an over-statement of work done by the main trades alone.

The conclusion it seems reasonable to draw from this is that the estimates for the main trades may be reasonably reliable in total (depending on the accuracy and comprehensiveness of the census and sample returns). But the breakdown by type of work is less reliable because on the one hand it understates, by virtue of partial coverage of each type of work, and on the other hand, it overstates by virtue of the mismatch between the site and other returns. But whichever way the balance lies its effect does not extend beyond the main trades analysis for it is taken up by the residual 'other work' (repairs and maintenance) category.

3.8.3.3. *Bowen's unofficial output estimates 1945–8.* In the early post-war years Bowen (Chief Statistical Officer of the Ministry of Works during the war) contributed a regular article on building and civil engineering output to the *London and Cambridge Economic Service Bulletin (LCES Bull.)* [B 269]—first published in Vol. 25 (2), 1947, pp. 55–59 and last published in Vol. 29 (4), 1951, pp. 119–20. Each article included a table of output statistics but it is important to appreciate the basis of these figures since for the period up to 1948 they predated the *regular* publication of official series for the period. Before 1949 only two official sets of data had been published: quarterly data for the period from the second quarter of 1945 to the end of 1946 in [QRL 335], Appendix III, and figures for the year 1946 in the National Income and Expenditure White Paper for that year [QRL 202] p. 8 (see footnotes to Table 3.7 above for comment). As Bowen describes, his series were estimates derived by applying output-per-man factors to the statistics of employment published in the *MDS* [QRL 195] (Section 3.9.2 refers); consequently, it should be noted, coverage extended to the 'main trades' alone. Subsequently the series included in the *LCES Bull.* [B 269] were based on the official series (see Table 3.7).

Table 3.7
MOW Output Time Series 1946–55* (Great Britain)

Classifications by Agency and Type of Work		Period Covered	Origin or Nature of Data
1. TOTAL OUTPUT—Total		1946–55 (1st qtr)	See Remarks
New Work			
Repairs & Maintenance ('other work')		1948–55 (1st qtr)	
2. FIRMS OTHER THAN THOSE IN THE SPECIALIST TRADES (i.e. the '13 Trades')—	Total	1946–55 (1st qtr)	Census and Sample
(a) Employing One or More Operatives:	Total	1946–52 (3rd qtr)	Census and Sample
All Work—by type		1946–52 (3rd qtr)	Site and Departmental Returns and Estimates
New Work—by type		1948–52 (3rd qtr)	
Repairs & Maintenance—by type		1948–52 (3rd qtr)	
(b) Employing No Operatives	Total	1946–52 (3rd qtr)	Census and Sample
3. FIRMS IN SPECIALIST TRADES ('7 Trades')	Total	1946–55 (1st qtr)	Census and Estimates
4. DIRECT LABOUR—Work done by Operatives employed by			
(a) Local Authorities	Total	1946–52†	Census and Estimates
(b) Government Departments	Total	1946–52† –1955 (1st qtr)	Estimate
(c) Public Utility Undertakings	Total	1946–52†	Census and Estimates
(d) Private Firms in Other Industries	Total	1946–52 (1st qtr)	Conjectural
5. WORK DONE BY PRISONERS OF WAR	Total	1946–48 (1st qtr)	Estimate
6. PREFABRICATION	Total	1946–48	Materials Cost

SOURCES AND FREQUENCY: Annual figures for 1946 and 1947 and quarterly series from 1948 were published in the *Monthly Digest of Statistics* [QRL 195] February 1949 *et seq.* Annual statistics, excluding analyses by type of work, were published in the *Annual Abstract* [QRL 31]. Quarterly series from 1946 are be found in [QRL 194] No. 38 *et seq.* (these have now been reproduced in the *Collection of MOW Statistics* [QRL 321]). Reference should also be made to [B 273] regarding definitions and explanatory notes.

  * A separate quarterly series by type of work for the period 1945 (2nd qtr) to 1946 (4th qtr) was included

Remarks
Coverage varied according to the periods for which statistics for the categories listed in the first column were prepared. The item 'repairs and maintenance' was a residual category covering new work for which separate figures were not available as well as repairs and maintenance—see notes below.
Statistics of total work done were obtained from censuses and samples. Analyses by type of work were based on site and departmental returns and estimates based on licences issued and census returns of employment by type of work. The coverage of these returns and estimates was affected over time by changes in the financial exemption limits for authorization or licensing. The difference between the total value of work done and the value of the subsidiary series was shown as a residual item—'other' (shown under repairs and maintenance when distinguished) which covered, in fact, new work as well as repairs and maintenance. Further details are given in the main text. The term 'new work' covered work of construction, reconstruction, extensions and alterations except in the case of housing for which conversions and adaptations were counted as repairs and maintenance rather than new work.
Labour force (monthly return from Department) × estimated gross output per man-month (weighted average of figures supplied by Departments).
Based on an assumed labour force and estimated gross annual output per man (from 1948: 100,000 operatives × £500 per man). The value was assumed to include 70 per cent of the value of annual maintenance licences issued to private firms, the rest being done by contractors.
Based on numbers employed.
Costs of manufacture of hulls, components and fittings for prefabricated houses (permanent and temporary) in those cases where they were not included in other headings.

he first MOW *Annual Report* [QRL 335] Appendix III and equivalent annual figures for 1946 in the *National Income and Expenditure* White Paper for that year [QRL 202] p. 8. The coverage of the data is not specified ut it is apparent that they refer to the 'main trades' alone. Their bases are probably the same as for the main rades above coupled with estimates based on employment. Subsequent *Annual Reports* [QRL 336] [QRL 37] [QRL 37] [QRL 38] either contained no output data or the series referred to in the table above.
† Separate series to 1952 (3rd qtr), then combined as shown.

3.9. Employment Time Series Compiled by the Ministry of Works 1941–55

3.9.1. *Introduction*

Most of the principal enquiries in which statistics of employment were obtained by the Ministry of Works have been considered in earlier sections since they were not confined to the collection of labour statistics. The purpose of this section is to consider the general time series of employment that are available, as distinct from the particular data obtained in specific enquiries. Much of the latter, as we have indicated, were not separately published but they were used, at least in part, in the compilation of time series which, for the post-war period at any rate, *were* published. Certain subsidiary employment series and other statistics relating to labour which were collected by the MOW in this period are considered in Section 3.10.

Particular care is required in interpreting the time series available for their coverage is not comprehensive and the subsidiary series (by type of work) suffer from marked discontinuities. Despite the fact that a great deal of information was collected about the number of operatives employed, no attempt seems to have been made to compile a comprehensive series for employment in the way that was done for output especially after the war (Section 3.8.3). In interpreting any particular series, therefore, it is crucially important to bear in mind the limitation in coverage to which it is subject and to appreciate the nature of the particular sources of information used in its compilation.

3.9.2. *MOW Employment Time Series 1941–5: the Series Available and Their Interpretation*

During the war-time period information about employment was obtained in two types of enquiry:

(1) the periodic censuses of contractors—considered in Section 3.3 and Appendix IV,
(2) monthly returns for individual sites made by Government Departments in connection with the 'Government Building Programme'—see Appendix VI.

A monthly series was compiled for the period September 1941–November 1945 and was regularly included by the Ministry in its departmental *Statistical Bulletin* [QRL 318] during the war and then, after the war, was published in the *MDS* [QRL 195] from issue No. 1, January 1946 (the published series covered the period from January 1944) in a table entitled at first: 'Number of Male Insured Workers in Building and Public Works Contracting', and then: 'Estimated Number of Insured Male Workers (Aged 16–64) in the Building and Civil Engineering Industries in Great Britain' (the change in title signified no substantive change in content). The full series from 1941 has now been reproduced in the *Collection of MOW Statistics* [QRL 321].

In this series an attempt was made to reconcile the MOW statistics with those relating to insured workers obtained by the Ministry of Labour and National Service (MOLNS)—for details of these statistics see the official *Guide* [B 241] and the *Historical Abstract* [QRL 58]. As we explained earlier the definition of the industry employed by the MOLNS—'Building and Public Works Contracting'—was one which most closely corresponded in coverage to the 'main' trades defined by the MOW (Section

3.3.2 refers). The first essential point to note, therefore, is that coverage did not extend to all workers engaged on construction activities. It excluded in particular those employed in the specialist trades, as direct labour and, in the main trades themselves, it would exclude Working Principals. The second essential point to note is that reconciliation between the two series was only achieved through the inclusion of a residual 'other' category. Moreover, the residual category embraced both operatives and clerical and administrative workers until the inclusion of a separate series for the latter. The various categories for which separate series are available and the periods covered are shown below (Table 3.8)

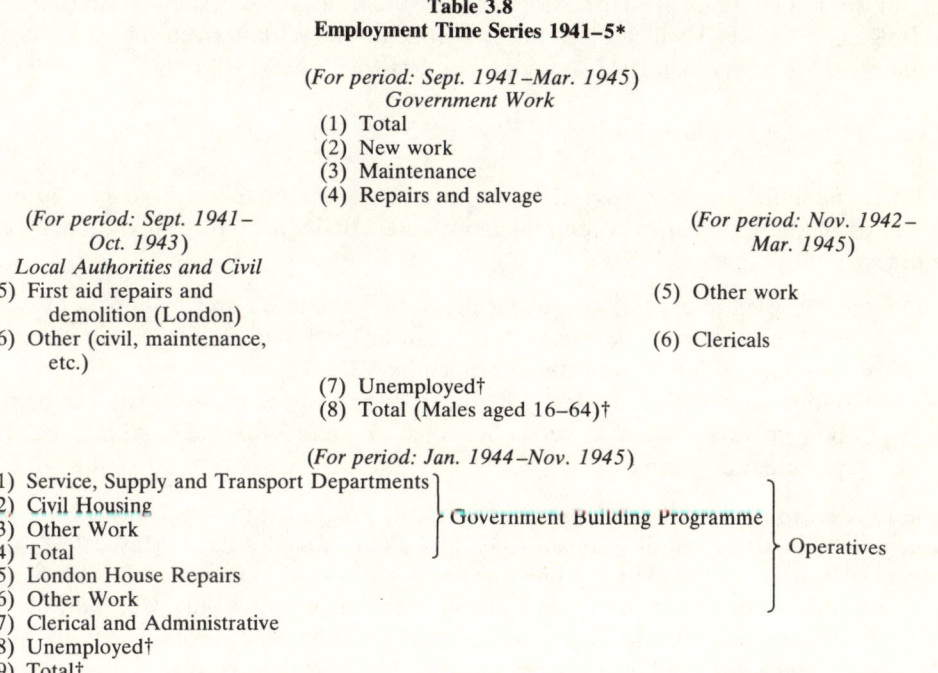

Table 3.8
Employment Time Series 1941–5*

(For period: Sept. 1941–Mar. 1945)
Government Work
(1) Total
(2) New work
(3) Maintenance
(4) Repairs and salvage

(For period: Sept. 1941– Oct. 1943)
Local Authorities and Civil
(5) First aid repairs and demolition (London)
(6) Other (civil, maintenance, etc.)

(For period: Nov. 1942– Mar. 1945)
(5) Other work
(6) Clericals
(7) Unemployed†
(8) Total (Males aged 16–64)†

(For period: Jan. 1944–Nov. 1945)
(1) Service, Supply and Transport Departments ⎤
(2) Civil Housing   ⎥
(3) Other Work   ⎬ Government Building Programme ⎤
(4) Total   ⎥   ⎥
(5) London House Repairs   ⎦   ⎬ Operatives
(6) Other Work   ⎥
(7) Clerical and Administrative   ⎦
(8) Unemployed†
(9) Total†

---

* Separate series confined to operatives employed on Government new building work and on work controlled under civil licences, which provide analyses by Department, type of work and region, are considered in Section 3.7.4.
† MOLNS Statistics (Section 6.2.1 refers).

With regard to the available breakdown (Table 3.8) notice should be taken of two further points. First, the breakdowns by type of work were based on the site returns; consequently the same problem of coverage is involved as in the output series, namely that whereas the total employment figures refer to the main trades, the site returns covered the specialist trades as well. As we explained earlier in connection with the output series, it was assumed that the on-site specialist labour covered on the site returns would be balanced by the off-site labour of the main trades not covered on the return, and thus it could be regarded as covering the labour force of the main trades contractors alone. However, statistics collected in one of the post-war censuses (February 1948) showed this assumption to be invalid. If these results were generally applicable, it would mean, other things being equal, that the site returns overstate the main trades labour in total by some 6 to 7 per cent (see Section 3.9.3 below for further details).

The second point concerns the monthly series for 'Clericals' or 'Clerical and Administrative' labour. The basis of this series is not clear for returns with the appropriate coverage are available only from the censuses of November 1942, October 1943 and November 1944 (site returns were naturally confined to clerical and administrative labour employed on site). It would appear that the series up to November 1944 represent merely interpolated estimates. The basis of the figures subsequent to November 1944 is less clear, however, since information for clerical and administrative labour was not obtained at all in subsequent censuses.[30] Reference should also be made to [QRL 320] Table 1 which attempts to reconcile MOW data from the censuses of January 1942, November 1942 and October 1943 with MOLNS data.

3.9.3. *MOW Employment Time Series 1945–55*

3.9.3.1. *The series and their sources.* In the post-war period up to 1955 the data used as the basis of the time series of employment were obtained by the MOW from four sources:

(1) the censuses of contractors—considered in Section 3.5 and Appendix IV,
(2) 'sample censuses' of contractors—considered briefly in relation to output statistics in Section 3.8.3 and fully in Appendix VII,
(3) monthly site returns made by contractors in respect of work subject to the building controls—considered in Sections 3.7.4 and 3.8.3 and in Appendix VI,
(4) departmental returns.

The full censuses provided statistics of operatives employed by type of work and by occupation, quarterly until August 1949 and then annually from May 1950. The 'sample censuses', initiated in September/October 1945, provided monthly statistics of total operatives employed but by contractors in the main trades only. Breakdowns by type of work were not introduced on this return until October 1954 (see Appendix VII). The site returns were also limited in coverage inasmuch as they were not obtained from all sites and covered on-site labour only, but they naturally allowed analysis by type of work in considerable detail. The departmental returns were summary returns for work subject to control but not covered by separate site returns (see Appendix VI). All these enquiries continued to require, it should be noted, a return of male operatives aged *16 years* and over (as in the 'war-time' enquiries) although this did not coincide with the school-leaving age (this had been raised from 14 to 15 years in 1947 and was not raised to 16 years until 1973). The reason for this limitation in coverage is not clear but it obviously introduces further scope for error in the completion of the returns. Statistics of the number of Working Principals were obtained in the censuses, and in the samples from January 1948; they were not incorporated into the time series but some of them were published from 1950 (see below). No statistics were collected about other types of labour (administrative, clerical, etc.) employed by contractors.

---

[30] The only apparent basis would be to take the difference between the MOLNS figures and the figure of total *operatives* employed in the main trades obtained in the MOW quarterly censuses, interpolating as necessary for the months not covered.

3.9.3.2 STATISTICS COLLECTED BY THE MINISTRY OF WORKS 1941–54

The employment series published in the period 1945–55 (see Table 3.9) were incorporated in the *MDS* [QRL 195] No. 2 *et seq.* in a table entitled initially 'Estimated Number of Male Employees in the Building and Civil Engineering Industries in Great Britain' and later 'Men Employed in the ...'. The table was identical to that included in the Ministry's *Monthly Bulletin* [QRL 194] except towards the end of the period (see Table 3.9). In this post-war series the attempt to reconcile the MOW data with the MOLNS data (see Section 3.9.2) was abandoned. But otherwise the same procedure was followed as in the war-time series, that is to say the site returns were generally used to provide a breakdown of employment by type of work with the difference between these and the total employment figure (in this case derived from the censuses and sample returns) being shown as a residual. The full series has now been reproduced in the *Collection of MOW Statistics* [QRL 321].

The categories of work for which separate series were produced were much fewer than in the case of output (cf. Section 3.8.3) but, as in the case of output, were gradually reduced in number as the coverage of the building controls changed. At the end of the period only one category, apart from the total, was published and only three, apart from the total, included in the Ministry's *Bulletin* [QRL 194]. The categories distinguished and the period over which each series was produced are shown in Table 3.9.

Table 3.9
MOW Employment Time Series 1945–55*

Descriptive Title	Period Covered
Total	Jan. 1945–55 (1st qtr)
Housing Work	
New house construction (later 'on new housing sites')†	Jan. 1945–Jan. 1955
Other housing work	
Conversions and adaptations to houses	Jan. 1945–Oct. 1949 ⎫
Repair and maintenance of houses	Jan. 1945–Oct. 1949 ⎬ Feb. 1953
War damage repairs to houses	Jan. 1945–Oct. 1949 ⎭
Non-Housing Work	
Industrial, agricultural and commercial work‡	Jan. 1945–Feb. 1953
War damage repairs	Jan. 1945–Oct. 1949
New industrial work§	1948–51,¶ Jan. 1952–Jan. 1955
Other new non-housing§	1948–51, Jan. 1952–Jan. 1955
'Other Work' (a residual category)	Jan. 1945–Jan. 1955

* Separate figures were produced for England and Wales and Scotland in slightly more detail for a number of months in the period July 1945–Jan. 1947 in [QRL 194] Nos. 7–14.

† N.B. The series described as 'men employed "on new housing sites"', introduced towards the end of the period, was said to cover the specialist trades as well as the main trades. But the figures for the overlapping parts of the new and old series remain identical (cf. *MDS* [QRL 195] Jan. 1951, Table 89 and *MDS* [QRL 195] Jan. 1953, Table 86). The explanation for this probably rests in the assumptions made about the coverage of site returns—on-site labour of specialist trades covered on the return was assumed to equal the off-site labour of the main trades not covered (see text below on this matter).

‡ Initially described as 'industry and agriculture'.

§ Included only in [QRL 194] Nos. 87–110.

¶ June and December each year and monthly averages.

3.9.3.2. *Interpretation of the MOW employment time series 1945–55.* The coverage of the series as a whole generally extended to the operatives employed by contractors in the main trades only (the exclusion of specialist trades and direct labour is clearly stated in all *MDS Supplements* [B 273] from 1950). However, separate figures for the total operatives returned in the May censuses from 1950 to 1954 by the specialist trades, local authorities, government departments and public utilities are to be found in footnotes to the building employment table published in the *MDS* [QRL 195] together with a figure for the total number of Working Principals in all firms—main and specialist trades combined. (It should be noted that the number of operatives employed in these other organizations was very substantial indeed amounting, in May 1950 for example, to 46 per cent of the number employed by the main trades alone, not counting Working Principals.)

Prior to the publication of the annual *MDS Supplement* [B 273] for 1950, general guidance about the coverage of the series was notably lacking. In interpreting any individual series, particular attention needs to be paid to the footnotes to the tables themselves, which document some of the detailed changes, as well as the information in the *Supplement* [B 273]. Their coverage was affected, of course, by changes from time to time in the scope of the building controls which defined the sites from which returns were obtained (see Section 3.2). In addition, attention needs to be directed once again to the problem of using the site returns as a means of breaking down the total employment figures obtained from the censuses and samples, due to the mismatch in coverage discussed earlier (Section 3.8.3.2): the totals were confined to the main trades but the site returns included on-site labour of both specialist and main trades contractors. As we have pointed out earlier, it was assumed that the site returns could be regarded as covering the main trades alone on the grounds that the off-site labour of these contractors missed from the return would be equivalent to the on-site labour of the specialist contractors. This assumption, however, was shown to be invalid by the statistics collected in the census for February 1948 (the only time apparently, that information was sought about on-site and off-site labour). The implication of the results (assuming them to be of general applicability) was that, other things being equal, the site returns would overstate the main trades labour force by some 6–7 per cent overall.[31] The overstatement was not likely to be the same for each category, however, and new housing work in particular seems likely to have been subject to a much smaller error on this score.

At the same time, it must be remembered that these errors may have been off-set or even enlarged further, by virtue of the estimates incorporated for sites which failed to submit returns. Without further information one can do no more than enjoin caution. In this respect, however, useful comparisons may be made between the census results (see Table 3.2) and the labour series considered in Section 3.7.4.

3.10. Miscellaneous Labour Statistics Collected by the Ministry of Works 1941–55

3.10.1. *Employment in the Mobile Labour Force and the Special Repair Service*

The Mobile Labour Force was formed by the Ministry in June 1946 on the basis of the war-time Special Repair Service which had been formed in 1940 to do war-damage

---

[31] The on-site labour of the specialist trades was shown to be almost three times as great as the off-site labour of the main trades; since the latter amounted to some 3 to 4 per cent of the total main trades labour force, the effect was to overstate by between 6 and 7 per cent overall.

repair and other jobs.[32] The members of the force undertook to go anywhere at any time to work on war damage repairs and to undertake housing work in war-damaged and rural areas and urgent Government building work where local labour resources were inadequate. It was also the practice in places where the force was at work to recruit men locally on a temporary basis. Few statistics seem to be available about the Special Repair Service. Some data may be found in [QRL 335]. For the Mobile Labour Force, referred to as 'Labour employed by the Directorate of Mobile Labour Services', separate monthly data for mobile and 'immobile' (i.e. local) labour broken down by type of work were included for the period July 1946–March 1950 in the *Monthly Bulletin* [QRL 194] last appearing in issue No. 52. A breakdown by occupation was also included but only for the period up to July 1949 (*Bulletin* [QRL 194] No. 44).

3.10.2. *Employment of Prisoners of War on Construction Work 1946–8*

Monthly series from May 1946 are available giving details of the employment of prisoners of war on construction by type of work up to May 1948 (last included in *Bulletin* [QRL 194] No. 30), and series provided by the War Office of the numbers 'allocated' and 'not allocated' to Ministries, broken down into a number of sub-categories, up to August 1948 (last included in *Bulletin* [QRL 194] No. 34).

3.10.3. *Employment on Opencast Coal Production from 1942*

Opencast coal production is classified to the construction industry because it is generally carried out by civil engineering contractors who have the plant required for this work. Details of the labour employed were obtained on the site returns (WB 1 and CPS 23—described earlier). A series, so obtained, was included for the period 1942–4 in [QRL 318] No. 27 along with figures for plant in use and coal produced. Subsequent series for employment are to be found incorporated in the analyses discussed in Section 3.7.4.2.

3.10.4. *The Housing Labour Force and Employment on Air-raid Damage Repairs to Houses in London 1944–5*

Special demands for labour for the repair of air-raid damage arose as a result of the flying bomb attacks on London and south-east England in June 1944 and the following months. Hence from this date (up to May 1945) separate monthly series were brought together in the *Statistical Bulletin* [QRL 318] No. 26 *et seq.* providing a detailed analysis of the number of operatives employed on housing work of all kinds nationally and, in particular, the total labour (including Forces and Civil Defence personnel) engaged on air-raid damage repairs in London.

3.10.5. *Statistics Relating to the Payment-by-results Scheme 1941–7*

A payment-by-results scheme was introduced at the instigation of the Government in July 1941. Regional Payment-by-results Advisers were appointed throughout Great

---
[32] For further details see Kohan [B 90].

Britain to advise on the practical application of the scheme at site level. Returns obtained from these advisers in respect of sites *visited* (not necessarily a representative sample) provided the basis for national statistics on such things as the output achieved in relation to basic output (in general and by operation), the bonus earned, the proportion of men earning bonus and the proportion of man-hours worked on bonused work. Data were included from time to time in the period 1943–4 in the Ministry's *Statistical Bulletin* [QRL 318] and an official Report on the operation of the scheme from its inception to its termination in March 1947 was published in 1947 [B 286]. Reference should also be made to a *Memorandum* [B 272] on the scheme, published in 1944, which included the schedules of trade operations for which bonus rates were fixed. Useful background information about the scheme, particularly relating to its introduction, may be found in [B 90] and [B 20]. Statistics about payment by results were also collected by the Ministry of Labour and National Service during this period—see Section 6.9.3.6.

3.10.6. *Surveys of Incentive Schemes 1951–5*

Surveys were made in June of each year from 1951 to 1953 and again (the last such survey) in 1955 to obtain information about the number of operatives paid under incentive systems of 'bonus payments related to output or targets', in order to measure the spread of such schemes which had become permissible under the terms of national industrial agreements which came into operation in November 1947. The scope of the 1951–3 surveys was confined to the labour employed by main contractors alone[33] (though some direct labour was included in 1953) on sites from which site returns were obtained (see Appendix VI for details). The 1955 enquiry was on a different basis, since site returns had ended, being conducted on a separate form in conjunction with the monthly sample return (see Appendix VII) and thus covering all contractors on the new (SIC-based) register (see Section 4.1). The return required information about the number of sites on which schemes were and were not in operation, the number of operatives covered by such schemes and the total number of operatives employed.

It is not intended to consider closely questions of interpretation for the results of these surveys are not generally available: they were presented to the National Consultative Council of the Building and Civil Engineering Industries, publication being confined to summary details in a Press Notice issued by the MOW. A report of the 1951 survey will be found in *MOLG* [QRL 190] Vol. 60, p. 7. A note of warning is in order, however, with regard to the use of the results, especially in view of the existence of alternative statistics collected by the former Ministry of Labour (see Section 6.9.3.6). First, the MOW and MOL results are not in close agreement. Secondly, comparison of the MOW surveys is beset by difficulties arising from limitations and changes in scope and varying response rates.

---

[33] In Scotland, however, the system of separate trades contracting used there meant in practice that the returns were wider in coverage.

CHAPTER 4

STATISTICS COLLECTED BY THE DEPARTMENT OF THE ENVIRONMENT AND ITS PREDECESSOR DEPARTMENTS SINCE 1954

4.1. Introduction

4.1.1. *The Changes Introduced in 1955*

Changes were introduced in 1955 which mark a clear division in the statistics relating to output, labour employed and the structure of the industry. These changes were brought about by the ending of the building controls which were introduced during the war and continued in force until 1953–4. Up to this time, as we have described in Chapter 3, there were two main sources of statistical information:

(1) returns, on both census and sample bases, from undertakings which had been required to register with the MOW, and render statistical returns, in accordance with Defence Regulation 56AB,
(2) returns in respect of individual sites covered by the scheme for the licensing and authorization of building and civil engineering work under Defence Regulation 56A.

The revocation of DR56AB in November 1953 ended the power of the Ministry to compel firms to register and to render statistical returns. Thereafter the Ministry relied on the general power conferred by the *Statistics of Trade Act* of 1947 to compel the provision of returns[1] but, as far as the compilation and maintenance of a register was concerned, it was left to its own devices (see Section 4.1.3). During 1954, however, the Ministry continued to maintain the register voluntarily and to use it as the base for continuing monthly sample enquiries and for taking a census in May. In November 1954 DR56A was revoked, finally ending controls over building operations and destroying thereby what remained of the base for obtaining site returns.

The scope of the register of building and civil engineering undertakings which had been maintained in accordance with DR56AB did not correspond with the definition adopted for the industry in the *Standard Industrial Classification* (SIC) [B 329] which had been issued by the CSO in 1948 to promote uniformity and comparability in official statistics. The revocation of the regulations made it opportune for the Ministry of Works to bring its own definition into line. Thus the major change in the statistics collected by the MOW in the period from 1955 is their classification in accordance with the SIC; henceforth the definition of the industry used for statistical purposes by the MOW and its successor Departments corresponds in principle with that used by other Government

[1] The *Statistics of Trade Act* appears to have been used for the first time in May 1954.

Departments. The application of the definition in practice, however, deserves more detailed attention and we comment upon this from time to time as appropriate in the Sections which follow. We first examine the principles of the classification in more general terms.

4.1.2. *Construction in the Standard Industrial Classification*

The SIC is drawn up not on the basis of the nature of an occupation or economic activity as such, but on the basis of industrial 'Establishments' which are classified to an Industry ('Orders' of the SIC) according to their principal activity. An establishment is defined as *normally* the whole of the premises (such as a farm, a factory or a shop) at a particular address. Thus if a firm carries out its activities at several different addresses, for each of which separate information is available, each will be treated as a separate establishment and classified accordingly. Further, if at a single address a firm operates separate departments, for which separate accounts are available, each may be treated as a separate establishment and again classified accordingly. Where a single establishment is responsible for different economic activities it is classified to an industry in accordance with its major activity.

In applying the principles to construction it is not the practice to treat each site as a separate establishment. The establishment will normally be the office address from which the firm operates and a single return will be sought from this address in respect of all of its site activities. It will be appreciated, however, that construction *work*, as such, is only embraced by the definition for the industry (called 'Building and Contracting' in the 1948 Classification—Order XVII) if it is carried out by an establishment whose major activity is construction. Thus the building labour directly employed by firms classified to other industries, and its activities, are excluded unless it is employed as part of a distinct building department with separate accounts. Conversely the non-construction activities of firms which are classified to construction, such as the off-site manufacture of components, are counted as part of construction unless they are carried on by a department for which separate accounts are kept and which, therefore, can be separately classified to an appropriate branch of manufacturing. The direct labour forces of government departments, local authorities and other public authorities are generally embraced by the SIC definition for the industry, but difficulties have been encountered in obtaining returns from all such authorities and there have been some differences of treatment over time (see below).

Since 1948 the SIC has been revised twice (1958 and 1968).[2] For convenience each of the definitions is reproduced in Appendix I, together with an analysis, for 1958 and 1968, of the activities expressly included or excluded (it is not possible to make a similar analysis for 1948 because of the lack of a detailed guide to the classification such as those issued for the 1958 and 1968 editions [B 330] [B 331]). The phraseology of the definitions differs but the only substantive change in 1958 was the transfer of certain Constructional Engineering firms from the engineering industry to which they were classified in the 1948 SIC (Order VI) to the construction industry, if the major part of their activity was erection on site as distinct from off-site fabrication. The only change in

---

[2] At the time of writing the classification is under review in connection with the industrial classification drawn up by the statistical office of the European Communities—NACE [B 231] (see Appendix XIII).

4.1.3 STATISTICS COLLECTED BY THE DEPARTMENT OF THE ENVIRONMENT

1968 was to remove from the construction classification the construction work carried out directly by gas, electricity and water undertakings.

There are a number of notable features about the general scope of the definition for the industry. Activities for instance which require the use of contractors' plant or analogous equipment are generally classified as Construction, although they do not necessarily serve to provide or maintain a structure of any kind, thus dredging, opencast coal mining, mineral boring (except for oil and gas) and mine sinking are included. Among the exclusions, shop and office fitting and parquet floor laying are the most notable. Fencing and drainage carried out by agricultural contractors are classified to Agriculture, but fence contractors and land drainage contractors as such are classified to Construction. Thatching is classified to Agriculture but stone-walling to Construction. We also note in Appendix I a number of activities related to the cleaning of buildings which are at present classified as Services.

In summary, therefore, it will be appreciated that as a consequence of the basis on which the SIC is drawn up and the way in which particular activities are classified, certain activities of a construction nature are not covered by the official statistics for the industry whilst other, non-construction, activities are included. In addition, of course, a substantial amount of repair, maintenance and alterations work to dwellings, and possibly also to buildings such as small shops, offices and workshops, is carried out by their owners or occupiers themselves and this too is not covered by the official statistics for the industry. Certain statistical information about expenditure in this field is available, however, and is referred to below (Section 4.4.5).

4.1.3. *The Register of Contractors since 1954*

The register maintained by the MOW in accordance with DR56AB (Section 3.2.2 refers) was wider in scope than that required under the SIC. The main action required in 1954, therefore, was to identify and remove from the register those firms or 'establishments' that did not fall within the scope of the SIC—i.e. those whose *major* activity was not construction. (Hitherto, as we have described, all firms who undertook building and civil engineering work under contract, irrespective of whether it constituted the major part of their activity or not, had to be registered.)

This was done by means of a special census taken in November 1954 (see Appendix IV) in which firms were asked to indicate whether the major activity of the undertaking was: '(a) Building and Civil Engineering' or '(b) Electric Wiring Contracting' (a note was included to indicate that category (a) was also to include all firms in the specialist trades (see Section 3.3.2) except for those electrical contractors who, where appropriate, were classifiable under (b)). No guidance was given as to the interpretation of the term 'major activity', but in subsequent enquiries it has meant the activity accounting for the major part of a firm's turnover. Non-active firms were required to indicate whether or not they were 'closed down permanently'.

Although the preparation of the new register mainly involved the removal of firms from the old register, the movement was not solely in one direction. In particular, building departments of non-construction firms could be treated, in principle, as separate 'establishments' and placed on the construction register (i.e. where they were able to supply the statistical information required, thus making separate classification feasible) whereas previously they were not registrable unless they carried out work under contract for persons outside the organization itself. Now, therefore, the direct labour forces of industrial firms came within the scope of the industry but for statistical purposes they were treated as contractors rather than direct labour. It is not known what action was taken to obtain the registration of such firms; some information may have been available from returns made to the Ministry in November/December 1941 (see Section 3.4) which would have provided a starting point, but whether or not this was utilized is not clear. Given the widespread existence of works departments—as revealed in the war-time enquiry in 1941—and the fact that the response to that enquiry is believed to have been incomplete, it is perhaps probable that the coverage of such departments remained incomplete. Action was also taken at this time to reconcile the MOW register with that maintained by the Board of Trade for census of production purposes. Henceforth these two departments maintained a joint register.

As we indicated earlier, however, the ending of compulsory registration created the problem of keeping the register up-to-date, a problem which remains to the present day, for it seems that the *Statistics of Trade Act, 1947,* does not provide adequate powers in this respect.[3] For an industry so large, so dispersed, consisting of so many small units and in which the annual turnover of firms entering and leaving the industry is also large, the problem is severe. In recent years the problem has been aggravated very considerably by the growth that has taken place in the practice of 'labour-only' sub-contracting in which a gang of men undertake part of the work on a contract, often by merely verbal agreement with the main contractor or another sub-contractor, by supplying their labour and perhaps some tools and equipment but not materials. Since the members of such gangs often remain as self-employed workers and their association is often both informal and transient, it is virtually impossible to ensure that they are covered on the register. (Further information about the practice of labour-only sub-contracting may be found in the report of the Phelps Brown Committee [B 307].)

The Ministry has used a variety of means in attempting to maintain a comprehensive register including the scanning of telephone directories and the trade press and various *ad hoc* enquiries from time to time. Some of these methods are described in [B 220] and, more recently, in [B 217]. But given the nature of the industry it remains extremely difficult, if not impossible, to ensure that a comprehensive register is, in fact, maintained in default of a system of compulsory registration. Unless such a register is maintained, of course, not only are deficiencies in it transmitted in some degree to the statistical series based upon it, but, if they are allowed to accumulate and revisions made only infrequently, then such revisions will introduce discontinuities into the series. Indeed this is precisely what has happened.

Substantial deficiencies in coverage were accumulated up to the early 1970s—these were officially acknowledged in 1973 in [B 217]. The scale of the problem may be appreciated by considering some of the figures put forward in [B 217]. There it is estimated that by 1971 the Register, consisting of some 70,000 firms, was deficient by some 30,000 firms not counting 'many thousands of self-employed workers who hire their labour to main contractors' (labour-only sub-contractors) who had been progressively under-recorded. The combined effect it is thought was a gradually increasing

---

[3] The post-war Working Party on Building Operations had recommended in its report in 1950 [B 349] that registration should continue for the purpose of compiling statistical information (para. 92) and it is understood that an appropriate clause was inserted in draft legislation; it did not advance further, however, because of the resignation of the government of the day and it appears that no further action was taken. In 1969 a committee [Forbes] on the registration of builders was appointed but in its report [B 304] did not concern itself with the question from the statistical point of view.

deficiency in the labour recorded rising from around 120,000 workers in 1963 to 260,000 in 1972. In terms of output it is estimated that this represented an under-recording of $7\frac{1}{2}$ per cent in 1963 rising to $13\frac{1}{2}$ per cent in 1972 (allowing for increased productivity). These additional firms were formally added to the main register in 1974, having been retained on a 'Special List' in 1972 and 1973 (see Appendix IV—Sections (e) and (h) (5)).

4.1.4. *General Review of the Enquiries Undertaken since 1954*

In the period since 1954 information about employment and output in the industry has been obtained solely from full censuses or sample surveys of contractors and censuses of direct labour organizations; no equivalent of the former site returns has existed.[4] These have provided the bases for time series of employment and output. The censuses, as before, have also provided the basis for analyses of the industry's structure. Unlike the earlier period, however, much more of the data collected has been systematically analysed and made available. At the same time the scope of the questionnaires, in terms of the information sought, has been expanded and the notes and guidance given to those making the returns have been amplified. A further development has been a greater use of sampling techniques. Major new enquiries have also been commenced on a regular basis. The most important of these is one into the value of new contracts and orders obtained by contractors for it provides, in principle, an important indicator of the future work load of the industry. More recently (1977) this has been supplemented with a qualitative 'state-of-trade' enquiry. Another enquiry with a similar intention of providing a forward-looking indication of demand has been one concerned with the value of work at the design stage in local authority offices, intended to supplement surveys by the RIBA of the volume of work in hand in private architectural practices (see Section 13.5.1). Certain subsidiary enquiries have also been instituted, e.g. on the overseas activities of British contractors. Each of these enquiries and the statistics available are examined in turn in this Chapter. In addition statistics about the operation of building controls, which were re-introduced for a short time in the 1960s, are also considered here.

4.2. MOW–DOE Censuses of Contractors in Great Britain since 1954

4.2.1. *Introduction*

Censuses were taken in September 1955 and April 1956 and then regularly in April and September each year from 1957 to 1970 when they were combined into a single annual census taken in October, commencing in 1971. The April census was used to obtain information about employment and output, and the September census was used to obtain detailed information about the composition of the labour force. In October 1976, to reduce the form-filling burden only a sample of the smaller firms was included in the annual enquiry: from 1977 onwards those firms not included in the October enquiry will be asked to complete a short form to provide basic information for classification of size and trade. Specimen copies of some of the questionnaires used

---
[4] Though it may be noted that a 'project-based' system of collecting output and employment statistics for new work may be introduced in the near future (at the time of writing—late 1977—it had been under investigation for some years) which would, once again, provide information about individual projects.

together with a brief commentary on the principal changes in their content over time will be found in Appendix IV. This section is devoted to a review of the available analyses and matters relating to their interpretation.

4.2.2. *Nature and Coverage of the Censuses*

Until the change in practice in 1976, referred to above, all firms on the register were covered in each enquiry, but it should be noted that from 1959 some categories of information were collected only on a sample basis from the smaller firms. Coverage is meant to extend to the activities of all contractors in Great Britain but, as noted above, severe difficulties, associated with the very large number of small firms and the growth in the practice of labour-only sub-contracting, have been experienced in maintaining a complete register of firms and ensuring comprehensive coverage of output and employment (see Section 4.1.3).

The large number of firms identified in the early 1970s as not having been included on the Department's register of firms (see Section 4.1.3 above) was not immediately incorporated in the censuses but was maintained as a 'Special List'. They were included for the first time in 1974. In April 1972 a Special Enquiry was made in respect of these firms (see Appendix IV for details) but the results were not published. In October 1973 they were sent separately-coded questionnaires and results were published on separate bases, including and excluding such firms. The difficulty of covering the output and employment of self-employed operatives working under labour-only sub-contract has remained as a continuing problem for which only estimates can be made—see Section 4.4.2.

Apart from the problems posed by small firms and labour-only self-employment there is the need to ensure that foreign contractors undertaking work in Great Britain are covered and, conversely, that British contractors undertaking work outside Great Britain do not include such activities in their returns. The means available for covering foreign contractors are essentially informal and depend upon the vigilance of the Department's staff in the regions who are responsible for the circulation and the collection of the questionnaires; since it would seem reasonable to assume that the contracts involved would be large in size but small in number this problem is probably much less acute than that of keeping track of all the small national contractors. The question of ensuring that only work within Great Britain is covered is one which depends on the instructions given in the questionnaires. In fact, no guidance was given with respect to geographical coverage until 1967 when specific instructions were added to say that the returns should relate to 'Great Britain (i.e. excluding Northern Ireland)'. These instructions were expanded in 1977 to specifically exclude the Isle of Man and Channel Islands as well.[5] With regard to work done overseas by British contractors it may be noted that a separate annual enquiry is made (see Section 4.6).

The coverage of the term 'contractors' extends to the direct labour departments of firms classified to other industries in the private sector on the basis we described earlier (Section 4.1.2) but only if such firms have a separate building department for which separate accounts are kept.

---

[5] The author is informed that this was not because of any evidence of error but merely part of a tidying-up of definitions.

4.2.3. The Available Analyses and Their Interpretation

4.2.3.1. *General guide to the data available.* A guide to the analyses of all the censuses taken from 1957 to 1976 is provided below (Table 4.1). At the time of writing the results of the census for 1977 had not been published but details of the scope of the enquiries will be found in Appendix IV; attention is drawn in particular to the changes introduced in 1977. Analyses of the data collected in the census taken in September 1955 were not published except for an analysis of apprentices according to craft in [QRL 64] Appendix 6 (this also shows operatives employed by craft but as the census return did not require this information, the figures must be presumed to be estimates). None of the results of the April 1956 census were published at the time but they are now available in the *Collection of MOW Statistics 1941–56* [QRL 321] recently compiled by the author with the assistance of the DOE.

We now turn to consider the available analyses more closely and to discuss the salient features of the data that are relevant for purposes of interpretation.

4.2.3.2. *Analyses of the number of firms.* The same general points apply to data relating to the number of firms as were made in respect of the earlier censuses. The use of the word 'firm' is ambiguous. Firms under common ownership or control may or may not make separate returns and some firms may make more than one return in respect of its activities in different parts of the country. Strictly speaking, therefore, the figures would be better described as the numbers of 'reporting units' or simply the 'numbers of returns', although it is understood that there are relatively few firms with more than one reporting unit. Changes in this number, of course, do not necessarily reflect changes in the number of firms in the industry. Indeed the interpretation of changes in the number must contend with the problems we noted earlier relating to the maintenance of a comprehensive register (Chapters 2 and 4.1.3). Changes in numbers may also reflect non-response; although the making of a return is compulsory under the terms of the *Statistics of Trade Act* a complete response is never obtained and after weeding out of the register those firms which are found to be no longer eligible, the remaining number may still be an over-statement of active firms on the register. It should also be noted that the number of firms includes those not trading at the time of the census (this is pointed out in the later editions of the *Supplement* [QRL 71] and in the latest census publications [QRL 240]). Hence in the analyses by size of firm it is possible for the figure for the smallest size group—nil operatives or (currently) nil–1 person (i.e. total employed manpower including Working Proprietors) to exceed the figure for total employment in the group.

Separate figures of entries to and exists from the industry (additions to and deletions from the Register) are not generally published although the author is informed that limited information prepared primarily for statistical and management purposes is available for some past years. Some figures were published in the *Supplement* [QRL 71] for April 1965 (Table 4) showing the numbers of firms closed down according to trade of firm and region of registration but the author is informed that the closures could not be related to any specific period of time and the table was discontinued because of the unreliability of the figures.

Table 4.1

MOW–DOE Construction Census Analyses 1957 to Date—Contractors Only (Great Britain)

Note: This table covers the regular analyses of the April and September census results from 1957 to 1970 and the October census results from 1971 to 1976—the latest available at the time of writing. Details of the April 1956 census results and certain supplementary analyses are given at the foot of this table.

Statistic / Cross-Classifications	Trade of Firm and Region	Trade and Size of Firm	Size of Firm and Region	Trade of Firm and Type of Work	Size of Firm and Type of Work	Type of Work and Region	Craft and Trade of Firm	Craft and Size of Firm	Craft and Region	Craft	Type of APTC Staff and Trade of Firm	Type of APTC Staff and Size of Firm	Type of APTC Staff and Region	Trade of Firm	Size of Firm	Region
Number of Firms: Totals	1957 to date†	1965 to date‡														
Employing APTC staff			1957 to date‡													
Value of Work Done (1st quarter only 1957–70) (3rd quarter only 1971 to date)	1957 to date			1957 to date§	1957 to date§											
Employment: Operatives						1957 to date§	1957 to date‡	1963 to date‡	1957 to date‡	1957 to date‡						
Apprentices (Trainees)	1963 to date‡	1965 to date‡														
APTC staff*											1965 to date‡	1965–9		1963 to date‖		
APTC staff under training		1965–9														
Working Principals (Proprietors)*														1963 to date‖		
Total Employment														1963 to date‖	1963 to date‖	1963 to date‖

104

PUBLICATION SOURCES. The primary sources are the Bulletin of (Construction) Statistics Supplement [QRL 71] for the period 1957–70 (April and September censuses) and Private Contractors' Construction Census [QRL 240] thereafter (October censuses). Historical series in summary form (no cross-classifications) are to be found in the ABCS 1970 [QRL 32] for the period 1959–70 and, for recent years back to the 1960s in [QRL 240] and also in HCS [QRL 163] from time to time. The ABCS [QRL 32] also included data for an extended range of size groups.

APRIL 1956 CENSUS. The results of this census—the first post-1955 census—were not published at the time. Selected analyses are now available, however, in Statistics Collected by the MOW 1941–56 [QRL 321]—a collection recently compiled under the author's direction with the assistance of the DOE—as follows: numbers of firms and operatives and value of work done (1st quarter of 1956) by size of firm, by trade of firm and by region and cross-classifications by size and trade of firm; number of Working Principals by size of firm and analyses of operatives employed and the value of work done each according to type of work and each analysed by size of firm, trade of firm and region of registration.

SUPPLEMENTARY ANALYSES. Analyses additional to those indicated in the table are available as follows:

(a) Number of Firms employing Apprentices.
(b) Number of Apprentices according to Craft and Type of Agreement } Available on request from DOE Statistics Construction Division; at one time published in Departmental *Press Notice* [QRL 230]. Data for the period 1957–68 and, for (b) only, for 1949, were reproduced in [QRL 121].

(c) *Ad hoc analyses:*
 (i) *April 1965 Census*—an analysis of the percentage of firms in each size group which reported undertaking maintenance work according to the percentage which such work represented in their total output, published in [QRL 68] Appendix IV, Table 18;
 (ii) *April 1969 Census*—an analysis of the value of work done by trade of firm sub-classified simultaneously by type of work and size of firm, published in *Bulletin of Construction Statistics Special Supplement, April 1969* [QRL 70].

* Statistics back to 1959 (totals only) were published in [B 307] Table 4.
† April censuses only in the period 1957–67, then both April and September censuses.
‡ September censuses only from the date shown up to 1970.
§ April censuses only from the date shown up to 1970.
‖ September censuses only in 1963 and 1964, then both April and September censuses.

The number of firms employing APTC staff. The definition of APTC staff was altered in 1971 resulting in the reclassification of around 10,000 persons as Working Proprietors rather than APTC. Analyses of the number of firms employing APTC staff will therefore have been affected from this date: many firms run by a Working Proprietor and employing no other APTC staff would have been included prior to 1971 but not subsequently.

4.2.3.3. *Employment analyses—General remarks.* Matters relevant to particular categories of labour are considered separately in the sections which follow. This section is concerned with general matters relevant to all the employment data. A comparison of the statistics themselves with those from other sources is made in Table 6.1 included as part of Section 6.2.4.1 below.

The statistics have continued to relate to employment at particular points of time—numbers on the payroll during a particular week—rather than averages over a period of time. But their coverage has been altered: in contrast to the earlier post-war censuses taken from May 1945 to May 1954, when only *male employees age 16 and over* were meant to be covered, the questionnaires from 1955 (indeed from November 1954) have referred to all persons, *both male and female, aged 15 years and over, whether full or part-time*. The reference to females is mainly of relevance to the series for non-manual labour since there are few females employed as operatives on construction work (though it should be noted that the term operatives covers canteen workers, cleaners, etc.). The age limit of 15 years was in accord with the school-leaving age; the reason for the former higher limit of 16 years (a limit adhered to in all the MOW enquiries from 1941) seems to have been connected originally with the object of achieving comparability with MOL statistics (see Section 3.3.3).

As in the enquiries for earlier periods, each contractor, regardless of whether he was a main or sub-contractor, was meant to provide a return only in respect of his own employees. In fact, however, no specific instruction to this effect was included on the questionnaire in relation to employment, as distinct from output, until April 1959. It is conceivable, therefore, that some double counting occurred by virtue of some main contractors including the labour employed by sub-contractors on some sites, though this is probably unlikely since they would not normally have a record of such labour.

Unrecorded labour. For reasons given earlier, some labour is missed altogether in the censuses. Estimates of this labour have been made for census months back to 1967 and published, not with the census results themselves, but in Supplementary Tables in *HCS* [QRL 168]—for further details see Section 4.4.2 below. There are two further points of general relevance about the employment statistics obtained in the census enquiries. First, the timing of the enquiries (formerly April and September, now October) is such that the seasonal influences to which the industry is subject are less marked than at other times: the other employment statistics are collected more frequently but in less detail. Secondly, the fact that the employment figures are not averages for a period of time needs to be borne in mind if relating them to figures of the value of work done which cover work done over a full quarter.

As with other series the information collected has become more detailed over time. We turn now to consider the statistics available for each category of labour separately.

4.2.3.4 STATISTICS COLLECTED BY THE DEPARTMENT OF THE ENVIRONMENT

4.2.3.4. *Analyses of operatives employed.* The term 'operatives' is meant to cover all *employees*, both full-time and part-time, who do *manual* work, including apprentices (for further details see Section 4.2.3.5), operatives engaged in transport work, stores and warehouses, and on the manufacture of goods for sale, canteen workers, etc. (cf. specimen questionnaire BIM3/AR8 *et al.* reproduced in Appendix IV). Working Foremen, as distinct from General Foremen who are counted as APTC staff, were meant to be counted as operatives, although prior to 1967 they were specifically referred to in the guidance notes in the September returns only (since then the distinction has been stressed in every census). Working Principals who, by definition, also do manual work, are not employees and thus are not counted as operatives (for details see Section 4.2.3.6).

Occupational analyses. Information about the occupations of operatives employed has been obtained only once a year, originally in the September censuses, and then in October from 1971 to 1976. In 1977 the occupational classification is being dropped from the DOE census and responsibility for the collection of craft data transferred to the CITB. The occupations for which separate statistics are available since 1957 are listed below together with particulars of apprenticeship statistics. It should be noted, however, that from 1975 data have been collected for all 'trainees', not just apprentices (further details are given below).

Crafts distinguished from 1957	Additional Crafts and Occupations distinguished from 1965
Carpenters and joiners	
Bricklayers	
Slaters and tilers	{ Roof slaters and tilers { Floor, wall and (from 1967) ceiling tilers
Plasterers	
Painters	
Plumbers and glaziers	{ Plumbers and gas fitters { Glaziers
Masons (except 1974)	
Electricians	
Heating and ventilating engineers	
Other B and CE crafts and occupations	{ Tunnellers (1974 only) Formwork erectors* (until 1974, then combined with carpenters and joiners) Paviours Steel benders and fixers* Scaffolders* Steel erectors and sheeters† Mechanical equipment operators† Crane drivers* Concrete erectors and assemblers* } combined from 1975 Other B and CE crafts All other occupations* } combined from 1971 for Labourers* } publication purposes

* There are no apprenticeship statistics for these occupations (see below).
† Apprenticeship statistics available from 1967 only.

These occupational categories represent, with only two exceptions, all those for which separate data were collected and published until 1975. The exceptions are that data for 'other B & CE crafts' and 'all other occupations' has been separately collected throughout the whole period and canteen workers have been separately identified since 1969. In October 1975 the number of categories were expanded in consultation with the CITB in order to harmonize the respective questionnaires. Although published tabulations have continued to present data for the same occupations as above separate data have been collected for the following additional categories:

Plant mechanics
Misc. craftsmen excl. mech. engineering services
Natural gas conversion workers
Other mech. eng. services workers

Earth moving plant operators
Other mech. plant operators
Demolishers
Other B & CE skilled workers
Unskilled labourers.

Guidance regarding the completion of the occupations return. With the earlier expansion in the number of occupational categories distinguished, in 1965, more precise guidance was included in the questionnaires about the category to which particular occupations should be classified—see specimen form BIM164 in Appendix IV for details. Before 1965 the only guidance given was in respect of the 'all other occupations' category (see Appendix IV). It may be noted in particular that this category, although differentiated from 'other B & CE crafts' since 1965, may also include craftsmen inasmuch as it also covers labour engaged on 'the manufacture of goods for sale'.

Certain other data about operative employment has been collected but not published and we refer briefly to these categories below.

Operatives under training. Information was requested in each September census from 1965 to 1969 about the number of operatives 'under training for additional or new skills' broken down according to the occupation for which they were being trained. This information may be made available on request. Reference should also be made to the statistics collected by the CITB—see Section 6.4.

Labour-only sub-contractors. No reliable information is available about the number of operatives engaged in labour-only sub-contracting (see [B 217], [B 307] and [B 308] for comment and estimates). Between September 1967 and September 1969 the question was asked on the questionnaires 'Are you wholly or mainly a sub-contractor supplying labour only to other contractors?', but the information obtained was not published.

Other analyses of operatives employed—by type of work, by trade and size of firm and by region—are considered later in this section.

4.2.3.5. *Analyses of apprentices (trainees) employed.* Statistics about apprentices as such were collected in each September census from 1957 to 1970 and in each October enquiry subsequently up to and including 1974. In the 1975 census the term 'apprentice' was replaced by 'trainee' which is, of course, wider in scope. Details of the analyses available, at the time of writing, are shown in Table 4.1. The occupations for which separate apprenticeship data were collected correspond with most of the skilled occupations for which operative employment data were collected—see above. Trainee statistics will cover all occupations. Information collected prior to 1957 which formed the basis for intake statistics has not been collected subsequently.

The information requested on the questionnaire categorized apprentices as follows:

(a) Apprentices with written indentures.
(b) Boys on probation for written indentures (from September 1959).
(c) Apprentices with verbal agreements and other probationers.

The full range of information collected was not regularly published but it is available on request from the DOE Statistics Construction Division. For details of the instructions regarding the completion of the returns see Appendix IV.

4.2.3.6. *Analyses of Working Principals (Working Proprietors).* Prior to 1971 statistics were collected in both the April and the September censuses of the number (total only) of Working Principals who were defined as self-employed owners, managers, partners, etc. who do *manual* work. With effect from the census for October 1971 the more comprehensive term 'Working Proprietor' (covering also those who do no manual work) has been used. Working Proprietors are defined as 'persons engaged in the business covered by the return who are regarded as self-employed persons for National Insurance purposes, e.g. self-employed owners, managers, partners, etc.' (including directors working in the business but not in receipt of a definite wage, salary or commission, but excluding part-time directors paid by fee only). The working partners in labour-only sub-contracting groups are also meant to be included in this category. Formerly, self-employed persons who did not do manual work were returned along with APTC staff. The change in definition in 1971 had the effect of transferring about 10,000 APTC staff to the 'Working Proprietors' category.[6] It should be noted that working partners in groups of labour-only sub-contractors should have been included as Working Principals throughout but a specific instruction to this effect was not included until September 1959.

4.2.3.7. *Analyses of Administrative, Professional, Technical and Clerical staff.* Statistics of the total number of such staff were collected in each September census from 1957 to 1964. Subsequently they were covered in both the April and September censuses, the September (and later October) censuses being used to obtain breakdowns by occupation. Details of the analyses available are set out in Table 4.1 above.

Until 1971 the return for these categories was meant to cover all persons who did not do manual work other than Working Principals (who do both manual and non-manual work and were returned separately) and directors paid by fee only. With effect from the census for October 1971, however, the return for Working Principals was widened to cover Working Proprietors, thereby embracing within that category certain persons who would formerly have been returned as APTC staff (see above under 'Working Principals').

[6] Census Report for 1971 [QRL 240] Table 5, footnote 4. Compare also the returns of the number of self-employed owners and partners obtained in 1969 and 1970—see under 'APTC staff' below.

Coverage has also been affected in practice by other factors. Prior to September 1965 the word 'Professional' was not used on the questionnaires, although such staff were meant to be included, and it is likely that as a consequence at least some professional staff were not covered. It is also likely that the specification of a separate occupational classification in the September returns from 1965 improved their quality by helping to ensure that certain staff were not overlooked. Certainly it is thought that the statistics collected in the April enquiries may be understated as a result of the fact that the information was sought in less detail than in September. Particular attention is drawn to this fact in the April *Supplements* [QRL 71] 1966–8; that for 1966 suggesting an error of about 8 per cent.

Difficulties in ensuring reliable returns are reflected in changes made in the wording of the questionnaires from time to time. A major potential source of error is the incorrect classification, or even double counting, of Working Principals at one time, for the fact that they do both manual and non-manual work may have led to their being classified to the APTC category instead of, or as well as, Working Principals. In September 1959, however, it was made explicit that persons returned as Working Principals should not also have been included as APTC staff. Other changes in wording suggest that other types of labour may possibly have been omitted altogether at particular times. Thus specific references were added regarding the inclusion of 'learners and trainees' in September 1960 and 'self-employed owners' who 'do not do manual work' as late as April 1968. Similarly General Foremen who 'do not do manual work' are specifically referred to for the first time in April 1967; Working Foremen by contrast are supposed to be returned as operatives.

Occupational analyses of APTC staff. As we indicated above, information has been collected in the September censuses since 1965 and the October censuses since 1971 about the occupational classifications of APTC staff. The categories which have been distinguished are listed below; it will be seen that since 1975 the professional staff category has no longer been sub-divided (its coverage has also been changed).

Managerial staff[7]
Professional staff
  Architects (up to 1974)
  Surveyors (up to 1974)
  Engineers (up to 1974)
  Other professional staff (up to 1974)
Training officers (full-time officers only up to 1974. Separate statistics for part-time training officers were collected in the period 1965–8 only).

Technical grades
  General foremen
  Draughtsmen and tracers
  Other technical grades
Clerical and sales staff

Details of the occupations included within each category are given on the specimen forms BIM164 included in Appendix IV (see also [QRL 240]). Until 1975 the general principle for classification, it should be noted, is that professional and technical staff should be recorded according to the main duties on which they are engaged, with the exception that professional staff engaged upon administrative or managerial duties for which they are required to be professionally qualified should be recorded under their professions and not as managerial; no guidance is given, however, regarding the

---

[7] Two sub-categories: 'Self-employed owners and partners' and 'Employed managerial staff' were separately distinguished in September 1969 and 1970.

4.2.3.8 STATISTICS COLLECTED BY THE DEPARTMENT OF THE ENVIRONMENT

interpretation of the term 'professionally qualified'. From October 1975 the undivided 'professional' category has covered only 'professionally qualified architects, surveyors and engineers engaged in these occupations', other professional staff (e.g. chartered accountants) have been included under 'managerial staff'.

APTC staff under training. In addition for the period 1965–9 separate figures were collected of the numbers of persons under training for each of the categories listed above (see Table 4.1).

4.2.3.8. *Analyses of output.* A return of output (the value of work done) broken down by type of work was called for in each of the April censuses from 1956 to 1970 and in each of the October censuses subsequently. Details of the analyses made are set out in Table 4.1 above.

Little comment is required here since the same general principles have been followed as in earlier enquiries. The value of output returned is supposed to represent an estimate of the amounts 'chargeable to customers' for work actually done during the specified period. Until 1973 each contractor was instructed to include only the value of work done directly by him, excluding that done by sub-contractors, the latter being returned by the sub-contractors concerned (if they were on the register). From 1974 the instructions have been amended to require contractors to provide separate information about the value of work done under sub-contract, whilst at the same time retaining the returns from sub-contractors on the register. The same applies to labour-only sub-contractors except that the value of materials supplied by the main contractor is returned by the main contractor, the labour-only sub-contractor returning only the payments received for the work done. Similar instructions, it may be noted, have been used in the quarterly sample enquiries (see Appendices IV and VII for further details and Section 4.4.5). The purpose of this change is to allow estimates to be made of 'unrecorded output' for incorporation in the overall output time series (Section 4.4). This is done on the basis of a comparison of the grossed-up estimates of sub-contracted work done *for* contractors with the work done by firms *as* sub-contractors. It should be noted, however, that the census results themselves, published in [QRL 240], include no allowance for 'unrecorded output'.

The value of work done is also meant to include that done on the contractors' own initiative on buildings destined for eventual sale or lease and on the construction or maintenance of their own premises (although specific instructions to this effect were not given until April 1965 and April 1964 respectively—see Appendix IV for details). The cost of land, legal charges and professional fees is meant to be excluded, as is the value of goods made by the contractor but not used on any of his contracts. It should be noted too that the values returned included VAT where appropriate (i.e. in relation to repair and maintenance work) in each census from October 1974 to October 1976. With effect from the October 1977 census VAT is to be excluded from the output returns: to provide an estimate of the effect of this change, contractors were asked to give an aggregate figure of VAT in this census return. For details of the application of VAT to construction work see [B 346] and [B 347].

It is important to appreciate, as we have stressed elsewhere, that the output value returned by each contractor is an estimate—see the general discussion of measurement and valuation problems in Section 2.

4.2.3.9. *Analyses by type of work and sector.* Breakdowns of the number of operatives employed and the value of work done according to type of work and sector have been required in each of the April censuses and subsequently in the October censuses. The types of work have remained the same over the whole period as follows:

Work on houses and flats:
    (1) New housing construction in the public sector,
    (2) New housing construction for private owners and developers,
    (3) Repair and maintenance of dwellings.

Non-housing work for private owners and developers:
    (4) New industrial construction,
    (5) New non-industrial construction,
    (6) Repair and maintenance.

Non-housing work for public sector clients:
    (7) New construction,
    (8) Repair and maintenance.

Prior to 1966, however, only three categories were distinguished in the published tabulations: total new housing, total new non-housing work and total repairs and maintenance. Since 1966 data for all the categories listed above have been regularly published. It should also be noted that further output data are published separately as time series—see Section 4.4.5. The wording used on the questionnaires has remained substantially unchanged over the period—details are given in Appendix IV. We turn now to consider some of the most important characteristics of the data.

First, it may not be possible to classify certain operatives by type of work (e.g. transport workers, stores and warehouse staff, canteen workers and operatives employed on the manufacture of goods for sale) and they are therefore returned as a separate total; the figure is not published separately, however, but is allocated *pro rata* among the various categories of work. Secondly, the employment and output data differ in timing. The statistics of employment refer to employment on the pay-day in one week each year whereas the output statistics refer to the estimated value of work done in the quarter up to the end of the preceding month. Thus if the two series are used in conjunction the potential effect of the difference needs to be borne in mind. Thirdly, there is a discrepancy in the treatment of goods manufactured for sale by the contractor. Contractors are instructed to exclude the value of such goods from the return but to *include* the number of operatives engaged on their manufacture.[8] The value of goods both made and used by the contractor, however, are included. Fourthly, it should be noted that the term 'repair and maintenance' is defined differently in respect of housing and non-housing work. For housing it includes work of 'improvements, house/flat conversions, extensions, alterations and redecorations' whereas on non-housing work 'extensions, major alterations and improvements' are defined as new construction (the term 'major alterations' is left undefined).

A final matter of importance is that the boundaries between the public and private sectors may be altered by measures such as nationalization affecting both the classification of output and employment by sector and the division between contractors and direct labour. The most important change during the period under examination

---

[8] Separate questions about the value of non-construction work done and the number of operatives employed on it were included in the October 1977 census—the first time such questions had been asked.

4.2.3.10 STATISTICS COLLECTED BY THE DEPARTMENT OF THE ENVIRONMENT

here was the renationalization of certain steelworks in 1967 which had the effect, from the April 1968 census, of transferring some work formerly returned as 'private industrial' to 'public non-housing'. Further, some steel companies had their own direct labour departments and also carried out construction work under contract for clients outside the industry. The act of nationalization, therefore, also affected the boundaries of the contractors and direct labour sectors. The practices adopted for the classification of this work, however, have varied. Initially these departments continued to be classified as contractors rather than direct labour. This practice was discontinued in (apparently) April 1970 but then re-established in 1973, when retrospectively revised series of output for the whole period from 1972 back to 1963 were published [B 217], on the grounds that these departments continue to carry out work under contract for clients outside the industry ([B 217] p. lxii refers).

4.2.3.10. *Analyses by trade of firm.* The types of firm for which separate analyses are made have been increased in number from thirteen in 1957 to twenty-one since 1968 as shown below. A detailed guide to the classification of firms by trade is included in Appendix III.

The terms 'main trades' and 'specialist trades' used before 1955 fell out of use after the reclassification of the industry in accordance with the terms of the SIC. However, in 1974 they were reintroduced, but with a different scope, in [QRL 240]: the term 'main trades' is there used to refer to the general builders and contractors listed as trades (1) to (3) below, the term 'specialist trades' to refer to all others. For details of the scope of the terms prior to 1955 see Section 3.3.2.

The trade classification of firms since 1957 *

Trades from April 1957
(1) General builders
(2) Building and civil engineering contractors
(3) Civil engineering contractors
(4) Plumbers
(5) Joiners and carpenters
(6) Painters and decorators
(7) Roofers
(8) Plasterers
(9) Glaziers
(10) Heating and ventilating engineers
(11) Electrical contractors
(12) Constructional engineers

Additional trades from April 1965 †
(13) Plant hiring contractors

Additional trades from September 1967 †
(14) Demolition contractors
(15) Scaffolding specialists
(16) Reinforced concrete specialists
(17) Asphalt and tar-spraying contractors
(18) Flooring contractors

Additional trades from September 1968
(19) Insulating specialists
(20) Suspended ceiling specialists
(21) Wall and floor tiling specialists

---

* In addition a group of 'other specialist firms' is defined for 1957–April 1967, together with an 'unallocated' group up to 1964 and one 'miscellaneous' group from September 1968, leaving a gap in the period September 1967 to September 1968 when no such group was defined: it is not clear how these non-specified firms were classified in this period.

† Data for the six additional trades, numbered (13) to (18), were subsequently published retrospectively for the period back to 1959 in the *ABCS* [QRL 32] but not for the full range of analyses (see Table 4.1 for details) included in the primary census publications—the *Supplementary Bulletins* [QRL 71]. Data are given only for: number of firms, value of work done, employment of operatives and total employment.

The principles and practice of classification by trade require explanation. In the past information on the trade classification of firms was sought routinely only for new additions to the register; these firms were required to indicate from a list of trades the one which was most appropriate. For firms already on the register up-to-date information was sought as follows:

(1) In November 1954 on a census questionnaire (BCE3/AR5) when firms were classified to:
   (a) Building and civil engineering, and
   (b) Electrical wiring contracting.
(2) In 1957 when over a period of some months a special form (BIM 124) was sent to all firms to classify them into eighteen trade categories. In addition a space for 'Remarks' was included which firms could use for amplification.
(3) In September 1968 on the census questionnaire (AR 31) which also specified eighteen trade categories together with a space for 'other' categories to be written in. As a result three additional trade categories came into use.
(4) In April 1970 on the census questionnaire (AR 34) when the classification was extended to twenty-one categories together with a space again for other categories.

A detailed guide to the scope of the classification is included in Appendix III.

Since 1971 information has been sought regularly in each census about trade of firm though it has been used for classification of the published results of the corresponding census only since 1974: the 1973 results were classified in accordance with the 1972 trade classification and the 1971 and 1972 results were classified in accordance with the April 1970 trade classification (the Introductions to the volumes of published results [QRL 240] refer—the reference to September 1970 in the volume containing the 1971 and 1972 results is an error since the census was taken in April 1970).

Thus it will be appreciated that up to the late 1960s the available trade analyses have rested upon out-dated classifications and that changes in the composition of the industry by trade taking place over a period may well have been obscured. How important this is with regard to the interpretation of the data is arguable. Switches by some firms from one trade to another are probably not likely on a wide scale; perhaps more likely is the situation where the *major activity* of a firm shifts from one trade to another (e.g. plumber to heating and ventilating engineer). At the same time it must be remembered that deficiencies in the coverage of the register of firms will also affect comparisons of the trade composition, especially inasmuch as new entrants are an important source of change.

The reviews of 1957 and 1968 resulted in changes in the classification of a number of firms. Hence there are discontinuities in the series at these points. In 1957 many of the firms who had been described previously as 'General Builders' were reclassified as specialist firms, notably as 'Painters'. Unfortunately, comparable figures on the old and new bases are not available. The reclassification was not introduced until 1958 so that the trade analyses for 1957 are not comparable with those following. For the 1968 reclassification, comparative figures on the old and new bases, the latter including three trades which were separately distinguished for the first time, were prepared for the September census and again in April 1969. Nearly all trades were affected by the reclassification. Similar comparisons for the 1970 and subsequent reviews from 1973

4.2.3.10 STATISTICS COLLECTED BY THE DEPARTMENT OF THE ENVIRONMENT

were not published. In 1973, however, analyses were affected by the inclusion of 25,000 additional firms on the register for the first time and separate analyses on the basis of the old and the new 'combined' register *were* published at that time—see [QRL 168] No. 10.

It will be noticed that the timing of the extensions in the number of trades classified in the available tabulations do not always coincide with the dates of the reviews. Particularly notable is the extension in 1967 which could only be based on the review for 1957.

As we have indicated, if a firm is engaged on more than one type of activity it is expected to classify itself on the basis of its major activity which is currently defined as meaning the greatest part of its turnover. But it is perhaps worth noting that in the review of 1957 a firm was merely required to indicate 'the category appropriate to the undertaking' without further guidance. Thus in principle the practices adopted by the firms in classifying themselves may not have been consistent.

The classification of the building departments of non-construction firms by trade may be a cause of difficulty. Currently such undertakings are required to identify themselves as such when first placed on the register but not in subsequent reviews—indeed they have not been distinguished as a separate category in any of the general reviews of the register that have been made. The author is informed by the Department that so far as can be ascertained they have been classified to the General Builders category.

Certain problems arise in connection with the analyses of employment and work done by trade of firm according to type of work and the practices adopted are worthy of note. The trades affected are the minor ones of demolition, plant hire and scaffolding contractors. The employment and work done by demolition contractors is attributed, in the analyses according to type of work, to the type of work which is to replace the structure being demolished but where this is not known the work (and employment on it) is assigned to the same type of work as that being demolished. Not all demolition work, of course, is carried out by demolition contractors. Plant hire firms are not generally able to specify the work on which plant has been used and the practice adopted is to distribute the figures of employment and work done over different types of work proportionately to the distribution of the figures for all other firms. Before 1968 the figures were distributed over new work only on the assumption that little plant was hired for repair and maintenance work; since then they have been spread over all work. Similarly in the case of scaffolding firms, employment and work-done figures are distributed proportionately over all work. The points are important when considering the work done by these trades analysed by type of work but it will be appreciated that the effects on the analysis by type of work for all trades combined is small since the activity of these particular trades is a small part of the total.

Another problem that arises in connection with plant hire is that of double counting. Plant hire firms are not in the same category as other specialist firms since they do not normally carry out work on a contract themselves. Consequently contractors will not exclude payments made to these firms, as they would in the case of other specialist firms working as sub-contractors. Hence total output will include the element of plant hire costs incorporated in the return of output of firms using hired plant and again in the returns of 'output' by plant hire firms themselves. Analogous situations do not arise in the case of goods supplied by one contractor to another—e.g. window frames supplied by a carpentry and joinery firm—because, as mentioned earlier, contractors are instructed to exclude the value of goods made for sale from their returns.

4.2.3.11. *Analyses by size of firm.* Firms have always been classified by size on the basis of employment but in 1965 a change was made from classification according to the number of operatives employed to one based on total employment (including Working Principals and all other administrative, professional, technical and clerical staff as well as operatives).[9] A discontinuity was thus introduced in the series, although the size group boundaries first chosen in April 1965[10] were modified in September to provide a greater degree of comparability. Comparative data on the new and the old bases is to be found in both the *Supplements* [QRL 71] for 1965. Summary data for an extended range of size groups (again including comparative data for 1965) over the period 1959–70 were published in the *ABCS* [QRL 32] for 1970.

4.2.3.12. *Analyses by region.* Regional analyses for building work present a major problem because of the fact that the production units do not occupy a fixed location but move about from site to site and many may work on more than one site at the same time. As we indicated earlier (Section 3.5.4) in the period 1946–54 contractors were required to make a return of the number of operatives employed according to the region in which they were working. In 1955, however, the practice was abandoned and, apart from an exception noted below, all subsequent regional analyses have been based upon the location of a firm's head office (except where separate returns are obtained from branch offices) and not the location of the work. The figures do not relate, therefore, to employment or work actually carried out within a region. From time to time, however, the DOE makes estimates of total employment and total output for each region on a location of work basis. These estimates are available on request, but the Department emphasizes that the figures must be regarded only as indicating approximate orders of magnitude of regional totals. (For background information about these estimates see [B 120].)

An exception to the normal classification, based on region of registration of the firm, is that for Scotland and Wales separate information about the number of operatives actually working in these countries was requested in each September census from 1957 to 1976. The data were not published but were used mainly to identify those firms from which additional information should be obtained in sample enquiries so that output statistics on a regional basis could be produced each quarter for Scotland and once a year in respect of the third quarter for Wales (see Section 4.4.5). It is understood, however, that in practice little use was made of the data and the question was dropped from the 1977 census.

It is also worth noting that, in contrast to the output and employment data, statistics of new orders received by contractors *are* analysed according to the location of the work (see Section 4.5).

Until 1965 the Ministry continued to use the former Civil Defence regions as the basis for its regional classifications although these differed in certain respects from the official 'standard regions for statistical purposes'.[10] In 1965 new standard—'Economic Planning'—regions were adopted. There are ten such regions but since the Department

---

[9] *N.B.* Following this change some published size analyses were incorrectly headed 'number of employees'.
[10] The differences were between the Southern and South-Western regions prior to May 1958, when the 'standard' region was revised and the division by the MOW of the standard 'London and South-Eastern Region' into two.

continued to sub-divide the South-East Region (into four), thirteen regions altogether are distinguishable as against twelve under the previous basis of classification. Five of the new regions remain identical with the old, namely Northern, West Midlands (former Midland), North-Western, Wales and Scotland. For comparative purposes classifications were made according to both the old and new regions when the changeover was made in 1965 and will be found in [QRL 71]. Since regional classifications were used in a variety of sources without definition, the definitions of both classifications are brought together for convenience in Appendix II. The regions were revised again on 1st April 1974—details of these changes and the timing of their introduction for classification purposes will be found in [B 250] 1975 edition.

4.3. MOW–DOE Censuses of Direct Labour Organizations in Great Britain since 1954

4.3.1. *Introduction*

As in the period up to 1954, information has been sought about the direct labour of local authorities, public utilities and government departments. The direct labour forces of non-construction firms on the MOW–DOE register have been treated as contractors. A multiplicity of returns have been used to collect the information but these have gradually been reduced in number and, since October 1975, only two forms of return have been used: one for government departments and the other a combined return for all other authorities within the scope of the enquiry. Before October 1975 local authorities were covered separately and at earlier periods New Town Corporations were treated separately from local authorities and each public utility received a separate form of return. A short history of the enquiries and selected specimen questionnaires are included as Appendix V. But it should be noted that the history of the enquiries is difficult to trace in detail for a complete set of the questionnaires used in successive enquiries does not exist and a lot of the data collected were not published.

For most of the period since 1955 the enquiries undertaken have broadly followed the pattern that was set for contractors from 1957 onwards; that is to say twice yearly censuses in April and September, statistics about employment and output by type of work being obtained in April and more detailed statistics about employment being obtained in September. But unlike the contractors' censuses, for which the bi-annual enquiries were replaced by a single annual enquiry from 1971, this bi-annual pattern has been retained throughout. There are also two major points of difference in content: in the case of Government Departments statistics of output are collected on an annual basis (for years ending 31 March) rather than the first quarter only, and in the case of local authorities (and other public authorities within the scope of the enquiry with effect from the third quarter of 1975) statistics of output and employment by type of work are collected in both enquiries (for the third quarter of each year as well as the first). Broadly speaking developments in the content of the returns have followed those for contractors (though often with a difference in timing).

The only detailed analyses of the data that have been made available, however, relate to local authorities. No separate data are published for Government Departments and Public Utilities; the only published statistics in which their activities are covered are combined output and employment series (see Section 4.4).[11] We turn now, therefore, to consider the statistics available for local authorities; we return at the end to consider other public authorities again briefly.

4.3.2. *Local Authorities' Direct Labour*

4.3.2.1. *The censuses taken and the nature of the data.* It is difficult to be certain about the nature, content and frequency of the enquiries made in the period 1955–60 because only a few of the questionnaires used in this period seem to have survived, virtually none of the data were prepared for publication and departmental records appear to be incomplete. It would seem, however, that the regular pattern of enquiries each April and September in the form described earlier was established in 1957 as it was in the case of contractors; these have continued up to the present day, except that since 1972 the September enquiry has been moved to October and a census was not taken in April 1974 because of the reorganization of local government in England and Wales at the beginning of that month. Prior to 1957 it seems that censuses were taken in July and September 1955 and in April 1956 (see Appendix V).

Detailed analyses of the data have been regularly published since 1961 and we examine these below. First we consider the nature and coverage of the returns in more general terms.

Coverage of authorities. The coverage of the enquiry extends to all local government authorities throughout Great Britain including, currently, the Commission for the New Towns and New Town Development Corporations. The bodies for the new towns were covered for the first time—initially by means of a separate enquiry—in September 1964, but they were not included in the published results until April 1966. The SSHA, it should be noted, is treated as a contractor and is therefore not covered in these enquiries (some data on the direct labour force of the SSHA may be found in its *Annual Reports* [B 178]).[12]

Operatives. In the returns made prior to 1955 it would seem that local authorities were required to include *all* male building and civil engineering operatives aged 16 and over (permanent and temporary) employed in *all* departments of the authority on a specified pay-day. After 1955 (from April 1956[13]) the returns have been intended to cover both male and female operatives aged 15 years and over 'wholly or mainly engaged on building and civil engineering work—i.e. work which otherwise would be undertaken by building and civil engineering firms' on a specific day. For details of the guidance given as to which particular types of labour should be included or excluded see the commentary and specimen returns in Appendix V. Each September enquiry has required the return of operatives to be broken down by occupation; this information

---
[11] Statistics are published by the CSO, however, though not based on the DOE sources, which provide an industrial analysis (including 'construction') of employment in the public sector differentiating between central government, local authorities and public corporations, in *Economic Trends* [QRL 147] from time to time—see Section 6.2.3.4.

[12] In contrast, however, it is included in the local authority design work enquiries (see Section 4.7). It may be noted too that dwellings built for SSHA ownership are included with local authorities' housebuilding figures and thus classified to the public sector.

[13] The terminology used in July 1955, for which the results are unpublished, differed.

4.3.2.2   STATISTICS COLLECTED BY THE DEPARTMENT OF THE ENVIRONMENT   119

was not published prior to 1968 but it is available from September 1957 on request from DOE Statistics Construction Division.

Apprentices. Statistics for apprentices have been collected in each September census (including that for September 1955) broken down by occupation and by type of agreement as for contractors (see Section 4.2.3) up to 1974. From 1975 statistics have been collected for 'trainees'. Statistics for new recruitment have not been collected since the September 1955 census. Again, as in the case of operatives, the results of this part of the census have been published only since 1968 but are available back to September 1957.

APTC staff. These have been covered in each census since September 1966 with a breakdown by occupation being required in each September/October enquiry only. Once again, publication of the results of this part of the census was not begun until 1968 but the earlier data back to September 1966 are available on request. There is an important distinction to be made between the statistics of APTC staff employed by local authorities and those for contractors. Whereas the activities of the latter are naturally related solely to the work being undertaken by contractors, in the case of local authorities such staff may be engaged on work which is carried out by construction firms under contract to the Authority and not by the Authority's own direct labour organization. Thus analyses, for example, of the relative proportions of APTC staff employed by contractors as against local authorities are not comparable. See Appendix V regarding the completion of the return.

Output. Output is an estimate of the value of work done during a specified period of three months by the operatives defined above—i.e. a sum calculated to cover the cost of materials, wages and the establishment charges attributable to the work carried out. It is not directly comparable with contractors' output statistics since, quite apart from differences in the type of work carried out, it does not include a profit element and there may be some doubt too about the appropriate allocation of overheads. The value excludes the cost of land, legal costs and professional fees.

4.3.2.2. *The available analyses.* The analyses of the results that are available are set out in Table 4.2 in a comparable form to that included for contractors in Table 4.1, i.e. in a form which indicates the cross-classifications of the data that are available and the periods of time covered—together with publication references. Details of the information provided within each particular analysis are given below.

Analyses by type of work. A distinction is made between new work and repair and maintenance on housing and non-housing respectively from September 1968. Prior to this date the repair and maintenance figure was not split in the sources referred to in Table 4.2. However, figures which were split (but for the value of work done at constant prices only) were published in response to a parliamentary question in *Hansard* [B 247], covering the period 1961–70 (1st and 3rd quarters combined).

Analyses of operatives, apprentices and APTC staff by occupation. The categories distinguished are the same as for contractors except that the subdivision of professional staff according to occupation (architect, surveyor, engineer)—abandoned in the case of

Table 4.2
MOW–DOE Construction Census Analyses 1961 to Date—Local Authorities' Direct Labour (Great Britain)*

(The entries in the body of the table indicate the analyses that are available, the particular census in which the data are collected (represented by A or S/O for April or September/October respectively) and the years of commencement and, where appropriate, termination of series. From 1972 the census formerly taken in September has been taken in October. No census was taken in April 1974)

Statistic \ Cross-classifications	By Region	By Type of Authority	By Size of Authority
Number of Authorities:			
Employing Direct Labour		A(1961–70) S/O(1961–)†	A(1969–70) S/O(1968–)
Not Employing Direct Labour (or Total)		A(1969–70) S/O(1968–)†	
Value of Work Done (1st qtr (A)) (3rd qtr (S/O))			
Employment:			
Operatives (incl. Apprentices)			
Apprentices (Trainees)			
APTC staff			

PUBLICATION REFERENCES. 1961–70: *Monthly Bulletin of Construction Statistics* [QRL 194]—generally six to eight months after the date of the census. The *BRS Collections* [QRL 120] and [QRL 121] include the series, for the period 1961–9, of the number of authorities, the value of work done and the number of operatives employed each analysed by region and by type of authority. 1971 to date: *Housing and Construction Statistics* [QRL 168].

* This table covers the published analyses of results from 1961 to 1976—the latest available at the time of writing. The results of local authority censuses taken in the period from 1956 to 1960 were not published at the time but certain analyses of the April 1956 census results have now been published and details are given below:

4.3.2.2 STATISTICS COLLECTED BY THE DEPARTMENT OF THE ENVIRONMENT 121

By Region	By Type of Work		By Craft of Operative and Type of Authority	By Type of APTC Staff and Type of Authority
	By Type of Authority	By Size of Authority		
A&S/O(1961–)		A(1969–70) S/O(1968–)		
A&S/O (1961–)	A(1961–70) S/O(1961–)	A(1969–70) S/O(1968–)	S/O(1968–)‡	
			S/O(1968–)	
				S/O(1968–)

APRIL 1956 CENSUS. Analyses of the results of this census have now been included in *Statistics Collected by the MOW 1941–56* [QRL 321] as follows: Number of authorities employing direct labour, number of operatives employed by type of work and value of work done by type of work (1st quarter 1956) each analysed by region, type of local authority and size of local authority.

† Analyses of the numbers of authorities employing direct labour according to region have not been published since 1973.

‡ An analysis by craft for 1963 will be found in [B 315] Table D.

contractors after 1974—has been retained (see Section 4.2.3). The data collected for apprentices according to type of agreement are not published but are available on request from DOE Statistics Construction Division.

Analyses by type and size of authority. Prior to September 1968 only County Councils were distinguished from other types of authority in England and Wales and in Scotland. Since then analyses have been published for each type of local authority in England and Wales and in Scotland. The analysis by size of authority refers to the size of the direct labour force as determined by the number of *operatives* employed. This contrasts with the size analyses for contractors which have not used operatives as the basis since 1965.

Regional analyses. These are naturally based upon the regional location of the local authority and, since their direct labour forces rarely (if ever) work outside the boundaries of the authority, the analyses are more reliable than those made for contractors who are classified according to an office location but may be at work in different regions.

4.3.3. *Government Departments' and Public Utilities' Direct Labour*

Detailed analyses of the censuses of Government Departments, Public Utilities and other Public Authorities are not published and very little summary information is available. It is possible, however, to derive some of the results for these authorities. Total operatives and total APTC staff may be derived for the period from 1967 by subtracting local authorities' direct labour figures from 'public authorities' totals given in *HCS* [QRL 168] in periodic 'supplementary tables'. Output data could be derived similarly until series for total public sector direct labour output were discontinued (see Section 4.4.5).[14] The DOE, however, are prepared to supply much of the data, in more detail than used to be published regularly, on request. In interpreting the public authorities' direct labour data it should be borne in mind that coverage of the sector is incomplete (see Appendix V and Section 4.4.5) and that it was altered in the revision of the SIC in 1968 (figures for total direct labour output on both the revised and unrevised bases for the period 1963-72, however, may be found in [B 217]).

One detailed analysis of public sector employment available in a published source is one for 1963 giving details of operatives, according to craft, employed by: government departments, the gas and electricity industries (separately) and other public utilities, as well as by local authorities and contractors (plus total APTC staff), included in [B 315] Table D. Hospital authorities are not covered by the DOE enquiries but a total employment figure (England only in September 1970) which may be helpful in gauging the size of the sector may be found in [B 249]. Reference should also be made to analyses of public-sector employment published by the CSO from time to time in *ET* [QRL 147], although these are not based on DOE sources—see Section 6.2.3.4 for details.

Government departments. Apart from the exceptions noted above, separate data for the direct labour of government departments are not published. But a major employer

---

[14] An alternative method, giving analyses by type of work, was to subtract the data for contractors (Section 4.2.3) and local authorities (Section 4.3.2) from total output (Section 4.4.5); this procedure is no longer possible, however, for the latter now includes estimates for unrecorded output.

4.4–4.4.1 STATISTICS COLLECTED BY THE DEPARTMENT OF THE ENVIRONMENT

amongst departments is the DOE itself, and statistics showing the numbers employed by the Department each year from 1965 to 1971, together with an estimated constant-price series of maintenance work done for the Department by direct labour and contractors respectively over the period 1964/5–1970/1, were given in a written answer to a parliamentary question in [B 248].

4.4. MOW–DOE Output and Employment Time Series for Great Britain since 1954

4.4.1. *Introduction*

The time series of output and employment that are available for private contractors (as distinct from direct labour) were based on quarterly and monthly sample enquiries, which continued along the same lines as those laid down before 1955, until 1978. That is to say the contractors in the sample were required to make a return of employment every month and output every quarter except (generally speaking) in months which coincided with the taking of a full census of the industry (for details see Appendix VII) and, from 1971, the month of June in order to avoid duplication of the DE employment census for construction and other industries (Section 6.2.3.2 refers). From the beginning of 1978, the returns of employment in the months between the quarterly enquiries have been discontinued.

Naturally the reliability of the data collected is dependent upon the sampling practices adopted and the adequacy of the sampling frame. Unfortunately, as we noted earlier, severe difficulties have been experienced in maintaining the register of firms which forms the base for these enquiries (see Section 4.1.3). Deficiencies in the register accumulated progressively from the early 1960s (and almost certainly earlier) into the 1970s. The problem still remains but by 1971 the DOE had succeeded in identifying by means of *ad hoc* investigations some 30,000 firms (mostly very small) as having been omitted from the register (consisting at that time of some 70,000 firms) besides 'many thousands' of self-employed persons who work as labour-only sub-contractors [B 217].

For a time the extra 30,000 firms were retained on a 'special list' and kept separate in subsequent enquiries (by the time they were incorporated in the main register, in 1973, the number had fallen to 25,000). As regards the sample enquiries, they were incorporated in the normal sample selections along with the other firms for the first time in July 1974. In order to deal with consequential continuity problems overlap figures have been prepared and, in addition, some retrospectively revised sets of estimates have been prepared back to 1963 (see below for details).

The problem of recording the output and employment of operatives working as 'self-employed' under labour-only sub-contract remains and only approximate estimates may be made—again see below.

As regards sampling practices, very little information has been made available in the past regarding sample size and sampling methods (some details were published in [B 220], [B 335] and [B 127] Appendix H), and virtually no information is available about sampling errors (a brief comment relating to the situation in 1960 was included in [B 220]). Currently very brief details about sampling practice are included in the annual *HCS Notes and Definitions Supplement* [B 250].

4.4.2. *Interpretation*

The monthly and quarterly sample enquiries lead, as one would expect, to the production of two types of series: a monthly series of the number of operatives employed by contractors and a quarterly series of output and employment according to type of work. Interpretation of the data obtained cannot be divorced from an examination of the questionnaires, details of which are given in Appendix VII. The purpose of the sample returns, however, is to provide more frequent, rather than different types of data than those obtained in the censuses. Consequently the questions asked in the census and sample returns correspond with each other, and reference may thus be made to the discussion of the nature of the data and its interpretation made earlier in Section 4.2. Full details of the development of the sample returns, particularly as regards content and the timing of changes, are provided in Appendix VII together with selected specimen questionnaires.

Before turning to consider the particular series available notice should be taken of the following particular factors relevant to their interpretation. First, as we explained earlier, no sample enquiry is made in those months which coincide with the taking of a full census.[15] Therefore, one would expect the output and employment figures published in the detailed analyses of the census results (see Section 4.2) to agree with the totals published as part of the time series. In fact this is not the case for the reason, the author is informed, that for the purpose of obtaining quick results, samples are extracted from the full census returns (a pre-selected sample contained within the 'census') and it is the figures based on this sample (separately processed according to the normal time-scale which operates for the quarterly returns) which are incorporated in the published time series. They naturally differ from the full census results but are not subsequently adjusted. The question of adjustment was reviewed, however, in 1973 when revised output series were produced (see [B 217]) with the result that adjustments were made for output back to 1963 but not for employment.[16] The discrepancy between sample and census results is 'kept under review'.

Secondly, the series available are not always directly comparable because of differences in coverage and changes in practice over time; care is required therefore to avoid the inherent pitfalls this factor presents. There are two relevant matters here. One is the fact that the employment and output series analysed by type of work are not always comparable due to differences in the treatment of public sector direct labour in the two series, and a lack of consistency in this respect over time. The other matter is that some of the series have been revised retrospectively since 1973 but again in the published series these revisions have been applied to output but not employment[16] (for further details see below).

Finally, in addition to the differences in coverage mentioned above, there are certain other differences in the scope and coverage of the output and employment series which are important for the interpretation of each series separately, but which also affect their comparability and are particularly important if the two series are used conjointly (e.g. as in the calculation of figures of output per man). There are four relevant factors here:

(1) The difficulties in maintaining a comprehensive register, referred to above, and in particular, the problem of recording the 'self-employed' men working as

---

[15] For exceptions to this statement see Appendix VII.
[16] The author is informed (July 1977) that the employment series have now been revised retrospectively and are to be published in future editions of *Housing and Construction Statistics* [QRL 168].

labour-only sub-contractors, has meant that the employment series understate to a greater extent than the output series, for the latter is supposed to include the value of materials supplied to labour-only sub-contractors by main contractors.[17] Estimates of output per man, therefore, will tend to be overstated and, of course, if such labour grows relative to the number of recorded 'employees', the overstatement will increase also; conversely if the number becomes relatively smaller the overstatement will be reduced. As far as the evidence goes there is no doubt that during the 1960s at least the relative importance of this labour grew considerably (cf. self-employment data available from the *Censuses of Population* of 1961, 1966 and 1971—see Section 6.3). Since 1971 it is thought that various measures taken by the government in an attempt to combat the evasion of tax, national insurance and other payments by the 'lump' may have reduced the growth, and possibly the total numbers,[18] of such labour but the statistical evidence is limited. 'Very approximate' estimates made by the DOE for census months from 1967 suggest a marked decline since 1973 (see, for example, *HCS* [QRL 168] No. 18, p. 69). These estimates are based partly upon the census of population data, referred to above, which provide basic benchmarks. Estimates of the change from year to year between census of population years is made up to 1974 on the basis of evidence obtained from DE/DHSS samples of Class 2 insurance cards exchanged at the end of the second quarter each year. Since 1974, provisional estimates are based on the movement of the number of working proprietors recorded in the DOE censuses; these are subsequently revised as necessary on the basis of evidence obtained in bi-annual Labour Force Surveys conducted by the OPCS on behalf of the DE and EEC. For further comment, particularly on primary source material, see Section 6.2.3.4 which considers published DE estimates for self-employment in construction and other industries.

(2) Working Principals (Proprietors) are not counted as operatives, although they do manual work, whereas the output return covers the work done by both. The extent to which Working Principals do manual work will vary, of course, from firm to firm but is likely to be greater in the smaller firms.

(3) It is important to note that the value of output is meant to exclude the value of goods made for sale, but that the employment series includes the labour employed on their manufacture.

(4) There is a difference between the series in timing in that the labour series refers to numbers on the pay-roll on a particular pay-day in one month each quarter, whereas the output series refers to the estimated value of work done in the whole quarter up to the end of the preceding month.

4.4.3. *Monthly Total Employment Series*

The DOE produced two monthly series of employment until monthly returns were discontinued at the beginning of 1978:

(1) Operatives employed by contractors on the DOE register—actual and

---

[17] But note, as indicated earlier, that the DOE plan to publish retrospectively revised employment series to include estimates of unrecorded labour.

[18] The slump in construction activity since 1973 will also have acted as a counteracting force.

seasonally adjusted series. The current source is [QRL 168] which provides monthly averages, quarter by quarter, back to 1966. Formerly the series were published month by month in *MBCS* [QRL 194] back to 1955 (actual) and 1958 (s.a.).

(2) 'Employees in employment'—operatives and other employees employed by contractors and direct labour combined. Actual and seasonally adjusted series are available in *HCS* [QRL 168] monthly back to 1971 and monthly averages back to 1967. Since direct labour statistics are not collected monthly the series incorporates estimates based upon census results (Section 4.3 refers).

It is important to note that series (2) above is not the same as the one produced by the Department of Employment under the same title (Section 6.2 refers). For a comparative discussion of the DOE and DE statistics, see Section 6.2.4.1 and for a comparison of the data from these and other sources see Table 6.1 included in the same Section. It is also most important to note that neither of the series to date have been revised to take account of unrecorded labour (see Section 4.4.1 above) but, as noted earlier, retrospective estimates have been prepared and are to be published in *HCS* [QRL 168] (very approximate estimates of the deficiency have already been published for census months back to 1967 in a periodic supplementary table in *HCS* [QRL 168]—e.g. No. 18 p. 69—for further details see Section 4.4.2 above).

Working Principals/Proprietors and APTC staff. Statistics have been collected in each monthly enquiry for Working Principals (Proprietors from November 1971) and from May 1965 in respect of APTC staff (see Appendix VII). The data are not published but may be made available on request. Census data for these categories are published (see Sections 4.2 and 4.3).

4.4.4. *Employment Series by Type of Work*

The principal series (and the only series currently published) relate to contractors only.

Contractors

The primary source currently is *HCS* [QRL 168], which includes quarterly data back to 1966, and formerly *MBCS* [QRL 194] which carries the series back to 1955. The whole series to date has also been published in the *MDS* [QRL 195]. It is important to note that, as with the monthly series, the data refer to recorded employment only—no adjustments are made for operatives working as self-employed under labour-only sub-contract or employed by firms not on the register. The types of work distinguished are:

New work:

Public sector	Private sector
Housing	Housing
Other new work	Industrial
	Commercial (i.e. all other new work)

Repairs and maintenance—Total (see below for further details).

Repairs and maintenance. Information is sought in the quarterly enquiries for repairs and maintenance broken down according to three categories: housing (total) and non-housing (public and private). It has not been published to date but the DOE are planning to do so in the near future. Data collected under these headings in the censuses, however (relating to one quarter each year), have been published with the census results since 1966 (see Section 4.2). In addition, quarterly data for the housing category for the period 1962–71 are to be found in [QRL 169] No. 6 *et seq.* as part of 'housing labour force' statistics.

Direct labour

Information about the employment of direct labour by type of work has been collected only in the full census enquiries—considered in Section 4.3. As noted there, published data have been largely confined to the direct labour of local authorities but particulars for other public authorities covered in the DOE enquiries are available on request from the DOE Statistics Construction Division. In the context of time series the following are worthy of note although they are now of historical interest and relate to housing alone:

(1) *All direct labour on housing* (one month each year)—estimated series of operatives employed by direct labour organizations in the scope of the MPBW/DOE enquiries (see Appendix V) differentiating between new work and repairs and maintenance—published for the period 1962–71 in [QRL 169] No. 6 *et seq.* (along with contractors' employment data) as part of the 'housing labour force' statistics referred to above.

(2) *Local authorities' direct labour*—quarterly series for England and Wales, as distinct from Great Britain, for new housing and a combined contractors' and direct labour series for repairs and maintenance work for the period January 1961–April 1966 in [QRL 169] No. 2 Supplementary Table VII.

4.4.5. Output Series

4.4.5.1. *Current price series.* This section should be read in the light of Chapter 2, which considers the conceptual problems of output valuation for construction work and the nature of the returns. Quarterly series of the value of output by type of work are collected in the same quarterly return from contractors as the employment data considered above (Section 4.4.4). Currently, however, the published employment and output time series are not directly comparable because the output series incorporates work done by direct labour and the retrospective revisions made in 1973 to allow for unrecorded output back to 1963, whereas the employment series relates to contractors only and has not, at the time of writing (July 1977), been adjusted to allow for unrecorded labour.[19]

The retrospective revisions made in 1973 were not carried back through the whole series to 1955 because it was felt, the author is informed, that revision of the earlier figures was not necessary, these figures being regarded as consistent with the revised later ones. Thus the period since 1955 is spanned by two sets of data overlapping for the period 1963–73 and particular care is therefore required in using long-run series to ensure that the appropriate series is taken. Full details of the series available, distinguishing those based on the 'new' and the 'old' bases, are set out in Table 4.3.

The revised series. The series were revised on account of three factors. First was the need

---

[19] Publication of such a series is planned for a future issue of *Housing and Construction Statistics* [QRL 168].

Table 4.3
MOW–DOE Output Time Series from 1955 (Great Britain)*
(Annual series are separately indicated in this table only if they provide information not obtainable by aggregation of the quarterly data)

Description of Series	Frequency	Period Covered	Price Basis			Coverage	
			Current Prices	Constant Prices		PC/DL	Wor All/N
				Actual	s.a.		
CURRENT SERIES—NEW BASIS* (incl. Retrospective Revisions) Values	Q A	1972 (Q₂) to date 1963 to date	Yes Yes	No Yes	Yes —	PC&DL PC&DL	All All
Indices	Q	1972 (Q₂) to date (see Remarks)	—	No	Yes	PC&DL	All
	A	1961 to date	—	Yes	—	PC&DL	All
FORMER SERIES—OLD BASIS Values	Q	1955–74 (Q₁)	Yes	No	Yes (1958–)	{ PC DL	Al Al
Indices	Q	1954–72 (Q₁)	—	Yes	Yes	PC&DL	All/N
	Q	1970–4 (Q₁)	—	No	Yes	{ PC DL	Al Al

* The following series (new basis) are available on request from the DOE, Statistics Construction Division (*Statistical News* [B 333] No. 27, November 1974 refers):
  (i) From 1963, annually, at constant (1970) prices with separate figures for work done by private contractors (PC) and by the direct labour departments (DL) in the public sector: New Work—Public New Housing (PC, DL, Total); Private New Housing (Total); Public New Works (PC, DL, Total); Private Industrial (Total); Private Commercial (Total); Total New Work (PC, DL, Total). Repairs and Maintenance—Housing (PC, DL, Total); Public Non-Housing (PC, DL, Total); Private Non-Housing (Total); Total Output (PC, DL, Total).

4.4.5.1 STATISTICS COLLECTED BY DEPARTMENT OF ENVIRONMENT 129

nalysis Type Work†	Publication (Primary Source)	Remarks
		A descriptive note about the revised series is provided in [B 217].
Yes Yes	HCS [QRL 168] No. 10 et seq. HCS [QRL 168] No. 13	Reproduced in MDS [QRL 195] and AAS [QRL 31]. Separate series (annual at current prices) for contractors and direct labour separately with an abbreviated breakdown by type of work (new housing, other new work, repairs and maintenance) for the 'recorded' element of the revised series were given in [B 217] for the period 1963–72.
Yes	HCS [QRL 168] No. 10 et seq.	Indices back to 1965 (without a breakdown by type of work) are published in HCS [QRL 168] Table 1—'Activity indicators' and in MDS [QRL 195] No. 334 et seq. from 1970.
Yes 69–)	HCS [QRL 168]	Published in table of 'Activity indicators'.
es No	{ MBCS [QRL 194] (1955–72) HCS [QRL 168] (1970–4 Q₁) }	The series at current prices were reproduced in MDS [QRL 195]. A breakdown of repair and maintenance work by type for contractors was published for 1956–70, annually at current and constant prices, in ABCS [QRL 32].
No	MBCS [QRL 194]	Called 'Index of Production' but not the same as the construction industry component of the official index of industrial production (see Section 5.1).
es No	{ HCS [QRL 168] to issue No. 9	

(ii) Output, by the above five types of new work and for repairs and maintenance in total, quarterly, at constant (1970) prices, seasonally adjusted, from 1963.

† The types of work distinguished are the five types of new work as in (i) above plus repairs and maintenance (total). In addition an annual series of total repair and maintenance output, by contractors and direct labour combined, has been included for the period from 1948 [QRL 201], as a footnote to the table of 'Gross Domestic Fixed Capital Formation by Type of Asset'.

Abbreviations: s.a.—seasonally adjusted; Q—Quarterly (Q_1—1st quarter, etc.); A—Annually; PC—Private contractors; DL—Direct labour.

to allow for the output of firms and self-employed workers working as labour-only sub-contractors, not covered on the DOE register—a deficiency which, as we noted above, had become progressively worse from the early 1960s through to the early 1970s (the problem still remains today but its severity may have eased—see Section 4.4.2). The second reason for revision was to deal with larger-than-expected discrepancies between census results and sample estimates of contractors' output. A third adjustment was made to allow for a revision which had been made to the SIC in 1968 but which had not been allowed for in the DOE series for the industry. This affected direct labour only: the 1968 SIC, as we observed earlier, expressly excluded the construction work carried out by employees of gas, electricity and water undertakings, but the DOE had continued to include them. They were then excluded from the revised series right back to 1963. In addition it should be noted that one direct labour force—that of the British Steel Corporation—was transferred from the direct labour sector to contractors on the grounds that part of their work is carried out for clients outside the employing organization.

Overall, therefore, the increase in the revised series of total output represents the net outcome of an increase on account of unrecorded output by contractors (an increase of 9 per cent in 1963 rising to 19 per cent in 1972, disregarding adjustment due to sampling/census discrepancies) and a decrease on account of direct labour output (from -17 per cent in 1963 to -28 per cent in 1972)—see [B 217] (Appendix III Table 1) for details. In addition, it should be noted that in converting the revised series to constant prices a separate (higher) cost index was introduced from 1971 for private housing 'to allow for the fact that the revised output series when deflated by the cost index for total new work was rising faster than would otherwise have been expected from estimates based primarily on the monthly statistics ... of private housing starts and completions' ([B 217] p. lxii, para. (d) refers). Statistics of new house prices, adjusted for changes in prices of building land, were used in this revised index. The net effect was to increase the overall construction output index from a former level of 117 in 1972 (1963 = 100) to 127 (an increase of $8\frac{1}{2}$ per cent).

But it must still be appreciated that the revised series itself remains open to error. A detailed account of the revisions is given in [B 217]. Essentially the revision methods rely on the conversion of employment estimates to output values on the basis of output per man ratios allowing for changes in productivity over time. All these factors require judgement (or, as the DOE admit in [B 217], 'guesstimation') rather than simply measurement, and are not therefore beyond dispute. Employment figures for periods between *Census of Population* 'benchmark' years are necessarily estimates. Output per man ratios can be based on recorded output and employment but the ratios *may* not be equally applicable to the unrecorded element, particularly if the unrecorded firms are not a 'representative' group, and if the self-employed (or nominal self-employed) earn different (probably higher) rates of remuneration than recorded employees. And, of course, the assessment of productivity change is necessarily conjectural (see Section 8.2). None of these remarks must be taken as denying the value of the revised series. They are simply meant to warn the unwary that, for very good reasons, the margins of error remain potentially high. Since the introduction of the revised series steps have been taken to improve the sources of information about unrecorded output by collecting data about sub-contract payments and work done from contractors on the register (see below for further details).

With regard to output revisions it should also be noted that in 1977 revisions were made to exclude work on steel oil-drilling platforms and a number of firms were removed from the construction register and reclassified as 'structural steel fabricators' (these revisions, of course, affect both output and employment).

4.4.5.2. *Constant price and seasonally adjusted output series.* The reliable measurement of price changes for construction work poses severe problems and it is doubtful whether these are surmounted satisfactorily by the index used officially for deflating current output values.[20]

These problems, and the various price indices available, are considered fully in Section 8.1. In the present context it is sufficient to note that, as a consequence, interpretation of the series at constant prices must contend with two important potential sources of error: first those arising from deficiencies in the original series, particularly those stemming from incomplete coverage of the industry which have been discussed above, and secondly, those introduced through the use of a price index which is itself open to error. It should be noted that a separate (higher) cost index was introduced in 1973 for the deflation of the private housing component from 1971 (see the discussion of the revised current price series in Section 4.4.5.1 above). Seasonal adjustments are made by means of a standard programme described in [B 145].

4.4.5.3. *Output time series for Scotland and Wales.* Regional analyses of the quarterly sample results, similar to those made for the censuses, are not made. Separate arrangements are made, however, to produce series for Scotland and Wales. Until the end of 1975 the samples were devised so that firms *working* in Scotland or Wales (as distinct from firms *registered* in the two countries) made a return of work done in each country. Unlike the regional analyses of output based on the censuses, therefore, these statistics relate to the actual location of the work. The samples were devised on the basis of firms which reported the employment of operatives in Scotland or Wales in answer to a question inserted in the census questionnaires (see Appendix IV)—a special 'sticker' being attached to the sample questionnaires for the collection of the data. The returns were made quarterly in respect of Scotland and once a year in respect of the third quarter for Wales.

At the end of 1975, however, this system was abandoned because of low response, delays before the information could be collected and processed and because it was felt that projections of output on the basis mainly, of new orders statistics (considered in Section 4.5 below), in which the value *and location* of new construction jobs are recorded, provided a quicker and, it is thought, 'reasonably accurate' method of estimating output. The figures now published for Wales and for Scotland are estimated from: (i) a 'forward-spread' of contractors' new work orders in the two countries, (ii) Welsh and Scottish contractors' repair and maintenance output (it is implicitly assumed that only such work done outside the borders by such contractors would be balanced by work by English contractors inside the borders) and (iii) direct labour output in the two countries.

[20] New output deflators were introduced in 1978 after the preparation of this text—see the Addenda, this volume, page 23.

The series for Scotland show: contractors' output broken down by type of work together with a separate undifferentiated series for direct labour, and are published currently in [QRL 306], formerly in [QRL 139]. These provide series annually or half-yearly for the period from 1957. The data for Wales are published as an annual series throughout (although originally collected for one quarter only each year) in [QRL 142] and [QRL 360]. Output by direct labour is included together with a breakdown by type of work for contractors but in less detail than for Scotland or Great Britain: new housing, other new work and repairs and maintenance only; the series is carried back, however, to 1951 (the precise basis of the pre-1955 part of the series is not clear). The series for Scotland and Wales are, of course, subject to the same deficiencies in coverage as the series for Great Britain discussed earlier (Section 4.4.5.1) and, as in the case of Great Britain, were retrospectively revised in 1973 back to 1963.

Separate employment series for Scotland or Wales are not published. Reference may be made, however, to [B 120] which provides estimates of employment (1970) and output (1966 and 1970) on a region of location basis for all regions of Great Britain; but note that the article was prepared before revisions of the statistics to allow for unrecorded output and employment.

4.4.5.4. *Value of sub-contracted work.* Separate statistics for such work have been collected in the quarterly sample and the annual census enquiries since 1974 (see Appendices IV and VII for details). Results have been published for each of the financial years from 1974/5 to 1976/7 in *HCS* [QRL 168] Nos. 18 and 22 Supp. Table II, showing: work done as sub-contractor, work done as labour-only sub-contractor, work done for firms by other sub-contractors, and payments made to labour-only sub-contractors on new housing, new non-housing and repairs and maintenance, all analysed by size of firm. Quarterly data for the year 1974/5 only, but analysed by trade as well as size of firm, showing the value of work done for firms on a sub-contract basis were included in *HCS* [QRL 168] No. 14 Supp. Table III.

4.4.5.5. *Construction work outside the scope of the SIC.* A good deal of construction work goes unrecorded. Some of this is nonetheless incorporated in the official statistics, some is not. One reason work goes unrecorded, already considered earlier, is the impossibility, under present arrangements, of maintaining a fully comprehensive register of firms and self-employed workers. As we have explained above, estimates for such work are now incorporated in the official series. Another reason is that some of the work falls outside the scope of the definition of the industry laid down by the SIC. Particularly important here is the work done to property by the owners and occupiers of the property themselves—'Do-it-Yourself' (DIY) output. This is quite apart from work of a construction nature which is in fact expressly excluded by the *Standard Industrial Classification* (see Section 4.1.2). DIY work is work of repairs, maintenance, decorations, alterations and improvements, mainly to housing, but also to small properties such as shops, workshops, etc. None of this work is included in official construction statistics. There is an analogy of course between DIY work on non-residential property and the direct labour employed by industrial and commercial firms; here too the work is not covered unless the direct labour is organized as a separate accounting unit within the firm and is recorded on the DOE register of firms.

Naturally if the DIY and private unrecorded direct labour work were carried out by contractors it would be included in the official statistics, so long as such contractors had not escaped registration. Thus, other things being equal, an expansion in the volume of DIY and private direct labour work will lead to an apparent decline in construction output recorded in official statistics. There is no doubt that a substantial amount of work is done within the DIY category and that it has grown in importance. Some statistical information about expenditure, on residential property at least, is available from the *Family Expenditure Surveys* [QRL 156]. These record expenditure on building and decorating materials separately from payments made to contractors and may be used, therefore, as the basis for making a rough estimate of the total value of work done. An estimate by the author, based on this information, for the year 1969 will be found in [B 188], Appendix VI. See also [QRL 68]. [B 188] also contains a rough estimate of expenditure on the cleaning of buildings other than dwellings (Appendix VI pp. 62–63)—work which is not classified to construction in the SIC.

4.5. Contractors' New Orders Statistics and EEC State of Trade Enquiry for Great Britain

4.5.1. *Introduction*

The main value of statistics about new orders received is for measuring changes in the level of demand in the industry and forecasting future output. Such statistics have been collected by the DOE and its predecessor Departments quarterly since 1956 (4th quarter) and monthly since January 1964. At the beginning of 1977 the DOE also initiated a qualitative 'state of trade' enquiry designed to give a quick impression of trends in the level of activity and to complement similar enquiries carried out in other member countries of the EEC. We consider this new survey in sub-section 4.5.4 below. The rest of this section is concerned with the new orders statistics.

4.5.2. *The Nature of the New Orders Enquiry*

4.5.2.1. *Scope and methodology.* Initially the new orders statistics were collected along with the output and employment statistics on the quarterly output and employment returns (see Section 4.4). This meant that the statistics were collected by means of a full census in April of each year for the first quarter but by means of a sample enquiry for the other three quarters. An article describing the new series soon after its introduction was published in [B 98] together with the results from the first five enquiries. The monthly enquiry instituted in January 1964 was also placed on a sample basis but was now made on a separate questionnaire (see Appendix VIII), except that use was also retained of the April census each year until 1969.

We now turn to examine the nature of the data collected in general terms before considering the series which are published (Section 4.5.3). The data cover new contracts and orders received by contractors only (direct labour organizations are not covered) for work in Great Britain. Work overseas is covered in a separate enquiry (see Section 4.6) and there is also a separate enquiry in Northern Ireland (see Chapter 9). The statistics relate to new work only—all repairs and maintenance work is excluded. The term 'new work' is defined, as in the case of output, to include such work as extensions, 'major alterations (i.e. improvements)', site preparation and demolition *except for housing*, for which extensions, alterations and conversions work is excluded. Also as in the case of output, the value of building sites and the costs of architects' and consultants' fees are meant to be excluded from the returns.

In contrast to the procedure used for the collection of output statistics, however, work done under sub-contract is dealt with differently. Whereas for output statistics such work is returned by the contractor concerned, i.e. the sub-contractor, for new orders statistics such work is meant to be returned by the main contractor—each contractor is instructed to exclude from his return any contracts obtained from other contractors. This practice, however, involves a difficulty concerning contracts obtained from contractors who are not classified as part of the construction industry. Clearly such contracts are not in the same category as other sub-contracts and ought not to be excluded by the sub-contractor since to do so would mean that they were not covered at all. Initially no distinction was drawn between contractors inside and outside the construction industry; but in July 1967 the instructions were amended to indicate that contracts obtained from contractors outside the construction industry should be included (see, for example, the current instruction—Form BIM/OR, Note 3(a)—reproduced in Appendix VIII). The question of whether or not a particular contractor is inside or outside the construction industry, however, remains at the discretion of the person making the return.

By their very nature statistics of new orders in construction are likely to be more reliable than statistics of output for the former can be precisely defined at a point of time whilst the latter, carried out over a period of time, will normally need to be based, at least partly, on estimates. In addition, since information about new orders is collected for the order as a whole, and not separately for such parts of it as are let under sub-contract, the problem of ensuring full coverage by collecting information from labour-only and other small sub-contractors is of much smaller significance. At the same time, however, it must be recognized that the series has not escaped altogether from the difficulties in maintaining comprehensive coverage of the industry that have beset the output statistics (see Sections 4.1.3 and 4.4.2).

Further, the procedure adopted for collecting the statistics since 1964 is one which makes the series of particular value. Contractors have been asked to record the geographical location as well as other details of each contract or order received including 'own initiative' work (above a certain low limit—see below). The enquiry is thus tantamount to a site return. Consequently the statistics can be precisely classified (except for the very smallest jobs) by type of work and, unlike output, the work can be classified precisely according to the region in which it is to be carried out. Prior to 1964 precise regional classification was impossible for the returns were made in the aggregate only and only five types of work were specified—the same five categories used for the classification of new work in output statistics (see Section 4.4.5). From 1964 to April 1976 larger contractors had to specify each job of £10,000 or more in value and smaller contractors each job costing £2,500 or more; from April 1976 the figure of £10,000 has been applied to all contractors. For jobs below these limits their total number and total value is returned together with, since April 1969, a description of the first and the last jobs only, information which is used for the purpose of classifying this segment of work by type.

Builders' 'own-initiative' work—work not covered by orders. As we have indicated, the coverage of the enquiry extends not only to contracts and orders obtained for new work from clients but also to work to be undertaken by the contractor on his own initiative. This will be work either on premises for the builder's own use or work on buildings destined for eventual sale or lease; a large component of it is speculative house-building but it may also cover such buildings as shops, offices, storage premises, etc. Cases where it is the builder's practice to sell plots of land and obtain a contract to build from the purchasers are also included in this category.

It should be noted, however, that 'own-initiative' work is in a different category from other work, inasmuch as it represents (currently) work actually started as opposed to orders *received* in the case of clients. In the original quarterly enquiries the builder was required to record the estimated *overall* value of projects 'expected to be started' in the quarter following the date of the enquiry—whereas for orders obtained from clients the data referred to orders obtained in the preceding quarter. But from January 1964 this was changed to 'projects started' in the same month as the enquiry (during 1964, however, certain detailed changes were made to the instructions for this part of the form which may possibly have affected the continuity of the data for this period—see Appendix VIII for details). A quarterly series of the value of this work, referred to as 'work not covered by orders', is published in the *MDS* [QRL 195] along with the series labelled 1 (a) in Table 4.4 below. It is not broken down by type of work although it is incorporated as an integral part of the series which *are* classified by type of work.

4.5.2.2. *The valuation of new orders.* The value of a new order will normally be explicit, being the price accepted by the client, but there are certain instances where this is not the case or where the value has to be estimated. Work undertaken on a contractor's own initiative, to which we have already referred, is one such case. Others are serial contracts, that is 'continuation' or 'run-on' contracts, in which the total value may not be known; in this case the actual value of work *done* in the period covered by the return is supposed to be included. In the case of 'package deals', that is work for which the builder is responsible for design as well as construction, the estimated value of the building, civil engineering and associated work should be included. Specific instructions on these matters were given for the first time in January 1964.

There is another aspect of valuation which it is important to note when using the statistics for forecasting purposes. New orders will be transformed into output over a period of time but the value of a particular job on completion (the price paid by the client) will not necessarily be the same as the original contract sum (the value which will have been recorded as a new order). There are two reasons for this. One is the fact that variations are commonly made to a job as it proceeds which allow the contract sum to be amended. The other is that contracts often contain fluctuation clauses which allow the builder to claim for increases in the unit costs of labour or materials, or both, which take place in the contract period. Cost reimbursement and measurement contracts too will generally have a completion value different from the original estimate. Some contracts, normally those which are expected to have a short duration, may be quoted at a 'firm price' but these may still be affected, of course, by variations. This means, therefore, that the aggregate value of orders over time represents a varying mix of orders priced on the basis of different pricing systems, particularly important being the difference between fixed and variable price quotations.[21] Factors such as these weaken the statistical correlation between the new orders and output series. However, it is essential to note that the new orders series which are published are adjusted by certain factors with the intention of bringing them into line with output figures (see Section 4.5.3 below).

4.5.2.3. *Contract duration.* Information has been collected in these enquiries about the expected duration of contracts since 1964 (see specimen questionnaire—BIM/OR reproduced in Appendix VIII) but it is not published. It is used by the Department for the purpose of estimating the forward load on the industry.

4.5.3. *The New Orders Series and Their Interpretation*

4.5.3.1. *The series available.* Details of the series available in published sources are set out in Table 4.4. This section is confined to amplification of the information given in the table and discussion of matters relevant to the interpretation of the series. Particularly important is a knowledge of the adjustments and revisions made.

Adjustments made to the new orders series before publication. Two types of adjustment are regularly made to the statistics before publication with the ostensible purpose of bringing the series 'into line' with output series. A knowledge of these adjustments, details of which are not normally published, is essential for a proper appreciation of the published series.

One adjustment is made on the grounds that the value reported as a new order will understate the amount payable by the time the work has been completed for the kind of reasons we discussed earlier (Section 4.5.2.2). The adjustment made is to increase the value of private industrial orders by 30 per cent and private non-industrial orders by 10 per cent. No adjustment is made for private housing and public sector jobs. Details of the basis on which the actual adjustment factors themselves were originally determined are not available.

The other adjustment made is one aimed at allowing for an overstatement of new orders which arises, it is believed, from a failure by specialist firms to exclude all repair and maintenance work and sub-contracts from their returns. At one time different factors were applied to specialists' orders reported in the monthly and quarterly enquiries—the factors being redetermined annually and applied to both the number and value series, each being reduced by the appropriate factor. Currently a common factor of 4 per cent is used.

The merits of these adjustments are, of course, arguable. The first in particular is open

---

[21] Contractors have been required to indicate whether contracts are at a 'fixed' or variable price only since April 1976; no data on this had been published at the time of writing (July 1977). Some information, collected separately, relating to housing contracts in the public sector in England and Wales, however, is available in [QRL 169] and [QRL 168].

to the objection that the new orders series may be of interest in its own right, rather than as an indicator of future output, and thus adjustment is undesirable. Quite apart from the desirability of adjustment, however, the use of constant factors over long periods of time is especially questionable. The second adjustment is perhaps more readily justified, always accepting that the factors used are themselves good indicators of the degree of adjustment needed.

Revisions of the published series. Substantial retrospective revisions were made to the pre-1964 series after the statistics on the new basis initiated in that year became available although users should note that this is not made clear in the published series. It then appeared that the previous system of reporting had involved an understatement of orders particularly for non-housing work. Revisions to the series (introduced in the *MBCS* [QRL 194] for March 1965) were therefore made as follows: (i) private industrial work—increased by 34 per cent, (ii) private miscellaneous (i.e. non-industrial, non-housing) work—increased by 15 per cent and (iii) public non-housing work—increased by 5 per cent. Strictly speaking, therefore, there is a discontinuity in these series at this point. No further information about the basis of these adjustments was provided; indeed the revisions themselves are only apparent through an examination of the series published in successive issues of the *MBCS* [QRL 194].

Further revision of the series to allow for unrecorded work arising from deficiencies in the register, parallel to that made retrospectively in respect of output over the period 1963–72 (see Section 4.4.2), has not been made. But it should be remembered that this problem is much less serious in the case of the new orders statistics because of the difference in the method of collection: sub-contracts being returned by the main contractor rather than the sub-contractor. Nonetheless it is to be expected that the series has been affected to some degree by the large number of firms omitted from the DOE register (see Section 4.1.3). The firms, reported as having been identified in this category by the early 1970s [B 217], were included in the normal sample selections for the new orders enquiry with effect from July 1974 and produced a discontinuity (said to be small) in the series from the third quarter of 1974.

It may also be noted that the adjustments made to the register early in 1977 (referred to earlier) to exclude firms reclassified as structural steel fabricators and, a related point, to exclude steel oil-drilling platforms, will affect the series.

4.5.3.2. *Classification by type of work and sector and regional analyses.* Before 1964, the classification of work by type was made by the contractor. Since then for jobs above a specified value (currently £10,000) the contractor has been required to provide a brief description or to select the category from a list provided (see Appendix VIII)—with the exception that up to April 1976 a brief description had to be provided for the largest jobs—i.e. those valued at £¼ million or more. For jobs below the size limits referred to earlier (£10,000 or £2,500—see Appendix VIII for further details) which are returned in the aggregate only, a classification by type is made on the basis of information about the first and last of such jobs obtained by each contractor in the period, the classification being made proportionately by value in the aggregate. The classification of work to the public or private sector is made by the contractor, a list being supplied of authorities in the public sector (again see Appendix VIII for details).

138   CONSTRUCTION AND THE RELATED PROFESSIONS

Table 4.4
Contractors' New Orders Statistics* Great Britain

Description of Series		Period Covered	Frequency	Analy... By Type of Work
VALUES				
1. At current prices—(i) National series (a)		1956 (Q$_4$)–1972 (Q$_1$)	Q	5 types
		1970 to date	Q	5 types
(b)		1964–72 (Q$_1$)	Q	18/19 types
		1970 to date	Q	18/19 types
(c)		1964–March 1972	M	5 types
		1964 to date	M	5 types
(ii) Regional series (d)		1964–72 (Q$_1$)	Q	5 types
		1970 to date	Q	5 types
2. At constant prices, s.a.		1960–72 (Q$_1$)	Q	5 types
		1970 (Q$_4$) to date	Q	5 types
INDEX NUMBERS				
3. At constant prices, s.a. (a)		1970 to date	Q	5 types
(b)		1963 to date	Q	No
NUMBER AND VALUE OF CONTRACTS BY SIZE				
4. Totals and percentage distribution by value ranges (a)		1966–71 (Q$_2$) (see Remarks)	Q	5 types
(b)		1968 to date	A	5 types

Abbreviations: s.a.—seasonally adjusted; M—Monthly; Q—Quarterly; A—Annually.
* *Unpublished statistics.* In addition the following statistics of contractors' new orders are available on request from the Department of the Environment, Statistics Construction Division:
    (i) Great Britain, monthly value figures, at current prices, by nineteen types of work, from January 1965.
    (ii) Regions, quarterly value figures, at current prices, by fifteen types of work, from first quarter 1964.

4.5.3.1 STATISTICS COLLECTED BY DEPARTMENT OF ENVIRONMENT

By ctor	Publication	Remarks
es / es	MBCS [QRL 194] May 1958 et seq. HCS [QRL 168] } MDS [QRL 195]	*Annual series* are included in *AAS* [QRL 31] and also, back to 1958, in *HCS* [QRL 168] No. 1 Supp. Table III. [QRL 148] includes Totals (a)—no breakdown—from 1963. *Work not covered by orders*—separate series is published in *MDS* [QRL 195].
es / es	MBCS [QRL 194] June 1965 et seq. HCS [QRL 168] } MDS [QRL 195]	*Annual series*: 1964–70 were included in *ABCS* [QRL 32] 1970; 1967 to date in *HCS* [QRL 168]. Annual series for Scotland, 1964 to date, are published in [QRL 306].
es / es	MBCS [QRL 194] Sept. 1965 et seq. MPBW/DOE *Press Notices* [QRL 235]	N.B. Currently the only published source is the DOE *Press Notice* [QRL 235].
es / es	MBCS [QRL 194] Sept. et seq. HCS [QRL 168]. [QRL 252]—annual series only. [QRL 306]—Scotland. [QRL 360]—Wales.	For Scotland, annual series, further broken down by Planning Regions (totals only), are published for the period 1968 to date in [QRL 306]; see also remarks against item 1 (b) above.
es / es	MBCS [QRL 194] June 1965 et seq. HCS [QRL 168]	Annual series back to 1958 were included in *HCS* [QRL 168] No. 1. Retrospectively revised series back to 1963 (using new deflators from 1970) were introduced in *HCS* [QRL 168] No. 9. *ETAS* [QRL 148] includes *Totals* (Q)—no breakdown—from 1963.
es / No	HCS [QRL 168] ETAS [QRL 148]. HCS [QRL 168] from 1964	Annual series back to 1967 also included. Included in table of 'Activity Indicators'—Annual series back to 1961—in *HCS* [QRL 168].
es / es	MBCS [QRL 194] Feb. 1970 et seq. HCS [QRL 168]	Quarterly figures from 1966 to 1968 were not published but are available on request. Annual series from 1966 to 1970 were included in *ABCS* [QRL 32] 1970.

(iii) Sub-regions (sixty-six in Great Britain), quarterly value figures, at current prices, total for all types of work, from first quarter 1967.

(iv) Great Britain, numbers and value (current prices) of new orders by five types of work, sub-classified by size of firm (in terms of total employment) annually from 1970 to 1975 and the first quarter of 1976 and by value group of firm (in terms of estimated annual new work as main contractor) from second quarter 1976.

Either five or nineteen categories of work are defined as follows:

5 Types

Public Sector	*Private Sector*
New Housing	New Housing
Other New Work	Other New Work:
	Industrial
	Non-Industrial

19 (formerly 18) Types*

Public Sector
New Housing
Other New Work:
  Public Corporations:
    Gas, electricity and coal
    Railways and air transport

  Education:
    Schools
    Universities
  Health
  Offices, garages, factories and shops
  Roads
  Harbours
  Water
  Sewerage
  Miscellaneous

Private Sector
New Housing
Other New Work:
  Industrial†
  Non-Industrial
    Offices
    Shops
    Entertainment
    Garages
    Schools and colleges
    Miscellaneous

---

* DOE numbering; in fact there are currently twenty types if housing in the public and the private sectors is treated as two separate categories (formerly nineteen types could be distinguished—work for public corporations not being sub-divided).

† A further breakdown of the private industrial sector is now shown in monthly press notices [QRL 235] with 'oil' separated from the rest.

A detailed guide to the categories to which particular types of work are currently classified for the purposes of new orders statistics is given in [B 250] (see also *Form BIM/OR*—reproduced in Appendix VIII). Note should be taken of a change in approach to classification with effect from 2nd quarter 1976—see [B 250] 1976 edition.

Regional analyses. As we noted earlier, the regional classification of new orders is based on the actual location of the job, unlike the output and employment statistics which are classified according to the location of the firm's head office (or regional office where separate returns are made)—except in the case of Scotland and Wales for which special series are produced (see Section 4.4.5.3). For a study of the relationship between regional new orders and regional output statistics see [B 120]. Comparative data on the basis of the old and the new regional classification introduced in 1965 is to be found in the editions of the *ABCS* [QRL 32] issued from 1968 to 1970. It should also be noted that statistics are available for sixty-six sub-regions of Great Britain on request from the DOE (see Table 4.4—footnote).

4.5.3.3. *Constant-price and seasonally adjusted series.* Details of the series available are given in Table 4.4; we are again concerned in this section with matters relevant to the interpretation of the series. The conversion of the current price new orders series to a constant price basis introduces a number of severe practical and conceptual difficulties. In the aggregate the current-price series each period will consist of a varying mix of essentially one-off projects differentiated not only by design and function, etc. but also by the basis upon which price has been determined. Reference should be made to Section 2.3 for a discussion of pricing and valuation questions. We may note here, however, that the price of each project will be determined not only by current factor costs but also by anticipated changes in factor costs, depending on the planned construction period and whether or not a firm or variable price is quoted, and also by changes in planned profit margins which in turn will be influenced by the tendering climate and perhaps by the nature of the work.

Ideally, therefore, a price index (or indices) is required to reflect adequately these twin sources of diversity and changes in them over time. This is no simple task and it cannot be pretended that the problem has been solved although undoubtedly improvements have been made in recent years by the development of indices which are directly based on tender price information rather than merely unit factor costs. Reference should be made to Section 8.1 for a full discussion of the problems and methods of measurement of construction cost and price indices and an appraisal of the indices available.

A major change of practice in the preparation of constant-price series for new orders was made in 1973 when tender price indices were used for the first time and retrospective revisions made to the previous series. A brief notice was included in *Statistical News* [B 334] Feb. 1974, p. 24.19 but no official published account is available and the detailed particulars given here are based upon information supplied by the DOE Statistics Construction Division.

Up to 1973 the index used for deflating new orders was the same as that used for the deflation of output—the DOE 'CNC' index (considered in detail in Section 8.1.2.1). Quite apart from its suitability as an output deflator, this index was not a satisfactory deflator for new orders inasmuch as it attempts to measure changes in the price level for currently-executed work rather than tendering levels for work yet to be started. At one time it is understood that adjustments were made to the labour and materials cost constituents of the CNC index in an attempt to allow for likely future price levels. It will be appreciated that such adjustments were necessarily speculative (although some information would be available about the dates of commencement of negotiated wage increases and some materials price changes) and that tender prices also depend upon changes in overheads, planned profit and productivity for which no forward-looking allowance was possible. It may be that the indices so devised proved satisfactory but undoubtedly the potential scope for error was large and variable. At one time also two separate indices were used (apparently until the rebasing of the CNC index on 1963 in 1969)—one for housing and one for non-housing—each being variants of the single 'CNC' index.

At the end of 1973, however, new indices were introduced based upon recently developed indices of tender prices as such (again considered in Section 8.1). The method used to devise the tender price indices has undoubted virtues over 'composite' or 'synthetic' methods based on factor costs (as in the CNC index) and are naturally more appropriate for the deflation of new orders. Currently, the author is informed, deflation is performed separately for different types of work as follows:

Type of Work
- (i) Public housing (E & W)
- (ii) Public housing (Scotland)
- (iii) Private housing
- (iv) Public works (building)
- (v) Public works (roads)
- (vi) Public works (civil engineering excluding roads)
- (vii) Private industrial
- (viii) Private commercial

The deflators are derived from the following tender price indices: DQSS and BCIS indices (Sections 8.1.2.6 and 8.1.2.7 refer), two indices for housebuilding (PILAH for England and Wales—described in [B 114]—and an unpublished index for Scotland) and a road construction price index (so far unpublished). For private housing, the housebuilding tender index is combined with an index of house prices adjusted for movements in land prices.

The retrospective revisions of the constant price series, made in 1973, were carried back to 1970 on the basis of the new tender price deflators (the 'CNC' index being used up to 1969) but other, minor, revisions were also incorporated back to 1963 at this time; these were published in *HCS* [QRL 168] No. 9. For purposes of publication the constant price series are prepared only for five categories of work (the public sector categories listed above being combined into housing and non-housing categories). This contrasts with the nineteen types distinguished in the current price series. It will be appreciated, of course, that to devise separate price deflators for each of these types would demand a much more extensive data-capturing system, especially in the private sector, than is at present available.

In summary, two points should be stressed with regard to interpretation. One is that even at current prices it is difficult to know what precise meaning may be attached to the 'value' of new orders in the aggregate due to the nature of pricing for work yet to be done and, in particular, variations in the mix of work with different anticipated construction periods and variations in the mix of firm and variable price quotations. At constant prices the difficulty is compounded by those involved in obtaining a satisfactory measure of price changes. It is essential, therefore, to interpret changes in the series in the light of the conceptual and practical problems involved in their compilation and the inevitable margins of error that must arise.

Seasonally adjusted series. With regard to seasonal adjustments, these are based on the method (basically the ratio to moving average method) developed by the US Bureau of the Census and known as the X-11 Variant of the Census Method II program (it is fully described in [B 145]).

4.5.3.4. *Number and size of contracts and orders.* The published statistics of the number of new contracts and orders are incomplete because the number of contracts each with a value of less than the cut-off points used in the returns (before April 1976, £2,500 for smaller firms and £10,000 for larger firms, now £10,000 for all firms) are not published although the total number of such contracts, unclassified by type of work, is obtained in the enquiries. Another fact to note is that the number and size of sub-contracts is not known since they are not recorded separately, the value of these being incorporated in the return from the main contractor. Further, extensions to existing jobs are treated as a new order and should therefore be recorded separately in the returns. It will be appreciated, of course, that the number of new building projects is also understated inasmuch as those parts undertaken by public authority direct labour forces are not covered.

The classification of new orders by size is in terms of value ranges expressed at current prices. Naturally the distribution of jobs by size, defined in this way, is affected by changes in building price levels over time.

4.5.3.5. *New construction work outstanding.* The statistics of new orders, coupled with the information about contract duration that is collected in the same enquiry, enable the DOE to make estimates of the future work load for contractors. In turn, these estimates coupled with the statistics of work done by contractors, provide a basis for estimating the volume of new construction work outstanding. Nothing is published currently but a quarterly index of this kind, seasonally adjusted, for the period from 1963 (4th quarter) to 1969 (4th quarter) was published in *ET* [QRL 147] from March 1965 to December 1969. It will be appreciated, of course, that the series covers contractors only and, given the dates of the series, will have been affected over time by shortcomings in the output and new orders series discussed earlier (Sections 4.4 and 4.5.3) arising out of an incomplete register of firms and the reporting practices of respondents.

4.5.4. *EEC State of Trade Enquiry for Contractors in Great Britain*

This enquiry was initiated on a quarterly basis by the DOE at the beginning of 1977 in order to complement similar surveys carried out by other members of the EEC. It is conducted on a sample basis covering all types and sizes of firm other than those employing less than twenty-five persons (the sample size amounting to about 1,500 firms) with the intention of obtaining a quick qualitative indication of current circumstances and trends in the industry. Information is collected under six heads (each subdivided by type of work) as follows: level of activity, delaying factors, work in hand, intake of orders, employment and prices. For further details see the specimen questionnaire (BIM 400) and the accompanying notes included in Appendix IX.

As yet no results have been published but it is hoped that, once the enquiry has been established, it will be possible to publish the results about one month after the end of the quarter concerned. It will not be possible to pass any judgement on the enquiry until it has run through a number of periods and the results can be compared with quantitative data, but the nature and proposed speed of the enquiry clearly make it a potentially very valuable economic indicator.

4.6. British Construction Work Overseas

A census of contractors undertaking construction work overseas has been taken annually each April since 1955. The questionnaires for this enquiry are sent only to those contractors who have stated that they undertake such work in reply to a question inserted on one of the previous quarterly returns of employment and output. A specimen copy of the questionnaire in current use—Form BIM 60—giving details of the information requested and the instructions given with regard to its completion is reproduced in Appendix X.

Part 1 of the form requires a return by country under each of the heads listed below and has remained the same since 1955 except for the introduction in 1974 (not repeated subsequently) of a division of the totals between Building and Civil Engineering. Information is requested for each year, ending 31 March, as follows:

(a) the total value of contracts obtained,
(b) the estimated value of work done,
(c) the value of work outstanding at 31 March.

The results for this part of the enquiry are available according to trading area (i.e. Sterling area, Dollar area, EEC, etc.) for the period from 1955, and according to geographical area from 1970. These are published, along with a commentary on some of the outstanding contracts obtained and the firms involved, currently in *Trade and Industry* [QRL 352], formerly *Board of Trade Journal* [QRL 48], generally in October or November each year; the first of these was published in the issue of [QRL 48] for 29 October 1955, Vol. 169, No. 3071, pp. 937–9. Currently the series are also published in *HCS* [QRL 168]; formerly they were included in the *ABCS* [QRL 32] and the *MBCS* [QRL 194]. All values are in current price terms; no constant price series are available. It will be appreciated that, given the international character of the work the preparation of constant price series is confronted by severe conceptual and practical difficulties.

The information collected in Part 2 of the Form, which requires a return of payments and receipts in respect of overseas contracts, was added in 1962 and is used in the compilation of balance of payments statistics. The net earnings of contractors plus the fees of consultants (consulting engineers, architects and quantity surveyors) engaged in projects overseas are published in [QRL 356] as one of a miscellaneous set of items entitled 'other services'—see, for example, Table 17 in the 1974 edition. Statistics relating to the overseas work of the professions are considered in Section 13.5. Details of separate annual series for overseas earnings and investment by construction and other industries is given in Section 7.2.6.

4.7. Local Authority Design Work in Great Britain

4.7.1. *Introduction*

Information about work at the design stage may serve a double purpose. First, it provides an indication of the level of activity at this part of the construction process. Secondly, it provides, in principle, an earlier indication of the future work-load for contractors than new orders statistics and thus should enable forecasts to be made for the more distant future; although in practice, apparently, difficulties have been experienced in making effective use of the available statistics for this purpose. In the private sector, design work is generally carried out by architects and engineers in private practice though some will also be done by staff directly employed by contractors and manufacturing firms (e.g. producers of prefabricated systems of construction). In the public sector, design work is carried out by the authorities' own professional staff as well as by designers in private practice. Statistics for the public sector were collected for the first time by the then Ministry of Public Building and Works in respect of local authorities in 1965.[22] In the private sector the collection of statistical information was begun by the Royal Institute of British Architects (RIBA) in 1958, in respect of private architects. The latter is considered in Section 13.5; this section is concerned solely with the official enquiry.

4.7.2. *The Statistics Collected and Their Interpretation*

4.7.2.1. *The scope of the enquiry and the available data.* The enquiry initiated by the MPBW, and continued by the DOE, covers all local government authorities in Great Britain including New Town Development Corporations and Commissions, County Councils, Road Construction Units and the Scottish Special Housing Association. It will be appreciated, therefore, that coverage of work being designed in the public sector is incomplete; for instance, Government Departments, Nationalized Industries, Hospital Boards, etc. are not covered. With regard to coverage it should also be noted that the enquiry covers work to be designed *by or for* the authority and thus overlaps with the returns obtained by the RIBA. Separate details are obtained, however, about work which is to be wholly or partially done by private firms and is available on request.

As regards the data collected, a major change was made in 1972, and a further change in 1975, both of which reduced the range of information required but, since a good part of it was not published, the published series were little affected. Initially information was sought about projects at more than one stage of the design process, but with effect from August 1975 the return was confined to projects at the working drawing stage only. A specimen copy of the questionnaire in current use—Form BIM 148—is reproduced in Appendix XI. Details of the published series are set out in Table 4.5 below. We discuss here those features of the data which are important from the point of view of their interpretation and use. Information about the more detailed data collected prior to 1972 is contained in the brief history of the enquiry included in Appendix XI. Reference should also be made to a special report [B 266], prepared by Lady Lea, formerly Chief Statistician at the Ministry, which provides a useful appraisal of the new series soon after their introduction.

4.7.2.2. *Valuation, coverage and continuity of the series.* It will be appreciated that at the design stage the estimated costs of projects are necessarily approximate and may be revised as the projects move from one stage of the design process to the next. It should be noted that the value is meant to represent the gross cost of construction work only—i.e. excluding site values, professional fees and the costs of furniture and equipment, but including site preparation.

[22] In fact the enquiry was initiated during 1964 but the initial response was low and thus the series effectively commences in 1965.

Table 4.5
Local Authority Design Work—Published Series (Great Britain)

Description of Series	Period Covered	Frequency†	Breakdown By Type of Work‡	Breakdown By Region	Publication	Remarks
Number and Value of Projects for New Work valued at over £2,500:*						
(a) Working drawings stage	1965–71 1970 to date	Thrice yearly Thrice yearly	Yes Yes	No Yes§	MBCS [QRL 194] Jan. 1969 et seq. HCS [QRL 168]	HCS [QRL 168] also contains series back to 1965 but not broken down by type of work.
(b) Sketch plan stage	1965–71 1970–5 (Apr.)	Thrice yearly Thrice yearly	Yes Yes	No Yes§	MBCS [QRL 194] Jan. 1969 et seq. HCS [QRL 168]	HCS [QRL 168] also contains series back to 1965 but not broken down by type of work. Collected for the last time in April 1975.
(c) Work in hand	1965–71	Thrice yearly	Yes	No	MBCS [QRL 194] Jan. 1969 et seq.	} No longer collected
(d) Work in abeyance	1965–8 (Jan.)	Thrice yearly	Yes	No	[B 266]	

* Except in the case of road works prior to 1972 and all projects in the first enquiry in 1972—see text. Data on numbers not published after April 1975.
† Four-monthly periods ending in January, May and September from 1965 to 1971 and then April, August and December except for the last enquiry of 1971 which covered three months to the end of December to avoid double counting.
‡ The types of work for which series are published are as follows (for details of the categories for which information is collected see specimen questionnaire BIM 148 reproduced in Appendix XI):
  Building   Civil Engineering
  Housing   Roads
  Education Other
  Other
§ Regional analyses for 1971–4 were published in HCS [QRL 168] Nos. 6, 10 and 14; earlier analyses, back to 1967, are available on written application to DOE, Statistics Construction Division.

4.7.2.3   STATISTICS COLLECTED BY DEPARTMENT OF ENVIRONMENT   147

The coverage and continuity of the series were affected by the changes made in 1972 and 1975. In general only projects valued at over £2,500 have been covered since 1965. However, the size limit was abolished in the first enquiry on the revised basis in 1972, only to be reintroduced in the second enquiry in that year, so that there is a discontinuity in the series at this point. A further break in continuity is caused by the fact that prior to 1972 County Councils were required to make a return of road works only when their costs exceeded £25,000 rather than £2,500. Furthermore this part of the return was required only once a year, in September, thus in interpreting the intra-year series prior to 1972 note must be taken of the fact that the roads and total figures were understated each January and May. It will also be appreciated that, since the limit of £2,500 has remained throughout the whole period, apart from the exception to which we have referred, the coverage of the enquiry in terms of projects will have gradually expanded as a result of rising costs. It is also possible, of course, that a project not reported at the sketch plan stage, because it fell below the limit of £2,500, may nonetheless be included at the working drawings stage if its estimated cost has been revised in the meantime to a level above this limit. With effect from August 1975, however, information about work at the sketch plans stage is no longer collected.

4.7.2.3. *Forecasting applications.* The main value of design work statistics is their potential for forecasting future output. We proceed, therefore, to consider the data further, briefly, in this particular context although, as we mentioned earlier, in practice it has not proved possible to make effective use of the data for this purpose officially. There are, of course, a number of practical problems relating to the nature of the data and the estimation of the statistical relationships.

The restriction of the series to the working drawings stage alone means that it now provides a potential indicator of the likely future work-load for the construction industry in the near, as distinct from the more distant, future only. From a statistical point of view, the series is probably most useful for forecasting contractors' new orders rather than output, inasmuch as the statistical relationship between the two series is likely to be a stronger one (since further valuation changes and variable time lags occur before the output stage is reached). And the working drawings series is probably more useful for this purpose than the former sketch plans series.

With regard to the relationship itself between these series and future output or new orders for the construction industry, there are a number of factors to take into account. One problem is that some of the work will be carried out not by contractors but by direct labour forces. Unfortunately, however, no statistics of new orders for direct labour forces are available. At one time the authorities were asked in the design enquiry to indicate the projects on which they expected to use direct labour—see [B 266] para. 48—but it was not normally published and is no longer collected.

Further, as far as the public sector is concerned, some of the design work is undertaken by private architects; this does not need to be taken into account separately inasmuch as the local authority design statistics cover all projects, including those on which the work is delegated to architects in private practice. On the other hand, it has to be borne in mind that the local authority design work statistics naturally cover only part of all work in the public sector. Thus if the similar RIBA series, which covers all work commissioned of private architects (see Section 13.5 for details), is used in conjunction with the DOE series the element of overlap between the two needs to be taken into account (data are collected separately for work designed 'wholly by a local authority design staff' and 'wholly or partially by private consultants' and are available on request).

Apart from the question of coverage of the data, their usefulness for forecasting purposes will depend on such factors as the accuracy with which construction costs (or tender prices) can be estimated at the design stage, the accuracy with which price changes can be eliminated from the series (there are no special indices available), the extent to which the element of abandoned work is subject to variation and the variability of the time lags (which are likely to be influenced by type-of-work mix and workload), all of which will determine the strength and stability of the statistical relationships. Some of these aspects were considered in the special report on the series by Lady Lea [B 266] paras. 14–29 and 43. With regard to time lags, in particular, information was regularly requested in the enquiry up to 1971 about the expected starting dates but no analyses were published.

4.8. Building Control Statistics 1966–8

Under the *Building Control Act 1966* it became unlawful to carry out any work in the construction or alteration of a building, or of any other fixed works of construction or civil engineering, which was not exempted by the Act, unless a licence had been obtained from the Minister of Public Building and Works, the purpose being to regulate the starting dates of certain large privately sponsored projects. The Act came into force on 9 August 1966 but the control applied to all schemes, not exempt, for which a contract had not been made or work started before 28 July 1965. The categories of work exempt from control were set out in sections 2–7 of the Act; in the main these were private dwellings, industrial buildings, all projects in development districts, development by or on behalf of the Crown and work carried out at the expense of local authorities and other public bodies as well as projects costing less than a specified limit. The limit specified in the Act was £100,000, but on 11 August 1966 it was reduced to £50,000; it was subsequently restored to £100,000 on 23 May 1968. The control was suspended altogether with effect from 20 November 1968.

Quarterly statistics were published in the *MBCS* [QRL 194] from April 1967 to December 1968 giving the value and number of projects authorized and refused analysed as follows:

(a) By Category (defined as in the New Orders statistics):

New Housing*	Entertainment
Industrial*	Garages
Offices	Schools and Colleges
Shops	Miscellaneous

(b) By Region.

---

* Although Housing and Industrial schemes as such were exempt, those which included more than the specified limit of non-housing and non-industrial accommodation were licensable.

Summary statistics were also published in reports by the Minister on the operation of the Act [QRL 66], [QRL 67]; these include, in addition to those referred to above, separate total figures of the number and value of schemes in the range £50,000–£99,999 authorized and refused. Both of these sources give statistics from the date of commencement of the Act.

In the interim period between the announcement of the intention to enact legislation in July 1965 and its passage in August 1966 applications were submitted to the Minister and advice was given on schemes which would be authorized or refused. Statistical analyses of these applications and those under consideration up to June 1966 were given by the Minister in the House of Commons [B 246]. Subsequent figures of this kind do not appear to have been published.

It should be appreciated that, since the intention of the control was to regulate starting dates, schemes could appear more than once in the statistics if for any reason, such as a failure to be licensed on previous applications, they were submitted more than once. Separate analyses of this element of double counting, if any, were not published and neither were analyses of the delays which were actually imposed on starting dates. In themselves, however, the statistics may give a misleading impression of the impact of the legislation for it is thought that some potential developers postponed or abandoned their plans without applying for a licence.

4.9. Miscellaneous Enquiries

4.9.1. *Site Lighting and Winter Building Precautions*

Surveys were conducted annually from 1965 to 1973 to obtain information about the measures taken by contractors to facilitate the progress of construction work during winter, the questionnaire being issued as a Supplement to one of the monthly sample returns on employment. Initially it was concerned only with the use made of site lighting, but in 1967 it was amplified to cover heating and a variety of other aids and protective measures. The information was collected for the use of the Winter Building Advisory Committee and was not published, though it may be made available.

4.9.2. *Industrialized Building*

The use of industrialized building methods is a subject of some interest and, although no statistics are available, it may be worth noting that an attempt was made to collect statistics about it for a time during the 1960s. Because of definitional problems, however, the enquiry was discontinued after a two-year trial period. In the housing field, it may be noted, much more statistical information is available particularly about proprietary building 'systems', which are much more amenable to statistical expression than 'industrialized building' as such which is wider in scope. For details of the housing data (which, it should be noted, is confined to the public sector) see the companion *Reviews* in this series [B 52] and [B 57]. Reference should also be made to the *HCS Notes and Definitions Supplement* [B 250] regarding the definition of 'industrialized building' applied in housing statistics.

CHAPTER 5

PRODUCTION STATISTICS OTHER THAN THOSE COLLECTED BY THE DEPARTMENT OF THE ENVIRONMENT AND ITS PREDECESSOR DEPARTMENTS

5.1. Introduction

The principal production statistics for construction in Great Britain, collected by the Department of the Environment and its predecessor departments, have been examined at length in Chapters 3 and 4. Those statistics, however, by no means exhaust the range of information available; there exist a variety of other types and sources of data relating to construction activity in either Great Britain or the United Kingdom and these are grouped together for consideration in this chapter. Data relating solely to Northern Ireland are considered separately in Chapter 9. The term 'production', it should be noted, is used here as an omnibus term to embrace all data relating to construction work whether completed, in progress or planned.

5.2. Construction in the Index of Industrial Production

5.2.1. The Available Series

5.2.1.1. The UK index. Since the Second World War index numbers of construction output have formed a constituent series of the official index of industrial production for the United Kingdom compiled by the CSO. The primary source of publication, currently, is *Trade and Industry* [QRL 352]. Convenient secondary sources are the *MDS* [QRL 195], *Ec. Trends* [QRL 147] and its *Annual Supplement* [QRL 148]. The annual series (only) are also reproduced in the *AAS* [QRL 31] and in the annual 'Blue Book' [QRL 201] in which it appears in a table of 'Index numbers of output at constant factor cost'. The output index published in *HCS* [QRL 168], it should be noted, relates to Great Britain and not the UK.

The post-war series for construction run from 1948 on a quarterly basis although the 'all-industries' index itself is prepared monthly—the monthly construction component is estimated since output data are only collected quarterly and it is not now published. Since its introduction in 1948 the index has been revised twice in accordance with the revisions to the SIC in 1958 and 1968 [B 329], with consequential changes in the name used for the industry (see Appendix I), and rebased on four occasions: 1954, 1958, 1963 and 1970. These changes, and the methods of compilation, are described in a series of official guides [B 259], [B 254], [B 255], [B 218], [B 256] and [B 271]. The first of these guides [B 259], it may be noted, dealt with an 'interim' index based on 1946 which was subsequently replaced by the index based on 1948 (described in [B 254]) as soon as the results of the first full post-war census of production became available.

Continuous series. Because of the breaks in continuity that the revisions referred to above have involved, valuable efforts have been made officially to link the data so as to provide reasonably continuous series. These cover the period from 1948 (annual series) and from 1952 (quarterly series, seasonally adjusted) up to 1971 on the 1963 base in [QRL 15] and up to 1972 on the 1970 base in [QRL 149]. However, it is crucial to note that in 1973, in between the publication of these two articles, major retrospective revisions were made to the estimates of construction output for Great Britain for the period 1963 to 1972 to allow for output which had previously gone unrecorded. Thus the evidence provided by the series given in [QRL 15] and [QRL 149] is markedly different. An account of these revisions will be found in [B 217]; see also Section 4.4.5 above. It may be noted that these revisions were such as to increase the construction output index for Great Britain for 1972 by 8.5 per cent above its former level (117 to 127), an increase which was sufficient to increase the overall index of industrial production for *all* industries (1963-based) by 1 per cent; 'there were corresponding but retrogressively smaller increases to the production index for previous years from 1965' ([B 217] p. lxiii refers).

Pre-war series. Before the 1939–45 war the official index did not include a separate series for construction but one in which 'building' was included along with 'building materials' (series from 1934 with 1930 as base). For this reason and because we are mainly concerned with the post-war period, no attention is devoted to this series here; the official description is to be found in [B 186] and the series themselves in [QRL 317]. Attempts to compile long-run, unofficial, series retrospectively have been made notably by Lomax for the period 1900–57 in [B 96] and by Feinstein, using Lomax's and other series, for the period back to 1855 in [QRL 13]. Given the data available, these series are subject to potentially large margins of error.

5.2.1.2. *Indices for Great Britain, Northern Ireland, Scotland and Wales—Great Britain.* The post-war series referred to above relates to the UK as a whole and is compiled by taking a weighted average of separate indices for Great Britain and Northern Ireland. Neither of these indices is published as part of the official industrial production series. For Great Britain, however, index numbers of construction output have been (and still are) published by the DOE and its predecessor Departments. Full details of these index numbers, which are available over various periods back to 1954, are set out in Table 4.3. Particular attention needs to be paid to the revised series, prepared in 1973 for the period 1963–72, to which we have already referred—these are clearly indicated in Table 4.3. It should also be borne in mind that the pre-1963 series may also be affected to some extent by the same problem of under-recorded output (though probably less severe in incidence) which was the reason for the revision of the post-1963 series. Under-recording of output in itself, of course, may not provide a misleading measure of proportionate *changes* in the volume of output, as is measured by the index, as long as the degree of under-recording remains constant. In the post-1963 period, however, this was certainly not the case and there would seem to be no reason to believe that the situation before 1963 was any different in kind (though it may have been different in degree). In addition, the interpretation of these series needs also to take account of differences and changes in the coverage of direct labour—see below under *Interpretation* (Section 5.2.2).

Northern Ireland. An index of industrial production for Northern Ireland including a construction constituent, has been prepared locally for the period since 1950 (compiled retrospectively in 1958)—details are given in Chapter 9. But the index incorporated in the UK series remained a separate estimate, made on the basis of employment by the CSO ([B 254] p. 54 and [B 255] p. 81 refer). Since then the Northern Ireland output index itself has been incorporated. The former CSO estimates were not published.

Scotland. A new index of industrial production for Scotland was introduced in 1976, the previous series having been suspended in 1971 because it was felt that the system then in use was 'no longer supplying reliable results'. The new system (described in the *SEB* [QRL 308] No. 10, 1976, pp. 8–26) provided annual series from 1970 and quarterly series (non s.a.) from 1973. Revisions to the earlier, 1958-based, index were made later in *SEB* [QRL 308] No. 12, 1977, pp. 19–26 and spliced to the 1970-based series. Seasonally adjusted series are described in *SEB* [QRL 308] No. 14, 1978, pp. 16–19. Currently the series itself is published regularly in the *SEB* [QRL 308], *SAS* [QRL 306] and *T & I* [QRL 352] (formerly it was published—quarterly from 1948—in the *Digest of Scottish Statistics* [QRL 139]).

The primary source of data for the calculation of the construction index is the data collected by the DOE and considered earlier in Section 4.4.5. Currently current-price estimates are made of contractors' output of new work on the basis of a 'forward-spread' of new orders received, together with additions for local contractors' repair and maintenance work and local direct labour output. A Scottish deflator is used for public housing but otherwise the same deflators are used as for the UK. Before 1971 the series were based on data about output collected directly from contractors carrying out work in Scotland—for further details see Section 4.4.5. General questions of interpretation are considered below but it will be appreciated that the same problems of data collection and interpretation apply as for the UK as a whole and that the system using the 'forward-spread' of orders is necessarily approximate (although it may, of course, be more reliable than the direct collection of output data). The derivation of suitable price deflators pose their own problems (see Section 8.1) with the added reservation here that the use of the UK deflator for part of the series may not appropriately reflect Scottish experience.[1]

Wales. As in the case of Scotland, the index for Wales has recently been revised using DOE 'forward load' estimates derived from the new orders statistics—see above. Unlike the Scottish method of estimation, however, which requires the use of price deflators, the Welsh estimates are taken as a proportion of the total for Great Britain—the proportion representing the Welsh share of the forward-load estimates.

---

[1] Since the preparation of this Review and the introduction of the revised Scottish index a major revision has been made to the UK construction output deflators—see Addenda at the front of this volume—which will not have been reflected in the revised production index referred to here.

The current series (1970 based) provides annual and quarterly (s.a.) estimates from 1970 and is described in [B 257] together with the series from 1970 to 1975 (2nd quarter); current publication sources are: *DWS* [QRL 142], *WET* [QRL 360] and *T & I* [QRL 352]. The former series, based on the direct collection of output data (see Section 4.4.5), ran quarterly from 1964 (1963 base)—a description and the series itself is contained in *ET* [QRL 147] Nov. 1970, pp. xxxiii–xliii. General questions of interpretation are considered below.

5.2.2. *Interpretation*

There are a number of important matters that need to be borne in mind in interpreting the evidence provided by the construction indices. In essence these relate to the coverage and reliability of the statistics used in their compilation and the method of compilation itself; naturally the indices can be no better than the data on which they are based.

The purpose of the indices is to measure changes in the amount of 'work done' by the industry in contributing to total industrial production. Ideally, therefore, this ought to be represented by a measure of net output (i.e. gross output less the inputs of materials and services from other industries) but in practice, as with other industries, such information is not obtainable frequently enough and a measure of gross output is taken instead. Because of the heterogenous nature of construction work it can be measured only in monetary terms, but since these will reflect changes in price levels as well as changes in output, the measurement of changes in the real volume of output requires the elimination of the effect of price changes. This means, of course, that the validity of the resultant index is dependent equally upon the reliability of the original output data and upon the reliability of the measure of price changes used for price deflation purposes. On both these counts construction poses difficulties whose importance cannot be overrated.

As we have pointed out above, the UK index is a weighted average of indices for Great Britain and Northern Ireland. Until recently the Northern Ireland constituent was an estimate based on employment rather than output; it will be appreciated however, that since the weight attributed to it is small its influence on the overall average for the UK will be slight. For Great Britain, which represents the major part of the index, the calculations are based on the output statistics collected by the DOE and its forerunners which have been considered at length earlier (Chapters 3 and 4). Until 1963 it was the practice to devise the index for Great Britain on the basis of a weighted average of three separate series for new housing work, new non-housing work and repair work ([B 254] pp. 53–54 and [B 255] p. 81 refer). Since 1963 it has been based on two separately weighted series: one for new work and one for repairs and maintenance.

Before 1955, however, the output returns which form the bases for these series did not provide breakdowns of the value of work done by type and it was therefore necessary to make estimates (see Section 3.8.3 for details of the returns and the estimates made; see also [B 254] p. 54). Since 1955 the index has been based upon the enquiries considered in Section 4.4 above in which quarterly breakdowns of output by type of work have been obtained directly. But since 1955 the reliability of the data has suffered because of the problems of maintaining a comprehensive register of firms and ensuring complete coverage of the increasing volume of work done under labour-only sub-contract by self-employed workers (see Section 4.1.3). In the context of an index concerned with measuring rates of change of output it is important to note that these problems grew progressively worse and led ultimately, in 1973, to the preparation of the major retrospective revisions to the series back to 1963, which were referred to above in discussing the published series for Great Britain (Section 4.4.5). The likelihood is that the series for the late 1950s and early 1960s may also have been affected by these problems to some extent at least and must be treated with caution. With regard to the revised series from 1963, although the output estimates on which it is based are perhaps the best estimates that can be made, it is well to bear in mind the size and nature of the revisions that were necessary (see Section 4.4.5) and thus the margin of error that must inevitably adhere to them.

There are two further aspects of the coverage of the series that are relevant to their interpretation. The industries covered by the index of industrial production are meant to be defined in accordance with the SIC. But until 1955, as we explained earlier, the construction statistics were not collected on this basis (see Section 4.1). There is an implicit assumption, therefore (not an unreasonable one) as far as the construction index was concerned, that the movement of output on one base was representative of the movement on the other. The second point concerning coverage relates to the work done by direct labour, in particular that done by employees of gas, electricity and water undertakings. Such work was not expressly excluded from the SIC 'Order' for the construction industry until the introduction of the 1968 SIC. But it is notable that for the purposes of the industrial production index the construction work done by these three bodies was counted as part of the SIC 'Order' for 'Gas, Electricity & Water', not as part of the Construction 'Order', whereas the output statistics published by the DOE and its forerunners included such work until 1973, when the series back to 1963 were retrospectively revised. For further details of the coverage of direct labour in DOE enquiries see Sections 3.6 and 4.3.

The estimation of price changes for construction work is particularly difficult and hazardous. We consider the nature of the problems involved at length in Section 8.1 below in conjunction with an analysis of the various indices that are available. Since the output index is a weighted average of separate indices for different categories of work separate price indices are required. These were not published officially but they were made available unofficially up to 1972 in a quarterly article published in the journal *Building* (formerly *The Builder*) [B 37]. The index published officially covers all new work and is referred to as the 'Cost of New Construction' (CNC) index (the repairs and maintenance index still used is not published). The CNC index was published for the first time in 1956, series being given for the period from 1949. It is discussed fully in Section 8.1 where it is emphasized that quite apart from the normal price index number problems (which are intensified in construction because of the one-off nature of the work) a number of factors relating to the methodology and the data available make the index vulnerable to error and possibly bias. The price indices used in the early years of the production index differed in at least one respect: whereas the CNC index incorporates an allowance for productivity change, the earlier indices did not (see [B 255] p. 54). Whether or not the production index was itself revised on the basis of the new price indices is not clear. The effect of the difference, of course, is that when productivity is increasing the price index will overstate price rises, other things being equal, thus leading to an understatement of real output change and vice versa.

It will be appreciated, therefore, that the interpretation of the construction output index is beset by difficulties partly on account of changes over time, but mainly arising from inherent problems of measurement and practical problems of data collection. Although steps have been taken to remedy some of the deficiencies in coverage that grew progressively worse after 1955, especially during the 1960s and early 1970s, there remains some unrecorded output for which estimates have to be made. The problem of price measurement remains unresolved.[2] The outcome in terms of the likely size and direction of errors is extremely difficult to judge and it would seem that all one can do is to enjoin caution.

5.3. Construction in the Censuses of Production

5.3.1. Introduction

As we have indicated in earlier sections, since 1941 the primary responsibility for the collection of statistics about the construction industry has rested with the MOW and its successor departments (currently the DOE) and a large number of enquiries have been carried out (these are considered fully in Chapters 3 and 4). At the same time, however, the industry has also been included in censuses of production covering 'all' industry carried out by the Board of Trade and its successor departments (currently the Department of Industry, Business Statistics Office). Thus for many years since the Second World War there are two sources of census information about the industry. Before the war the 'census of production' provided the only source.

The basic reason for maintaining two parallel enquiries since the war is that they serve different purposes. Both sets of enquiries provide data about output and employment, but the scope of the census of production is wider, covering in addition the costs of inputs and capital expenditure. The purposes served by the census of production in the post-war years have been described in [B 32]. These include analyses of the size and structure of industry for purposes of economic analysis and the preparation of the national income and expenditure accounts [QRL 201] (see Section 7.1), the construction of input–output tables (see Section 5.3.4) and the provision of bench-marks for the measurement of output changes and weighting systems for index numbers of production and prices amongst others. (The original purposes of the census are described in [B 239] and [B 93].) The purposes served by the MOW–DOE enquiries, on the other hand, were originally related to the operation of controls over building. Since then they have continued to serve MOW–DOE needs as the 'sponsoring' department for the industry as well as providing information required by other government departments for purposes related to economic management generally (including the measurement of industrial production—see Section 5.2) more frequently and quickly than that available from the census of production.

The existence of two sets of data, however, is a mixed blessing for, perhaps inevitably, they provide conflicting evidence. In this section, therefore, after outlining the types of information available from the various census inquiries we devote particular attention to its interpretation in relation to the MOW–DOE data.

---

[2] New output deflators were introduced in March 1978 after the preparation of this text—see the Addenda at the front of this volume.

5.3.2. *The Censuses Taken and Subjects Covered*

5.3.2.1. *Pre-war censuses.* Before the Second World War construction ('building and contracting') was covered in five censuses: 1907, 1912, 1924, 1930 and 1935. These are not considered in detail here. A guide to the subjects covered and publication references is given in [B 239]. The use of the data involves certain problems, due especially to deficiencies in coverage, and the interested reader should refer to the amendments to the 1935 census data made by Bowen and Ellis in [B 23] and to the critical appraisal of the census data provided in [B 21], [QRL 5] and [QRL 12].

5.3.2.2. *Post-war censuses—The general pattern of enquiries.* Since the war a census covering construction ('building and contracting' until 1958) was taken in each year from 1946 to 1969 inclusive with the exception of 1947 and 1950. Since 1969 a 'new system of industrial statistics' has been devised, under the control of the BSO (see [B 149] for details) to meet criticisms made by the Estimates Committee in its report on Government Statistical Services in 1966 [B 230]. The new system is designed to replace all or most of the enquiries conducted by 'sponsoring' departments for particular industries, as well as the old-style periodic detailed censuses, but at the time of writing (July 1977) no announcement had been made about the timing of the transfer of responsibility for construction from the DOE to the BSO. However, the construction industry has been covered, along with other industries, in the BSO censuses from 1974 (it was not covered in the 1970–3 enquiries). But at the same time the DOE censuses (Section 4.2 and 4.3 refer) have continued, so that the dual system of censuses in operation up to 1969 has been re-established.

An official guide, which deals in general terms with all the censuses taken up to 1960, was published in [B 239]. Construction, however, is often an exception with regard to subjects covered and in other respects and it is important to study the *Introductory Notes* for each census—see references [QRL 50], [QRL 157], [QRL 116], [QRL 268] to [QRL 277] inclusive, and [QRL 353] (published as a separate volume in 1948, 1949, 1951–8 inclusive, 1963 and 1968)—and especially the introductory notes included in each particular report for the industry.

In brief, the pattern of enquiries established after the war was to take a census once every few years in which information was sought in some detail, especially about purchases (and sales for manufacturing industries), whilst in other years information was obtained in less detail. The detailed census years were: 1948, 1951, 1954, 1958, 1963 and 1968. The full range of information was sought only from firms above a size exemption limit (twenty-five or more persons in the case of construction), firms below this size receiving simplified forms—full details of the practices adopted for construction (which differ from those applied to most other industries because of the relatively high proportion of output and employment accounted for by small firms) are to be found in the introductory notes to the relevant reports (see Table 5.1).

Until 1952 each enquiry was a full census (in the sense of covering all firms on the register). In 1952 and each subsequent enquiry, with the exception of 1954 and 1959, sampling methods have been used, generally for obtaining information from smaller firms—*all* larger firms being included. For 1954 a full census was taken and in 1959 smaller firms were not covered at all. Fuller details about the sampling practices will be

Table 5.1
Subject Guide to Censuses of Production for Larger Firms in Construction 1946–69
(A cross 'x' signifies the availability of data)

	1946	1948	1949	1950	1951	1952(i)	1953(i)	1954(j)	1955(i)	1956(i)	1957(i)	1958	1959	1960	1961	1962	1963	1964	1965	1966	1967	1968	1969	Remarks
SCOPE AND COVERAGE																								
Area	(a)	GB	UK		←——————————————————————— United Kingdom ———————————————————————→																			For details of N. Ireland reports see Section 9.2.2. Certain data for N. Ireland are shown separately in the UK reports.
Industry—Firm Size(b)		←— 11 or more persons —→			←— 11 or more persons —→				←— All firms —→			25+	←— All firms —→				25+	←— All firms —→				25+	All	
Classification (SIC)	See [QRL 51]	←— 1948 SIC —→			←————————— 1948 SIC —————————→							←————————— 1958 SIC —————————→										←— 1968 SIC —→		
MAJOR SUBJECTS REPORTED																								
Reporting units (No.)	x	x			x			x				x					x					x		Establishments and/or Enterprises and/or 'Returns'.
Output—Gross(c)	x	x	x		x	(x)	(x)	x	(x)	(x)	(x)	(x)					x					x		Broken down by type of work in 1946, 1948, 1951 and 1954.
Net	x	x	x		x	(x)	(x)	x	(x)	(x)	(x)	x					x					x		
Purchases and Payments for:																								
Materials and fuel	x	x	x		x	(x)	(x)	x	(x)	(x)	(x)	x					x					x		Broken down by commodity in 1948, 1951, 1954, 1963, 1968. Until 1954 'materials and fuel purchased and used' as distinct from 'purchased' (stock figures have been collected separately since 1955).
Goods for merchanting and canteen purchases																	x					x		
Transport(d)	x		x		x	(x)	(x)	x	(x)	(x)	(x)	x					x					x		Outwards transport only before 1951 then inwards and outwards transport, but the costs of transport carried out by 'own employees', or included with the cost of materials purchased, is excluded. Note, however, detailed analyses made in 1963 and 1968.(d)
Hire of plant and machinery	x		x		x	(x)	(x)	x	(x)	(x)	(x)	x					x					x		
Work done on contracts sub-let	x	x	x		x	(x)	(x)	x	(x)	(x)	(x)	x					x					x		
Employers' contributions		x	x		x			x				x					x					x		National Insurance and, in 1954 and 1963, private pension schemes. Breakdowns made in detail for 1963 and 1968.(e)
Certain services(e)									(x)	(x)	(x)	x	x	x	x	x	x	x	x	x	x	x	x	
Stocks						(x)	(x)	x	(x)	(x)	(x)	x					x					x	x	
Employment—Total incl. W.P.s	x	x	x		x	(x)	(x)	x	(x)	(x)	(x)	x					x					x	x	Broken down by age (under/over 18) and sex in 1946, 1948, 1951 and by sex only, in 1954 and 1958. Monthly analysis of employment given for 1946 and 1948. Separate figures of the numbers 'mainly employed on transport' were collected in 1963 and 1968—see [QRL 277] Part 156.
Operatives	x	x	x		x	(x)	(x)	x	(x)	(x)	(x)	x					x					x		
Other employees	x	x	x		x	(x)	(x)	x	(x)	(x)	(x)	x					x					x		
Wages & Salaries (Ops/Other)	x	x	x		x	(x)	(x)	x	(x)	(x)	(x)	x	x	x	x	x	x	x	x	x	x	x	x	
Capital Expenditure (By type)(f)								x				x					x					x		New building; plant and machinery; vehicles.
Output Carried In/Out(g)					x			x				x					x					x		
ANALYSES MADE																								An analysis of concentration for 1958 was given in [QRL 273] Part 133.
By Size of Firm	x	x			x			x				x					x					x		Size of 'establishment' or size of 'enterprise'.
By Trade of Firm								x				x					x					x		'Sub-divisions' of the industry—Trades 1–18 of those listed in Section 4.2.3.10. A distinction is also drawn between 'main' and 'sub'-contractors (see text regarding interpretation). Analysed by 'Industrial Areas'.
By Country or Region		x	x		x			x																
Degree of Specialization		x																						
PUBLICATION REFERENCE	[QRL 51] (h)	[QRL 157] Vol. 12 Trade A	[QRL 268] Vol. 12		[QRL 269] Vol. 12 Trade A	[QRL 270] Vol. 4		[QRL 271] Vol. 12 Ind.A and Summary Tables	[QRL 272] Vol. 4			[QRL 273] Part 128					[QRL 274]					[QRL 275] Part 126	[QRL 276]	[QRL 277] Parts 151, 156, 158	[QRL 353]
Years for which comparative figures included	1935	1935 and 1946	1935 and 1948		1948			1951	1951 and 1954			1954					1958					1958	1963	1963	—
SEPARATE DATA FOR SMALL FIRMS	x	x			x	(x)	(x)	x				x					x					x		

Column 1950: Construction ('Building and contracting') not covered

(a) Said to cover 'work done in the UK by private firms domiciled in Great Britain'.
(b) The size exemption limit below which firms were not required to make returns in full detail. In the years where 'All' appears estimates are given for all firms, no distinction by size being made.
(c) The term 'gross output' is used here as a convenient short-hand expression for production data; it is used more strictly in the census to refer to sales (work done in construction) adjusted for stock changes. Separate data are also given for 'Value of work done and goods produced' in 1954, 1958, 1963, 1968 ('gross output' is not given in 1958) and 'Sales of merchanted goods and canteen takings' in 1958, 1963 and 1968.
(d) Payments for transport were broken down in considerable detail in 1963 and 1968 under the following heads: wages and salaries; derv fuel and motor spirit; tyres and other spare parts; payments to other organizations for transport; by road (1968), by rail and other means (1968); cost of operating road goods vehicles: insurance, vehicle licences, depreciation, payments to other organizations for repairs and maintenance—full details were published in [QRL 277] Part 156.
(e) Separate data for: repairs and maintenance to: buildings, road goods vehicles, plant, machinery and other capital equipment; hire of plant and machinery; insurance, licensing and depreciation of road goods vehicles; rates, postage, telephone, etc.; advertising; market research; professional services; royalties; commercial insurance premiums; receipts from royalties—full details were published in [QRL 277] Part 156.
(f) Data also collected for acquisitions and disposals of: plant and machinery (1951–68); vehicles (1951–68); land and existing buildings (1963 and 1968).
(g) Construction work done by establishments classified to other industries and 'Sales of other than principal products by larger firms in the industry'.
(h) Reports [QRL 53], [QRL 55] and [QRL 52] also give details of construction and installation work carried out by firms in the Electrical, Mechanical and Constructional Engineering Trades respectively.
(i) Combined figures only available: private firms combined with certain direct labour organizations.
(j) Full details only available for firms employing twenty-five or more persons.

Table 5.2
Guide to the Coverage of Public Authorities' Direct Labour in Censuses of Production 1946 to Date
(The entries refer to the report in which data were included)

Year	PUBLIC AUTHORITY									
	Government Departments	Local Authorities	Hospital Authorities (Building and Civil Engineering)	Railways (Civil Eng.)	Tramway Trolley-bus and Omnibus Undertakings (Civil Eng.)	Canal, Dock and Harbour Undertakings (Civil Eng.)	Gas Supply Industry	Electricity Supply Industry	Water Undertakings	Other*
1946	[QRL 51]	[QRL 54]	—	—	—	—	—	—	—	—
1948	[QRL 157] Vol. 12 Trade A	[QRL 157] Vol. 12 Trade B	—	[QRL 157] Vol. 12 Trade C	[QRL 157] Vol. 12 Trade D	[QRL 157] Vol. 12 Trade E	[QRL 157] Vol. 12 Trade F	[QRL 157] Vol. 12 Trade G	[QRL 157] Vol. 12 Trade H	—
1949	[QRL 268] Vol. 12	[QRL 268] Vol. 12	—	[QRL 268] Vol. 12	[QRL 268] Vol. 12	[QRL 268] Vol. 12	—	—	—	—
1951	[QRL 269] Vol. 12 Trade A	[QRL 269] Vol. 12 Trade B	[QRL 269] Vol. 12 Trade A, App. A	[QRL 269] Vol. 12 Trade C	[QRL 269] Vol. 12 Trade D	[QRL 269] Vol. 12 Trade E	[QRL 269] Vol. 12 Trade F	[QRL 269] Vol. 12 Trade G	[QRL 269] Vol. 12 Trade H	—
1952	†	} [QRL 270] Vol. 4	†	} [QRL 270] Vol. 4	†	†	—	—	—	—
1953	†		†		†	†	—	—	—	—
1954	[QRL 271] Vol. 12 Ind. A	[QRL 271] Vol. 12 Ind. B	[QRL 271] Vol. 12 Ind. A, Part B	[QRL 271] Vol. 12 Ind. C	[QRL 271] Vol. 12 Ind. D	[QRL 271] Vol. 12 Ind. E	[QRL 271] Vol. 12 Ind. F	[QRL 271] Vol. 12 Ind. G	[QRL 271] Vol. 12 Ind. H	—
1955	†	} [QRL 272] Vol. 4	†	—	—	—	—	—	—	—
1956	†		†	—	—	—	—	—	—	—
1957	†		†	—	—	—	—	—	—	—
1958	[QRL 273] Part 128	[QRL 273] Part 128	—	—	—	—	[QRL 273] Part 129	[QRL 273] Part 130	[QRL 273] Part 131	[QRL 273] Part 128
1963	[QRL 275] Part 126	[QRL 275] Part 126	—	—	—	—	[QRL 275] Part 127	[QRL 275] Part 128	[QRL 275] Part 129	[QRL 275] Part 126
1968	[QRL 277] Part 151	[QRL 277] Part 151	—	—	—	—	[QRL 277] Part 152	[QRL 277] Part 153	[QRL 277] Part 154	[QRL 277] Part 151
1970–3	—	—	—	—	—	—	—	[QRL 77]	—	—
1974 to date	Results published annually in *Business Monitor PA 500* [QRL 76]. Public undertakings are grouped together as a single category. In the 1974 report (the only one published at the time of writing) coverage is said to extend to local authorities, public authorities and government departments but to exclude construction work carried out by the employees of nationalized industries and transport and water undertakings except for the building and civil engineering work of the British Steel Corporation and the housing departments of the National Coal Board.									

* Principally the National Coal Board (housing departments and opencast coal mining activities—but see the relevant reports regarding differences in treatment of the latter) and, in 1968, the British Steel Corporation. Coverage of other authorities in the public sector is not specified.
† Results combined with those for private firms—see Table 5.1.

found in the introductory notes to the appropriate reports (see Table 5.1). Information about sampling errors has been published on only two occasions: for 1952–3 in [QRL 270] Vol. 4, p. 79 and for 1955–7 in [QRL 272] Vol. 4, Appendix.

Private firms and direct labour. As in the case of the MOW–DOE enquiries (Chapters 3 and 4), it is important to make a distinction between private firms of contractors and direct labour organizations and to be clear about the precise coverage of the latter. Unfortunately the coverage of the latter has varied over time and for some years (1952, 1953, 1955–7 incl.) the results for these two parts of the industry were not published separately.

Private firms. Details of the subjects covered, and analyses made, in each of the 'old style' censuses for private contractors from 1946 to 1969, together with publication references, are set out in Table 5.1. The table refers to the data available for firms above a certain size (as shown) but for many years data are also available for smaller firms (in less detail) and where this is the case this is also indicated in the table. The data generally relate to the UK but in the case of small firms coverage is sometimes confined to Great Britain alone. Statistics for Northern Ireland are sometimes shown separately in the UK reports but full details are published in separate reports for the province (details are given in Chapter 9).

As indicated above, after 1969 construction was not included in the new system of annual censuses of production conducted by the BSO until 1974. The results, published in *Bus. Mon. PA500* [QRL 76], provide information broken down by trade of firm ('sub-divisions of the industry') for Great Britain, together with total data for Northern Ireland, on the following subjects:

Number of undertakings

Building and civil engineering work carried out:
   As a main or direct contractor
   As a sub-contractor

Receipts for plant hire

Other work done and sales of goods produced

Goods merchanted or factored
   Total work done and goods sold

Change in year in goods on hand for sale
   Gross output

Purchases of materials for use in construction

Cost of fuel and electricity*

Purchases of goods for merchanting or factoring

Other purchases*

Change in year in stocks of materials, stores and fuel

Cost of industrial services received
   Net output

---

* For undertakings in the UK employing twenty or more persons purchases of fuel and electricity are broken down by type (value and quantity) and other purchases are broken down into: replacement parts and tools (by type), stationery and 'other'.

Total employment
  Net output per head
Operatives:
  Average number employed
  Wages and salaries
Other employees:
  Average number employed
  Wages and salaries
Capital expenditure
  New building work
  Acquisitions and disposals of: land and existing buildings; motor cars; other vehicles; plant and machinery
  Buildings constructed and capital goods produced by undertakings' own staff for their own use.
Stocks at the beginning and at the end of the year of:
  Materials, stores and fuel
  Goods on hand for sale

In addition, for undertakings in the UK employing 100 or more persons, separate analyses of the payments made for 'industrial' and 'non-industrial' services are made as follows:

Amounts payable to other organizations:

  Payments for work sub-contracted out

  Payments for repairs and maintenance
    to own buildings
    to road goods vehicles
    to plant, machinery and other capital goods

  Other industrial services
    Total cost of industrial services

  Rent, hire of plant, machinery and vehicles

  Commercial insurance premiums

  Bank charges

  Postage, telephones, telex, etc.

  Road transport

  Rail, etc. transport

  Other non-industrial services
    Total cost of non-industrial services

Separate analyses are provided for undertakings in the UK employing twenty or more persons classified to construction under the NACE classification (see Appendix XIII for details). These include, in respect of the undertakings employing 100 or more persons, additional statistics on the following subjects: employers' insurance and welfare contributions; licensing of motor vehicles; rates, excluding water rates.

Directory of businesses. Until 1968 particulars of the firms on the register remained confidential. In 1968 the names and addresses of those enterprises participating in the census, *which agreed to their disclosure*, were published in [QRL 277] Part 159.

Direct labour. Table 5.2 shows the types of direct labour undertaking which have been covered in the post-war censuses and gives publication references. Each of these reports generally includes background notes specific to the particular industry, or sub-division of industry, which are important for interpretation purposes. Apart from the exception noted below, the enquiries have generally conformed to the same pattern as for private firms with regard to the coverage of larger establishments, the subjects about which information was sought and the publication of results and analyses. Unlike private firms, however, coverage in some censuses and for some types of undertaking only extends to Great Britain. Further, results for small undertakings are not always published separately for each type. The major exception to the above regarding subjects covered concerns Gas, Electricity and Water undertakings for which information has been sought only about the value of work done by their direct labour forces.

Unpublished data and data retention practices. Special analyses of census data not included in the published reports are provided on request subject to the rules regarding disclosure and the payment of a fee to cover the costs involved. For details of the periods of time for which the results of various censuses are to be retained see [B 80].

5.3.3. Interpretation

The purpose of this section is to consider some of the most important factors relating to the interpretation of the census of production (henceforth referred to as COP) results and their comparison with the corresponding statistics of output and employment collected by the DOE and its predecessor departments (referred to as 'MOW–DOE').

5.3.3.1. *Industrial definitions and the registers of firms.* The first matter of importance, of course, is the scope of the enquiries in terms of industrial definitions and the adequacy of the registers on which the enquiries are based. Until 1955 the industrial definitions used in the two sets of enquiries differed. Whereas the COP has been based on the SIC (see Section 4.1.2 for discussion of the classification of construction in the SIC) from 1948 onwards, the SIC was not used by the MOW until 1955 (see Section 4.1.1) and both departments maintained separate registers.

In 1955 a joint register was drawn up (see Section 4.1.3) and was subsequently maintained by the MOW and successor departments. For reasons set out earlier, however (Section 4.1.3), this register grew increasingly deficient. It is difficult to quantify the extent of this deficiency but reference may usefully be made to the estimates of unrecorded output and employment made retrospectively by the DOE in 1973 [B 217]. Note also the addition of 30,000, hitherto unregistered, firms to the DOE register in 1973 (reduced to 25,000 in the census of that year—see Section 4.1.3). Compare also the number of 'persons' registered for VAT (see Section 7.6.4).

It is also worth noting perhaps that the major deficiency in the register is of small firms whereas the most detailed information in the COP is only collected from larger firms. In a sense, therefore, the influence of the deficiency is limited; certainly this is true if one is interested in the composition of inputs rather than levels of output and employment. On the other hand it is also important to note that part of the problem of ensuring comprehensive coverage of the industry has arisen because of the growth of the practice of labour-only sub-contracting to self-employed (or at least nominally self-employed) workers. Insofar as firms of all sizes employ labour-only sub-contractors this deficiency in coverage affects the results for all firms. In particular, the deficiency affects the labour returns, and hence any comparisons (such as productivity comparisons) which involve the use of the labour figures, for the labour returns relate only to employees whilst output figures relate to *all* work done (including sub-contracted work). Current enquiries by the DOE are attempting to quantify the relative importance of labour-only sub-contracting—see Section 4.4.5; see too [B 307] for earlier estimates and general discussions of the practice.

Whether the register used for the COP before 1955 was comprehensive is difficult to say, for little information has been made available as to how the register was maintained. During the war the census office was disbanded and in the first census taken after the war, in 1946, the names of larger firms at least (those employing fifty or more persons) were taken from the MOW register. But the practices adopted with regard to other firms and at later dates is not specified in published reports.

Coverage of direct labour. The difficulties in maintaining a comprehensive register, referred to above, concern private firms rather than direct labour organizations. Interpretation of the direct labour figures, however, does need to take account of the scope of the enquiries in this sector, changes over time, differences in the coverage of this sector by the DOE (MOW) and differences in practice between the two departments. The coverage of direct labour organizations in the COP is indicated in Table 5.2. As may be seen the tendency over time has been for the extent of the coverage of this sector in the COP to diminish. In contrast, the DOE (MOW) in their enquiries have continued to collect data from a wider range of authorities in this sector, although separate details for each type of undertaking (except local authorities) are not normally published (see Sections 3.6 and 4.3). A notable difference in coverage is that the direct labour of hospital authorities, covered in the COP in 1951 and 1954, appear not to have been included in any MOW–DOE enquiry except the September 1955 (unpublished) census. Certain differences in classification practices also need to be noted. Currently the direct labour of the BSC is classified as part of the public sector in the COP, but with contractors by the DOE, and the direct labour of New Town Corporations are classed with local authorities by the DOE but with 'other' public authorities in the COP. Unfortunately, it is not possible to give an account of all the points of difference that there may be between the two sets of data because details of the coverage of the MOW–DOE data at different points of time are not available (for further details see Sections 3.6 and 4.3).

5.3.3.2. *Other aspects of coverage and definitions.* As far as the COP is concerned it is not necessary to consider at all closely here the definitions of the terms used since these are defined together with relevant background information in the *Introductory Notes* to each census and/or in the introductory notes to each specific industry report (the appropriate references are listed at [QRL 50] to [QRL 55] inclusive, [QRL 157], [QRL

116], [QRL 268] to [QRL 277] inclusive and [QRL 353]. Specimens of all the census forms used since 1930 are available for inspection in the Library of the BSO[3] and recent introductory reports also include a specimen questionnaire (though not for construction specifically). Certain aspects of the statistics, however, deserve attention, particularly those relating to output and employment.

Output. Because a substantial volume of construction work is carried out by one contractor for another under sub-contract, the danger of duplication in output returns is acute. A general discussion of output measurement problems for construction is contained in Section 2.3 above. In the COP, firms are required to distinguish work which they carry out as main contractors or sub-contractors respectively but, unlike the MOW–DOE enquiries, the COP requires a contractor working under 'main' or 'direct' contract to return the total value of work done on such contracts inclusive of any work sub-contracted. Consequently, there is duplication in the gross output figures for the industry to the extent that such sub-contract work is carried out for other contractors making returns in this industry. Separate information is obtained about the payments made by contractors for contracts sub-let including payments for work done on materials supplied (of particular relevance to work done under labour-only sub-contract in construction), but this may overstate the degree of duplication in the construction returns inasmuch as some payments go to firms which are not classified to construction under the SIC, and some to persons not otherwise covered in the census returns at all—particularly important here being the payments made to men working as 'self-employed' under labour-only sub-contract arrangements.[4] In contrast, the DOE and its predecessor departments have always attempted to avoid the duplication problem by adopting the practice in their enquiries of asking contractors to exclude the value of work sub-contracted from their returns altogether—each contractor being responsible for returning the value of work which he himself has carried out. But in this case, of course, work which is sub-let to firms which are not classified to the construction industry (or to construction firms or labour-only gangs not on the register) is missed entirely.[5] On this score the COP has (or at least had until the recent development of DOE practice regarding sub-contract work) an advantage since such work is covered in the return from the main contractor and, in detailed census years, information was also obtained about the value of construction work done by firms classified to other industries (sometimes referred to as 'carry in' or 'carry out' items as the case may be). Likewise information is also sought about the work done by construction firms which represents the principal products of other industries ('carry-out' items from construction). The more recent censuses also obtained a return of 'sales of merchanted goods and canteen takings' separately—see Table 5.1. It is therefore possible to obtain a measure of the value of work done on *construction* as such, subject always, of course, to any deficiencies in the register, deficiencies in the returns themselves and the element of duplication, discussed above, for which separate allowance cannot be made. In the MOW–DOE enquiries to date no information has ever been obtained about work other

---

[3] In Newport, Gwent. Copies of current forms are also normally available on request from the BSO. For these reasons no specimen census of production forms have been included in this Review.

[4] Separate information about payments to labour-only sub-contractors, however, is now requested in the new system of COP enquiries under the BSO initiated, for construction, in 1974 [QRL 76].

[5] It may be noted, however, that since 1974 DOE have required sub-contract work and payments to be separately returned in order to cover work missed through an incomplete register—see Sections 4.2.3.8 and 4.4.5.

than construction but it is planned to include a question about such work in the October 1977 census (see Section 4.2).

As regards the value of work done under sub-contract it may also be noted that the results in the last four detailed censuses of production for construction under the 'old system' of enquiries (1954, 1958, 1963, 1968) were sub-divided between 'main contractors' and 'sub-contractors'. But since the classification to these categories was made according to the one which represented a contractor's major activity, measured in terms of the proportionate value of each category, it provides no guide to the value of sub-contract work as such done within the industry. Likewise the first BSO census for construction relating to 1974 has been analysed in this way [QRL 76] but unlike earlier censuses, however, the actual values of work carried out as a main contractor and as a sub-contractor are also given.

Net output. Care is required in the use of the figures of 'net output' presented in the COP reports. They do not represent the net contribution of the construction industry to national output—'value added' (and therefore differ from the estimates made in the *Blue Book* [QRL 201]—for they remain gross of certain inputs—e.g. payments for certain services provided by other industries such as insurance, advertising, etc. about which information has not normally been collected (see Table 5.1).[6] The method of calculation is made plain in every census report, but the limitations of the measure need to be recognized, especially in the interpretation of ratios in which it is used, such as 'net output per person' which are also presented in the census reports. The estimates published in the *Blue Book* [QRL 201] are made by a different method (aggregating factor incomes)—see Section 7.1. Further discussion of the pitfalls in the use of net output statistics will be found in [B 148].

Employment. A comparison of the employment data from the 1974 census of production (the latest available at the time of writing) with that from other sources is made in Table 6.1 included as part of Section 6.2.4.1.

Operatives. The returns of operatives employed suffer particularly from the problem, discussed earlier, of covering that part of the labour force working as 'self-employed' operatives under labour-only sub-contract—a practice which grew in importance considerably between the early 1960s and the early 1970s. None of this labour is covered in either set of enquiries (COP or MOW–DOE) unless they are recorded as contractors on the register and submit returns but there is no ready means, of course, of ensuring their registration. The user of the COP results also needs to face the problem that whereas the value of output of a non-construction nature is defined (at least in the detailed census years) the employment of labour on such work is not separately specified. The validity of the labour returns as a measure of *construction* labour are therefore subject to two opposing forces, one tending to understate construction labour as such, the other tending to overstate. The MOW–DOE enquiries do require a separate return of labour not employed on construction work (see Section 4.2.3.9 and Appendix IV—specimen questionnaire AR8 *et al.*) but the data are not published.

Other employees. These are referred to as 'administrative, technical and clerical' employees in the COP but as 'administrative, *professional*, technical and clerical' by the DOE. Professional staff are meant to be covered in the COP and this seems reasonably

---

[6] The BSO census reports, however, [QRL 76] do now include separate figures for 'value added'.

clear in the census forms although the word 'professional' as such is not used (see Section 4.2.3.7 regarding DOE data). Comparison of these two sets of data also needs to take account, however, of differences in the treatment of Working Proprietors—see below.

Working Proprietors. The COP returns have always used the term 'Working Proprietor' but until 1971 the MOW–DOE collected data for 'Working Principals'—a category which is narrower in scope. Prior to 1971 some persons now classified as Working Proprietors would have been classified as APTC staff in the MOW–DOE enquiries (see Section 4.2.3.6).

5.3.3.3. *Other differences between the COP and the MOW–DOE enquiries.* Two other factors may help to explain differences between the COP and the MOW–DOE statistics, both of which relate to timing. One is that the COP data cover a period of twelve months whereas the MOW–DOE censuses currently cover only one quarter—output and employment data for the rest of each year are based on samples (at one time, however, censuses were taken more frequently—see Sections 3.5 and 4.2). Since 1952 part of the COP has been based on samples, of course, so that differences also reflect sampling errors in each case (in this respect, it may be noted, however, that the COP is grossed up on the basis of the MOW–DOE data). The other factor is that firms responding in the COP enquiries are allowed to provide returns for a 'business year' rather than a calendar year (analyses of the proportion of returns covering different periods of time are given in the census reports); the MOW–DOE returns, on the other hand, are obtained for the same periods of time or, in the case of labour, points of time.

5.3.4. *Input–Output Tables*

A major use of the census of production data is the compilation of input–output analyses showing the inter-relationship among industries throughout the whole economy.

UK Tables. Tables for the UK, showing construction as a separate sector, are available as follows:

Year	Publication	Remarks
1935	[QRL 1]	Unofficial analysis
1948	[QRL 25] [QRL 201] 1952 edn.	[QRL 25] contains an unofficial analysis prepared with the collaboration of the Board of Trade. [QRL 201] contains a summary analysis only.
1950	[QRL 201] 1953 edn.	Summary table. See [B 275] pp. 52–55 for background details.
1954	[QRL 176]	First official detailed analysis. An analysis consistent with the 1963 tables (1958 SIC basis) is provided in [QRL 29].
1960	[QRL 311]	Up-dated analysis based on 1954.
1963	[QRL 177]	
1968	[QRL 178]	See also [B 64] which presents aggregates in broad industry and commodity groups.

From 1970 up-dated tables based on the analysis for 1968 have been published in the *Business Monitor PA 1004* series [QRL 79]; summary tables are published in *Economic Trends* [QRL 147] April edition.

Accounts of the methods of devising the tables are given in the sources referred to. As far as construction is concerned it needs to be appreciated that its inputs of materials, etc. are drawn from a wide variety of other industries and that the amount of detailed information collected in the censuses of production about these inputs is limited—as much as 60–70 per cent of the value of materials purchased by the construction industry remains unclassified—[QRL 177] p. 16 and [QRL 178] p. 6 refer. As a consequence, the incorporation of construction into the input–output framework does require a good deal of estimation. An 'up-dated' table, it may be noted, means that the analysis is not based on detailed information for the year in question but is projected on the basis of an earlier analysis—an account of the method used for the official up-dated series, which are now being prepared annually, is given in *ET* [QRL 147] April 1975. A general account of recent developments in this field will be found in [B 14].

The analyses contained in the official tables referred to above are inevitably confined to broad industrial and commodity groupings as a consequence of the nature of the statistical sources on which they are based. Some research by the Building Research Station into resource use has provided estimates of materials inputs for building work at a lower level of aggregation which may be of interest, although it is not specifically couched in an input–output framework. Some results showing inputs required in different types of building have been published in [B 32] and [QRL 18].

Input–output tables for Scotland and Northern Ireland. Work on the preparation of input–output tables for the constituent countries of the UK is confronted by severe statistical difficulties. Unofficial tables have recently been compiled for Scotland, however, and are due to be published in 1977 [QRL 175]. Details for Northern Ireland are given in Section 9.2.2.2.

5.3.5. *Official Uses of the COP Data for Construction—Summary*

Many of the uses to which the COP data are put officially are considered elsewhere in this Review and a summary guide may be found useful. The principal uses and cross-references are as follows:

(a) Weights for official index numbers—e.g. the index of industrial production (the construction constituent is considered in Section 5.2) and indices of material prices (construction materials are considered in Section 11.1).
(b) National income and expenditure accounts—Section 7.1.
(c) Input–Output statistics—Section 5.3.4.

5.4. Statistics of Expenditure on Construction Work

5.4.1. *Introduction*

Expenditure on new buildings and other construction work is, of course, a major constituent of capital expenditure in both the private and public sectors of the economy.

Capital expenditure data, therefore, provide an important additional source of information about construction output as well as information about investment in buildings and works as such. The most comprehensive statistics are those incorporated in the official national accounts for the UK [QRL 201] as part of 'gross domestic fixed capital formation' and consequently this section is mainly devoted to a consideration of this series. However, attention is also devoted to the primary sources on which the capital formation series are based, for these provide useful supplementary sources of information, and to sources of 'current' (as distinct from 'capital') expenditure statistics.

Official national accounts for the UK were drawn up for the first time in 1941, but separate estimates for expenditure on 'buildings and works' were not included until 1951 [QRL 203], when annual series from 1946 were presented. Very considerable work has also been done unofficially to compile retrospective series; these are now available going back to the eighteenth century (considered in Section 5.4.4). Apart from their importance as an integral part of the national accounts statistics, the capital formation data are of particular importance from two points of view. First they provide a largely independent source of information about the volume of construction activity in the country, which may be contrasted with the production data obtained in the censuses of production (Section 5.3) and in the MOW–DOE enquiries (Chapters 3 and 4). Secondly, the capital formation data provide analyses by industry and sector not available from other sources. The unofficial historical series are especially valuable inasmuch as they provide the only summary evidence available about construction work for most of the period they span.

Interpretation of the official series demands special attention, particularly in view of the differences that exist between them and the series derived from the output enquiries. Therefore, after defining the series available, an extended discussion is devoted to their interpretation in relation to the output series (Section 5.4.3). The unofficial series are noted, briefly, in Section 5.4.4. The primary sources of capital expenditure data are considered in Section 5.4.5 and, finally, sources of current expenditure data are noted in Section 5.4.6.

5.4.2. *Capital Formation Statistics—Official Series, 1938 and 1946 to Date*

5.4.2.1. *The series available.* There are two basic series, one for 'gross' and one for 'net' capital formation (these terms are defined below) and each of these in turn differentiates between dwellings and 'other buildings and works' (as well as other assets). Both series are produced at current and constant prices. The gross series are available annually for the whole of the period from 1946 (except that no breakdown between dwellings and other work was made for 1946) together with a retrospective estimate for 1938, and quarterly from 1954, at both current and constant prices. The net series are available for 1938 and annually from 1948. For more recent years analyses have been made of the gross series by sector (public/private and institutional sector, i.e. companies, public corporations, etc.), and by industry (or industry group). The net series differentiate dwellings only by sector.

The primary source of publication of the annual series is *National Income and Expenditure* [QRL 201] (often referred to as the 'Blue Book') and for the quarterly series *Economic Trends* (*ET*) [QRL 147] (introduced in issue No. 39, January 1957).

Convenient secondary sources (although these do not all reproduce the full detail) are the *MDS* [QRL 195] and the *ET Ann. Supp.* [QRL 148] (introduced recently with the intention of providing long runs). Annual series only are also included in the *AAS* [QRL 31] and (periodically) in *HCS* [QRL 168].

Details of the sources and methods used in the compilation of the series are set out in an official guide first published in 1956 [B 275] and revised in 1968 [B 100]. Changes that have taken place since the 1968 edition are described in notes included in the annual *Blue Book* [QRL 201]. Thus detailed questions concerning the derivation of the series may generally be settled by reference to these sources. We confine our attention here to more general matters of interpretation.

5.4.2.2. *The definition and scope of the capital formation (expenditure) series*. The term 'capital formation' is defined as investment in physical productive assets that yield a continuous service beyond the period of account in which they are purchased. The term 'gross' signifies that no deduction is made for wear and tear, obsolescence and accidental damage (as regards 'net' statistics see below). The term 'domestic' denotes that the statistics are confined to those assets located in the UK.

Within the bounds defined by these definitions there are two important points of principle to note at the outset regarding the scope and nature of the series. The first is that investment in buildings and works is measured at the purchasing end of the transaction in terms of the cost to the purchaser—largely independently from the output statistics which are measured from the opposite, 'supply', side of the transaction on the basis of returns provided by producers (contractors), of the value of work done. The capital formation series thereby form part of an integrated set of accounts dividing expenditure between consumption and investment. Henceforth, for convenience, we refer to the capital formation statistics as the 'expenditure series' to distinguish them from output data.

The second point of principle concerns the question of how far all expenditure on construction work ought to be included in the series, for it can be argued that not all construction work represents an addition to the nation's stock of productive assets. In particular, work of repairs and maintenance may be regarded as merely maintaining the existing stock of buildings and works intact and thus does not represent a net addition to the stock. In practice, however, maintenance work often involves an element of improvement which *can* be regarded as enhancing the stock. To accept the distinction between ordinary maintenance and improvement in practice, however, involves the difficulty of distinguishing one from the other and renders the definition of capital expenditure somewhat imprecise. Despite this problem the convention followed *in principle* in the UK accounts is to include the expenditure on improvements (including extensions and structural alterations, etc.), as well as all new building, but to exclude all expenditure on routine repairs and maintenance. For an extended discussion of this question see [B 275] pp. 281–3.

In practice the part of repairs and maintenance expenditure included in the industrial and commercial field is determined by the accounting conventions adopted by businesses in allocating expenditure between capital and current accounts (we discuss this question further below). For privately-owned dwellings all such expenditure is excluded, except for that which is grant-aided, because of the difficulty of obtaining adequate information. Before leaving this question it should be noted, however, that in the series published up to 1952 repairs and maintenance expenditure was included in the capital formation series—but shown as a separate item. Currently, an estimate of total repairs and maintenance (provided by the DOE—and therefore based on output returns, rather than expenditure, and relating to Great Britain alone) is shown as a footnote to the tables in [QRL 201].

A further important aspect of the scope of the expenditure series is that it extends not only to the costs of the buildings and works themselves but also to expenditure incurred in the course of their acquisition, e.g. the professional fees of architects, surveyors, consulting engineers, solicitors, etc. and items such as the cost of a clerk of works on large projects, etc. They also include the capitalized value of interest charges incurred during long periods of construction, but expenditure incurred in arranging the supply of finance, e.g. the cost of share issues, are regarded as part of current expenditure and are not included. Likewise, the costs of land, which are merely a transfer payment, are not included, but the costs incurred in the transfer of the land *are* included.

Sources of information. Details of the sources used in compiling the expenditure estimates are given in [B 275] and [B 100]. In brief, these are returns of capital expenditure from businesses in the private sector and from the various authorities in the public sector. This leaves out of account private housing for which there is no adequate source of expenditure data. Until 1973 the main source here was the DOE output statistics. Thus the private housing series is an exception to the general rule that the capital formation statistics represent expenditure. From 1973 an important change was made in the calculation of the series—see [QRL 201] 1964–74 edition, p. 123 for details. It is also worth noting that in the early years of the capital formation series, in general more reliance was placed on 'supply side' data because of the lack of expenditure data at that time (see [B 275] for details). Some of the primary sources of capital expenditure data used in the compilation of the capital formation series are published separately. These provide supplementary statistics which are useful in a number of respects and we devote separate attention to them in Section 5.4.5 below.

5.4.2.3. *Analyses by sector and industry.* Details of the methods used for making the classification by sector and industry may be found in [B 275] and [B 100]. An essential point to note about the classification is that it is based upon sector or industry of ownership, rather than of use. Thus expenditure on, for example, office building by property developers will be classified to the services sector while the user of the offices may, of course, be found in any industry or sector.

Capital formation in the construction industry. It is important to note that the statistics of capital formation in the construction industry itself do not cover the building and civil engineering establishments of central government, local authorities and public utilities (see [B 100] p. 374).

5.4.2.4. *Reliability gradings.* The official guides [B 275] and [B 100], published in 1956 and 1968 respectively, include reliability gradings for the estimates for dwellings (public/private) and roads (1968 edition only) but not for other buildings and works. It should be noted, however, that figures for the most recent year are always subject to revision as more information becomes available and are therefore open to a wider margin of error than is indicated by the reliability grading. The quarterly series are subject to greater error than the annual series. The constant price series are especially open to error on account of the difficulties of devising satisfactory price indices, although it is possible, of course, that errors in the price index may work to offset errors in the original current price series.

5.4.2.5. *Constant price series.* The measurement of price changes for construction is fraught with difficulties (considered fully in Section 8.1), so that the constant price series need to be regarded with great circumspection. The price deflator used is the DOE's 'CNC' index (considered in detail in Section 8.1.2.1). Until 1969 two sub-indices were used—one for dwellings and one for all other buildings and works; in 1969 the preparation of these sub-indices was discontinued but then from 1971 a separate deflator for private housing was reintroduced (Section 4.4.5.2 refers). It is therefore assumed implicitly that price changes for all types of non-housing work (and for part of the period, all work) move together by the same amount. The inherent difficulties in measuring price changes satisfactorily together with this bold assumption naturally introduce further scope for error.[7]

5.4.2.6. *Net capital formation.* The series for net capital formation—i.e. gross domestic fixed capital formation less capital consumption—were introduced in the *Blue Book* [QRL 201] in 1956 (estimates for 1938 and annual series from 1948). Capital consumption represents depreciation by wear and tear, obsolescence and uninsured losses (insured losses by fire or accident are treated as negative capital formation and deducted before arriving at gross fixed capital formation). The measurement of capital consumption is confronted by enormous difficulties and these estimates therefore are subject to even wider margins of error than the gross series (see Section 12.1 and [B 100]).

5.4.3. *Comparison of Official Expenditure and Output Statistics*[8]

The difference between the gross capital formation series and the construction output series is substantial. The capital formation series is consistently higher than the output series and, over the last decade at least, the difference has been widening in almost every year. A number of reasons can be put forward that help to explain the difference. But it is not possible to account for it very readily in quantitative terms nor to explain the systematic tendency for the difference to increase, although there are some special factors in the most recent years (we return to this point below).

One point to note at the outset is that the capital formation and census of production data relate to the UK but the MOW/DOE data relate to Great Britain. Apart from this difference in geographical coverage, the reasons for the difference between the expen-

---

[7] New price deflators were introduced by the DOE in March 1978 after the preparation of this text—see the Addenda at the front of this volume.

[8] In writing this section the author has been allowed to draw upon an unpublished report prepared for the former Ministry of Public Building and Works by Lady Eleanor Lea in April 1970 [B 92].

diture and output data can be classified as partly conceptual differences and partly differences relating to the nature and coverage of the original sources. We adopt this distinction here for purposes of exposition because of its convenience; it should be appreciated that the conceptual and other differences do not fall neatly into self-contained compartments but are in fact inter-related. All or most of the explanations that can be offered for the difference between the two series ultimately stem from the conceptual difference between expenditure by the purchaser and output of the supplier when viewed from the standpoint of one particular sector of economic activity, as in the case of construction. At the level of the whole economy, of course, the problem of reconciling expenditure and output over all economic activities does not give rise to the same difficulties.

5.4.3.1. *Conceptual differences between construction expenditure and output.* As a consequence of the definition of the capital formation data as an expenditure series, certain categories of expenditure are included that do not form part of the output series. One of these categories is the expenditure on professional fees, transfer payments and capitalized interest charges, etc. incurred in connection with the acquisition of the assets. Separate data are not generally available about the value of fees; but estimates for the year 1958 will be found in [B 45] (regarded in [B 92] as being too low) and for 1963 in [QRL 177] p. 23. The transfer costs of land and existing buildings are shown as a separate single item in the *Blue Book* [QRL 201].[9]

Another category of expenditure not covered in the output return relates to work carried out by agencies which are not classified to construction under the SIC (the scope of the SIC is considered in Section 4.1.2). Firms in a wide range of industries carry out construction work for clients. Information about this is obtained periodically in the 'detailed' censuses of production and the results shown as a 'carry in' item to construction (see Table 5.1). This work will generally not be covered at all in the MOW-DOE enquiries; it may not be missed entirely for if the work is carried out by an establishment organized as a separate contracting unit then it is possible for this establishment to be included on the MOW-DOE register. This is simply a reflection of the distinction, discussed in Chapter 2, between the construction 'industry' and construction 'activity', the expenditure series naturally tending to be more comprehensive with regard to 'activity'. Further, certain categories of work of a construction nature are expressly excluded from the SIC, definition for the industry (e.g. shopfitting) but again may be covered in the expenditure series. Similarly, the work of some direct labour organizations in the public sector, as well as the direct labour of non-construction firms, is not covered in the construction output series but will be covered in the expenditure series insofar as it is of a capital nature.

Then there is the contrary case to that just discussed, where work is recorded as construction output but is not classified as capital formation. The major items here are buildings and works for military purposes which are conventionally treated as current expenditure (there are certain exceptions—see [B 100] pp. 362–3), work by contractors on open-cast coal production, and other work which may be carried out by contractors but which is not construction—e.g. the painting of plant by building firms, the erection

---

[9] It may be noted that the size of this item was very considerably underestimated prior to 1972 when it was retrospectively revised—see [QRL 201] 1972 edition, p. 110.

of scaffolding for plant erection, etc. Statistics of 'current' expenditure by public authorities on construction for military and other purposes are not available on a regular basis. Details of the statistics that are available are given in Section 5.4.6 below.

5.4.3.2. *Differences in the nature and coverage of the sources.* As we indicated earlier, differences in the nature and coverage of the sources may be inseparable from the conceptual distinction between expenditure and output. Some factors of this kind have been discussed above. Other factors, however, relate more specifically to the characteristics of the primary sources and it is these with which we are concerned here.

First there is the possibility that expenditure may not be coincident in timing with the execution of the work due to the fact that construction projects generally take a long time to complete. In practice the effect of this timing difference is alleviated to some extent, for it is the normal practice for the client to make regular progress payments (generally monthly) to the contractor for new construction work; thus the correspondence between 'output' and 'expenditure' series should thereby be improved. On the other hand, the contractor in the MOW–DOE enquiries is required to make an estimate of the work done in a period—an estimate which may or may not be based upon valuations made for the purpose of progress payments (the valuation practices adopted by contractors in making their output returns are discussed in Chapter 2). Further, from the clients' side, expenditure may be recorded as payments made rather than payments due; of particular relevance here is the fact that it is normal practice to retain part of the payment due until the end of the contract or until the end of the subsequent maintenance period. Moreover, payment for variations to the work ordered during the construction process may be delayed due to problems in negotiating an acceptable price or for other reasons. Thus correspondence between 'expenditure' and 'output' series may not be realized due to differences in timing and the element of estimation involved in output returns.

Secondly, the accounting conventions adopted by construction clients in the private and public sectors may not produce an allocation of expenditure to capital account in accordance with the principles of the national income and expenditure accounts. As we have indicated, new work and 'improvements' are regarded as capital expenditure. In practice, however, the allocation of expenditure between capital and current account may be determined to some extent by essentially arbitrary rules rather than by reference to the nature of the expenditure (e.g. expenditure below a certain limit may always be allocated to current account rather than capital). These practices will differ from one organization to another and also perhaps from time to time. Even if the attempt were made to classify expenditure in the appropriate manner, consistency would be unlikely because of the difficulty of distinguishing between improvements and ordinary maintenance.

In the private sector the allocation may also be influenced by tax considerations: there is an incentive to classify expenditure to current, rather than capital, account wherever possible since this reduces the profits base on which tax is levied. In the public sector, tax considerations may not apply, but the basic problem of allocation between capital and current accounts remains. There is, apparently, no legal definition of capital and although accounting recommendations and standards are made by the accountancy bodies, and accounts are subject to audit, there remains room for legitimate variability of practice with regard to those items of expenditure that are capitalized and those charged to revenue. For further discussion reference should be made to the statement of general principles for the standardization of accounts by the *Chartered Institute of Public Finance and Accountancy* [B 332] and a recent 'situation report' [B 267].

On the output side the contractor faces a similar kind of classification problem in the MOW–DOE enquiries. These call for a return by type of work distinguishing new work from repairs and maintenance; in the case of housing, 'improvements, conversions, extensions, alterations and redecorations' are meant to be classified as repairs and maintenance, but in the case of non-housing work, extensions and 'major alterations and improvements' are meant to be classified as new work (for further details see Appendix IV). Two points should be noted: first, the difference in treatment between housing and non-housing work, and second, the difficulty that contractors (and even more sub-contractors) must face in distinguishing 'improvements', etc. The scope for divergence between the expenditure and output series is thereby further increased. The likelihood is perhaps that contractors will tend to return work as repairs and maintenance rather than improvements. Purchasing agencies, however, may tend to vary in practice depending on whether they are in the private or public sector. In the private sector there is the tax incentive to classify the work as current rather than capital, in which case it would be in line with the contractors' assumed practice. In the public sector, practice may be more variable.

Thirdly, a similar kind of classification difference may arise between the expenditure and output data in that expenditure on demolition and site clearance may be classed as part of expenditure on land rather than buildings whereas the work done is included as part of construction output.

A fourth major source of difference may arise in making a distinction between 'building' and 'plant'. As far as the purchaser is concerned the boundary between the two is not necessarily well defined. For instance, some construction work, such as the foundations for heavy plant or chimneys forming an essential part of plant, etc., is so closely associated with the plant that the work may be suitably classified as either one or the other, even though it may be carried out by a construction contractor. Similarly, the purchaser may classify some work, such as the provision of fixtures and fittings in shops, as building expenditure because of its close association with the acquisition of the building although such work may or may not be carried out by building contractors (shop-fitters in particular are expressly excluded from the SIC order for construction). Again, it may be noted that tax considerations may bias the allocation of expenditure between plant or building inasmuch as tax allowances or investment grants may be available for one but not the other, or be available at a higher rate for one (in fact discrimination in this way has generally favoured plant over building). A useful account of the development of the investment incentives available in the UK for manufacturing industry over the period 1946–74 will be found in [B 102].

A fifth source of discrepancy arises from the fact that in some contracts materials are supplied to contractors by clients. In these cases the contractors' output returns will not cover the value of materials but the capital expenditure returns will (although, of course, it may be treated as plant in the latter). Cases where this is important are where it is essential that the materials should satisfy certain performance standards. Principal examples would be the provision of pipes for water supply purposes, gas and oil pipelines and electrical cables.

Yet another factor that may contribute to the difference between the expenditure and output series is the fact that the coverage of the output returns is deficient because of an incomplete register of firms on which the enquiries are based. Estimates for unrecorded output are now included in the published series (see Section 4.1.3 for details) but they are naturally subject to error. On the other hand part of the output data relates to dwellings not yet sold and, therefore, ought not to appear in the expenditure series, and from 1973 estimates of their value, previously included with fixed investment in private dwellings, have been included as part of the value of construction industry stocks ([QRL 201] 1966–76 edition, p. 134 refers and gives figures of the amounts involved).

Finally, it should be noted that in recent years special factors associated with the prospecting for and exploitation of oil and natural gas in the North Sea have affected the correspondence between the output and expenditure statistics. Construction contractors are involved in the building of drilling platforms and pipelines[10] but, unlike all or most expenditure on construction in the past, a substantial part of expenditure by the petroleum and natural gas industry, which has grown enormously over the last few years, has gone on imports. For instance, in 1970 this industry's expenditure on new building was £15m: in 1975 it had grown to £1299m of which about half consisted of imports—oil platforms, pipelines, etc. ([QRL 201] 1976 ed. p. 76). Corresponding statistics of the value of exports by UK contractors are not available but information about the value of orders placed by companies operating on the UK Continental Shelf, including estimates of the UK share, broken down by type (including fabrication, design and consultancy, etc.) are given in [QRL 214].

5.4.3.3. *The classification by sector and type of work in the output and expenditure series.* The classification of the MOW–DOE output statistics is made by sector (public/private) and building type (Section 4.4.5). The classification by sector is open to error since it is made by the contractor and there is certainly scope for misunderstanding about the status of many organizations in this respect. The classification of the expenditure series, on the other hand, is made by the CSO and may therefore be regarded as more reliable and consistent. Both will be affected, of course, by changes in the boundary between the sectors from time to time. The classification of the output figures by type should not be regarded as precise. Apart from the problem of classifying improvements and alterations work, discussed earlier, and the difference in the treatment of housing and non-housing work, it should be appreciated that developments consisting of mixed categories of work are generally classified to the dominant category, rather than sub-divided. Thus, for example, shops incorporated as an integral part of a housing development are likely to be returned as 'housing', and offices built as part of a factory development are likely to be returned as 'industrial' rather than 'non-industrial'. The expenditure series are only sub-divided between 'housing' and 'other buildings and works' but the housing expenditure series is also likely to reflect the same classification practice referred to above.

[10] In the national accounts tables, production platforms (but excluding modules which are included with plant and machinery), wells and pipelines are regarded as new building and works; drilling rigs and floating structures are included with ships [B 129]. It may be noted in this connection that certain firms working on the fabrication of *steel* oil-drilling platforms were taken out of the construction industry classification in 1977—see Section 4.4.5.

5.4.4. *Capital Formation Statistics—Unofficial Historical and Regional Series*

The compilation of historical series of capital formation by type of asset is a difficult task because of the lack of adequate comprehensive information. Nonetheless, estimated series have been devised for the period back to 1856 and decade-by-decade estimates for the period back to the 1760s. The prime source of reference in this field is the work done by Feinstein. The principal work on capital formation covers the period 1920–38 and is reported in [QRL 12]. These estimates were subsequently carried back to 1856 and forward to 1965 (using, for the post-war period, the official series) in [QRL 13]. Both volumes include a full discussion of sources and methods, an evaluation of the reliability of the estimates, a comparison with estimates made by other workers in the field and a full bibliography. Reference should therefore be made to these volumes for further details. The work on the period back to the 1760s is to be reported in [QRL 20]. This subsequent work has led to some 'minor revisions' to the gross domestic fixed capital formation series for the period 1856 to 1914.

The thoroughness of the work presented in these volumes and the scrupulousness with which attention is drawn to the nature of the problems, the way they have been tackled and the limitations of sources, make these volumes exemplars of their kind. Whilst it must remain possible that *some* of the estimates could be improved upon here and there it must be doubtful whether these could be other than marginal. Needless to say, perhaps, the constant price series are open to an additional source of error because of the difficulties in devising satisfactory price index numbers for construction, especially over the long retrospective periods involved in these studies. For a critical review of these problems and the indices available reference should be made to the author's study in [B 58].

Regional estimates. Unofficial regional estimates of gross domestic fixed capital formation in buildings and works have been made in connection with the preparation of regional income and expenditure accounts: Woodward made estimates for each region of the UK in 1961 in [QRL 28]; Begg *et al.* have made estimates for Scotland for each year from 1961 to 1971 in [QRL 2] and Tomkins made annual estimates for Wales over the period 1965–8 in [QRL 27]. The references cited provide details of methodology and sources; the statistical sources are considered elsewhere in this Review and no further discussion seems called for here. Further particulars of the series themselves are given in the Quick Reference List at the end of this volume. Regional accounts, including recently introduced official series, are considered further in Section 7.1.2: the official estimates do not contain asset analyses of capital formation.

5.4.5. *Capital Expenditure—Supplementary Sources and Analyses*

A full account of the sources of capital expenditure data used in the compilation of the official capital formation series is given in [B 100] (pp. 369–79 and Appendix II). Not all of these sources are published but those that are published are considered briefly here for they provide supplementary sources of information which are useful in a number of respects: they provide data by industry at a lower level of aggregation than the capital formation series, some of it is available sooner and some of it provides the base for additional analyses, in particular regional analyses of expenditure. Statistics on expenditure on purchases and sales of land and *existing* buildings, as opposed to *new* buildings, are considered in Section 12.5 since these relate simply to transfers of the existing stock as opposed to new construction.

5.4.5.1. *Private sector—capital expenditure by industry.* The primary sources here are the censuses of production and distribution and more frequent sample enquiries conducted, currently, by the BSO. It will be appreciated, of course, that the data returned in these enquiries need to be interpreted in the light of the same considerations about the accounting practices adopted for classifying expenditure as capital, rather than current, and in distinguishing buildings from plant, as were discussed earlier (Section 5.4.2.2). Whereas the capital formation series summarizes the information collected according to broad industry groups ('Orders' of the SIC) the census reports provide data at a finer level of classification and also regional analyses.

Censuses of production. The censuses of production have covered capital expenditure in the mining and quarrying, manufacturing; construction, gas, electricity and water supply industries in each year since 1948 (except 1950 when capital expenditure questions were not asked) in both Great Britain and Northern Ireland (separate censuses are taken in Northern Ireland—see Section 9.2.2). In addition to the general accounting considerations, referred to earlier, interpretation of the capital expenditure data obtained in the COP, particularly in comparison with the capital formation series, needs to take account of the fact that, unlike that series, the data exclude expenditure on professional fees, legal charges, agent's commissions between 1948 and 1957.

The relevant reports run into several hundreds and it is not convenient, therefore, to list them all here. References to all of the reports published up to the census for 1958 will be found in the official guide [B 239]. For each subsequent census up to 1969 a list of references (and the data themselves for non-detailed enquiries) will be found in [QRL 274] (1959–62); [QRL 275] Part I (1963); [QRL 276] (1964–7); [QRL 277] Part I (1968) and [QRL 353] (1969). Since 1970 censuses have been conducted by the BSO and the results published in the *Business Monitor PA* series [QRL 75]; summary results are given in serial *PA 1002*. In the case of 'energy' industries—coal mining, mineral oil refining, gas and electricity—the results are reported in [QRL 141]. Data for 1950 (not covered in the census) were obtained in a special sample enquiry and reported in [QRL 49].

Regional analyses. The *Statistics of Trade Act 1947* requires that separate results should be produced for Scotland and for Wales for each census. Separate analyses for the regions of England were generally confined to the less frequent detailed censuses from 1948 to 1968. Under the 'new system' of annual censuses of production under the BSO, regional analyses of capital expenditure have been prepared annually [QRL 75] serial *PA 1002*, but without a breakdown by type of asset. For Northern Ireland, statistics are collected separately—see Section 9.2.2.

It should be appreciated that there are certain problems in obtaining a suitable regional classification of expenditure since reporting units which operate at more than one geographical location are not always able to provide separate information for each. This problem has been growing worse over time (a discussion of the problem in the context of the new BSO enquiries is given in [B 53]). The regional analyses, therefore, are subject to an additional source of error, though one which it is not possible to quantify. In some cases multi-establishment reporting units are able to provide capital expenditure on all types of asset in total for the parts of the unit in each region but are able to provide an asset split only for the unit as a whole. In these cases, the author is informed,[11] the practice currently in deriving estimates for Scotland and Wales is to allocate reporting units with 80 per cent or more of their total net capital expenditure in these countries to the country concerned for the purposes of the asset split.

Detailed industry statistics for Scotland and Wales are given in the various census reports for each year from 1948 (with the exception of 1949 and 1950 in the case of Wales when separate details were given only for manufacturing and non-manufacturing industry). References to publications in which the large number of relevant reports, running into hundreds, are listed were given above in considering the census reports in a non-regional context. Series for 'all manufacturing' industry in Wales are included in the *DWS* [QRL 142] and a similar series for Scotland, broken down by industry, in the *SAS* [QRL 306]. Analyses for the regions of England have been published as follows (all appear in 'Summary Volumes' except for 1951):

   1951   [QRL 115]—analysis by trades in manufacturing only, and [QRL 56]—aggregates for all industry.
   1954   [QRL 271] Summary Tables.
   1963   [QRL 275] Parts 131–3.
   1968   [QRL 277] Parts 156 and 158.

Censuses and large-scale surveys of distributive and service trades. Censuses of distribution cover most of the distributive and service trades in Great Britain but are only conducted periodically, and have included questions on capital expenditure only since 1957. The relevant results (i.e. capital expenditure by asset) have been published as follows: 1957 (confined to larger traders only) in [QRL 264], 1961 in [QRL 265] Part 14 and Supplement; 1966 (sample census) in [QRL 266] Vol. 1 and 1971 in [QRL 83] Part 13. These generally provide analyses in terms of kind of business and form of organization. For Northern Ireland sources see Section 9.2.3.

The trades not covered in the censuses are covered in periodic large-scale enquiries, as follows:

   Wholesale trades—1959, 1965 and 1974.
   Catering trades—1960, 1964, 1969 and 1977.
   Motor trades—1962, 1967 and 1972.

Details of the reports of these enquiries, each of which provides data for capital expenditure on new building work, as well as other assets, are given in the *Quick Reference List* which precedes the Appendices in this volume. The results of these periodic large-scale enquiries provide the benchmarks for the more frequent, smaller-scale enquiries which are considered below.

It should be appreciated that in this sector, the large number of establishments, a large proportion of which are small, pose particular problems for these enquiries in terms of the compilation of a register, reliability of returns, and level of response. The results, therefore, are subject to a considerable margin of error. An interesting account of the technical problems and conduct of the 1966 census of distribution is given in [B 140] and an account of more recent developments and plans in [B 334]. The use in the

---
[11] Private communication from the Department of Industry, June 1976.

latest enquiries of the new VAT-based register of businesses (first used in the 1974 Wholesale Trades enquiry) has led to a substantially more comprehensive coverage of firms (see *T & I* [QRL 352] 28 Oct. 1977, p. 201).

Annual and quarterly small-scale enquiries for manufacturing, distribution and services. Since 1955 the enquiries referred to above have been supplemented by regular smaller-scale enquiries conducted by the Department of Industry and its predecessors (initially the Board of Trade). In the manufacturing sector quarterly returns of capital expenditure by type of asset have been supplied on a voluntary basis by a panel of companies (details about the enquiry given upon its introduction were given in [B 182]). In the distribution and services sector (including the construction industry itself) an annual sample enquiry has been conducted under the *Statistics of Trade Act* and quarterly and monthly data have been obtained voluntarily from a panel of contributors. Since 1975 coverage has been extended to cover expenditure on assets for leasing, hiring or renting out by leasing subsidiaries of banks, finance houses and specialist leasing companies (reported in *T & I* [QRL 352] 24 Sept. 1976, pp. 801–2). The results of these enquiries (at constant prices, s.a.) are given in a *Press Notice* [QRL 230] issued by the Department of Industry and a quarterly article in *Trade and Industry* [QRL 352]; the results at current prices (together with the constant price series) are given only in the *MDS* [QRL 195]. Secondary sources are *ET* [QRL 147] and *ETAS* [QRL 148] both of which give summary constant price series for manufacturing industry only.

The coverage of the distribution and services sector has gradually been extended and the results thereby improved but, as noted earlier, the results for this sector have been weak in the past due to the difficulties of maintaining an adequate register and because of difficulties in obtaining reliable accounting information, especially on a quarterly basis. The constant price series (deflated by the DOE's 'CNC' index—see Section 8.1) are, of course, particularly open to error on account of the heterogeneity of the work and difficulties in devising suitable price deflators[12]—these difficulties are discussed fully in Section 8.1.

Quarterly regional series for manufacturing. Regional analyses were made between 1974 and 1976 (2nd quarter) on the basis of returns obtained from the panel of manufacturing firms referred to above. Analyses were confined to the four countries of the UK and three regions of England in which the 'assisted areas' are concentrated (North, North West and Yorkshire and Humberside). The series were published in *T & I* [QRL 352]: introduced in Vol. 22, 1976, pp. 609–10.

Capital expenditure on construction by the agricultural industry. Regional analyses of capital expenditure on construction by the agricultural industry in the UK based on grant payment data from the Agricultural Departments is published annually in *Regional Statistics* [QRL 252].

5.4.5.2. *Public expenditure on construction—National data.* There are two sources of national summary information for capital expenditure on construction by public sector agencies. First, the capital formation statistics for the UK—published in [QRL 201] and

---

[12] New price deflators were introduced in 1978—after the preparation of this text—and the constant-price expenditure series revised back to 1970; for further details see the Addenda at the front of this volume.

considered in detail in Section 5.4.2 of this Review—are sub-divided by institutional sector, providing separate data for central government, public corporations and local authorities. Secondly, more recently, the construction component of expenditure incorporated in future public expenditure programmes—details of which are published as a White Paper each year—have been made available along with corresponding details of actual investment in earlier years. The White Papers themselves do not specify the buildings and works component as such, but the relevant data which go to make up the White Paper estimates are published separately by the DOE in *HCS* [QRL 168] from time to time commencing with a breakdown of the programmes in the 1976 White Paper [QRL 245] in *HCS* [QRL 168] No. 16, Supp. Table III (giving figures for financial years back to 1970–1 and forward estimates to 1979–80, all at constant 'survey prices'). Similar details from the programmes in the 1977 White Paper [QRL 161] (revised only to 1978–9) were published in *HCS* [QRL 168] No. 21. Although it is not specified in the published source, it should be noted that both these analyses relate to Great Britain, not the United Kingdom. Analyses from the 1978 White Paper [QRL 162], however, will cover the United Kingdom for the period up to 1981–2 with separate figures for Northern Ireland (except those for nationalized industries). Background information about the methodology employed in the compilation of the White Papers was published by the Treasury in 1972 in [B 295]; a related study of interest by Goldman, dealing with the development of the system of public expenditure control, will be found in [B 62].

Regional data. For the years from 1962/3 to 1974/5 regional analyses of public investment in new construction in the UK were included in *Regional Statistics* [QRL 252], providing a breakdown under a number of service headings. These statistics are now published only for Wales in the *DWS* [QRL 142].

Expenditure by agency. Apart from the analysis of the capital formation statistics by institutional sector referred to above little information is available for different agencies in the public sector. Whilst the accounts of such bodies record capital expenditure they do not generally provide analyses by asset (local authorities are now an exception) and the primary sources on which the capital formation series are based (see [B 100] for details) are not published. Capital expenditure by local authorities in England and Wales on new construction and works (distinguishing dwellings and other construction assets) and expenditure on the acquisition of land and existing buildings broken down according to service (education, highways, trading services, etc.) separately for England and for Wales have been published in *Local Government Financial Statistics* [QRL 187] annually from the report for 1969–70. Separate data for Wales have also been published in a similar publication for Wales alone [QRL 361] introduced in 1977. Separate statistics for each County Council in England and Wales, providing a 'subjective analysis' of capital expenditure by type of asset, are published by the Society of County Treasurers in *Capital Expenditure of County Councils* [QRL 84].

Relevant details for public corporations and other bodies in the public sector may be contained in their published accounts but we have made no attempt to survey all of them for the purpose of this Review. Statistics of the following nationalized industries, however, are the subject of other Reviews in the series: Coal [B 68], Electricity [B 113], Gas [B 107] and Rail [B 1]. Reference should also be made to Section 5.5 with regard to expenditure on particular types of work: educational building (Section 5.5.2), road building (Section 5.5.5) and health service buildings (Section 5.5.6).

Unit costs in public expenditure. An earlier *ad hoc* analysis of construction in public expenditure published in 1968 [B 324] gave details of the unit costs (construction and running costs) over several years up to the mid-1960s for various types of building in the public sector: housing, schools and colleges of education, universities, roads, hospitals and prison establishments.

Public financial assistance to industry for construction purposes. Government financial assistance towards industrial building has been available over most of the post-war period as an incentive towards regional development. Details of 'regional development grants' available currently under the *Industry Act 1972* are published in *Annual Reports* on the operation of the Act [QRL 172]. Regional analyses of the grants made are published in *Regional Statistics* [QRL 252]. Separate details of the assistance given in Scotland and Wales are also given in [QRL 306] and [QRL 142] respectively. A useful summary of the assistance provided under earlier legislation for the period from 1960 will be found in [B 11]; this also provides references to sources for the post-war period prior to 1960.

5.4.6. *Current Expenditure on Construction Work*

Current expenditure on construction is mainly work of routine repairs and maintenance and minor improvements. But, as we have indicated earlier, the distinction between capital and current expenditure is not clear cut and it is dependent upon accounting conventions. Statistics are not systematically collected, as they are for capital expenditure, but there are a few sources of information to note. It should also be remembered that statistics of the output of contractors and certain direct labour organizations on repair and maintenance work have been regularly collected in MOW–DOE enquiries (see Section 4.4.5); indeed it is these statistics that are regularly reported as a footnote to the capital formation tables in the *Blue Book* [QRL 201].

With regard to expenditure statistics as such, information about expenditure on repairs and maintenance to buildings and works was collected in the detailed censuses of production taken in 1948, 1963 and 1968—details of the reports for these censuses will be found in [QRL 157] Vol. 1, Part 1, [QRL 275] Part 1 and [QRL 277] Part 1 respectively. In the public sector, data about current expenditure in the years: 1963, 1968, 1970 and 1971 will be found in [QRL 177], [QRL 178], [QRL 79] (1970 and 1971 editions) respectively (reference should also be made to [B 216] for data for 1968 and 1969 and background information). It should be noted that these analyses include some expenditure on *new* construction work which is conventionally treated as current expenditure in the public sector (e.g. construction work for defence purposes and work by contractors on the extraction of opencast coal). Separate data on the payments made to 'contractors' on opencast coal production were published by the NCB in its annual accounts [QRL 279] until 1973/4 (Schedule 7).[13] Separate data were also collected

---

[13] The author is informed by the NCB Opencast Executive that the data refer not only to building and civil engineering contractors, but also to drilling and haulage contractors, and to contractors involved in the construction of the Executive's coal preparation and distribution plants. The accounts up to 1971/2 gave a breakdown of the payments.

from contractors on opencast coal work in the 1948 census of production [QRL 157] Vol. 12, Trade A. Other sectors do not appear to be systematically covered: the only regular returns appear to be for repair and maintenance expenditure on university buildings in the UK—reported annually in [QRL 325] Vol. 6. For *ad hoc* analyses see Section 12.5.2.

5.5. Production Data for Specific Types of Building

5.5.1. *Introduction*

In addition to the various sources of information about the value of output or expenditure on construction work considered in Chapters 3 and 4 and Sections 5.3 and 5.4, there are a number of independent sources of information which provide data, some of it in physical units, for specific types of building. These statistics all arise out of the administration of schemes of control in different sectors and provide information not only about work completed but also about projects at earlier stages of the planning and construction process. We also consider here information about the way contracts are let to construction firms for different types of project.

5.5.2. *Educational Building in Great Britain*

Educational building projects in England and Wales and in Scotland require the approval of the appropriate Government departments and it is from the operation of this control, and the subsequent monitoring of progress, that the statistical series available result. It should be noted that the series do not provide comprehensive information about educational building, for work at independent schools, direct grant schools, universities and certain other educational institutions such as theological colleges is not covered. With this limitation, series have been published quarterly since 1946 to show the value of projects by type (e.g. schools, further education, teacher training, etc.) at different stages of progress and also to show the number of new places provided in grant-aided or 'maintained' primary, secondary and, more recently, 'middle' schools.

Currently the primary sources are [QRL 325] Vol. 5 for England and Wales, [QRL 309] for Scotland and [QRL 153] for the UK (data for Northern Ireland are considered in Section 9.2.5). For the post-war period as a whole the primary source is the *MDS* [QRL 195] though this now contains less detailed data than the publications referred to above. Summary series for Scotland and Wales are included in the *SAS* [QRL 306] and *DWS* [QRL 142] respectively.

Detailed notes about the series, important for purposes of interpretation, are set out in footnotes to the tables and in the annual *MDS Supplement* [B 273]. It is important to note in particular that there are significant differences in the basis of the figures for Scotland as distinct from England and Wales.

University building. For university building in the UK brief details of the value of starts are given by the UGC in *Annual Surveys* [QRL 358]. Reference may also be made to a special report on development in the period 1967–72 in [B 345].

5.5.3. *Industrial Building—Industrial Development Certificates*

Statistics in physical terms (area) about industrial building in Britain originate from statutory controls over industrial development which have been administered by the Board of Trade and its successor Departments (currently DOI) since 1945. Up to July 1948 it had been necessary to notify developments, as defined, to the BOT under the terms of the *Distribution of Industry Act* of 1945. From July 1948 development could not proceed without an industrial development certificate (IDC) having been issued in accordance with the *Town and Country Planning Acts* of 1947. This control applied to the whole of Great Britain until July 1972 when it ceased to be necessary for developers to obtain an IDC for development in 'Development Areas' and 'Special Development Areas' (as defined from time to time). Until the revision of the control in July 1972 the principal sources of publication were *T & I* [QRL 352] (formerly the *BOTJ* [QRL 48]) and the *MDS* [QRL 195]. Some regional statistics were published in [QRL 195], with more detail in [QRL 252] and additional analyses for Scotland and Wales in the separate statistical *Digests* for the two countries [QRL 139] and [QRL 142]. A regional analysis of the data for Great Britain over the period 1948–58 in conjunction with employment and output data was published in [B 99]. A special analysis for Scotland over the period 1965–71 was published in *SEB* [QRL 308] No. 3, 1972. Since 1972 the detailed statistics have only been available on request from the DOI; published data are confined to summary information in *Annual Reports* on the operation of the *Industry Act 1972* [QRL 172].

Interpretation. For discussion of the scope and nature of the IDC data and its interpretation in relation to other floorspace statistics reference should be made to the companion Review in this series on *Town and Country Planning* [B 60].

5.5.4. *Office Development Statistics*

Under the *Control of Office and Industrial Development Act* of 1965 (and later, the *Town and Country Planning Act 1971*) planning applications for the development of offices of more than a specified size in certain designated areas have to be accompanied by office development permits (ODPs) issued, currently, by the DOE (formerly by the BOT). Statistics arising from the administration of this control are published quarterly in [QRL 352] (the series was initiated in [B 185]) and in *Annual Reports* on the administration of the Acts [QRL 134]. As in the case of IDCs the control provides a source of information in physical units but its geographical coverage is limited, never having extended beyond London, the Midlands and the South East of England.

Interpretation. For further consideration of the data reference should be made again to the companion Review in this series on *Town and Country Planning* [B 60].

5.5.5. *Road Building*

Statistics relating to the value and mileage of new road building are published in [QRL 354] with further details being given in annual reports: *Roads in England* [QRL 288] and *Roads in Scotland* [QRL 289]. Further particulars about the series available will be found in a planned companion volume in this series on *The Road System* [B 136].

5.5.6. *Health Service Buildings*

The most detailed published sources of statistics are annual accounts under the National Health Service Acts for England and Wales [QRL 197] and Scotland [QRL 199] which contain details of capital expenditure on hospital building and some other health service buildings. Summary data for England and Wales were also included up to the early 1970s in the DHSS annual volume of health statistics [QRL 163]. It should be noted that the statistics cover not only construction work, strictly defined, but also related fees and equipment. The definition of capital spending, revised with effect from 1 April 1977, will be found in *DHSS Circular HC(77)6* [B 199]. Until the mid-1960s analyses of expenditure on hospital building according to Hospital Regions were regularly published in a series of *Progress Reports* for England and Wales [QRL 198] and for Scotland [QRL 165] covering the periods from July 1948 to September 1965 and to September 1962 respectively. Similar data for Northern Ireland are considered in Section 9.2.5.

5.5.7. *Surveys on the Methods Used for Placing Contracts*

Following the report in 1964 of the Banwell Committee [B 287], which had been appointed to examine the effects of the practices adopted for the placing and management of contracts for building and civil engineering work on efficiency and economy, surveys were conducted by the building and civil engineering EDCs to find out what use was made of different methods of placing contracts. The results from these surveys were published in [B 176] for housing (MOHLG data) and schools, and in [B 208] for roads, water and sewerage schemes. The information is summarized, together with unpublished data for factories and offices (and for large firms and small firms) by Hillebrandt in [B 73]. A later survey of 2,000 public sector building and civil engineering projects is reported in [B 297] providing data for education, housing, 'other building', roads and 'other civil engineering'. For local authority housing in England and Wales, it may be noted, statistics are regularly collected and published from time to time in *HCS* [QRL 168].

5.6. Current and Forward Indicators and Forecasts of Construction Activity

5.6.1. *Introduction*

Information is collected by a number of different bodies which provides an indication of the current level of activity or which is relevant for assessing the forward workload for construction. Some of the information is quantitative and some of it is qualitative. Most, though not all, of the quantitative information is considered at various different places, as appropriate, in this *Review*, but the qualitative information—in the main 'state of trade' enquiries—has not been considered elsewhere. The purpose of this section is to bring together the references to the various sources of data and to consider the information which is not dealt with elsewhere. Section 5.6.2 is concerned with the available statistical series, the information collected in investment intention surveys and their limitations for future output estimation purposes; Section 5.6.3 considers the various 'state of trade' enquiries; Section 5.6.4 refers to unofficial surveys of construction contracts (the official survey was considered in Section 4.5) and Section 5.6.5 refers to actual forecasts of future levels of activity. A final section considers subsidiary information relating to the planning and erection time-scale of construction projects.

5.6.2. *Forward-looking Statistical Series and Investment Intentions Surveys*

5.6.2.1. *The statistical series.* The statistical series, as such, record projects at various stages of the pre-construction process. The relevant series are:

(a) Contractors' new orders—considered in Section 4.5.
(b) Local authority design work—considered in Section 4.7.
(c) Private architects' design work—considered in Section 13.5.1.
(d) Forward indicators for specific types of building, in particular, housing, educational building, industrial building, office building and roads, all of which were considered in Section 5.5.

The contractors' new orders series is the most important immediate indicator of future levels of output. It provides a very short-run indication, of course, since it represents work already awarded, and work on site on most contracts can generally be expected to start within a few months of the contract being signed. The series is considered fully in Section 4.5 but in the present context the following points are particularly worthy of note. First, the series is not comprehensive, for it does not cover repairs and maintenance work, it does not cover work to be done by direct labour at all, and it may be affected by deficiencies in the register of contractors (though these are likely to affect the output more than the new orders series—see Section 4.5). Secondly, the correspondence between the new orders and the contractors' output series needs to be interpreted in the light of the adjustments made to the new orders series prior to publication (again see Section 4.5). Thirdly, changes in the value of new orders in the aggregate may be affected by changes in the proportion of fixed and variable price contracts. Fourthly, the implications of changes in the level of new orders for future construction employment and materials consumption is dependent upon changes in the composition of demand according to type of work so that it is potentially misleading simply to consider changes in the level of new orders in the aggregate. A recent attempt to forecast output from the orders data is reported by Sugden and Wells in [B 155].

The two design enquiries—that conducted by the DOE for local authorities and that conducted by the RIBA for private architects—both provide, at least in principle, an earlier indication of the construction work-load than the new orders series. In practice, as we have noted earlier, neither series has apparently realized its potential in this respect. Apart from the technical problems involved in their use, involving the interpretation of values which at the pre-tender stage can be nothing more than estimates and the adjustment once again for price changes over time, with the associated difficulty of devising an appropriate index, perhaps the salient factor to note is that the coverage of these series is partial, for some work in both the public and private sectors is outside the scope of the enquiries and other work is not architect-designed at all. For further discussion of the series see Sections 4.7 and 13.5.1 respectively. At one time quantitative information was also collected about the value of work being handled by quantity surveyors; currently qualitative enquiries only are made (see Section 13.5.2).

The production series for specific types of building, considered in Section 5.5, also incorporate forward indicators of future output—some of them at even earlier stages of the pre-construction process than design and some of them in physical, as opposed to monetary, terms. Apart from the fact that the data are confined to particular types of building, their main limitations are restrictions in scope either geographically or in terms of coverage of the particular type of work. For further details see Section 5.5. For house-building, which is outside the scope of this study, reference should be made to the companion *Reviews* in this series on the housing statistics of Great Britain [B 52] and Northern Ireland [B 57].

5.6.2.2. *Investment intention surveys.* There are three relevant surveys, two of which are quantitative and one qualitative.

Public expenditure plans. Since the publication of the 1976 White Paper on public expenditure [QRL 245], which gave details of expenditure plans up to 1979–80, and actual expenditure in earlier financial years, the construction component of the plans (which is not included in the White Paper itself) has been released by the DOE—details are given in Section 5.4.5.2. These statistics are, of course, particularly valuable in that they cover the public sector comprehensively but it should be noted that they refer to Great Britain (coverage is to be extended to the UK—see Section 5.4.5.2) and to new work only; repairs and maintenance expenditure is not included. It should also be appreciated that the data will cover contracts already in progress as well as new contracts to be let. They are also inevitably subject to changes in government policy.

DOI Survey of Investment Intentions. This survey was initiated in 1955 (by the Board of Trade) and is conducted three times a year on a sample basis covering firms in manufacturing and the distributive and service industries. As far as construction is concerned the results are of interest inasmuch as it regularly constitutes a major part of total investment: separate results according to type of asset are not published. Originally the enquiries were conducted in respect of each calendar year but since the mid-1960s they have been extended to cover intentions for two years and supplemented with qualitative information about likely expenditure. Currently, the quantitative results are grossed-up and published three times a year as a *Press Notice* [QRL 232] and in *T & I* [QRL 352] (January, June and October); a summary is also included in *Economic Trends* [QRL 147]. Originally the actual results were not published but only an official interpretation. A full description of the survey and an analysis of its use for forecasting purposes will be found in Lund *et al.* [B 97]; it may be noted that this study does incorporate disaggregated analyses at the asset level. Reference may also usefully be made to a study by Savage [B 138] for a valuable discussion and assessment of the survey. Further references are contained in a detailed bibliography in [B 97].

CBI Industrial Trends Survey. The CBI (formerly FBI) survey covers its member firms only and is confined to manufacturing. The number of participating firms has gradually increased from around 500 to nearly 2000 currently, employing between a third and a half of the manufacturing industry labour force. The survey was started in 1958 on a thrice yearly basis up to and including 1971 and then quarterly. The enquiry is wholly qualitative, each firm being asked whether it *expects to authorize* more, the same or less capital expenditure in the next twelve months than in the last twelve months. The reference to 'expected authorizations' contrasts with the reference to 'expenditure intentions' in the DOI enquiry referred to above. Building expenditure is distinguished separately. General results, which are weighted to take account of the industry and size of respondents, are published in a *Press Release* [QRL 237] and summary details are included in *Economic Trends* [QRL 147] as part of a table of 'indicators of fixed investment...'; more detailed results by industry and separate results for Scotland are available from the CBI on subscription. Special enquiries into the answering practices of respondents, the results of which are important for interpretative purposes, were carried out in 1967 and 1976 and are reported in [B 61] and [B 123] respectively. Recent studies of the usefulness of these surveys for forecasting purposes are contained in [B 97], [B 138] and [B 85].

5.6.3. *State of Trade Enquiries*

5.6.3.1. *Background and interpretation.* This section is confined to the enquiries carried out by private trade organizations among their own members. An official enquiry, initiated by the DOE at the beginning of 1977, is considered in Section 4.5.4. Several associations in the construction industry as such conduct enquiries. In addition to these, we also consider here enquiries carried out amongst building materials producers and merchants for, naturally, these too provide an indication of trends in construction activity.

The purpose of these enquiries is to provide a quick qualitative impression of the current situation and trends in particular sectors of the industry. This fact and the methods used for conducting the enquiries need to be borne in mind if the results are not to be mis-interpreted. All of the enquiries depend upon the voluntary co-operation of members; none of them are based on formal sampling methods and the results are not 'weighted' or 'grossed-up' to allow for the relative importance of respondents (though it should be noted that results are often sub-divided by size of respondent). It follows that the respondents and the results may not be representative of the membership. But of course, even if formal sampling methods were adopted the membership of a particular body will not *necessarily* be representative of a particular industrial sector. These qualifications, I would stress, are not meant to deny the usefulness of the enquiries. Insofar as the wind blows the same way for all producers in the sector concerned, it is likely that these enquiries cannot fail to reflect changes in its direction. Beyond that, however, quantitative assessment of its force is naturally subject to error.

5.6.3.2. *NFBTE State of Trade Enquiry.* The National Federation of Building Trades Employers (NFBTE) is the central organization of employers in all sections of the building industry in Great Britain including main contractors, sub-contractors and private house-builders. Most large building firms (i.e. those employing around 250 operatives or more) are members and a substantial proportion of medium and smaller sized firms. Membership extends down to small firms employing less than twenty-five operatives but the proportion naturally diminishes as one moves down the range of sizes. In 1975 membership was almost 12,000 compared with around 88,000 firms on the DOE register at that time. State of trade enquiries were initiated on a quarterly basis in the early 1960s. Currently questionnaires are circulated to a panel of about 1,000 member firms (not a random sample) broadly representative of the membership, both by size of firm and location, throughout the country. The published results are normally based on the first 700 or so replies.

As regards the future workload, respondents are asked to say whether enquiries from clients (by 'physical volume of work') are more, less, much less, etc. compared with the previous quarter (the information being broken down by type of work). They are also asked to state whether they anticipate the volume of work to be done in the forthcoming year to be more or less etc. than in the preceding year. Other questions are concerned with success in tendering, capacity working and the availability of labour and materials. The results (including details of the number and size of respondents) are issued by the NFBTE as a *Press Notice* [QRL 234], which is widely reported in the building and national press, and a summary is regularly included in the Federation's journal [B 274]. Interesting attempts by Turin to assess these enquiries in relation to the official DOE new orders statistics (Section 4.5 refers) will be found in [B 165] and [B 166], although it should be noted that the conclusions of the first study were disputed by the Federation (see correspondence in the issues of the journal *Building* [QRL 60] for 17, 24 and 31 July 1970).

5.6.3.3. *HBF State of Trade Enquiry.* The House-Builders Federation (HBF) is affiliated to the NFBTE and began a separate quarterly state of trade enquiry amongst its members in England and Wales in the middle of 1976. Although housebuilding is outside the scope of this Review, this enquiry is considered here since it was initiated after the publication of the volume on housing statistics for Great Britain [B 52]. The questions asked in the enquiry relate to the level of demand for housing compared with the position three months previously, the main factors limiting the demand for private housing, mortgage availability, factors affecting the ability of the respondents to meet demand and their anticipations regarding their employment of operatives in the year ahead. The results, including details of the number and size of respondents, are issued as a *Press Notice* [QRL 231]. It may be noted too, briefly, that an official enquiry into anticipated levels of housebuilding activity in the private sector is made by the DOE (the 'private enterprise housing enquiry'): the results are published in *HCS* [QRL 168]; for further details see the companion Review on housing statistics [B 52] and the *HCS Supplement* [B 250].

5.6.3.4. *FCEC Civil Engineering Trends Survey (UK Work).* The Federation of Civil Engineering Contractors (FCEC) has carried out surveys amongst its members for a number of years. In the past these were organized by individual sections of the

Federation on a regional basis and not published. In 1977, however, the enquiry was reviewed and since November of that year has been run from the central office in London, on a quarterly basis and covering (at least initially) all members, although some sections of the Federation still retain their local enquiry. The questions asked are on the usual 'better, same, worse' basis, as in other enquiries of this type, and cover the following subjects: the state of the order book, employment (operatives and staff separately), the amount of plant idle, the number of invitations to tender being received and the number of tenderers on lists, and the future outlook for their business (estimated future business and estimated employment trend), all compared to the position twelve months previously, except in the case of order books for which a comparison with the situation six months previously is also made. In addition information is collected about the materials supply position together with general observations about regional variations or about specific types of work, etc. At the time of writing (November 1977) the question of the distribution of the results outside the membership of the Federation was under consideration.

5.6.3.5. *HVCA State of Trade Enquiry.* The Heating and Ventilating Contractors' Association (HVCA), representing heating, air conditioning, ventilating, refrigeration, piping and domestic engineering employers in the UK, initiated bi-annual state of trade enquiries in 1975. The subjects covered are: the trend in the real volume of orders, the level of capacity working currently and anticipated, the volume of output compared with one year before and one year ahead, the availability of craft labour and views about tender prices. In the enquiries to date (late 1977) between 120 and 230 members have participated in each enquiry. The detailed results are issued by the Association along with a summary *News Release* [QRL 210].

5.6.3.6. *NFBPM Builders' Merchants Index and Business Confidence Survey.* The National Federation of Builders' and Plumbers' Merchants (NFBPM) carry out two surveys. One is a monthly survey of a 'major portion' of its membership by class of trade (heavy, light and mixed) and by region throughout the UK. Each member returns its total turnover/sales figure and these are aggregated, according to the divisions referred to above, and the results shown as a 'rolling annual index'—i.e. the value for the previous twelve months compared with the corresponding period one year earlier. The index is produced in two forms: one using the current values as returned and one using the values deflated to constant prices, using for this purpose the official DOI construction materials price index (see Section 11.1.1). Currently returns are obtained from around 200 members (representing, the author is informed, around 20 per cent of the membership in terms of numbers and 50 per cent in terms of turnover). The results are not formally published but are circulated to participants and to certain subscribers who pay an annual fee (the Federation reserves to itself the right to accept or reject applications for subscriber status from outside organizations); a summary statement of the results is incorporated in *BMP Statistical Bulletin* [QRL 47] which is a collection of construction statistics compiled by the NCBMP from official and other sources.

The NFBPM business confidence survey, carried out quarterly, includes questions on trends in the level of trade: the level of enquiries received and the value of orders placed with manufacturers, and feelings over trade for the next six months and twelve months. A question is also asked about shortages of particular materials and how members see these evolving. Results are published in the trade and national Press.

5.6.4. *Unofficial Surveys of Construction Contracts*

In addition to the comprehensive official DOE survey of new orders obtained by contractors (Section 4.5), information about contracts awarded or out to tender, etc. is collected together in a number of trade publications. The coverage of these is very far from being comprehensive but they provide information about individual contracts and may be of interest for that reason. *Trade Digest* [QRL 351], for example, is devoted entirely to collating details of individual contracts (and also planning permissions) throughout the British Isles and is issued fortnightly, in UK and separate regional editions, on subscription. Surveys of public works programmes have been regularly included in *Surveyor—Public Authority Technology* [QRL 344] for many years and until 1967 a *Tabular Summary of Civil Engineering Contracts* was printed as an annual supplement to *The Engineer* [QRL 154].

Other journals, providing contract details amongst other information, are *Tenders and Contracts Journal* [QRL 347] which gives details of both UK and overseas contracts, *New Building Projects* [QRL 206], *Construction News* [QRL 129], *Building* [QRL 60] and *Contract Journal* [QRL 131]. The publishers of the latter also make a monthly analysis of the number and value of projects by type reported each month compared with the previous year—a brief summary is included in the journal and full particulars are made available on subscription [QRL 133]. Interpretation of the data as a guide to trends is, of course, problematical since coverage is patchy and the values are at current tender prices and subject to the varying influence of the factors that go to determine such prices (see Section 4.5.2 regarding valuation and pricing).

5.6.5. *Forecasts of Construction Output for Great Britain*

No official (by which is meant government) forecasts for the construction sector as such are published. Since the late 1960s, however, more information has been made available than before about the government's short-term macro-economic forecasts which may be of interest inasmuch as they provide separate forecasts for fixed investment in which construction is always a major part. No distinction between construction and other assets is made in these forecasts, although it will be recalled that since 1976 the construction component in *public* expenditure plans has been published separately—see Section 5.6.2.2. The forecasts have been published in the *Financial Statement* [B 227] which accompanies the Budget since 1968 (first included in House of Commons Paper 151, Session 1967–8); more recently separate publication of the Treasury's forecasts has been initiated in accordance with the *Industry Act 1975* (Schedule 5)—the first of these appeared in *Economic Trends* [QRL 147] No. 278, Dec. 1976. It is also the case that macro-economic forecasts prepared by various other organizations of which the National Institute of Economic and Social Research (NIESR) is probably the most well-known—do not differentiate between investment in construction and other assets (apart from forecasts of investment in dwellings).[14] For this reason we devote no further attention to these forecasts here, although they do, of course, provide the essential framework for anyone concerned with forecasting for the industry, particularly over the longer-term. Those who wish to pursue the matter further should refer to Surrey [B 156] for a description of the NIESR forecasting model, to Renton [B 132], which includes several papers providing further details of the NIESR model and descriptions of other econometric models of the UK economy, and to Ash and Smyth [B 4] who describe other forecasting services[15] and make an assessment of the accuracy of many of the forecasts made over various periods up to the early 1970s. The rest of this section is concerned with unofficial forecasts that are made specifically for the construction sector.

5.6.5.1. *NEDO construction forecasts.* Regular forecasts of construction output have been made by the Building and Civil Engineering EDCs and published since at least 1967. Since 1972 the forecasts have been made at regular six-monthly intervals, supplemented as necessary by intermediate revisions to take account of major policy changes and other developments. These have been made available on subscription through HMSO since January 1975 [QRL 128], previously they were issued by the NEDO directly. Details of early forecasts, prepared in the period 1967–70, seem to have been released by NEDO in brief press notices only.

With one exception (referred to below) all the forecasts are short-term, covering a period of two or three years ahead, and are national forecasts for Great Britain. Regional forecasts have been made on one occasion only in the past (these too are referred to below). The methodology for making the forecasts has apparently changed somewhat over time and is not documented in the published reports. Our attention here, therefore, is confined to the methodology currently used.[16]

The essential point about the methodology is that it is not based upon a formal econometric model. The forecasts are determined by informal consensus amongst groups of forecasters in a two-stage process. First, three panels (referred to as 'sub-groups') of people, drawn in the main from construction companies, building materials producers and employers and trade associations but acting in a private capacity, prepare forecasts for three separate sectors: housing, private non-housing and public non-housing. Each member of these three sub-groups is required to make his or her own estimate for their particular sector. These estimates are then discussed at a meeting during which each member is free to change his estimate in the light of the discussion until a consensus emerges. No guidance is given to members as to how their initial estimate should be made, but prior to the meeting each member is circulated with a 'data base' of forward-looking statistics such as those we have discussed in earlier parts of this section. These are now supported by an explicit macro-economic assessment. At one time no such assessments were made. Recently, a fourth macro-forecasting sub-group has been formed and a summary of its views is provided to the members of the three other sub-groups to provide the broad economic framework for their discussions.

[14] It should be noted, however, that the NIESR does also make disaggregated forecasts of output by industry including construction (as opposed to investment in construction)—see Section 5.6.5.2.
[15] A useful up-to-date survey of economic forecasting services in the UK was published after the preparation of this text in [B 146].
[16] My thanks are due to NEDO staff for supplying the information on which this section is based.

There is one refinement to this process in the case of housing. Here, the sub-group forecast not output as such but the number of housing starts. These are then converted to equivalent completions and values by the DOE using a particular computer-based model developed by the Department for this purpose.

The second stage of the process is for the reports from the three sub-groups to be considered by the Joint Forecasting Committee of the Building and Civil Engineering EDCs, who may alter the forecasts made by the sub-groups, particularly in the light of developments that may have taken place subsequent to the work of the sub-groups. It is this committee (its membership is listed in the published reports) which gives formal approval to the forecasts as published.

Naturally, the most important question with any set of forecasts is their accuracy and their consistency over time. At one time the published reports included comparisons of previous forecasts and actual out-turns but, unfortunately, these were discontinued several years ago. But anyone, of course, can make such a comparison for himself. As usual with such comparisons, however, their interpretation raises the difficult problem of allowing for the influence of developments during the passage of time between the making of the forecast and the period to which it relates which were not foreseen at the time the forecasts were made. In other words, they can only be evaluated within the confines of their own particular assumptions. But in practice one has to judge how far differences between forecasts and out-turns are due to poor forecasting on the one hand, and to errors in the assumptions on the other. Although the principal macro-economic assumptions are now spelt out, the problem of subsequent evaluation of the forecasts remains because they are not founded upon any formal statistical model. If they were so based, errors in the assumptions could be more readily evaluated.

Whatever the degree of accuracy and consistency achieved by the forecasts, the question also arises of how far alternative, more formal methods would prove more satisfactory. One obvious possibility would be to develop a formal model relating the official DOE new orders and output series. It is known that the DOE prepares forward-load estimates, using this information, but they are not published. Private research workers have encountered difficulties in relating the two series satisfactorily—see Sugden and Wells [B 155]. Likewise, many of the other forward indicators referred to earlier (Section 5.6.2) seem to offer the potential for formal econometric work but a potential which seems not to have been realized in practice or to have gone untapped.

The forecasts discussed above are short-term national forecasts. Regional and longer-term forecasts have each been made on one occasion in the past. These are now out-dated and we do no more, therefore, than note their existence here. The reports in each case give full accounts of methodology, some of it partly econometric, which may be of interest. The regional forecasts were published in 1974 in [B 301] for the year 1977 relating to Scotland and three groups of regions in England and Wales; these had been preceded by a pilot study for Yorkshire and Humberside reported in [B 302]. The attempt to assess the prospects for the industry over the longer-term was made in 1971 in [B 204] for the period up to 1979.

Finally, reference should be made to two more recent studies concerned with the longer-term prospects for construction, although they do not provide forecasts as such. They both explore the implications for manpower and materials of *possible* high and low levels of demand in the early 1980s. Full details will be found in the reports—one for Great Britain [B 205] and one for Scotland [B 320].

5.6.5.2. *Other forecasts for construction.* Other forecasts are made by the National Council of Building Materials Producers—referred to as BMP forecasts—specifically for the construction industry and by NIESR for construction and other industries as part of its regular economic assessment for the economy as a whole referred to above.

BMP forecasts.[17] The BMP forecasts are published in *BMP Information* [QRL 46] and provide a breakdown into six categories of work (five for new work and one for repairs, maintenance and improvement) for two or three years ahead (the final year in qualitative terms). Like the NEDO forecasts, these are also prepared by a 'forecasting panel' but are of longer standing than the NEDO series. In the case of BMP, forecasting panels were started in 1956 and meet two or three times a year. They consist of a small panel of experts and industrialists from firms and trade associations in the construction industry, as well as the staff of BMP. Like the NEDO forecasts too, the methodology depends partly upon statistical evidence and partly upon subjective assessments. Analyses are made of trends in the DOE series for construction output and new orders (Sections 4.4 and 4.5 refer) and these, together with consideration of the general economic and political situation and probable future trends, and trends being experienced in forward demand for the main product sectors, coupled with the experience and expertise of panel members, are 'distilled' into the final forecasts.

From the point of view of comparing NEDO and BMP forecasts it should be appreciated, perhaps, that the two sets of forecasts cannot be regarded as completely independent of one another: both rely, naturally, to some extent on the same statistical evidence; both sets of forecasts are published and therefore, given the methodology, may influence the thinking of panel members; and, further, it is also worthy of note that members of the NCBMP also serve on the Joint Forecasting Committee of the Building and Civil Engineering EDCs. It may be, of course, that a consequence is an improvement in the quality of the forecasts that are made by both bodies.

NIESR construction forecasts. As mentioned earlier, industrial forecasts do not constitute an integral part of the National Institute's macro-economic forecasting model, but disaggregated forecasts for various industries, including construction, are made twice a year for a period two years ahead and published along with the quarterly economic assessment in the *National Institute Economic Review* [QRL 204]. The construction forecast is based mainly upon the macro-economic forecasts for gross domestic fixed capital formation but the final predictions are often modified in the light of the evidence from leading indicators for construction considered in Section 5.6.2. Unlike the other forecasts, considered above, no breakdown by type of work is made (though it may be noted that dwellings are separately distinguished as a component of the investment forecasts).

5.6.6. *The Time Scale of Construction Projects*

The work from the conception of a construction project to its realization on site generally extends over a lengthy period of time, often over several years. Information about the time lags involved, therefore, is an important adjunct to information about

---

[17] This section is based on information kindly supplied by NCBMP.

work at various stages of the pre-construction process if it is to be used as an indicator of future work-loads. The purpose of this sub-section, therefore, is to consider the information available on this subject. In fact, no comprehensive enquiries are made and the data available consist of little more than bits and pieces of information from *ad hoc* surveys that have been carried out at different times.

For the construction stage of the process, the only regular enquiry in which information about time lags is obtained is the DOE's contractors' new orders enquiry (considered in Section 4.5) which requires a return of expected completion dates but, unfortunately, no analyses of this part of the return are published. No regular enquiries are made of actual, as opposed to expected, construction periods. In the house-building field (strictly outside the scope of this Review) estimates are regularly made of the time-lag from start to completion though these are not based on actual returns or observations—the data are published in, currently, *HCS* [QRL 168]; background details will be found in [B 250]. Other information comes from *ad hoc* surveys. A recent survey of ninety-five hospital building projects, carried out by the Building Research Station, obtained information about their duration, amongst other things, and is reported in [QRL 19]. Also at the construction stage a one-off analysis of possible interest, though now out-dated, was made by Pascoe [B 116] of the *estimated* duration of civil engineering contracts reported in *The Engineer* [QRL 154] in the early 1960s, covering over 500 contracts and broken down into seven categories.

At the pre-contract stage, information used to be collected in the official local authority design work enquiry (considered in Section 4.7); it was not regularly published but an analysis of nearly 2,000 projects on which design work was started during the two years ended September 1966 is reported in [B 266] paras. 30–39. This shows the average time taken to the completion of sketch plans, to the completion of working drawings and to the start of construction on each of three types of work (housing, education, other). The only other information available for this stage of the process comes from *ad hoc* surveys covering various sectors from time to time. The surveys are all generally small-scale, but they provide useful insights into the size and variability of the time-lags frequently involved. We give what appear to be the principal references below (it is possible that some surveys in this area have escaped our notice).

The most recent information of this kind comes from case studies carried out for the Building and Civil Engineering EDCs in the early 1970s and reported in [B 297]. These studies covered fifty projects (forty-four public and six private) covering housing, education, roads, government buildings and a miscellaneous group of private buildings, and provide information on the time-lag experienced on each project between various defined stages of the pre- and post-contract periods. Earlier information about the pre-construction time-lags on a number of hospital schemes in the late 1960s was included in [B 284] Appendix 2. Some relevant information was also collected in a survey of factory and office building commissioned by the EDC for Building but printed in *RIBA Stat. Bull.* [QRL 249] No. 24. A still earlier survey was carried out by the RIBA at the request of the Ministry of Works in the late 1950s covering 311 building projects: architects in private practice or in employment with public authorities or in private industry were asked to provide details of the time-lag at a number of stages from the receipt of first instructions from the client through to the start or completion of building work. The results, giving information by type and size of project, were published in [B 316]. However, it was subsequently reported that the size of the sample was too small for reliable statistical conclusions to be drawn, given the variability of the data ([B 338] Vol. 1, para. 1.11 refers). Research on the building timetable was also carried out by the Building Economics Research Unit at University College London over a number of years from 1966 covering a large number of building projects, see [B 339], [B 131] and [B 130].

CHAPTER 6

LABOUR STATISTICS FOR GREAT BRITAIN OTHER THAN THOSE COLLECTED IN MOW–DOE ENQUIRIES AND IN CENSUSES OF PRODUCTION

6.1. Introduction

This section is devoted to statistics of all kinds relating to labour in the construction industry other than the employment statistics collected by the DOE and its predecessor departments (considered in Chapters 3 and 4) and those collected in the censuses of production (Section 5.3). In these cases employment data were collected as part of broader-based enquiries covering output and other subjects as well as employment, and for this reason they have been considered separately. In addition to these sources there are three other sources of employment data:

  (1) Department of Employment (DE) and its predecessor departments,
  (2) Censuses of Population,
  (3) Construction Industry Training Board (CITB).

We examine each of these sources in turn in the next three sub-sections (6.2, 6.3 and 6.4) paying particular attention to the nature of the differences that exist among these sources and the two other sources considered earlier. We then turn to examine all other labour-related statistics as follows:

  (1) Labour training and education statistics (Section 6.5),
  (2) Qualified manpower statistics for construction (Section 6.6),
  (3) *Ad hoc* labour enquiries (Section 6.7),
  (4) Unemployment, vacancies and labour mobility (Section 6.8),
  (5) Wage rates, earnings, hours and labour costs (Section 6.9),
  (6) Accident statistics (Section 6.10),
  (7) Strike statistics (Section 6.11),
  (8) Trade union statistics (Section 6.12).

6.2. Employment Statistics Collected by the Department of Employment and Its Predecessor Departments

6.2.1. *Introduction*

The DE is the department with the primary responsibility for the compilation of labour statistics for the whole economy, a responsibility which it and its predecessor departments have had since 1886. We confine our attention here, however, to the statistics collected since 1948. Details of the sources and nature of earlier series will be found in the *Guide to Official Sources* for *Labour Statistics* [B 241] and in the *Historical Abstract* [QRL 58] which brings together the principal series for the period 1886–1968. Before the Second World War, these statistics were the only regular source of employment data. From 1941, however, they were supplemented, as far as the construction industry was concerned, by the data collected by the then MOW (for further details see Section 3.9).

6.2.2. *Methodology*

The statistics compiled by the DE and its predecessors since 1948 fall into two distinct periods: 1948–71 and 1971 onwards. Until 1971 the DE employment series were derived from the administration of the extended National Insurance scheme introduced in 1948. In 1971 censuses of employment were introduced in anticipation of the discontinuance of national insurance cards, which were used for the purpose of recording contributions under the scheme, and counts of which had been the basis of the former series. Major discontinuities occur in the series, therefore, at these two points.

The methodology used for these enquiries has been dealt with in general terms elsewhere. The main focus of our attention here, therefore, is on the factors of relevance for the compilation and interpretation of the data for the construction industry in particular. Details of the National Insurance scheme itself will be found in the companion Review in this series on *Social Security Statistics* [B 170] and in the earlier official guide on the same subject [B 327]; further details of their use for compiling employment statistics will be found in a general review of *British Employment Statistics* by Buxton and MacKay [B 35] and in the earlier official guide to labour statistics [B 241]. Buxton and MacKay [B 35] also give an account of the new census of employment; an official account was published in *DEG* [QRL 135] January 1973 issue (reprinted in the labour statistics *Yearbook* [QRL 59] for 1972). A brief account to serve the purposes of this Review is given below in considering the available series and their interpretation.

6.2.3. *The Published Series and Their Interpretation*

In the next three sub-sections we consider the principal employment series compiled since 1948 and in a fourth sub-section (6.2.3.4) consider various subsidiary employment series compiled by the DE.

6.2.3.1. *The card-count series 1948–71.* Under the card-count regime three employment series, on GB and UK bases, were compiled:

(1) Numbers in employment='employees in employment' (category (3) below) plus the self-employed (estimated since not all self-employed were covered by the insurance scheme). This series was discontinued after November 1965.

(2) Employees=employed persons (as distinct from the self-employed) for whom cards were exchanged (*including the unemployed*) sub-classified by sex, region and two age groups (under/over 18 years).

(3) Employees in employment=employees (category (2)) minus *registered* unemployed (see Section 6.7 for unemployment statistics) sub-classified by sex.

The series were published monthly but only the June figures were derived from a direct count; for months between one June count and the next estimates were made—see below. The primary publication source was the *DEG* [QRL 135] (formerly the *MOLG* [QRL 190]). The series up to 1968 were reproduced in the *Historical Abstract* [QRL 58] and continued in the subsequent *Yearbooks* [QRL 59] thereafter. The *MDS* [QRL 195] and the *AAS* [QRL 31] are the most important secondary sources. Full details of the series and publication sources, especially for regional data, are given in the *Quick Reference List* which is given at the end of the text in this volume.

There are several salient points to note about the nature and coverage of the employment series derived from the counts of national insurance cards. First is the fact that it provided a count of 'insured persons' rather than 'employed persons'. On the one hand, some persons were not insured under the scheme, and on the other hand, some of the persons for whom cards were exchanged may not necessarily have been at work at the time, for cards were exchanged not only for the employed, but also for the unemployed and those absent from work due to sickness and other causes. For the purpose of employment series, therefore, adjustments were made to the basic card-count data to provide series covering different groupings of the labour force and a particular terminology was adopted to describe them, a terminology in which, as indicated above, the word 'employee' covered unemployed as well as employed persons.

Coverage of the new scheme was more comprehensive than the one it replaced but not complete, excluding certain categories of self-employed persons. In principle, this was not a major limitation as far as construction was concerned since the exceptions were self-employed men aged 70 and over, women aged 65 and over and self-employed married women who took the option of not being insured under the scheme, and none of these categories is of major importance for the industry. Apart from these exclusions, coverage was very full, in principle, covering all other persons 'who work for pay or profit' and all persons in 'unpaid work under a contract of service'. Coverage even extended to cases where employment amounted to only a few hours a week (in these cases a small insurance contribution had to be paid to cover the risk of industrial injuries). On the other hand, it was possible for some people to evade their obligations under the scheme and not pay contributions (hereafter referred to as 'non-compliance'). This certainly became a problem for the construction series in particular, from the 1960s onwards, if not earlier, because of non-compliance by 'self-employed' construction workers working under labour-only sub-contract (LOSC).

A second point of importance with regard to the accuracy of the series is that they were not based on complete counts of cards. Even within the confines referred to above, therefore, the series were estimates. A 'bench-mark' count was made of cards exchanged in June (approximately one-quarter of the total) supplemented by a *voluntary* return (return CF 205, later ED 205) from employers (to the Ministry administering the national insurance scheme—not the DE) of the total number of cards held. The fact that not all cards are exchanged on time, that cards exchanged for any one industry may not represent precisely one-quarter of those *held* in the industry and that the return of total cards held was voluntary, all introduce sources of potential error.

In addition, the adjustments needed in order to compile the three principal series based on the June count provide further potential sources of error. The series for total employment required an addition for the self-employed not covered by the insurance scheme but the only information available was that obtained in the intermittent censuses of population (1951, 1961, 1966 and 1971—see Section 6.3). The adjustment therefore is very approximate and this particular series was discontinued after November 1965 (published in *MOLG* [QRL 190] 1966, p. 31)—background information is given in *MOLG* [QRL 190] 1966, pp. 214–15. A subsequent annual series of estimates for the self-employed from 1961 were made retrospectively in 1976—see Section 6.2.3.4 below. The construction industry poses a particular problem because of the substantial growth of 'self-employment' in the industry (sometimes purely nominal and often referred to as the 'Lump'), the men involved supplying their labour on a labour-only sub-contract basis (for a full discussion see the Report of the Phelps-Brown Committee [B 307]; see too Section 4.4.2). The series for 'employees in employment' required the deduction of the numbers unemployed from the card count of 'employees'—the only data available, however, related to the numbers of *registered* unemployed which may not necessarily be the same as the numbers actually unemployed (see Section 6.8.1).

The series for months inbetween successive June counts was derived using the employment data collected by the DOE and its predecessors (Sections 3.9.3 and 4.4.3 refer). These data, however, grew increasingly deficient to a substantial degree over the years because of the difficulties experienced in maintaining a comprehensive register of employers and a failure to cover the growing number of self-employed through the 1960s and early 1970s—see Section 4.4.2. For this reason, if for no other, the monthly series must be treated with great circumspection. Finally, interpretation of the series needs to take account of the methods used for classification by industry and then by region.

Industrial classification. Since 1948 the DE statistics have been classified in accordance with the successive editions of the SIC. The general principles of the SIC as they apply to construction were considered above in Section 4.1.2. The basic principle is that 'establishments' (as defined) are classified according to the nature of their principal activity. The mechanics of the classification process are that each card is coded according to the industrial classification of the employer's establishment when it is received for exchange at the local office of the department responsible for administering the national insurance scheme. The general principle of classification is that *all* employees of the establishment are classified according to the major activity of the establishment. But where at a single address there are two or more departments engaged in different activities, each of which forms a distinct industrial unit, it is possible for each unit to be treated as a separate establishment and coded accordingly. This requires, however, the co-operation of the employer in presenting the cards for exchange in separate groups. Undoubtedly, however, construction employees, particularly those in works departments working on repair and maintenance of the firms' own premises, but also possibly those doing work for clients under contract, were not always separated out in this way, but were returned under the firms' main activity which could be in a wide range of different industries.

A similar problem arises in the case of the direct labour employed by public authorities which may not always have been separated out for classification to construction. Lastly, differences in classification may occur due to differences in the precise application of the SIC principles—in particular classification according to an establishment's principal product (measured in terms of output or turnover—as in the MOW–DOE enquiries) may differ from one based upon 'activity' measured in terms of the labour employed.

Regional and local classifications. Regional and local classifications raised a special problem for all industry since some cards were exchanged centrally. To deal with this problem, information was sought (on the voluntary ED 205 returns) about employees working in areas other than the one in which their cards were exchanged. The coverage of these returns was partial and the information collected was used to adjust the card-count estimates only if ten or more persons were involved. For construction, of course, regional classification poses a special problem because of the nature of site work—even though a construction firm may comprise a single establishment, most of the labour employed will not be working at the establishment's address and may not even be working in the same region, indeed at any one time its labour force may be distributed over several different sites in different regions. Although considerable efforts were made to include site workers in the region and local area in which they were working, this action was not always successful, and the MOL–DE regional figures for construction labour need to be used with the greatest of caution, as do those collected by the DOE (Chapters 3 and 4).

6.2.3.2. *Census of employment series from 1971.* On the census of employment basis, initiated in June 1971, only one series has been produced, namely for 'employees in employment' (sub-classified by full-time/part-time workers and by sex and region) on both GB and UK bases as before. It must be remembered, however, that the identity in title with one of the card-count series (category (3) above) does not signify identity of coverage. The DE has prepared a 'continuous series' but it must be used with caution—for details and comments see Section 6.2.3.3 below.

The first proper census (after earlier trials) was held in June 1971. This was held in parallel with the last detailed count of national insurance cards in order to provide a link with the earlier series. Subsequent censuses have been taken in June of each year, but a full census is held only every third year, the censuses in the two intermediate years not covering employers who had fewer than three employees in the previous full census. For the purpose of the count the numbers employed by these firms in the full census are incorporated in the figures for the next two censuses. The censuses for 1971 and 1972 were partial censuses in this sense—the excluded firms being defined on the basis of returns provided in a trial census taken in June 1970.

In brief, the censuses are taken by means of a postal enquiry of employers. For this purpose the list of employers used is the list of 'pay points' from which employers send their PAYE payments to the Inland Revenue. Each pay point is asked to show on the return the numbers of *employees* for whom it holds pay records (not merely those for whom it pays tax—some employees, of course, may not come above relevant tax thresholds). Coverage extends to employees who are temporarily absent due to sickness, holidays, short-time, stoppages or any other reason, whether or not they are being paid. Employers are also asked to include employees who did not work on the census day but whom they employ regularly and who would work for them on some other day in the census week. In addition to the unemployed, who are automatically excluded, the following categories (amongst others not relevant to construction) are specifically excluded from the returns: working proprietors; partners; the self-employed; directors not under a contract of service; wives working for husbands; husbands working for wives; and former employees still on the payroll as pensioners only.

Some of the problems discussed above in connection with the card-count series raise their head again under the census of employment basis. The scope in terms of categories of labour covered is less of a problem in the sense that it is confined to employees. It is unfortunate, however, that so much of the labour force in construction is consequently not covered—returns in the 1971 census of population (10 per cent sample), for instance, suggest that nearly a fifth of the construction labour force (322 thousand out of 1,669 thousand) were self-employed ([QRL 94] Part II, p. 171 refers). The DE have subsequently compiled an estimated annual series of self-employment in the industry—see Section 6.2.3.4 below.

At a national level, the reliability of the series, even as an indicator of employees, is open to a number of potential sources of error. One is the fact that a complete census is not taken each year. The assumption that the aggregate number of employees at pay points with one or two employees does not vary significantly between full censuses has been checked and justified but at present there is no means of testing the validity of this assumption in the construction or any other individual industry. The tax evasion problem posed by the 'Lump', discussed earlier, also means that some employers in the construction industry will not appear on the Inland Revenue list of pay points and their employees may not be counted in the census. Another source of error concerns census information supplied by non-construction firms which may not identify separately a construction department and the employees concerned will then be wrongly classified to a non-construction activity. The monthly series is open to the same source of error as before since it has continued to be based on the DOE monthly sample estimates for the months between each June census, and these too remain subject to error.

Prima facie the regional classification as such (i.e. taking the national totals as being accurate) seems likely to be more reliable than hitherto because more employers are now asked to give the numbers of employees working at each of their business addresses (sites in construction). This no doubt gives better results than the procedure adopted in the card-count (see Section 6.2.3.1). But at the regional and local level an important consequence is the creation of substantial discontinuities between the old and new series (see especially the study by Allen and Yuill [B 2] referred to below).

The discontinuity between the card-count and census of employment series. The card-count series most closely comparable with the census series is, of course, the series of 'employees in employment' since the census does not cover labour other than employees. There are two major points of difference in principle between the old and new series. First, the card-count covered, as explained earlier, holders of cards whether or not they were in employment when the cards were due for exchange; some of these would be 'part-year workers' who take only seasonal or occasional work, others may be sick and without a job when the cards were due for exchange. The census, on the other hand, includes only workers who have jobs in the census week—part-year workers, therefore, are only covered if they were in employment in the census week. Secondly, the card-count statistics measured people rather than jobs—i.e. an employee may have had more than one job but he would only be counted once—whereas the census of employment measures jobs rather than people; for a person with, say, two regular jobs with different employers in the census week would be counted twice. The first of these factors would lead to a higher figure, and the second factor a lower figure, on the card-count compared with the census. In the event the census returns for construction in June 1971 gave a result 27,000 (over 2 per cent) less than the card-count figure.

For a critical account of the statistics, based on an analysis of local area data for Scotland, reference should be made to a study by Allen and Yuill [B 2] which draws attention to 'massive, widespread and erratic discontinuities at the local level' which, it is felt, arise partly out of inaccuracies in the card-count system. Whatever their cause, however, the Department is confident that the inaccuracies are likely to be relatively smaller as the level of aggregation increases.

6.2.3.3. *Continuous series 1959–73*. The DE has attempted to overcome the discontinuity in the series by using the information provided by the parallel enquiries of June 1971 to adjust the earlier series so as to provide continuous series at both the national and regional level. Adjustments are also made to allow for earlier sources of discontinuity including revisions to the SIC. An account of the adjustments (together with the series for Great Britain) is given in *DEG* [QRL 135] March 1975; a series for the UK was published in October 1975 and a regional series (covering the period 1965–75 only) was published in August 1976, both in the *DEG* [QRL 135]. However, the estimates provided in these series must be used with great caution for they depend, as is stressed in the article itself, upon the assumption that the relationship between the old and the new series at the time of the discontinuity can be applied retrospectively to the whole of the earlier series. This is a questionable assumption for it implies that whatever the reasons for the difference (definitional or otherwise) it would have remained comparable in its incidence over the whole of the earlier period. The regional series for construction are especially open to doubt for the reasons discussed earlier.

6.2.3.4. *Subsidiary employment series—Series for the self-employed from 1961*. The DE published an annual series of estimates of the number of self-employed persons (i.e. persons working on their own account with or without employees) for construction and other industries in Great Britain for the period 1961–74 in *DEG* [QRL 135] December 1976 (extended to 1975 in the issue for June 1977). A full account of the methods of estimation are given in these two articles and reference should be made to them for full details especially bearing in mind the lack of reliable sources and the particular growth of self-employment in the construction industry.

In brief, the data obtained in the censuses of population of 1961, 1966 and 1971 are taken as benchmark figures and estimates are made for other years by interpolation using such other information as is available. No such source is available for the period 1961–6 and the annual series is based on the assumption of a linear change between the two dates. From 1966 to 1974 use was made of a $\frac{1}{2}$ per cent sample of Class 2 national insurance cards due for exchange in June by employers and self-employed made by the

DHSS. For 1975 (the latest estimate) use has been made of unpublished data obtained in the 1973 and 1975 EEC Labour Force Surveys [QRL 313] and [QRL 183] to give a percentage change.

A number of comments are in order. First, the census of population bench mark data (considered in Section 6.3) are themselves open to error, particularly since self-employed construction workers may have chosen not to record themselves as such (especially if they were evading tax and national insurance contributions and felt that their status, despite the strictly confidential nature of the census, might be revealed to the authorities). Secondly, the information from the DHSS sample of Class 2 cards is open to error, not only because of sampling, but also because of non-compliance by members of the 'Lump'. Likewise the straight line interpolations for years prior to 1966 are naturally open to error since there are no grounds, as far as the author is aware, for believing the growth to have been linear (it will be noticed that the subsequent estimates between 1966 and 1971 are not linear). Since 1971 the estimates for construction in particular have been agreed each year with the DOE ('which had access to other sources of information') but it is well to bear in mind that the DOE itself had no satisfactory means of estimation (the DOE sources are discussed in Sections 4.2 and 4.4.3). Likewise, since 1974 the EEC Labour Force Surveys may not provide a reliable indicator of change either because the sample element of self-employed construction workers was small or because of a failure of such workers to report their true status or both.

Lest the remarks made here be misinterpreted, it should be stressed that they are not meant to deny the value of the efforts made to provide a statistical series for the self-employed. On the contrary, having criticized this very deficiency in the series derived from censuses of employment, they are to be welcomed. The remarks are meant to do no more than to warn the unwary of the potential defects of the estimates, especially those for the construction sector where the number of self-employed has been subject to such a pronounced change over the last two decades or so. The DE itself does not pay particular attention to the construction sector, but in general terms it has set out clearly the basis of its estimates.

Direct labour—local authorities. From 1952 to 1974 three separate annual series for the employment of construction workers by local authorities (classified by full-time/part-time and sex) in England, in Wales and in Scotland separately were compiled by the DE on the basis of a special return from local authorities which was issued in order to allow construction labour to be appropriately classified to construction under the SIC and not under 'Local Government Service'. For England and Wales, the series was replaced in 1975 with quarterly data obtained in 'Joint Manpower Watch' surveys established in accordance with a circular on *Local Government Manpower* [B 268] and conducted by LACSAB. For Scotland similar surveys have been conducted since 1976 by the National Joint Council for Local Authority Services in Scotland. The results are published in *DEG* [QRL 135] and former *MOLG* [QRL 190]; the new quarterly data are also published as a *Press Notice* [QRL 233], in *MDS* [QRL 195] and, for Wales alone, in *Welsh Local Government Financial Statistics* [QRL 361]. These data differ from those obtained in censuses carried out by the DOE (considered in Section 4.3.2) ostensibly because the DOE attempt to cover employment of all building and civil engineering workers in all departments of the authority whereas the statistics referred to here are narrower in scope, being confined to employment in separate direct works departments as such.

Central government, local authorities and public corporations. Since 1959 an annual series has been compiled by the CSO, based partly on DE statistics, showing employment of construction direct labour by each of these three parts of the public sector separately (together with a fourth series for the private sector) and published in an article (currently annual) on 'Employment in the public and private sectors of the UK economy' in *ET* [QRL 147]. The series for local authorities and the private sector are based on *DE* sources. The other series are CSO estimates (again they differ from the data collected by the DOE—see Section 4.3.3).

Age analyses. Annual analyses of the age distribution of employees by sex in Great Britain were made on the basis of 1 per cent samples of national insurance records from 1950 to 1971 and published in the *MOLG* [QRL 190] and later the *DEG* [QRL 135], last appearing in Vol. 80, 1972, p. 535. Industrial breakdowns were not made for the following year (1972) and since then no analyses at all have been made due to changes in the administration of the national insurance scheme. It is understood that analyses by age and industry for some years before 1950 are available from the DE Statistics Division on request (see [B 241] p. 4 for further details).

Young persons entering employment. An annual series was compiled for the period 1951–74, classified according to region, sex and class of employment, based on analyses of national insurance cards. The series were published in *DEG* [QRL 135] and labour statistics *Yearbooks* [QRL 59]; series for Scotland and Wales were included in [QRL 306] and [QRL 142] respectively. The series was terminated due to the abolition of cards; it is understood that alternative methods of collection are being investigated.

6.2.4. *Comparison of MOL–DE and Other Employment Series*

6.2.4.1. *The MOL–DE and the MOW–DOE series.* Reconciliation of the DE (and former MOL) series with the MOW–DOE employment series raises some difficult problems since the series differ not only in level but also in rate of change. Needless to say, these facts pose a highly inconvenient dilemma for the potential user. All that one can do here is to summarize what would appear to be the major factors that help to account for differences and to suggest possible reasons for different rates of change being shown. The following factors would help to account for differences in level:

(a) Before 1955 the MOW series were not classified in accordance with the SIC. Partial figures were published based on the 'main trades' because these more closely coincided with the then MOL series, but the correspondence was not precise. The MOW series tended to provide a more comprehensive coverage of construction labour.

(b) The MOW series covered *male* operatives aged *16 years* and over (despite the fact that the school-leaving age was 15 years) until November 1954 when coverage was changed to *male and female* aged *15 years* and over 'whose national insurance cards are held by you' whereas the MOL series covered persons, male and female, aged 15 years and over throughout (until the raising of the school-leaving age to 16 years in 1973 when both series were changed accordingly).

(c) Coverage in terms of categories of labour has also been at variance. The MOW monthly series has been confined to operatives employed, whereas the MOL–DE covers manual and non-manual employees (as well as the unemployed up to 1971). Adjustment can be made to deduct the unemployed from the MOL–DE series but, unlike manufacturing industry, data are not available in the MOL–DE series for non-manual workers. In the MOW–DOE series separate figures for Working Principals were collected throughout (published only from 1959) but figures for A(P)TC staff were not collected until 1965 (Section 4.4.3 refers).

(d) Differences in classification by industry are likely to be present now and to have been present in the past. Currently it is possible that the register of PAYE pay points used for the census of employment may well differ from the register maintained by the DOE. In the past the methods used for classifying to industry under the card-count system were not likely to produce a classification identical with that obtained in the MOW–DOE surveys.

(e) Differences in the classification of direct labour. An insight here is given by the data collected in the two enquiries for local authority direct labour which is a clearly defined sector presenting no 'register problem'. Comparison of the two sets of data reveals that some labour is classified to construction in the MOW–DOE enquiries that is not similarly classified in the MOL–DE series. As indicated above, the tendency is for the MOL–DE series to be less comprehensive than the MOW–DOE series. However, a special enquiry in 1964 revealed that a substantial volume of labour was being wrongly classified under the then MOL system to 'Local Government Service' rather than Construction (see *MOLG* [QRL 190] February 1965, p. 59). Differences also occur in the classification of other direct labour—compare the public sector analyses compiled by the CSO referred to in Section 6.2.3.4 above and the MOW–DOE data (Section 4.4).

(f) The differences in the timing of the respective enquiries.

(g) Random effects arising from sampling errors, inaccuracies in returns, and, possibly, processing errors which would not lead to systematic bias in either series.

It is difficult to offer explanations for differences in rates of change of the two sets of data (the monthly series should not differ since the MOL–DE series were moved by reference to the MOW–DOE series). The major systematic factor at work in the construction industry over recent years has been the trend towards 'self-employment' on the part of many former 'employees', but for this to be a factor here would require it to have had a differential incidence in the two sets of data over time. To the author's knowledge there is no evidence on which to make any judgement about this and it is also difficult to speculate. A comparison of the data themselves from these and other sources for 1971 and 1974 is made in Table 6.1 below.

Table 6.1
Construction Employment Statistics for Great Britain—Comparison of Sources

Source:	Census of Population (10% sample)	DOE*		Dept. of Employment		BSO Census of Production†
		Sample	Census	Card Count Series	Census of Employment Series	
Section reference:	6.3	4.4.3	4.2 and 4.3	6.2.3.1	6.2.3.2	5.3

EMPLOYEES (Thousands)

1971 April	1347	1462		1243		
June		1473		1249	1222	
Oct.		1454	1405		1222	
1974 Avge.		1409			1288	1419
June		1394			1290	
Oct.		1410	1448		1292	

TOTAL EMPLOYMENT (Thousands)

1971 April	1669					
June				(1573)‡	(1546)‡	
Oct.			1486 (1770)			
1974 Avge.					(1718)‡	1475
June						
Oct.			1560 (1822)			

* The figures are of recorded employment of contractors and direct labour except those shown in parentheses which include DOE estimates of unrecorded labour. The figure for 'employees' excludes self-employed 'Working Principals' but it is thought that some self-employed labour may have been returned as operatives or APTC staff. The June figures are DOE estimates since they make no enquiry in June. Figures after June 1974 were based on a more comprehensive register of firms (Section 4.1.3 refers); the average for 1974 is also estimated on the new basis.

† The figures show average numbers during the year of return; they are not entirely independent of DOE data—a large part of the figure is estimated (41 per cent on a UK basis), the estimate being based on DOE statistics.

‡ These figures represent employees in employment plus the DE's estimate of the number of 'employers and self-employed' in construction (*DEG* [QRL 135], December 1976, p. 1347).

Sources: *Census of Population:* [QRL 94] Part II, pp. 171 and 176; *DOE data: HCS* [QRL 168] Nos. 3 and 17 (Table 12) and No. 18, p. 69; *Department of Employment data: DEG* [QRL 135] various issues; *BSO Census of Production:* [QRL 76] 1974, pp. 8 and 10.

6.2.4.2. MOL–DE employment statistics and Censuses of Production. Currently the following factors would help to account for differences between the construction employment data in the COP and the DE series:

(a) Differences in timing: data for a point in time (DE census) contrasted with averages over a period of twelve months (COP).
(b) Classification differences: the enquiries are not based on the same register of firms.
(c) Probable differences in the coverage of public sector direct labour.
(d) Errors due to sampling, non-response and inaccuracies.

The same factors apply to the former MOL–DE series based on card-counts up to 1971, although in this case classification differences may have arisen from the nature of the card-count system and the information available to classify cards by industry. Unfortunately it is not possible to attribute orders of magnitude to these potential causes of difference. A comparison of the figures from the 1974 census of production (the latest available at the time of writing) with those from the DE employment census and the DOE construction census is made in Table 6.1 above.

6.3. Construction in the Censuses of Population in Great Britain

6.3.1. *Introduction*

Apart from a brief reference below to sources of information for pre-war censuses, consideration here of the statistics collected in the censuses of population is confined to the four censuses taken in the post-war period in Great Britain: 1951, 1961, 1966 and 1971. Censuses taken at the same time in Northern Ireland are considered in Chapter 9. The next census of population is due to be taken in 1981, plans for a mid-term census in 1976 having been cancelled.

General guides to the censuses are available elsewhere: an official guide to the censuses taken before 1951 has been provided in [B 240] and updated to 1966 in [B 233]; a useful study covering censuses up to 1966 has also been made by Benjamin [B 13] and the subject will also be covered in a forthcoming review in the present series [B 158]. We focus our attention here on the availability and interpretation of information of relevance to construction and on the points of difference with other sources. Background information about the conduct of each census, the processing of results and other explanatory material is contained in *General Reports* on each census, except 1966, as follows: [B 194] for 1951, [B 196] for 1961 and a forthcoming report for 1971 [B 195].

Two aspects of the census make it an extremely important source of information. First, the means by which it is conducted—particulars being recorded in respect of each individual with completed schedules being collected by enumerators with a duty to ensure that they have been properly completed—makes it possible to collect particularly detailed information and, generally speaking, particularly reliable information. Secondly, the information collected provides statistics of a kind which are either not available from other sources or which, although duplicated elsewhere, provide a valuable check on the accuracy of other sources.

6.3.2. *The Available Data*

The analysis of the 'occupied' population rests on a basic distinction between 'occupation' and 'industry'—i.e. on a distinction between the occupations of *individuals* and the particular *industries* in which the individuals follow their occupations. The analysis by occupation is made in accordance with a classification which is published separately for each census—[B 193], [B 200], [B 201] and [B 202] respectively. These follow a system in which certain occupations are grouped together including one group for 'construction occupations'. However, it should be appreciated that, as a consequence of the distinction between industry and occupation, persons in construction occupations may be occupied in a variety of non-construction industries and likewise, persons occupied in the construction industry may be classified to non-construction occupations. Classification by industry in the post-war period has been in accordance with the SIC (see Appendix I). For the 1951 census, but not subsequently, a separate guide to the industrial classification was issued [B 192].[1] Within these classifications subsidiary analyses are made according to a number of characteristics of the labour force: age, sex, employment status (employed/self-employed and various sub-divisions of these categories), social class, socio-economic group, marital condition of female workers, nationality, etc.

Regional and local data. Many of the industrial and occupational analyses are broken down according to region and local administrative areas. These analyses, unlike some of those available from other sources, classify each individual, as far as possible, according to the actual place of work (including building sites in the case of construction) specified on the census forms. In some cases, however, place of work is not specified, in which case the classification is made according to area of usual residence, if known, or to the area of enumeration. Generally, however, the census statistics provide the most accurate source of regional and local area employment data for construction. Since 1961 information has also been obtained about the migration of labour from one region to another over defined periods prior to the census.

Education and qualifications. A major development in the range of information collected in the census of population in recent years has been the inclusion of questions about qualifications since 1961. The analyses according to industry provide data for the number of qualified persons analysed according to subject and type of qualification. For further details reference should be made to Section 6.6.3.2. Education tables provide information about the ages at which full-time education ceased.

Publication references. References to the various volumes in which the results are published are given in the *Quick Reference List* which precedes the Appendices in this volume. More detailed, unpublished, tabulations are often also available from the OPCS on payment of a fee to cover the costs of reproduction.

6.3.3. *Interpretation*

The principal merits of the census of population data follow from the fact that information is recorded, as we stressed earlier, separately for each individual in the population. This makes possible classifications of the labour force in greater detail and with a greater accuracy than is generally possible in other types of enquiry in which returns are made in respect of whole groups of persons, rather than individuals, and which may be critically dependent upon the adequacy of sampling frames, sampling methods and levels of response, etc.

The census statistics themselves, however, are not without error. There are three

---

[1] In the 1951 census (under the 1948 SIC) construction was sub-divided by MLH and the civil engineering MLH was further sub-divided between civil engineering contracting and open-cast coal mining; in subsequently revised SICs the construction Order has not been sub-divided.

principal sources of actual or potential error. First, there are sampling errors. Although the decennial censuses (1951, 1961, 1971) were indeed censuses in the sense of being based on 100 per cent enumerations of the population, much of the detailed information relating to occupation, industry and qualifications in 1961 and 1971 was based on samples (generally 10 per cent). In 1961, 10 per cent of households received more detailed questionnaires; in 1971, 10 per cent of completed questionnaires were analysed in greater detail than the other 90 per cent. The 1966 census was taken wholly on a sample basis. Details of the sampling methodology are given in the relevant reports coupled with further background information in *General Reports* [B 196] and [B 195] (no such report has been published in respect of the 1966 census). The second source of error is bias. This was detected in the sample element of the 1961 census and 'bias correction factors' (printed in the census reports) need to be applied to the published results.

A third source of error arises from inaccuracies in the completion of the returns and errors of subsequent classification. Inaccuracies in the completion of the forms are, of course, difficult to detect but some information is available from quality checks (post-enumeration surveys) held following the 1961 and 1966 censuses—particulars are given in [B 196] and [B 63]. In addition, comparisons were made after the 1951 and 1961 censuses of death registration records for a sample of those dying soon after the census in order to check the occupational classification. This showed a disturbingly low level of agreement. However, this evidence cannot be taken at its face value as evidence of mis-classification in the census, since death registration records may themselves not necessarily be valid. The fact that the informants in each case differ (the man himself at the census, a relative at death) tend to make discrepancies likely. Details of these checks are given in [B 194] and [B 196]. It is felt that the accuracy of the occupational classification has improved over the years (see [B 13]).

The classification by industry is made by matching information about the name, address and business of employer to an industrially classified register in the census office. The classification, therefore, is not solely dependent upon the information provided about industry on the census form. Nonetheless, it is not likely that absolute accuracy is achieved—the possibilities remain of inaccurate or incomplete information on the census forms and deficiencies in the register. *A priori*, however, it would seem plausible to suggest that the twin sources of information in the census of population make it more, rather than less, likely that the industrial classification obtained in the census is superior to other sources. Certainly the 1961 post-enumeration survey found very little error of response, in general, for this category.

6.3.4. *Comparison of the Census of Population and Other Employment Data*

In general the reasons which can be put forward for the differences that exist between the census of population statistics for employment in the construction industry and those available from other sources are partly definitional differences and partly hypotheses that seem plausible but are not readily open to verification, certainly not in any quantifiable way. A comparison of the results themselves from the latest—1971—census of population with other available sources for that year is made in Table 6.1 included as part of Section 6.2.4.1 above.

6.3.4.1. *Comparison with MOL–DE data.* To date all the post-war censuses were taken during the currency of the system based on counts of national insurance cards (Section 6.2 refers) and the discussion here is couched in terms of that system. The differences between the card-counts and the DE censuses of employment (by which they were replaced in June 1971) were examined in Section 6.2.3.2. A general discussion and comparison of differences between the census of population and MOL–DE statistics, although not from the point of view of particular industries, will be found in [QRL 89] Appendix A and [QRL 58] Appendix A. From the point of view of particular industries, comparison is best made of the MOL–DE 'employees' series since the MOL–DE data for employers and self-employed persons are themselves estimates based on the census of population. As far as construction is concerned, the following factors may help to account for the differences:

Differences of definition:

(a) Persons who held national insurance cards, and were therefore counted (in principle) in the MOL–DE data, would only be classified as 'economically active' in the census if they were actually working in the week before the census.

(b) Persons who were temporarily out of employment because of sickness or injury would normally still have a national insurance card, and because they were not available for work would not be registered as unemployed; they are therefore included in the MOL–DE estimates of employees in employment. However, in the census figures they would be classified as 'out of employment, sick' (from 1961; in 1951 no distinction was made between 'out of employment, sick' and 'out of employment, other').

(c) Persons covered in the MOL–DE card-count would not be covered in the census if they were out of the country on census night.

Other differences. Other differences arise out of the nature of the card-count system which leads to the inclusion of certain groups of persons who would normally not be classified as 'economically active' in the census of population:

(d) Full-time students and school pupils over the school-leaving age who work in their free time and held national insurance cards would be included in the MOL–DE data but excluded from the census (in which they would be classed as 'economically inactive').

(e) Seasonal and irregular workers who were not working in the week before the census and were not intending to get work in the immediate future.

(f) Persons with national insurance cards who also had jobs but failed to declare them at the census.

(g) Some persons may describe themselves as self-employed in the census but hold an *employee's* national insurance card and are thus counted as employees in the MOL–DE data. This could well be the case in the construction industry with persons who may have been working under labour-only sub-contract and who may regard themselves (rightly or wrongly) as self-employed.

(h) The MOL–DE statistics are not based on full counts and are thus open to error on account of that fact, as well as possible industrial mis-classification. Likewise, the census statistics are also subject to error (see above).

(i) Finally there are differences in timing between the censuses (taken in April) and the card-counts (counts by industry in June with subsequent monthly figures estimated on the basis of MOW–DOE employment data).

6.3.4.2. *Comparison with MOW–DOE data.* Consideration of the differences between the census of population statistics for employment in the construction industry and the MOW–DOE series may be aided perhaps by reference to the respective comparisons between the MOL–DE and MOW–DOE series (Section 6.2.4.1) and the MOL–DE and the census of population above. Once again, it is only possible to suggest the kinds of reason why differences occur without being able to quantify them. Some of the principal factors are as follows:

(a) In 1951 the then MOW statistics were not classified in accordance with the SIC (as were the census of population statistics) and were restricted to male operatives—see Section 6.2.4.1 above, sub-paras. (a)–(c).
(b) Deficiencies in coverage of the MOW–DOE data due to an incomplete register of firms.
(c) Some persons may be covered in the MOW–DOE data since they were on the pay-roll of a construction firm on the pay-day in a particular week, but may not be classified as 'economically active' in the census of population—e.g. full-time students who work in their free time (classed as 'economically inactive').
(d) Finally, there are, once again, potential differences due to differences in the timing of enquiries and errors due to sampling and other causes including inaccuracies in the returns.

6.4. Construction Industry Training Board (CITB) Statistics—Great Britain

Broadly speaking the statistics collected by the CITB for Great Britain, which was established in 1964 under the terms of the *Industrial Training Act 1964*, fall into three categories:

(1) Manpower statistics obtained from all firms on the CITB register in the 'Levy Return'.
(2) Training statistics.
(3) Information from *ad hoc* surveys.

In addition, financial information is published about the levy itself and the grants made for training purposes. We deal with each of these categories in turn below. Data collected by the CITB for Northern Ireland are considered in Section 9.3.6.

6.4.1. *CITB Levy Return—Employment Statistics*

The levy return is obtained in April and October each year and provides information about the number of employees (trainees shown separately), the number of self-employed labour-only workers employed and information about the degree of difficulty being experienced in filling vacancies, all broken down by occupation (distinguishing thirty-four categories including APTC staff, operatives and canteen workers—the same categories, since 1975, as in the DOE censuses—Section 4.2 refers). Summary results are published in the *CITB Annual Report* [QRL 255]. Information is also collected on the levy return about the size of the payroll in monetary terms and labour-only payments made and received but no analyses are published.

Quite apart from their relevance to the activities of the CITB itself, the employment statistics collected in the levy return are of special interest because they provide information not available from other sources (e.g. employment of self-employed LOSC workers). However, it is important to note their limitations: the data obtained relate solely to firms registered for the levy and must be interpreted, therefore, in the light of the scope and coverage of the register.

6.4.2. *The CITB Register*

It is essential to note that the scope of the industry, as defined for the purposes for which the CITB was established, does not coincide with that currently defined in the SIC (see Appendix I). There are a number of notable differences. For instance, certain aspects of structural engineering that come within the scope of construction in the SIC come within the scope of the Engineering Industry Training Board rather than the CITB. On the other hand, joinery manufacturers producing industrialized building components and prefabricated buildings or sections of buildings, and firms constructing shop and office fittings do come within the scope of the CITB but are not classified to construction in the SIC. Likewise, the activities of local authority and other direct labour organizations, some of which are embraced by the SIC definition, are excluded from the scope of the CITB. For precise details of the scope of the definition of the industry for CITB purposes, reference should be made to the statutory authority.[2]

How far the CITB register succeeds in covering all firms within scope is naturally difficult to assess, but it would be surprising if the CITB achieved greater success than the DOE, whose construction register has suffered from admitted deficiencies (see Section 4.1.3). For firms which undertake training there is, of course, a financial incentive to register in order to obtain training grants. But for others there is the disincentive that registration entails an obligation (with the exception noted below) to pay the training levy. Certain firms, however, are expressly excluded, namely firms *without employees* (whereas the DOE endeavours to be more comprehensive covering all firms). There is, further, less incentive to cover firms below a certain size in that the levy is payable only on payrolls above a defined sum (currently £15,000). The incentive exists, however, to the extent that small firms can grow during a year, and CITB grants are payable to all firms on the register whether or not they are excluded from levy.

The CITB register was initially compiled in 1964 on the basis of one maintained by the then Ministry of Labour. This was confined almost entirely to employers with five or more employees—a total number of 37,000 which was eventually reduced to 34,200 upon registration (details are given in the first *Annual Report* [QRL 255] for the period to 31 March 1965—*House of Commons Paper 281 Session 1964/5*—paras. 14–17). Comparison with the construction register maintained by the DOE and its predecessors

---

[2] Currently this is SI 1973 No. 160 as amended by SI 1974 No. 2081. The initial definition appeared in SI 1964 No. 1079 and subsequent amendments in SI 1967 No. 924 and SI 1971 No. 1766. Further amendments may be made from time to time.

is of interest although direct comparison is not appropriate because of the difference in scope. As at April 1964, the then MPBW register recorded 62,000 firms employing one or more *operatives*. The current comparison is similar: approximately 37,000 on the CITB register (*Annual Report 1975/6* [QRL 255] p. 41) as against 60,000 employing two or more persons (October 1975) on the DOE register. The situation may change in the near future, however, for action has recently been taken under the *Statistics of Trade Act* to allow the DOE to pass the names and addresses from its register to the CITB.

6.4.3. *CITB Training Statistics*

In addition to the Levy Return statistics about the number of trainees employed, information is also collected about the number of trainees, on 'off-the-job' apprentice training schemes (returns from CITB regional offices) and numbers in training at CITB national training centres. Data are also collected about the numbers on first-year craft courses in colleges of further education (also in returns from CITB regional offices). Most of these data are collected for the use of the CITB itself, but summaries appear in the *Annual Reports* [QRL 255].

6.4.4. Ad hoc *Surveys*

The CITB undertakes a certain amount of survey work on an *ad hoc* basis. Such work is generally directed at a specific internal policy area, and is not therefore published or made widely available. Recent surveys, for example, have covered the specialist building sector, the electrician labour market and the qualifications of building services staff. The first covered a 50 per cent sample of specialist sub-contracting firms in the scope of the CITB in February 1976, obtaining information on employment by craft, training, turnover and age structure. The second survey, taken in July 1976, was a 1 in 30 sample of skilled electrician members of EETPU and covered current employment status (employee, self-employed, unemployed, etc.) and duration, type of work done, industry and mobility between industries, training, grading (if any) and age. The third survey, taken in February 1977, covered all medium and large heating, ventilating and plumbing and certain other firms on the CITB register obtaining information about the number of managerial, supervisory and technical staff employed, according to level of qualification and occupation. Other questions were concerned with expected future trends in the employment of graduates. Unpublished reports on the second and third surveys may be made available to '*bona fide*' enquirers on request—[B 215] and [B 309] respectively.

The results of a series of 'Regional Manpower Surveys' carried out between 1972 and 1974 under NFBTE auspices were published by the NFBTE in [QRL 188]. These covered NFBTE members in the London Region in 1972 and in both the London and Midland Regions in 1973 and 1974, and provided information about numbers employed, trainees and LOSC in the main building trades and other occupations, labour turnover and labour requirements. The results of an earlier manpower study carried out in the Northern Region in 1970 were reported in [QRL 211]. This study was essentially an exploratory one concerned with methodology for assessing future manpower needs. The report itself provides background information and the employment statistics obtained for APTC staff, operatives and apprentices, providing a much more detailed occupational breakdown than that required in the DOE censuses.

6.4.5. *Grant and Levy Payments*

Statistics of grants received and levies paid analysed according to the main activity of the firms are published in the *Annual Reports* [QRL 255]. These include analyses of the types of training leading to grant aid.

6.5. Labour Training and Education Statistics for Great Britain

6.5.1. *Background*

In 1943 a Building Apprenticeship and Training Council (BATC) was appointed by the Minister of Works 'to observe and advise on all matters concerning the recruitment, education and training of young persons for craftsmanship and management in the building industry and to encourage the development of apprenticeship schemes on a comprehensive basis'. The Council established a National Apprenticeship Scheme and, with effect from 1 November 1945, a system for the registration of apprentices employed in accordance with the terms of the scheme. It also recommended that regular surveys of the number of apprentices employed in the industry should be made and, acting on this recommendation, the Ministry of Works conducted the first of an annual series of censuses in August 1949. These continued until 1975 when the scope of the enquiry was widened to cover all trainees.

The BATC continued to carry out the registration functions until January 1953 when arrangements were made for the work in England and Wales to be taken over by the National Joint Council for the Building Industry (NJCBI), and in Scotland by the equivalent Scottish Council.[3] The BATC itself remained in existence until 1956. In 1964 responsibility for the training needs of the industry was placed in the hands of the newly established Construction Industry Training Board (Section 6.4 refers).

6.5.2. *Apprentice Registration Statistics*

Statistics of the numbers of apprentices registered (according to craft and region) were published in the reports of the BATC: [QRL 62], [QRL 63] and [QRL 64] for the period up to mid-1955. These also included some data on apprenticeships completed. Since 1955 registration statistics have not been published but they are available on request from the registration bodies referred to above. It should be noted that the scope of these registration statistics is limited. First, they refer only to those apprentices undergoing training under certain approved conditions and who are formally indentured, whereas the census statistics (see below) cover apprentices employed under

---

[3] Administered by the *National Joint Apprenticeship Board* of the Council in England and Wales (renamed *National Joint Training Commission* in 1971) and by the *General Council Administering the Apprenticeship Scheme of the Building Industry in Scotland* (renamed *Scottish Building Apprenticeship and Training Council*.)

unwritten, as well as written, agreements. Secondly, they refer to 'building' trades narrowly defined. For other trades (e.g. civil engineering, electrical, plumbing) apprenticeship schemes are administered by other bodies (a list of these bodies is available from the CITB, since to qualify for training grants from the CITB trainees must be registered with these bodies). Thirdly, even for 'building' trades as such certain apprentices *may* not be registered (e.g. those employed in the maintenance departments of non-construction firms and public authorities).

Finally, it should be noted that apprentices are not necessarily registered in their first year of training; thus series showing the number of registrations in a twelve-month period do not provide an accurate indication of entry to the industry at this level. In this connection an allied series of interest (now discontinued) was provided in the analyses of young persons entering employment (which distinguished apprenticeship and other classes of employment) compiled annually by the DE and its predecessors from 1951 to 1974—see Section 6.2.3.4.

6.5.3. *Employment of Apprentices/Trainees*

The annual censuses of apprentices (later 'trainees') conducted by the MOW and its successor departments from 1949 were carried out as integral parts of the censuses of employment and output covering contractors and direct labour which are considered fully in Sections 3.5 and 3.6 (pre-1955) and Sections 4.2 and 4.3 (post-1955). In brief, statistics have been collected as follows:

(1) 1949–74 (except 1956): Apprentices employed by craft and type of agreement—see Sections 3.5.4.3, 3.6.2.2, 4.2.3.5 and 4.3.2.2.
(2) 1949–55: Intake of apprentices by craft over the preceding twelve months—see Sections 3.5.4.3 and 3.6.2.2.
(3) From 1975: Number of trainees by occupation. These statistics cover persons in all occupations (manual and non-manual, apprentice and non-apprentice crafts) and of all ages—see Sections 4.2.3.5 and 4.3.2.2. With effect from 1977 responsibility for the collection of these data from contractors is to be transferred to the CITB. Earlier statistics of 'operatives under training for new or additional skills' were collected in the censuses from 1965 to 1969 but the results were not published.

In addition to the census data the BATC reported statistics for 1939, 1944 and 1946, based on limited surveys, in [QRL 61] and [QRL 62].

6.5.4. *Government Training Statistics*

In addition to the training carried out by employers, referred to above, training is also carried out in Skillcentres, formerly called Government Training Centres (GTC), and in educational institutions under government vocational training schemes which were administered by the Department of Employment and its predecessors until 1974 when responsibility was transferred to the newly established Manpower Services Commission (MSC). These schemes have been in operation for the whole of the post-war period (and earlier—a useful account of their development up to 1973 will be found in [B 117]).

After the stimulus provided in the early post-war years by the resettlement needs of ex-servicemen, little training was undertaken until the 1960s. The schemes were then expanded considerably, placing particular emphasis upon training for the construction industry, and then again from 1972 with the initiation of the Training Opportunities Scheme (TOPS). Summary statistics of the numbers *completing* training in various building crafts under government training schemes in the years from 1959 to 1970 were given in *ABCS* [QRL 32] 1970 edition; subsequent data are available from the DE (training statistics were at one time regularly published in *MOLG* [QRL 190] but these did not provide craft breakdowns). Currently, occupational analyses of the numbers trained under the TOPS are available on request from the TSA. A report of a survey of the post-training careers of GTC trainees, carried out in 1968 and 1969 by the Government Social Survey, giving separate analyses for construction and other trades was published in [B 77].

Training in construction trades is also given in centres run by the CITB. Relevant statistics are given in CITB *Annual Reports* [QRL 255] along with figures for those undergoing training in public educational establishments and within companies. CITB statistics in general are considered in Section 6.4.

6.5.5. *Education Statistics*

6.5.5.1. *Official compilations.* Official statistics are compiled annually to show:

(a) Numbers following courses at grant-aided establishments leading to recognized qualifications in building according to the type of qualification (from City and Guilds qualifications to degree) and mode of attendance (full-time, part-time, etc.).
(b) Numbers released by construction employers to follow part-time day courses.
(c) Entries and successes in examinations according to subject and qualification.

These are published in [QRL 325] Vol. 3 for England and Wales, and [QRL 309] for Scotland. Summary statistics for the UK are published in [QRL 153].

Interpretation. The volumes referred to above contain notes on the statistics which need to be read before using them. Perhaps the most important point bearing on their interpretation is that the count of numbers on the courses refers to the numbers *enrolled*; since it is possible to enrol for more than one course there may be an element of double-counting. It should also be noted that an enrolment does not imply that a complete course is being followed.

The Further Education Statistical Record. The statistics referred to above are based upon returns, obtained from colleges, in which the total numbers of students under certain pre-determined headings are given. Recently a new scheme has been initiated, known as the 'Further Education Statistical Record', in which data are recorded individually for each student. The advantage of this system is that particular analyses and cross-classifications can be made as the need arises and do not need to be arranged in advance. Further details will be found in [B 12]. A similar system operates for universities—the Universities' Statistical Record—for details see [B 42].

6.5.5.2. *Unofficial compilations—Institute of Building (IOB) Surveys*. This survey has been conducted by the Institute annually since 1966/7 on the basis of a questionnaire sent to universities, polytechnics, colleges of technology and further education and technical colleges in the UK and, since 1970/1, the Irish Republic. The survey covers students on Degree and other General Building courses but does not cover students on craft or specialist technician courses. The results are published in the IOB journal [QRL 69] showing the numbers on each type of course and year by country (currently England and Wales, Scotland and Ireland) together with separate statistics for students on courses for IOB examinations. In some earlier years analyses were also made in terms of the students' actual or intended (as far as this could be ascertained) field of employment.

SAAT Education Facilities Surveys. The Society of Architectural and Associated Technicians (SAAT) has conducted a similar survey to the IOB since 1967 except that it is confined to the UK and covers only ONC and HNC courses. The results are not formally published but are brought together in [QRL 150] showing a summary by year and course together with the return made by every institution covered in the survey.

ILEA Survey of Technician Students 1975. This survey was commissioned by the ILEA in connection with the development of technician-level courses in the construction field. The results, published in [QRL 24], provide a profile of the ILEA student population studying subjects concerned with the 'built environment' at technician level. The specific subjects covered are: sex, age, residence, origins and mobility of students; school and college background; details of employment, attitudes and preferences in relation to teaching methods and curriculum; careers choice and advice, and future studying intentions. Brief details of a similar study carried out by the East Anglian Regional Advisory Council for Further Education in 1972 are given in an article describing the findings of the ILEA survey in *Building* [QRL 60] 24 June 1977, pp. 99, 101.

6.6. Qualified Manpower in the Construction Industry in Great Britain

6.6.1. *Introduction*

The term 'qualified manpower' may be used in more than one sense. When enquiries were initiated in this field, in the mid-1950s, it was narrowly defined in terms of persons possessing certain precisely defined scientific and technological qualifications. The term is now used more widely, however, to cover all persons with qualifications at a level above GCE 'A' level or equivalent. Useful surveys of qualified manpower statistics in general are given in [B 173], [B 171] and [B 34]. In construction the main demand for qualified manpower arises in connection with the design of buildings and other structures and related engineering and surveying services. This demand is partly filled by employment within construction firms and direct labour undertakings, but much of this labour is employed in independent architectural, engineering and surveying practices. Statistics about the latter are considered separately in Part IV of this Review which deals with information about the construction professions in general. In this Section attention is confined to the statistics relating to the construction industry in a narrow sense, i.e. contracting and direct labour organizations.

In the construction industry the Institute of Building (IOB) has evolved as an institution performing a professional role for persons concerned with building in various managerial, technical, administrative and educational positions and setting its own examinations. However, the Institute is not a 'qualifying association' in the same sense as other professional institutions are and for this reason it is not considered in Part IV of this Review along with other professional institutions related to the construction industry. For the same reason statistics relating to IOB membership are less comprehensive than other more general official enquiries relating to the employment of qualified manpower in the industry. We examine these sources first and then note special surveys of employment on R & D and of the earnings of qualified manpower.

6.6.2. *Institute of Building Statistics*

Details of the membership of the IOB are given in an annual *Yearbook and Directory of Members* [QRL 364]. Surveys of the membership have been conducted in 1966—reported in the *Yearbook* [QRL 364] showing details of the functions performed, field of employment and analyses by size of firm—and in 1975 providing similar information but reported in greater detail than the previous survey in [QRL 338]. The later survey also obtained information about the members who were also members of other professional institutions. IOB education statistics are considered in Section 6.5.5.2.

6.6.3. *General Statistics Relating to the Employment and Supply of Qualified Manpower in the Construction Industry*

Statistics about numbers employed are available from three sources:

(1) Triennial sample surveys, 1956–68.
(2) Censuses of Population, 1961–71.
(3) Annual DOE Censuses, 1965–74.

Information about the total supply (including the unemployed) is available from the censuses of population. The TSA National Training Survey in 1975 also included questions on qualifications, occupation and employment (or unemployment) but the results are as yet unpublished—see Section 6.7.6 for further details.

6.6.3.1. *Triennial sample surveys 1956–68.* These surveys were voluntary employer-based surveys of the employment of qualified scientists and engineers (QSEs) —defined, briefly, as persons holding degree or equivalent qualifications in engineering, technology and science. For the precise definition used see the reports referred to below. Architecture and surveying, both of particular relevance to construction, were not covered. The scope of the enquiries was later extended to cover technicians (see below). The enquiries were carried out by the MOL for the Committee on Scientific Manpower of the Advisory Council for Scientific Policy (later the Committee on

Manpower Resources for Science and Technology) in every third year from 1956 to 1968. The results were published as follows: 1956 [QRL 302], 1959 [QRL 303], 1962 [QRL 304], 1965 [QRL 281], 1968 [QRL 224].

Information was sought in each survey on numbers employed, vacancies and forecast requirements three years ahead. Employment was generally analysed according to field of employment (including construction), type of work or function (R & D/Other) and subject of qualification together with ratios of QSEs to total employees, but those given for construction are generally more limited than those given for manufacturing and other fields of employment. In particular, the vacancies, forecasts and ratio analyses are not given for several of the enquiries.

Technicians. The 1965 and 1968 surveys included a question about the employment of technicians and other technical supporting staff. Since the majority of those acting as technicians do not possess nationally recognized qualifications the survey had to be conducted on the basis of a description of function. This gave rise, however, to some difficulties in answering the questionnaire (for further particulars see [QRL 281] Ch. V and [QRL 224] p. 60).

The samples for the construction industry were drawn from the then MOW's (later MPBW's) register of contractors stratified by size. The coverage of firms, however, has varied: in 1956 it was limited to firms employing 100 or more persons, in the subsequent surveys the limit was lowered to thirty persons until 1968, when it was raised to thirty-five persons. It should be noted that in certain respects the results of the various enquiries are not directly comparable because each has been a development of the last: either a widening of the range of the sample, the fields of employment, or of the types of qualification covered. These differences are defined in the reports, and wherever possible the data are enumerated so as to facilitate the comparison of one survey with another, but generally speaking they are not such as to affect the comparison for the construction industry. The surveys are considered further in relation to other enquiries in Section 6.6.3.4 below.

6.6.3.2. *Censuses of population 1961–71 as sources of qualified manpower data*. Statistics of qualified manpower have been collected in each of the censuses of population conducted in 1961, 1966 and 1971. There are differences, however, in the information collected. In the 1961 census the question referred to the possession of degrees or equivalent qualifications in engineering, technology and science only—the same classification as in the triennial surveys referred to above; as we noted earlier, this excluded architecture and surveying. In the 1966 census the question was extended to cover all qualifications obtained after reaching the age of 18 and entailing study at a level above that required for GCE 'A' level or SCE. The 1971 census asked the same question (with only slight amendments) as in 1966. It was supplemented, however, by a question asking whether a person had obtained GCE 'A' level or its equivalents which enabled the 'non-qualified' population to be sub-classified by academic level (as well as by industry, etc.).

Separate qualified manpower reports provide analyses according to industry and occupation and by type of qualification, subject and academic level as well as other characteristics. The results for 1961 were published in [QRL 98]. In 1966 and 1971 two volumes were published for each census: one giving the results on the basis of the extended coverage defined above—[QRL 296] and [QRL 97] respectively—and one for each census giving tabulations on a basis which is 'as nearly as practicable' comparable with that produced in 1961—[QRL 297] and [QRL 225] respectively. In addition two further volumes, prepared by the CSO—[QRL 246] and [QRL 247]—provide summaries and commentaries on the data in the context of the population as a whole.

Interpretation. Apart from the widening in the scope of the enquiries from 1966, a number of factors are relevant for the interpretation of the results, particularly those in the full reports for 1966 and 1971 [QRL 296] and [QRL 97] compared with the more limited QSE tables [QRL 297] and [QRL 225]. First, surveying is counted under 'technology' in the full reports but not in the other volumes. Secondly, where people have more than one qualification they are classified according to the most recent highest attainment listed in the full reports, but in the other volumes they are classified according to the *first* science or technology qualification obtained at degree or equivalent level. Thirdly, the 'QSE' tables do not include some qualifications which are not accepted for membership of some professional institutions.

With regard to the accuracy of the returns themselves, it should be noted that evidence was obtained of under-recording in the quality check made after the 1966 census (see [B 63]) and that there is evidence that qualifications recorded in 1966 were not recorded in 1971 ([QRL 97] p. viii refers). Finally, it is important to note that all the results are subject to sampling error (the analyses in each case are based on 10 per cent samples) and that bias was detected in the 1961 and 1966 results (for further details see Section 6.3.3 above, the reports themselves and, especially, [QRL 224] pp. 125–6).

6.6.3.3. *DOE censuses 1965–74 as sources of qualified manpower data.* These censuses have been considered fully in Sections 4.2 and 4.3. The relevant information from these enquiries is the breakdown by occupation of the APTC staff category which has been required annually since 1965 in the case of contractors and 1966 for public authorities' direct labour. The relevant categories in the present context are: architects, surveyors and engineers which were separately specified in the contractors' enquiries up to 1974 (they have remained separately specified in the direct labour enquiries). Further details of the classification are given in Section 4.2.3.7 and Appendix IV (which includes specimen forms) for contractors, and in Section 4.3 and Appendix V for direct labour undertakings. We consider the data further in relation to the other sources below.

6.6.3.4. *Comparison of the surveys—The census of population and the other surveys.* The data on qualified manpower collected in the census of population of 1961 and that contained in corresponding analyses of those with scientific and technological qualifications in 1966 and 1971 are broadly comparable in scope to that obtained in the triennial manpower surveys. A precise account of the reasons for differences in the results is given in the census report for 1961 [ORL 98] pp. xiii–xiv and the survey report for 1962 [QRL 329] Appendix B.

Comparison of the census of population and the DOE censuses is hindered by the fact that they are not defined in the same way: the scope of the census of population data is defined precisely in terms of certain qualifications; the DOE census is more concerned with employment rather than qualifications and the breakdown by occupation is not defined in terms of qualification as such. (For precise details of the return see the specimen forms included in Appendix IV.) In this respect the DOE data are best compared with the general occupational analyses of the censuses of population as opposed to the qualified manpower tables (see Section 6.3).

Other factors that would help to account for differences are as follows. One is the fact that the census of population data are subject to sampling error but the DOE data are based on censuses of construction firms and may, for that reason, have greater accuracy; they will not have precise accuracy because of deficiencies in the register on which the enquiries were based (see Section 4.1.3) but in so far as these deficiencies have been mainly of small firms which may not employ many qualified staff (in the sense used here at any rate) the influence of this factor is probably limited. A second potential reason for difference is that the census relies on information from the person himself (or at least the head of the household) whereas the DOE data rely on returns from the employer who may not be aware of the qualifications held by employees particularly if the person concerned is engaged in an occupation for which the qualifications are not relevant. Thirdly, there may have been discrepancies between the register used by the census of population authorities for classification to construction (mainly based on information from the Ministry of Labour) and that maintained by the MOW–DOE (classification of public sector construction labour in particular may perhaps have been less likely to be classified to the construction industry in the censuses of population). In addition there are also differences in timing.

The triennial manpower surveys and the DOE censuses. Both of these enquiries were employer-based and used the same register of firms (the MOW–DOE register). The only category that may be compared is that for the employment of engineers in the surveys for 1965 and 1968. In these two instances there are in fact very marked discrepancies between the two sets of figures (even allowing for the fact that the census enquiry covers firms of all sizes, whereas the triennial manpower surveys are confined to larger firms). Apart from the sampling error to which the triennial surveys were subject (those relating to the construction industry were not published) and the effect of timing differences, the only explanation it would seem possible to offer for this are that there may have been differences of interpretation. The DOE census at this time referred to 'all qualified engineers' without any further definition, and it would seem reasonable to believe that this must have led to differences in interpretation by firms responding to this enquiry compared with those responding to the triennial surveys in which qualifications were precisely defined. Clearly, whatever the explanation, the results of these enquiries for the construction sector, at any rate, can only be used with caution.

6.6.3.5. *New supply of qualified manpower.* After the census of population of 1961, in which statistics about the total supply of persons with qualifications in science, engineering and technology (QSEs) were obtained for the first time (Section 6.6.3.2 refers), an official annual time series was developed by adding year by year the estimated net increment. These statistics were published in [QRL 281], [QRL 328], [QRL 329],

[QRL 330] and recently updated, covering the period 1958–74, in *ET* [QRL 147], 1976, pp. 98–123. Reference may also be made to [B 198], in which the series are updated to 1976 (though without a detailed subject breakdown) for discussion of the sources and methodology. As we emphasized earlier, however, it is essential to note in the context of construction that the definition of QSE excludes architects and surveyors.

Wider information about new supply in terms of qualification is available from education statistics which are considered in Section 6.5.5. In addition, statistics are compiled annually by the UGC in respect of university graduates in [QRL 160] showing first destination (where known) according to subject of qualification and sector of employment. It is important to note that these statistics show the *first* appointments taken up shortly after graduation and include both first and higher degrees. There is no similar series for CNAA graduates or for non-graduates, although records are being developed for polytechnic students: some results for 1975 covering twenty-seven of the thirty polytechnics giving details of the first destination of people getting first degrees and HNDs according to subject (distinguishing, in the construction field, architecture, surveying and civil engineering and building) were published in [QRL 226]. Statistics are also compiled by the DES of the number of students qualifying each year according to qualification (see Section 6.5.5.1) and by the IOB for students on building courses (see Section 6.5.5.2).

6.6.3.6. *Employment on R & D*. Information on the manpower (of all kinds—'qualified' and 'unqualified') employed on scientific research and development has been collected as part of surveys of industrial research and development expenditure, carried out annually by the DOI and its predecessors from 1967 to 1972, and again in 1975, covering private industry, public corporations and research associations (central government was included for the first time in 1975). The expenditure surveys, which were commenced earlier, are considered separately in Section 7.3. In 1972 and 1975 the results were sub-divided by product group (including construction); before 1972 the product group classification was confined to private industry and the published results did not distinguish construction as a separate category. The surveys for the private sector are based on the COP register of enterprises employing over 100 employees and reporting expenditure on R & D in a preliminary enquiry.

The results for 1972 and 1975 were published in *Trade and Industry* [QRL 352] Vol. 18, 1975, pp. 397–401, and Vol. 27, 1 July 1977, pp. 692–5 respectively. These provide, for construction, analyses of employment by: sector (as defined above) and by occupation (scientists and engineers; technicians, laboratory assistants and draughtsmen; administrative and clerical staff and others). The results of both the expenditure and employment parts of the surveys up to 1972 have been brought together, along with further background information, in a report by the CSO [QRL 283].

6.6.4. *Earnings of Qualified Manpower in the Construction Industry*

Information about the earnings of qualified staff in the construction industry as such is very limited. One of the most important sources of information is a voluntary enquiry carried out after the 1966 census of population based on a sub-sample of qualified people enumerated in the census in England and Wales, together with a smaller sample of 'unqualified' people who were included 'as an aid to interpreting the results'. The results were published by the DES in [QRL 327] and provide analyses of earned income according to industry (including construction as a separate category) by age (separate figures for qualified and unqualified), subject of qualification and status. Further analyses are made according to occupation but not cross-classified by industry.

A similar follow-up enquiry, as yet unpublished, was made following the 1971 census of population but, in this case, one which was not focused primarily on qualified manpower—further details are given in Section 6.9.4.3. Annual *New Earnings Surveys* [QRL 208] also cover labour generally but provide a certain amount of occupational data by industry (see Section 6.9.3.1).

It may also be noted that a large number of surveys covering the earnings of members of the construction professions have been carried out by different bodies at different times but only a few of them provide separate data about earnings in the construction industry. Since they are concerned with the construction professions generally they are considered in Part IV of this Review.

6.7. *Ad hoc* Labour Enquiries

6.7.1. *Background*

In addition to the regular employment statistics which have been considered in the preceding sections, *ad hoc* enquiries are made from time to time which provide information about various aspects of employment in the industry. Some of these enquiries are primarily concerned with employment, others obtain information about characteristics of the labour force incidentally in connection with some other related subject. Studies of this latter type are considered elsewhere in this Review: especially noteworthy are *ad hoc* earnings enquiries carried out by NEDO and the NBPI in the past (considered in Section 6.9.4) and, currently, the annual New Earnings Surveys (considered in Section 6.9.3). The CITB also carry out *ad hoc* surveys from time to time—see Section 6.4.4. In this section we are solely concerned to note studies of the first type. All but one of the enquiries are concerned with various aspects of the use of labour in the industry including training, recruitment and operatives' attitudes. The remaining study reports the results of large-scale surveys of labour supply and requirements on construction sites in London during the early 1970s.

6.7.2. *BRS Survey of Building Operatives' Work 1963–4*

The BRS study was mounted in 1963 at the request of the NJCBI to survey the work done by operatives in relation to their training and experience and to the current and potential future demand made by different sectors of the industry and is reported in [B 189]. A separate 'guide' to the report and 'discussion papers' were published in [B 81] and [B 109] respectively. The study was carried out by means of interviews with operatives engaged on new construction, repairs and maintenance and those employed in trades shops and factories and the results are reported separately for these three sections. These provide a great deal of detailed information relating to the training and origins of operatives and the work undertaken by them. Detailed appendices provide separate data for individual trades and age distributions.

6.7.3. *GSS Survey of Building Operatives 1965*

The GSS survey, carried out in 1965, is a related study to the BRS operative skills enquiry, referred to above, and was concerned with the social factors which influence or arise out of employment in the construction industry. The report [B 163] provides detailed information about operatives' current jobs (including the employer, length of service, whether living at home or away, etc.), recruitment, training, employment record, pay and attitudes towards training, towards various current issues in building, towards staying in the industry and towards wages.

Questions covering some of the same ground as in this enquiry were also asked in the National Training Survey considered below (Section 6.7.6).

6.7.4. *Surveys for the Phelps-Brown Committee 1967*

The Phelps-Brown Committee was appointed jointly by the Ministers of Labour and Public Building and Works in 1967 to enquire into the engagement and use of labour in building and civil engineering with particular reference to labour-only sub-contracting and reported in the following year [B 307]. The Committee commissioned a survey to obtain information about the continuity and discontinuity of employment throughout the industry and about labour-only sub-contracting.

The survey was conducted by Research Services Ltd during the period October–December 1967 on the basis of interviews with the management of 774 construction firms sampled from the then MPBW register, 102 local authorities having a direct labour building force, supplemented by interviews with foremen and management on 527 construction sites (the latter being confined, however, to sites of large main contractors only). A summary report was issued as a *Research Supplement* to the Committee's report in [B 308]. The main body of tabulations together with the questionnaire schedules and other survey documents, however, were bound together [B 263] and these are now available for consultation in the main library of the Department of Employment in London. The subjects covered are: the characteristics of the companies in the sample according to their size, their specializations, their contracts and their clients; managerial policy on employment (including use of incentive schemes, etc.); particular policies and practices regarding the recruitment and discharge of operatives; labour turnover and stability; use and general experience of labour-only sub-contracting; employment conditions for labour-only sub-contractors; trade union membership and employers' liaison with trade unions.

Subsequently, the data were re-examined at the request of the Manpower Working Party of the Civil Engineering EDC and a fresh set of tabulations produced [B 224] relating to civil engineering firms. This report, which is also available for consultation in the main library of the DE in London, is confined to information about the characteristics of the sample and policies towards the recruitment, maintenance and termination of employment.

6.7.5. *PEP Survey of Building Operatives 1967*

This survey was carried out as part of a study of security of employment in the construction industry reported in [B 143]. It was confined to a sample of operatives employed by one large construction company (on five different sites) which was known to be anxious to decasualize employment. The survey was conducted by interviews (371 men were covered) which were designed 'to explore their attitudes towards working in a "casual" industry, and their reactions to the company's efforts to decasualize employment and improve working conditions'. Apart from classification data (age, nationality, type of worker, etc.), the interviews covered matters relating to recruitment, conditions of work, work history, attitudes to work and to the company and future plans. An analysis was also made of records relating to current employees and to former employees paid-off to obtain information about the pattern of labour turnover.

6.7.6. *The National Training Survey 1975*

A 'National Training Survey' was commissioned in 1975 by the Training Services Agency—an executive arm of the Manpower Services Commission (MSC). It was designed to provide information on each respondent's first employment, and all employment since 1965, including occupation and industry. Information was also collected on the training which individuals (not only construction workers) had received throughout their working life. The survey was conducted by personal interview of 54,000 people—roughly 2 in 1,000 of the working population. At the time of writing no results had been published but an initial report is planned for publication in 1979 [QRL 205].

In brief, the subjects covered in the enquiry were: economic status; work history (occupation, industry, number of employers, dates of employment, size of employer, secondary jobs, etc.); training (details of all training occasions since leaving full-time education); attitudes towards training and classification data (age, sex, country of origin, membership of trade union/associations, earnings, etc.).

6.7.7. *GLC Surveys of Labour Availability and Requirements on London Local Authority Construction Sites 1973 and 1974*

Two surveys were carried out, one on 21 November 1973 and one on 30 October 1974, initially in response to concern over the effect of shortages of skilled labour on London local authority construction programmes during the construction 'boom' of the early 1970s. The purpose of the surveys was to obtain information about the structure of the labour force and shortages. The surveys covered local authority sites operated by both contractors and direct labour organizations in the Greater London area, returns being obtained from the Clerk of Works on each site. The second survey was confined to sites above a certain size (project values of £20,000 or more); in the first survey, however, the coverage was left to the discretion of the boroughs supplying returns with the result that it varies from one to another. The results of this, first, survey were not formally published but they are available in the GLC Intelligence Unit. The results of the second survey were published in [B 121]. Both provide detailed analyses of the occupational composition of the labour force according to type of work and corresponding figures for immediate labour requirements (in so far as this question could be answered) on the date of the survey.

6.8. Unemployment, Vacancies and Labour Mobility—Great Britain

6.8.1. *Unemployment Statistics*

Unemployment statistics are available from two sources: the DE, who compile a regular series, and the periodic censuses of population. Further information is sometimes collected in *ad hoc* enquiries such as the National Training Survey (Section 6.7.6).

6.8.1.1. *The DE unemployment statistics.* The bases of the DE series available for pre-war and post-war years is set out in the official guide to labour statistics [B 241] and in the *Historical Abstract* [QRL 58], which also contains the principal series up to 1965. Reference may also usefully be made to the report of a working party on the nature of the unemployment statistics [B 344] and a recent paper by the Director of Statistics at the DE [B 161].

The current series by industry runs from 1948 on a monthly basis until June 1976 and thereafter quarterly, but for the construction industry, in particular, some data continue to be compiled monthly (details are given below). The statistics record the numbers of persons on the registers of local offices of the Employment Services Agency (ESA) of the MSC (formerly Employment Exchanges), Careers Offices of the local education authority (formerly Youth Employment Offices) 'who were unemployed and capable of and available for work'[4] on the day of the count, with the exception of some persons who were severely disabled and unlikely to obtain work other than under special conditions and a small number of persons who were not claiming any benefits and who were registered only for part-time work.

The essential point to note about the series, therefore, is that it does not cover persons who are unemployed but not registered. There is, of course, an incentive to register in order to obtain unemployment benefit but some people do not bother to register for a short period or are ineligible for benefit—some temporarily (until a certain time has elapsed), others because of non-compliance with the national insurance scheme. As with the employment statistics for the construction industry, therefore, non-compliance by nominally 'self-employed' construction workers is also likely to lead to understatement in the unemployment statistics. A valuable discussion of 'the unregistered unemployed' and national estimates will be found in *DEG* [QRL 135] December 1976, pp. 1331–6.

Interpretation of the statistics also needs to take account of the basis of the industrial classification. This is made on the basis of the industry in which the person was last employed for more than three days. The construction industry is one which provides employment opportunities for many unskilled workers (often for brief periods) and also employs, briefly, people discharged by other industries who may be prepared to accept a

---

[4] The methods used to classify as 'capable and available' are said to be based on case law developed by national insurance decisions—see [B 344].

job in construction for an interim period until more familiar employment becomes available. At the end of such a period of employment such persons would be classified to the construction industry on registering as unemployed although they would not normally regard themselves as primarily construction workers.

The percentage rates of unemployment for the industry need to be interpreted with particular care. The number of registered unemployed are expressed as a percentage of the total number of *employees* (employed and unemployed). As we have explained earlier, however (see Section 6.2.3), the construction employment series has been influenced in a downwards direction by the marked growth of self-employment in the industry, some of it purely nominal. Thus, other things being equal, unemployment *rates* are likely to be biased in an upward direction. Since 1973 it appears that the numbers of self-employed may have declined but for at least a decade before that their numbers grew very considerably indeed.

Further, regional unemployment figures in particular need to be interpreted with special care since those registered as unemployed in a particular region need not necessarily have been previously employed in that region.

The available series and sources for construction—Industrial analyses. For the construction *industry* (as opposed to construction occupations) the statistics available are:

(a) *National series*. Monthly data until June 1976 and then only in February, May, August and November each year showing numbers by sex in Great Britain and the UK. Seasonally adjusted numbers and percentage rates are published for Great Britain.

   The primary publication source is *DEG* [QRL 135] (formerly *MOLG* [QRL 190]). The main series of numbers unemployed are reproduced in the *Yearbooks* of labour statistics [QRL 59] and in *HCS* [QRL 168]. The *Historical Abstract* of labour statistics [QRL 58] is a convenient source for the whole period from 1948 to 1968 (quarterly figures only).

(b) *Regional series*. These have not been regularly published by the DE and former MOL, but the construction series has been regularly incorporated in statistical publications by the DOE and its predecessors. Currently, analyses with the same frequency as in (a) above are given in *HCS* [QRL 168]—series back to 1971 and annual averages back to 1967. Before the introduction of *HCS* monthly series were regularly incorporated in *MBCS* [QRL 194] and the series for two months each year (June and December) in *ABCS* [QRL 32]. The DE itself now publishes an analysis sub-classified by sex, for two months each year in the *Yearbooks* [QRL 59]. In the early post-war years up to 1950 regional/industrial analyses for all industry were published in [QRL 346]. *Regional Statistics* [QRL 252] now gives data for one month each year and details for Scotland and Wales appear in [QRL 306] and [QRL 142] respectively.

(c) Temporarily stopped workers claiming benefits in Great Britain, by sex and industry, are given with the same frequency as in (a) above in *DEG* [QRL 135] and formerly in *MOLG* [QRL 190]. These workers are persons who are suspended by their employers on the understanding that they will shortly resume work but who register in order to claim benefits. They are not now regarded as part of the unemployed. At one time they were so regarded—a distinction being drawn between 'wholly unemployed' and the 'temporarily stopped' in the same table.

Occupational analyses. In contrast to the industrial analyses, in which a person is classified to the industry in which he last worked, the occupational analyses refer to the occupation in which a person is seeking work. Since November 1972, these analyses have followed the CODOT [B 203] system of classification; before that they were based on an internal guide used by local employment offices for placing purposes. The continuity of the series is therefore affected by this change.

For construction, two sets of data are available, one general and the other specific:

(a) General occupational analyses of all unemployed persons prepared quarterly and published, in conjunction with a corresponding analysis of unfilled vacancies (see Section 6.8.2), in the *DEG* [QRL 135] and, formerly, the *MOLG* [QRL 190] since May 1958. Sub-classifications by region were introduced with effect from the analysis for September 1963 in November 1963.
(b) For the construction *industry*, in particular, regular and more frequent occupational analyses have been published for the whole post-war period. At the present time, despite the change to a quarterly frequency for industrial analyses of the unemployed with effect from July 1976, analyses for construction *craftsmen* have continued—special analyses being prepared for the DOE and published, by craft, in *HCS* [QRL 168]. The DOE and its predecessors also regularly incorporated occupational analyses of unemployed construction workers in its monthly and annual *Bulletins* [QRL 194] and [QRL 32] respectively, for the whole post-war period—as for the regional 'industry' series referred to in (b) above—until they were superseded by *HCS* [QRL 168]. It should be noted that these analyses, in contrast to those referred to under (a) above, are confined to those workers who last worked in the construction industry.

Characteristics of the unemployed. Analyses of the characteristics of the unemployed are not normally made on an industrial or occupational basis. However, a special analysis, now of historical interest, was made of unemployed skilled construction workers in June 1964. The results were reported in *MOLG* [QRL 190] Vol. 73, November 1965, pp. 483–6 providing information about: age and duration of unemployment, standard of skill, prospects of employment, mobility (geographical, industrial and occupational), training received and suitability for training. The only other information available comes from periodic censuses of population (referred to below) and *ad hoc* surveys, e.g. the National Training Survey—considered in Section 6.7.6—and CITB enquiries—see Section 6.4.4.

Redundancy statistics. Statistics of the numbers of redundancies and the amounts paid in accordance with the Redundancy Payments Acts are compiled quarterly by the DE and are available on request. Published information is confined to a summary showing industries having the highest number of redundancies each quarter in the *DEG* [QRL 135]. In the context of the unemployment statistics it needs to be appreciated that not all persons made redundant necessarily become unemployed. A study of the impact of the 1965 *Redundancy Payments Act*, based on a survey carried out in 1969 covering construction and other industries, is reported in [B 115].

6.8.1.2. *Unemployment statistics from the censuses of population.* The censuses of population (1951, 1961, 1966 and 1971) provide analyses according to occupation but not by industry. These are to be found in the 'occupation' and 'economic activity' tables, references to which are given in the 'Employment' section of the *Quick Reference List* at the end of this volume. These statistics do not coincide with the DE statistics of registered unemployment for a number of reasons: a detailed discussion of the points of difference will be found in [QRL 89] pp. xxviii–xxix. It should also be noted that post-enumeration surveys conducted by the OPCS have shown that the census figures are open to error, caused particularly by persons who were in employment but sick, wrongly returning themselves as unemployed.

6.8.2. *Statistics of Vacancies and Placings*

Industrial and occupational analyses of vacancies follow much the same pattern as the unemployment statistics in the post-war period: industrial analyses compiled monthly until June 1976, and thereafter quarterly, and occupational analyses compiled quarterly throughout the whole period. The current series runs from October 1947 (details of earlier statistics will be found in [B 241]). The DE publish the series for construction, along with other industries and occupations in the *DEG* [QRL 135] and former *MOLG* [QRL 190]. The labour statistics *Yearbooks* [QRL 59] also include regional analyses for two months each year and the quarterly national series. Full regional and local area figures are available on request from the DE. For construction in particular, however, a full monthly analysis by craft cross-classified by region (as for unemployment) was regularly incorporated in the *MBCS* [QRL 194] until April 1972 and by craft and by region (not cross-classified) for two months each year in the *ABCS* [QRL 32] up to 1970. Unlike the unemployment analyses, however, these analyses have not been continued currently in the *HCS* [QRL 168]; the latter simply reproduces the national totals only (on actual and s.a. bases).

With regard to the interpretation of these data, perhaps the salient point to note is that they are not a total count of vacancies. They merely represent the vacancies which have been notified by employers to Local Employment Offices and Careers Offices (the latter are not added in to the analyses—see below) and which, at the date of the count, remain unfilled. A large proportion of vacancies are not in fact notified; nevertheless it is claimed that in general: 'experience has shown that the changes in the series of statistics of vacancies for adults reflect changes in the pressure of demand in the labour market' ([QRL 58] p. 18). It should also be noted that there may be duplication of notification to the two types of office and thus the two sets of figures should not be added together. Finally, as a time series, certain discontinuities have been caused by administrative changes—details of these may be found in [QRL 58] p. 18.

Industrial analyses of the number of placings—i.e. persons placed in employment through the Employment or Careers Offices—were compiled monthly and published in *DEG* [QRL 135] and in the former *MOLG* [QRL 190] until January 1970. Since then information on placings has been collected quarterly on an occupational basis for those placed by Employment Offices (but not by Careers Offices). Publication was resumed in the *DEG* [QRL 135] of May 1973.

6.8.3. Labour Mobility

In contrast to manufacturing industry, no regular series are compiled relating to labour turnover (i.e. the movement of workers into and out of employment with one particular employer) in construction. The only evidence available about this and about inter-industry mobility comes from *ad hoc* surveys. Two general labour mobility enquiries, carried out by the GSS, which provide data for construction and other industries about the nature and frequency of occupational and industrial mobility and some of the factors associated with it are: [B 162] covering the period 1945–9 and [B 67] covering the period 1953–63. Research by the Building Research Station in the 1960s into matters concerning building workers and their jobs, including an associated study by the GSS [B 163] (considered in Section 6.7.3), also provided information about labour mobility which has been briefly summarized in [B 108] giving details of length of service with current employers and reasons for job changing. Relevant information has also been obtained in the National Training Survey in 1975 (Section 6.7.6) and in *ad hoc* enquiries by the *CITB* (Section 6.4.4). A valuable summary and discussion of the evidence up to 1967–8, including references to some unpublished sources, will be found in the report of the Phelps-Brown Committee [B 307].

Relevant information is also available from various other sources. Data about inter-occupational mobility is available from the 1971 census of population [QRL 94] which required information about a person's occupation one year prior to the census as well as at the date of the census. Analyses of the returns made in the NES (considered in Section 6.9.3.1) enable estimates of labour turnover to be made (some of these were presented in *DEG* [QRL 135] January 1975, pp. 25–26). Further, whilst national insurance cards were in existence, analyses of a sample of cards enabled estimates to be made of inter-industry flows—an analysis for the period from 1959–60 to 1967–8 was published in the *Employment and Productivity Gazette* (as it was then called) [QRL 135] Vol. 78, April 1970, pp. 303–7. A discussion of these and of information available from other administrative records is contained in *DEG* [QRL 135] December 1975, pp. 1264–8.

6.9. Wage Rates, Earnings, Hours and Labour Costs

6.9.1. Introduction

Statistics about wages and earnings are the subject of a separate study in this series [B 44]; we focus our attention on these subjects here, therefore, only as is necessary to serve the purposes of this Review. The geographical coverage of the data considered here vary: some refer to Great Britain and others to the UK. Separate data that are available for Northern Ireland are considered in Section 9.4.3.

Statistics of labour costs have a number of dimensions: standard or minimum rates of pay agreed between organizations of employers and workers at the national or local level; actual rates, which may be in excess of the agreed rates; actual earnings, which reflect overtime pay and bonuses, etc. as well as the agreed time rates for normal hours. From the side of the employer, however, the costs of employing labour are generally greater than the payments made to employees because of a variety of labour on-costs which must be borne, e.g. national and other insurance contributions, labour-related taxes such as SET and, in the construction industry, regular HWP contributions[5] amongst others and this adds a further dimension to the subject. One might also be interested in total labour costs in the aggregate as opposed to unit costs per man. The principal statistics are compiled by the DE but it should also be noted that information is available from other sources and we also refer to these as appropriate below, with the exception that income statistics relating to the construction professions are considered separately in Part IV of this Review. The arrangement of this section is as follows:

Section 6.9.2. Wage rates and normal hours of work
Section 6.9.3. Actual earnings and hours of work (MOL–DE enquiries)
Section 6.9.4. Supplementary sources of income and hours of work
Section 6.9.5. Total labour costs.

6.9.2. *Wage Rates and Normal Hours of Work*

Statistics of wages and hours have a long history and for some building trades, in particular, can be carried back for several centuries. A brief reference is made to historical sources below but otherwise attention here is confined to current (post-war) statistics.

6.9.2.1. *Current sources—Actual wage rates and hours.* For the whole of the period since 1946 (except 1953) details of *national* basic rates of wages, normal basic hours and general conditions of employment of manual workers, determined by collective agreements between employers and trade unions for various sectors of the construction industry, have been set out annually in [QRL 348] (including details of HWP rates in separate appendices since 1951). Time series of the principal rates (from 1947) are given in the *Historical Abstract* [QRL 58] and the *Yearbooks* [QRL 59]. Details of changes from month to month are given in [QRL 117] and a summary in *DEG* [QRL 135] and former *MOLG* [QRL 190].

Monthly estimates are also given of the total number of workers affected by changes and the estimated change in the basic wage element in the weekly wage-bill and in total normal weekly hours, but these must be treated with caution. Fuller information and discussion are provided in the companion volume on *Wages and Earnings* [B 44].

Index numbers. Although official indices for basic weekly and hourly wage rates and normal hours have been published for many years covering 'all industry', based on the information described in the previous paragraph, the constituent indices for each industry were not published until recently. These were made available, monthly from June 1947, in the *Historical Abstract* [QRL 58] and are now carried forward in the *DEG*

---

[5] Contributions paid weekly by employers in respect of each operative under the holidays-with-pay scheme. This scheme was set up to meet the particular circumstances of the construction industry in which a large proportion of the labour force moves frequently from one employer to another. The employer affixes, each week, a stamp purchased from the company set up to manage the scheme (Building and Civil Engineering Holidays Scheme Management Ltd) to a card (similar to National Insurance Cards) for each employee. Payment to the face value of the stamps on his card is made to the worker by the employer for whom he is working when he takes his holiday, the employer being reimbursed by the management company.

[QRL 135] and in the *Yearbooks* [QRL 59]. Convenient secondary sources are the *HCS* [QRL 168] and the *MDS* [QRL 195] though they reproduce the index of *weekly* wage rates only. Prior to the publication of these series only unofficial indices had been produced—for details see [B 48], [B 47] and [B 49].

Interpretation. The use and interpretation of the data, particularly the index numbers, is not quite so straightforward as might seem to be the case at first sight. The basic rates, it should be emphasized, are nothing more nor less than nationally agreed minimum or standard rates. Quite apart from the fact that the rates paid in practice may be in excess of the nationally agreed rates by virtue of over-time pay, bonus and incentive payments, etc. additions to the basic rates may be made for work in certain special conditions or involving extra skill or responsibility, etc. Calculation and use of indices is more problematical. The agreed rates vary, not only over time, but also between one area of the country and another and between different categories of labour, especially, in the construction industry, skilled and unskilled labour. Over time the differential paid for skill has been reduced and thus the rate for unskilled labour has shown a greater relative increase than skilled rates. Many of the differences between one area of the country and another have been eliminated by a gradual process of upgrading so that the rates of increase for the same type of labour have been greater in some areas than others. A single index number is, therefore, an amalgam of all these factors and measures the relative rate of change for neither any particular category of labour nor for any particular area of the country. In practice, of course, the influence of these factors on the index number itself depends upon the way it is calculated, but details of the weights applied for skilled and unskilled rates and different regions are not published.

6.9.2.2. *Historical sources.* The construction industry is particularly well served with historical sources of wage rate data and these have been investigated by a number of writers. We do no more here than direct attention to principal sources.

A guide to official sources for the period back to the mid-nineteenth century has been provided in [B 241]. Some of the data themselves are reproduced as time series in the official *Historical Abstract* [QRL 58]. This provides: series of wage rates and weekly hours for bricklayers and bricklayers' labourers in selected towns for selected years from 1810 to 1968 and, for the period 1914–38, averages for thirty-nine large towns of weekly and hourly rates for various building trades. Although no official index numbers were published, a series for building and other wage rates for the period from 1920 to 1938 was published by Ramsbottom (a former Director of Statistics at the MOL) in [B 126] and subsequent supplements. Reference may also be made to the works of A. L. Bowley for data on the building trades throughout the nineteenth century in various parts of the UK in [B 25], [B 26] and [B 27]; for the nineteenth century and earlier in [B 29]; for the period from 1880 to 1914 in [B 28] and from 1914 to 1920 in [B 24]. For the inter-war period, and later, series compiled by Bowley for building and other trades were published in the *LCES Bulletin* [B 269]—for further details see Dean [B 44]. A valuable study of regional differences in building and other sectors from 1850 up to 1914 has also been made by Hunt [B 78]. Over the much longer period, evidence on building wages back to the thirteenth and fourteenth centuries has been provided by Phelps-Brown and Hopkins in [B 31] and by Beveridge in [B 15]. The references given here do not claim to be exhaustive; further references will be found in the works cited together with a consideration of the nature and sources of the primary data. A convenient source of long-run series for building and other industries, based on some of the sources cited here, is the *Abstract of British Historical Statistics* by Mitchell and Deane [QRL 21], which gives building data for the period from 1795 to 1938 together with an extensive bibliography. A *Second Abstract of British Historical Statistics* [QRL 22] has carried the index of weekly wage rates forward to 1965.

6.9.3. *Actual Earnings and Hours of Work (MOL–DE Enquiries)*

A major development in the range of information collected about actual earnings and hours of work took place in 1968 with the initiation by the DE of *New Earnings Surveys* (NES) covering construction along with other industries; previously much less detailed information was collected (Section 6.9.3.2 refers). An official description of the new survey written soon after its introduction is provided in [B 160] and again, the subject is covered in detail in the companion volume by Dean on *Wages and Earnings* [B 44]; our treatment here is therefore brief. A similar survey has been carried out in Northern Ireland since 1971 and is considered separately in Section 9.4.3.2.

6.9.3.1. *New Earnings Surveys (Great Britain) 1968 to date.*

The first survey for Great Britain was carried out in September 1968; subsequent surveys have been carried out annually since 1970, each relating to an April pay-period. They are made under the *Statistics of Trade Act 1947* and cover a random one per cent sample of employees. The results are reported in [QRL 208] in great detail; summary information is reproduced in *DEG* [QRL 135] and *Yearbooks* [QRL 59]. The full reports also contain accounts of the execution of the surveys. The main advantage of these surveys over other earnings enquiries is that information is collected (from employers) in respect of individuals, rather than in the form of aggregate data covering groups of employees. Consequently it is possible to make analyses according to a variety of characteristics relating to the individual and the nature of his employment. However, it should be noted that they relate only to employees—the self-employed (of particular importance in construction) are not covered.

The surveys provide a wealth of statistical information which it is difficult to summarize. A full account has been provided by Dean [B 44]. Briefly, each survey provides statistics about the level, the distribution and make-up of the earnings of employees classified according to age, sex, adult/juvenile, full-time/part-time, manual/non-manual, occupation (classified according to KOS—based on CODOT [B 203]), area of employment (this can be the construction site)[6] and collective agreement (at the time of writing—mid-1977—ten agreements are listed in the private sector for construction and three in the public sector—agreements for local authorities in England and Wales and Scotland and for electricity supply—but results are not published in this degree of detail). The information about the make-up of earnings distinguishes: (i) overtime pay, (ii) PBR and other incentive payments, bonuses and (iii) premium payments for shift,

---

[6] The question currently reads 'enter the names of the town or district and also the county, etc. in which the employee works or, if mobile, is based'.

night and week-end work. Information is also collected about normal basic hours of work and paid overtime hours.

Supplementary questions, which make these surveys useful sources of additional information about the labour force, are also asked from time to time, covering, for example: types of incentive payments, holiday entitlement, length of service, types of collective agreement, sick pay schemes and pension schemes, etc.

From the point of view of measuring changes over time a particularly valuable feature of the NES is the practice of including 'matched samples' of persons covered in successive enquiries.

6.9.3.2. *Earnings and hours of manual workers (UK) from 1946.* Until the introduction of the *NES*, surveys were conducted each April and October until 1970 and then in October only each year, based upon a panel of firms willing to supply information. Details of the numbers covered are given in the reports; in the latest enquiry for which information is available at the time of writing (October 1976 enquiry), for example, the number of adult males covered was 401,000—equivalent to 52 per cent of all operatives recorded in the DOE census of *contractors* (excluding direct labour) in the same month (Section 4.2 refers). In these enquiries data are provided on an aggregate basis only, i.e. data for total amounts paid, total hours worked and the total number of workers covered, enabling averages to be calculated. These particular series can be carried back to October 1946 but enquiries were also made for some earlier years, details of which will be found in Dean [B 44] and in the official guide [B 241] (data from these earlier enquiries have been reproduced in the *Historical Abstract* [QRL 58]). Unlike the NES, referred to above, the results for this enquiry are given on a UK basis. For details of the Northern Ireland constituent, which remained unpublished for many years, see Section 9.4.3.2.

The published series for the post-war period show average weekly and hourly earnings and average hours:

(1) for full-time men (21 and over), youths and boys (under 21) and women (18 and over) and part-time women (18 and over),
(2) according to region—full-time men only—since 1960.

The primary source of publication is the *DEG* [QRL 135] and former *MOLG* [QRL 190] but the whole time-series for the principal categories are conveniently summarized up to 1968 in the *Historical Abstract* [QRL 58] and carried forward in the subsequent *Yearbooks* [QRL 59]. The *MDS* [QRL 195] has also reproduced the whole post-war series of average *weekly* earnings.

Distribution of earnings. In the October 1960 enquiry an additional question was included to obtain details of the numbers of full-time manual men and women whose gross earnings in a particular week fell into certain ranges—analyses of the results for construction and other industries were published in *MOLG* [QRL 190] in 1961. Subsequent information about the distribution of earnings of both manual and non-manual employees is available from the New Earnings Surveys—see Section 6.9.3.1 above.

From time to time these enquiries were also used to obtain information about payment by results—this part is considered in Section 6.9.3.6 below.

6.9.3.3. *Occupational earnings and hours of work of adult male manual construction workers (GB) 1964–70.* Enquiries to obtain occupational data for men in certain manual occupations in construction were initiated in June 1964 and repeated in each subsequent January and June until January 1970 except in the case of the heating, ventilating and domestic engineering sector of the industry, for which a further special enquiry was held in June 1970 (reported in [QRL 135] November 1970). Since then, occupational data have been available from the NES (Section 6.9.3.1). Unlike the other earnings and hours enquiry, referred to above, this survey was compulsory under the *Statistics of Trade Act*, and covered all large firms and a sample of smaller firms on the then MOL register—further details are given with the results. The enquiry was conducted separately for constructional engineering firms and other construction firms.

The results provide data in respect of those receiving adult rates of pay (which includes young labourers aged 18 and over in the construction industry) for weekly and hourly earnings (including and excluding overtime premium payments), and hours of work according to occupation, differentiating between constructional engineering and construction other than constructional engineering. The results for the latter are also broken down by region as far as possible (separate data being given for firms unable to provide a regional breakdown—'multi-regional firms') and by size of firm (from January 1965). For further background information reference should be made to the commentary which accompanies the published results.

The results were published in the *MOLG* [QRL 190]—those for the first 'pilot' enquiry being published in the issue for January 1965, pp. 21–23. A summary of the weekly earnings data for construction other than constructional engineering up to 1968 was included in the *Historical Abstract* [QRL 58] and in subsequent *Yearbooks* [QRL 59] to 1970. As with the other earnings enquiries referred to above, it should be appreciated that these results do not cover the earnings of men working as self-employed under LOSC arrangements which, in all probability, would tend to be higher.

6.9.3.4. *Average earnings of non-manual employees (UK) 1959 to date.* An enquiry into the earnings of non-manual (ATC) employees in the UK covering construction and other industries and comparable to that for manual workers (Section 6.9.3.2) was conducted in October of each year from 1959 to 1970 when the enquiry was discontinued because of the advent of the NES (Section 6.9.3.1) providing similar information. In October 1973, however, the enquiry was reintroduced—though with the difference that, unlike the enquiries up to 1970, only full-time employees are covered (details are given in the *DEG* [QRL 135] Dec. 1975, pp. 1274–5)—and has been continued in October of each year since then. This enquiry, unlike the corresponding enquiry for manual workers, is conducted under the *Statistics of Trade Act* and is based upon a sample of larger firms only (twenty-five or more employees originally, now fifty or more employees). A full account will be found in Dean [B 44]. The results, providing separate data for males and females, are published currently in *DEG* [QRL 135], formerly the *MOLG* [QRL 190]; the earlier series were brought together in the

Historical Abstract [QRL 58] up to 1968 and continued in the *Yearbooks* [QRL 59]. Separate statistics for Northern Ireland, which are combined with results for Great Britain to provide statistics with a UK coverage, are considered in Section 9.4.3.2.

6.9.3.5. *Monthly index of average earnings (Great Britain) 1963 to date.* All of the earnings enquiries referred to above provide the basis for indices of average earnings. From January 1963, however, they have been supplemented by a further enquiry, on a smaller scale, to obtain information on a monthly basis covering construction and other industries in Great Britain. Details of the methodology, including retrospective revisions, are given in *MOLG* [QRL 190] March 1967, p. 214. From January 1976 new series have been introduced which, for construction, include hitherto uncovered employees in the national and local government fields (see *DEG* [QRL 135] April 1976). Again a full account is given by Dean [B 44]. The monthly index covers all workers—manual and non-manual, full-time and part-time of both sexes without distinction (until 1966, however, separate indices were published for weekly-paid and monthly-paid employees). The results are published currently in the *DEG* [QRL 135] formerly in the *MOLG* [QRL 190] and reproduced in the *Historical Abstract* [QRL 58] for the period up to 1968 and subsequently in the *Yearbooks* [QRL 59], in the *MDS* [QRL 195] and (quarterly) in the *HCS* [QRL 168].

6.9.3.6. *Payment by results (PBR)—MOL enquiries.* Currently the *NES* (see Section 6.9.3.1) provides statistics about PBR in construction and other industries. Formerly information was sought on the numbers of wage-earners paid under systems of PBR periodically in the manual earnings enquiries (Section 6.9.3.2) as follows: April and October 1947 and then once every other year until April 1961. The results were published in the *MOLG* [QRL 190] initially in conjunction with the earnings results. These enquiries required a return simply of the number of men paid at time rates and those paid wholly or partly under any system of PBR (e.g. piece-work arrangements, output bonus schemes, etc.). The enquiries were ended in 1961 because of the problem of devising an adequate working definition of PBR. It may also be noted that, for construction, enquiries were also conducted by the MOW on the basis of returns from individual sites in the period 1951–5 (referred to in Section 3.10.6). Little information was made available from the MOW enquiries but it appears that the two sources are in conflict. Apart from the NES enquiries, referred to above, later *ad hoc* information has also been collected in surveys by the NBPI in 1968 (see Section 6.9.4.2).

6.9.4. *Supplementary Sources of Income and Hours of Work*

In addition to the regular surveys, considered above, there are a number of supplementary sources.

6.9.4.1. *NEDO survey of operatives' earnings and hours 1973.* This survey was carried out by the Building EDC, in order to provide information for the negotiation within the National Joint Council for the Building Industry of a new wages structure, and provides information and analyses not available elsewhere. Information was collected in one payweek in May 1973 about the composition of earnings and hours, the pay of apprentices and adult trainees, the operation of pension schemes and length of service. In addition, information was collected for comparative purposes, about *annual* earnings in contrast to weekly earnings. The results were analysed according to size of site and type of contractor. A summary of the results and details of the survey itself, which was not based on any official register of firms but on that held by the Building and Civil Engineering Holidays Scheme Management company, were published in [QRL 145]. Full tabulations are said to be available on request from NEDO.

6.9.4.2. *NBPI surveys 1968–71.* During its existence the National Board for Prices and Incomes produced a number of reports on various sectors of construction and related industries for which special surveys were often conducted. The relevant sectors and reports are as follows:

Sector	Date	Publication		Remarks
1. Building	1968	[QRL 217]		These surveys are notable for providing
2. Civil engineering	1968	[QRL 219]	[QRL 218]*	separate information for private
3. Construction other than building and civil engineering	1968	[QRL 220]		contractors and public authorities (direct labour). Analyses are provided in considerable detail about the composition of earnings and hours (according to grade and occupation, region, size of firm and type of work) and about conditions of service (holidays, PBR, profit sharing and pension schemes).
4. Electrical contracting	1966	[QRL 359]		Special MOL analysis of earnings and hours.
5. Electrical contracting	1968	[QRL 222]		Pay and conditions in private and public sectors as under (1–3) above.
6. Electrical contracting (Scotland)	1968	[QRL 223]		
7. Thermal insulation contracting	1968	[QRL 218]		Composition of earnings and hours by occupation.
8. Contract cleaning	1971	[QRL 221]		

* Statistical Supplement covering the three sectors.

6.9.4.3. *OPCS Voluntary Income Enquiry 1972.* This survey was linked to a 1 per cent sample of the 1971 Census of Population but conducted separately on a voluntary basis. This is a development of some considerable importance, although the level of response obtained was not high, because of its wide coverage of the labour force, but at the time of writing the results of this enquiry had not been published. It will cover categories of the labour force not covered in other enquiries, or for which separate information is not available (e.g. the self-employed), and also allow analyses according to characteristics of the labour force not covered elsewhere (e.g. according to educational attainment and qualifications). A similar type of enquiry was carried out after the 1966 census of population in England and Wales but confined in the main to qualified manpower (considered in Section 6.6.4).

6.9.4.4. *Family Expenditure Surveys 1964–9.* The Family Expenditure Surveys [QRL 156] are not normally thought of as a source of income data for different industries, but it is perhaps worth noting that the respondents in these enquiries were classified by industry in the results of each of the annual enquiries from 1964 to 1969. For construction, separate analyses are provided of the distribution of earnings for men employees and men manual workers. It should be noted, however, that the numbers involved are extremely small.

6.9.4.5. *Hours of work by occupation and industry—Census of Population data.* A further source of information about hours of work is the census of population (considered as a source of employment data in Section 6.3). The first census in which such information was collected was that for 1961 but in this and the subsequent 1966 census it was confined to part-time workers only. The 1961 results [QRL 99] provide analyses by occupation; the 1966 results [QRL 295] provide analyses by occupation and by industry. In 1971 coverage was widened to all workers and the published results [QRL 94] Part IV, provide frequency distributions of hours worked classified by industry, occupation and sex for the whole labour force. They provide therefore, since they are not confined to employees alone, information not available from other sources.

6.9.5. *Total Labour Costs*

Two aspects of total labour costs are of interest. At the level of the firm, costs are incurred in the employment of labour additional to wages and salaries. These costs are considerable, amounting in construction currently to around one-tenth of total labour costs. Secondly, interest may focus not on levels of earnings or total labour costs per man, but on the total wage and salary bill for the industry as a whole.

6.9.5.1. *Labour cost surveys (Great Britain).* Between 1964 and 1975 four surveys of total labour costs in construction and other industries were conducted by the DE and its predecessors on the basis of its own register of firms. From UK entry into the EEC, such surveys are required to be held in construction and various other industries at intervals of three years under Council Regulations. The next survey will relate to costs in either the calendar year 1978 or a firm's 1978/9 twelve-month accounting period. Results from the first four surveys have been published as follows:

Year of
Survey   Publication References
 1964 *MOLG* [QRL 190] December 1966 and March 1967. Reprinted in [QRL 181].
 1968 *DEG* [QRL 135] August and October 1970. Reprinted in [QRL 182].
 1973 *DEG* [QRL 135] September and October 1975. Summary data were reproduced in the *Yearbook* [QRL 59] 1974.
 1975 *DEG* [QRL 135] September, November and December 1977.
Other results are being published in EUROSTAT publications by the SOEC.

The content of the enquiries is best explained, briefly, by reference to the latest (1975) enquiry. Earlier enquiries were on broadly similar lines; the exceptions are noted in the reports themselves which provide detailed background information. In 1975 information was collected for eight broad categories of labour costs: (i) wages and salaries (with separate figures for the parts attributable to bonuses not payable regularly, holidays, other time off with pay and wages and salaries in lieu of notice, sickness and wages and salaries of apprentices and full-time trainees); (ii) statutory national insurance contributions; (iii) provision for redundancy (net); (iv) employers' liability insurance; (v) private social welfare payments; (vi) payments in kind; (vii) subsidized services to employees and (viii) vocational training. In addition, information was collected about amounts received, where applicable, for regional employment premium. The results are analysed in terms of average expenditure per employee per hour, according to size of firm, separately for manual (operatives) and non-manual (administrative, technical and clerical workers), as well as all employees combined. The results are also analysed in terms of average annual amounts per employee; in these calculations it should be noted that part-time workers are counted as full units.

Firms with ten or more employees were included in the 1975 survey and will be included in the next (1978) survey. The lower threshold varied in earlier enquiries; in 1973 it was fifty employees, in 1968, twenty-five employees and in 1964, eleven employees. However, although small firms dominate the construction industry in terms of numbers, it needs to be remembered that in terms of employment they are relatively less important. On the other hand there is some evidence that the level and composition of labour costs is influenced by the size of firm and this needs to be borne in mind when the general results for different years are compared. It also needs to be borne in mind that, by virtue of the fact that the returns relate to 'employees', the statistics do not reflect payments for the services of 'self-employed' labour obtained under LOSC arrangements and therefore need to be interpreted in the light of this fact too.

6.9.5.2. *Total wage and salary bill.* Estimates of the total wage and salary bill in construction are included as an integral part of the national accounts statistics in [QRL 201]—these are considered further in Section 7.1.1. Separate estimates are also given for total 'employers' contributions'—i.e. to national and other insurance schemes, redundancy payments, etc. (for full details see [QRL 201] and [B 100]; the latter also gives a reliability assessment (p. 141) for the wages and salaries item). Further aggregate information is available from the Censuses of Production which provide separate figures of expenditure on wages and salaries for operatives and other employees and also, for some years, 'employers' contributions'—references are given in Table 5.1. For the inter-war years, detailed estimates of the wage and salary bill will be found in Chapman [QRL 5] together with a full commentary on the sources and nature of the figures; see also Feinstein [QRL 13].

A further source of information is provided by taxation returns [QRL 173] (formerly [QRL 258]) in which data are given, according to industry, of income charged under PAYE (i.e. in the main wages and salaries) but it should be remembered that PAYE comes into operation only where pay exceeds a certain limit (the 'deduction card limit'). These statistics are used as the basis of the national accounts and in this connection information is given in the official guides [B 275] and [B 100]. Figures are also given of tax deducted and the number of 'deduction cards' (not the same as the number of employees). For further particulars relevant to interpretation reference should also be made to the notes included in the reports.

Regional estimates. No official regional estimates of the total wage and salary bill by industry have been available until recently. They are now compiled by the CSO in connection with the preparation of regional accounts for the UK. These are considered further in Section 7.1.2 along with earlier unofficial estimates.

6.10. Accident Statistics for Great Britain

Official statistics about accidents in the construction industry are available from two sources: the Health and Safety Executive (previously from HM Factory Inspectorate) and the Department of Health and Social Security (DHSS). The former relates to accidents reported to the Executive, of which the Inspectorate now forms part, under factories legislation. The DHSS statistics relate to accidents compensated under social security legislation relating to industrial injuries. We first consider the sources and nature of the information available from these two sources and then turn to consider its accuracy and reliability. We confine our attention, once again, to the information available for the post-war period; an account of earlier statistics will be found in the official guide to labour statistics [B 241]. See too [B 242] for a discussion of the historical record in construction since the beginning of the century.

6.10.1. *The HM Factory Inspectorate (HMFI) Statistics*

Notification of accidents which occur on 'building operations' or 'works of engineering construction' (as well as in factories and other places) has been a statutory requirement under Factories Acts (currently the *Factories Act 1961*)[7] for the whole of the post-war period (and indeed very much earlier). Reports are legally required to be made to HMFI by the occupiers[8] of such premises on accidents which cause the death of a person employed there or which prevents him, as a result of injury, from earning full wages at the work at which he was employed for a period of *more than three days*. It should be noted that the legislation applies to construction processes rather than the construction industry as such, so that the primary statistical material is not coincident in scope with the boundaries of the construction industry. It is important to distinguish, therefore, between analyses of the data made on an industrial basis and those based on the process classification—for further comment see below under 'Interpretation' (Section 6.10.3).

In addition 'dangerous occurrences' (e.g. the collapse of a crane) have to be notified whether death or injury occurs or not. There is also a fourth requirement relating to the notification of industrial diseases (not to be confused with prescribed industrial diseases under the Social Security Acts which have been prescribed in relation to insured persons employed in particular defined occupations). This is of less relevance to construction, but the industry does not escape altogether; for instance, cases of lead poisoning in particular are reported especially in the demolition sector of the industry (see *Annual Report of HM Chief Inspector of Factories* for 1974 [QRL 36] Ch. 4).

For statistical purposes analyses of reported accidents are made in considerable detail

---

[7] In due course new regulations on the notification of accidents will be made under the *Health and Safety at Work, etc. Act 1974*.

[8] In the construction industry, the contractor, though not necessarily the main contractor, is the occupier (see [QRL 36] 1963, p. 53 for a note on the allocation of legal responsibilities). See too [B 312].

according to type of accident, nature of injury, etc. and also incidence rates. In addition, since 1969, further information has been obtained from a 5 per cent sample of accidents about injury severity. It should be noted that in all these cases the unit of measurement used in the statistics is the injured person, not the event, thus one event which leads to the injury of three persons, for instance, would be recorded as three not one. At one time 'frequency rates'—defined as 'numbers of lost-time accidents per 100,000 man-hours worked'—for construction and other industries were also published in the *Annual Reports of the Chief Inspector of Factories* [QRL 36] but it should be noted that these were based on voluntary returns received from a small number of employers and, therefore, not necessarily representative of the whole industry. Further particulars about the statistics will be found in a guide issued by the Inspectorate in 1960 [B 238] and in current reports by the Health and Safety Executive [B 243], [B 242] and *Health and Safety Statistics* [QRL 164]. We consider the interpretation of the data in Section 6.10.3 below after considering DHSS statistics and publication sources.

Publication sources. From 1975 the primary source of statistical series is *Health and Safety Statistics* [QRL 164] (this also includes industrial analyses of 'notifiable' and 'prescribed' diseases). Before 1975 statistics were published in *Annual Reports of HM Chief Inspector of Factories* [QRL 36]. For construction in particular, reference may also be made to a number of special reports on the industry: [B 242] and [B 283] (a special survey of fatal construction accidents) both published in 1978; a survey of construction accidents made in 1966 [B 175] and a report covering the period 1954–8 in [B 312]. Details used to be given also (in [QRL 36]) of the number of places subject to the Acts according to Factory Inspectorate Divisions (defined in [B 244]) although it is doubtful how far these figures could be taken as comprehensive indications of the total number of building and construction sites in operation.

Summary statistics are also published with a greater frequency than in the principal sources referred to above in the *DEG* [QRL 135] and former *MOLG* [QRL 190]: monthly for fatal accidents and quarterly for both fatal and non-fatal accidents. Convenient secondary sources for the annual fatal accident series are the *Historical Abstract* [QRL 58] up to 1968 and then the *Yearbooks* [QRL 59]; it is also included in the *AAS* [QRL 31]. The *Yearbooks* [QRL 59] also contain the series for the number of 'severe injuries'.

6.10.2. *The DHSS Accident Statistics*

The DHSS statistics, which are based on records arising from the administration of social security legislation relating to industrial injuries (currently the *Social Security Act 1975*), cover persons in 'employed earner's employment' (currently)—formerly 'insurable employment' (for further details see the official guide to *Social Security Statistics* [B 327] and the companion Review in this series by Whitehead [B 170]).

Two basic sets of data are compiled, one relating to accidents which attract the award of Industrial Death Benefit (not payable if there are no dependants) and one relating to accidents accepted as 'industrial accidents' for Industrial Injury Benefit purposes. Analyses of the latter by industry (including construction) provide series for the 'number of spells of certified incapacity resulting from fresh industrial accidents' and duration of incapacity; these, unlike the fatal accident series, are based on samples of claimants (5 per cent to 1968–9, then 2½ per cent to 1974–5—in 1975–6 the sample size was reduced to 2 per cent but at the time of writing these data had not been published).

Publication sources. The primary publication source is *Social Security Statistics* [QRL 312] but series from 1970/1 are also reproduced in *Health and Safety Statistics* [QRL 164].

6.10.3. *Interpretation*

Little needs to be said about the fatal accident statistics. The only doubt about the accuracy of the HMFI figures that would occur would be in marginal cases where there was some doubt about the cause of death. The DHSS statistics may under-record to the extent to which death benefits were not payable. The HMFI injury and dangerous occurrence statistics, however, are known to be seriously deficient. It is possible for both under-reporting and over-reporting to occur but it is generally agreed that the Factory Inspectorate statistics suffer seriously from under-reporting. A special survey carried out in October 1962 in conjunction with the then Ministry of Pensions and National Insurance, based upon claims for industrial injury benefit terminating in a particular week, showed that in construction only 43 per cent of the accidents which appeared to be reportable to the Factory Inspectorate had in fact been reported (*Annual Report* for 1963 [QRL 36] p. 20 refers) and it is still felt that under-reporting in the construction industry is of the order of 50 per cent (*Health and Safety Statistics 1975* [QRL 164], p. 10). It is generally recognized that the DHSS statistics provide a more reliable measure of the number of accidents because they do not suffer from under-reporting in the same way as the Factory Inspectorate statistics, but they also include incidents which would not be 'accidents' for Factory Inspectorate purposes and the sources of information available (basically doctor's statements) are much less amenable to analysis by cause.

However, the fact that the DHSS statistics are much greater than the Factory Inspectorate figures is not due solely to under-reporting in the latter. There are differences in the scope and coverage of the two sets of data and, in practice, differences in industrial classification occur—cases classifiable to construction by the Factory Inspectorate may not be so classified by the DHSS (see Shipp and Sutton [B 144] para. 47). The discrepancy that arises, therefore, is the outcome of several conflicting forces. An extremely valuable discussion of the reasons why under-reporting (and mis-reporting) occurs and of the reasons for, and extent of, other errors will be found in the study by Shipp and Sutton [B 144], referred to above, which was made for the Robens Committee on Safety and Health at Work. The Committee's report [B 317] also discusses the available statistics.

Scope—employees and the self-employed. For construction in particular, the interpretation of the statistics also needs to take account of the numbers at risk in the industry who work as 'self-employed' operatives under labour-only sub-contract, since the legal reporting requirement for accidents does not extend to the self-employed. In construction too Working Principals or Working Proprietors also undertake manual work on site. To the extent that such workers are not in 'employed earner's employment' they would also not appear in the DHSS industrial injury statistics. Under new regulations to be made under the *Health and Safety at Work, etc. Act*, the author is informed that the reporting requirement in future is likely to apply to the self-employed only in certain cases—those on a construction site where they come under overall control of a firm—but are unlikely to apply to those working *entirely* on their own.

Incidence rates. With regard to incidence rates, it needs to be appreciated that data on the numbers at risk—on which the incidence rates are based—have themselves to be estimated, for official employment statistics for the industry cover persons who are not at work on construction processes and therefore not within the scope of the legislation. Details of how the estimate of the numbers at risk in construction in particular is made have not been published. For manufacturing industries special surveys were made prior to the introduction of incidence rate series in 1959 to establish the relationship between numbers employed and numbers at risk (*Annual Report* [QRL 36] for 1959, Cmnd. 1107, pp. 10–12 refers) but incidence rates for construction were not introduced at that time and were published only irregularly in subsequent reports. Series for construction from 1959, however, have been published by Eden [B 51] using previously unpublished data. Naturally, the point about the non-coverage of self-employed labour, made above, also has a bearing on the interpretation of the published incidence rates—and in this connection it should be noted that marked changes have taken place in the numbers of self-employed workers in construction (see Section 6.2.3.4).

Industrial and process classification. Interpretation of the HMFI statistics also needs to take account of the distinction, referred to earlier, between the classification by process and the classification by industry. For instance, accidents on building operations carried out by the maintenance staff of a factory would appear under construction in the process classification, but in the industrial classification it would be recorded under manufacturing industry. Conversely accidents on joinery work, for example, carried out by a builder in his own workshops would be classified as a factory process but could be classified to construction in the industrial classification (depending on whether the workshops were regarded as a separate manufacturing 'establishment' for SIC purposes).

A final point concerns the value of the data as indicators of trends rather than levels. This depends, of course, upon the extent to which the degree of over-reporting or under-reporting remains constant. It appears, however, that it has in fact varied: there was a sharp rise in reported accidents, for example, in the early 1960s and it is suggested that this was not entirely due to there being more accidents, but arose partly from improved reporting resulting from publicity and changes in the law—see the *Annual Report* [QRL 36] for 1961 (Cmnd. 1816) and *Construction Health and Safety 1976* [B 242]. There have also been changes in the scope of the regulations relating to construction processes from time to time—details are given in [B 242] and the *Annual Reports* [QRL 36].

6.11. Strike Statistics—United Kingdom

Current series. Strike statistics form the subject of a separate *Review* in this series [B 50] and our treatment here, therefore, is brief. Reference should be made to that work for fuller discussion; a useful brief official account of the data will be found in [B 323] pp. 5–8. Statistics relating to stoppages of work due to disputes concerning terms and conditions of employment have been compiled by the DE and its predecessors for the whole of the post-war period and earlier. The primary series show the number of stoppages beginning in a defined period and, for all stoppages in progress, the number of workers involved (both directly and indirectly involved but at the establishment where the stoppage occurred only) and the number of working days lost. These are given monthly in the *DEG* [QRL 135] and the former *MOLG* [QRL 190]. Secondary sources are the *Historical Abstract* [QRL 58], which reproduced the annual series by industry for the period 1960–8, and subsequently the *Yearbooks* [QRL 59]; the *AAS* [QRL 31] which includes annual series for all three categories, and the *MDS* [QRL 195] which includes monthly series but of the number of working days lost only. Separate analyses of the data in respect of the disputes known to have been official are now also made regularly and published in the *DEG* [QRL 135] each month, though annual data only are given for individual industries—the series extends back to 1960 but was published for the first time in 1972 (*DEG* [QRL 135] Vol. 80).

Additional information and analyses are provided in an annual summary article in the *DEG* [QRL 135] and former *MOLG* [QRL 190]. This has provided particulars about individual 'principal' or 'prominent' stoppages over the whole period. In addition, regional analyses of the primary series for construction and other industries have been included since 1955 (first published in *MOLG* [QRL 190] Vol. 65, 1957, pp. 153–6) and industrial analyses by cause of the dispute have been published for the period since 1959 (first published in *MOLG* [QRL 190] Vol. 68, 1960, pp. 181–6)—earlier analyses by cause did not provide an industrial breakdown. A description of the classification system used for the analyses by cause will be found in *DEG* [QRL 135] Vol. 81, 1973, pp. 117–20. Incidence rates, showing the number of working days lost per 1,000 employees (as recorded in the DE series of 'employees in employment'—Section 6.2.3 refers) have been published annually in the *DEG* [QRL 135] and former *MOLG* [QRL 190] since 1959.

The scope of the data, it should be noted, is expressly limited: stoppages involving fewer than ten workers and those which lasted less than one day are excluded unless the aggregate number of working days lost exceeds 100. Interpretation of the data also needs to take account of certain difficulties involved in compiling the data with precision. There is no statutory obligation to report stoppages and it is possible for some to occur which go unrecorded. This may be particularly important in construction given the large number of scattered sites of widely varying sizes in operation at any one time and the constant flux in the situation as some sites close down and new ones open up. Further, the distinction between workers directly and indirectly involved must often be difficult to make for construction bearing in mind the fact that sub-contractors' labour may be prevented from working on a particular site by a dispute involving another contractor's employees—and thus be directly involved, apparently, in the dispute—but in fact they may not be put out of work since they may simply transfer to another site. For the same reason determination of the number of days lost may be difficult.

With regard to the incidence rates, it should be noted that they are not entirely satisfactory as indicators of 'strike-proneness', as the total number of days lost, on which the calculations are based, includes days lost at the establishments concerned by workers who were both directly and indirectly involved; also the employment series, constituting the denominator in the calculations, includes ATC workers who are normally less involved in stoppages and the proportion of these varies considerably from one industry to another.

In the light of the above, it should also be appreciated that accuracy of reporting is also likely to be greater for some industries than others so that a comparison between one industry and another cannot always be taken at its face value. Clegg [B 40], in particular, has also pointed out the limitations of these statistics as indicators of industrial disputes inasmuch as no account is taken of forms of pressure other than strikes, e.g. the 'work-to-rule', the 'go-slow' and the 'over-time ban'.

Details of the number of cases dealt with by the Advisory, Conciliation and Arbitration Service (ACAS) are given in its *Annual Reports* [QRL 33].

Historical series. For details of historical (pre-Second World War) statistics reference should be made to the companion volume in this series by Durcan [B 50], the official guide to labour statistics [B 241] and to the critique by Knowles [B 89]; the latter also contains series for building and other industries for the period 1911–47.

6.12. Trade Union Statistics—United Kingdom

6.12.1. *Membership and Industrial Relations*

Accurate analyses of trade union membership according to industry are not available. Many trade unions have members in more than one industry and figures which would enable an allocation by industry to be made are not readily available. Nevertheless, the attempt was regularly made in official statistics until 1968, to produce an industrial analysis as far as possible. Except for special *ad hoc* estimates made for 1964, however, it is most important to note that this was done by assigning the *total* membership of each union to the industry with which the majority of its members were believed to be connected. But in cases of unions with widely dispersed membership (e.g. the TGWU) industrial assignation in this way is unrealistic and the figures were left unclassified. Many 'unskilled' and 'semi-skilled' labourers in the construction industry are included in the membership of such general unions.

The statistics themselves were compiled by the DE (and former MOL) on the basis of data supplied by trade unions to the appropriate registration authority (Registrars of Friendly Societies until 1971; the Registrar of Trade Unions during the operation of the *Industrial Relations Act 1971*; the Certification Officer under the *Employment Protection Act 1975)* or directly to the Department and published in an annual article in *DEG* [QRL 135] and former *MOLG* [QRL 190]. They related to all organizations of employees (manual and non-manual, wage earners and salary earners) 'which are known to include in their objects that of negotiating with employers with a view to regulating the wages and working conditions of their members' with head offices in the United Kingdom. In some cases, it should be noted, membership of UK-based unions extends to the Irish Republic. It should also be noted, particularly if comparison is made with the total number of employees in the industry, that the figures may also include retired members and members working overseas. It should also be appreciated that any person belonging to more than one union is counted more than once. Further particulars of the data will be found in the articles themselves.

The special estimates referred to above were made by the Ministry of Labour for the Royal Commission on Trade Unions and Employers' Associations for the year 1964 and were published in [B 323] p. 23. These estimates, it should be noted, excluded retired members, but no further particulars are given of the basis of the estimates.

The only other information available about trade union membership on an industrial basis comes from *ad hoc* enquiries. Questions on trade union membership were included in the National Training Survey carried out in 1975 (see Section 6.7.6), in the construction survey carried out for the Phelps-Brown Committee [B 307] (Section 6.7.4) and in a survey of small firms carried out for the Bolton Committee [QRL 227] (Section 7.2.5 refers). Estimates of 'density' of union membership in construction and other industries in 1948 and 1974 have been made by Price and Bain in [B 124] using, it should be noted, information obtained directly from unions for the purpose of making estimates of membership according to industry.

Information about the membership of individual trade unions is available in the annual reports of the Certification Officer for Trade Unions [QRL 34] currently (formerly in those of the Chief Registrar of Friendly Societies [QRL 256]) and details for those affiliated to the TUC are given in its annual reports [B 341] but, as stressed above, it needs to be remembered that trade union membership cuts across industrial boundaries. In construction this is true not only of unions which represent unskilled workers but also those which represent craftsmen. Currently the principal unions for construction workers are UCATT, TGWU, GMWU and FTATU; these, however, do not represent some important crafts—e.g. plumbers and electricians (EETPU).

For details of historical data in this field reference should be made to the official guide to labour statistics [B 241].

Industrial relations. There are no formal statistics as such relating to the conduct of industrial relations in the industry but some information of interest is available from a series of surveys carried out for the Royal Commission on Trade Unions and Employers' Associations, and reported in [B 350], which were designed to find out how industrial relations are actually conducted at 'workshop' level in construction and other industries and about the attitudes of, and part played by, shop stewards, local full-time trade union officers, works managers, personnel officers and supervisors, as well as workers themselves.

6.12.2. *Finance*

Information about the finance of 'listed' trade unions is contained in the reports of the Certification Officer [QRL 34] and, prior to 1976, in those of the Chief Registrar of Friendly Societies [QRL 256]. It should be noted that until the passage of the *Trade Union and Labour Relations Act 1974* returns were required only from registered trade unions and then from all trade unions. The reports of the Chief Registrar [QRL 256] provided an industrial grouping but this was subject to the same lack of precision as the membership statistics, referred to above, and has now been discontinued.

CHAPTER 7

FINANCIAL STATISTICS

First, a word of explanation is perhaps necessary about the scope and content of this chapter. Its purpose is to consider all statistics of a financial or accounting character which are not examined elsewhere in this Review. The first part of the section is concerned with construction in the context of the national income and expenditure accounts for the whole economy and associated regional accounts which are now being developed. This is followed by a sub-section dealing with company income and finance in the construction sector. Four further sub-sections are concerned with R & D expenditure (by both private and public agencies), acquisitions and mergers by construction companies, statistics of bankruptcy and company liquidation and taxation statistics.

7.1. Construction in the National Income and Expenditure Accounts

7.1.1. *Accounts for the UK*

7.1.1.1. *The official accounts 1946 to date.* Accounts for the whole of the UK have been compiled by the CSO for the whole of the post-war period and are published annually as *National Income and Expenditure*—the 'Blue Book'—[QRL 201]. Quarterly accounts, introduced in the mid-1950s, do not provide relevant information for construction except for capital formation data and these were considered earlier in Section 5.4.2. The basic purpose of these accounts is to provide a measure of total economic activity—gross domestic product (GDP). They also reveal something of the anatomy of the economy by providing analyses of: the contribution to total output made by each industry, the incomes generated and the flows of expenditure—each being an alternative way of looking at total economic activity but each being integrated into a single set of accounts. Construction, of course, forms an integral part of these accounts and indeed represents one of the country's major industries in terms of its contribution to GDP and, especially, because of its pre-eminence in the provision of capital goods.

The compilation of these accounts naturally follows certain conventions and draws upon a very wide variety of statistical sources, many of which we consider elsewhere in this Review. A detailed explanation of the conventions and the sources and methods used is set out in two successive editions of an official guide [B 275] and [B 100] published in 1956 and 1968 respectively; developments since 1968 are noted in the 'Blue Books' themselves. It is not proposed, therefore, to consider these fully here. The objective of this section is to define the scope and nature of the information available for construction and to consider its use and interpretation.

Construction is represented in the accounts under each of the three ways of looking at economic activity referred to above—output, income and expenditure—and we examine each of these in turn.

Output. With regard to the contribution of the construction industry to total national output (series from 1948), interpretation needs to take account of two points. First, the contribution made by the industry is not the same as the value of its gross output—statistics about which were dealt with earlier (Chapters 3, 4 and 5.3)—for this value incorporates the contribution of goods and services supplied by other industries. Rather it is a measure of net output—the value added by construction activity itself. Secondly, it should be noted that the estimate included in the 'Blue Book' [QRL 201] is not derived from output statistics at all, but is based upon the aggregation of factor incomes generated in the industry. Statistics of net output published in the census of production reports are not the same—see Section 5.3.

Income. Separate figures are given for 'income from employment' and 'gross profits of companies and income from self-employment', the former being sub-divided into two categories: wages and salaries and 'employers' contributions' (further sources of information for this item and the total wages and salaries bill were considered in Section 6.9.5). Company profits are also given separately on a gross and net basis (i.e. gross profits less the statutory depreciation allowances granted for tax purposes) in a separate table. All of the income figures are based upon the statistics compiled by the Inland Revenue as a consequence of its taxation functions, after due allowance is made for the income of people who are not subject to tax. These statistics are considered in Section 7.6 below. It is worth noting here, in connection with this series, however, that the construction estimates may be affected particularly once again by the success achieved by many of the large number of self-employed construction workers in slipping through most of the statistical nets and that the estimates of self-employed income rely on Inland Revenue assessments under Schedule D plus an estimate for tax evasion.

Expenditure. Expenditure can be looked at from two points of view: expenditure by other industries and sectors of the economy on the products of the construction industry and, secondly, expenditure by the construction industry itself. The products of the construction industry are primarily capital goods and are distinguished in accounts of 'gross fixed capital formation'. These provide separate data for expenditure on 'buildings and works' broken down in considerable detail according to industry and sector for whom the work is carried out. These statistics are an important source of information about construction work and, therefore, they are considered at some length as part of the chapter dealing with production above (Section 5.4). As we note in that section, expenditure on repairs and maintenance to buildings and other construction works is not regarded as part of capital formation but a separate figure for this item is shown as a footnote to the tables (based, however, on output rather than expenditure returns and relating to Great Britain rather than the UK).

Expenditure by the construction industry. Expenditure by the construction industry itself on capital formation is also shown, but it is important to note that for this purpose the industry is not defined in accordance with the SIC—all public sector direct labour departments being excluded. Expenditure by the industry on the products of other industries for non-capital purposes are not given in the Blue Book. Relevant analyses are available, however, in separate input–output tables; these are derived from the censuses of production and were also considered earlier (Section 5.3.4).

Capital stock. Finally, in addition to current expenditure on capital formation the national accounts also include estimates of: the accumulated capital stock of buildings and works and other assets, the capital stock of the construction industry itself and related figures of 'capital consumption'; these are considered later in Chapter 12.

7.1.1.2. *Unofficial historical accounts for the UK 1920–38.* We direct attention here to historical sources but provide no further discussion since, strictly speaking, they are outside the scope of this Review; the primary sources in any case provide detailed accounts of methodology. But we would emphasize that the attempt to compile retrospective series is attended by substantial difficulties due to limitations in the primary statistical source material and that the results are consequently subject to potentially greater margins of error than the official post-war estimates.

Retrospective accounts of national income, expenditure and output have been compiled for the period 1920–38 by Feinstein and reported in [QRL 13] (together with a very detailed commentary on sources and methods of estimation) and [QRL 14] (tables alone, without the commentary). Tables relevant to construction (called 'Building and Contracting') show the estimated contribution by the industry to GDP each year sub-divided into: (a) income from employment (further sub-divided into wages, salaries, and employers' contributions), and (b) gross trading profits and other trading income (further sub-divided, for the years 1927 and 1937 only, by type of enterprise). Earlier estimates of profits in building and contracting and other industries, with which comparisons may be made, are reported by Hart, also for the period 1920–38, in [B 70] and by Worswick and Tipping for the period 1909–38 in [B 172].

Feinstein also provides estimated series of capital formation and capital stocks in buildings and works over the period back to 1856 and 1855 respectively, both of which are referred to elsewhere in this volume—Section 5.4.4 and Chapter 12 respectively.

7.1.2. *Regional Accounts*

The preparation of official regional accounts is still in its infancy. As yet the only figures at an industrial level that have been prepared show the estimated contribution to GDP in each of the four constituent countries of the UK and the regions of England sub-divided by type of income as in the national accounts (except that no separate figures are given for company profits on a regional basis). These were presented for the first time, covering the period 1971–4, in [QRL 17] together with brief background notes about the methods of estimation. The statistics alone are also published in *Regional Statistics* [QRL 252]. A full account of the methodology is due to be published by the CSO in its *Studies in Official Statistics* series [B 300].

One problem in estimating regional incomes is drawing a distinction between region of residence and region of work. The official series attempt to measure the former (though it is suggested that, given the size of the regions, there is little difference between the two approaches). The primary source of material is considered elsewhere in this Review and there is, therefore, no need to consider it closely here. It is stressed in the descriptive article [QRL 17] that the figures are estimates subject to error and some broad orders of magnitude are quoted, although no special attention is devoted to the individual industry components.

Finally, we note, briefly, earlier unofficial attempts to compile regional accounts. All of these provide two categories of information of relevance for construction: estimates of the contribution by construction and other industries to regional GDP and estimates of capital formation in buildings and works (as well as other assets) in the region. Since capital formation statistics were considered earlier (Section 5.4) we confine our attention here to the industrial analyses of GDP only. The only regional estimates covering the whole UK were made for the year 1961 by Woodward and reported fully in [QRL 28]. This provides estimates for the same categories as the CSO now provide for more recent years and was based on similar sources and methods. It will be appreciated that the same difficulties in covering the incomes earned by self-employed workers, but not declared to the Inland Revenue, arise with these earlier estimates as with the CSO figures, although the incidence of this factor may have been less severe in 1961. Assessments are made of the orders of magnitude of margins of error (pp. 145-6) but since there is no discussion of the self-employment problem in construction it is doubtful whether these are meant to encompass this potential source of error or not.

The only other regional estimates come from studies confined to constituent countries of the UK. Estimates for Wales were made by Tomkins for the years 1965-8 in [QRL 27]. Like other studies these too are based on the sum of incomes method. Unlike the other studies, however, the Welsh study was based on alternative sources to the Inland Revenue data (in the main census of production data and data on employment and average earnings)—a full account is given in the published report [QRL 27]. It also provides estimates in more detail than the other studies, differentiating between wages and salaries and between income from self-employment and gross profits of companies. Estimates for Scotland for the years 1961-71 were made by Begg, Lythe and Sorley in [QRL 2] including estimates of expenditure on buildings and works (capital formation) but no estimates of income according to industry; a discussion of earlier studies for Scotland to which reference may usefully be made is also provided. Studies for Northern Ireland are considered separately in Section 9.6.1.

The only other source of regional income data by industry would appear to be Phyllis Deane's work, for the year 1948, in [QRL 8]; this covered all constituent countries and regions of the UK but was confined to income from employment. The basic data sources used, details of which are given in the study itself, are discussed elsewhere in this Review.

7.2. Statistics of Company Income and Finance

We are mainly concerned here with analyses based on published accounts covering the major construction firms, but the scope of the section also extends to related financial statistics available from other sources, in particular: analyses of returns to the Price Commission (Section 7.2.2), bank advances (Section 7.2.3), statistics relating to quoted securities (Section 7.2.4), surveys of the small firm sector not covered in the regular analyses of company accounts (Section 7.2.5) and surveys of overseas earnings, investment and assets (Section 7.2.6). Further financial information, based upon returns for taxation purposes, is considered separately in Section 7.6.

7.2.1. *Statistics from Company Accounts*

7.2.1.1. *Summary analyses.* Until recent years the only summary analyses of company accounts were those based on the accounts of public companies quoted on UK Stock Exchanges. The construction industry, however, is dominated by private companies, partnerships and sole traders. Given the size of the industry, the proportion of public companies is extremely small and the proportion quoted on the Stock Exchanges infinitesimal. Since 1967 the analyses have been extended in scope to cover both quoted and non-quoted companies (now referred to as 'listed' and 'unlisted' companies) back to 1960 but confined to those above a certain size (for details see the reports referred to below). As far as construction is concerned, however, the published analyses have remained limited to the few listed companies, those for unlisted companies being consolidated as part of a larger industrial group and available separately only on request (see below). It should also be remembered that, despite the expansion in coverage, the construction companies included still constitute a small part of the construction industry.

The analyses available run from 1949 and provide three separate summaries of the accounts: an income appropriation account, a balance sheet and a statement of sources and uses of funds. Summaries of further information, which companies have been required to include in their annual reports since 1967, are referred to below. It should be appreciated that these analyses are not simple aggregations of published accounts. First, variation in accounting practices between one company and another means that adjustments have to be made to place these accounts on as comparable a basis as possible. Secondly, as companies do not always include a sources and uses of funds statement, the provision of a summary has to be based upon an analysis of the other two accounts.

Early work in bringing the published accounts together and compiling summaries in a standardized form was carried out at the NIESR and the results, covering the period 1949–53, were published by the Institute in [QRL 127]. This also contains a general discussion about the data and the preparation of the summary accounts. An analysis and discussion of the data for the construction companies quoted at that time (less than 50 companies) will be found in a related work: [B 159] Ch. 12. After 1953 the analyses were continued by the BOT and its successors (currently the DOI) on the same lines until 1960 when certain changes were made (see below). However, the analyses published for the period 1953–60 (included periodically in *ET* [QRL 147]) provide separate details for manufacturing industries but not construction. For construction, the information is available only in separate tabulations issued by the BOT Statistics Division [QRL 171]; these cover the whole period from 1949 to 1960.

In 1960 changes were introduced in the scope and presentation of the analyses. First, the scope of the data have been confined from 1961 onwards to companies above a certain size only (the size limit was subsequently changed—details will be found in the reports). Secondly, the analyses have been confined to a fixed population of companies—previously all companies had been covered, but in order to provide a basis for comparisons over time, it had been necessary to prepare figures each year for 'comparable sets of companies' for the current and the previous year. Details of the changes were given in the *BOTJ* [QRL 48] Vol. 183, 1962, p. 1153. From 1961 the analyses were also made every quarter until 1968 when the previous annual frequency was resumed.

From 1960 separate figures for construction were published in *SIPEP* [QRL 331] until it was discontinued in June 1969 (covering the period up to 1968) and then in *Business Monitor M3* [QRL 72] (the first issue containing figures back to 1964) although, as we noted above, this continues to identify separately only listed construction companies. Summaries of the results for the unlisted construction companies included in the extended analyses, referred to earlier, are available on request, however, from the DOI (Economics and Statistics Division).

The *Business Monitor* [QRL 72] also includes summaries of the information which certain companies have been required to include in annual reports since the passage of the *1967 Companies Act*: turnover, exports, political contributions, charitable contributions, contracts for capital expenditure placed but not provided for, aggregate remuneration paid to UK employees per year and the average number of employees per week in the UK.

Overseas-owned construction companies. Since 1969 separate analyses have been prepared for those companies operating in the UK which are owned by a company overseas. A comparison and general commentary on the accounts of such companies, analysed according to whether such companies are overseas-controlled or UK-controlled, will be found in *ET* [QRL 147] No. 238, 1973. Subsequent figures are available on request from the Statistics Division of the DOI. The number of construction companies concerned is very small indeed.

Unofficial summaries. We may also note that unofficial analyses of company accounts are also published regularly, the most notable being those prepared by the *Financial Times (FT)* [QRL 159] and *The Economist* [B 222]; the latter are now available (quarterly) only on subscription but at one time analyses were regularly published in the journal itself. These analyses are generally available more frequently than the official summaries, but it should be realized that they represent simple summaries of the accounts received up to a short time before publication. Consequently they are not comprehensive and comparisons over time may be affected by changes in the composition of the group covered from one period to the next. Further details of the *FT* analyses are given in [B 235].

Interpretation. We have already emphasized the marked limitation in the scope of the data as far as the construction industry is concerned. One further aspect of their scope is also important. It is important to appreciate that the accounts reflect all the activities of the companies. Many large construction companies carry out work overseas and some of them have interests in other fields of economic activity (a company is classified to construction if that represents its major field of activity). There is a contrast, therefore, with most of the other official statistics for the industry considered elsewhere in this Review, which are confined to domestic activity and in which the collection of statistics from constituent 'establishments' of a company permits a more accurate industrial classification.

It is also perhaps necessary to stress that company accounts suffer from certain defects. This is not the place to consider this question in detail, but certain drawbacks of the data central to their interpretation must be emphasized. Traditionally, company accounts are drawn up on the basis of historic costs. One consequence, and one of major importance when costs and prices do not remain stable over time, is that the values attributed to the various constituent items in the accounts are not on a comparable basis. This affects particularly the values attached to fixed assets. Further, although accounts are drawn up on the basis of commonly agreed principles meant to ensure objectivity, and accounts have to be independently audited, there exists nonetheless room for a certain diversity in the way the principles are applied in practice.

The interpretation of one company's accounts, therefore, needs to be based partly on a knowledge of the particular accounting practices adopted. As regards the summary analyses considered here, problems of non-comparability between one set of accounts and another are intensified in trying to aggregate the accounts of several companies. It is for this reason, as we noted above, that steps have to be taken to try to standardize the accounts as far as possible.

For two reasons, perhaps the most acute problem is that of asset valuation. First, the assets of most companies will have been built up over long periods of time and, therefore, inevitably at different price levels. Secondly, the interpretation of performance ratios based on assets, such as rates of return on capital, are inevitably critically dependent upon the valuation of the assets. Analyses based on turnover are more amenable to analysis since turnover is necessarily on a current price basis, but it was not until the passage of the *1967 Companies Act* that the inclusion of turnover figures in published accounts became a legal requirement. (For an earlier source of information about turnover see Section 7.4 below.) A fuller discussion of the nature and limitations of historic cost accounting will be found in the report of the Sandilands Committee [B 258] Ch. 7, which recommended its replacement by a system of current cost accounting. Further valuable discussion of the nature and limitations of the official standardized accounts in general terms has been provided by Singh and Whittington for the period 1948–60 in [B 147] Appendix A and by Meeks and Whittington for the period since 1960 in [B 101] Appendix B.

Interpretation of the accounts of construction companies in particular is also affected by certain specific factors. For instance, differences in the amount and value of land held for speculative building or investment purposes may introduce marked divergencies between accounts which may otherwise be similar. Differences in the classification of this item in the accounts—it may apparently be included under stocks or fixed assets for instance—may also be important and will certainly influence measures of return on capital employed, depending upon how capital is defined. Also important is the fact that companies may vary considerably in the proportion of plant hired; this too will alter the apparent return on capital employed and make comparisons between companies difficult. Likewise different practices adopted by construction companies in taking profits—i.e. during contracts or at the end of contracts—also make comparisons difficult. Further, differences in the degree to which contracts are sub-let will influence apparent rates of return and the pattern of the accounts. Still further scope for divergence is introduced by differences in the treatment of retention monies and the value of work in progress. For further discussion of these matters reference may usefully be made to the study by Carter of the original analyses of accounts prepared by NIESR in [B 159].

7.2.1.2. *Financial statistics for individual companies.* Since the passage of the *1967 Companies Act* every limited company, public or private, has been required to file copies of its accounts with the Registrar of Companies and these are open to inspection by the public. Before the 1967 Act some private companies had been exempt from this requirement. Lists of large companies classified by industry and according to certain size variables are available from a number of sources. The analyses of company accounts initiated by the NIESR and continued by the BOT, referred to above, led these bodies to publish such lists on a number of occasions: the NIESR listed the larger quoted companies (assets over £2.5 million in 1953–4) included in its analyses in [QRL 119] and the BOT listed the larger companies included in its analyses in 1957, 1960 and 1963 in [QRL 124], [QRL 125] and [QRL 126] respectively. In addition *The Times* newspaper has published a list of large companies annually ranked according to size together with key figures from their accounts for a number of years in [QRL 350]. Private commercial organizations also compile data banks of company accounts and prepare analyses for particular sectors from time to time; we have made no attempt to cover these in this Review but we may perhaps note that some organizations provide a service to subscribers of regular up-to-date company information on cards for filing in card indexes for the use of stockbrokers and others. The most well-known service provided currently is that by Extel Statistical Services Ltd, London.

7.2.2. *Turnover and Profit Margins of Large Companies—Price Commission Returns, 1973 to date*

Since 1973 information about turnover and profit margins of certain large companies has had to be provided to the Price Commission which was established under the *Counter-Inflation Act* of that year. For this purpose companies were divided into three groups according to their size (in terms of turnover). In the case of construction, companies with a turnover of more than £5 million had to report up to 1 August 1977 when the limit was raised to £9 million. The information available from this source is therefore very restricted. Analyses, based on samples of these returns, are published quarterly in *Price Commission Reports* [QRL 238]. It should be noted that the method of calculating profits for this purpose is not that generally used for published accounts (see the Reports cited).

7.2.3. *Bank Advances*

Analyses of the value of advances (amounts outstanding) made by banks to construction and other industries are compiled by the Bank of England for four quarterly months each year for Great Britain and Northern Ireland. These are published in *Financial Statistics* [QRL 158] and, on a UK basis, in *MDS* [QRL 195], with annual series in *AAS* [QRL 31]. The series is available for the whole of the post-war period but note should be taken of discontinuities that occur in 1972 and 1973 owing to a reclassification in 1972 affecting the construction industry *et al.* and the inclusion of six finance houses for the first time in November 1973 although these had been recognized or confirmed as banks some time earlier. Further information is given in [B 228] and in [B 273].

7.2.4. *Statistics Relating to Quoted Securities*

This section is concerned with the statistical information and analyses available about the securities of construction companies listed on the Stock Exchange. Details of the securities themselves are given in *The Stock Exchange Official Yearbook* [B 337].

Share prices, price indices and related information. Actual share prices for each company and related information (dividends, dividend yields and price/earnings ratios, etc.) are published in the daily press, principally the *Financial Times* [QRL 159] and *The Times* [QRL 349]. For the construction sector, share price data are also included in *Construction News* (weekly) [QRL 129]. An index of the share prices of quoted construction companies is compiled jointly by the *Financial Times* newspaper, the Institute of Actuaries and the Faculty of Actuaries and published daily in the *Financial Times* [QRL 159] as one of a series of 'FT-Actuaries Share Indices' which cover various industrial sectors. Background information and details of the method of calculation are given in [B 235]. Since 1972 the journal *Building* [QRL 60] has also published its own 'Building Share Index'. In contrast to the FT-Actuaries index, however, this index covers not only contractors but also companies which supply building materials or services to the construction industry (covering initially thirty companies and then fifty companies). The indices were introduced in the issues of *Building* [QRL 60] for 4 February 1972, pp. 60–61 and 5 May 1972, p. 67 but details of the method of calculation were not given.

Nominal and market values. Statistics of nominal and market values, interest and dividends of the total of listed securities grouped according to industry, including separate groups for 'contracting and construction' and 'building materials' (divided into several sub-categories) are published quarterly in *The Stock Exchange Fact Book* [QRL 332].

7.2.5. *Small Firms in the Construction Industry—Financial and Other Data*

As we indicated earlier, most firms in the construction industry are either small private companies, partnerships or sole traders and very little statistical information of a financial character, or indeed non-financial character, is available for this highly important sector of the industry. An important source of information of both kinds has now been provided in a survey carried out for the Bolton Committee on Small Firms which reported in 1971 [B 326]. This was carried out by the BSO by means of a postal questionnaire addressed to a sample of small firms in construction and other industries. In construction, 438 firms responded to the enquiry—a response rate of 29 per cent from a sample of 1,500. The results have been published in two separate reports providing financial and non-financial data respectively.

The financial analyses, reported in [QRL 26], do not provide separate details for construction for every subject covered, most of the analyses being confined to manufacturing and non-manufacturing groups. Construction is separately distinguished in analyses of the following subjects: asset structure, trade debtors and profitability. Some financial data are also given in the 'non-financial' report referred to below.

Non-financial data were reported in [QRL 227]. For construction, the subjects are: legal status; history of chief executive; source of main competition; training of: clerical staff, management and other staff; proportion of firms covered under the *Industrial Training Act* and relationship between levy and grant payments; trade union membership amongst their labour force; membership of employers' federations/associations; relationship of wage rates to those paid by large firms; strike experience in the previous two years; firms which had merged or been taken over in the previous five years; possession of overdrafts; attempts to obtain additional finance and success achieved; profit margins on sales; trends in trading ratios (debtors/sales and debtors/creditors); pressure on liquid assets; effects of Town and Country Planning Acts; dividend distribution policy (companies only) and the effect of the SET on the use of labour and on business organization.

The Bolton Committee also commissioned a special study of small firms in the construction industry from Hillebrandt—reported in [B 75]. This made use of many of the statistics about the structure of the industry, output, manpower, earnings and characteristics of the labour force referred to elsewhere in this study including some special analyses of DOE statistics (these were separately reported in [QRL 70]).

7.2.6. *Overseas Investment, Earnings and Assets*

Surveys are conducted (currently by the Departments of Industry, Trade and Prices and Consumer Protection) annually to obtain statistics of overseas earnings and investment and every three years to obtain information about the book value of assets. Currently, analyses of the results by industry (construction *et al.*) are given in detail in *Bus. Mon. M4* [QRL 73] providing, in respect of inward and outward investment, statistics of net earnings and net investment according to area and country. The results of the latest census of assets were published as a Supplement to the 1974 edition of *Bus. Mon. M4* [QRL 73]. Summary results are published in *T & I* [QRL 352]. The series were initiated in *BOTJ* [QRL 48] 1963, pp. 877–83, providing annual data back to 1958 but providing aggregates only, without a country breakdown, for earnings and direct investment overseas only, in the early years of the series.

7.3. R & D Expenditure Surveys

R & D statistics are to be the subject of a separate Review in this series [B 174] and our attention to the subject here is, therefore, brief. Statistics of expenditure on R & D have been collected for many years but data for the construction sector is not available until the year 1966/7. The industry had been covered in an earlier enquiry in 1964/5 but the results were published only as part of a larger industrial grouping (in [QRL 328]). Since 1966/7, construction has been separately distinguished in all enquiries. Each of these provides details of: current expenditure by type of expenditure (wages and salaries, materials, etc.) and by type of work (i.e. type of research—'basic'/'applied'/'development'), capital expenditure (analysed, in some enquiries, by type of asset) and sources of finance. Since 1967 the surveys have also been used to obtain statistics about employment on R & D—these were considered in Section 6.6.3.6.

These surveys cover not only private industry but also public corporations and research associations, but are confined to firms affirming, in response to an earlier enquiry, that they carry out R & D work (generally larger firms). Data are given separately for each of these categories. Separate data are also given for central government expenditure on R & D classified by function (now referred to as 'EEC objectives') including, originally, a separate category for 'construction, building and town planning' (these data are also available from the 1964/5 survey referred to above), and currently for 'construction and planning of buildings'. Details of the dates to which the surveys relate and the publication sources are as follows:

```
Year         Publication
1966/7   [QRL 329]  ⎤
1967/8   [QRL 330]  ⎬  [QRL 282]
1968/9              ⎦
1969/70             ⎤
                    ⎬  [QRL 283]
1972/3              ⎦
1975/6   T & I [QRL 352] 24 June 1977, pp. 638–44
```

As indicated above, the results for the enquiries up to 1972/3 have been brought together in two summary reports—[QRL 282] and [QRL 283]. These were compiled by the CSO and contain some revisions of earlier figures as well as detailed notes on the definition and scope of R & D and the execution of the surveys. Reference should be made to these, therefore, for further details as well as to the *Review* of R & D statistics planned as one of the present series. With regard to interpretation, it is emphasized in the case of construction that the figures do not include the sums for 'the appreciable development work undertaken on sites, particularly work undertaken in civil engineering'. It should also be appreciated that much R & D work of relevance to construction is undertaken in building materials industries.

7.4. Company Acquisitions and Mergers

Statistics of expenditure on, and the numbers of, acquisitions and mergers by construction and other companies in the UK are compiled by the DOI. The data on this subject extend back to 1954 but series according to industry have been published only for the period from 1960—annually up to 1967 and then quarterly (an important change in coverage was made in 1969—see below). The primary source of publication currently is *Business Monitor M7* [QRL 74] introduced in 1971 (the third issue—November 1971—contained the full annual series back to 1960); formerly the series were included in the *BOTJ* [QRL 48] and its successor publication *Trade and Industry* [QRL 352] which still provides summary information each quarter. A summary and discussion of the earlier data from 1954 (up to 1961), including a summary by industry for the period, will be found in *ET* [QRL 147] No. 114, April 1963.

Interpretation. The first point to note is that the analyses are restricted to acquisitions of companies: they do not cover the acquisition of unincorporated businesses which, of course, are particularly important, numerically, in the construction industry.

Secondly, it is important to appreciate that there is no statutory reporting requirement and that the series have had to be compiled, therefore, using incomplete sources of information. Up to 1969 the series were compiled on the basis of the accounts of *quoted* companies included by the BOT in its analyses of company income and finance (Section 7.2.1.1 refers)—analyses which also showed figures of expenditure on the acquisition of subsidiaries. From 1969 coverage was widened on the basis of reports in the financial press to cover companies generally (the quarterly series introduced in 1968 to supplement the previous annual series had also been based on reports in the financial press). The change in 1969 showed that the previous figures for construction had been seriously understated. Comparative results on the basis of the old and new statistical populations showed that the effect of the change was to increase the construction series in 1969 by factors of well over two—the expenditure series increasing relatively more than the numbers series—in contrast to manufacturing industries for which the increases were very much less and for which the expenditure series were least affected (overall numbers being raised by 28 per cent and expenditure by only 4 per cent—*BOTJ* [QRL 48] Vol. 198, 1970, p. 526 refers).

The series compiled since 1969, however, still remain incomplete, excluding in particular many small acquisitions. Given the large number of small firms in the construction industry it would seem reasonable to believe that the series for this industry is still particularly affected. Of the two types of data provided—numbers (companies acquiring and companies acquired) and expenditure—it is likely that the latter is less open to error proportionately than the former (in contrast to the earlier period) since it is the smaller mergers that are now more likely to be missed. It is not being suggested here that the errors are necessarily substantial. But, unfortunately, any assessment of the magnitude of the errors that still remain is impossible on the basis of the existing sources of information.

Finally, it should be appreciated that the classification by industry is limited in that it is made only on the basis of the acquiring company. Thus the classification for construction shows the number of acquiring companies classified to the industry, the number of companies acquired (not all of which may be construction companies) and expenditure on acquisitions. Information on the number of construction companies taken over either by other construction companies or by companies in other industries is not given.

7.5. Bankruptcy and Company Liquidation (Insolvency) Statistics

7.5.1. *Introduction*

Insolvency, which normally occurs when a person or company is unable to pay debts on the due date, is recorded in statistics only when it has been acknowledged voluntarily or has been determined by the courts. A distinction is drawn between persons and companies for they are dealt with under separate legal arrangements. Insolvent persons, who are said to become bankrupt, are dealt with under the *Bankruptcy Act 1914* or they may make arrangements with their creditors under the *Deeds of Arrangement Act 1914*.

Insolvent companies, who are said to go into liquidation, are dealt with under the *Companies Acts* of 1948 and 1967. Insolvent partnerships are dealt with in conjunction with the insolvencies of the individual partners under the Bankruptcy Acts.

Statistics of the number of bankruptcies and company liquidations analysed according to industry have been compiled for many years on an annual basis, and for the period since 1969 on a quarterly basis (England and Wales only). A guide to the nature of the information and the way it is compiled, which is useful for interpretative purposes, will be found in [B 219].

7.5.2. *Bankruptcy*

England and Wales. Annual bankruptcy statistics for England and Wales are published in [QRL 45] and provide analyses of the number of failures and the value of assets and liabilities divided between 'receiving orders' (under the bankruptcy arrangements) and 'deeds of arrangement'. Quarterly series show the number of failures only (not differentiated as above); these were published for the first time in *ET* [QRL 147] March 1975 covering the period 1969–74 and since then have been carried forward quarterly in *T & I* [QRL 352] (first published in the issue for 2 May 1975, pp. 330–2). The analysis by trade, it should be noted, relates to self-employed workers. Employees who go bankrupt are not so classified.

Scotland. Statistics of bankruptcies in Scotland, comparable with those for England and Wales, are not available because of differences in the legal arrangements and no statistics are published.[1]

7.5.3. *Company Liquidations—England and Wales and Scotland*

There are two types of company liquidation that involve insolvency: company liquidations which stem from winding-up orders by the courts following petitions to them, and creditors' voluntary liquidations in which the company and its creditors come to terms without court proceedings. Separate statistics of the number of liquidations under these two categories for England and Wales and for Scotland separately are published annually in [QRL 123]. Quarterly series, for England and Wales only, of *total* liquidations is published, together with the quarterly bankruptcy statistics noted above, in *ET* [QRL 147] March 1975 for 1969–74 and subsequently in *T & I* [QRL 352] once a quarter. These statistics do not cover, it should be noted, members' (i.e. shareholders') voluntary liquidations, in which the company winds up for reasons other than insolvency.

7.5.4. *Interpretation*

Information about the compilation of the data, relevant for purposes of interpretation, has been set out in [B 219] to which reference should be made. As far as the construction

---

[1] Further particulars may be obtained from the Accountant of Court, Bankruptcy Department, Parliament Square, Edinburgh.

industry is concerned, one additional matter requires emphasis for the figures for this industry are frequently ill-used. The construction industry generally records a higher number of failures than any other industry and this fact alone often seems to be taken in isolation as a fact of some significance. Meaningful comparison with other industries, however, can only be made in relation to the number of businesses at risk (also a very large number in the construction industry). In addition, it is also desirable to consider the size of the businesses that fail in relation to the size of the industry as a whole but unfortunately, there are difficulties in the way of providing satisfactory size analyses of insolvencies and no such figures are published (see [B 219] for comment). With regard to the interpretation of the series over time, it should be noted that interpretation of the quarterly series in particular is complicated by seasonal variations to which the series are subject due to irregular sittings of the High Court. A useful study which attempts to place the statistics for the construction industry and some others within the context of their relative size has been made recently by Hillebrandt in [B 74].

7.6. Taxation Statistics

7.6.1. Introduction

This section is concerned with the statistics prepared by the Inland Revenue for the UK arising from its work in the collection of taxes levied on the construction industry and the persons who work in it. Statistics about the taxation of capital and the valuation of property for rating purposes, which are also the responsibility of the Inland Revenue, both relate to the construction stock and are therefore considered separately as part of Part III of this Review. Analyses are made as far as possible in accordance with the SIC, but it is important to appreciate that the classification may not be precisely comparable with output and employment statistics because the 'financial units' which form the basis of the taxation data may not coincide with data classified on an 'establishment' basis. A financial unit, of course, may consist of several establishments. The same point applied, it will be recalled, in connection with the statistics derived from analyses of company accounts which were considered earlier (Section 7.2.1). With regard to the industrial classification, it should also be noted that the term 'construction', used in the current SIC, is not used in the IR statistics—these have retained the term 'building and contracting' throughout.

A further general point to note at the outset is that the growth of self-employment in the construction industry in recent years has been accompanied by tax evasion on a scale which may be substantial. The recent statistics for income from employment and self-employment need to be regarded in this light. (There are no adequate statistics about the numbers of men working on a self-employed basis in the industry—for details of the estimates available see Section 6.2.3.4.) A special tax deduction scheme was introduced in April 1972 (under the *Finance Act 1971*) to combat evasion by self-employed workers working under labour-only sub-contract, under which contractors making payments to sub-contractors had to deduct tax and pay it to the Inland Revenue as an advance of the sub-contractor's personal liability, unless the sub-contractor was a limited company or other corporate body or had been issued with a sub-contractors' tax certificate. The scheme was widened and tightened up in the *Finance (No. 2) Act*

1975. Details of the initial scheme will be found in [B 252] and [B 253] and, for the modified scheme, in [B 251]. The new measures did not come into full operation until 6 April 1977 so that it is too soon to judge what effect they have had. But in this connection, interpretation will have to take account of the effect that the severe decline in construction activity that took place after 1973 is likely to have had in reducing the numbers working on a self-employed basis quite independently of the new tax arrangements.

7.6.2. *Personal and Corporate Income Tax*

Analyses of tax assessments classified by industry are published for each financial year as shown below. Since 1970 they have been published in [QRL 173]; previously they were published in [QRL 258].

(a) *Income from Employment (UK)*

This refers to income assessed under 'Schedule E' and collected under the PAYE scheme. Coverage extends to all employees taxed whilst in employment in construction but is confined, of course, to persons whose income exceeds the non-taxable limit. Thus coverage is not comprehensive and will have varied over time with changes in taxation allowances and as a result of inflation. At one time statistics were also published of the number of tax deduction cards but this figure is not an indication of employment (especially in construction where labour turnover is high) because a fresh card was prepared whenever an employee changed his employment.

(b) *Income from Self-employment (Assessments under Schedule D)*

Analyses by trade group are made of the number of assessments, gross true income, capital allowances, net true income and tax deducted separately for England and Wales, Scotland and Northern Ireland as well as for the UK as a whole. Currently, separate analyses are also made for professional earnings and the number of assessments separately for individuals and partnerships providing separate data for architecture (reference should also be made to Section 13.4 regarding professional earnings).

(c) *Company Income*

Analyses by trade group are made on a UK basis of the number of assessments, analyses of 'agreed assessments' (including gross trading profits, other income, etc.), net amount chargeable to tax and tax deducted. In addition, percentage analyses were also made, until 1965, of companies' appropriation of income based on the tax assessments and company accounts, showing the relation between turnover and trading profit (as assessed for tax) and the way in which total income was allocated between dividends and interest, tax, reserves, etc.—these were published annually in [QRL 258].

(d) Analyses of the capital allowances due to sole traders and partnerships and to companies (including separate data for allowances made to all industries on industrial buildings).

(e) Estimated distributions (dividends, etc.) and annual payments made by companies in construction and other trade groups under the corporation tax system (further details are given in [QRL 173]).

7.6.3. *Selective Employment Tax (SET)*

The SET, described in [B 325] and imposed under the *Selective Employment Payments Act 1966*, applied to construction and other industries until it was abolished in 1973. But statistics analysed by *industry* of the numbers of employees covered and the amount collected were not published and the author is informed that none are available. Estimates of inpayments and refunds for the year 1970, however, will be found in the study by Reddaway [B 127] p. 160. It is perhaps worth noting briefly that the tax was aimed at the stimulation of productivity growth in the economy, rather than the raising of revenue, and that it had a number of important incidental effects on the construction industry.

Since the tax was levied on the number of *employees* (self-employed were exempt) and was refundable in the case of manufacturing activities, the tax stimulated self-employment in the industry and also measures to ensure the classification of as much of the work undertaken by construction firms as 'manufacturing', rather than 'construction' as such, under the provisions of 'split-establishment' and 'separate establishment' rules. A discussion of these 'anomalies' will be found in the Reddaway Report [B 127] Ch. XVI. This report also provides an extremely valuable appraisal of official construction (then MPBW) statistics of employment, output and prices in the context of their usefulness for assessing the effect of the tax on prices and productivity in the construction industry (a task which had to remain largely unaccomplished).

7.6.4. *Value Added Tax (VAT)*

VAT was introduced on 1 April 1973 but as yet the statistical information available from its administration is limited. Because of its comprehensive nature, however, the information obtained in its administration will provide an important new source of economic statistics; in particular, information will be obtained about the economic transactions of each firm throughout the economy in terms of sales and purchases (taxable purchases). Since anyone carrying on a business (with a small exception) has to register as a 'taxable person' this source provides important information about the number of 'firms' in the construction industry. The exception referred to above is that businesses with a turnover of less than a certain amount per year are exempt. The amount remained unchanged at £5,000 or less from 1 April 1973 until 1 October 1977 when it was raised to £7,500. Traders are also able to cancel their registration if their turnover falls below a certain level—initially £4,000, now £6,000. These size limits are so small as to exclude very few businesses.

Businesses registered have been classified by trade and also by legal status. Construction is defined in accordance with the SIC [B 329] but sub-classified into twenty-three separate trades (the same as in the DOE analyses but with the addition of a separate category for opencast coal mining)—details are given in [B 348] and [B 112]. At present the only statistics published have been to show: the number of 'registered persons' and details of tax due, tax deductible (i.e. tax paid on inputs) and net tax payable (for construction as a whole). These have been published in the *Customs and Excise Annual Reports* [QRL 257] 66th Report *et seq*. As we noted above, the potential of the information obtained in the administration of this tax is considerable: a useful discussion has been provided by Noyce [B 112].

One important part of the potential which seems to have been realized already is that relating to a compilation of a comprehensive register of businesses. Having remarked upon the difficulties faced by the DOE in the maintenance of a comprehensive register of contractors since 1955 (Section 4.1.3) it is of particular interest to compare the two sources. This reveals a very marked disparity of the order of two to one, the VAT register being twice as large as that of the DOE (the latest available figures show 88,000 firms recorded in the DOE contractors' census for October 1975 [QRL 240] as against 182,900 'persons' on the VAT register at 31 March 1976 [QRL 257] 67th Report, Cmnd. 6694, p. 99).

Certain reasons may be advanced to explain why a discrepancy should exist between the two figures. One is that it is possible for a single firm (reporting unit) on the DOE register to have more than one VAT registration number and consequently to be recorded as more than one unit on the VAT register. Another reason is that persons may be registered for VAT purposes, and classified to construction, who only carry out construction work in their spare time and are not recorded on the DOE register. How far the discrepancy can be explained by factors such as these it is impossible to say at present (it may be noted that the DOE now obtain details of VAT registration numbers and, with effect from the census for October 1977, details of the amount of VAT paid, on its census returns—see Appendix IV—to provide the basis for comparison of the two registers). *Prima facie*, the discrepancy seems very large and would appear to emphasize the difficulties that the DOE face in maintaining a comprehensive register. Reconciliation of the two registers, therefore, would appear to be an urgent task.

With regard to the interpretation of the tax data, perhaps the most important point to note is that, generally speaking, VAT is not payable on new construction work (zero rated) but is payable at the standard rate on repairs and maintenance work. Full particulars of the application of VAT to construction work will be found in [B 346] and [B 347].

CHAPTER 8

CONSTRUCTION COSTS, PRICES AND PRODUCTIVITY

This chapter is concerned with output costs and prices, rather than input costs and prices, and mainly with the indicators that are currently produced. Unfortunately the indices that are currently produced cannot be carried far back in time, although with such a long-lived product as construction goods represent, long time series are often needed. Because of the interest of long time series, brief attention is devoted to historical sources, after considering the current series, in Section 8.1.4. Statistics relating to changes in the costs and prices of inputs of labour and materials are considered in Sections 6.9 and 11.1 respectively. Section 8.2 below is concerned with the problems and pitfalls of productivity measurement for the construction industry in relation to the available statistics—no official index of productivity is published.

8.1. Indices of Construction Costs and Prices

Several series of index numbers are prepared currently (and even more are available for various periods in the past) which attempt to measure changes in building costs or prices. These indices, and the conflicting evidence they provide, are partly reflections of differences in the methods which have been used in the face of severe problems of measurement, and partly differences in concept. Interpretation of the indices available must rest upon an appreciation of the nature of these problems and the related differences in concepts and methodology. We consider these matters first, therefore, before turning to examine the indices that are currently produced.

8.1.1. *Problems and Methods of Measurement*

8.1.1.1. *The nature of the problems and the methods.* The measurement of changes in the costs or prices of construction work poses the most severe difficulties because of its extremely varied nature. In any one year the output of the industry is a mixture of widely varying types of work, including the construction of new buildings of all kinds, civil engineering works and a wide variety of repair and maintenance jobs. Within each of these categories, projects vary in scale, design, complexity and methods of construction, and even similar jobs vary according to differences in site conditions, so that in some sense each job tends to be unique.

Further problems, of a conceptual nature, influence both the approach to measurement and the interpretation of the indices which have been devised. First, there is a simple distinction to be made between building costs and building prices. These two expressions are sometimes used synonymously as meaning the cost of the completed building to the building's owner—the purchase price. However, the term 'building costs' may be used with reference to the costs of the principal factors of production incurred by the builder—labour, material and plant inputs—the difference between these and the price paid by the client representing profit.[1] But quite apart from this distinction, the terms may be used with greater or lesser precision depending on the stage of the building process at which they are measured. They may refer to prices for work yet to be carried out, that is to say tender prices, or to the level of costs for work currently being executed, or to the costs or prices of work which has been completed—i.e. complete projects ready for use. Clearly, measurements which relate to these three stages may be expected to differ and likewise the rates of change over time of such measurements may not be equivalent.

We turn now to consider the methods of measurement which may be used for devising indices, and then use the distinctions we draw as a means of classifying the indices available. Since most work in the field has been concerned with the cost of work to the building owner, we shall use the unqualified expressions 'building costs' and 'building prices' in this sense; use of them in a more restricted sense will be made clear in the particular context in which they are used.

Broadly speaking there are two approaches to the problem of devising an index of construction costs. One is to utilize price data for actual contracts, either in the form of total prices related to the size of the job, or in the form of unit rates for particular items of work abstracted from priced schedules of the operations involved (bills of quantities). The other is to construct an index on the basis of changes in the elements which determine price, namely unit labour and materials costs, overheads, profits and productivity. Within these two categories a number of sub-categories may be defined and we now turn to examine each of these.

8.1.1.2. *The use of actual price data*—(a) *Total prices.* It is generally necessary to draw a distinction between two prices—the tender price and the final account price. The tender price is the price at which the contractor is prepared to execute the building works at the time of acceptance, and, if a 'firm' price, is likely to reflect not only current prices but expectations about future changes in costs during the construction period. Regardless of the basis of the quotation, however, the two prices may differ because at the tender stage certain specialist work and other items will only be priced provisionally and, if the tender is not quoted as a firm price, 'fluctuation clauses' will allow changes in the cost of labour or materials or both, occurring during the life-time of the contract, to be recouped. Further, variations to the design or specification of the work ordered during the process of construction naturally allow the original tender price to be revised. Hence final costs of construction may differ from initial tender prices for a variety of reasons. It is possible, of course, that the trend of tender prices may not diverge from the trend of final account prices though this may be unlikely in periods of unstable prices and high levels of uncertainty.

Whichever price basis is used the indices need to be based on a sufficiently representa-

---

[1] Profit, of course, is also a factor income but it may be regarded as a residual which is not determined until the final account is settled. How it relates to planned profit is critically dependent upon the builder's ability to estimate the costs that any particular contract will involve.

tive number of contracts for work as closely identical in type as possible. This is a major difficulty, and over long periods of time it becomes less and less possible to satisfy this condition because of changes in standards, technical requirements and design. The 'Venning' index (published from the First World War until 1975 [B 167]) was based, informally, on total tender prices but no current indices are so based—current tender price indices are based on disaggregated (unit rate) data—see below.

A method which has been suggested (it has not been used in Britain) to overcome the problem of the lack of a standard product would be to invite tenders periodically from builders for a building of a standard design and specification, even though it was not intended to erect the building. Such a method would be faced, of course, with the need to allow for the changes in standards that do take place over time and with the more severe problem that, since the builders tendering would have no prospect of gaining a contract, there could be no assurance that the prices quoted were reasonable reflections of current cost levels and the tendering climate. A further potential method is to use regression techniques to develop a model which 'predicts' prices on the basis of given physical characteristics of projects in a base period. The model can then be used to reprice current projects at base year prices and a comparison of the two values yields an estimate of the percentage change in price allowing for differences in physical characteristics. Again, therefore, given a sufficient number of projects a general price index could be devised in this way. It is not used in this country but some exploratory work has been carried out, some particulars of which have been given by Bryant in [B 33].

(b) *Unit rates and the repricing of tenders.* An alternative to using total prices is to use unit rates for particular items of work extracted from the priced bills of quantities of accepted tenders. The use of unit rates helps to overcome the lack of homogeneity over time, but requires access to a sufficiently representative selection of bills. It requires too, a reasonably large sample of bills for the reason that the rates inserted by different builders vary considerably not only because of differences in their levels of efficiency and in the labour, materials and plant costs used by the estimator, but also because of differences in the practices adopted by firms in arriving at a total tender price.

There are basically two ways in which unit rate data may be used. One is to take the rates in current bills and compare them directly with those quoted in base-period tenders. This method, of course, depends on the regular quotation of comparable rates and presents the familiar index number problem of devising appropriate sets of weights for averaging the prices extracted. The method is not used to obtain a general building tender price index but it is used to obtain a price index for local authority house building (PILAH) in England and Wales (excluding Greater London). We simply direct attention to this index here in the context of methodology since housing is outside the scope of this Review—further particulars will be found in [B 114]; the index itself is published in *HCS* [QRL 168].

Rather than comparing unit rates directly, the other way in which the information may be used is for repricing tenders. Two basic approaches are possible: either to use standard rates from a base period to reprice current bills or to use the current rates to reprice a standard bill. Comparison of the values of the bill at base-period and current prices yields an index of price change for each bill which then have to be averaged over several bills to produce a single index. The former, of course, produces a Paasche type (currently weighted) index as far as the individual bill indices are concerned, whilst the latter, based on a standard bill, naturally involves the use of fixed base weights. In either case the method may be used for full repricing of the whole bill or partial repricing by taking a sample of items only from the bill. This method is used to compile both official and unofficial general building tender price indices. A study which explored the practical application of these methods prior to the development of the official index is reported in [B 30].

A method analogous to the use of rates extracted from priced bills is to use unit rates published in builders' estimating manuals (price books) or trade journals. Such rates, however, are only estimates built up on the basis of certain standardized formulae for combining input costs and as such are more appropriately considered later.

The use of methods based on actual prices has a disadvantage from the point of view of studies concerned with total construction work, in that it will generally be possible to cover only certain well-defined classes of work, the price movements for which may not be representative of all work. Studies concerned with construction work as a whole require a more general measure of price movements. Such a measure is most conveniently built up on the basis of changes in input costs—the constituents of prices—although here too severe practical and conceptual difficulties are involved.

8.1.1.3. *The use of input costs data—composite indices.* Indices based on changes in the costs of inputs representing the constituents of prices may be derived in three ways. First there are those which may be based upon separate indices for labour and materials costs, possibly incorporating some allowances for changes in overheads, profits and productivity. Secondly, one may distinguish an indirect method using labour and materials costs indices to reprice the input of factors of production. Thirdly, there are those based upon published unit rates which are themselves based on factor price movements.

(a) *Averages of labour and materials costs indices.* This method consists of averaging separate indices of labour and materials costs and may or may not incorporate some allowances for changes in productivity, overheads and profit. Failure to allow for changes in profits means that the index will be insensitive to changes in market conditions and will be a measure of costs to the builder (treating profits as a residual rather than a factor cost), rather than prices to the client. Failure to allow for changes in productivity means that, other things being equal, the index over-estimates price changes when productivity is rising and vice versa.

The measurement of changes in labour and materials costs requires, of course, satisfactory information about the actual costs of labour—i.e. average earnings and associated labour on-costs as opposed to wage rates—and about the wide range of materials used in construction. Much depends on the reliable measurement of these two inputs for in general they constitute a very substantial part of total costs. In principle it is also desirable to incorporate a separate allowance for changes in the costs of using plant but there are difficulties in the way of obtaining satisfactory information and, in general, they constitute a small proportion of total costs; they are generally subsumed, therefore, in the allowance made for changes in overheads.

In practice the most severe difficulties are presented in allowing for changes in productivity, overheads and profits. Little satisfactory information is available on changes in overheads and profits and what there is, is only available retrospectively—either periodically from the Censuses of Production (considered in Section 5.3) or Inland Revenue statistics (Section 7.6). Since the proportion of total costs represented by overheads and profits is generally small, the effect of changes in these factors on prices is proportionately much less, of course, but this is not to say that they may not be important particularly at times of marked fluctuations in the level of demand on the industry.

Perhaps more important, certainly in the long run, is the need to allow for changes in productivity since changes in labour costs per man will not necessarily be reflected proportionately in overall construction costs if, for whatever reason, the rate of output per man changes. The index of labour costs required is one of labour costs per unit of output. The difficulties involved in measuring changes in productivity, however, are formidable. The character of these difficulties is the same as that involved in the direct measurement of price movements, for the need to obtain a representative standard of comparison over time is the same, but with the added problem of requiring information about inputs as well as output. Further, the sole means of comprehending all output in a single measure—monetary units—is now ruled out as a means of measuring changes over time unless a satisfactory *independent* means of eliminating the effect of price movements from it is available. This brings one back full circle, of course, to the problem with which one started. But in any case, output in money terms, whether measured in current or constant prices, remains a heterogeneous mixture of work, the constituents of which have different input requirements, so that apparent changes in output per man at constant prices may be due to changes in the output mix rather than productivity change as such. As a consequence, no satisfactory index of productivity has been devised even for the most recent times—for further discussion see Section 8.2 below.

Despite the difficulties, this method is used to compile the official 'CNC' index and we consider the methodology and, in particular, the conceptual problems further in the context of this particular index in Section 8.1.2.1 below.

(b) *Repricing factors of production.* This method has not been used for Britain or the UK, but it has been used by the author to devise an index for Northern Ireland and is fully described in [B 55]. Briefly, the method consists of revaluing aggregate factor inputs in terms of base year prices. It is to be distinguished from the repricing of bills of quantities which involves the repricing of specific construction tasks in the bills. The required indication of the change in building prices over the base year is then represented by the ratio between the value of gross output at current prices to its estimated value at constant prices. The method depends upon the availability of independent information about the make-up of gross output according to the input of the factors of production and about changes in their costs.

(c) *Published unit rates ('Measured rates').* This method is analogous to that using unit rates from priced bills, described above, the difference being that the rates used are those published in 'price books' or trade journals. These rates are meant to represent the going rates for carrying out specific items of building work. *To the extent to which this is the case* they possess certain advantages from the point of view of devising an index. As with unit rates from priced bills, they facilitate the maintenance of a comparable standard over time reflecting both changes in costs and productivity and incorporating a built-in weighting of labour and materials (they do not eliminate the comparability problem because steps still have to be taken to cope with technical change). It is also possible to derive indices for separate building trades (as was done in published series) which may then be suitably averaged to produce index numbers applicable to different sorts of work. They would also possess the advantage over unit rates from priced bills of enabling the compiler of the index to avoid the trouble and expense of obtaining a representative selection of bills and extracting equivalent rates from them.

In practice, however, it is extremely doubtful whether published unit rates can support the weight of evidence which this would place upon them. Generally, the rates are calculated on the basis of labour and materials 'constants', i.e. the quantities of materials and the estimated man-hours (and possibly plant-hours) required to carry out the item of work in question. Changes in productivity may be allowed for when the rates, or more particularly the constants, are revised. But this may be infrequent, indeed a study by the author [B 59] of one of the most long-standing series going back to the nineteenth century has shown that it is very rare for the constants to be changed. Overheads and profits are commonly allowed for in these rates through the addition of a fixed percentage. Certain reservations, therefore, need to be emphasized. One relates to representativeness, for published rates are generally drawn up by one or a few estimators whose experience can only be limited. Others concern their sensitivity to change: the use of labour and materials constants to describe a changing situation is obviously unsatisfactory, and the incorporation of a fixed percentage to allow for overheads and profits means that the rates must also fail to reflect fluctuations in market conditions. In the post-war period, the BRS Measured Work index was based on this method, but it has now been discontinued—for details see [B 58].

We now turn to examine the indices that are available in the light of the various methods of calculation discussed above.

8.1.2. *Currently Compiled General Indices of Construction Costs and Prices*

In this section we are concerned solely with *general* indices that are compiled at the present time. Special indices that are prepared for price adjustment purposes on contracts do not provide 'general' measures and are considered separately in Section 8.1.3. The scope of this section is also restricted in a number of other ways. No attention is devoted to indices which relate solely to housing (details for this sector are given in the companion review on housing statistics [B 52]), or to indices which are not currently produced (several indices have ceased publication in the recent past—brief references to these and other historical series are given in Section 8.1.4). In addition, there are some indices to which we devote no attention because they are not regularly published; many of these are specialized indices produced by organizations for their own purposes.[2]

Details of the indices available, classified according to the methods of measurement used, are set out in Table 8.1. The variety of indices available presents the user with a difficult problem of choice. Not all of the indices, of course, cover the same period of

[2] For example, indices are prepared for road tender prices by the Department of Transport (some further particulars of this are given in [B 317]), for hospital building by the Hospital Authorities, and by the CEGB relating to the costs of power stations. It is likely that several such specialized indices are prepared by organizations in the public and private sectors for their own use.

Table 8.1
Currently Compiled General Indices of Construction Costs and Prices[a]

INDEX	PERIOD COVERED AND FREQUENCY	BASIS OF INDEX				PUBLICATION REFERENCES		Text Reference Sect. No.	REMARKS
						Descriptive Articles	Index Numbers (Primary Sources)		
		COMPOSITE INDICES *Factor Cost Constituents*							
		Materials	*Labour*	*Productivity*	*Overheads and Profit*				
1. DOE. Cost of New Construction (CNC) Index	1949–(Q)	Official (DOI) construction materials price index.	Index of average earnings (DE data) in construction.	Trend index of estimated materials input per man at constant prices.	Percentage per unit of output.	[B183] [B250]	*T & I* [QRL 352] and *HCS* [QRL 168].	8.1.2.1	Published in *T & I* [QRL 352] and also in *MDS* [QRL 195] and *AAS* [QRL 31] as one of a series of 'Index Numbers of Wholesale Prices—Output of Broad Sectors of Industry'.
2. RICS (BCIS) Building and Elemental Price Indices[b]	1950–(Q)	Official (DOI) materials indices and other sources (manufacturers and suppliers, etc.).	'All-in' hourly wage rates and on-costs[c].	Adjusted for 'market conditions' and 'fluctuations risk' (see text—Section 8.1.2.2).			Generally available only on subscription[d]. Series for 1963–74 were reproduced in [B 141].	8.1.2.2	Likely to be discontinued in favour of 'Factor Cost Indices' (as distinct from estimated tender level indices).
3. RICS (BMCIS) Maintenance Costs: General Maintenance Redecoration Fabric Maintenance Service Maintenance	1970–(Q)	Official (DOI) materials price indices as appropriate and VAT.	Official earnings data for contract labour and various wage rates for 'direct' labour plus ancillary payments (HWP, insurance, etc.) and VAT (on contract labour).	—	—	—	Available only on subscription[d].	8.1.2.3	The General Maintenance index is a weighted average of the other three indices.
4. Spon's Cost Indices (i) Building Costs	1956–(Q)	Official (DOI) construction materials price index.	Hourly wage rates and labour on-costs.	—	—	—	[QRL 314] and [QRL 43].	8.1.2.4	Labour and materials are weighted 40:60.
(ii) M & E Services Costs	1965–(Q)	Official (DOI) materials price indices as appropriate.	Hourly wage rates and labour on-costs for the appropriate labour.	—	—	—	[QRL 315].	8.1.2.4	Labour and materials are weighted 30:70 in the case of mechanical services and 50:50 in the case of electrical services.
5. EIU Costs Index	1938–(Q)	Official (DOI) construction materials price index.	Official (DE) average earnings in construction.	—	—	—	Available on subscription only[e].	8.1.2.5	Index for 'Industrial Buildings' covering 'most types of non-residential buildings': one of a set of 'Capital Replacement Cost' Indices. Labour and materials are weighted 55:45.
		ACTUAL PRICES							
6. DOE (DQSS) Tender Price Index	1968–(Q)	Based on accepted tenders for certain types of new work[f] accepted by the DOE Property Services Agency.				[B103] [B250]	*HCS* [QRL 168].	8.1.2.6	Based on the partial repricing method using standard (base) rates [B 318] and [B 319]. The published index represents the geometric mean of the 'bill' indices. Separate trade indices are also prepared but not published.
7. RICS (BCIS) Tender Price Index	1974–(Q)	Based on accepted tenders for both public and private sector work[g].				[B 134]	Available on subscription only[d].	8.1.2.7	Methodology is the same as for the DOE (DQSS) tender price index (*q.v.*). Separate indices are also published for firm and fluctuating price contracts (less reliable—see text).
8. Spon's Tender Price Index	1966–(Q)	Based on accepted tenders for new work[h] in the London area handled by one firm of chartered quantity surveyors (Davis, Belfield & Everest).				—	[QRL 314] and [QRL 43].	8.1.2.8	Methodology is the same as for the DOE (DQSS) tender price index (*q.v.*) except that the standard base rates are taken from *Spon's Price Book* [QRL 314].

(a) Special 'price adjustment formulae' indices are excluded from this table and considered in Section 8.1.3; references to non-current general indices are given in Section 8.1.4.
(b) Prepared for: Four Building Types—steel frame construction, concrete frame construction, brickwork construction and light frame construction and Six Group Elements—foundations (by building type), superstructure (by building type), internal finishes, fittings, services and external works.
(c) Covering nationally agreed wage rates in the building, mechanical engineering, heating and ventilating and electrical contracting industries and labour on-costs in accordance with national working rules.
(d) Building Cost Information Service, 85/87 Clarence Street, Kingston-upon-Thames, Surrey, KT1 1RB. £45 per annum (£35 for Chartered Surveyors) as at October 1977 for indices (2) and (7) and £45 p.a. for the maintenance cost indices (3).
(e) Economist Intelligence Unit, Spencer House, 27 St James's Place, London, SW1A 1NT. £40 plus £15 p.a. (annual series subscription) or £20 p.a. (quarterly series subscription).
(f) Projects over £50,000 (originally £30,000) but excluding housing work, work of a mainly civil engineering nature, mechanical and electrical work and complex works of alterations and extensions.
(g) Projects over £25,000 (originally £20,000) for new buildings or horizontal extensions priced in competition or by negotiation excluding work of a mainly civil engineering nature and complex works of alterations.
(h) Projects over £30,000 excluding work of a mainly civil engineering nature, mechanical and electrical work, complex works of alterations and extensions and negotiated contracts.

time but for those that do two basic preliminary distinctions can be drawn. One of these concerns the scope of the index—whether it refers to construction work in general or to a particular type of work or building. The other relates essentially to timing, that is the question of whether the index refers to the costs (to the builder or to the client) of work currently being executed or whether it is based on estimates or tenders for work yet to be started—the question of current $v.$ future costs and prices. Having made these distinctions, a particular series must be judged in relation to how successful it seems to be, or likely to be, in surmounting the problems we have discussed. This requires an appraisal of the methods of measurement and the data used. Choice of an index to use in practical applications will depend partly upon judgement about the respective merits of particular series and partly upon the particular purpose for which the index is required. We turn now, therefore, to examine the indices available. We consider first the merits and demerits of particular series and then devote some attention to their suitability for particular applications. The discussion of each series below needs to be read in conjunction with the details given in Table 8.1.

8.1.2.1. *DOE 'Cost of New Construction' (CNC) index.* This index is of the composite type based on changes in each of the elements which go to determine price; that is to say it is a weighted average (base weights are employed) of labour and materials costs indices adjusted for estimated changes in productivity, overheads and profits. It is calculated for the purpose of deflating the official (DOE) statistics of new construction output (and at one time new orders) and also the CSO statistics of investment in new buildings and other construction works (gross fixed capital formation—considered in Section 5.4) to a constant price basis in order to measure 'real' movements over time.[3] It is meant to measure changes, therefore, not in tender prices for future work but in the current costs (to the client) of new work (as opposed to repairs and maintenance) as it is executed; it will be recalled that in any particular period, expenditure represents progress payments on work under construction (as well as released retention monies for completed projects), and output is meant to represent the amounts chargeable to customers for work done in the period.

In effect, therefore, the index for any particular period should reflect the movement of an amalgam of prices for various *parts* of contracts passing through the construction process in that period. These prices, of course, will have been set at various periods in the past depending on the length of the construction process, but in some cases will have been adjusted in line with movements in labour and/or materials costs since the tender date under VOP arrangements.

As with other indices of the composite type, any merit the index possesses depends on the reliability with which each of its constituent elements is measured and on how far their combination can be regarded as providing a valid representation of the underlying economic reality which we wish to measure. Given the uses to which the index is put, it is particularly important to make an appraisal of these matters. We now turn, therefore, to examine the methodology and the primary data used in the calculation of the index more closely.

---

[3] New price deflators were introduced in March 1978 after the preparation of this text and earlier constant price series based on the CNC index were retrospectively revised—see the Addenda at the front of this volume.

Changes in the major constituents—materials and labour costs—are based on official series considered elsewhere in this Review. The index is dependent partly, therefore, upon the reliability of these series. We consider the official index of construction materials prices in Section 11.1. During the currency of the CNC index it has covered, in contrast to earlier periods, a fairly comprehensive range of construction materials but it is important to appreciate that it does remain open, nonetheless, to potential sources of error—for further discussion see Section 11.1. From the point of view of measuring current construction cost levels, it should also be borne in mind that whereas the materials index does attempt to reflect current price levels to the builder, part at least of the materials currently used on site will have been purchased at earlier periods. Furthermore, the movement of current materials cost levels may not in any case coincide with those incorporated in the charge to the client because these will depend upon the tender prices in the way we have described. Any divergence between the two levels will affect the builders' profits. Thus, as far as the overall price index is concerned, any differential movement in the two must be picked up in an offsetting movement in the allowance made for profits.

Labour costs are measured, appropriately, on the basis of changes in average earnings (originally covering manual workers only but now covering all employees) as opposed to wage rates, and also labour on-costs such as national insurance contributions. It will reflect, therefore, actual labour costs incurred by contractors in respect of their own employees. But again, it should be appreciated that the series is open to potential sources of error and it will not reflect, in particular, any differential movements in the payments made to self-employed operatives working under labour-only sub-contract. Further details of the earnings statistics are given in Section 6.9.3.2. Any differential movements over time in labour on-costs (a very substantial proportion of total costs) not allowed for in the labour costs index have to be picked up in the allowance made for overheads. This was also true with respect to differential movements between the earnings of operatives and other employees at the time when only operatives' earnings were covered in the official earnings series. Although, unlike materials, the builder has necessarily to pay current prices for the labour he employs, it remains possible that an index of earnings for all employees fails to reflect the movement of labour costs charged to clients on the basis of the tender. Again from the point of view of a reliable price index any differential movement here has to be picked up in the allowance made for profits.

In the nature of the case, it is not possible to say how large a potential source of 'error' these factors may represent. Perhaps the main problem, however, is that of allowing for changes in productivity and in overheads and profits. In default of a better measure, the index of productivity used is a proxy measure based on estimated materials input per man at constant prices. Such a measure suffers from the deficiency that economy in the use of materials would be reflected as a fall in productivity and vice versa. Probably more important, however (certainly in the short-run), is that the figure of materials input is not an independent statistic but one which itself has to be estimated and, given the data available, the scope for error here may be significant.

The estimate of materials input represents the residual after deducting from gross output (DOE statistics) estimates of the value of labour costs (DOE employment × DE average earnings) and overheads and profits (percentage of gross output). For a time the output and operative employment series became subject to a downward bias due to the marked growth in the numbers of self-employed operatives working for contractors under LOSC arrangements whose numbers and output went largely unrecorded in official statistics. Consequently, the estimate of materials input tended to be overstated because, although both the numbers and the work of the self-employed tended to go unrecorded, the returns of output provided by contractors *included*, in principle, the value of materials supplied to LOSC. The consequent index of materials input per man (at constant prices) is thus inflated for this reason and also because the employment series, used as the divisor, understated the true labour force. Errors here may be offset by errors in the allowance made for overheads and profits, but it would seem inherently unlikely that they would be large enough, or work systematically in the opposite direction.

The information that is available about the extent of self-employment suggests that there was a marked growth from at least the beginning of the 1960s through to the early 1970s (see Sections 4.1.3 and 6.2.3.4). Since 1973 the calculations referred to above have incorporated an estimate for unrecorded output and employment. In that year too, the published gross output series were retrospectively revised back to 1963 (Section 4.4.5 refers) but the author is informed that the CNC index was not modified retrospectively on this account.

Overstatement of the true productivity increase, arising from the overstatement of materials input per man would, of course, transmit a downward bias to the index of construction costs itself, other things being equal, since the productivity index is used to deflate indices of labour costs per man (a major component) and overheads and profits per man to a costs-per-unit-of-output basis: overstatement of productivity increase producing a corresponding understatement of costs per unit of output. At this stage it should perhaps be added that irregular movements in the index of materials input per man at constant prices are smoothed for the purpose of using it as a productivity index.

For overheads and profits there are no satisfactory statistics and in practice a percentage mark-up is taken. The only statistical evidence available in this field is that which may be derived periodically from the census of production (Section 5.3) in which the difference between gross output and certain categories of input may be taken as a measure of apparent overheads and profit. In the intervening periods partial information about profits may be obtained *retrospectively* from Inland Revenue statistics (Section 7.6). Apart from the time-lag before these statistics become available, they are not wholly satisfactory because they also embrace an element of non-profit income—e.g. the 'salaries' of working proprietors. Up to 1970 the overheads and profits proportion was revised periodically. Since 1970 it has been altered each quarter in accordance with such information as is available at the time.

It should be appreciated, therefore, that due to the nature of the information available, the adjustment made for changes in overheads and profits may be insensitive and thus the index itself may lack sensitivity to market conditions. Errors on this account alone are not normally likely to be large for the reason that overheads and profits are generally a relatively small proportion of output and thus the size of error transmitted to the index is proportionately much smaller. On the other hand, it is perhaps well to note that cases are on record of successful tenders incorporating an addition for overheads and profits amounting to 30 per cent during boom periods as in the early 1970s. More important in the context of the CNC index is the fact that the estimate of overheads and profits does not stand alone but is itself used in the estimation of materials input (as described above) which in turn determines the adjustments made for productivity change. Thus the estimate of overheads and profits has a two-fold influence and errors in this estimate have a relatively much larger influence on the final index of prices than the relative importance of overheads and profits themselves would imply.

The CNC index, therefore, suffers from a number of limitations, the effect of which may, on occasion, be substantial. It has been the subject of critical attention in the past both from this author in 1966 in [B 58], from Bowley and Corlett in 1970 in a report commissioned by the then MPBW itself [B 30] and in the final Reddaway report on SET in 1973 [B 127]. The latter provides a thorough evaluation of the index and the data on which it is based (as in the late 1960s) and also makes an assessment, on the basis of certain plausible assumptions, of the possible size of the error to which the index may have been subject, suggesting that in 1969 the index may have erred on the low side by some 6–7 per cent.

We have felt it necessary to devote particularly close attention to this index here because of the uses to which the index is put. Given these uses it will be appreciated that the interpretation of all the official constant-price series for construction output and expenditure are dependent as much upon an assessment of the validity of the costs (price) index as upon an assessment of the reliability of the primary current-price data. Further, given the importance of investment as a key economic variable and, in turn, the dominance of construction, as opposed to other types of asset, in total investment (approximately half the total) it will be appreciated that the accuracy of the CNC index is of far-reaching importance. In so far as the index fails to reflect true changes in construction price levels it may, by consequentially distorting the apparent movement of investment in real terms, have an important influence on government decision making about the management of the economy.

The officially sponsored report by Bowley and Corlett [B 30], referred to above, went so far as to conclude that 'unfortunately it has been shown that the method of construction of the existing index is highly unsatisfactory and the index should only be used with the greatest caution for specific purposes' (p. 208). But lest the impression should be given that construction suffers from faults that other sectors manage to avoid, it is perhaps well to record that the price indices for other capital assets are also open to substantial margins of error. Whether or not these are greater than those for construction it is not within our competence to judge nor, fortunately, is it within the scope of this Review. In the official guide [B 100] published in 1968, the CSO itself give all the constant-price investment series a reliability grading of C ('for periods more than 3 or 4 years away from the base date') which implies an error of ±10 per cent ([B 100] p. 381 refers).

Desirable improvements. Although suggestions for improvement have generally been left to the concluding section in this Review it would seem useful to add something specific at this particular point. Unfortunately, it is easier to provide a critique than to make practicable suggestions for improvement. In this author's view the most fruitful avenue would seem to be to utilize direct price information from contracts as the means of developing an index of *current* price levels. To reiterate a point made earlier, this would not be the same as tender prices. It would involve the use of information derived from the valuations made for the purpose of progress payments. Naturally the analyses would need to be based on large and representative samples to obtain reliable results, particularly in the construction field where prices from one contract to another are subject to such a high degree of variation. If carried out on a sufficient scale, however, it would offer the potential advantage of providing the base for indices for different types of work and thus make it unnecessary to assume, as is done currently, that the prices for all work move by the same relative amount.

In the meantime, one useful step that could be taken would be to examine the effect on the index each quarter of varying the constituent elements on which it is based within plausible margins of error and to publish the results. This is a well-established routine of sensitivity analysis. This could be part of a critical commentary which was something recommended by Bowley and Corlett [B 30]—a recommendation which we would support. Finally, in all fairness it must be acknowledged that the problems are very severe. The DOE are naturally aware of these problems and the author is informed that attempts are being made to improve both the methodology and the estimation procedures.

Sub-indices of the CNC index. The only index published officially has always been the CNC index itself covering all new construction. Until 1969, however, two separate sub-indices of the CNC index were compiled using the same methodology: one for new housing work and one for new non-housing work. In addition, a third index for repairs and maintenance work is compiled (again using the same method except that the assumption is made that productivity on repairs and maintenance remains constant); this, combined with the CNC index for new work, provides an index for 'All Building'. These indices were published for many years, unofficially, in [B 37].

8.1.2.2. *BCIS building and elemental price indices.* These indices are compiled using the composite method based on factor costs but, unlike the CNC index, are meant to reflect current tender price levels. They are produced primarily for adjusting BCIS elemental cost analyses of buildings to constant prices. Since these analyses are based on the priced bills of quantity submitted in successful tenders and provide a breakdown of the price under a number of sub-headings ('elements') a variety of indices are ideally required to represent *tender* price changes for each element for various forms of construction. With this aim in view, separately weighted indices are prepared for four building types and six group elements, details of which are given in Table 8.1 above. Each index represents a weighted average of indices for labour and materials costs coupled with adjustments for 'market conditions' and 'fluctuations risk'.

The adjustment for market conditions (originally shown separately) is a single adjustment meant to reflect the combined effect of changes in productivity, overheads and profits which are neglected by simply averaging the principal factor cost components of prices. It is very important to note that initially this adjustment was not made on any formal basis but was an essentially subjective assessment (influenced by a knowledge of the general tendering climate, tender levels in particular contracts and available statistics—e.g. of house tender prices). Currently the adjustment is based on a comparison of the BCIS Tender Price Index (Section 8.1.2.7) with the movement of factor costs.

It will be appreciated, therefore, that the current methodology makes the indices heavily dependent upon the BCIS general tender price index (the primary tender price data is subject to very wide variability—see Section 8.1.2.7), the separately weighted data on costs only producing a benchmark for each index category, but these in turn, of course, are dependent upon the reliability of the cost data and the weightings adopted for each category. The earlier methodology, involving a substantial subjective element, makes the indices inherently less reliable for that period.

The allowance for 'fluctuations risk' is not incorporated into the indices but is shown separately. Its relevance is that since the indices are based on current factor costs they would not reflect the level of prices likely to be submitted in firm price tenders. The allowance represents, therefore, an assessment of anticipated cost increases (phased over an eighteen month contract period). Needless to say, therefore, the allowance can only be regarded as conjectural.

In principle, given the purpose for which the indices are compiled, indices based directly upon information in priced bills of quantity (as in the tender price index also produced by the BCIS) would eliminate these difficulties. But in practice this solution is confronted by the problem of obtaining a satisfactory number of bills to maintain a sufficiently large sample when sub-divided according to building type, etc.

8.1.2.3. *BMCIS maintenance cost indices.* Four specific series are produced (details are given in Table 8.1) which are meant to reflect movements in the costs of various types of building maintenance as distinct from new construction. Like the indices considered above, they also represent weighted averages of materials and labour costs but, in this case, without any further adjustments for changes in productivity or overheads and profits. The need for any further adjustment is, of course, arguable. It is sometimes claimed (justifiably) that the scope for productivity improvement on maintenance work is limited, but it is doubtful whether the scope is so limited as to offer no improvement at all over time, especially in the context of innovations in materials and fixing methods. Similarly, it would also seem doubtful whether changes in market conditions, in terms of profits per unit of output, and changes in overheads do not influence the level of maintenance prices as they do for new building work. Having said this, however, the practical difficulty has then to be confronted of finding a suitable measure of these factors and for this there is no ready solution. The indices need to be interpreted, therefore, with these limitations in mind.

It should also be appreciated that devising a suitable weighting pattern itself presents problems because of wide differences in the pattern of maintenance expenditure on individual buildings. In any particular application, therefore, the indices can be expected to give only the broadest indication of price changes. Indeed inappropriateness of the weights when the indices are applied to particular cases may well outweigh or, conversely, reinforce the potential 'bias' introduced by a failure to allow for productivity changes and market conditions in general.

8.1.2.4. *Spon's building and M & E services costs indices.* Three separate indices are compiled: one for building costs (published in *Spon's Architects' and Builders' Price Book* [QRL 314]) each year and quarterly in the *Architects' Journal* [QRL 43], and one each for mechanical services and electrical services respectively (published in *Spon's Mechanical and Electrical Services Price Book* [QRL 315]). The calculations are made by Davis, Belfield and Everest, a London-based firm of chartered quantity surveyors. Each is a composite index based *solely* on movements in the costs of labour and materials (details are given in Table 8.1 above). No allowance is made for changes in productivity, overheads, profits or for payments to labour additional to the basic rates. It will be appreciated, therefore, that these indices merely reflect general changes in contractors' primary factor costs and not current costs of construction nor tender prices. A tender price index is produced, however, by the same organization (see Section 8.1.2.8 below). The attempt is also made to forecast the movement of the building costs index (and the tender price index) for a period two years ahead and the results are published in the *Architects' Journal* [QRL 43]—again, see Section 8.1.2.8.

8.1.2.5. *EIU capital replacement costs index for industrial buildings.* This index is available to subscribers only and no information about its calculation is published, but the author is informed[4] that it is of the composite type based on official statistics of average earnings in construction and construction materials prices (see Table 8.1). No allowances are made for changes in overheads, profits or productivity. It will be appreciated once again, therefore, that the index suffers from the same limitations as the Spon's index referred to above although, mitigated in this case to some extent by the use of average earnings statistics rather than wage rates for the labour costs constituent.

8.1.2.6. *DOE (DQSS) tender price index (public sector).* This index is based upon information about tender prices for new work accepted by the Property Services Agency (PSA) of the DOE. It thus represents public sector building work only—in particular: post office and telecommunications buildings, defence buildings, offices and other government building projects. The method used is that of partial repricing of current tenders on the basis of standard rates discussed earlier in Section 8.1.1.2. For each bill examined, a sample of items is selected for repricing from each trade or section of the bill according to their relative importance (in terms of value) to represent a total value of 25 per cent of each trade or section. These trades or sections are then weighted according to the total value of each trade or section relative to the total value of the bill (i.e. the weights are current weights and peculiar to each bill). Some further details are given in Table 8.1.

This index (first published in 1972—extending back to 1968) represents the most promising development in the compilation of building price index numbers for many years. Its main virtues are that it relies on actual price data and the fact that, since it is based on the comparison of quotations for comparable items of work from each trade or section of the bill of quantities, it is able to meet the problem of the non-standard product. A potential difficulty is the fact that the rates inserted by different contractors in bills for tendering purposes may differ considerably, for a variety of reasons, and thus introduce an erratic influence, unless the index is based on a large sample of bills. The DQSS does have access to a reasonably large number of bills, the aim being to analyse at

---

[4] Information has been kindly supplied by the Economist Intelligence Unit.

least eighty contracts each quarter whenever possible. It should also be noted in this connection that the practice is adopted of truncating the sample by removing the top and bottom deciles in order to remove the 'rogue' tenders and the index itself 'smoothed' before publication on the basis of a moving average. Information about the number and the variability of the indices for the repriced bills each quarter is not regularly published but a study of the data, reported in the early 1970s, indicated a coefficient of variation at that time of 11 per cent ([B 10] para. 4.2 refers). The use of the geometric mean for averaging the 'bill indices' (Table 8.1 refers) might also be expected to reduce the degree of variability that would otherwise be reflected in the ultimate tender price series but the author is informed that in practice the effect, compared with the use of the arithmetic mean, is negligible and that the geometric mean is retained simply for the sake of consistency of practice over time.

A potential limitation of the index is that since it is only based on work for which the PSA is responsible, it may not be representative of the trend of tender prices for types of work not represented in its contracts; it will be noted that certain categories of work are specifically excluded in any case (see Table 8.1). In the private sector, however, a comparable index (based on both public and private sector work) is now maintained by the BCIS using the same methodology—see Section 8.1.2.7 below.

Another possible limitation arises from the fact that the index is based on contracts of over a certain size (Table 8.1 refers) so that it *may* not be representative of price trends for smaller contracts (due perhaps to a marked difference in the composition of the two groups in terms of forms of construction and the proportion of firm price contracts). Further, changes in the composition of the contracts which *are* included in the analyses, according to type of contract may also have some influence upon the index; in particular it should be noted that the inclusion of a larger number of VOP contracts since 1974 tends to introduce a downwards influence on the series. It should also be appreciated that regional price variations may mean that the index does not necessarily reflect experience in any one region of the country.

8.1.2.7. *BCIS tender price index (public and private sectors).* Brief details of this index (available on subscription only) are set out in Table 8.1 along with the other indices that are currently produced. The methodology used—partial repricing of bills of quantity—follows that used in the official DQSS tender price index referred to above (Section 8.1.2.6). The priced bills for analysis in this case are supplied by BCIS members. As is common, the prices obtained from the sample of bills each quarter exhibit very wide variability and a quarterly sample of eighty bills is aimed at (not always achieved) in order to produce a reasonably reliable average index. Publication of each index number is accompanied by information about the sample size and the 70 per cent sample range—a practice which serves as a useful antidote to any belief in precision in this field and could be imitated with benefit in the publication of the corresponding official tender price index. A further valuable innovation in the BCIS index is the publication of separate indices for firm price and VOP tenders (although these sub-indices are less reliable because of the smaller samples upon which each is necessarily based). Separate indices are also calculated for public sector and private sector work but these are not normally issued.

As we have stressed above, the repricing of tenders method offers great advantages in the derivation of an index of building prices by virtue of the fact that it is directly based on detailed price data, and is able to avoid the difficulties that confront the synthetic approach based upon factor costs. Perhaps the most important development that is now needed is the disaggregation of the index to measure price movements for different types of building and in different regions of the country. To do this,of course, would require a greatly enlarged sample.

8.1.2.8. *Spon's tender price index*. Like the Spon's 'Building Costs Index' (Section 8.1.2.4) this index is compiled by Davis, Belfield and Everest and published in *Spon's Architects' and Builders' Price Book* [QRL 314] each year and quarterly in the *Architects' Journal* [QRL 43]. It is based on exactly the same methodology as the DQSS and the BCIS tender price indices referred to in the two preceding sections (*q.v.*) except for the facts that Spon's base rates [QRL 314] are used for repricing and that it represents the arithmetic mean of individual bill indices rather than the geometric mean. The number of bills covered, however, is smaller than in the other indices, being based on contracts handled by Davis, Belfield and Everest itself. It should also be noted that these contracts are confined to work in the London area (mainly, but not solely, for housing). Further details of scope are given in Table 8.1.

It may also be noted that the attempt is made, as referred to above, to forecast the movement of this index for a period two years ahead and the results published, in the form of 'minimum' and 'maximum' limits, quarterly in the *Architects' Journal* [QRL 43]—the series and methodology were introduced in Vol. 162, 12 November 1975, pp. 1017–18. No formal statistical model is employed. On this question, the difficulties involved in trying to devise a formal statistical model for forecasting construction price movements has been examined, with particular reference to primary data problems, in a paper by Fildes and Wood [B 34].

8.1.3. *Price Adjustment Formulae Indices*

Brief attention is devoted to these indices for they were devised for a special purpose and do not provide a single measure of *general* construction costs. They were devised for use in the adjustment of prices in contracts let under price variation arrangements as an alternative to the conventional methods, in which reimbursement for price changes requires the repricing of each item of work involved separately and, it is argued, is therefore costly to operate, and, at a time of rapid and unpredictable inflation, has deleterious consequences on contractors' cash flows. Under the 'formula' method, reimbursement is merely calculated by reference to the movement of the appropriate index numbers. The relevant contractual provisions under the Standard Form of Building Contract relating to the use of the formulae are contained in *Practice Note No. 18* of the Joint Contracts Tribunal [B 288] and the related *Formula Rules* [B 328].

8.1.3.1. *NEDO price adjustment formulae indices*. These indices are compiled monthly by the DQSS (formerly DQSD) division of the PSA but the methodology itself was devised by the EDCs for Building and Civil Engineering. They were introduced into new building contracts for the first time in 1974. Three sets of index numbers are published relating to building works (sometimes referred to as the 'Osborne indices'), civil engineering works (sometimes referred to as the 'Baxter indices') and specialist engineering installations in [QRL 191], [QRL 192] and [QRL 193] respectively. Except for civil engineering work, a variety of indices for different 'work categories' are published together with separate indices for skilled and unskilled labour and plant (cost of providing, operating and maintaining constructional plant and equipment), the work-category indices representing composite rates for labour, materials and plant. In the case of civil engineering works, indices are given for labour, materials, fuel and plant (provision and maintenance only); composite rates are not compiled. The specialist engineering formulae make separate provision for electrical engineering; heating, ventilating and air conditioning; lifts and structural steelwork.

Details of the indices themselves were given in [B 212] for the original series and in [B 290] for revised series introduced in 1977. Guides to their practical application will be found in [B 292] (revised in 1977 in [B 291]) and, for civil engineering work in [B 293] and [B 294]. Reports of the original investigations carried out into the practicability of the scheme were published in [B 229], [B 311], [B 298] and [B 299].

The 'work category' indices are meant to reflect changes over a base period in the current costs of specific items of work arising from changes in the costs of labour, materials and the cost of using plant and are composite indices for these items weighted together according to their relative contribution to costs in a base year. They do not reflect, and are not meant to reflect, changes in overheads, profits and productivity over time (although it may be noted, incidentally, that 'productivity deductions' from allowable cost increases were required to be made under counter-inflation legislation from April 1973 until August 1976).

Interpretation of the evidence provided by these indices needs to be made at two levels, the general and the particular, bearing in mind the specific purposes for which they were devised. Given the general nature of index numbers it is, of course, virtually inevitable that their use to calculate cost reimbursement payments on an individual contract will not yield amounts which equal exactly the cost increases the contractor has actually incurred on that contract: both under-recovery and over-recovery of cost increases will occur. In principle, this should even-out in the aggregate over several contracts. This depends in part upon the reliability and 'representativeness' of the data and methods used to calculate the index numbers and in part upon the way the contractor prepares his tender. Consideration of the latter would carry us beyond the sensible confines of this Review but a valuable study, commissioned by the NFBTE, which examines the sensitivity of the formula method in this context will be found in [B 8].

At a more general level, how accurately the indices reflect changes in costs depends upon the reliability of the methods and the data used. It is not easy to judge these matters, but a number of points would seem worthy of note. Of the indicators used for measuring the movement of the costs of the constituent items, it is notable that changes in labour costs are assessed by reference to the movement of wage rates rather than earnings (except in the case of engineering categories where there was no national wage agreement applicable to the labour) and other costs based on *National Working Rules* applicable to various sectors of the construction industry (details are set out in the reports of the working groups referred to above). This is justified in the case of the purposes for which these indices were devised, but it needs to be taken into account should the attempt be made to use them for any other purpose—as in the calculation of a general costs index. Changes in materials and plant costs are based on the official DOI series considered in Chapter 11. The weights used—labour, materials and plant 'constants' valued at base year prices—were derived initially from an analysis of fifty bills of quantity (*prima facie*, a small number, given the variety of forms of construction and types of building that need to be covered and the variability in the performance and pricing of different contractors, but the individual categories represented by each index were covered many times over and the working parties, representative of industrial interests, clearly felt the number to be adequate). Any base-weighted index, of course, must be revised periodically, if it is to remain representative of contemporary conditions. It was originally stated that the constants 'will not be varied' ([B 298] p. 42) but, as noted above, revisions covering the weights and the work categories themselves were made in 1977 [B 290] and [B 291] and arrangements have been made to keep the working of the method in practice under review.

8.1.3.2. *GLC, ILEA building contract fluctuations clause indices.* These indices are prepared by the GLC Quantity Surveying Division for use in the adjustment of prices in GLC contracts let on a VOP basis with effect from October 1973; they therefore perform the same function as the NEDO formulae indices referred to above (Section 8.1.3.1). But unlike the NEDO building formula, which is based on separate indices for various 'work categories', the GLC formula is based on single adjustments for labour (including at one time 'productivity deduction', as above) and materials. The labour index is based on wage rates, national insurance and other costs agreed in *National Working Rules* [B 276] (separate calculations for craftsmen and labourers being weighted together in the ratio of 2:1) and the official DOI index of housebuilding materials prices (Section 11.1). These are published monthly in [QRL 137]. A guide to the application of the formula is set out in an internal note available from the GLC Quantity Surveying Division [B 197].

8.1.4. *Historical Indices of Construction Costs and Prices*

A large number of indices has been prepared relating to various periods in the past as far back as 1845. References to these, together with an analysis of the methods of calculation used and the evidence they provide, have been provided by the author elsewhere [B 58]. Since that article was written there have been two notable developments. One is the discontinuance of many of the indices which were then being regularly prepared (e.g. the BRS Measured Work Index, the Venning Index [B 167] and also the constituent sub-indices of the official CNC index (Section 8.1.2.1) which were published quarterly in [B 37]). The other development has been the initiation of series systematically based on data derived from large samples of priced bills. In addition it may be noted that the CSO now publish an index going back to 1888 as one of a series of *Price Index Numbers for Current Cost Accounting (PINCCA)* [QRL 239]. No background details are given about this index but the author is informed that it is the index compiled by Redfern in [B 128] coupled with the 'CNC' index for more recent years.

Redfern's index is in fact a combination of several others, all of which are discussed in the article referred to earlier [B 58].

8.1.5. *Use and Interpretation of the Indices*

Our attention here is confined to currently compiled series, once again, since the historical series were considered fully in [B 58]. The discontinuance of many of the historical indices may be a result of the recognition by their compilers of the superiority of the tender-based indices recently introduced. Certainly these indices constitute a valuable improvement, although they do not provide a solution to the need for measures reflecting current construction costs (i.e. the prices paid by clients for *current work*) as distinct from changes in the level of *current tenders* for work yet to be carried out. Further, the variety of evidence hitherto available did serve to engender a healthy scepticism about the evidence provided by any one index and a caution in its use. This caution is no less needed today.

Interpretation of the available indices obviously needs to take account of the inherent problems involved in attempting to produce a single measure of price changes for such a heterogeneous mixture of non-standard products, and the nature of the methods and sources of information used. These have been fully discussed above. The use of the available indices must also depend partly upon the purpose for which the index is required. Broadly speaking, perhaps four purposes may be distinguished:

(1) For use in converting value series expressed in terms of current prices to an equivalent volume (i.e. constant price) series by eliminating from it the effect of price changes;
(2) for converting figures of construction costs or tender prices for a particular building or category of construction work from one time base to another;
(3) for the calculation of price adjustments in contracts including variation of price clauses;
(4) for studying price movements as such, as in studies of building cycles and economic fluctuations or comparative studies of industrial performance and trends.

Except for the third, rather specialized use, each of these purposes may be said to require an index of prices rather than costs, although the latter purpose might also find information about costs useful.

The main purpose, as far as official statistics and the general user are concerned, is generally the first defined above. Here a distinction may be made between series of the value of work done (output) and work to be done (new contracts and orders). Both require indices coincident in timing with the valuation of the work. Thus in so far as building output statistics record the value of work at the time it is done (as distinct from the time when the whole contract is complete), as is the case in Britain (and Northern Ireland), the index required for deflation purposes is one reflecting current costs as defined above. The deflation of value series of new orders, on the other hand, requires an index of tender prices allowing for the incidence of firm price and VOP contracts.

As far as the revaluation of output is concerned, it is essential to bear in mind the conceptual problems which were discussed earlier (Section 2.3) for these determine both the choice of index and the interpretation of the results. These problems, it will be recalled, reside essentially in the nature of construction work itself and its pricing. Thus the current valuation of output cannot be regarded as being founded on an unambiguous time base because of the length of construction periods and the prior determination of prices (albeit adjusted in some cases under VOP clauses). The derivation of a suitable price index must contend not only with this problem but also with the great heterogeneity of construction work.

The index used officially for the deflation of construction output and related series—gross fixed capital formation (Section 5.4.2) and capital stock statistics (Section 12.1)—the CNC index, has been considered fully in Section 8.1.2.1 above. As we note there, the index suffers from a number of very important potential limitations arising from its method of calculation and the information on which it is based. No other index, however, is available. The various tender price indices are, of course, not directly suitable (they might conceivably be used for output deflation purposes on a suitably lagged basis if such indices were regarded as being suitably representative of the whole range of construction work though such a procedure would itself be open to error).[5]

The official new orders statistics, as we noted in considering the series earlier (Section 4.5.3), have been deflated by tender price indices since 1973—the previous constant-price series being retrospectively revised back to 1963 (see Section 4.5.3 for precise details)—previously the CNC index had been used. Tender-based price series are obviously more suitable in principle for this purpose than others, though for reasons discussed earlier (Sections 4.5.3 and 8.1.1) the constant-price series must inevitably remain open to margins of error which may be substantial.

The second purpose identified above mainly concerns the construction client and his advisers. The index required for this purpose would generally be one reflecting changes in tender prices and thus one of the tender price indices now compiled would seem the most suitable, although as yet they cover only a very short period of time. On the other hand, in this particular use, one is concerned with the repricing of a particular building, or building type, in a particular location and it is essential to recognize that the available tender indices do not necessarily apply equally to different building types and locations. Again, therefore, their use must unavoidably involve potentially substantial margins of error. A useful discussion of the use of price indices in this context has been provided by Azzaro [B 6].

The use of indices for the third purpose identified above is an innovation of the 1970s and has involved the compilation of indices specially for the purpose. These are considered in Section 8.1.3 and no further discussion seems called for here.

Under the fourth purpose—studies of economic fluctuations and comparative performance—cost and price indices may be not so much intermediate tools of analysis as the subject of analysis themselves. Hence known deficiencies in the indices, and disagreements among them, make it either impossible to arrive at definite conclusions or necessary to attach important qualifications to them. Yet again, therefore, it is necessary to express reservations, but of the indices available the tender price indices would again seem to offer the more reliable source of evidence bearing in mind their potential limitations in scope across the industry.

---

[5] New output deflators based upon lagged tender price series were introduced in 1978 after the preparation of this text—see the Addenda at the front of this volume.

8.2. Productivity

8.2.1. *General Measurement Problems and Interpretation*

The problems involved in trying to devise a satisfactory indicator of productivity change for the construction industry as a whole are even greater than those involved in obtaining an overall indicator of price movements and, although a proxy index of productivity is used in the compilation of the official costs (CNC) index, no official index for productivity as such is published. The problems involved are so severe as to seem insurmountable. Nonetheless putative measures are produced from time to time. This being so, and since the subject is of great economic importance, it would seem desirable to devote further attention to it here.

It is a simple matter, of course, given statistics of employment, the value of output and a price index, to calculate an index of output per man at constant prices, and it is not uncommon to see the results of such calculations quoted in the trade, academic and general press[6] and even officially from time to time. Such calculations are open to objection on grounds of principle and also because of deficiencies in the data employed.

The objections of principle are that estimates of the value of gross output per man are not an indicator of changes in the productivity of the construction industry as such, for they reflect the value of materials and components bought in from other industries. Since the input of materials is a large proportion of total output, the ratio is critically dependent upon changes in the proportion they represent. Increased purchases of prefabricated components, for example, may serve to increase the value of these inputs and also to reduce site labour requirements. An index of gross output per man, therefore, may show a marked increase. Yet all that has occurred has been a transference of work from site to factory with, possibly, no change in the total men employed (indeed it is possible to conceive of an increase through more roundabout methods of production and increased transport), and a level of *net* output per man on construction work proper which may have changed in any direction or not at all. In any case, changes in output per man over time are also affected naturally by changes in the number of hours worked so that measures of output per man-hour are strictly more appropriate.

Further, the use of such broad measures as gross output which, for the construction industry, encompass such a heterogeneous mixture of work is also inherently misleading, for differences in the labour and material requirements of different sorts of work (e.g. road building as against say, hospitals) means that the 'productivity' index changes merely in response to changes in the output mix. Therefore, interpretation of measures of this kind requires, at the very least, further information about the composition of output and about changes in the relative consumption of materials. It needs too, information about the costs and use of plant, for capital substitution may not only be the cause of improved 'labour productivity' but also absorb the benefits in extra costs.

At the practical level, the deficiencies in the primary data are such as to make the calculations of extremely doubtful validity, quite apart from the objection in principle. The deficiencies have been fully discussed at appropriate places in this Review. In summary, the principal (DOE) output and employment series have been affected by

---

[6] An index of this kind was regularly published in *The Guardian* newspaper [B 232] for a time during the 1960s.

deficiencies in coverage varying in their incidence over time and in their effects on the output series and the employment series respectively so that differences in ratios of output per man may be as much a reflection of deficiencies in the data as in the underlying reality. Needless to say too it is also dependent on the reliability of the price index used for deflation purposes. For further consideration of the output and employment data, and the difficulties of collection, reference should be made to Sections 4.1.3 and 4.4. The limitations of the CNC index were considered above (Section 8.1.2.1).

In the present context two further points need to be noted. One is that the index of construction costs is itself dependent upon the estimate of productivity used in its calculation. Thus even if the output and employment data and the costs index itself were open to no objection, statistics of the ratio of output per man at constant prices would still be largely meaningless as a productivity index, for they would be reflecting little more than the prior productivity assessment integrated into the original data. The second point is that, whilst the DOE statistics now include estimates for unrecorded output and employment, they are necessarily approximate and can scarcely be used for fine judgements about productivity change over time. No doubt calculations of output per man will continue to be made despite the practical and theoretical difficulties; one can only enjoin that they should be interpreted within bands of error which must be potentially very wide.

For particular types of building work a number of *ad hoc* studies of productivity levels, and of the factors which affect them, have been made and we direct attention to them below. It will be appreciated, however, that by their very nature they provide snapshots at particular points of time rather than measures of trends.

8.2.2. Ad hoc *Sectoral Studies of Productivity*

We do no more than direct attention to relevant studies for particular sectors of construction here since the reports cited contain particulars relevant to their interpretation. Housebuilding productivity has been the subject of special attention: in Great Britain several studies have been made by the Building Research Station since the war—for discussion and references see Bishop [B 16]—and for Northern Ireland a study by the author in the mid-1960s is reported in [B 56]. Similar sample studies of labour requirements for other types of building construction have been reported by the Ministry of Education in respect of school buildings completed in 1954 [QRL 65] and by the Building Research Station in respect of hospital building projects completed in 1968 [QRL 19].

Efficiency in other construction sectors has been the subject of studies by the Economic Development Committees of the NEDC; these tend to be more concerned with steps that may be taken to improve productivity than with its measurement as such but they naturally provide information of interest in the present context. Efficiency in road construction, for instance, was studied by the Civil Engineering EDC in reports issued in 1966 [B 223] and in 1967 [B 321]; a study of performance on engineering construction projects by the Mechanical and Electrical Engineering Construction EDC was reported in 1976 in [B 225] and an earlier study of related interest dealing with the organization of, and industrial relations on, large industrial plant construction sites was reported in 1970 in [B 264].

CHAPTER 9

CONSTRUCTION INDUSTRY STATISTICS FOR NORTHERN IRELAND

9.1. Introduction

This chapter is comparable in scope to Chapters 3–8 inclusive which relate to statistics about the construction industry in Great Britain or the United Kingdom as a whole. Statistics relating to building materials, the construction stock and the construction professions are dealt with as appropriate in Chapters 10–13 inclusive. As in the case of Great Britain, the scope of this chapter is also confined to construction *other than housing*, the latter being covered in a separate *Review* in this series [B 57].

Separate treatment of the statistics for Northern Ireland is both convenient and necessary. Most of the statistics are collected or compiled separately by departments of the Northern Ireland Administration and their scope, coverage and timing do not always coincide with those collected for the rest of the United Kingdom. Further, since attention is often focused on Northern Ireland separately from the rest of the UK, separate treatment in a self-contained section would seem to offer advantages to the user. Many of the problems, however, are the same as in Britain and this chapter should be read in the context of the general discussion of the problems of definition, collection and measurement included as Chapter 2.

There is a marked difference between Northern Ireland and Great Britain, as far as construction statistics are concerned, in that the amount of statistical information available is very much less extensive in Northern Ireland. This is particularly true for the period up to the mid-1960s.

As we have described in earlier sections, a considerable volume of detailed statistics were collected by the former MOW in Great Britain during the war-time and early post-war years under powers conferred in Defence Regulations 56A and 56AB, which related to the licensing of building operations and the registration of builders. No comparable statistics are available, however, for Northern Ireland. The Regulations applied to the whole of the UK, but were administered separately in Northern Ireland, and remained in force until 1953 and 1954 respectively. It is known that registered undertakings in Northern Ireland were required to make returns of the number of employees, their occupations and the types of work on which they were engaged (it is not clear whether this continued for the whole period that the regulations were in force) but official searches undertaken on behalf of the author have failed to reveal the existence of these statistics now. It is assumed, therefore, that they have been destroyed.

The ending of enquiries conducted under defence regulations was not followed, as it was in Great Britain, by the institution of regular enquiries under the *Statistics of Trade Act* (a similar Act with the same title was passed in Northern Ireland in 1949) until the mid-1960s and then only on a more limited basis than the corresponding British enquiries. There still remains no census corresponding to that conducted by the DOE in Great Britain (Section 4.2).

The relative paucity of information for the province is probably a consequence in part of the fact that there is no one Department which has performed the same function as the DOE and its predecessors in Great Britain as the 'sponsoring' department for the industry, although the Department (formerly Ministry) of Finance has long performed a number of similar functions.[1]

As in the case of Great Britain, the available statistics are considered by subject, rather than source, under the following headings:

Section 9.2. Production Statistics
9.3. Employment Statistics
9.4. Labour Statistics other than Employment
9.5. Industrial Structure
9.6. Financial Statistics.

Attention is confined almost entirely, as before, to the period since the Second World War.

9.2. Production Statistics for Northern Ireland

There are three sources of information about the output of construction work in Northern Ireland:

(1) Quarterly surveys of output, employment and new orders. These enquiries were initiated in 1966 on broadly comparable lines to surveys conducted for Great Britain by the DOE and its predecessors (Sections 4.4 and 4.5 refer).
(2) Censuses of production for all industry including construction—conducted annually since 1949 in the post-war period.
(3) Capital formation in buildings and works—estimates of total capital expenditure—annual series from 1950.

We deal with each of these sources in turn.

9.2.1. *Quarterly Surveys of Output and New Orders—Northern Ireland*

This enquiry was initiated in 1966 by the Department of Commerce, on behalf of the Economic Section (now the Statistics and Economics Unit)—located in the Northern Ireland Cabinet Office but now part of the Department of Finance—modelled on the similar enquiries undertaken by the then MPBW for Great Britain. Since the beginning of 1976 responsibility for the enquiry has rested with the Department of Finance. As in the British enquiries, the industry is defined in accordance with the SIC. Up to and including the second quarter of 1976 two forms of return were used, one for contractors and one for the direct labour organizations of public authorities, specimen copies of which were reproduced in the companion Review in this series on *Housing in Northern*

---
[1] Recently, however, a Northern Ireland Construction Industry Advisory Council has been established under the chairmanship of the Minister responsible for the Department of Finance and it has devoted special attention to the statistics collected. An early outcome has been a reform of the enquiries referred to above.

Ireland [B 57]. With effect from the third quarter of 1976 a major change was made in the contractors' part of the enquiry, the former single questionnaire being replaced by two separate returns. Specimen copies of these new returns are reproduced in Appendix XII.

The revised enquiry affects in the main the method of collecting output statistics. The former enquiry required each contractor to return an estimate of the value of work carried out by himself (as in the corresponding British enquiry, main contractors were instructed to exclude the value of work carried out *for* them by sub-contractors—such work being covered in principle by returns from the sub-contractors concerned). The comprehensiveness of the statistics obtained depended, therefore, on covering all contractors regardless of whether they were operating on a particular contract as a main contractor or a sub-contractor. The revised enquiry replaces this method with a project-based, as opposed to a contractor-based, system. Each *main* contractor is now required to return the value of work carried out each quarter on each individual contract (for *new* work) for which he is responsible covering the work done both by his own directly employed labour and by all sub-contractors including labour-only sub-contractors. The new system depends upon the availability of information about new construction projects. This is obtained from the new orders returns, referred to below. These, it should be noted, are obtained from all firms employing twenty or more operatives but a 20 per cent rotating sample of those employing five to nineteen operatives. Thus at any one time not all main contractors will necessarily be covered by the project-based enquiry.

We now turn to consider the information collected and publication sources. The question of the reliability of the statistics is considered further in the section headed 'Interpretation' below. Suffice it to say at this stage that the new system is likely to provide more reliable output statistics than the one it has replaced.

Output—Northern Ireland. On the basis of the new project-based output returns it will be possible to provide much more detailed analyses by type of work than were available in the past when these were predetermined by the categories specified on the questionnaires. With one exception (noted below), however, the same classification as before has been retained as follows:

Contractors:
  New Housing—for public sector.
      —for private sector.
  Roads—new work and repairs and maintenance combined up to and including the
      2nd quarter of 1976, than new work alone.
  Other New Work—for public sector
          —for private sector
              non-industrial
              industrial
  Repairs and Maintenance—all types except roads prior to 1976 (3rd quarter).
Public Sector Direct Labour: Total all work.

This classification, it may be noted, is identical to that used in the corresponding British enquiry apart from the treatment of roads and direct labour (the British direct labour statistics are considered in Sections 4.3 and 4.4).

New Orders—Northern Ireland. No change of substance has been made to the new orders enquiry since it was initiated in 1966 on a similar footing (apart from a difference in frequency) to the corresponding British enquiry (the frequencies are quarterly in Northern Ireland and monthly in Great Britain). Throughout the whole period contractors (there is no corresponding enquiry for direct labour organizations) have been required to return details of individual projects above certain exemption limit values; below these values aggregate figures only are required—for full details see the specimen of the current questionnaire which is reproduced in Appendix XII and the earlier specimen reproduced in [B 57]. Coverage extended down to firms on the register employing seven or more operatives until mid-1976 and then down to five or more operatives (partly on a sample basis—again for full details see Appendix XII). For a full discussion of the nature of the data reference should be made to Section 4.5.2 above, which deals with the corresponding British enquiry.

The published results (publication sources are considered below) are not broken down in comparable detail to those for Great Britain (Section 4.5.3). Instead the same six categories of work are distinguished as for output, defined above, except for repairs and maintenance work which, of course, is not within the scope of the enquiry. Until mid-1976 some work remained unclassified by type: it was the practice to group 'work not covered by orders'—i.e. work undertaken by the contractor on his own initiative—together with work below the exemption limit (returned in the aggregate only)—although a large part of the former is private housing. Separate details of these categories were only given from time to time in *Economic Reports* [B 280]. Since mid-1976 it has been classified to the appropriate type of work—details are given in [QRL 140] September 1977 edition, p. 56.

Publication sources for output and new orders—Northern Ireland. The quarterly series of output and new orders statistics are published in the *Northern Ireland Digest of Statistics* [QRL 140] and annual series in the British publication: *Housing and Construction Statistics (HCS)* [QRL 168]. All series are published at current prices only. Until very recently the employment statistics collected in the same enquiry were not published in any Northern Ireland publication (see Section 9.3.3).

Interpretation. The collection of output and new orders statistics for Northern Ireland must contend with the same difficulties as have to be faced in Great Britain. Consequently, many of the same comments and criticisms apply to these data as were expressed in relation to the British series. But further, the interpretation and use of these statistics, and many others also for Northern Ireland, is hindered by the dearth of background information such as would help the user to interpret the data and make a sensible appraisal of their nature, coverage and limitations. The principal statistical publication—the *Northern Ireland Digest of Statistics* [QRL 140]—for instance, is not accompanied by a 'Notes and Definitions' supplement comparable to those issued in Britain to accompany the *Monthly Digest* [B 273] or the *Housing and Construction Statistics* volume [B 250]. Unlike some deficiencies, this is one which could be remedied fairly easily and inexpensively.

As in Britain, the primary problem afflicting these statistics must be the maintenance of a comprehensive register of contractors (see Section 4.1.3). Obviously the scale of the problem is much less since the size of the province in terms of area and population is much less but there is no reason to suppose that in relative terms the problem is any the less. Certainly the nature of the problem is the same: no compulsory registration requirement, a large number of small firms with relatively high rates of entry and exit (there are no official statistics available about this but it would be surprising if this were not the case), and a growth in the practice of sub-contracting on a labour-only basis to self-employed (or nominally self-employed) men.[2] Northern Ireland faces the added problem of covering firms operating only temporarily in the province from a base across the border in the Irish Republic or from Great Britain; no systematic means exist whereby information is obtained about such firms, but the author is informed that use is made of trade journals, newspapers and public sector clients as sources of information.

Unfortunately no information is made available about the methods used to compile and maintain the register. Until the revision of the output and new orders enquiry in 1976, the register used in practice was the same as that used for annual censuses of production (Section 9.2.2), both enquiries being conducted by the same Department (the Department of Commerce). It is possible that this register was *initially* based on that compiled under the war-time statutory registration requirements, as in Britain, but no information is available to confirm this supposition. Since mid-1976 the enquiry has been conducted by the Department of Finance on the basis of a register maintained by the Department of Manpower Services, a register which is regarded as being more comprehensive (for further details see Section 9.3).

It is important to appreciate, as far as the output statistics are concerned, that the change to a project-based system in 1976 helps to remove some of the deficiencies caused by the failure to cover many small firms and self-employed workers since the system requires a return from the main contractor (generally larger firms) for each project in respect of work by *all agencies* on that project. This potential improvement, however, only affects the output statistics for new work. Repairs and maintenance output statistics are still collected in the same way as before since no information is collected about orders received for repair and maintenance work which could form the basis of a similar project-based enquiry. This fact, plus the fact that much repair and maintenance work is undertaken by small firms, must mean that the repair and maintenance statistics are likely to be open to a much larger margin of error than the new work statistics.

Unfortunately the revised enquiry was not run in parallel with the old system for even one period so that it is impossible to compare the old and the new series directly. A major discontinuity occurs, therefore, between the second and third quarters of 1976.

It is also important to note that when the 'old system' was in operation questionnaires were only sent to firms employing seven or more operatives (this fact was never noted in the regular publication source) whereas under the 'new system' coverage extends down to firms employing five operatives including a sample element on a rotating basis (see Appendix XII for further details). Information about the response rates and related estimation practices is not published. The type of information obtained in terms of definitions, the valuation of output, etc. are comparable to the equivalent British

---

[2] Information was sought under the 'old system' of output and employment returns from contractors up to mid-1976 about the value of wage payments made to, and number of, self-employed operatives engaged on a 'labour-only' basis but the author is informed that it was not used in the compilation of output statistics and it was not published. The same problem does not arise under the 'new system' of enquiries.

enquiries and reference should be made to the discussion of these in Section 4.4 for output and Section 4.5 for new orders. The British new orders returns, it will be noted, are adjusted in certain ways prior to publication (see Section 4.5.3); as far as the author is aware no such adjustments are made to the Northern Ireland series.

Finally, the statistics relating to public sector direct labour organizations must be regarded with a certain reserve for two reasons. First many authorities carry out construction maintenance work as part of more general maintenance and service functions and do not maintain separate construction 'establishments' as such. Returns for construction activities alone, therefore, may often necessitate speculation as much as anything else. Secondly administrative reorganization in 1973 when many local functions were placed in the hands of new Boards, acting as agents of the central administration, introduced difficulties in identifying the authorities in scope and disrupted the previously established channels of communication as far as the construction returns were concerned.

9.2.2. Censuses of Production and Input–Output Analyses for Northern Ireland

9.2.2.1. *Censuses of Production.* Censuses of production have been conducted annually by the Department (formerly Ministry) of Commerce since 1949 in the post-war period in accordance with the *Statistics of Trade Act (Northern Ireland) 1949*. The results of these censuses are published as a series of separate reports [QRL 278] and are also incorporated with the British censuses to provide results for the United Kingdom—these are considered in Section 5.3.

Scope and coverage. Up to 1972 the censuses taken in Northern Ireland differed in certain respects from those taken in Great Britain. The pattern established in Great Britain of taking a 'detailed' census every few years, in which additional detailed particulars were sought, particularly about payments for the purchase of inputs, was followed in Northern Ireland with the same timing since 1951—i.e.: 1951, 1954, 1958, 1963 and 1968 (1968 was the last of the 'detailed' censuses in both Northern Ireland and Great Britain). In other years, however, the content of the censuses in Northern Ireland was different, for throughout the whole period information was sought each year about the full range of topics (although in less detail than in the 'detailed' census years), whereas the scope of the British census was narrowed down and after 1959 was confined (in non-'detailed' years) to the collection of data solely about capital expenditure and stocks (cf. Table 5.1). Thus the following major subjects were reported in the Northern Ireland censuses every year:

Gross output (sub-classified by type of work in 1951 and 1954).
Payments for materials, fuel, services and sub-contracted work (breakdowns in greater detail were obtained in 'detailed' census years and, in some cases, quantity figures as well as values).
Net output.
Employment (Working Principals, ATC staff, operatives).
Wages and salaries.
Capital expenditure by type of asset (not in 1949 and only from public sector undertakings in 1950).

Analyses by geographical location of the establishment (not necessarily location of the work) and by size of establishment were also prepared in detailed census years.

Except in detailed census years the census was confined to larger firms: this meant firms employing eleven or more persons until 1958 when the size limit was raised to twenty-five or more persons. Firms below these limits were covered in the detailed census years (with one exception, noted below) but they were required to provide less than the full range of information; in construction, however, unlike other industries, firms in the size range eleven to twenty-four persons were also required to provide less than the full range of information prior to 1958 and in 1951 the smallest firms (employing less than 11 persons) were excluded altogether.

Industrial definitions and direct labour. The classification of industry in each census is said to be based on the Standard Industrial Classification—see Appendix I (it should be noted that the name applied to the industry has differed in successive editions of the SIC but for convenience here we use the current term, 'construction', to refer to the industry throughout the whole period). But particular care is required in the use and interpretation of the construction data because of the treatment of direct labour organizations (i.e. the construction works departments of public authorities and public utilities—the term 'direct labour' is not used in the census reports). The coverage of these organizations has varied over time and the results for the organizations which were covered were not always grouped with the results for private contractors—construction data for gas, electricity and water undertakings, in particular, were regularly included with the results for these industries although, under the SIC prior to 1968, they were classifiable to the Construction 'Order'. Up to 1954 separate data are provided for the construction activities of: transport undertakings and of local authorities, harbour, dock and canal undertakings (combined). Since then no separate data have been given for direct labour but it is possible to infer the figures by comparing census reports for the UK [QRL 273] Part 128, [QRL 275] Part 126, [QRL 277] Part 151 with the corresponding Northern Ireland reports [QRL 278]: the former provide separate data for private firms which may be subtracted from the combined public and private figures which are given in the latter.

Interpretation. As so often seems to be the case, the existence of more than one source of statistics proves to be a mixed blessing. In this case the statistics of the value of output obtained in the census of production differ substantially from those obtained in the quarterly surveys considered in Section 9.2.1. It is to be expected that the figures should differ since although the enquiries were based, until recently, on the same register, the firms covered were defined by a different size exemption limit: seven or more *operatives* in the quarterly surveys, twenty-five or more *persons* in the censuses. Contrary to expectation, however, the more narrowly based census does not produce results which are lower than the quarterly enquiries and, in particular, there is a conflict between the results for employment and those for output—the census results for employment are regularly lower while those for output (gross output) are regularly higher.

With regard to output, the major part of the difference is probably attributable to double counting of sub-contract work in the census, since, unlike the quarterly enquiries, the contractors in the census are not required to exclude sub-contract payments from their returns. The same applies to the comparable data collected in the

British census of production and by the DOE and reference should be made to the discussion of the British census statistics in Section 5.3.3.4 for further comment. As we stress there, the closest comparison that can be made between the two sets of data is to deduct the value of payments made for work sub-let including work done on materials given out (of relevance to LOSC in construction) from gross output in the census results (although this means the deduction of some work which is then not covered at all, either because the sub-contractors are below the size exemption limit or because they are not on the register). There are, of course, also differences in timing—as in the corresponding British enquiries.

With regard to employment, the most likely explanation for the difference between the two sources would seem to be the difference in the scope of the two enquiries because of the different firm size exemption limits.

Finally, it is necessary to stress doubts about the comprehensiveness of the register upon which the enquiries are based. We discussed this question earlier in connection with the quarterly series (Section 9.2.1). Ironically, however, the fact that main contractors *include* the value of sub-contract work in their returns in the census of production, in contrast to their quarterly returns, means that the effects of deficiencies in the register are less in the census of production. On the other hand, this advantage is offset by the unknown element of double counting that this practice involves. Fortunately, the new project-based enquiry recently introduced for the collection of the quarterly output data possesses great potential for improving the quality of the quarterly data—at least for new construction work.

9.2.2.2. *Input–output tables for Northern Ireland.* Only one set of input–output tables has been prepared for Northern Ireland—for the year 1963 published in [QRL 174]; tables for the year 1968 are in course of preparation. For most industries the tables are based on the information collected in the census of production. Construction, however, is an exception. No information is given in the published report about the derivation of the construction components of the matrices and the brief account given here is based upon information kindly supplied by the staff of the Statistics and Economics Unit of the Department of Finance.

There are severe difficulties in compiling such tables, especially for the construction component of the matrices because of the deficiencies and limitations in the scope of the census and the wide variety of materials used by the industry but about which only limited information is collected, information which is itself likely to be subject to considerable margins of error. For construction, therefore, starting from an estimate of total expenditure on construction work (divided into eight categories: housing; factories; schools and hospitals; offices; agricultural improvements; water projects; roads; repair and maintenance) estimates were made in physical terms of the quantities of different materials required in each of these types—these were then valued and allocated to the appropriate producing industry. In total the eight types of work stand for total construction expenditure.

The information about the inputs required for the first four categories of work listed above was taken from materials usage estimates for Great Britain prepared by the Building Research Station [QRL 7]; these, of course, may not be appropriate for Northern Ireland inasmuch as materials specifications and forms and methods of construction used in the two countries may differ. Given the fact that many materials have to be imported into Northern Ireland, this could well be the case. Lack of information about the extent to which materials are imported rather than locally produced also presents difficulties and in allocating the input estimates to producing industries the two are combined (this, of course, does limit the use of the tables for estimating the impact of changes in construction demand on domestic industry).

Given the nature of the estimation process employed, and the fact that the whole sector is represented by eight categories of work, it is to be expected that the estimates should be open to potentially large margins of error. No attempt is made to quantify these in the report [QRL 174] but the fact that the outcome is the appearance of an estimate for 'profits and depreciation' which is much *larger* than the wages and salaries bill for the industry would suggest, especially in view of its labour intensive character, that the margins of error to which the estimates are subject are unacceptably high. This comment, however, should not be taken as detracting from the extremely useful nature of this investigation. The publication itself makes plain that the work was initially undertaken as an exploration of the adequacy of existing statistics. Investigation of the reason for this particular discrepancy would require access to the working papers but the supposition of this writer would be that the source of error may lie not so much in the materials input estimates as in a failure to allow for payments made to men employed under labour-only sub-contract.

9.2.3. *Statistics of Expenditure on Construction Work in Northern Ireland*

9.2.3.1. *Capital formation statistics.* As in Britain, statistics of capital expenditure provide an extremely useful additional source of information about building and construction work, particularly because they do not depend upon returns from contractors, with all the difficulties that involves, but are derived from the clients' side of the transactions. Separate estimates are made of gross fixed capital formation in building and works (and other assets) based upon the same concepts and conventions as in the UK (see the discussion of the UK series—Section 5.4.2). These statistics, however, are *not* a constituent of the UK series (they are devised independently by the Department of Finance in Northern Ireland) and they do not form part of an integrated set of national accounts as do the UK series.

The available series. The analyses are prepared in much less detail than for the UK as a whole and are of more recent origin. The series published are as follows:

(1) Dwellings/Other Buildings and Works from 1950 annually at current prices in *NI Digest* [QRL 140] No. 10, September 1958, *et seq.*
(2) Analyses of the above by sector (public/private) from 1961 annually at current prices in *NI Digest* [QRL 140] No. 32, September 1969, *et seq.*

In addition, capital accounts for the 'central government' (meaning in this context the Northern Ireland administration) provide figures of the value of capital expenditure on roads and factory building, and local authority accounts provide data for housing.

Constant price series are not now published; they were included at one time in

Economic Reports [B 280]. It is well to note, however, that the price index used for deflation purposes in this series was the same as that used for the UK (Section 8.1.2.1 refers) and not one peculiar to the Province.

Capital stock. No official estimates are made of the accumulated capital stock in construction and other assets in Northern Ireland and the only unofficial attempt to make any estimates appears to be that reported in [B 82] for manufacturing industry only.

Interpretation. The conceptual basis of statistics of capital formation, and the nature of the statistics themselves, were discussed earlier in considering the equivalent series for the UK (Section 5.4.2) and for a full discussion reference should be made to that Section. In the context of construction it is important to note that, as in the UK series, repairs and maintenance work is excluded but that, in principle, major improvements are included. But in practice it is not possible to make this distinction with precision and it is, in any case, an economic rather than an accounting distinction, whereas the statistics depend upon accounting information. Further, the accounting distinction between capital and current expenditure is determined in practice by certain conventions rather than by reference to the nature of the expenditure as such. Thus, however good the original sources of information may be, the resultant series will rarely if ever measure up to intention. Quite apart from these conceptual considerations, however, the reliability of the series also depends upon the scope and coverage of the primary sources of information.

Unfortunately, judgement of the reliability of the Northern Ireland series is hindered by the lack of an official guide to the sources and methods used to devise the series comparable to those available for the UK—[B 275] and [B 100]. The sources of information available, however, are certainly less complete than those in Britain for no returns of capital expenditure are obtained in the private sector other than those obtained annually in the census of production [QRL 278] and this is confined of course to larger firms operating, in the main, in manufacturing industry.

Statistics for service and distributive trades have been obtained on only two occasions —1965 (on a voluntary basis) [QRL 267] and 1975 (results not yet published). It is true, on the other hand, that a substantial part of capital expenditure is directly in the hands of the government and other public authorities, including a large part of factory building, and that some private work is grant-aided by the government. In these cases the estimates, which are provided by the government departments concerned, ought to be reasonably reliable. But in other cases there are no statistical sources and the estimates are likely to be highly conjectural. The capital formation series for housing were examined in the companion Review on *Housing in Northern Ireland* [B 57]—these too, it should be noted, are open to error (being estimates based on completions and prices data).

Over time it is probable that the quality of the series has improved. It is difficult to put dates on such improvements but it should be noted that the early series were devised retrospectively and that for some time, the author is informed, the final series was based to some extent merely on the use of ratios comparing, for example, Northern Ireland's population with that for the UK as a whole and using these as an indicator of the local share of UK capital formation. Although it is difficult to put a date on improvements in a general sense, it would seem likely that the series from the early to mid-1960s, when development plans for the province first began to be prepared, are perhaps somewhat more reliable than those that went before.

Comparison with other series. As with the UK series, comparison with the statistics of output is salutary for it acts as a healthy reminder of the magnitude of the errors that are involved in the preparation of both sets of statistics. It is not possible to make a direct comparison because it is not possible to identify all *new* work separately from repairs and maintenance in the output statistics (though it may be noted that this deficiency has now been remedied in the recently initiated project-based system for the collection of output statistics—Section 9.2.1 refers). On the capital formation side, no figures are available of expenditure on professional fees and transfer costs of land and buildings, or improvements work (for data for housing see [B 57]) so that it is not possible to deduct this element from the capital formation series. The difference between the series, however, is very large—the capital formation series is bigger than both of the output series—and too big to be readily accounted for by the factors we have mentioned. Indeed the factors tend to intensify the difference rather than reduce it. For further discussion of the potential causes of difference reference should be made to the discussion of the corresponding UK series in Section 5.4.3.

In view of the lack of information both about the sources and methods used for the capital formation series and about the likely reliability of the output statistics (in particular lack of information about the register) it is not possible to suggest with any assurance that greater credence should be attached to one series rather than another. A personal view, however, would be that the capital formation series, particularly perhaps from the 1960s, may be the more reliable. But, at the same time, it must also be stressed that it is undoubtedly open to error which may be substantial. In conclusion, therefore, the user of these statistics is well advised, yet again, to regard the statistics with circumspection and to bear in mind that they will not stand the weight of fine judgements. Needless to say, an official account of the means used to devise the series is badly needed together with reliability gradings on the UK model.

9.2.3.2. *Other capital expenditure statistics for Northern Ireland.* Statistics of capital expenditure on construction work other than the estimates presented in the gross fixed capital formation series, considered in the previous section, are only partial. The principal source is the annual census of production, reported in [QRL 278], but this is confined to manufacturing and process industries (i.e. manufacturing, construction, gas, electricity and water) and to larger firms only within these industries. They are useful as an additional source, however, in giving separate information by industry. From 1960 they also provide statistics of expenditure on acquisitions and disposals of land and existing buildings.

The reliability of the information naturally depends on the adequacy of the statistical registers for each industry, the levels of response attained and the reliability of the returns themselves. Unlike the register for the construction industry, it is probably reasonable to assume that the registers for other industries do not suffer from serious deficiencies given the fact that most other industries operate at a fixed location and that the enquiries are confined to the larger firms. No information is given about levels of response and, as far as the author is aware, no studies have been made of the reliability of the returns received. But it will be appreciated, of course that the classification of expenditure to 'capital' or 'current' accounts is affected by the accounting practices adopted and that the boundary between 'construction' and 'plant' cannot always be sharply defined—we discussed these aspects fully in Section 5.4.3 in the context of the UK series. One further point to note with regard to the interpretation of the data is that the census of production figures do not cover the substantial volume of expenditure on industrial building borne directly by the government (see Section 9.2.5).

As indicated earlier, statistics for non-production industries have been obtained on only one occasion—in the first census of distribution in 1965 [QRL 267]—and then only on a voluntary basis so that the results are incomplete. Another census of the distributive and service trades was taken in 1976 but at the time of writing no results had been published.

Capital expenditure by the construction industry in Northern Ireland. The only data available are those collected in the censuses of production—see Section 9.2.2.1.

9.2.3.3. *Current expenditure on construction.* The only information about current, as opposed to capital, expenditure on construction comes from recent censuses of production [QRL 278] and from official accounts for certain types of buildings in the public sector. The former required a return of expenditure on the repair and maintenance of buildings in 1963 and in 1968. As regards coverage and interpretation, etc. see Section 9.2.3.2 above. For expenditure in the public sector see Section 9.2.5. Statistics of repair and maintenance output by contractors, as distinct from expenditure by clients, have been collected regularly since 1966 and were considered above—Section 9.2.1.

9.2.4. *Construction in the Northern Ireland Index of Industrial Production*

In the account which follows it is necessary to draw two distinctions, one between the series compiled currently and that compiled prior to 1966, and one between an index incorporated historically by the CSO in London into the index of industrial production for the UK as a whole and an index compiled locally in the Province. We deal first with the current, and then the historical, positions.

Currently an output index for construction is compiled by the Department of Commerce on the basis of the quarterly enquiry which is considered in Section 9.2.1 and is published in the *NI Digest* [QRL 140]. This index forms part of the construction index for the UK compiled by the CSO (considered in Section 5.2). For the purpose of compiling the *monthly* overall index of industrial production covering all industry, both in Northern Ireland and in the UK as a whole, construction is incorporated at its quarterly value since monthly data are not available. It is understood that the whole series back to 1966 is now based on the quarterly output data. The price index used to convert the current price series to a constant price basis is the 'CNC' index compiled by the DOE for Great Britain. It needs to be appreciated that there are great difficulties in devising a reliable general measure of construction price movements—these, and the 'CNC' index in particular, are considered at length in Sections 8.1.1 and 8.1.2.1

respectively. It is also worth noting that quite apart from the reliability of the 'CNC' index itself, its application to Northern Ireland may be inappropriate.

Historically the position is more complex. An official index of industrial production for Northern Ireland, incorporating a separate index for construction output, was first published in 1958 when an annual index, based on the census of production, was published for the years 1950–7 in the *NI Digest* [QRL 140]. This was followed by the regular publication of a monthly index—also in [QRL 140]. An account of the sources and methods used in the compilation of the monthly index was issued by the then Ministry of Commerce in [B 282]. Briefly, for the purpose of the monthly index, returns were obtained from a number of contractors of the cost of materials purchased and the amount paid in wages and salaries each month. These were adjusted to a constant price basis by dividing the first by the official UK price index for building materials (Section 11.1.1) and the latter by an index of 'pay' rates (*sic*). The sum of these two adjusted items was taken as an indicator of the value of production at constant prices and used to calculate the index (after an adjustment for length of month). The index numbers for each year (based on the monthly series) were revised as soon as the results for the census of production became available, and, if necessary, the monthly figures were amended accordingly.

The reliability of the monthly index was critically dependent on the representativeness of the returns obtained. Information was not published about this but the number of firms supplying returns is known to have been very small, consisting only of large firms which had agreed to co-operate. The method itself is also open to objection inasmuch as the inputs of labour and materials are affected by changes in the composition of work, no allowance is made for changes in overheads, profits and productivity (probably a small factor in the measurement of month to month changes) and the deflators may not be wholly appropriate (the labour deflator was apparently based on wage rate changes). The annual index, based on the census of production, is more reliable inasmuch as it covers the industry more comprehensively. But it may still have been affected by deficiencies in the coverage and reliability of the census of production data (see Section 9.2.1) and by the possible inappropriateness of the CNC price deflator. Suspicions about the validity of the index at this time are reinforced by observation of the erratic movement of the monthly index and movements of the annual index which are at odds with official employment series (considered in Section 9.3.1) below.

The index was not used as a constituent of the index prepared by the CSO for the UK as a whole—for this purpose an independent estimate prepared on the basis of employment statistics was used—see [B 254] p. 54 and [B 255] p. 81.

9.2.5. *Production Data for Specific Types of Building in Northern Ireland*

9.2.5.1. *Educational building statistics for Northern Ireland—Schools and Institutions of Further Education.* Statistics for schools and Institutions of Further Education are compiled by the Department of Education (NI) and published in [QRL 151]. Annual statistics for the post-war period for projects started, under construction and completed show new accommodation provided and also the value of building work—the latter is also given for work done in each year. These values include professional fees and site values. There are certain exclusions from the scope of the data, details of which are given in introductory notes to the tables. Some of the data relating to new accommodation provided in schools is also given in the *NI Digest* [QRL 140] and in [QRL 153].

University building. Statistics of capital expenditure on building work and repairs and maintenance of buildings at universities in Northern Ireland are published in [QRL 151].

9.2.5.2. *Health and personal social services building programme in Northern Ireland.* Statistics have not been published on a regular basis but an official summary of the hospital building programme in 1963 with estimated costs was published in [B 340] and this was followed by a series of periodic reviews: [B 245], [B 313] and [B 322]. Planning has now been widened to cover personal health and social services more generally—details are given in *Strategy for the Development of Health and Personal Social Services in Northern Ireland* [B 303], published in November 1975, to which is appended a list of the major capital projects in the health and personal social services field (on site or contracted at October 1975).

9.2.5.3. *Industrial building statistics for Northern Ireland.* There is no counterpart to the IDC statistics available for Great Britain. But since the war a major part of industrial building has been carried out directly by the Department of Commerce under Industries Development legislation and series are published in the *NI Digest* [QRL 140] to show the number and area of government factory building projects approved, started and completed. The expenditure on this programme is recorded in central government capital accounts also in [QRL 140]—referred to in Section 9.2.3.1 above. Industrial development was also carried out by three Development Commissions (now dissolved) from the late 1960s to the early 1970s and expenditure was recorded in their accounts [B 211], [B 179] and [B 270]. In the private sector, details of capital expenditure (and for some years, repairs and maintenance) by larger firms within the scope of the annual census of production, are reported in [QRL 278]—see Sections 9.2.3.2 and 9.2.3.3.

9.2.5.4. *Road building in Northern Ireland.* Annual statistics for expenditure on 'new construction and improvement' and 'operation and maintenance' are compiled by the Department of the Environment (Northern Ireland) and published in the *NI Digest* [QRL 140]. Figures for total expenditure on roads are also to be found in *Regional Statistics* [QRL 252].

9.3. Construction Employment Statistics for Northern Ireland

9.3.1. *Introduction*

There are five sources of construction employment statistics for Northern Ireland:

(1) Statistics compiled by the DMS and its predecessor departments comparable to the DE statistics for Great Britain.

(2) Quarterly surveys covering employment along with output and new orders conducted by the Department of Finance (formerly Department of Commerce) since 1966.
(3) Censuses of production conducted by the Department of Commerce annually from 1949.
(4) Censuses of population taken in 1951, 1961, 1966 and 1971.
(5) Manpower surveys conducted for the Construction Industry Training Board for Northern Ireland by the DMS.

Each of these sources has its counterpart in Great Britain but the statistics collected in Northern Ireland are generally much less detailed. This, as we suggested earlier, seems to have been associated with the lack in Northern Ireland of a Department with central responsibility for the collection of statistics about the industry comparable to that exercised by the DOE and its predecessors in Britain. Thus there has been no equivalent to the detailed DOE censuses in Britain which have provided detailed occupational data for the construction labour force annually for many years. In Northern Ireland this gap has been filled to some extent by enquiries conducted for the CITB (NI) since 1964 (Section 9.3.6 refers) although many of these data have remained unpublished. We consider each of the sources in the following five sections and then turn to examine the differences among them and the problems of interpretation. A final section brings together references to *ad hoc* construction manpower surveys.

9.3.2. *Department of Manpower Services (DMS) Employment Statistics for Northern Ireland*

9.3.2.1. *Principal employment series.* These statistics are largely comparable to those compiled by the DE and its predecessors in Great Britain (Section 6.2 refers). That is to say, for the period from 1948 to 1971 series were devised for each industry upon the basis of counts of national insurance cards exchanged each June, supplemented by returns from employers (a few specific employers in Northern Ireland) to show the total number of cards *held*. Since 1971 a census of employment has been taken each June. As in Great Britain a major discontinuity occurs in the series at this point as a result, but both systems were run together in June 1971 for comparative purposes. It should be noted that there is a substantial discrepancy between the two series. Since (with one exception) the scope and nature of the data are the same as in Britain reference should be made to the discussion there for further background information—Section 6.2. The exception is that the June census in Northern Ireland is a full census every year whereas in Great Britain a full census is only taken every third year.

Briefly, the series available are as follows:

(1) Numbers in (civil) employment (i.e. employees in employment plus employers and self-employed) from 1948 to 1974 (continued beyond 1971 by including information about the self-employed available from card counts until 1974)—in *NID* [QRL 140].
(2) Employees (employed plus unemployed) from 1950 to 1971 in *NID* [QRL 140] and *British Labour Statistics Yearbooks* [QRL 59].
(3) Employees in employment from 1949 in *NID* [QRL 140] and the *Yearbooks* (as above) [QRL 59].

Further particulars, including details of the breakdowns and frequency of the series, are included in the Quick Reference List at the end of this volume.

Continuous series. An official attempt has been made to prepare a 'continuous series' of estimates for employees in employment (by sex) on a consistent basis from 1959. The series from 1965 to 1975 were published in *DEG* [QRL 135] for August 1976. The earlier series for Northern Ireland back to 1959 may be obtained as the difference between series for Great Britain and the UK published in the *DEG* [QRL 135] for March 1975 and October 1975 respectively. This series attempts to allow for various causes of discontinuity including in particular, the major discrepancy caused by the change to censuses of employment in 1971 (an account of the methodology is given in *DEG* [QRL 135] March 1975), but it is well to remember that it is not possible to remove the basic cause of discontinuity and that it involves, in particular, the bold assumption that the relationship between the old and new series at the time of the discontinuity also holds for the whole of the previous series. The series must not be regarded, therefore, as in any sense truly continuous, especially bearing in mind the size of the discrepancy caused by the changeover in 1971.

Historical employment series for Northern Ireland. Series for the number of insured workers in construction ('building and contracting') and other industries for the period prior to 1948 (series back to 1923) have been conveniently brought together in [B 79] p. 578. Interpretation of the pre-1948 data needs to take account of the differences in the scope of the National Insurance scheme and changes over time—for details reference should be made to [B 241].

9.3.2.2. *Subsidiary DMS employment series for Northern Ireland.* Of the subsidiary series published for Great Britain (see the *Quick Reference List*) only one is regularly published for Northern Ireland—that for young persons entering employment.

Young persons entering employment. Figures for boys and girls by class of employment were published in *NI Digest* [QRL 140] until 1974. The same points apply to the interpretation of these data as for the British series—see the introductory notes to [QRL 59].

Age analyses. An age analysis of insured male employees based on a 5 per cent sample is to be found in *NI Digest* [QRL 140] No. 10, September 1958 relating to June 1957; it appears not to have been repeated subsequently.

Local authorities' direct labour. No figures are published for Northern Ireland as such but it is possible to derive them for figures are published for both Great Britain and the UK—see Section 6.2.3.4.

9.3.3. *Quarterly Construction Employment Surveys for Northern Ireland from 1966*

These surveys, conducted currently by the Department of Finance (formerly Department of Commerce), cover output and new orders as well as employment and have therefore already been considered earlier (Section 9.2.1). Attention was drawn in the earlier section to two crucial matters relating to the coverage of the data which bear repetition here. First there is the fact that up to the second quarter of 1976 the surveys were confined to firms on the register employing seven or more operatives only, although this fact was never publicized in the regular source of publication. Secondly, it is important to recognize that the register itself was rarely, if ever, likely to be complete because of the difficulties of maintaining an up-to-date and fully comprehensive register for the construction industry.

It is also notable that the labour statistics collected in the enquiries were not regularly published in Northern Ireland itself until September 1977 when the latest results (third quarter of 1976) were included for the first time in the *NI Digest* [QRL 140]; these statistics were the first results from the newly initiated project-based enquiry—for details see Section 9.2.1. Formerly the statistics were regularly published only in the British publication *Housing and Construction Statistics* [QRL 168]—though for the months of June and December each year only, not the full quarterly series. The introduction of the project-based enquiry has created a major discontinuity in the series.

Both series are published in the same format: the number of *operatives* employed classified by type of work (as for output—Section 9.2.1 refers) together with a figure of the number employed by public sector direct labour organizations—this is published in the aggregate only although it is obtained broken down by type of work. Specimen copies of the questionnaires used for the contractors' part of the enquiry up to mid-1976 and for public authorities (this has remained unchanged) will be found in the companion Review on *Housing in Northern Ireland* [B 57] Appendix I. Under the new system two forms are sent to contractors and specimen copies of these are reproduced in Appendix XII of this volume.

It should be noted that under the new system returns are obtained from main contractors in respect of *all* labour employed on particular sites where *new* building work is taking place covering sub-contractors' labour (including labour-only) as well as their own directly employed labour. The enquiry is therefore more comprehensive in coverage than the one it replaced since it is not confined to larger firms and overcomes the problem of having to obtain separate returns from sub-contractors (many of whom are small firms or gangs or individuals working under labour-only arrangements). This enquiry does not cover, however, the labour employed off-site or on repairs and maintenance and housing improvements work. It is to cover this labour that a second form of return, as referred to above, is used. Since this return is required from the small firms of sub-contractors as well as the main contractors it is possible that the coverage is less complete than that obtained in the site returns; it is in any case confined to firms employing five or more operatives.

The statistics published to date from the new enquiry relate, it is important to note, solely to site labour (including repairs and maintenance) and relate to operatives only. The use and interpretation of the data should also take account of the fact that Working Principals are not covered in the data although they perform, in part, operative functions. Statistics of the number of Working Principals have been collected throughout the whole history of this enquiry but not published. Likewise no statistics have yet been published about the number of APTC staff employed (covered for the first time in the new system). The separate statistics about 'labour only' operatives obtained in both the old and new enquiries have also remained unpublished (though they are incorporated in the total employment analyses).

There are a number of further matters that are relevant with regard to the interpretation of the employment data, particularly if they are to be considered in conjunction with the output data for purposes such as comparing relative movements over time or calculating labour productivity ratios, etc. Since the old enquiry system was modelled on that used by the DOE in Great Britain, reference may usefully be made to the discussion of these matters included in the final part of Section 4.4.2. With regard to the new system, there is likely to be a better match between the coverage of work done and the labour employed on it as far as *site work* is concerned. The main limitation arises from the inability to differentiate between the activity of off-site labour in preparing materials and components for use on-site (and therefore recorded in the value of output return, though the labour is not) from its activity in preparing goods for sale (the value of which is not recorded in the enquiry).

9.3.4. *Employment Data from the Censuses of Production for Northern Ireland*

These enquiries too have been considered earlier since, like the quarterly enquiries referred to above, they also provide output statistics. Reference should be made to Section 9.2.2 for publication references and for comment on the scope of the census: it is affected by the same register problems as the quarterly enquiries and is also restricted to larger firms except in the detailed census years (1951, 1954, 1958, 1963 and 1968). The census of production is a useful supplementary source of information (ignoring possible deficiencies in coverage) for, until recently, it was the only regular source of information about the employment of employees other than operatives (other sources are considered in Sections 9.3.3, 9.3.5 and 9.3.6) about remuneration (see Section 9.4.3) and also about direct labour organizations of public authorities (see Section 9.3.3). The reports of the detailed censuses also provide the only published analyses by size of firm (apart from one *ad hoc* analysis of CITB (NI) data—see Section 9.3.6) and their location.

9.3.5. *Censuses of Population Data for Construction in Northern Ireland*

As far as industrial and occupational analyses are concerned, the Northern Ireland censuses are essentially the same as those taken in Great Britain (considered in Section 6.3). The major points of difference relate to the omission of certain questions rather than differences in the nature of the data. Unlike pre-war censuses their timing since the war has also coincided with those for Great Britain (1951, 1961, 1966 and 1971); a major difference, however, is that the 1966 census was a full census, rather than a sample. As we stressed earlier, when considering the reports for Great Britain, the principal virtues of the census data are its comprehensiveness and the degree of accuracy which can be achieved by virtue of the way the census is taken—viz. the completion of returns by individuals or the heads of households and the employment of enumerators in the field with responsibilities for ensuring complete and, as far as possible, accurate returns. Complete accuracy is not achieved in the census—this has been made evident by post-enumeration surveys in Britain—but in all likelihood the census is more reliable than other sources, which rely on returns from employers.

Publication references for the principal industrial and occupational tabulations for the province as a whole are as follows: 1951—[QRL 113]; 1961—[QRL 110]; 1966—[QRL 111] (occupational data not collected); 1971—[QRL 108]. These are generally analysed with reference to age, sex, employment status, marital condition, etc. As in Great Britain, information about scientific and technological qualifications was collected for the first time in 1961 (published in [QRL 110]) and extended to cover qualifications more generally in 1971—published in *Education Tables* [QRL 109]. The subject was not covered in Northern Ireland in 1966. In addition the 1971 census also provides separate analyses by occupation and industry of migrants [QRL 112] and of work place movement [QRL 114]. The latter, it should be noted, defines 'work place' in terms of sites in the case of construction workers as opposed to the location of the employers' offices. It may also be noted that information about hours of work was also collected in the censuses of 1961 and 1971, although occupational and industrial analyses of the data have not been published.

Interpretation. Little discussion is required of the Northern Ireland data additional to that devoted to the British data in Section 6.3.1. Full attention was given there to the nature of the data collected and reference should be made to that section. Perhaps the most important point of difference that needs to be noted is that, unlike the British census, none of the data relating to occupation, industry or qualifications has been obtained by sampling. Thus the sample errors (and also the bias that occurred in the 1961 census) are not present in the Northern Ireland data.

9.3.6. *CITB (Northern Ireland) Manpower Surveys*

Since 1964 annual surveys have been conducted for the Northern Ireland CITB under the terms of the *Industrial Training Act (Northern Ireland) 1964*, first by the Ministry of Health and Social Services and now by the Department of Manpower Services. As in Britain, however, the definition of the industry is wider in scope than that defined in the *SIC* (see Appendix I). The precise definition will be found in the *Industrial Training (Construction Board) Order (Northern Ireland) 1964* [B 336]. Like the definition adopted for the CITB in Great Britain (Section 6.4.2 refers) the scope of the definition extends to certain manufacturing processes, particularly the production of timber components and prefabricated structures. There are certain differences, however, between the Great Britain and Northern Ireland definitions. Particularly notable are the inclusion of structural steelwork erection in Northern Ireland but its exclusion in Great Britain and the inclusion of local authorities' construction activities in Northern Ireland (these were expressly excluded in an amendment to the British definition).

The annual surveys provide the only regular detailed source of occupational statistics. Unfortunately, much of the data remains unpublished, but it is possible that it would be made available on request for serious research purposes subject to the usual rules regarding disclosure. Statistics are collected for:

(1) *Employment*
    (a) APTC staff, Working Principals and operatives all broken down by occupation and cross-classified by type of work as follows: housing, other building, roads and bridges, other civil engineering work (each of which is sub-

divided between new work and repairs and maintenance with the exception of roads and bridges).
   (b) Young persons employed in age group 15–17 by occupation.
(2) *Apprentices, recruitment and training*. Number of apprentices employed by year of apprenticeship by occupation (APTC and operatives) and apprenticeships completed and discontinued.
(3) *Labour requirements*—return by occupation requested.
(4) *Labour mobility and stability*. Statistics are collected for the number of persons recruited in the last twelve months (plus the number of those requiring training and the number in training on a certain date) and the number who left in the last twelve months—all by occupation for all categories of labour.

The only data regularly published are summary analyses in the *Annual Reports* of the CITB (NI) [QRL 254]. These show:

(1) Employment: numbers by occupational group and percentage distribution according to type of work.
(2) Apprentices: numbers employed by trade and year of apprenticeship.
(3) Firms' estimates of labour requirements by occupational group. In addition an analysis of employment according to size of firm from the 1966 survey distinguishing: ATC staff, 'skilled' operatives, 'mainly semi-skilled' operatives and 'other workers', was published in the *Northern Ireland Economic Report* on 1966 [B 280] p. 26.

Interpretation. An essential point to bear in mind is the fact that the industry is not defined in accordance with the SIC. Obviously the validity of the statistics collected depends upon the reliability of the register of firms used and the level of response and accuracy of the returns obtained. As regards the latter, no information is published. As regards the register, the CITB faces the same problems in compiling and maintaining a comprehensive register as the Departments of Finance and Commerce who conduct the enquiries considered in Sections 9.3.3 and 9.3.4 above, and it would seem reasonable to believe that it may suffer from some deficiencies (some evidence of deficiencies in 1964, when the register was first compiled and the first enquiry made, were obtained incidentally in a housing study made by the author—see comment in [B 57] p. 35). Unlike the CITB register in Great Britain, however, its scope is not confined to firms *with* employees.

An interesting feature of the data, without parallel in any British enquiry, is the classification of labour of *all* types (including APTC) by type of work. This must be regarded with some reserve because of the difficulties that many contractors must face in allocating APTC labour in this way since, even at any one time, it may be employed on a range of activities not related solely to one type of work.

9.3.7. *Comparison of the Construction Employment Series for Northern Ireland*

The scope and nature of each of the five principal sources of construction employment statistics has been considered in the Sections above. Direct comparison of the statistics from each source cannot be made in every case because allowances have to be made for differences in terms of the scope of the enquiries or of the categories of labour covered. The information available, however, is enough to give rise to substantial misgivings, for the differences between the series are large enough not to be explicable solely in terms of ostensible differences in coverage. Details of the size of these differences may be seen from Table 9.1. Comparisons are made for the year 1971 in this table because this is the year of the latest census of population and also the year when the DMS old system of card counts and new system of censuses of employment were run in parallel.

We suggested earlier that the most reliable source is probably the census of population and it is notable that the figures from this source are much higher than any of the others. Some of the major points of difference between census of population data and DMS statistics (DE statistics in Great Britain) have been considered in a British context in Section 6.3.4 above, to which reference should be made since the nature of the data is the same in each case. Of particular concern, however, is the large difference between the DMS card count and those based on the census of employment in June 1971 especially since it is three times as large, proportionately, as the difference that occurred in Great Britain. Two official reasons have been put forward to explain, in principle, why a difference should exist—one of which acts to offset the other. These are discussed in the final part of Section 6.2.3.2.

The two Department of Commerce surveys—the census of production and the quarterly construction survey (now the responsibility of the Department of Finance)—cannot be compared directly either with other sources or with each other because of the limitations in their coverage. Allowing for the explicit restriction in the census of production, however, it does seem that coverage is still markedly below other sources. Part of the difference may be due to a difference in timing since the census of production data are averages over 'business years' whereas the others are point estimates all taken at times of the year when employment levels would normally be higher than at some other times due to seasonal factors. But, given the size of the discrepancy, it is doubtful whether this could be a sufficient explanation. It does seem, therefore, as if the census of production survey for 1971 (and presumably others) may have been deficient (although a reconciliation exercise between the COP and CITB registers was carried out for the 1968 census—see below). Since the enquiry is of central economic importance this conclusion, if it is true, must be a cause for no little concern. Since the quarterly survey was also based on the same register (until 1976) it would seem reasonable to entertain the same reservations about that series too.

Comparison with the CITB data is again difficult because of the difference in scope of the CITB register: on the one hand it is wider than the SIC definition because of the inclusion of manufacturing activities, but on the other hand all direct labour organizations, other than those of local authorities, are excluded. How far these factors may be held to account for the difference from the census of population 'benchmark', however, is impossible to say.

The reconciliation exercise, referred to earlier between the CITB and COP registers, showed, naturally, that some firms on the CITB register belonged to non-construction trades; others were shown to be 'not firms at all in the ordinary sense but merely employees of other firms engaged in short-term private enterprise ventures', whilst others were construction units of manufacturing firms (and therefore classifiable in principle to construction under the SIC) which were able to supply employment figures

9.3.7 CONSTRUCTION INDUSTRY STATISTICS FOR NORTHERN IRELAND

Table 9.1
Construction Employment Statistics for Northern Ireland—Comparison of Sources
(Thousands)

Survey:	QUARTERLY SURVEY	DMS EMPLOYMENT SERIES		CENSUS OF PRODUCTION	CENSUS OF POPULATION	CITB (NI) MANPOWER SURVEY
		CARD COUNT	CENSUS			
Section ref:	9.3.3	9.3.2		9.3.4	9.3.5	9.3.6
Department:	Commerce (now Finance)	DMS		Commerce	Gen. Register Office	DMS*
Coverage:	D.L. and Private firms employing seven or more operatives	Complete		D.L. and Private undertakings employing twenty-five or more persons 1971	Complete	Complete*
Date:	June 1971	June 1971	June 1971		April 1971	Sept. 1971
Operatives:	34.0	42.8	39.9	25.5		37.2
All employees:		50.8	47.9	29.2	49.8	43.9
Total persons†				29.6 (35.3)‡	58.1	46.4

* Non SIC-based register (see Section 9.3.6).
† Including self-employed (Working Principals/Proprietors).
‡ Author's estimate for *all* firms assuming that the ratio between employment in larger and smaller firms remained the same as in the 1968 census of production.

for CITB surveys but not the full range of data required in the COP. How many additions were made to the COP register as a result of the exercise has not been revealed.

9.3.8. Ad hoc *Construction Manpower Surveys for Northern Ireland*

A special survey of skilled manpower in the building industry was conducted by the then MOLNI in November 1963 through local employment offices using a list of firms 'prepared from several sources', in order to obtain information about labour shortages in the industry. Information was sought about the number of craftsmen and the number of apprentices in each of the trades of bricklayer, plasterer and joiner (these figures were meant to include LOSC labour). Firms were also required to state whether or not they could employ more of such labour if it were available and, if so, how many. The results as such were not published but are referred to in [B 214] p.78.

More recently a Working Party has been appointed by the Chairman of the Northern Ireland Construction Industry Advisory Council to assess the extent and effects of labour-only sub-contracting in Northern Ireland. A survey has been conducted but at the time of writing (July 1977) no decision about the publication of the results had been taken.

9.4. Labour Statistics for Northern Ireland other than Employment

Data relating to features of the construction labour force other than the numbers employed can be dealt with briefly for the statistics available are sparse. Those that are available, however, are (with a few exceptions) comparable to those collected for Great Britain.

9.4.1. *Labour Training and Education Statistics for Northern Ireland*

Apprenticeship and training statistics. Relevant sources are as follows:

(a) Numbers employed by occupation, year of apprenticeship, etc. have been obtained in CITB manpower surveys since 1964—see Section 9.3.6 above for further details.
(b) CITB (NI) statistics, reported in [QRL 254], show the numbers sponsored (by firms or officially) for off-the-job training at CITB centres each year.
(c) Young persons entering employment in the construction industry by class of employment including apprenticeship were recorded up to 1974 and reported in the *NI Digest* [QRL 140]—Section 9.3.2.2 above refers.

Education statistics. Statistics are published in [QRL 151] covering the following subjects of relevance to construction:

(a) Numbers of students in advanced and non-advanced courses (separate data) by subject of course (distinguishing building, civil engineering, surveying, architecture and planning) by mode of attendance and sex,

(b) Numbers by type of course (HND, HNC, etc. by subject) and qualification on entry,
(c) Analyses of employed students by industry of employer (including construction as a separate category) and also by occupation of student.

Northern Ireland is also covered in an unofficial survey conducted by the Institute of Building but the published results do not differentiate Northern Ireland (currently the data are combined with those for the Republic of Ireland)—for details see Section 6.5.5.2. See also details of the SAAT survey in the same section.

9.4.2. Unemployment, Vacancies and Labour Mobility in Northern Ireland

9.4.2.1. *Unemployment statistics for Northern Ireland—Current series.* Unemployment statistics are compiled, currently, by the DMS on the same basis as those compiled by the DE in Britain (Section 6.8.1.1 refers). Monthly series for the wholly unemployed (males and females) have been published in the *NI Digest* [QRL 140] for the period since 1950. The series may also be derived as the difference between data for Great Britain and the UK included in the *DEG* [QRL 135] and *British Labour Statistics Yearbooks* [QRL 59] (quarterly data).

Occupational analyses. Published analyses are confined to a broad classification according to KOS groups [B 203] in which construction occupations form part of a larger group—these are published periodically in *DEG* [QRL 135]. More detailed analyses are available, however, on request from the DMS.[3]

Historical series. A convenient source of historical series spanning the whole period from 1926 to 1953 (monthly) is [B 79] p. 580.

9.4.2.2. *Vacancies statistics for Northern Ireland.* Statistics about *notified* vacancies in the industry, as in Britain, are published together with British regional data in the *British Labour Statistics Yearbooks* [QRL 59] for January and July each year from 1969. Earlier figures, from 1957 onwards, are available from the DMS on request. Currently, occupational analyses according to KOS groupings [B 203] are published periodically as part of regional analyses for the UK, along with corresponding unemployment data, in the *DEG* [QRL 135].

9.4.2.3. *Labour mobility statistics for Northern Ireland.* As in Great Britain, statistics about the mobility (inter-firm, inter-industry or inter-occupational) of construction workers are not systematically compiled and much of the information that is collected is not published. The most important source of information about labour turnover in construction firms is the CITB (NI) manpower surveys, considered in Section 9.3.6, which include a question on the number of employees entering and leaving employment during the preceding twelve months; the data are not published but it is possible that they would be made available for serious research purposes. New Earnings Surveys

---

[3] Netherleigh House, Massey Avenue, Belfast, BT4 2JS.

(considered in Section 9.4.3.2) obtain information for employees who have been with their current employer for less than twelve months but small sample problems make the results for individual industries and occupations unreliable and the data are not published. Information about inter-occupational mobility is available from the 1971 census of population for Northern Ireland [QRL 108] which provides a comparison of occupation at the census with the occupation one year previously.

9.4.3. Wage Rates, Earnings, Hours and Labour Costs in Northern Ireland

A distinction needs to be drawn, as in Britain, between negotiated minimum rates of pay and hours of work and actual earnings and hours. The following categories of information are available:

(1) Wage rates and normal hours of work—manual workers.
(2) Average earnings and actual hours and periodic analyses by occupation—manual workers.
(3) Earnings of non-manual (ATC) employees.
(4) Aggregate wage and salary payments—operatives and other employees.

The sources are similar to those for Britain but the information available for Northern Ireland is much less detailed and is not available for the whole post-war period in some cases. We deal with each of the categories in turn below.

9.4.3.1. *Wage rates and normal hours of work in Northern Ireland.* Details of negotiated rates and hours are published along with the same information for Britain in [QRL 312], annually, and in [B 40] monthly. No official index numbers are published but an unofficial series of weekly wage rates for the period 1948–65 (annual) will be found along with indices for Great Britain in [B 48]. General matters regarding interpretation were discussed in Section 6.9.2.1. For details of historical sources see [B 241]; see too [B 26] which provides data for the nineteenth century and earlier.

9.4.3.2. *Average earnings and actual hours of work in Northern Ireland.* The pattern of enquiries in this field in Northern Ireland is similar to that for Great Britain although the information available is much less. Until recently the only information collected about actual earnings and hours of work was aggregate data which only provided the basis for the calculation of a single average figure. This is now supplemented by the much more detailed New Earnings Surveys conducted annually and periodic total labour costs surveys (Section 9.4.3.3 refers).

New Earnings Surveys (Northern Ireland)—All employees. New Earnings Surveys (NES) based on 1 per cent sample surveys of *employees* have been conducted in Northern Ireland by the DMS since 1971 on the same lines as those carried out in Great Britain by the DE (Section 6.9.3.1 refers). Small sample problems tend to make the results for individual industries and occupations unreliable and only summary results for all industry are published [QRL 140]. However, occupational and industrial data for

9.4.3.2 CONSTRUCTION INDUSTRY STATISTICS FOR NORTHERN IRELAND

construction and other sectors are available on request from the DMS. A full account of the nature and content of the surveys will be found in the companion Review in this series by Dean on *Wages and Earnings* [B 44].

Average earnings and hours of manual workers in Northern Ireland. Northern Ireland has been covered in the enquiries conducted by the British Department of Employment and its forerunners throughout the whole post-war period and earlier which were considered in Section 6.9.3.2. Separate figures for Northern Ireland, however, were not regularly published until recently. Details are now given for adult male (i.e. aged 21 and over) manual workers of average weekly and hourly earnings and actual hours worked. The results for each April and October enquiry from 1960 to 1969 (except October 1960) and then October each year have been made available in *NI Digest* [QRL 140]—introduced in issues No. 19, 1963 and No. 21, 1964 and in the *MOLG* [QRL 190] and subsequent *DEG* [QRL 135] from March 1963—except for the 1961 results which were included in *SIPEP* [QRL 331] (this publication also included other figures in the series until 1969). The figures are now also published in the *British Labour Statistics Yearbooks* [QRL 59].

For the period prior to 1960 the only data published are:

(a) Index of average weekly earnings from 1950 in *NI Digest* [QRL 140] No. 23, March 1965.
(b) Average weekly earnings and hours for the MLH 200 part of the 1948 SIC [B 329] published for the period from October 1948 in [B 55].

Information is also available from special labour cost surveys carried out in 1968, 1973 and 1975—see Section 9.4.3.3 below.

Occupational earnings and hours of male manual workers. Enquiries were conducted annually from 1967 to 1972 and the results published in *NI Digest* [QRL 140] (introduced in No. 30, 1968 and terminated in No. 41, 1974). These enquiries were carried out independently from the regular average earnings enquiries referred to above. They were based on voluntary returns submitted by firms employing twenty-five or more persons covered in the CITB (NI) manpower surveys (Section 9.3.6).

Interpretation. Perhaps the major point to bear in mind about the interpretation of all the statistics about the earnings of manual workers in the construction industry is the fact that they do not reflect payments made to self-employed operatives engaged on a labour-only sub-contract basis. In so far as such labour receives different levels of remuneration and the extent of the practice has changed over time, total labour costs and thus average earnings will have been affected accordingly.

Earnings of non-manual (ATC) employees in Northern Ireland. Corresponding enquiries to those for Britain (i.e. annual enquiries each October—considered in Section 6.9.3.4) were carried out by the Ministry of Commerce from 1959 to 1970 on behalf of the MOL in Great Britain for their use in compiling statistics for the UK. Separate results for Northern Ireland were not published until 1967 (data for 1959 and from 1963 onwards) in *NI Digest* [QRL 140] No. 28 (but it should be noted that the information obtained was grossed-up and published in the Northern Ireland census of production reports—Section 9.2.2 refers—the relevant question being dropped from the census, except in detailed census years, in order to avoid duplication). The enquiry was ended in 1970 with the advent of the New Earnings Survey, referred to above, but then reintroduced in 1973 (as in Britain—see Section 6.9.3.4) under the auspices of the DMS. Separate results from the new enquiry, however, have not been published.

Wage and salary payments—Northern Ireland Census of Production data. Returns of the amounts paid to operatives and 'other' employees respectively have been published in annual census of production reports for Northern Ireland [QRL 278] (unlike the corresponding censuses for Great Britain) from 1949—Section 9.2.2.1 refers. In association with the employment data for these two categories annual averages can be calculated for each. It may be noted, however, that from 1959 to 1962 and from 1964 to 1967 the data for employees other than operatives was based upon the separate surveys of ATC employees referred to above. It should also be noted that the figures relate to larger firms only and that there are reservations about the extent of the coverage of the census—see Section 9.3.7. Indices based on this source, however, for the period 1949–62 will be found in [B 55] p. 54. Again, it should be remembered that the figures will not reflect changes in the payments made to self-employed workers or to nominally self-employed operatives working on a labour-only sub-contract basis. Reference should also be made to Section 9.4.3.3 below regarding total labour cost surveys.

9.4.3.3. *Total labour costs in Northern Ireland—Labour Cost Surveys (Northern Ireland).* In addition to the statistics of wages and salaries referred to above, surveys of total labour costs, including those costs that are incurred in the employment of labour additional to wages and salaries, have been carried out in Northern Ireland on a comparable basis to those carried out in Great Britain (Section 6.9.5.1 refers). Results for Northern Ireland have been published as follows: 1968—*Employment and Productivity Gazette* [QRL 135] October 1970, pp. 872–9 (this includes a full account of the survey); 1973—*N. Ireland Digest* [QRL 140] No. 46, 1976 *et seq.* (summary results only). An enquiry was also conducted, by the DMS, for 1975, as in Great Britain, but the results are not yet available. No survey comparable to that carried out in Great Britain in 1964 was carried out in Northern Ireland.

Total wage and salary bill in construction in Northern Ireland. Estimates of the total wage and salary bill and of total income from self-employment are made by the Statistics and Economics Unit of the Department of Finance and published as an integral part of regional accounts for Northern Ireland—these are considered in Section 9.6.1 below. Other, less comprehensive, information is available in the reports on the census of production for Northern Ireland—considered in Section 9.2.2.1 above.

9.4.4. *Construction Accident Statistics for Northern Ireland*

Accident statistics are published in *Annual Reports* of the Chief Inspector of Factories for Northern Ireland [QRL 155]. Like those for Great Britain, the nature of these statistics is such that it is likely that they understate the number of accidents (other than fatal accidents) considerably. For discussion reference should be made to the British data in Section 6.10. Statistics comparable to those for Britain based on claims for industrial injury benefit (administered by the DHSS for Northern Ireland) analysed by industry are not available.

9.4.5. Strike Statistics for Northern Ireland

The fullest information about strikes in Northern Ireland now comes from regional analyses of UK data which have been made since 1969 and published in the *DEG* [QRL 135]—for details and discussion of the nature of the data see Section 6.11. The only published data for earlier periods are monthly statistics of 'industrial stoppages' published in the *NI Digest* [QRL 140] from issue No. 25, March 1966, for the period from 1956, showing the total number of working days lost. Figures for the number of workpeople affected were only published from time to time in [B 343].

9.4.6. Trade Union Statistics for Northern Ireland

Most of the trade unions operating in Northern Ireland, including those relevant to construction, are branches of unions registered in Great Britain. Separate industrial analyses of the number and local membership of unions operating in the province, whether registered locally or not, are not published.

9.5. Structure of the Construction Industry in Northern Ireland

The only regularly published source of statistics about the structure of the industry is the Census of Production [QRL 278]. Analyses are made of the principal results in 1949 and in the 'detailed' census years (1951, 1954, 1958, 1963 and 1968) according to size of firm (establishment) and also according to county. Unlike the British censuses, no analyses according to trade of firm are made. As we have mentioned several times, there are doubts about the comprehensiveness of the coverage of firms in the census which need to be noted—see Section 9.2.2.1 and 9.3.7.

Obviously the quarterly enquiries made into the employment and output of the industry in Northern Ireland (Sections 9.2.1 and 9.3.3 refer) and the CITB (NI) manpower surveys (Section 9.3.6 refers) provide potential sources for structural analyses, but they appear to have remained largely unexploited. Certainly no statistics are regularly published. The CITB returns in particular would seem to offer the most fruitful means of supplementing the existing data although their industrial scope does not coincide precisely with the SIC definition. Only one analysis based on this source, however, is available: an analysis of employment according to size of firm (distinguishing ATC staff from three classes of operative—'skilled', 'mainly semi-skilled' and 'other')—published in [B 280] 1966, p. 26. Mention may also be made perhaps of an additional source of 'structural' information that arises from the administration of taxes. Separate information was published in [QRL 258] giving the number of income tax 'assessments' (not the same as the number of persons or firms assessed) made on trading profits for individuals and partnerships and also for companies and local authorities, etc. but this particular series was discontinued in 1968 (see Section 9.6.2.1).

Direct labour. Statistics for direct labour organizations are very scanty. The censuses of production [QRL 278] provided separate analyses up to 1954—see Section 9.2.2.1. No further information was published until 1974 when separate results for public undertakings in Northern Ireland were included, together with the results for Great Britain, in

Business Monitor PA500 [QRL 76] for that year. Otherwise information is largely confined to the output and employment aggregate figures obtained in the quarterly enquiries (Sections 9.2.1 and 9.3.3 refer). Such information about direct labour as is obtained in other enquiries can only be inferred—see Section 9.2.2.1 regarding the census of production and Section 9.3.2.2 regarding DMS employment series (local authorities component).

9.6. Financial Statistics for Northern Ireland

The amount of information of a financial character about the industry in Northern Ireland is very limited. There are no analyses of company accounts equivalent to those for Britain and the preparation of national income and expenditure accounts for the province is still in its infancy.

9.6.1. *Construction in Regional Accounts for Northern Ireland*

The relevant accounts for Northern Ireland consist of estimates of gross domestic product (GDP) and estimates of gross fixed capital formation. The latter are considered in Section 9.2.3.1 above. The official estimates of GDP showing the contribution of each industry including construction were introduced in [B 214] (Appendix I) in 1965, for the years 1950, 1954, 1958 and 1960–2, and subsequently carried forward in the *NI Digest* [QRL 140] (introduced in No. 28, 1961). Little background information about the sources and methods used has been published and the account given here is based upon information kindly supplied by the Statistics and Economics Unit of the Department of Finance.

The series currently published has been revised back to 1963 and for construction, unlike that for manufacturing industries, is based upon estimates of factor incomes generated in the industry. The estimates for manufacturing are based in part upon census of production data. Separate figures are estimated for: income from employment, income from self-employment and gross profits. The estimates for income from employment are both based upon Inland Revenue statistics together with an allowance for incomes below the tax limit and tax evasion. How the allowance for tax evasion is calculated has not been revealed, but for construction, the evasion of tax especially by the self-employed is an important problem in Northern Ireland just as it is in Great Britain. The Inland Revenue statistics of income from self-employment in the industry are published but not those for income from employment—see Section 9.6.2.1 below.

The final element in the contribution to GDP—gross profits—is a rough approximation made by the CSO and is made by distributing the estimate for the UK as a whole [QRL 201] over the regions according to the regional/industrial distribution of employees in employment. It assumes therefore that gross profits per employee are equal over all regions of the UK.

The official estimates for the period before 1963 are very approximate, being derived, as far as the construction industry is concerned, largely as ratios of the official accounts for the UK as a whole [QRL 201].

Before the preparation of official accounts for Northern Ireland, unofficial attempts had been made to compile such accounts. Details of statistics compiled for the year 1952 are reported in [B 38] and this was followed by annual estimates in more detail for the years 1950–6 showing GDP by industry of origin—published in [B 36] p. 149. These statistics should be contrasted with the subsequently published official data referred to above. Reference may also be made to the discussion of regional accounts for the UK as a whole in Section 7.1.2.

9.6.2. Miscellaneous Financial Statistics for Construction in Northern Ireland

9.6.2.1. *Inland Revenue statistics for construction in Northern Ireland.* Very little information relating to the administration of taxes in Northern Ireland is published. Statistics were published for a time in *Inland Revenue Annual Reports* [QRL 258] of assessments on trading profits under Schedule D showing: the number of assessments, and gross and net (net of capital allowances) true income for individuals and partnerships and for companies and local authorities, etc. but this series terminated in 1968. The only data now published relate to income from self-employment given in [QRL 173].

9.6.2.2. *Bank advances in Northern Ireland.* Statistics of bank advances to the construction industry are compiled by the Northern Ireland Bankers' Association for four quarterly months each year, as in Britain, and published in the *NI Digest* [QRL 140]—series from 1959. Current data are also given in *Finanical Statistics* [QRL 158].

9.6.2.3. *Insolvency statistics for Northern Ireland—Bankruptcy.* Industrial analyses of bankruptcy data have been regularly made since 1962. Estimates for the year 1962 itself were included in [B 281] p. 70. Subsequent data giving numbers, liabilities and assets are available on request.[4]

Company liquidations. Analyses according to industry of company liquidations in Northern Ireland are not available.

---

[4] From: The Official Assignee, Royal Courts of Justice (Ulster), Belfast, BT1 3JF.

PART II

CONSTRUCTION MATERIALS AND PLANT

CHAPTER 10

CONSTRUCTION MATERIALS AND PLANT—STATISTICS RELATING TO PRODUCTION, CONSUMPTION AND FOREIGN TRADE

10.1. Introduction

The amount of information available about the production and use of construction materials is very limited. This is largely a consequence of the fact that, with a few exceptions, many materials and components are suitable for use in construction but are not solely used for construction purposes and their producers and merchants are not necessarily able to specify the end-uses of the products they supply. As a consequence the information available about end-uses is generally confined to that prepared for special studies—we refer to the relevant sources in Section 10.2.1 below. Statistics are collected from users (contractors) directly in censuses of production but not on a regular or comprehensive basis (again see Section 10.2.1). The only statistics collected regularly are those obtained from producers and generally related to total production, sales or deliveries for certain well-defined construction materials.

In the early post-war years, when price and production controls continued in operation over many building materials, statistics were compiled in some detail. Limitations of space, however, prevent any detailed consideration of these data. Our attention here is confined to series that are currently compiled. A collection of the non-current series, however, has been compiled under the author's direction in [QRL 321]. These were originally included in the MOW's *Monthly Bulletin of Statistics* [QRL 194] which was prepared at the time mainly for official purposes; most of the series terminated in the late 1940s or early 1950s.

For most of the post-war period, responsibility for the collection of most of the building materials statistics has rested with the DOE and its predecessors. But from the 1960s onwards these functions were gradually transferred to the BSO and at the time of writing (August 1977) the DOE remain responsible for statistics on cement, gypsum, plaster and plaster-board only (steel statistics have remained the responsibility of the DOI). Nonetheless, the DOE has continued to compile a collection of relevant tables [QRL 196], in the same form as those prepared when it was the sponsoring department, which are available on subscription. In addition supplementary information is also available from various sources other than the BSO.

The information available about the use of plant by contractors is more limited than that available for materials. We consider the sources and nature of the data available for these two subjects separately in Sections 10.2 and 10.3 respectively.

10.2. Construction Materials

We consider the data available about construction materials under three headings:

(1) *Consumption statistics*—data collected from consumers and also estimates of construction materials usage.
(2) *Production and related statistics*—this covers data collected from producers about sales, deliveries, stocks, etc. as well as production.
(3) *Overseas trade statistics*.

10.2.1. *Consumption Statistics*

Few statistics are prepared about the consumption of building materials. The major source is the information collected in censuses of production in which contractors are required to return the value of materials and fuel purchased supplemented, in 'detailed' census years, with information about specific materials. Table 5.1 provides relevant publication references and Section 5.3 contains a discussion on the scope of the censuses. It will be appreciated, of course, that some materials are consumed by the DIY market or by the Works departments of private firms and public bodies which may also fall outside the scope of the SIC definition of the industry (see Appendix I), and are consequently not covered in the censuses. Further information about materials inputs is provided by the input–output analyses, considered in Section 5.3.4, which are themselves based upon the census of production results. These analyses, however, are limited in two ways: they rely very heavily on estimates as far as construction is concerned because of the limited amount of information obtained in the censuses of production (as much as 60–70 per cent of the value of materials purchased by the construction industry remains unclassified—[QRL 177] p. 16 and [QRL 178] p. 6 refer), and secondly, they provide estimates in terms of broad industrial groups rather than particular materials.

At a less aggregated level work has been carried out by the Building Research Station (BRS) and the EDCs for building and civil engineering into the usage of building materials in different forms of building. Early estimates for six types of work were prepared by BRS in the early 1960s and published in [QRL 7] together with a description of the method of estimation. More recent work has provided estimates of the overall usage of specific materials: aggregates in [QRL 18] (see too the *Report of the Advisory Committee on Aggregates* [B 177]) and limited information about timber in [QRL 4] (early post-war estimates for timber consumption will be found in [B 306] and the *BOTJ* [QRL 48] vol. 159, p. 697). A recent study has also been made for the Building and Civil Engineering EDCs which has enabled estimates to be prepared on the end-uses of some eighty materials in the period 1974–5 on the basis of invoice analyses and informed judgement—details are to be published in a report [QRL 170] in the near future. The end-uses to be specified are mainly: housing, public non-housing, private non-housing and repair, maintenance and house improvement (including DIY). Limited historical information is also available from surveys conducted from time to time in the past (now discontinued) by a commercial research and consultancy organization (Building Statistical Services): reports have covered industrial buildings completed in Great Britain in 1965, 1967 and 1969 [QRL 339] and school buildings

Table 10.1
Current Building Materials Statistics—Summary Guide[a]
(Key to abbreviations used for types of data available: P.—Production. S.—Sales. D.—Deliveries. ST.—Stocks.[b] E.—Exports. I.—Imports.)

Material[c]		Commencement of Current Series[d]	Current Frequency[e]	Primary Sources — Current DOI Bus. Monitors[c] [QRL 81] (Ser. Ref. No. ...) UNITED KINGDOM	Primary Sources — Orig. DOE M. Stats. [QRL 196]	Primary Sources — Orig. DOE MBCS [QRL 194]	Secondary Sources — HCS [QRL 168]	Secondary Sources — MDS [QRL 195]	Secondary Sources — AAS [QRL 31]	Secondary Sources — UK Min. Stats. [QRL 357]	Availability of Regional Data (see Table 10.2)	Remarks
General Category	Sub-classified by Type											
1. AGGREGATES AND OTHER MINERALS												From 1974 Annual Mineral Inquiries (reported in *Bus. Mon. PA 1007* [QRL 80]) provide the most detailed source of production data for various minerals analysed by end-use and region. Detailed sand and gravel production statistics are published in [QRL 241].
1.1 Sand and gravel	Yes	1938/1945	Q	S. (PQ 103)						P.	P.	
1.2 Crushed rock	Yes	1963	A	P. (PA 1007)	—	—	—	—	—	P.	P.	
1.3 Mftd. lt.-weight aggs.	—	1969	Q	S. (PQ 469.2)	P.	P.	P.	P.	P.	P.		
1.4 Gypsum	—	1945	M	S. (PQ 109.2)	P.	P.	P.	P.	P.	P.		
1.5 Slate(s)	Yes	1945	M	S. (PQ 102) P. (PA 1007)	P.D.ST.	P.D.ST.	P.D.ST.	P.ST.	P.ST.	P.	P.	
1.6 Stone	Yes	1973	Q / A	S. (PQs 102 & 469.2) / P. (PA 1007)	— / —	— / —	— / —	— / —	— / —	— / —	P.	
2. ASBESTOS CEMENT GOODS	Yes	1938/1945	M	S. (PQ 469.2)	P.D.ST.	P.D.(E.)	P.D.	P.	P.	P.		
3. BRICKS	Yes	1938/1945	M	S.E.I. (PQ 461.2 & 469.2)	P.D.ST.	P.D.ST.	P.D.ST.	P.ST.	P.	P.	P.D.ST.	Monthly production and deliveries (actual and s.a.) and stocks are issued in a *DOE Press Notice* [QRL 228]. Various pre-current series going back to 1938 and earlier were included in the *MBCS* [QRL 194] and the *MDS* [QRL 195] until the early 1970s.
4. CLAY GOODS (Other than bricks)	Yes	1962	Q	S.ST.E.I. (PQs 461.2, 462 & 469.2)	—	See Remarks	—	—	P.	P.		
5. CEMENT	Yes	1938/1941	M	S.E.I. (PQ 464)	P.D.ST.E.	P.D. ST.E.	P.D. ST.	P. ST.	P.	P.	D.	United Kingdom data. Weekly averages of production and home deliveries of cement (actual and s.a.) and of clinker stocks and cement stocks are issued in a *DOE Press Notice* [QRL 228].
6. CONCRETE GOODS		Part 1945 / Part 1960	M	S. (PQ 469.2)	P.D.ST. (part)	P.D.ST. (part)	P.D.ST. (part)	P.ST. (part)	P.	P.	P.	
6.1 Precast goods	Yes											
6.2 Readymixed concrete	—	1961	Q	S. (PQ 469.2)	P.	P.	P.		P.	P.		United Kingdom.
7. GLASS	Yes	1971	Q	S.E.I. (PQ 463)	—	—	—	—	—	—		Statistics relating solely to flat glass are not published.
8. METALS AND METAL GOODS												
8.1 Steel	Yes	1950	Q	The primary source is [QRL 170]. There are two basic categories of data: (i) deliveries of finished steel (tons) by type of product by producers to consuming industries, merchants and exports and (ii) estimates of receipts by consuming industries which allow for deliveries by merchants to these industries—these estimates are based upon returns from larger consumers, but those from the construction industry are thought to represent only a minor part of the consumption of the industry. Separate estimates are also made of stocks and changes in stocks of finished steel by category by consuming industry. Currently data for receipts, consumption and stocks are reproduced in *M. Stats.* [QRL 196] and *HCS* [QRL 168], and for consumption and stocks quarterly in *T & I* [QRL 352].								
8.2 Metal windows, doors and curtain walling	Yes	1938/1945	M	S.E.I. (PQ 399.2)	P.D.ST.E.	P.D.ST.E.	P.D.ST.	P.	P.			
8.3 Cast iron goods	Yes	1945	Q	Not yet introduced	P.	P.	—	P.	P.			
8.4 Copper and brass tubes				Statistics have been collected by the World Bureau of Metal Statistics since 1946 and published in [QRL 362]. Data are reproduced currently in [QRL 196] and [QRL 31] (copper pipe, sheet, strip and plate). End-uses are not solely in building.								
8.5 Lead semi-manufactures (sheet, pipe, etc.)	—	1972	Q	S.E.I. (PQ 323)					P.			Statistics for the consumption of lead by end-uses are collected by the World Bureau of Metal Statistics and published in [QRL 362].
9. PLASTER	—	1938/1945	M	S. (PQ 469.2)	P.D.	P.D.	P.D.	P.	P.	P.		Excludes plaster used in plasterboard.
10. PLASTERBOARD	—	1939/1945	M	S. (PQ 469.2)	P.D.ST.E.	P.D.ST.	P.D.ST.	P.ST.	P.	P.		
11. PAINT, etc.	—	1962	Q	S.E.I. (PQ 274)	—	—	—	S.	S.			
12. PLASTICS PRODUCTS	Yes	1970	Q	S. (PQ 496)	—	—	—	—	—			
13. SHOP AND OFFICE FITTINGS	Yes	1970	Q	S. (PQ 474)	—	—	—	—	—			
14. TIMBER AND TIMBER GOODS												
14.1 Timber and boards, etc.	Yes	Pre-1945	M & Q	S. (PQ 471, PM 471.1 & PM 476)	D.ST.	—	D.ST.	D.P.ST.				
14.2 Builders' woodwork	Yes	1962	Q	S.E.I. (PQ 471)	—	—	—	—	—			
15. OTHER MATERIALS												
15.1 Building board	Yes	1939/1945	Q	S.E.I. (PQ 481)	—	—	—	P.	P.			Products of paper and board industry (insulation board), laminated wallboard and hardboard).
15.2 Felt	—	1973	Q	S. (PQ 469.2)	—	—	—	—	—			
15.3 Insulation materials	—	1973	Q	S. (PQ 469.2)	—	—	—	—	—			Thermal and acoustic insulation.
15.4 Pitch fibre pipes, etc.	—	1956 and 1964	M	S. (PQ 469.2)	P.D.ST.E.	P.D.ST.E.	P.D.ST.	P.ST.	P.	P.		
15.5 Wallcoverings	Yes	1970	Q	S.E.I. (PQ 484.1)	—	—	—	—	—			

(a) Great Britain unless indicated otherwise (*Business Monitor* series are on a UK Basis).
(b) *Manufacturers'* stocks.
(c) A detailed index for the *Business Monitor* series is published as *Bus. Mon. PQ 1000* [B 190] and a *Guide* to the enquiries as *Bus. Mon. PQ 1001* [B 191]. These enquiries are confined to establishments above a given size.
(d) The dates shown are the earliest dates of the *current* series but do not necessarily apply to every constituent series for particular categories of data nor to every publication: the early series will generally be found in *MBCS* [QRL 194] or *MDS* [QRL 195]. The *Business Monitor* series generally commence later, having been introduced from the early 1960s. The series for the period up to the late 1950s originally included in the *MBCS* [QRL 194] have been reproduced in the *Collection of MOW Statistics* [QRL 321].
(e) The *greatest* frequency is shown—it does not apply to the series in every publication. The DOE sources generally contain the series with the greatest frequency; most of the *Business Monitor* series (which are collected separately) are quarterly. Annual series only are reproduced in *AAS* [QRL 31] and in *UK Min. Stats.* [QRL 357].

in England and Wales in 1969 [QRL 340] and housing (for which details are given in the companion Review in this series on the *Housing Statistics of Great Britain* [B 52]).

10.2.2. *Production and Related Statistics*

10.2.2.1. *Data for Great Britain or the United Kingdom.* The type of information available varies according to the particular material: either production, sales or deliveries (home or total) supplemented in some cases with statistics of stocks (held by *producers*) and exports and imports (in some cases collected separately from the official foreign trade statistics—for which see Section 10.2.3 below). In some cases information for each of these categories is collected.

Given the great diversity of the materials themselves and the industries from which they are drawn it is difficult to summarize the information available. But concise guides to the series that are currently compiled on national and regional bases are presented below in Tables 10.1 and 10.2 respectively. Table 10.1 lists fifteen broad categories of materials and components and thirty specific types of materials and components as sub-categories. It is emphasized, however, that the list provides a general, rather than a detailed, guide to *current* series and is designed to act as a point of reference to the range of data available and their location. Thus the list indicates the categories of materials and components for which series are available, whether or not more detailed sub-classifications by type (type of use or type of material) are made, the type of information included in each source and the commencement dates of series. All of the sources provide data in physical units but the *Business Monitors* [QRL 81] mainly provide data in monetary units.

Currently, as we indicated earlier, most of the enquiries (the exceptions were noted at the end of Section 10.1) form part of the system of sales enquiries run by the BSO, the results of which are published in the *Business Monitor* series [QRL 81]—an index to the commodities for which information is available in the series (providing more detail than Table 10.1) and a guide to the enquiries themselves have been published as *Business Monitor PQ 1000* [B 190] and *Business Monitor PQ 1001* [B 191] respectively. The most convenient general source of statistics, however, is the collection compiled monthly by the DOE in *Monthly Statistics of Building Materials and Components* [QRL 196] which combines data from BSO, DOI and their own enquiries. *Housing and Construction Statistics* [QRL 168] also reproduces some of the data, though in less detail than the monthly collection referred to above, and for some materials the *MDS* [QRL 195] and the *AAS* [QRL 31] provide convenient secondary sources—further details are given in Table 10.1.

For some materials, however, minerals in particular, much more detailed sources are available. Especially useful here are the annual *UK Mineral Statistics* [QRL 357], which bring together data from a wide range of sources and provide estimates for the usage of some minerals not available elsewhere, and, from 1974, *Business Monitor PA 1007* [QRL 80] which presents data, obtained in a special annual minerals enquiry conducted by the BSO, for production in Great Britain (broken down by county and Scottish region) by type of mineral and end-use.

Table 10.2
Sources of Current Regional Building Materials Statistics*

Material	Scotland	Wales	English Regions	Northern Ireland†	Remarks
Aggregates					
Sand and gravel	[QRL 241]‡ [QRL 196] [QRL 357]	[QRL 241]‡ [QRL 196]‡ [QRL 357] [QRL 142]	[QRL 241]‡ [QRL 196]‡ [QRL 357]	[QRL 189] [QRL 140] [QRL 357]	[QRL 241] provides very detailed statistics for both marine-dredged and land-won production (by type) according to 'Gravel Region' (defined in [B 305]) and smaller 'Service Areas' and also production by county.
Crushed rock	[QRL 357] [QRL 80]	[QRL 357] [QRL 80]	[QRL 357] [QRL 80]	†	
Bricks	[QRL 168] [QRL 196]	[QRL 168] [QRL 196] [QRL 142]	[QRL 168] [QRL 196]		Deliveries *from* Economic Planning Regions. Production, Deliveries and Stocks. Production.
Cement	[QRL 168] [QRL 196] [QRL 357]	[QRL 168] [QRL 196] [QRL 357] [QRL 142]	[QRL 168] [QRL 196] [QRL 357]	See Remarks	Deliveries *into* Economic Planning Regions. Deliveries data for Northern Ireland may be inferred by comparing series for the UK and GB in [QRL 168] and [QRL 196]. Separate production and trade statistics for Northern Ireland are collected by the Dept. of Finance (NI) but not published.
Concrete blocks	Regional production statistics for Great Britain are available from the Dept. of the Environment, Statistics Construction Division, on request.				
Limestone	[QRL 80]	[QRL 80]	[QRL 80]		
Slate	[QRL 6]	[QRL 6]	[QRL 6]	—	Series from 1895 to 1973 (incl. English counties—analyses from 1967).
Roofing slates		[QRL 142]			

* Production of various minerals by county are given in reports on an annual Minerals enquiry introduced by the BSO in 1974—*Bus. Mon. PA 1007* [QRL 80].

† The principal Northern Ireland publication for mineral statistics is [QRL 189] (with series reproduced in the *N. Ireland Digest of Statistics* [QRL 140]. This includes production data (quantity and value) for several minerals used for building purposes (e.g. clay and shale, granite roadstone, limestone) as well as the sand and gravel series indicated in this table.

‡ 'Gravel Regions' (defined in [B 305]). Separate data for Wales (as distinct from the Welsh Gravel Region) will be found in [QRL 241] from the issue for 1970 and 1971 (series from 1960) and in [QRL 142].

Additionally, the supply and demand for aggregates, in particular, have long been the subject of special attention. Detailed supply statistics for marine-dredged and land-won production (by type) according to 'Gravel Regions' (defined in [B 305]), smaller 'Service Areas' and also by County are presented in a separate bulletin: *Production of Aggregates* [QRL 241] as well as in *Business Monitor PA 1007* referred to above. From time to time in the past the special publication on aggregates [QRL 241] also contained forecasts of future demand—these are now available on request from the Statistics Construction Division of DOE. It is well to note, however, that previous forecasts made during the post-war period have been highly inaccurate. Reference may usefully be made to the recent *Report of the Advisory Committee on Aggregates* [B 177] which reviews previous forecasts and the problems involved in making such assessments, considers questions related to the usage and long-term supply of aggregate resources and includes a full bibliography on these subjects.

Further valuable sources of reference with regard to the production and use of minerals have been provided in a series of *Mineral Dossiers* prepared under the auspices of the Mineral Resources Consultative Committee. These contain long-run series going back, in some cases, to the nineteenth century and provide useful commentaries on the resources and uses of the minerals and about the statistics themselves. Up to December 1977 relevant volumes had covered sand and gravel [B 3], slate [QRL 6], gypsum and anhydrite [B 111] and sandstone [B 69].

Prior to the initiation of the current BSO enquiries, the main general source of statistics about the sale or production of specific commodities was the 'detailed' census of production. A guide to the nature and coverage of the censuses up to 1958 and references to the large number of individual industry reports and *Indexes of Products* has been provided in [B 239]; for subsequent detailed censuses (1963 and 1968) reference should be made to Part 1 of the respective *Reports* [QRL 275] and [QRL 277]. These enquiries supplemented those conducted regularly in the case of specific building materials by the DOE and its predecessors to which we have already referred.

It may also be worth noting that trade associations sometimes provide useful supplementary sources of statistical information which may be made available to non-members on request, although being collected from Association members only it may not always provide comprehensive coverage of the industry. Up-to-date information about the data collected by different associations is not available but a useful review carried out in 1966 will be found in [QRL 120].

10.2.2.2. *Data for Northern Ireland.* Currently sales enquiries are carried out in Northern Ireland by the Department of Commerce on the same lines as those carried out by the BSO in Great Britain. The results of these enquiries are not published separately but are combined with the British data to provide the figures for the UK published in the *Business Monitors* [QRL 81]. No enquiries comparable to those carried out in Great Britain by the DOE and its predecessors were carried out except in the case of cement for which returns relating to domestic production, exports and imports have been regularly obtained by the Department of Finance (the data are not published but may be made available on request). Statistics for the output of minerals are regularly obtained under mines and quarries legislation and reported in [QRL 189] and [QRL 140] (see too *UK Mineral Statistics* [QRL 357]) but these are less detailed than those obtained in the BSO annual minerals enquiry in Great Britain [QRL 80]. The only other information for specific commodities is limited to that collected in censuses of production for Northern Ireland [QRL 278] in 'detailed' census years: 1951, 1954, 1958, 1963 and 1968.

10.2.2.3. *Reliability and interpretation.* Unfortunately, it is not possible to make any statement about the reliability of the official series since, except for the current BSO enquiries, information about relevant matters, such as the way in which enquiries were conducted (sample or census), the comprehensiveness of the register of firms and the degree of, and allowances made for, non-response, etc. was not made available. There is little doubt, however, that some, at least, of the series are open to error (certainly by virtue of non-response if for no other reason) and that some series are more affected than others. This is particularly likely to be the case perhaps where production is not concentrated in the hands of few producers and where part at least may be carried out on a small scale by producers for whom it does not represent their major activity (the production of concrete building blocks would perhaps provide an example) for in these cases the comprehensiveness of both registers and returns is more likely to be in doubt. But it is not possible to provide more precise information about the materials most affected at different times over the period of thirty years that has elapsed since the end of the Second World War nor about the magnitude of possible errors.

It may also be relevant to note that most of the series originally collected by the MOW and its successors were collected on a voluntary basis. Legal powers to require returns to be made were conferred initially under Regulation 55AA of the General Defence Regulations during the Second World War and, after its revocation in the early post-war years, by the *Statistics of Trade Act* but it is understood that these were relied upon in few cases to compel the provision of returns.

Currently, the sales and production enquiries conducted by the BSO, the results of which are published as *Business Monitors* [QRL 81], are made with the backing of the *Statistics of Trade Act* but they are expressly restricted to larger firms (generally the cut-off level is establishments employing twenty-five or more persons but some enquiries extend down to smaller sizes—reference should be made to the reports themselves [QRL 81] or to the general *Guide* [B 191] for precise details; it should also be noted that changes were made to the cut-off levels for some of the enquiries in 1976).

The initiation of the BSO sales and production enquiries has been accompanied by a number of salutary changes in the provision of background information about levels of response, maintenance of registers and other matters relevant to the interpretation of the data. Information about the extent of response (by employment) to each enquiry is given in the notes at the beginning of each *Business Monitor* [QRL 81], but it should be noted that this figure is not applicable to individual commodity headings and that no indication is given of the element of estimation in the figures for individual commodities except that where response is below 50 per cent the item is marked with an 'E'. For further details of collection and processing practices, definitions, etc. reference should be made to the official guide—*Business Monitor PQ 1001* [B 191].

10.2.2.4. *Historical sources.* The statistics considered above are generally confined to the period since the end of the Second World War although some of the former MOW series include a comparable figure for the last full pre-war year—1938. Earlier data are strictly outside the scope of this Review but because of the interest of long time series in this field we provide a brief account here, simply directing attention to sources of the principal data.

For the war-time period it is known that tabulations of data relating to building materials were brought together for use within the MOW in a bulletin known as the 'Sixth Floor Bulletin'; it has not been possible, however, to trace any surviving copies of this Bulletin and the only data that now appear to be readily available are some which were reproduced in the more general *Statistical Bulletins* [QRL 318], a set of which are available for consultation in the Statistics Construction Division of the DOE. These contain data at various times for asbestos cement, bricks, cement, roofing slates, bitumen felt, fireclay, chalk and chalk lime. An account of the 'Sixth Floor Organization' itself, which was the part of the MOW responsible, *inter alia*, for the control of the building materials industries during the war, will be found in Kohan [B 90].

Prior to the war, some commodity details for construction and other materials were, of course, collected in the periodic censuses of production taken from 1907 onwards, details of which will be found in the official guide [B 239], and for the production of minerals, in particular, data collected under mines and quarries legislation are available back to the nineteenth century—see the references given in the discussion of minerals statistics in Section 10.2.2.1 above.

Earlier commodity data appear to be confined to materials which were at one time chargeable to excise duty. Series for bricks, for the period 1785–1849, and 'white glass' (glass other than that used for bottles), for the period 1747–1845, are especially notable. Both relate to England and Wales and are reproduced in the *Abstract of British Historical Statistics* [QRL 21] together with comment on the reliability of the series and relevant references. The series for bricks in particular has been analysed at length by Shannon in [B 142]. A further series of interest is one for 'stained paper' (i.e. wallpaper) chargeable to duty—see Ashton [B 5].

10.2.3. Overseas Trade in Construction Materials

There are two sources of statistics about foreign trade in building materials and components. The most comprehensive source is the official overseas trade statistics which provide details of imports and exports monthly in [QRL 215] and annually, in somewhat greater commodity detail, in [QRL 39].[1] A description and guide to the classification used is provided in [B 234]. The DOE and its predecessors regularly extract information from [QRL 215] for the principal materials and components suitable for construction purposes and present a summary, currently in *HCS* [QRL 168], formerly in *MBCS* [QRL 194]. Currently, import and export figures are also reproduced in the *Business Monitors* [QRL 81]. Further information about exports of some materials is also available from the production enquiries conducted by the DOE—see Section 10.2.2.

[1] More detailed information than that published is available, subject to rules regarding disclosure, from the Statistical Office of HM Customs and Excise, Bill of Entry Service, Portcullis House, 27 Victoria Avenue, Southend-on-Sea, SS2 6AL.

10.3. Construction Plant and Equipment

10.3.1. *The Use of Plant in the Construction Industry*

Official estimates of investment by contractors (excluding direct labour organizations) on plant (as well as on other assets) form an integral part of the national income and expenditure accounts [QRL 201]. Annual series are available (at current and constant prices) from 1948. The place of construction in these accounts is considered in Section 7.1. Investment expenditure in particular forms part of the tables of 'gross fixed capital formation'. This concept has been considered in the context of investment in buildings and works in the economy as a whole in Section 5.4. The estimates rest partly upon data collected in censuses of production for construction (Section 5.3) to which reference may also be made. Further details about sources will be found in the official guide [B 100].

The only information currently available about the total amount of plant and equipment used in the construction industry is that included as part of the official estimates of gross capital stock which are also included as part of the national accounts statistics in [QRL 201]. These figures are estimates devised using the perpetual inventory method and are subject to a substantial margin of error. The concepts and methodology employed are considered more fully in Section 12.2.1 where the statistics for the stock of buildings and works are discussed. As before, reference may also be made to the official guide [B 100]. At one time censuses of construction plant held by contractors, direct labour organizations and other users were taken by the MOW. Over thirty censuses were carried out in the period 1942–52 but the results were not normally published. Some particulars of the early censuses will be found in Kohan [B 90].

10.3.2. *Production and Overseas Trade Statistics for Construction Plant*

Statistics about the production and sales of particular types of plant are collected currently in the enquiries conducted by the BSO the results of which are published in the *Business Monitor* series [QRL 81]—the principal part is PQ 336. An index to the commodities covered is provided in *Business Monitor PQ 1000* [B 190] and a guide to the nature of the enquiries themselves in *Business Monitor PQ 1001* [B 191]. Summary data from these and earlier enquiries are reproduced in the *MDS* [QRL 195]. Information is also available from the censuses of production of the relevant industries—guides to the censuses will be found in [B 239] for those taken up to 1958 and in [QRL 275] Part 1 and [QRL 277] Part 1 for the detailed censuses of 1963 and 1968 respectively—1968 being the last of 'old style' detailed enquiries. The results of censuses taken under the new system of enquiries conducted by the BSO are published in the *Business Monitor PA Series* [QRL 81].

Sources of statistics about foreign trade in construction plant are the same as for construction materials considered in Section 10.2.3 except for the DOE sources referred to there.

CHAPTER 11

CONSTRUCTION MATERIALS AND PLANT PRICES

11.1. Construction Materials Prices

Construction work involves the use of a wide variety of materials and components all of which have to be transported, often over considerable distances, to the sites of particular construction projects. Since many of the materials are heavy and bulky, transport costs may constitute a substantial part of the costs of materials as delivered to site. Thus a reliable index of the costs of construction materials to the contractor must be representative of the wide range of materials used and reflect 'delivered' prices rather than 'ex-works' quotations. Since the incidence of transport costs will vary from one material to another and the movement of transport costs themselves is unlikely to be similar to the movement of 'ex-works' materials prices, these considerations are particularly important in evaluating the usefulness and reliability of the general indices available and the indices for particular materials or components.

An official general index of construction materials prices has been published monthly for the period from 1930 to the present day by the Board of Trade and its successor Departments as part of its series of Wholesale Price Indices. The first index, however, was based on a narrow range of materials and a limited number of price quotations taken from published sources. It was eventually replaced in 1951 with a much broader-based index (the series being carried back to 1946); since then the series have been regarded as the authoritative measure of price movements for construction materials and indeed the only indices prepared. In fact two series have been prepared for the post-war period, one for construction materials in general (originally referred to as 'building and civil engineering' materials) and the other representative of the materials used in housebuilding. More recently more specific indices have been compiled for current cost accounting (CCA) purposes to reflect the price movement of materials and fuel held as stocks by various sectors—the relevant ones in the present context being construction, builders' merchants and building materials producers.

Because of the limitations of the early Board of Trade index for building materials the Ministry of Works prepared indices for its own internal use during the war and early post-war years which were more broadly based than the BOT (1930) index, and with a weighting pattern more appropriate to the greatly changed pattern of materials consumed for war-time and, later, post-war construction activity. This index was continued until the introduction of the BOT's revised index of 1951.

We now turn to consider these two official sources followed by a very brief note on earlier unofficial series and finally an examination of sources of actual price data as distinct from index numbers.

11.1.1. *Department of Industry (and Former Board of Trade) Indices*

11.1.1.1. *Price indices for materials purchased by the construction industry.* Currently the official series are compiled monthly by the DOI and form part of a set of tables entitled 'Wholesale Price Indices—Price Index Numbers of Materials Purchased' covering various sectors of industry. No significance should be attached to the word 'wholesale': the prices are meant to reflect prices paid by the industrial user—in the present context the contractor—rather than prices at an earlier distributive stage. Since the replacement of the earlier, 1930-based, index in 1951 revisions have been made to the weighting pattern and composition of the indices on three occasions. The indices available, therefore, constitute not one continuous series but a series in a number of discontinuous segments. Fortunately the series for each pair of segments are always prepared concurrently over a lengthy period and the effects of the changes may be observed. Further details of the series themselves are given in the *Quick Reference List*.

Publication references. The primary source of publication for the two general indices is *T & I* [QRL 352] but the series are reproduced in a variety of secondary sources, the principal ones being the *MDS* [QRL 195], *HCS* [QRL 168] and the *AAS* [QRL 31] (annual series only). Not all of the constituent indices for specific materials and components are published but the most complete sources currently are *HCS* [QRL 168] and *Monthly Statistics of Building Materials and Components* [QRL 196]. The *Business Monitors* [QRL 81] for particular commodities also include relevant indices.

Interpretation. Valuable general accounts of the new scheme of index numbers introduced in 1951 and the methods used to compile them will be found in [B 150] and [B 119]. In contrast to the 1930-based index described in [B 187] which was a geometric mean of price relatives, the series introduced in 1951 [B 184] have all been base weighted arithmetic means of price relatives. The weights are said to be based on data obtained in the detailed censuses of production (considered in Section 5.3) supplemented as necessary with information from other sources but, as we noted earlier (Section 10.2.1), a very substantial part of the materials purchased by the construction industry remain unclassified. It is understood that estimates are made on the advice of the DOE and its predecessors as the sponsoring department for the industry, but no further particulars have been revealed. 'Errors' in the overall index may be introduced, of course, by inaccurate weights but it is well to bear in mind that the number of constituents is large and that unless the errors for any important constituent are large and allied with a price movement which is markedly different from that of other constituents, and not offset by contrary errors elsewhere, the effect on the overall index may be slight. In other words, it is possible for some latitude to exist in the specification of weights without the overall index being unduly affected, if at all.

The purpose of the construction materials indices, as we have already noted, is to measure movements in the purchase prices of the materials used. It is important to note, however, that none of the price data is obtained from users. In practice a mixture of ex-works and delivered prices are used (the distance and area of delivery vary) the latter usually including discount appropriate to the firms' most common selling quantities. The prices are obtained in the main from producers but some are obtained from Trade Associations and a few are still based on published sources. All prices are taken exclusive of relevant taxes (i.e. VAT and, before its abolition, purchase tax). Details of the type and number of price quotations actually used for each of the materials incorporated in the two general indexes and the sample of firms from whom the data are collected are not published.

In practice, of course, the prices actually paid in particular transactions may be affected by rebates and discounts that are not reflected in these particular quotations and may also differ from producers' prices if the materials are obtained, as many building materials are, through builders' merchants. The assumption is implicit, therefore, that the movement of the price quotations will faithfully reflect the movement of actual transaction prices. With relatively stable trading practices this assumption is perhaps not unreasonable. But it may well not be reasonable if trading practices change. And significant changes have in fact taken place in the UK since the mid-1950s due to the ending of restrictive trade practices in many industries, especially price fixing agreements, as a consequence of the operation of the *Restrictive Trade Practices Act 1956* and, later, legislation against the practice of resale price maintenance. The latter removed the previous rigidity of prices in different outlets and the former also provided latitude for transactions to take place at less than manufacturers' list prices (list prices themselves being maintained in order to hide price-cutting behaviour).[2]

Thus quite apart from the usual problems of index number construction, relating to the appropriateness of fixed weights and problems of changes in quality and specification and the like, the reliability of the indices is dependent on how far the sample of price quotations used is representative of all producers and how far they reflect actual delivered prices to users throughout the UK, especially at a time when trading practices are suddenly changed. The use of ex-works prices for some materials is an important limitation in principle in the case of construction, given the necessity for distribution to sites throughout the whole country and the importance of transport costs for many of the materials used. Delivered prices are preferable but need to reflect the geographical pattern of construction activity. Information collected directly from users (contractors) would be better still but, of course, would be more difficult and costly to collect.

These comments are meant to imply not that the indices are necessarily faulty but that their accuracy should not be regarded as beyond question. This is true of both of the general indices and of those for specific materials—the user of the latter, especially those based on ex-works quotations, needs to be aware of their limitations as indicators of price movements to contractors in different areas of the UK.

11.1.1.2. *Price indices for stocks held by contractors, builders' merchants and building materials producers.* Following the report of the Sandilands Committee on *Inflation Accounting* [B 258] a variety of special indices were introduced for current cost accounting (CCA) purposes and published by the CSO in a special volume of *Price Index Numbers for Current Cost Accounting (PINCCA)* [QRL 239]. In the context of construction materials, 'industry-specific' indices—intended to reflect the price movements of stocks of materials held in three sectors—are of relevance, namely the construction industry, builders' merchants and the 'building materials industry' (as

---

[2] For detailed case-studies of the effects of the *Restrictive Trade Practices Act* of 1956 in particular industries (incl. cement, standard metal windows, glazed tiles, roadstone, sanitary ware, baths, sewage and drainage pipes, galvanized tanks, wire mesh, sand and gravel, and black bolts and nuts) see [B 157].

defined—see below). In the case of the latter two series are produced: one for 'stocks held as materials and fuel' and one for 'stocks of goods on hand for sale'. Each index represents a base-weighted average of appropriate combinations of indices in the family of wholesale price index numbers discussed above—details are given in appendices to *PINCCA* [QRL 239]. The building materials industries, it should be noted, are defined as those falling within the scope of MLH 461, 464 and 469 which embrace bricks, fireclay and refractory goods, cement and such other goods as are not specified under other headings of the 1968 SIC [B 329] (the principal products covered in the miscellaneous category are concrete products, plaster, plasterboard, asbestos cement goods and also abrasives).

It should be appreciated that these indices are prepared for the convenience of companies who wish to use them for CCA purposes. Warnings are expressed in *PINCCA* [QRL 239] about the possible inappropriateness of the indices for individual companies. At a general level too it should be appreciated that the series may suffer from the same kind of potential limitations as were discussed in Section 11.1.1.1 above, although in this case the same considerations may not apply equally in each sector in the sense that a limitation for one sector may be an advantage for another. For instance, the revaluation of stocks using indices based on ex-works price quotations may be inappropriate from the contractors' point of view, for the reasons discussed earlier, but appropriate from the point of view of their producer. Again, therefore, the reliability of the indices depends upon how well the behaviour of the price quotations in combination do manage to achieve a satisfactory representation of the experience of each sector. In the nature of the case, of course, it is not possible to make any external judgement about this.

11.1.2. *Ministry of Works' Series 1939–51*

These indices were prepared monthly by the Ministry for its own use, as we indicated earlier, because of the limitations of the then current BOT index. Details are as follows (see also the *Quick Reference List*):

	Descriptive title	*Base date*	*Period covered*	*Remarks*
1. (a)	5 materials 'sensitive' index	Aug. 1939	Aug. 1939–Oct. 1945	General indices only.
(b)	46 materials index		Aug. 1939–Mar. 1944	1942 weights.
(c)	44 materials index		Aug. 1939–Oct. 1945.	
2.	Building materials	1946 and 1939	Dec. 1945–Apr. 1951	General index (both bases) and constituent indices (1946 base).

The war-time series were originally included in the MOW's internal *Statistical Bulletin* [QRL 318] November 1943 *et seq*. The post-war series were included in the successor *Monthly Bulletin of Statistics* [QRL 194] from the issue of April 1948. All have now been brought together in a *Collection of MOW Statistics* [QRL 321] compiled by the author for the DOE.

Details of the sources and methods used for the compilation of war-time series other than the fact that they were based mainly on London delivered price quotations (at least initially) are not available. Details of the post-war series were given in the *Bulletin* [QRL 194] for April 1948 referred to above. In brief they were based on 'several hundred' price quotations relating to ninety-two materials and components (thirty-six sub-indices). The prices are said to relate 'wherever possible, to average prices throughout the country for normal merchanting quantities of typical specifications delivered to site less normal trade discounts'. Most of the prices at this time, it may be noted, were subject to some form of control. The weights used for the 1946-based series were originally based on the values of deliveries to the home market during 1946, but from January 1947 onwards current weights (a moving chain weight based on deliveries to the home market during the preceding twelve months) was adopted. The 1939-based series was linked by means of such comparable series as were available for both dates (taken mainly from published sources) weighted by average 1939 and 1946 deliveries.

In this context it may also be of interest to take note of indices which were prepared after the war by Bowen (Chief Statistical Officer of the MOW during the war) and published in [QRL 43] Vols. 103–12, 1946–50. As in the MOW series themselves, separate indices appropriate for 'war-time' and 'peace-time' conditions were prepared covering the period 1939–45 and 1939–50 respectively. A description of these indices is given in [B 22] and [QRL 43] Vol. 103, 1946, p. 393.

11.1.3. *Unofficial Historical Series 1845–1939*

It is not the purpose of this Review to give any detailed consideration to historical sources but it may be useful to bring together the principal references. Apart from Bowen's indices referred to above, series have been compiled by: Maiwald for the period 1845–1938 in [B 98], by Jones for the period 1845–1922 in [B 83] and by Saville for the period 1923–39 in [B 139] (Saville's index was a direct extension of Jones' using the same sources of information). For further details reference should be made to the sources cited and to a discussion by the author in [B 58]. It may also be noted that an index was compiled by *The Economist* [B 222] as a constituent of a composite index of construction costs for the period 1924–39 but not published (for details see the issue for 11 November 1933, Vol. 117, pp. 907–8).

11.1.4. *Actual Price Data*

Actual prices for a range of materials are regularly quoted (as either ex-works prices or prices delivered to certain areas) in the trade press and builders' price books. The principal journal is *Building* [QRL 60]; the most well-known and long-established price books are *Laxton's Building Price Book* [B 265] and *Spon's Architects' and Builders' Price Book* [QRL 314]. In the context of the discussion of the official price indices above (Section 11.1.1) it will be appreciated that the prices quoted in these sources are not necessarily representative either of prices in different parts of the country nor of the prices which buyers actually pay: many of the quotations are representative list prices quoted either ex-works or delivered to a particular town (generally London). A more comprehensive source of information about *list prices* is lists prepared since the early 1960s by Building Materials Market Research Limited (based in Brighton) replacing, apparently, similar lists prepared previously by the British Federation of Plumbers Merchants. These lists are 'Trade Price' lists available to members of appropriate Trade Associations and professions on subscription only. Three types of list are prepared covering 'light' and 'heavy' building materials respectively in different regions of the country (monthly) and a quarterly list for domestic heating equipment. Further information is made available to subscribers.

Northern Ireland. Although the DOI wholesale price index numbers are presented as UK series, no separate information is collected in Northern Ireland. Published data are limited to list prices for selected materials in the Belfast market included in the *Ulster Builder* [B 342] since 1953. As an indicator of prices to users, this source suffers from the same limitations as the published sources for Great Britain referred to above. It was used by the author, however, as the basis of price index numbers for the period 1954–64 published in [B 55].

11.2. Construction Plant Prices

Price indices for construction plant and equipment are compiled by the DOI currently as part of the same 'Wholesale Price Indices' series of which the construction materials price indices form part (Section 11.1.1 above). Currently, indices are compiled for several types of plant and published in *T & I* [QRL 352], incorporated in *Business Monitors* [QRL 81] (various numbers in the PQ series 336–9—see the *Index of Commodities* [B 190]) and also reproduced as part of a set of 'asset-specific' indices for current cost accounting in *PINCCA* [QRL 239]. The latter also includes general 'industry-specific' indices, including one for capital expenditure on plant and machinery by the construction industry (quarterly series from 1956 to 1971 and then monthly), constituting base-weighted averages of appropriate indices in the family of wholesale price index numbers—details of the composition and weights are given in *PINCCA* [QRL 239].

In addition, it may be noted, indices covering the costs of providing, operating and maintaining constructional plant and equipment are compiled as part of the series devised for use in the NEDO price adjustment formulae—see Section 8.1.3.1.

PART III

THE CONSTRUCTION STOCK

CHAPTER 12

STATISTICS OF THE CONSTRUCTION STOCK

12.1. Introduction

The purpose of this introductory section is to indicate the purposes for which statistics of the construction stock are, or may be, required and to outline the scope of the chapter as a whole.

Interest in statistics about the construction stock may be said to arise for two basic sorts of reason. One is the fact that, owing to the durability of construction goods, the demand at any time for the facilities and services they provide is satisfied in the main by the existing stock rather than new supply. As a consequence, the demand for new construction is determined in some degree by the size and characteristics of the existing stock. And in turn, therefore, statistics about the stock may be of value to those concerned with the assessment of future levels of demand for new work, with the analysis of their determinants and with their industrial and resource implications.

Secondly, at a more general level, there is the fact that construction goods constitute a major part of the nation's total stock of fixed capital assets. And thus economic analysis which requires the use of measures of capital is particularly dependent upon the reliable measurement of the construction constituent of the total stock. Two major examples of areas in which such measures play a central role would be the study of the process and determinants of economic growth and fluctuations and in the analysis of the distribution of income and wealth. There is too their use, referred to above, in studies of future levels of demand for new construction.

Apart from their relative importance as a constituent of the capital stock, another characteristic of construction goods which distinguishes them from most other capital assets is the fact that they are not mobile or transportable. Interest in the size and valuation of the stock, and in additions to it, therefore, is almost inevitably bound up with the land on which it is, or is to be, located. Thus students in this field must inevitably touch upon questions relating to land use and development (town and country planning). However, these are large subjects in their own right and strictly outside the scope of this Review; indeed each is the subject of separate Reviews in this series by Coppock [B 41] and Gebbett [B 60] respectively. In this Review, therefore, we devote no more than cursory attention to these subjects and only insofar as they are relevant to construction.

Finally, given the importance of the existing stock in satisfying the major part of construction demand at any one time, statistics about transactions in the existing stock—i.e. the level of trade and costs for different types of building—may be regarded as within the scope of this Review. We therefore devote brief attention here too to the, rather limited, information available in this field.

We now turn to examine each of these subjects in turn. Statistics relating to the size, composition and characteristics of the stock demand most attention and are considered in the next section (Section 12.2). Section 12.3 is concerned with changes to the stock. This is followed by two small sections dealing in turn with relevant land use and development aspects of construction and then statistics about transactions in, and costs of, the existing stock.

12.2. Size, Composition and Characteristics of the Construction Stock

12.2.1. *The Total Stock of Buildings and Works*

In this sub-section we are solely concerned with data relating to the construction stock as a whole. Separate information relating to different parts of the stock is considered separately in sub-section 12.2.2.

12.2.1.1. *Problems and methods of estimation.* Measurement of the total stock of buildings and works may be approached in two ways—directly, using a census method, and indirectly, using the perpetual inventory method. The official statistics for the UK are based on the latter method. As the name implies, this involves the maintenance of a total stock figure, starting from a benchmark year, by adding in new investment each year and subtracting an allowance for capital that has reached the end of its life. In practice, severe practical and technical difficulties are involved and the series, especially for buildings and other construction works, is acknowledged to be open to very wide margins of error.

The difficulties that arise apply generally, but are felt particularly sharply in the case of construction work. As we indicated above, application of the perpetual inventory method requires information to start with about the stock of capital at a point in time to act as a benchmark. Such an estimate is perforce difficult to make and open to a very wide margin of error. The basis of the estimate actually used for the official series is described in [B 46] and justified by comparison with the only estimates available using the direct 'census' method made by Barna [B 7]. Over time, of course, the importance of errors made here recedes as the stock comes to consist more and more of subsequent additions for which reasonably reliable statistics may be available. Ultimately none of the original stock is left and the current stock will consist solely of capital which has been directly measured (at least in an annual investment series). For the whole of the post-war period, official statistics of gross fixed capital formation provide the data for this purpose; they themselves are not devoid of error (see Section 5.4.2) but are infinitely superior to anything available for earlier periods. There still remains, however, the need to allow for capital retirements each year and in this area no direct statistics are available. The practice adopted is to deduct an allowance based on an assumed length of life for different assets, but again very little direct information is available about the lives of different assets. For buildings an average life of eighty years is assumed (100 years in the case of dwellings)—[B 100] p. 386 refers. Therefore, the allowances made currently for capital retirements are dependent upon estimated investment back in the nineteenth century, estimates which can only be of the roughest kind.

Finally, it will be appreciated that capital assets are not homogeneous and can only be measured, therefore, in money terms. This introduces the further difficulty of allowing for price changes over the long periods of time involved. The difficulties here are very considerable and still further increase the scope for error. These difficulties are considered in Section 8.1.1.

The method described above produces estimates of 'gross' capital stock. That is to say, a capital asset is retained in the valuation of stock at its original value (adjusted for price changes) right up until the end of its assumed life, when it is retired. Alternatively, a 'net' measure may be defined which is one in which the original value of an asset is deemed to decline gradually over its service life. This is analogous to the conventional depreciation of capital in business accounts. But it should be appreciated that the allowances made (referred to as 'capital consumption') are not the same as those actually used by businesses in their accounts nor by the Inland Revenue for taxation purposes. Further non-technical discussion of the usefulness of the measurement of capital stock on the gross and net bases will be found in Griffin [B 66], where it is emphasized that neither can claim to be more intrinsically correct than the other.

Fuller information about the perpetual inventory method itself will be found in Ward [B 168], who provides a useful review of the methodology of capital stock estimates in the UK and other OECD countries, and in Redfern [B 128] and Dean [B 46] whose work forms the basis of the official UK series. Redfern compiled estimates of capital consumption and stock for 1938 and for each year from 1947 to 1953 analysed by several groups of assets including separate estimates for housing, roads and other buildings and works. Dean revised some of Redfern's earlier estimates. The methodology used by Redfern and Dean was used unchanged up to 1974 and is described briefly in the official guide, *National Accounts Statistics—Sources and Methods* [B 100]. The revised methodology introduced in 1975 is described by Griffin in [B 65]. The main change has affected the allowances made for capital retirements—the previous practice of retiring all assets with the same average life altogether in the same year being replaced by the practice of distributing retirements over a number of years around the mean expected life of the relevant asset group. A useful stock-taking of the current methodology and deficiencies in the present estimates for the UK has been provided by Hibbert et al. in [B 72].

12.2.1.2. *The official series, 1948 to date.* The official series for buildings and other construction works cover the UK and are published annually in the national income and expenditure 'Blue Book' [QRL 201] as follows:
  (1) Gross capital stock at replacement cost (constant prices)
     (a) for dwellings (public/private), roads and other buildings and works—annual series from 1948,
     (b) analysis by industry (manufacturing, construction, distribution and other services)—annual series from 1948.
  (2) Net capital stock at current replacement cost—dwellings/other buildings and works, each by sector—annual series from 1948.
  (3) Capital consumption—dwellings/other buildings and works at current and constant prices—annual series from 1948. First published in 'Blue Book' [QRL 201] 1956 edition, but subsequently revised.

(4) Capital retirements—dwellings only—annual series from 1965. First published in 'Blue Book' [QRL 201] 1976 edition.

Age distribution. The only other data of note relating to the stock as a whole are estimates of its age distribution (by industry), as at the end of 1961, which were published by Dean along with his original estimates in [B 46]. These estimates too, it will be appreciated, are subject to considerable margins of error.

12.2.1.3. *Interpretation.* As we have emphasized above, the estimates of the stock of buildings and works are subject to very wide margins of error because of the very long length of life of most buildings and construction works and the lack of adequate statistical series. Dean himself emphasizes [B 46] p. 332 that the estimates for building in particular are 'highly suppositious' and need to be checked by direct estimates; no such check, however, has yet been made.[1] Official assessments of the reliability of the gross capital stock estimates are not sub-divided according to type of asset but gradings given to the roads and private dwellings component suggest an error in excess of ±20 per cent and for public dwellings in the range of ±10–20 per cent [B 100] p. 387. It would seem likely that the assessment for non-dwellings would be higher. With regard to roads in particular, Prest [B 122] pp. 240–1 has made alternative estimates, based on the mileage of roads and official figures of the costs of road-building, which are very much at variance with the perpetual inventory estimate and serve to emphasize the margins of error that are involved.[2]

It should be stressed, however, that the estimates of error cited above naturally apply to the series as defined for the purpose of the study. These are not comprehensive. As far as construction works are concerned, certain parts of the stock are expressly excluded because it was impossible to estimate them by the perpetual inventory method. This part embraces much or all of the building and other construction works which have survived from the distant past such as 'historic buildings' (cathedrals, castles, churches, Elizabethan houses, Oxford and Cambridge colleges, etc.) and public works such as embankments. In the case of roads, no foundation work (which, it is argued, lasts indefinitely) carried out before 1887 has been incorporated. The inclusion of these parts of the stock could only be done by direct estimation, as opposed to the indirect perpetual inventory method, though this would naturally pose the major problem of valuation at current prices.

A number of further points are relevant to the interpretation and use of the data. First, although it is true in principle that the quality of the estimates should improve over time as more and more of the assets which pre-date the availability of reliable capital formation statistics are retired from the stock, it is well to remember that the capital formation statistics themselves are open to error. Further discussion of the capital formation series is included in Section 5.4.2.

[1] An interesting attempt to use the valuation of property for rating purposes (Section 12.2.2.1 refers) to arrive at a total estimate is reported in Revell [QRL 23] (see too [B 106]), but it should be noted that, unlike the official estimates, land is included as well as buildings. Official analyses of the rating valuation records that are now made in terms of total floorspace by building type would seem to offer very great potential indeed for making a direct valuation of a substantial part of the building stock but seem to have remained unexploited.

[2] Prest's comparison was made with the estimates prepared by Redfern [B 128] but the discrepancy would remain if the same comparison was made with the subsequently revised series introduced by Dean [B 46]—for further comment see Revell [QRL 23] p. 311.

Secondly, an important source of error may arise from errors in the assumptions made about the average length of life of assets, for these determine the annual allowance made for capital consumption (straight line methods of computation are followed for all assets) and the timing of retirements from the stock. Overestimation of mean asset lives, of course, produces estimates of the capital stock which are themselves too high. It may also influence, depending on the time-profile of capital formation, the estimate for capital consumption: given that the tendency has been for capital formation to increase then the estimate will be too low. Errors in the estimation of capital consumption are, of course, of wider consequence in that the estimates are required in the estimation of national income as well as for net capital stock itself. With regard to the construction stock, there is very little evidence available to verify or refute the life assumptions made; it has been claimed officially, however ([B 66] p. 139), that limited data obtained in a recent survey (mainly concerned with plant) tend to support them.

Thirdly, errors may arise from a failure to measure changes in construction prices adequately. Over the short-term, of course, errors in the price index may be of more significance in the measurement of investment at constant prices from year to year than in the measurement of capital stock or capital consumption because new investment in any year represents but a small increment to the total. But errors over the long-term, of course, will transmit bias to the estimates of capital stock and capital consumption at constant prices: underestimation of price increases, for example, means that too little weight is attached to the older parts of the capital stock and too great a weight to the newer parts. The measurement of price changes for construction, especially over the long period required for capital stock estimation purposes, presents severe difficulties. These difficulties, and the series currently compiled, are discussed in Section 8.1. A discussion of the difficulties and a review of the long-run evidence for the UK has also been provided by the author elsewhere in [B 58]. It is shown that over the long run there is a fair measure of agreement among the alternative indicators available, but it will be appreciated, of course, that this does not prove conclusively that the measures are therefore satisfactory. The index used in the UK accounts for the years before 1948 is one compiled by Redfern [B 128] on the basis of the indices reviewed in [B 58] (part is now regularly reproduced, for the period back to 1888, in *PINCCA* [QRL 239] albeit with a warning that the series prior to 1948 at least is not very reliable; for years since 1948 the DOE's 'CNC' index is used—see Section 8.1.2.1).

Finally, care is required in interpreting the sub-classification of the stock according to industry and sector. Because of the way the statistics are compiled the classifications relate not to the industry or sector of use but to the industry or sector of ownership. Thus some of the capital used, say, in manufacturing industry may be owned by a property company and therefore classified not to manufacturing but to the finance sector of the economy. A further complication is that even on an ownership basis the classification of the stock of buildings is open to error because there is no way in the perpetual inventory method of allowing for the transfer of ownership of buildings, from one industry or sector to another (the total costs of transfer are allowed for in the accounts but the industries or sectors to or from which the transfers are made is not known—it may be noted, however, that more information is now becoming available about *current* transfers from surveys of conveyancing—see Section 12.5). As far as construction is concerned, the importance of this problem has grown in recent years with the growth in the practice of selling factories and office buildings to property leasing companies which then lease the property back to the original owners.

12.2.1.4. *Unofficial historical series and estimates.* Only brief reference is made to historical sources here once again since they are strictly outside the scope of this Review; fortunately the nature of the data available is considered fully in original sources.

The major source of pre-war series is the work of Feinstein (utilized, incidentally, by Dean [B 46] in initiating the official post-war series). This is reported in [QRL 12] together with a full description of the basis of the estimates and comparisons with earlier work. Before describing the series included in this volume, however, it should be noted that they were originally published with 'loud warnings as to their margin of error' ([QRL 12] p. 198) and that subsequent research by Feinstein has shown that substantial revisions are required to the series for the period 1855–1920 such that 'for the present the series ... should be regarded as withdrawn' ([QRL 14] p. viii refers).

The estimates included in [QRL 12]—and reproduced in [QRL 14] without the supporting commentary on sources and methods—provided annual series of gross and net reproducible capital stock at both current and constant replacement costs by type of asset (including a separate series for dwellings and one for other buildings and works) over the period from 1855 to 1965 (the post-war series are the official estimates considered earlier). In due course Feinstein hopes to provide revised estimates for the period 1855–1920; in the meantime one indication of the orders of magnitude of the likely error is provided by the statement that 'it seems likely that the estimates for the *gross* stock should be reduced by about 25 per cent at the beginning of the period, with the correction diminishing steadily to perhaps 5–10 per cent by 1914' ([QRL 14] p. viii).

Analyses of the capital stock by industry are also presented in the work referred to above but the construction industry as such is not separately distinguished.

Feinstein has also prepared estimates of the capital stock for the period back to 1760. These are to be published in Volume VII of the *Cambridge Economic History of Europe* [QRL 20] and will provide estimates of the gross stock in the years 1760, 1800, 1830 and 1860 with a number of separate categories for buildings and civil engineering works but without a strict classification by type of asset.[3] In due course it is hoped to provide a complete and consistent series covering the whole period 1760–1948.

Other unofficial data, to which we would direct attention, provide estimates for a particular point, or small period, of time rather than series. Barna [B 7] prepared estimates of the replacement cost of fixed assets (by type—including separate data for buildings) in British manufacturing industry in 1955, using a direct method of estimation on the basis of fire insurance valuations. Full details and a discussion are included in the reference cited. Barna's estimates were made soon after the official estimates made by Redfern [B 128] using the indirect perpetual inventory method and turned out to be substantially larger; it should be noted, however, that the disparity was much reduced in the revised official estimates, later made by Dean [B 46], considered earlier.

A major study of relevance too is one by Revell [QRL 23], covering the period 1957–61, concerned not simply with the stock of fixed capital assets but with the

---
[3] I am indebted to Dr Feinstein for providing this information in advance of publication.

preparation of a 'national balance sheet' for the UK encompassing the stock of physical assets of all kinds owned by all economic units in the various sectors of the Economy and also the financial claims outstanding between economic units. As far as construction is concerned this study also employed a direct method of estimation based on rateable valuation records (Section 12.2.2). As a consequence, it is essential to note, the study covers both land and buildings combined and provides estimates of *market values* (as distinct from replacement costs used in the other studies referred to above).[4] A full discussion is provided in the work itself [QRL 23] to which reference should be made for further details. Reference may also be made to work by Moyle [B 106] who collaborated with Revell on this part of the study. The results provide estimates of the value of land and buildings by eight classes of property and fourteen sectors of ownership (the latter are further sub-classified between dwellings and other buildings, and between sub-sectors, in balance sheet summary tables) for each year from 1957 to 1961 inclusive.

12.2.2. Stock Statistics for Particular Types of Buildings

The estimates of the total stock of buildings and works considered above do not provide data for particular buildings and works apart from dwellings and roads in the official series and dwellings and certain classes of property in the unofficial calculations. But there are a number of separate sources of information about the stock of particular types of building and the purpose of this section is to bring together the appropriate references. Unlike the total stock statistics, which are inevitably in monetary units, these sources provide data in physical units.

12.2.2.1. *Rating and floorspace statistics—Numbers of properties and rateable values.*
The most comprehensive source is the analyses of the records of the valuation of properties prepared by the Inland Revenue for rating purposes. For many years analyses have been prepared of total rateable value for a large number of different classes of use (currently over forty) and, for England and Wales, related information about the number of properties assessed (hereditaments), all broken down according to local authority areas. More recently this source has been exploited to provide particularly useful analyses of total floor space (see below). The most detailed analyses of the number of properties and their rateable value by type of use for England and Wales are published in [QRL 173] (formerly in [QRL 258]) together with brief background notes about the data. Information for each local authority area in England and Wales (rateable value only for broad use classes) is published in [QRL 250] (separate data for Wales are now also given in [QRL 361], with corresponding data for Scotland in [QRL 251] and for Northern Ireland in [QRL 186]).

In the context of the construction stock, perhaps the most important point to bear in mind about the rateable value statistics is that they relate to the land on which the buildings stand as well as the buildings themselves. Background information about the

[4] It is worthy of note, perhaps, that an attempt to obtain direct information about the value of buildings and land occupied was made officially in the 1948 Census of Production but 'the results showed the difficulty of obtaining information ... in a form suitable for aggregation' and they were not published ([B 239] p. 19 refers).

rating system is contained in the references cited above. Reference should also be made to the work of Revell [QRL 23], referred to in Section 12.2.1.4 above, in which use is made of the rateable valuation statistics to obtain estimates of the total market value of land and buildings, and which provides an appraisal of the nature of the data.

Floor space statistics. The initiation of regular, comprehensive floor space analyses based on the rating valuation records constitutes a most important improvement in the information available about the stock of buildings. A complete analysis of the records was made for the first time in 1967; subsequent censuses have been taken annually since 1974. Analyses of the floor space *changes* for intervening years are also made, including one for the three years preceding the 1967 census (although in this case it is felt that the data may be unreliable since it was the first time such information had been collected). The results of these surveys, analysed by use-classes, size groups, region and local authority areas are published in [QRL 323] including relevant background information about the principles of measurement and classification by use-class, etc. The results are also now included in *Regional Statistics* [QRL 252]; separate data for Wales are included in [QRL 142] and [QRL 360]. Further discussion of these data is contained in the companion Review by Gebbett on *Town and Country Planning* [B 60]. Reference may also be made to a recent analysis of these data as indicators of change in the building stock in commercial and industrial use by Black [B 17].

In addition to this source, information about floor space is also available from two other sources. The reports on the censuses of the distributive and service trades in Great Britain for the years 1966 [QRL 266] and 1971 [QRL 83] provide figures of total floor space according to type of business in considerable detail. And information about *additions* to the stock of industrial floor space is available from the records of completed projects for which IDCs were issued (Section 5.5.3 refers). A comparison of the information available from this source with that from the Inland Revenue and a discussion of the reasons for the differences between the two series will be found in [B 181].

12.2.2.2. *Characteristics and miscellaneous stock statistics for particular types of buildings*. All of the statistics about the construction stock considered above have been almost wholly concerned with its size. Information about its characteristics in terms of age, condition, etc. is very limited. Indeed the only parts of the stock which appear to have been the subject of full surveys are dwellings and schools. Our purpose in this section is to survey these sources and to note further supplementary sources of stock statistics. We attempt to survey these sources as comprehensively as possible but given the wide diversity in the constituents of the stock it is possible that data, particularly if they have remained unpublished or have been obtained as part of some other study, may have been overlooked. Dwellings and schools are considered first and then other categories in alphabetical order.

Dwellings. More information is available about the size and characteristics of the housing stock in Great Britain and Northern Ireland than for any other type of building; it is considered fully in the two companion Reviews in this series on housing in each of the two countries: [B 52] and [B 57] respectively. Since the Review for Great Britain was written, however, three developments have taken place: a summary of the results of the second House Condition Survey of England and Wales, taken in 1971 (the first was taken in 1967), has been published (*HCS* [QRL 168] No. 1); a third survey has been undertaken (in 1976—the results have yet to be published) and an annual series of official estimates of the age distribution of the stock by region from 1971 has been initiated in *HCS* [QRL 168]; an article setting out the basis of these estimates has been published in [B 133].

Schools. With the exception of housing, more information is available about the stock of school buildings than for any other constituent of the construction stock. Two official surveys (both confined to England and Wales) have been carried out, one in 1962 [QRL 301] and one in 1975–6 [QRL 334]. Both provide information about the age and condition of the stock and the cost of making good deficiencies. The latter also provides an estimate of the replacement value of the stock.

Time series of the number of schools by size (in terms of number of pupils) will be found in [QRL 325] Vol. 1 for England and Wales, in [QRL 326] for Wales alone, in [QRL 309] for Scotland and in [QRL 151] for Northern Ireland. Summary data for each of the four countries are also given in [QRL 153] and *AAS* [QRL 31] and for Scotland and Wales in [QRL 306] and [QRL 142] respectively.

Factories. The only survey known to the author providing information about the characteristics of factory buildings is a sample survey carried out by the Building Research Station in the late 1950s in the Midlands and the Home Counties, reported in [B 154], which provides data on age, size and other physical characteristics. Information about the numbers of industrial 'establishments' is also given in reports on censuses of production (for references see Section 5.4.5.1) which may be of interest inasmuch as it provides data for individual industries, but it needs to be appreciated that many 'establishments' will comprise a complex of buildings of great diversity. Since 1971 the BSO have published annual analyses of the number of larger manufacturing establishments on its register according to size (persons employed), region and industry in [QRL 78] (formerly in *DEG* [QRL 135]). Also of possible interest are summaries prepared by HMFI of the number of 'places registered under the Factories Acts'—see Section 6.10.1.

Hotels. Statistics about the stock of hotels in the UK in 1970 are available from a study [QRL 167] commissioned by the Hotel and Catering EDC. This provides data on size and location and also covers caravans, holiday camps and university accommodation. Some information about additions to the stock are published in [QRL 209] for England and [QRL 305] for Scotland. Reference may also be made to the companion volume in this series on *Tourism* [B 95].

Leisure facilities. Relevant information is contained in the companion volume in this series on *Leisure* [B 94].

Shops, offices and railway premises. Information about the number of shops of various types in Great Britain is available from the censuses of the distributive and service trades which have been carried out periodically since 1950. The results of the first direct count, carried out preparatory to the taking of the first census in 1950 [QRL 107] covering both retail and wholesale establishments, were published separately in [QRL 57], together with relevant background information about the enumeration procedures and the interpretation of the data (separate data are included for England, Wales and Scotland). References to subsequent censuses will be found in the *Quick Reference List* under 'Capital Expenditure'. As we noted earlier, the last two censuses (those for 1966 and 1971) have also obtained data on floor space. Equivalent censuses for Northern Ireland were taken in 1965 [QRL 267] (but excluding floor space data) and in 1975 (not yet published).

In addition, it may be noted, registration records have to be maintained by local authorities under the terms of the *Office, Shops and Railway Premises Act* of 1963 for Great Britain and the *Office and Shop Premises Act* of 1966 for Northern Ireland. Details of the numbers registered are given in *Annual Reports* under the Acts: [QRL 213] and [QRL 212] respectively.

Transport facilities. Analyses of the mileage of public highways and information about new schemes, etc. is given in annual reports on *Roads in England* [QRL 288] and *Roads in Scotland* [QRL 289]. Statistics of the lengths of various types of road are also given in a number of other publications. The most detailed source (containing data by type of road for each administrative area in England, Wales and Scotland) is *Transport Statistics* [QRL 354]. Data for Northern Ireland are included in the *Northern Ireland Digest of Statistics* [QRL 140], for all four countries of the UK in *Regional Statistics* [QRL 252] and for Wales alone in [QRL 142]. Data for Great Britain are also reproduced in [QRL 31]. Further details are given in the companion Review on *Town and Country Planning* [B 60] and in a separate Review on *The Road System* which is in preparation [B 136]. Statistics about other transport facilities—railways, ports and inland waterways, and airports—are considered in three separate Reviews in the series: [B 1], [B 9] and [B 118] respectively.

12.3. Changes to the Construction Stock

Many of the relevant sources of information here have already been considered at various places elsewhere in this Review. The purpose of this section is merely to bring together the relevant references.

Additions to the stock. Direct information is available from the floor-space statistics considered in Section 12.2.2.1 which provide details of net increases or decreases in the particular use-classes covered. The most general source, used in the maintenance of the of the official capital stock estimates, is the series for gross domestic fixed capital formation considered in Section 5.4.2. Other sources of 'production' statistics for particular types of buildings or construction in total are considered throughout Chapters 3–5 inclusive.

Losses from the stock. Direct information about losses is extremely limited. Demolition statistics appear not to be available for any part of the stock except housing (considered in [B 52] and [B 57] for Great Britain and Northern Ireland respectively). Conventional allowances of 'consumption' and 'retirements' from the construction stock are computed by the CSO for the purposes of the national income and expenditure accounts [QRL 201] but they are not based on direct statistical evidence and are subject to wide margins of error—for further details see Section 12.2.1. The only other source of relevance would appear to be information about destruction and damage that is available from detailed analyses that are made about fires in buildings [QRL 355]. The published figures of the cost of damage are early estimates of loss (not final settlements) based on insured values and cover buildings and contents but a split between the two can be supplied for serious research purposes.

Changes of use. Statistics in this field too are extremely limited. Planning statistics for England and Wales [QRL 322] and for Scotland [QRL 307] provide figures of the *number* of *applications* for change of use granted or refused and indicate only the use *to which* the application refers. For further discussion of these statistics reference should be made to the companion Review by Gebbett on *Town and Country Planning* [B 60].

12.4. The Construction Stock and Land

12.4.1. *Land-use Statistics*

This work would not be complete without reference to statistics about land-use since the latter is so closely bound up with construction development. The subject is a large one in its own right, however, and is dealt with in a separate Review in this series by Professor J. T. Coppock [B 41] to which reference should be made for details of the sources and limitations of the data available. As far as construction is concerned there are perhaps three main subjects of interest: statistics about the amount of land devoted to urban uses, about the rate of conversion of land from one category of use to another and, thirdly, about the types of use to which urban 'developed' land itself is put. Despite the importance of these questions, however, it is in these areas especially that the amount and quality of statistical data available are particularly limited.

12.4.2. *Development Control Statistics*

A natural counterpart to statistics about land-use and construction development is information about proposed developments available from the administration of planning and development controls. The statistical sources are considered fully in a separate Review in the series by Gebbett on *Town and Country Planning* [B 60]. In fact the amount of information available here is also very limited.

In brief, the principal source for England and Wales, published in [QRL 136] (formerly in [QRL 322] and [QRL 324]), is confined to information on the number of planning applications and the decisions taken (including the results of planning appeals) analysed according to class of use (including separate data for change-of-use applications) and by region. These data are available annually for the period from 1962. No details are given about the size of building developments proposed nor of the amount of land involved. Summary information for Scotland in less detail is contained in [QRL 307]. For further discussion of the nature and limitations of the data see the companion review by Gebbett [B 60].

Supplementary sources of information arise from the administration of controls over office development (ODPs), considered in Section 5.5.4, and over industrial development (IDCs), considered in Section 5.5.3. Both of these, however, are partial: ODPs have never applied to the whole country and IDCs have only applied to part of the country since 1972 and have always been confined to developments above a certain size limit. Again, further information is given by Gebbett [B 60].

12.5. Construction Stock Transactions and Costs

12.5.1. *Sales and Purchases of Existing Buildings*

Until recently, the statistical information available about the level of activity in the market for the existing stock of buildings and the prices at which particular types of property change hands was very scanty. Much fuller information has now become available as a result of surveys of conveyancing in England and Wales conducted by the Board of Inland Revenue on the basis of information which has to be provided for administrative reasons connected with the assessment of stamp duty and valuation purposes. We consider this source first and then turn to note other sources of expenditure data.

12.5.1.1. Surveys of conveyancing. Surveys have been carried out in February 1968 (reported in *Inland Revenue Statistics* [QRL 173] 1970 edition, p. 210), in June and October 1973 (reported in [QRL 10] together with relevant background information) and in October 1974 and November 1975[5] (reported in [QRL 9]—again with detailed background information). The surveys from October 1973 onwards have been the most detailed, providing information about the number and value of transactions by price range, by type of property (land, residential, commercial) and by tenure (freehold/leasehold) together with analyses by region and by sector of buyer and sector of seller. The surveys cover England and Wales only. Corresponding statistics for Scotland and Northern Ireland are not available but series (monthly) of the value of conveyancing over £15,000 in these countries are given for comparative purposes with the results of the latest surveys for England and Wales in [QRL 9].

Relevant information about the interpretation of these data is provided in the references cited above. A number of points are worthy of emphasis. First, it is important to note that each survey refers to one week's conveyancing only. Grossed-up results for the last three surveys, however, are given in [QRL 9]. Secondly, there is a problem of regional bias (which affects not only regional comparisons but also the average level of prices overall), for which adjustments are made. Thirdly, with regard to prices it should be noted that the data used are not necessarily coincident in timing with the dates of the surveys, for the reason that prices may have been agreed at contract at a considerably earlier period than the transaction completion date, and that for leasehold property, rentals have not been taken into account but only the consideration paid on completion of the transaction. It will be appreciated, of course, that the price data, given in terms of average price per transaction, are difficult to interpret without further information about the size and other characteristics of the buildings and land involved and, in the case of land in particular, whether it is building land or not. Nonetheless, the information provided in these surveys is a great advance on anything available hitherto.

[5] A further survey, for November 1976, was reported in [QRL 11] after the preparation of this text.

12.5.1.2. *Other sources of data on the acquisition and disposal of land and existing buildings.* Until the initiation of surveys of conveyancing the only sources of information were: (a) returns obtained for the private sector of industry in censuses of production and distribution and other smaller-scale enquiries in these sectors, (b) summaries of accounts in the public sector—particularly for local authorities—and (c) statistics about house prices and housing land.

The relevant sources for the private sector are considered in the context of capital expenditure on new building in Section 5.4.5.1. As far as buildings are concerned, these returns were generally confined to the purchase of *new buildings*, as opposed to land and existing buildings, until the 1960s or late 1950s, depending on the enquiry. In the censuses of production the subject has been covered regularly since 1959. Previously it was covered on only one occasion—1948—and the results were not published in the census reports—a summary for manufacturing industry is to be found in [B 239] p. 19. In the censuses of distribution relevant information has been collected since 1961 (see references in Section 5.4.5.1). In other enquiries the subject has been included at various dates from the 1960s onwards—for precise details see the *Quick Reference List* under 'Capital Expenditure'.

In the public sector, the principal source of information appears to be annual series for local authorities in England and Wales from 1969–70—for further particulars see Section 5.4.5.2. With regard to the third category referred to above—housing and housing land—relevant particulars are given in the companion Review on *Housing in Great Britain* [B 52]. But since that Review was written, much fuller information about private sector housing land has become available: regular regional analyses for England and Wales are now made by the DOE of the number of transactions, the area of land and prices and reported periodically in *HCS* [QRL 168]. A descriptive article appeared in *Economic Trends* [QRL 147] February 1974.

12.5.1.3. *The treatment of land and existing buildings in the National Accounts.* The information about expenditure on buildings and land is used by the CSO in the compilation of the capital accounts in the annual 'Blue Book' [QRL 201]: a summary table gives the value of 'purchases *less* sales of land and existing buildings' analysed by the institutional sector (annually from 1959). These transactions, of course, represent the opposite sides of a balance sheet which, in the aggregate, would balance, and thus sum to zero each year, were it not for the inclusion of transfer costs in the costs of acquisition. In the aggregate, therefore, the difference represents total transfer costs and these are counted as part of gross fixed capital formation (Section 5.4 refers). It should be noted, however, that the new surveys of conveyancing considered above (Section 12.5.1.1) revealed that these costs had been very considerably understated hitherto (see [QRL 201] 1972 edition, p. 110).

12.5.2. Building Rents and Occupancy Costs

Information about the rents paid for particular categories of property, other than housing, is very sparse. The only official statistics published provide assessments in index number form of the movement of rents for three types of property—offices (in London (three areas) and in the Provinces annually from 1965); shops (three classes annually from 1965) and factories (annually from 1969)—based upon information obtained by the Inland Revenue (Valuation Office) about transactions involving *new* leases. Further background information is given in [QRL 122] together with the series themselves. Reference may also be made to a fascinating official study by Neuburger and Nichol [B 110] which explores the causes of the great boom in land and property prices which occurred, roughly, in the period 1970–3.

Also of interest in this context is a regular quarterly survey which has been conducted jointly by the RICS and the *Financial Times* since 1976 in which RICS member firms and investing institutions are asked if there is a rising, falling or static trend in rents, investment yields, capital values and investment activity for different classes of commercial and industrial property throughout the UK (Northern Ireland was covered for the first time in 1977). The results, analysed by region, are published in the *Financial Times* [QRL 159] in a quarterly article under the title 'Property Market Indicators'.

Rent is, of course, a major form of factor income and as such constitutes an important component of the *National Income and Expenditure* accounts for the UK [QRL 201]. In this context rent denotes the income derived from the ownership of land and buildings, reckoned after deduction of actual expenditure by the owners on current repairs, maintenance and insurance. In addition, it is most important to note, where the owner of property not used for trading purposes is also the occupier, an equivalent rent is imputed to him. On this basis the annual 'Blue Book' [QRL 201] provides analyses of rent income according to sector. For further particulars reference should be made to the full account which is provided in *Sources and Methods* [B 100] pp. 473–7.

Apart from rent, the occupation of buildings also involves considerable expenditure on their upkeep and associated operational and running costs—cleaning, lighting, heating, etc. The large volume of resources devoted to these purposes is not commonly appreciated. Since it is so closely bound up with construction and, in particular, with the nature of the original investment and professional design decisions we have regarded the subject as worthy of note but as otherwise outside the scope of this Review.

On the statistical side, the most important development has been the establishment, with official support, of the BMCIS in 1971. Since its establishment this body has been building up a data bank of analyses about the full range of property occupancy costs for particular buildings in a comparable, standardized, form.[6] Apart from public sector housing (for which see [B 52]) the only other information which appears to be regularly collected and made available in this area relates to the running costs of hospital buildings published in [QRL 166], [QRL 200] and [QRL 30] for England and Wales, Scotland and Northern Ireland respectively (an analysis and commentary on the usefulness of some of the data contained in these returns in the early 1960s will be found in [B 153] and [B 43]). Other sources are generally *ad hoc* studies, rather than regular statistical returns, analysing either running costs fairly generally or a particular category of costs in some detail (energy costs are a particular focus of attention). Of the general studies, the most notable are a study of school buildings over the period 1952–61,

---

[6] Further details are available from the Building Maintenance Cost Information Service, 85/87 Clarence Street, Kingston-upon-Thames, Surrey, KT1 1RB.

reported in [B 39], a study of government offices in the early 1970s, reported in [B 125] and an earlier case study of such buildings reported in [B 210]. Other more specific references will be found in [B 209], in a bibliography compiled for the *Committee on Building Maintenance* [B 188] (para. 1.6 refers) and in publication digests compiled as part of the service offered by the BMCIS referred to above.

PART IV

THE CONSTRUCTION PROFESSIONS

CHAPTER 13

STATISTICS OF THE CONSTRUCTION PROFESSIONS

13.1. Introduction

The professions with which we are mainly concerned here are architecture, surveying (particularly quantity surveying) and the various kinds of engineering which are related to the design of buildings and other structures and engineering services installations. In many respects the statistical information available about these professions is ill-organized and incomplete. A major difficulty in the collection, and the interpretation, of statistical data in this field is one of definition, for the provision of professional services is not necessarily confined to those with defined qualifications nor to those who have been admitted to membership of a professional association. A distinction has to be drawn, therefore, between the qualified and the unqualified. Qualification may be controlled by a statutory registration body or by one or more professional associations. The statistical information available is generally derived from the membership records of such associations or surveys of their members. In some cases there exists more than one professional association with overlapping memberships so that counting the numbers in each in order to obtain an estimate of the total numbers in each profession may involve multiple-counting. Even where a statutory registration body is established, as in architecture, it does not necessarily become illegal for those who are not registered to provide the relevant service, for the restriction may apply to the assumption of a particular title and not to the exercise of a particular function.

Much of the statistical data available comes from *ad hoc* enquiries made on different bases at different times so that the information is disparate in character; there are few regular series. It is hoped that this review of sources is reasonably comprehensive but this cannot be stated with assurance; it is possible in particular that surveys made by private bodies or research workers will have escaped notice especially if they have not been formally published. The statistics available for each of the three professional sectors are considered in turn according to subject as follows:

Section 13.2. Numbers, characteristics and employment.
          13.3. Organization and structure of professional practice.
          13.4. Financial statistics—earnings and professional practice costs and incomes.
          13.5 Work undertaken by the professions.

13.2. Numbers, Characteristics and Employment of the Construction Professions

13.2.1. *General Sources*

The one general source of information about the numbers in professional occupations is the reports of the national census of population which has been taken every ten years since 1801, with the exception of 1941, together with an additional mid-term 'sample census' in 1966. The census has attempted to record and classify the occupations of individuals since 1841 and since 1961 has recorded additional information about qualifications. Official guides to the information collected in the censuses are available in [B 240] for censuses up to 1931 and in [B 233] which extends the coverage up to 1966. We confine our attention to the four censuses taken since the Second World War: 1951, 1961, 1966 and 1971.

Unfortunately, as far as the construction professions are concerned, the occupational classification is not as fine as one would wish: in the 1961 and 1966 censuses architects and surveyors were grouped together as one category; in 1951 and 1971 they were separated but architects and town planners were grouped together as one category and surveyors were not further sub-divided by type. Civil, structural and municipal engineers have remained one category throughout. Full details of the classification used in each of these four censuses will be found in [B 193], [B 200], [B 201] and [B 202] respectively. For details of the relevant statistical sources reference should be made to Sections 6.3 and 6.6.3.2 above, which consider the information available in the context of the construction industry and provide references to all the relevant reports. It will be noted that since 1961 qualified manpower (Section 6.6.3.2 refers) has been subject to special attention and a number of special analyses of the data have appeared as well as the census reports themselves.

For the period before the Second World War the relevant census statistics covering architects for the period 1841–1931 have been collected together in the major historical study of the development of the profession by Kaye [B 84] and for surveyors and civil engineers for the period 1841–1951 by Thompson [B 164], together with brief commentaries on the data.

13.2.2. *The Architectural Profession*

A statutory registration body, the Architects' Registration Council of the United Kingdom (ARCUK), was established for the architectural profession in 1931 under the terms of the *Architects' Registration Act* of that year. Under a subsequent Act (1938), the legal use of the term 'architect' has been restricted to those who are legally registered, registration being limited to those who are suitably qualified, but no restriction as such was imposed on the provision of architectural services. The establishment of a register, therefore, coupled with the restriction on the use of the term 'architect', provides a good source of information about the numbers qualified to practise as 'architects'. It will be appreciated, however, that not all those on the register will be practising in the UK and some may not be practising at all. Further, some people who satisfy the qualification requirements may not register.[1] At the same time it must be remembered that it still remains possible for building design work to be carried out by persons who are neither formally qualified nor registered.

13.2.2.1. *Membership statistics (RIBA and ARCUK).* The principal professional association for architects is the Royal Institute of British Architects (RIBA) and it is the only examining body recognized by the ARCUK other than the 'Schools' of architecture, both within and without the Universities, which are themselves 'recognized' by the RIBA. Many of the architect members of other professional bodies which cater for architects and surveyors are also members of the RIBA, as are most (if not all) members of allied societies in Scotland (RIAS) and Northern Ireland (RSUA). A good deal of the statistical information about the profession, and those in training for it, is either produced by the RIBA or comes from surveys of its membership.

Statistics of RIBA corporate and student membership are published in *Annual Reports* [QRL 35] (time series—totals and new elections/enrolments were also included for a while, 1960–70—in the *RIBA Stat. Bull.* [QRL 249]). Corporate membership statistics by class for every fifth year for the whole period from 1835 to 1945 are reproduced in Kaye [B 84]. The RIBA also publish an annual *Directory of Members* [QRL 143] which contains an alphabetical list of corporate members and their addresses. The ARCUK is bound by law to publish an annual list of names on its register; this also includes addresses and a note on the numbers added and removed in the year [QRL 253].

SAAT membership. Membership statistics of the Society of Architectural and Associated Technicians (SAAT) which caters for the unqualified architectural staff were at one time published in the *RIBA Stat. Bull.* [QRL 249] last appearing in No. 4 for the period 1966–9.

13.2.2.2. *Fields of employment and other characteristics.* Information about the fields of employment of architects and about other characteristics of the profession and its supporting staffs, such as employment status, age, etc., has been collected from time to time in a variety of enquiries. The most general and important source of information is the qualified manpower analyses drawn from the censuses of population in 1966 and 1971 (considered in Section 6.6.3.2) though as we noted above (Section 13.2.1) architects are grouped in the occupational analyses either with surveyors or town planners. Information about qualifications obtained in the earlier, 1961, census (the first time the subject had been covered) was confined to 'scientific and technological' qualifications, the definition of which *excluded* architecture. For 1951 and 1961, therefore, the only relevant information in the censuses of population is contained in the general occupational analyses—see the *Quick Reference List* under 'Census of Population Employment Data'. Other information is available either directly from surveys of registered architects or of RIBA members, or as a by-product of enquiries

---

[1] After the establishment of the register it took some time for the numbers on it to build up since there was a time lag before those qualified to register did in fact do so, registration being voluntary. An appraisal of the figures for this period is to be found in Bowen [QRL 3].

concerned primarily with some other subject such as earnings or the organization of the profession.

Since 1964 a regular source of information has been provided by surveys of earnings conducted by the RIBA (with one exception) every third year from 1964 to 1973 inclusive and then annually from 1975; the exception is the year 1967 when a survey was made by the NBPI [QRL 41]. Publication references and further details are given in Section 13.4. In addition, information is available for the year 1969, from the report by the Monopolies Commission on professional services in general published in 1970 [QRL 244] which provides a breakdown of the membership of various professional bodies (RIBA and other) according to broad fields of employment and status. Information will also become available from surveys conducted by the RIBA in 1976, but as yet unpublished, in connection with a 'Structure of the Profession' study covering samples of registered architects, SAAT registered technicians, private architectural practices and public offices. For private practice, in particular, information is also available from censuses which were carried out every other year between 1962 and 1972—see Section 13.3 for details.

Prior to 1964 the following surveys are of relevance:

(1) 1949. RIBA (Percy Thomas Committee)—census of all members with a 63 per cent response rate for corporate members—reported in [QRL 259].
(2) 1952. Bowen—3 per cent sample of registered architects with 83 per cent response rate—reported in [QRL 3]. (Includes a comparison between the type of employment in 1938 and 1952 for that group of architects responding who were employed in both years.)
(3) 1955. RIBA in conjunction with the Pilkington Commission [QRL 261] and [QRL 290]—20 per cent sample of corporate members stratified by class in 1958 with 75 per cent response rate. Only architects practising in 1955/6 were included, the analysis being based on their employment in that year.
(4) 1957. RIBA census of all members with a 47 per cent response rate for corporate members—reported in *RIBAJ* [QRL 180] 1959–60, 3rd Ser., Vol. 67, p. 160. (This also includes a summary comparison of the results of the first three surveys listed above.)

Staffing in private practice. Since the second quarter of 1977 information has been obtained each quarter by the RIBA about changes in the number of Principals, salaried architects and other architectural staff employed in private practices as part of the design work enquiry (Section 13.5.1.2 refers). As yet, published analyses (*RIBA Stat. Bull.* [QRL 249]) have been confined to percentage analyses of changes between one period and another. Information about employment in private practice is also available from a number of separate censuses and surveys conducted by the RIBA and other bodies—see Section 13.3.1.

Architects employed by contractors and local authorities. Architects were separately distinguished as a category in DOE censuses of contractors from 1965 to 1974 and in censuses of local authority direct labour organizations from 1968 to date (data collected for other public authorities are not published). For further details see Section 6.6.3.3. It should be noted that the term 'architect' was not defined in these enquiries so that the data are not necessarily confined to registered architects. Surveys of local authority architects' departments conducted by the RIBA are referred to in Section 13.3.1.2 below.

RIBA Student Membership Survey 1969. Detailed analyses of the student membership according to a variety of characteristics (including date of election to student membership, age, qualification stage, type of employment, etc.) as at 1st April 1969 will be found in the *RIBA Stat. Bull.* [QRL 249] No. 4.

Women in the architectural profession. An analysis of the numbers and characteristics of women in the architectural profession, drawn from a variety of sources, is to be found in the *RIBA Stat. Bull.* [QRL 249] No. 14.

Job mobility. Information about the mobility of those in architectural employment is not regularly collected but an analysis of data for the period 1967–70 collected by the RIBA as part of the 1970 Earnings Enquiry is reported in *RIBA Stat. Bull.* [QRL 249] No. 13, and a special question included in the fifth RIBA Regional Chairmen's Survey [QRL 287] (Section 13.5.1.3 refers) in March 1977 obtained information about the reduction of architectural staff in private and local authority offices and their fields of redeployment. See too the surveys of staffing in private practice referred to above.

13.2.3. *The Surveying Professions*

The major professional bodies for surveyors are the Royal Institution of Chartered Surveyors (RICS)—the principal body, covering a wide range of surveying specializations—and the Institute of Quantity Surveyors (IQS) which represents in the main the quantity surveyor in employment with contractors. Most of the information available relates to the membership of these bodies. It should be noted, however, that, unlike architecture, there is no statutory registration body and no restriction on the use of the term 'surveyor'. Quantity surveyors may practise, therefore, without formal qualification or membership of professional associations. It may be noted too that some architects offer quantity surveying services as do civil engineers and mechanical and electrical engineers in their respective fields. For background information about the development and organization of the profession reference should be made to the major study by Thompson published in 1968 [B 164]. Recent brief accounts are given by the Monopolies and Mergers Commission in [QRL 345] and by Steel on the organization of the 'real estate profession' in the UK in [B 152].

RICS membership statistics. Members of the RICS are listed according to professional practice division and the name of firm or office in which the member practises is given annually in the *RICS Yearbook* [QRL 291]. Statistics of membership of the Institution for the period since its foundation (at five-yearly intervals from 1871) up to 1966 have been brought together in Thompson [B 164] and extended to 1975 and back to 1960 on an annual basis in [QRL 345] though not broken down by practice division ([QRL 345] also carries the series back at ten-yearly intervals to 1870). More detailed analyses of employment have been published for the building surveying and quantity surveying branches of the profession in 1947 and 1949 in [B 289] and for various branches of surveying, including these two, in 1955 in [B 87] (reproduced in Thompson [B 164]), in 1975 in the report of the Monopolies and Mergers Commission cited earlier [QRL 345] and in 1976 in [B 152]. An analysis of fields of employment of QS membership over the period 1962–72 was included in [QRL 333]. RICS members were also covered in the survey made for the Pilkington Royal Commission in 1955, although it should be noted that this excluded surveyors employed in the public service and did not provide a separate analysis for quantity surveyors (earnings and age analyses were included in [QRL 261] and [QRL 290]).

As in the case of the architectural profession, separate earnings enquiries and surveys into private practice have also been undertaken. These are considered in Sections 13.3 and 13.4 below.

Membership statistics of the IQS and other associations of surveyors. Members of the IQS are listed alphabetically (no statistical summaries are given) together with details of private practices where the Principal or at least one Partner is a member of the Institute in its *Yearbook* [QRL 363]. Again, it should be appreciated that membership of the IQS and other associations—particularly the RICS and the IOB—overlaps to some extent. The IQS conducted a survey of its membership in 1969 [QRL 248] producing information about the ages, employment and income of its members—further particulars are given in Section 13.4 below. More recent details of fields of employment have been given by the Monopolies and Mergers Commission [QRL 345] p. 99. Other relevant associations including surveyors among their members are the Faculty of Architects and Surveyors (FAS), the Incorporated Association of Architects and Surveyors (IAAS), the Construction Surveyors Institute and the Guild of Surveyors. Details of their membership are given in the Monopolies Commission's report on *Professional Services* in 1970 [QRL 244] and the subsequent report on *Surveyors' Services* in 1977 [QRL 345] (the former also gives broad analyses of fields of employment or employment status (Appendix 7) along with details for the RICS, IQS and other professional associations).

Surveyors employed by contractors and local authority direct labour organizations. Statistics of the number of surveyors employed by contractors from 1965 to 1974 and by local authorities' direct labour organizations from 1968 (continuing) were obtained in DOE census enquiries—see Section 6.6.1.3. It will be appreciated that the persons recorded as surveyors will not necessarily have been quantity surveyors nor necessarily members of any of the associations referred to above.

13.2.4. *The Engineering Professions*

The engineering professions associated with the construction industry consist broadly of two groups, one comprised of civil and structural engineers and the other a more heterogeneous group with responsibilities for services installations. The principal professional institutions for the first group are the Institution of Civil Engineers (ICE) and the Institution of Structural Engineers (ISE). Engineers in the second group may be members of the Institution of Mechanical Engineers (IME.) or the Institution of Electrical Engineers (IEE)—institutions not primarily concerned with the construction industry—and/or the Institution of Heating and Ventilating Engineers (IHVE) or the Institute of Municipal Engineers. There is no statutory registration body but in 1962 a Council of Engineering Institutions (CEI) was established as a federation of some fourteen professional engineering institutions (including all those mentioned above with the exception of the IHVE), and this has established an Engineers' Registration Board to operate a register of chartered engineers, technician engineers and engineering technicians. A further association of relevance in the context of construction is the Association of Consulting Engineers (ACE) to which many of the consulting engineers in private practice belong.

Membership statistics. Bare statistics of membership of the professional institutions are generally available from *Yearbooks* and *Directories* issued by the relevant bodies (e.g. [QRL 185] in the case of civil engineers, [QRL 365] in the case of structural engineers and [QRL 184] for members of the ACE) but, as indicated earlier, such statistics are of limited value for they may embrace members both at home and overseas, employed and unemployed/retired and members who may not be necessarily associated with construction. And, again, it must be remembered that membership of many of the institutions may overlap.

Fields of employment and other characteristics. Information about fields of employment and other characteristics of the labour derives either from surveys directed at the individual as in the censuses of population and surveys of the membership of the professional bodies or from surveys directed not at the individual but at the employing establishment. Unfortunately, these do not always distinguish the various categories of engineer separately.

Censuses of population. The data on qualified manpower available from the censuses of population, which constitutes the most important source, are considered in Section 6.6.1.2. Unlike architects and surveyors, qualified engineers were covered in the censuses from 1961 (i.e. 1961, 1966 and 1971) when questions on scientific and technological qualifications were first included. Prior to 1961, as noted in the introductory section on the professions in general (Section 13.2.1), occupational analyses were the only relevant statistics available from the census.

Membership surveys. Regular *Surveys of Professional Engineers* have been conducted since 1966 covering corporate and graduate members in the UK of the constituent institutions of the CEI as follows: 1966 [QRL 341] (with additional analyses in [QRL 329]), 1968 [QRL 342], and every other year from 1971 [QRL 343]. The subjects covered and analyses made have varied, but age, qualifications and training, field of work (including construction/installation as a category), income and nature of work (managerial/administration, etc.), unemployment, have been features in all or most of the surveys. For further details of these surveys reference should be made to the reports cited, each of which provides a full account. A further general source of information about the fields, or status, of employment of members of the professional engineering institutions *circa* 1969 is, as for architects and surveyors, the Monopolies Commission's report on *Professional Services* [QRL 244]. In the case of the ICE further information about fields of employment is available from sample surveys of the membership carried out in 1976 and 1977 primarily to collect earnings data (reported in [QRL 207]—Table 13.1 below refers). The published results also provide analyses of the respondents according to age and type of work.

Surveys of employers. Two enquiries are of relevance here although both have now been ended and are thus of interest as a historical source only. Each has been considered separately elsewhere in the Review and comment here is therefore brief. First is the triennial survey of engineering, technological and scientific manpower conducted over the period 1956–68—considered in Section 6.6.3.1. These surveys, it should be noted, were confined to certain fields of employment including construction firms and firms of consulting engineers but excluding private professional persons. The 1965 and 1968 surveys were extended to include information on technicians or technical supporting staff associated with the employment of the qualified manpower. For further details reference should be made to Section 6.6.3.1. Secondly the censuses for construction carried out by the DOE (Sections 4.2 and 4.3 refer) included, for a time, a question on the number of engineers employed, as they did for architects and surveyors referred to above, namely from 1965 to 1974 in the case of contractors and from 1968 (continuing) in the case of local authority direct labour organizations (the data obtained for other direct labour organizations in the public sector are not published)—this part of the DOE censuses is considered further in Section 6.6.3.3. The two sources—DOE and triennial manpower surveys—are compared in Section 6.6.3.4. It should be noted that they provide markedly different evidence.

13.2.5. *New Entrants to the Construction Professions and Education Statistics*

Education. Relevant statistics of the number of students attending courses and obtaining qualifications according to subject are contained in the official compilations of education statistics for the constituent countries of the UK: [QRL 325] for England and Wales, [QRL 326] for Wales alone, [QRL 309] for Scotland, [QRL 151] for Northern Ireland and in summary, for the UK as a whole, in [QRL 153]. These statistics were considered earlier in Sections 6.5.5 for Great Britain and 9.4.1 for Northern Ireland (*q.v.*). In addition, for architects, the RIBA also make an annual survey, the results of which have been published in the *RIBA Stat. Bull.* [QRL 249] from time to time (see Nos. 4, 8, 14, 21 and 24) and most recently, for the year 1977–8 and some earlier years, in a separate bulletin of *Education Statistics* [QRL 152]. It may also be noted that unpublished analyses available from an 'individualized data' survey of architectural students (as distinct from general counts) carried out in 1970 are listed in *RIBA Stat. Bull.* [QRL 249] No. 24. The objective of this survey was to produce 'a dynamic picture tracing each individual entrant to architectural education through to eventual departure from the system' (cf. the Further Education and Universities Statistical Records referred to earlier—Section 6.5.5) but it should be noted that the scheme was never fully implemented.

New entrants. As regards new entrants, a distinction needs to be drawn between subject of qualification (i.e. new supply) and field of employment. Information about new supply may be gathered from the official education statistics, referred to above (although these include overseas students and, of course, do not reflect new supply from immigration), and from the membership statistics of relevant professional bodies referred to earlier–Sections 13.2.2–13.2.4 inclusive. The interpretation of new membership statistics presents problems however, for the same reasons considered earlier in connection with their usefulness as an indicator of the total stock of qualified manpower in these sectors: incomplete membership, overlapping membership, members located overseas or retired or unemployed and the fact that some members may work in fields completely unrelated to construction. With regard to the supply of civil engineers in particular, a useful recent analysis of trends has been made by Head in [B 71].

Since 1959 official series have been compiled of changes in the population of persons in Great Britain with degrees or equivalent qualifications in engineering, technology and science (QSEs); as noted earlier, these embrace certain of the engineering professions but exclude architecture and surveying—for further details see Section 6.6.3.5.

As regards fields of employment, reference should also be made to Section 6.6.3.5 for details of series relating to the first employment taken up by university graduates and polytechnic students, both of which are more comprehensive with regard to qualification than the QSE data referred to above.

13.3. Organization and Structure of Professional Practice

13.3.1. *Architectural Practice*

13.3.1.1. *Private architectural practices.* As well as publishing a *Directory of Members* [QRL 143], referred to earlier, the RIBA also publish a *Directory of Practices* [QRL 144]. Inclusion in the *Directory*, however, depends on the payment of a fee and applies only to those practices which have an RIBA member as a Principal. It does not provide, therefore, a comprehensive register.

RIBA Censuses of Private Architectural Practices 1962–72 and their interpretation. On the basis of the register referred to above and a list of such other practices as the RIBA was able to identify, it conducted a regular census at two-yearly intervals between 1962 and 1972—initially in Great Britain (up to 1964) and then in the UK. They were carried out, however, largely to provide the frame for other enquiries and the results were not regularly published. The analyses that are available provide information about the number of practices according to their size and regional distribution and about staff employed. Details are as follows:

   1962/6—see reference for 1968 below.
   1968—reported in *RIBA Stat. Bull.* [QRL 249] Nos. 1 and 2 (staff ratio tables) and No. 5 (practices cross-classified by size and region). Bull. No. 1 also includes comparative data on number of practices and employment by size of practice for each of the surveys to 1966 (including data for 1958) and information about practices with branch offices.
   1970—see reference for 1972 below.
   1972—reported in *RIBA Stat. Bull.* [QRL 249] No. 27 together with some comparative data from the 1970 census.

Evaluation of the reliability of the results obtained in these censuses is difficult to make for, as is so often the case, there are no external yardsticks to which to appeal for comparison. But a number of matters seem worthy of attention from a qualitative point of view. Of crucial importance is the fact that the register may not have been complete for any one census and that its coverage over time may have changed. Judging by the increase in the number of practices that the results reveal, it would seem likely that coverage was less complete in the early censuses, but how far the increase is a reflection of this fact rather than a genuine creation of new practices, it is impossible to say.

One problem in compiling and maintaining a comprehensive register is the fact that the number of practices is large (currently, it would appear, of the order of 4,000) and that entry (in the sense of establishing a practice) and exit are relatively easy. A further problem, though probably of lesser importance, is the fact that some architectural practices are operated on a part-time, and perhaps irregular, basis. This increases still further the difficulty of maintaining a comprehensive register, and also has implications for the interpretation of the employment figures, for at other times the persons running such practices may be in employment with another private architectural practice, in which case the employment figures involve an element of duplication.

Duplication of the labour return may also occur to the extent to which partners who have interests in more than one firm are recorded more than once, and to the extent to which firms share staff and record the same labour in their returns. Finally, of course, it will be appreciated that the results include an element of estimation on account of non-response. Since the second quarter of 1977 information about staffing in private practice has been obtained in quarterly sample enquiries—see Section 13.2.2.2 above.

Other surveys of private architectural practice. Other surveys of private architectural practice have been carried out from time to time by the RIBA and other bodies on a sample basis. The relevant references are listed here in chronological order; further background information will be found in the references cited.

1957/8—RIBA surveys reported in *RIBAJ* [QRL 180] 3rd ser. Vol. 66, 1959, pp. 201–3 and 273–5. Based on a sample of private practices in 1958 and on RIBA membership survey in 1957—for details see the report cited—p. 273. This also included data on the average annual value of work certified over the period 1955–7 according to size of practice.

1960/1—RIBA postal survey of one in five private offices on the RIBA index of practices and all local authority architects' departments supplemented by personal visits carried out in connection with the report on *The Architect and His Office* [QRL 40]. This report contains a considerable volume of statistical information about the structure of the profession and the organization, staffing and work of private and local authority offices.

1967/8. NBPI survey—one in five sample of RIBA list of practices—reported in [QRL 41]. Most of the survey was concerned with financial matters and is referred to below in Section 13.4.

1975. MMC survey—one in seven sample drawn from list of architects and firms believed to be in practice in the UK based on telephone directories, and directories maintained by RIBA and other professional bodies—reported in [QRL 44].

1976. RIBA 'Structure of the Profession' study—as yet unpublished—for further details see Section 13.2.2.2.

13.3.1.2. *Local authority architects' departments.* Apart from the survey made by the RIBA in 1960/1, referred to above, for the report on *The Architect and His Office* [QRL 40], the only other published information appears to be from a survey of local authority architects' departments in England and Wales, carried out in 1958, which is reported in *RIBAJ* [QRL 180] 3rd ser. Vol. 67, 1959–60, pp. 160–3, giving number of departments making returns, the number of qualified and unqualified staff employed and the average annual value of work certified (1955–7) by type of work. Other enquiries have been made from time to time by the SCALA and by the RIBA, who conducted an 'enquiry into local authority staffing' in 1970 (largely on the subject of earnings and gradings). The results of these enquiries have remained unpublished but it is possible that some information would be made available for research purposes.

13.3.2. Quantity Surveying Practices

Statistical information about quantity surveying practices is available from three surveys. One for 1960, based on a questionnaire sent to every firm of private chartered quantity surveyors in Great Britain, is reported in the journal of the RICS [QRL 118] Vol. 93, 1960, pp. 130–1, and provides analyses of the number of firms and staff employed (professionally qualified/other technical) according to size of office. A more detailed survey was carried out for the RICS in 1972, covering the employment of chartered quantity surveyors not only in private practice but also those in employment in the public sector and in the private sector other than quantity surveying practices throughout the UK and the Republic of Ireland. The results were published in [QRL 333] together with full background details. In addition to providing organizational and structural statistics, considerable attention was devoted to the range and nature of the tasks undertaken by the quantity surveyor in each of these sectors. Two relevant surveys were also carried out by the Monopolies and Mergers Commission in 1974 and 1975 in connection with an investigation of the supply of surveyors' services. The first survey was not confined to quantity surveyors, but was directed at all potential suppliers of surveyors' services in general, but some of the results are given separately for quantity surveyors including an analysis by size of the number of offices included in the survey. The second survey was confined to quantity surveyors but was undertaken to obtain financial information only (see Section 13.4). The results, together with full details about the scope and conduct of the surveys, are given in [QRL 345].

13.3.3. Engineering Practices

The only survey that appears to be generally available is one covering all member firms of the Association of Consulting Engineers (with the exception of one-man firms and those based overseas) made in connection with an enquiry into the costs and earnings of these firms over the period 1963–71 reported in [QRL 260]. Apart from financial data (Section 13.4 refers) the report contains analyses of the number of firms and staff employed analysed by size of firm and specialization.

13.4. Financial Statistics for the Construction Professions—Earnings and Professional Practice Costs and Incomes

This section is concerned with two categories of statistical data about the construction professions: the earnings of individuals employed in this sector (whether professionally qualified or not) and financial statistics relating to the operations of professional practices—turnover, costs, assets, etc. More data are available for the architectural profession than the others and much more about earnings than anything else. Much of the data comes from *ad hoc* surveys and appears to be of an uneven quality. A common fault is a failure to publish any assessment of the errors to which sample survey results are subject, a fault which may be particularly important when results are broken down and analysed in terms of a variety of characteristics and sub-groupings for which the sub-samples may be exceptionally small.

The clearest way to present details of what is a fairly substantial body of data is in tabular form and this we do in Table 13.1 below. For convenience, however, we also summarize in the next paragraph the sources which are currently compiled on a regular basis. The practice followed in the preceding sections of dealing with each profession in turn is not followed here since in some instances a single source provides data for more than one profession. Instead the surveys are listed generally in chronological order, the only exceptions being that all surveys carried out by the same agency are grouped together and related engineering surveys are placed in juxtaposition. The date given refers to the year(s) to which the information relates rather than the date when a survey was undertaken. An indication is provided of the type of information available from each survey, and the analyses made, but no attempt has been made to define in detail the full range of these analyses, for in many cases they are extensive. Notes to the table, however, provide an indication of the availability of further information of this kind and also serve the purpose of defining the coverage and nature of the surveys.

Although Table 13.1 provides a comprehensive guide to sources, it may be useful, in view of its length, to pinpoint separately those sources which provide regular current series. There are two official sources, one quasi-official source and three private sources. Official sources are listed in the table as serial numbers 7 and 10. Both of these, it will be noted, are limited. The nature of these sources is considered further in two companion Reviews in the present series on *Personal Incomes* [B 151] and *Wages and Earnings* [B 44] respectively. Quasi-official data are published three times a year in respect of persons on the PER register–listed as serial number 15 (PER is an official agency but the data are published privately); these data are also discussed more fully in [B 44]. Private surveys are conducted currently by the RIBA for architects' earnings and fee income (serial nos. 2(iii) and 2(v)), by the CEI in respect of engineers (serial number 5) and annually by the ICE (serial number 16) in respect of civil engineers.

The surveys noted in the table are confined to those carried out officially, or by or for professional bodies. One source not noted in the table is the survey of the architectural profession made by Bowen in 1953 [QRL 3]. This did not formally cover earnings but some respondents (134 in all) volunteered information and an analysis of the distribution of these among different income ranges was published [QRL 3] p. 125. It is difficult, of course, to say how representative these data were. Other surveys are carried out from time to time by commercial organizations concerned with the recruitment and selection of staff. These are generally a by-product of the work of these organizations and cover only those persons who have registered with the agency. Hence they are of a different character from those listed in the table and not likely to be representative of a profession as a whole (the PER analysis, which *is* listed in the table, is similar but more comprehensive). References to these and other private surveys are given from time to time in

[B 237]. For further comments see the companion volume by Dean on *Wages and Earnings* [B 44].

13.5. Statistics of Work Undertaken by the Construction Professions

Information about the work undertaken by the construction professions serves at least two distinct purposes. First it complements the other information available in providing a statistical picture of this part of the construction industry: the most well-documented sector once again is the architectural profession. Secondly such information may also provide a particularly valuable forward indicator of trends in construction activity in the sense that information about work at the design stage provides an earlier indication of the future construction work-load in the field covered by the data than contractors' new orders statistics. Most attention will be devoted here to the usefulness of this information for this purpose.

In the private sector, design work is generally carried out by architects and engineers in private practice, though some will also be done by staff employed by building firms and possibly too by producers of prefabricated systems of construction. In the public sector a good deal of the design work is carried out by the authorities' own professional staff although they do, of course, also commission private designers to undertake work for them. Statistics for part of the public sector were collected for the first time officially by the then MPBW in respect of local authorities in 1965 (Section 4.7 refers). Surveys have also been undertaken by the Society of Chief Architects of Local Authorities (SCALA) into the building programmes handled by architects' and other technical departments of local authorities in England and Wales in 1976 and 1977, and these may be placed on a regular footing in future; the information from them may be made available subject to the approval of the SCALA Council. Information for the private sector has been collected by the RIBA since 1958 in respect of private architects. For the other professions only very limited information is available. We consider each professional group in turn once again.

13.5.1. *Private Architects' Design Work Statistics*

13.5.1.1. *Introduction.* Most of the statistical data available come from surveys conducted by the RIBA since 1958 and relate to the work carried out by architects in private practice. The principal series provide quantitative data on the workload. More recently the chairmen of the RIBA's regional organizations have commenced a qualitative survey of trends in the workload in their regions. We consider each of these sources separately and then consider the limited information available about overseas work. We naturally devote most attention to the principal data including a discussion on their use and interpretation. We also refer to the limited information available about design work done outside private practice.

13.5.1.2. *RIBA enquiries into private architects' new building work.* The statistics about the value of work at the design stage have been collected by the RIBA on a sample basis

Table 13.1
Construction Professions—Surveys of Earnings and Professional Practice Costs and Incomes
(A cross (×) signifies the availability of data)

Source		Profession	Date	Earnings	Turnover (Fee Income)	Costs Salaries	Costs Overheads	Profit	Assets	Sector Private Practice	Sector Private Other	Sector Public	Profession Principals	Others
1. Govt. Social Survey		Architects	1954/5 and 1955/6	×						×	×	×	×	
		Chartered Surveyors		×						×	×	×	×	
		Engineers		×						×	×	×	×	
2. RIBA	(i)	Architects	1957/8 and 1958/9	×	×	×	×	×		×			×	×
			1960/1	×		×	×					×	×	×
	(ii)	Architects	1964	×	×					×		×	×	×
	(iii)	Architects	1964–73 (Triennially) 1975 to date (Annually)	×						×	×	×	×	×
	(iv)	Architects	1956–68	×	×	×	×		×	×			×	
	(v)	Architects	1977		×									

Other trades of Staff	Publication Reference	Notes	
	[QRL 261] and [QRL 290]. See also *RIBAJ* [QRL 180] 3rd ser. Vol. 67, pp. 195–200 and 233–5.	1 in 5 sample of RIBA corporate members in UK stratified by class of membership. 1 in 3 sample of RICS corporate members in GB excluding those in public service and those qualified as mining engineers. 1 in 5 sample of corporate members of the ICE, IME, and IEE in GB.	Aggregate figures for 1954/5; more detailed data for 1955/6 including separate figures for Quantity Surveyors and Civil Engineers. More detailed analyses for Architects in RIBA ref. cited [QRL 180]. Comparative data for other professions. Age/income cross-classification in [QRL 290].
× ×	[QRL 40].	GB except local authorities (E & W). Information obtained either from a highly selective sample of sixty-nine offices, visited in 1960/1, or a postal survey of a 1 in 5 random sample of private offices on the RIBA index (42 per cent response) plus the 136 local authority architects' departments (87 per cent response). Extensive breakdowns and analyses indicating whether based on visited or postal samples. Not all data available for each year; earnings data mainly relate to 1960/1.	
	RIBAJ [QRL 180] 3rd ser. Vol. 72, 1965, pp. 9–10.	GB. An attempt to bring up-to-date some of the data in source 2(i) above but based on a very small sample restricted to offices originally visited in that enquiry. Medians and distribution by income group by level of responsibility. Ratio of turnover per head.	
×	See notes.	UK. *RIBA Earnings Surveys*. Sample surveys of registered architects initiated by the RIBA in 1964 to keep up-to-date the income data collected in source (1) above (in 1967 the NBPI survey [QRL 41]—source (6) below—was substituted). The content of the surveys and analyses have been extended over time and now include data according to age, region, size of practice, fields of employment, etc. Publication references are as follows: 1964—*RIBAJ* [QRL 180] Vol. 72, 1965, pp. 279–80. 1970—[QRL 146] with summary details in *RIBA Stat. Bull.* [QRL 249] Nos. 10 and 11. 1973—*RIBAJ* [QRL 180] Vol. 81, 1974, pp. 16–29 and *RIBA Stat. Bull.* [QRL 249] Nos. 21 and 22. A full report was prepared [QRL 286] but not published—further particulars are available from the RIBA Statistics Section. 1975—*Architects' Journal* [QRL 43] 31 December 1975, pp. 1332–5. 1976—[QRL 42].	
×	*RIBA Stat. Bull.* [QRL 249] No. 7.	'Surveys of Private Practice Cost and Income Trends' carried out by or for the RIBA in 1966 (interview) for 1956–65 [QRL 280] and in 1969 (postal) for 1966–8, with probability of selection proportional to size in terms of technical staff employed. Results most accurate for years in which sample was representative—i.e. 1964 and 1968. Data mainly expressed in ratio or index form. Breakdowns for practices inside and outside London and size. A further survey of office costs is in progress (1977).	
	RIBA Stat. Bull. [QRL 249] Nos. 32 and 33—see notes.	*Ad hoc* surveys of fee income from work in Great Britain (distinguishing non-building from building work) and from work overseas (by country)—conducted as part of the RIBA quarterly design work enquiries (Section 13.5.1) in 1977. Published data give percentage analyses—no values.	

(continued overleaf)

Table 13.1 (cont.)

Source	Profession	Date	Type of Information						Analyses				
			Earnings	Other Financial Statistics					Sector		Sta...		
				Turnover (Fee Income)	Costs		Profit	Assets	Private	Public	Professiona...		
					Salaries	Overheads			Practice	Other		Principals	Others
3. EIU	Chartered Surveyors	1962/3	×						×			×	×
4. Engineers' Guild	Engineers (Civil and other)	1959/60 1962/3	× ×										
5. CEI	Engineers (Civil and others)	1965/6 1967/8 1970/1 1972/3 1974/5 1976/7	×										
6. NBPI	Architects	1964–6/7	×	×	×	×	×	×	×	×	×	×	×
7. Inland Revenue	Architects Engineers	1966–7 to date (Annually)	×						×			×	
8. DOE (Reddaway enquiry)	Consulting Engineers	1963–71		×	×	×	×	×	×			×	×
9. DES	Architects/ Surveyors Engineers	1966/7	×										
10. DE New Earnings Surveys	Architects and Planners Q. Surveyors Civil, Structural and Municipal Engineers	1968 and 1970 to date (Annually)	×										

STATISTICS OF THE CONSTRUCTION PROFESSIONS

Other trades of Staff	Publication Reference	Notes
	See notes.	UK. Unpublished report [B 310] prepared for RICS but quoted in [B 164] p. 348. Sample of 50 per cent of firms in private practice in England and all such firms in Wales, Scotland and NI (60 per cent response rate overall). Separate figure for Quantity Surveyors. Other figures for all surveyors analysed by status, location and age. Some figures for 1946 and 1949 which may be compared are to be found in [B 88].
	[QRL 242] [QRL 243]	UK. Sample of members of the Institutions of Civil, Mechanical, Electrical and Chemical engineers. Medians and quartiles according to age, *institution*, field of employment and comparative figures for graduates and non-graduates. A sample survey was also conducted in 1948 but is said to have been too small to be of national value. For subsequent surveys see source (5) below.
	[QRL 341] and [QRL 329] [QRL 342] [QRL 343]	Surveys of UK corporate and graduate members of constituent institutions of the CEI (sample-based prior to 1971). Data for the construction professions is not always separately distinguished but detailed analyses of the civil engineering group (civil, structural and municipal) were reported in [QRL 329] for 1965/6 and analyses by age and *institution* and field of employment (incl. construction/installation) are reported in the surveys from 1973.
	[QRL 41]	UK. 1 in 5 random sample of registered architects and 1 in 5 sample of architectural practices. Income and earnings data generally relate to 1966/7. Extensive analyses according to various characteristics of practices, employment or the person.
	I.R. Stats. [QRL 173]	UK. Analysis of all assessments for income tax under Schedule D: number and average value for individuals and partnerships separately including analysis of size of partnerships and by value ranges of assessments. Problems of interpretation of the architectural series are discussed in [QRL 249] No. 5 and [QRL 44] Appendix 9.
×	[QRL 260]	Survey of all ACE member firms (excluding one-man and overseas-based firms).
	[QRL 327]	Survey linked to the 1966 census of population. Data for architects and surveyors (grouped together) by age and subject of qualification for employees plus self-employed and employees alone. Data for civil, municipal and structural engineers (employees and self-employed combined) by age.
	[QRL 208]	Sample surveys of earnings of *employees* only (self-employed are excluded) recorded in a single week each year. Information is also given for 'Town planning assistants, architectural and building technicians' (single group). Heating and ventilating engineers are not separately specified. Statistics are only published if the number of persons covered is 100 or more. Further details are given in Section 6.9.3.1.

(continued overleaf)

Table 13.1 *(cont.)*

Source	Profession	Date	Earnings	Turnover (Fee Income)	Costs		Profit	Assets	Sector		Public	Professional	
					Salaries	Overheads			Private			Principals	Others
									Practice	Other			
11. IQS	Quantity Surveyors	1969	×						×	×	×	×	×
12. OPCS	See notes	1971/2	×										
13. MMC	Architects	1971–3		×			×	×	×			×	
14. MMC	Surveyors Quantity Surveyors	1972–3 1973/4		× ×			×		×			×	
15. PER	Civil and Structural Engineers. Quantity Surveyors	1975 to date (3 times a year)	×										
16. ICE	Civil Engineers	1976 1977 1978		×									

from private architectural practices since 1958 and the results published in the *RIBA Stat. Bull.* [QRL 249] (for a time—1959–63—the results were also published in full in the *RIBAJ* [QRL 180]). The sample is drawn from all practices that can be identified, not merely those run by RIBA members, although the large majority of private architects are members of the Institute. Naturally the data cover building work only, unlike the series for local authorities' design work (considered in Section 4.7) which cover civil engineering also (it should be noted that there is an element of duplication

	Publication Reference	Notes
Other trades of Staff		
	[QRL 248]	Survey of members during first three months of 1969 (65 per cent response). Covers in the main people in employment with contractors but includes some self-employed quantity surveyors. Income ranges only—actual earnings not asked for. Analyses according to age, type of employment and personal experience.
	[QRL 263]	Voluntary income enquiry linked to 1971 census of population. Analyses for employees and self-employed by a variety of characteristics including occupation and qualifications.
	[QRL 44]	Sample survey (details are given in the reference cited) conducted by the Monopolies and Mergers Commission. Analyses of fees and profit according to size of job and size of practice.
	[QRL 345]	Sample surveys (details are given in the reference cited) conducted by the Monopolies and Mergers Commission in connection with an investigation of the supply of surveyors' services. Information about the value of business and type of service for each of several groups of suppliers of such services (including separate data for Quantity Surveyors, Architects and Consulting Engineers) is given together with separate data for Quantity Surveyors—as shown (collected in a separate survey)—analysed by size of job and size of fee income.
	Reward [QRL 284].	Analyses of existing salary levels of persons seeking new jobs and registered with PER. Analyses are made by age (including separate data for the professionally qualified) and by region.
	[QRL 207] 4 March 1976 pp. 15–39. [QRL 207] 17 March 1977 pp. 33–45. [QRL 207] 23 Feb. 1978 pp. 31–45.	'ICE Salary Surveys'—sample surveys of ICE members in Great Britain and Ireland. Analyses of remuneration and numbers employed by age (cross-classified by field of employment, qualification and type of work) and by location. Some comparative data for other professional bodies are also included.

between the two series for the latter also covers work which is delegated to private architects).

Principal Series—Commissions received and work in progress. Returns are obtained about the value of work according to type and sector at two stages: new commissions received and work entering the production drawings (formerly referred to as the 'working drawings') stage. Regional analyses are included in the published results but based on the location of the architects' offices, not the location of the work (before the second quarter of 1977, when the form of return was simplified, information was obtained about site locations but it was not used in the published results). Some information about work according to location of site *and* location of design office is available, however, from series dealing with the progress of metrication and dimensional co-ordination between 1969 and 1976 (see under 'subsidiary series' below). Before 1964, the geographical coverage was confined to Great Britain; it was then extended to the UK until the beginning of 1976 when it was confined once more to Great Britain.

The simplified enquiry, introduced with effect from the second quarter of 1977, has covered all new work and 'rehabilitation work' (i.e. work carried out on existing buildings) exceeding £2,500 in value sub-divided between housing and non-housing work in the public and private sectors. In the case of new commissions, a return of rehabilitation work by type (but not sector) is also obtained separately but the information is not published. Previously all new work was covered together with extensions, alterations and conversions work except for such work to houses and flats costing less than £2,500 (a separate question was asked about the total value of such work, together with one about the value of repair and maintenance work, but this information was also not published) and private non-housing work was sub-divided into 'industrial' and 'other' in the published results. We next describe certain subsidiary series that are available before turning to examine the use and interpretation of the data.

Subsidiary Series—Progress of metrication and dimensional co-ordination. From 1969 to 1976 the production drawings series was utilized to monitor the progress of metrication and dimensional co-ordination. Analyses of the proportion of such work dimensionally co-ordinated in metric by value and of the number of projects by size according to type of work, sector and location were regularly reported in the *RIBA Stat. Bull.* [QRL 249] up to the end of 1976. Doubts about the quality of the information provided were raised, however, in an important review included in the *RIBA Stat. Bull.* [QRL 249] No. 16, April 1973 to which reference should be made for further details.

Partial service work. Not all work involves the design and supervision of a project through to completion—for some only partial services are required. The returns used for compiling the principal series, referred to above, have been utilized to obtain separate details of such work and the data have been published from 1970 to 1977 (1st quarter) in *RIBA Stat. Bull.* [QRL 249] Nos. 8–31 (earlier unpublished data go back to 1964).

Work certified. Information is also collected about the value of new work (including extensions and major alterations to buildings other than houses) certified by private architects throughout the whole period from 1958 and published in the *RIBA Stat. Bull.* [QRL 249] (some earlier data, collected in surveys of private practice, go back to 1955—see Section 13.3.1.1). These figures exclude, of course, work designed but not supervised or certified by private architects, consultancy work undertaken, abortive design work, etc. The figures are also expressed as a proportion of an official estimate of the total annual value of all new *building* work (excluding civil engineering) based on DOE data (Chapter 4) to give an indication of 'market share'. These proportions, however, must be regarded as approximate orders of magnitude only, first because the grossed-up values of work certified are necessarily estimates, and secondly, because the output series is open to error due to difficulties experienced in compiling comprehensive output data (Section 4.4 refers) and also because the *building* component of construction output has to be estimated (no separate statistics being collected for civil engineering work).

Work abandoned or postponed. Statistics of the value of work abandoned or postponed were collected each quarter from the fourth quarter of 1973 to the first quarter of 1977 (included in *RIBA Stat. Bull.* [QRL 249] Nos. 20–31).

Work revived. Information about projects revived is naturally of allied interest to series for work postponed, but at the time of writing has been collected on only two occasions (3rd and 4th quarters of 1977)—the first results (summary particulars only) were included in *RIBA Stat. Bull.* [QRL 249] No. 33.

Interpretation

Although the principal data on new building work have been collected regularly since 1958 (1960 in respect of production drawings), the series cannot be regarded as strictly continuous because of problems associated with a falling rate of response to the survey in the early 1960s which led to its recasting in 1964. We deal here briefly with the changes made in 1964 and matters relevant to the interpretation of the series.

The sample of offices on which the survey is based is stratified by size and, more recently, by regional location also. Since 1964 it has been revised every two years in order to try to maintain the level of response (and, until 1976, extended to cover the UK). The introduction of a new sample every two years can produce discontinuity because of a difference in reporting practices by new respondents and an attempt is made to differentiate between changes arising for this reason from actual changes in the workload by running the old and new samples concurrently for one quarter. The sample results are grossed-up on the basis of statistics of the numbers of architectural staff employed and estimates, derived from the survey results, of work per head of architectural staff according to type of work and region.

A particular problem arises when grossing-up the results of surveys of this kind in allowing for the incidence of abnormally large projects which may distort the results for a particular quarter. In response to this problem, and also because of the degree of variability exhibited in the results for other reasons, it is important to note that, from 1964, the practice was adopted of basing the published results for any quarter not on the actual survey results for that quarter but on the average of the results for the quarter in question and the one preceding it in order to try to reduce the degree of variation. (Sampling errors are not published but at one time attention was drawn in the published tables to those statistics for which the error exceeded ± 14 per cent.) For these reasons, therefore, it is unwise to regard the post-1964 series as being continuous with that which preceded it.

Given these problems and those associated with levels of response, coupled with the unavoidable approximation in the valuation attached to projects at the design stages (especially new commissions on which design work may have scarcely commenced) and the further hazard of attempting to convert the series to a constant-price basis for inter-temporal comparisons, it will be appreciated that great caution is required in the use of these data (see the further discussion below under 'Uses of the design work statistics').

Uses of the design work statistics. There are two principal uses for these data. One is in the straightforward assessment of the market situation for architects' services (in this connection the RIBA regional chairmen's surveys, referred to in Section 13.5.1.3 below, are also of relevance as an indicator of trends). It needs to be remembered, however, that the RIBA data refer solely to architects in private practice; some design work is carried out by architects employed by contractors or elsewhere in the private or public sectors and some is carried out by persons other than architects. Apart from the local authority design enquiry (Section 4.7) little information is available about the extent of the demand for design services which is satisfied outside private practice. In this connection, however, two sources are of interest. For local authority housing work in England and Wales the DOE regularly collect data (currently published in *HCS* [QRL 168] and formerly in [QRL 169]) showing the extent to which technical advice is employed, differentiating between the employment of an architect for layout or for building, and between private architects and architects employed by the local authority or by the contractor. Secondly, an *ad hoc* enquiry into the design and construction of office and factory building in the period 1968–72, commissioned by the EDC for building in connection with its report *Before You Build* [B 180], provides, *inter alia*, information about the involvement of architects with this work. In addition to the report cited above, reference may be made to the *RIBA Stat. Bull.* [QRL 249] No. 24 where the results of this study are examined in more detail.

The other main use of the design work statistics—at least potentially—is for forecasting future levels of demand on the building industry. In this connection a number of factors need to be borne in mind. One, regarding the valuation of work, is common to other series discussed earlier: the value of a project in its progress from initial conception to realization on site will change as a result of changing price levels and variations to brief and specification. At the new commission stage, in particular, it should be appreciated that the valuation may be a very rough estimate. The relationship between the series of new commissions and work entering the production drawings stages will also be affected by the proportion of work in new commissions for which only a partial service is to be given and by postponements and cancellation of work.

In addition, it is important to bear in mind that the series provide only partial coverage of construction work since civil engineering work and work designed outside private practice are not covered. From the point of view of forecasting, the series for work in the private, as opposed to the public, sector is probably more useful because its coverage is more comprehensive, and within this sector for non-housing work rather than housing, since a large proportion of the latter is not architect-designed.

For public sector work a number of problems face the forecaster, for the data suffer from a number of deficiencies. The coverage of work at the design stage in this sector can be improved by amalgamating the local authority design work series (Section 4.7 refers) with the private architects' series, after allowing for work carried out by private architects for local authorities (information about the work delegated by local authorities to private architects is available from the DOE on request). Coverage of the RIBA series for the public sector extends, of course, to work delegated by other public bodies (e.g. public corporations, government departments, hospital boards, etc.) but this still leaves out of account work not so delegated as well as work delegated to private consulting engineers.

From the point of view of future construction demand, it also needs to be borne in mind that not all work in the public sector is carried out by contractors. Statistics of the amount of work covered in the local authority design enquiry to be let to direct labour forces were at one time collected ([B 266] para. 48 refers) but they were not published and the practice has now ceased. At the same time, statistics of 'new orders' *received* by direct labour forces are not collected so that in both cases information which would permit the correlation of comparable series—i.e. series for design work on the one hand and for new orders on the other each with comparable coverage (either for contractors alone or for contractors plus direct labour)—is lacking.

Further, apart from deficiencies in the data to which we have already referred, the reliability with which they can be used for forecasting purposes is affected by two further factors. One, to which we also referred earlier, is bound up with changes in price levels and the valuation of work. The confidence limits of forecasts will be influenced by the accuracy with which price changes can be allowed for and by the extent to which the relationship between the initial and subsequent valuation of work at different stages remains a stable one over time. The RIBA series are deflated to constant prices using the official 'CNC' index (Section 8.1.2.1 refers). But this index is meant to reflect changes in the current costs of construction *output* and is, therefore, not conceptually appropriate for the conversion of values at the *design* stage which are more likely to reflect current tender prices or estimates of future tender prices, rather than current costs. The other factor is the reliability with which the time lags between the design stages and the start of work on site can be allowed for. The information available about this aspect is limited—see Section 5.6.6.

13.5.1.3. *RIBA Regional Chairmen's Surveys.* These surveys were commenced at the end of 1974 to obtain information about trends, on a qualitative basis, about the workload in both private practices and the architects' departments of local authorities throughout the UK and have been repeated twice a year since then. Questions are asked about the number of months' work on hand (design and working drawings) and on the value of commissions in the period in relation to those received in the preceding period (higher, same, lower, etc.). A question was also asked about the percentage of fee income received from overseas work in the early enquiries. In addition special questions are asked from time to time; for instance, the fifth survey (March 1977) included a question on changes in staffing. The results are published as a *Press Notice* [QRL 287]. Details of a similar survey undertaken in June 1974 prior to the initiation of the regular series are reported in *RIBA Stat. Bull.* [QRL 249] No. 21.

It is too soon perhaps to appraise the value of these surveys since only a handful of results are available. As usual with 'state-of-trade' type enquiries like this one, however, one of the main problems in interpreting the results, assuming that reasonable levels of response are maintained, will be in allowing for the relative importance of different respondents.

With regard to trends in domestic workload, it is worth noting finally an *ad hoc* survey of a similar kind carried out by the *Architects' Journal* [QRL 43] by means of a questionnaire circulated with its issue of 6 April 1977. Questions were asked about the number of months' work considered to be on hand in the offices in which the respondents worked, the number of months they anticipated to continue in their present employment and about earnings. The respondents to the survey (1450)—covering architectural assistants and technicians as well as qualified architects in all fields of employment—were, of course, self-selected and, therefore, may not be representative. For this reason an additional random sample survey was commissioned. The results of both surveys were published in the *Architects' Journal* [QRL 43] Vol. 165, 8 June 1977. It will be appreciated that surveys of this kind can do no more than give a quick impression of the subjective views held by those responding. The intention of this survey was to try to crystallize feelings about prospects at a time of depression in the industry.

13.5.1.4. *Overseas work and earnings of British architects.* Information about overseas commissions was collected regularly by the RIBA as part of the new commissions sample enquiry (Section 13.5.1.2) from 1970 to 1977. Analyses were not regularly published but an estimate of the total value was published in an article on the work of consulting engineers, architects and surveyors overseas published around August each year in *Trade and Industry* [QRL 352]. It should be appreciated that the figures are approximate because they were based on samples and because the response to the relevant question tended to be poor. Information about fee income from overseas work was obtained in the Regional Chairmen's surveys referred to above (Section 13.5.1.3) and is now obtained from time to time in the new building work enquiry (Section 13.5.1.2) from the second quarter of 1977—as yet summary details only have been published in percentage terms in the *RIBA Stat. Bull.* [QRL 249] Nos. 32 and 33. An estimate of the overseas earnings of architects is made by the CSO (with the assistance of the RIBA) for balance of payments purposes and incorporated in the 'Pink Book' [QRL 356] but architects do not constitute a separate category. An estimate for architects and surveyors combined for 1970 will be found in [B 285].

13.5.2. *Work Undertaken by Private Chartered Quantity Surveyors*

Quantitative data were collected for a time during the 1960s about the work received by private chartered quantity surveyors (last published in [QRL 118] April 1965, pp. 567–8). Currently, the only information is qualitative 'state of trade' data collected in quarterly returns by the RICS from quantity surveying practices in England and Wales, in which they indicate whether the volume of work, as compared with the previous quarter, is 'more', 'the same' or 'less', etc. This information has been collected since the beginning of 1975 in three sections: 'early preliminary estimate commissions', 'bill of quantity commissions', and 'total load of all work on hand', each broken down by type of work. Summary results are published in 'Q.S. Notes' in [QRL 118]. In Scotland less detailed information of this kind has been obtained for a longer period (since the mid-1960s) by the Scottish Branch of the RICS but the results are not published.

Other information about the demands for quantity surveyors' services is limited either to a particular field or to that obtained for a special purpose in *ad hoc* enquiries and we simply note what would appear to be the principal references here. In the local authority house-building field in England and Wales regular series are compiled by the DOE to show the extent to which private quantity surveyors are employed as against quantity surveyors in the direct employment of contractors or the local authority itself and published, currently, in *HCS* [QRL 168]—formerly in [QRL 169]. Sample surveys were undertaken by the Monopolies and Mergers Commission in connection with an investigation into the supply of surveyors' services with reference to scale fees and these provide statistical data about the volume of business undertaken by firms in the sample in the 1972–4 period—further background information and the results themselves are given in [QRL 345]. Some further information of interest in this context, about the range of tasks undertaken by quantity surveying practices today, was obtained in the survey of the profession reported in [QRL 333].

Work overseas. The quantitative enquiries referred to above included data on the number and value of overseas commissions received but no current data are collected. As in the case of architects, considered above, the current work of British surveyors overseas is described in an annual article in *Trade and Industry* [QRL 352] and an estimate of their overseas earnings is incorporated into the official balance of payments statistics [QRL 356] but not separately distinguished; a separate estimate for surveyors and architects *combined*, however, will be found in [B 285] for the year 1970.

13.5.3. Work Undertaken by Consulting Engineers

The only statistics collected regularly are for overseas work obtained by members of the ACE which are published annually in [QRL 216]. A total value figure, and a commentary on the major projects, is included in the annual article referred to above in connection with architects' and surveyors' work overseas in *Trade and Industry* [QRL 352]. A detailed analysis of the ACE data together with information about other overseas contracts—contracts awarded to non-members of ACE and contracts awarded to British contractors overseas—was made by the NEDO in 1969 and published in [QRL 262]. The only information about the volume of domestic work comes from an *ad hoc* survey of members of the ACE conducted for the Reddaway Enquiry [QRL 260] which provides *inter alia* statistics about revenue over the period 1963–71 and on the number of commissions, by size and type, completed in the latest complete accounting period at the time the survey was carried out (early 1972)—full details are given in the report cited [QRL 260].

PART V

CONCLUSION

CHAPTER 14

DESIRABLE IMPROVEMENTS AND FUTURE DEVELOPMENTS

14.1. Introduction

The scope of the statistics surveyed in this volume is very wide and a large number of detailed subjects are covered as comprehensively as possible. Given the size and nature of the field it seems most convenient and useful in this section to focus attention on those major areas where the statistics currently collected seem most in need of improvement. There are, in any case, limits to the extent to which comprehensive treatment of desirable improvements and future developments is possible for there are inevitable limits to the breadth and depth of vision and foresight of any single author.

The nature of the improvements which it may be desirable, in principle, to make may vary from the general to the particular. But these are not all of equal importance and they are not all equally discernible. For instance, improvements of a technical nature may be desirable in some cases but one is rarely in a position to make observations at this level of detail. At more general levels, various kinds of improvement may be desirable ranging from the filling of gaps in the existing range of data to improvements either in the quality of the existing statistics or in the availability of background information about them which is relevant to their use and interpretation. Even here there are limits to the extent to which comprehensive treatment is possible. With regard to future developments it is, of course, impossible to foresee—even for the immediate future—every requirement for statistical information which does not at present exist but which will be needed by someone, somewhere, for some purpose.

In the rest of this chapter, therefore, we focus attention on some of the most important problems and deficiencies as we see them, coupled with observations of a more general nature, taking each main subject area in turn. Numerous comments in relation to particular series or sources are also made in the course of the Review itself.

14.2. The Construction Industry in Great Britain

As far as the construction industry is concerned, the main subject areas are, of course, output, employment and statistics relating to its organization and structure.

One improvement which is of a general nature and can perhaps be put at the forefront of all suggested improvements concerns the availability of information about the methods used to compile published series and a clear expression of the nature and, if possible, the size of errors to which series may be subject. The printed statistic, even more than the printed word, seems to possess a magic of its own, especially if printed in an official government publication, impressing upon its reader a sense of accuracy which it is difficult to resist or dispel. Undoubtedly the establishment of the Government

Statistical Service and the development of a new 'open-ness' in government have led to many improvements over recent years. As far as construction is concerned, the main improvement has been the publication of more information of a definitional kind. But few steps have been taken in the more sensitive and difficult area of providing the user with the minimum of information which could enable him to make some assessments of the reliability and usefulness of the statistics for his own particular purposes. In this connection a demand for the development of 'quality labelling' for official statistics has recently been foreseen by Sir Claus Moser, Head of the Government Statistical Service at the time, in an article looking towards likely developments in the next decade [B 105]. Such a development is one which we would strongly support.

A second outstanding matter of general importance concerns the comparability and the reconciliation of differences between statistics on the same subject collected by different agencies. There are many instances, both in the past and currently, where series collected by different agencies provide different results but no official attempt at a reconciliation is made, or if it is, it is not made public. We refer to instances of this kind at appropriate places in this Review. The major areas of concern are the employment statistics where substantial differences occur among the data collected in enquiries conducted by the Department of the Environment and the Department of Employment and in Censuses of Production and Censuses of Population. On the production side, differences between the output series and the capital expenditure series are a particular matter for concern, especially since the difference has grown consistently larger year after year over a long period of time. Although there are good reasons why the two series should differ to some extent and reasons why the difference should have grown larger over recent years (discussed in Section 5.4.3), it is a worrying feature of these two series, given their importance as indicators of the level of investment. We have taken pains to attempt to provide an explanation of the kinds of reason that may account for differences of this kind at various places in this Review, but in the absence of detailed official background information in many cases this is no easy thing to do. It is certainly no substitute for accounts written contemporaneously with the collection of the statistics by those acquainted with the collection procedures and subsequent processes and with access to the returns themselves. Ideally what is required, of course, is reconciliation in quantitative terms.

At the same time, however, it is perhaps worth stressing a view expressed earlier. Namely, that the existence of more than one series does serve to counteract the sense of accuracy otherwise conveyed by the 'official' statistic. That in itself is salutary but it does not, of course, provide the user with the guidance necessary for sensible use of the data. In this respect, the proposal to centralize the collection of most industrial statistics in the hands of one agency, the BSO, possesses the disadvantage of replacing diversity by a single source with no assurance that accuracy will be improved or even maintained, given the severe difficulties in maintaining a comprehensive register of businesses in the construction industry. Certainly the degree of estimation that has been incorporated in the first census of production for construction conducted by the BSO (that for 1974—[QRL 76]) gives cause for concern,[1] particularly if these enquiries become the principal source of statistical information about the construction industry.

---

[1] Estimates for unsatisfactory returns, non-response and unsampled small undertakings account for 41 per cent by employment and 37 per cent by turnover of the total figures shown—[QRL 76] p. 4 refers. How much of these estimates arise from sampling and how much from the other factors is not specified.

14.2 DESIRABLE IMPROVEMENTS AND FUTURE DEVELOPMENTS

We now turn to more particular matters. We devote most attention to the statistics about the construction industry as such, considered in Part I of this Review.

The Register of Contractors. The basic problem in compiling reliable statistics in this area since 1954 has been the maintenance of a comprehensive register of contractors. This problem is of unrivalled importance since the basic series of output and employment are critically dependent upon it. In default of a compulsory registration requirement, as existed prior to 1954, it is difficult to see how a comprehensive register can be maintained in view of the large size, geographical dispersion and high rates of entry to and exit from this industry.

The accumulation of a deficiency of some 25,000 firms, added to the DOE register in 1973 (out of a total, including these firms, of 96,000) provides an indication of the magnitude of the problem. But there can be no assurance that similar deficiencies will not recur nor that the register, even now, is complete. One reason for particular doubt on this score is given by the information which has recently become available about the number of 'persons' registered with HM Customs and Excise for VAT purposes. This gives a number which is almost twice as high as the number of firms on the DOE register. In principle the VAT register provides a most fruitful source of information for there is a legal requirement to register (applying to all businesses above a low size limit) and also some financial incentive to do so arising out of the administration of the tax. It is to be hoped, therefore, that it will be exploited to the full in updating and maintaining the register used by the DOE and BSO. Certainly the enormous disparity between the VAT and the DOE registers needs to be investigated. In relation to the register problem, other desirable improvements are of lesser importance inasmuch as it is the quality of the register that must determine the quality of the data.

Output and Employment. As we suggest above, the main difficulties experienced in the past in the collection of reliable statistics about output and employment have arisen out of the difficulties of maintaining a comprehensive register of businesses. Currently, however, a new 'project-based' method of collecting output and employment data is under investigation by the DOE and is likely to be introduced as the principal collection method in the near future. In contrast to the 'contractor-based' system used up till now, with its dependence on a comprehensive register of firms, the new system will be based on returns from *main* contractors in respect of individual projects, details of which are obtained by DOE in its new orders enquiry (Section 4.5 refers).

In principle the proposed new system will have two virtues. First, it will overcome, certainly for most contracts for new work, the difficulty of ensuring comprehensive coverage of the large number of small sub-contractors and individual men working under labour-only sub-contract arrangements. It depends, of course, upon reliable information about contracts let to start with, but this is much less likely to suffer from deficiencies (see Section 4.5.2). Secondly, the collection of details of work done and employment on individual projects is likely to ensure the provision of more reliable information than the collection of data about all contracts in the aggregate.

Two further desirable improvements would be the collection of statistics about the composition of output by type of work in greater detail than is at present available and more reliable information about its regional location. Currently output data are collected for only five types of work in which all new non-housing work is put into one amorphous group (apart from a sub-division between the public and private sectors). A more detailed breakdown, preferably parallel to that provided for new orders, would be valuable. The usefulness of the regional analyses of output and employment data currently compiled by the DOE is severely limited since (with exceptions in the case of Scotland and Wales—Section 4.4.5.3 refers) it rests on the registered office location of contractors and not the location of the work.

In both these respects the proposed project-based system also offers the potential for improvement for, in contrast to returns for output and employment in the aggregate, returns for individual projects can be readily classified by both type of work and location.

Thus in terms of more reliable output and employment series and more detailed sub-classifications of the data, the proposed project-based system holds considerable promise. It remains to be seen, however, whether reliable series can be compiled by this method and, in particular, whether labour employed under labour-only sub-contract can be adequately covered. The problem of collecting reliable repair and maintenance statistics will also be left untouched by this method, for the returns of projects are confined to new work and much of repair and maintenance work is carried out by small firms—a sector of the register which is particularly likely to be deficient.

A further particular problem as far as output is concerned is that of ensuring that contractors supply reliable information about the value of work done. This problem arises out of the nature of contract work and related costing and payment practices; it was discussed fully in Chapter 2 and there is no need, therefore, to repeat the discussion here. As far as improvement is concerned, the salient point we would make is that the questionnaires used for the collection of output data do not give specific guidance on how the return of output should be completed beyond referring to 'the amounts chargeable to customers for work done'. In particular, they do not specify whether costing records or valuation certificates should form the basis and, if the latter are used, whether it is values certified or payments received (i.e. certified amounts less retentions) that are relevant. For a fuller discussion of these matters reference should be made to Section 2.3. The matter is raised again here only to suggest that the inclusion of more precise notes of guidance might be beneficial.

The Self-employed and Labour-only Sub-contractors. A further major deficiency in the official employment series for construction is the failure to obtain adequate information about the self-employed, including men employed under LOSC. The growth of this practice has meant that a large part of the labour force—and a part subject to considerable change over time—has gone unrecorded and makes the employment series of limited value. The current censuses of employment conducted by the Department of Employment only set out to cover employees but the point remains that employment series which fail to cover a significant part of the labour force are of limited use and difficult to interpret. Of course, this does not only apply to Construction, but it is particularly important for this industry given the extent of self-employment (genuine or otherwise) and apparent changes in the extent of the practice over time.

Direct Labour Output and Employment. A further improvement in the output and employment area which could be made immediately concerns the publication of data for the output and employment of direct labour organizations. First, it is useful to have data published separately for the direct labour sector. It is a pity that the DOE has stopped doing this in its time series. Secondly, it is of the greatest importance to know precisely how the sector is defined at any time. The DOE historical series is impossible to interpret because of a lack of information about its coverage (i.e. which bodies are included) and changes in its coverage over time. The same is true with respect to the current census of production data for construction: although separate results are published for public authorities, no precise information is given as to which authorities are included. This is particularly important because coverage is not comprehensive and the *Standard Industrial Classification* is not explicit here.

The Public Sector and the Standard Industrial Classification. The guidance given in the current SIC about the extent to which the construction departments of public bodies should, or should not, be included within the Construction 'Order' appears unsatisfactory and the rationale (to this writer at any rate) is difficult to discern. Reference is made to the inclusion of the building and civil engineering departments of government departments, local authorities and New Town Corporations and Commissions, and currently (1968 SIC) to the exclusion of the direct labour of gas, electricity and water undertakings (see Appendix I). But why the latter should be excluded and whether or not the direct labour of other public bodies should or should not be included is not clear. The definition in this area, therefore, lacks clarity.

Further, our examination of the available statistics appears to show that there is no effective machinery for ensuring consistency of practice amongst Departments. It certainly seems likely that there are differences in the practices employed by the DOE and the DE for classifying public-sector labour to the construction industry. And certainly there are notable differences between the statistics for directly employed construction labour in the public sector published by the CSO as part of an industrial analysis of public sector employment (Section 6.2.3.4 refers) and those published by the DOE. This is simply another instance of a failure to reconcile conflicting statistics compiled or published by different agencies.

Undoubtedly there are difficulties in collecting satisfactory information in this sector. These difficulties themselves make it important, particularly with the expansion of the public sector, that the scope of the data should be defined and that it should be suitably distinguished from the private sector.

Constant Price Series and Price Indices. Perhaps of equal importance to the improvement of the employment and output series is the need for a better index of construction costs. The current official index (the 'CNC' index—discussed at length in Section 8.1.2.1) is open to serious criticism and thus all the series which involve its use are open to a further important source of potential error.[2] These are, in particular, the index of industrial production, the series of output at constant prices and the statistics of gross fixed capital formation in buildings and works at constant prices.

Informational Needs and Available Series. Returning to more general matters, the lack of information which is of value for interpretative purposes is perhaps nowhere more keenly felt than in the field relating to the construction industry as such. Despite the improvements made over recent years, particularly in the introduction of a *Notes and Definitions Supplement to Housing and Construction Statistics* [B 250], it would be

---

[2] It should be noted, however, that after the preparation of this text new output deflators were introduced by the DOE (in March 1978) and the series, to which we refer here, retrospectively revised—see the Addenda at the front of this volume for further particulars.

highly beneficial if the information given in that publication were to be amplified so as to include information about such things as sampling practices, processing operations, the ways in which series are adjusted (if any)—as, for instance, with the series of new orders—non-response, grossing-up practices and any other information which would enable the user to gain a better appreciation of the nature and quality of the published data.

It would also be useful to print copies of the questionnaires used, and the notes for guidance, along with the results, regularly in the case of major enquiries (e.g. the DOE censuses) and perhaps intermittently, as necessary, in the case of other enquiries, drawing attention from time to time to any significant changes. It is surprising that, as far as can be ascertained, not a single questionnaire has ever been published for any of the fifty censuses, nor for any of the numerous other enquiries, carried out by the DOE and its predecessor departments since it first obtained powers in this field in 1941. In this connection, however, we would draw attention to the Appendices to this volume which include a number of specimen questionnaires.

14.3. The Construction Industry in Northern Ireland

The statistics available about the construction industry in Northern Ireland are less detailed than those collected in Great Britain and less information is published. But the collection processes are confronted by the same difficulties as those encountered in Britain.

As in Britain, the collection of data from contractors is entirely dependent upon the reliability of the register of firms. No information has been made available about the steps taken to maintain the register but the practical difficulties are certainly the same in kind as those encountered in Britain. Whether or not the deficiencies are the same in degree, it is not possible to say. Again, as in Britain, similar disparities occur in the series collected by different agencies (this is particularly true in the case of employment—see Section 9.3.7) but yet again little or no attempt is made to provide the user with official guidance about the reasons for the differences.

With regard to the background information made available in Northern Ireland, the situation is worse than it is in Great Britain. Northern Ireland benefits from no *Notes and Definitions Supplement* of any kind and even introductory notes or footnotes to published tabulations are notable for their paucity. Improvements have begun to be made in recent years by the inclusion of slightly more detailed notes in the *Northern Ireland Digest of Statistics* [QRL 140] but much still remains to be done. As we suggested earlier in connection with the data for Great Britain, guidance needs to be sufficiently detailed to enable the user to make his own judgements about the usefulness of the data for his own particular purposes. Thus information is required of the kind detailed above, viz. register maintenance practices, industrial classification practices, levels of response, sampling and grossing-up practices, etc.

To turn to more particular matters, the main areas where the points made above mainly apply are the output and employment statistics. For further particulars reference should be made to the sections in which the data themselves are discussed (Sections 9.2 and 9.3 respectively). In this connection it should be noted that a project-based method of collecting statistics on similar lines to that being investigated by the DOE (referred to above) was introduced in Northern Ireland in 1977. For reasons discussed earlier in connection with the British data the new system possesses a number of potential advantages.

On the production side, however, a further difficulty confronting the user of Northern Ireland statistics is the lack of any guide to the sources and methods used for compiling the official estimates of gross fixed capital formation. These statistics have now been regularly published for over a decade and such a guide would obviously be helpful. It is possible that the historical series of gross fixed capital formation in buildings and works may be a more reliable indicator of new construction work than the output statistics collected from contractors, but without information about the basis of the estimates this cannot be judged.

Finally, with regard to production in general, all construction constant-price series—output and expenditure values and the index of industrial production—are subject to an additional source of error introduced via the index of costs used for deflation purposes. For this purpose the official index compiled by the DOE for Great Britain is used; no official index of construction costs for Northern Ireland is calculated. As we have indicated, this index suffers from important limitations, but even if it did not, its applicability to Northern Ireland would naturally remain questionable.[3] The development of separate price deflators for both output and new orders in Northern Ireland would seem particularly worthy of investigation.

14.4. Construction Materials and Input–Output Analyses

Construction materials are, of course, an extremely difficult field to cover adequately because of the fact that many materials are suitable for use in construction but are not specifically construction materials. Comprehensive data can only be collected therefore from the users of the materials rather than their producers. There is, however, a major gap in the information available about consumption. Data have been collected from consumers (contractors) from time to time in Censuses of Production, but covering only large contractors and only a few specific materials and therefore only part of total consumption.

Information here is of direct relevance to the development of input–output models. In the official input–output tables for the UK the major part of inputs to construction remain estimates. These tables in any case only include Construction as a single component. Given the diversity of construction work, more detailed sub-division is ideally required: since construction represents such a major part of national investment, a more detailed input–output model would provide a tool of enormous value in analysing the implications of changes in the level and in the pattern of construction investment on the materials industries. Even less information is available about the labour requirements of different sorts of construction work—information which is of great potential value for manpower planning purposes.

As regards the published statistics of production and sales, etc. of building materials extending back over the whole of the post-war period, a major fault has been a failure to

---

[3] It should be noted that new output deflators were introduced in Great Britain after the preparation of this text (see Addenda at the front of this volume) but their applicability to Northern Ireland, of course, still remains open to question.

provide any information yet again about how the data were collected: whether statutory powers were used or not (it is known that *some* enquiries were voluntary in the early post-war years); how the register of producers, from whom returns were obtained, was maintained; whether or not sampling was employed, etc. Undoubtedly the series for some materials is better than for others: it would seem likely that in cases where production is highly concentrated, the series are more likely to be reliable, but the user of these statistics is left to infer these things for himself. If adequate records still survive in the DOE about these matters the publication of an historical account of the data for which it, and its predecessors, were responsible until the recent transfer of these responsibilities to the BSO would be of considerable interest and value, particularly to those who require long time-series. More background information is now published about the BSO enquiries but here too 'quality labelling' still remains an aspiration.

Building Materials and Input–Output Analyses for Northern Ireland. On the building materials side in Northern Ireland, very little information is available about the production and consumption of materials in any detail either by type of material or type of work. At the very least it would seem desirable to collect statistics from local producers about the production, deliveries and stocks of the principal building materials. It is known that some information of this kind is collected but it is not published. An attempt has been made to compile an input–output model for Northern Ireland covering Construction along with other industries in some detail, but it is clear that the estimates for Construction are subject to very substantial margins of error (see Section 9.2.2.2). Given the economic development needs of Northern Ireland and the central position occupied by the construction industry in this context, the need for a reliable model of this kind is very great.

14.5. The Construction Stock

Estimates of the stock of buildings and other construction works are extremely difficult to make and are open to wide margins of error. Buildings and works are such a large part of the total stock and open to such wide margins of error that it would seem highly desirable that any opportunity for improving the estimates should be exploited. We suggested earlier that data now available from analyses of the rating valuation records of property in commercial and industrial use coupled with separate survey information about other major components of the stock (housing and schools are already covered) offer great potential for making a direct assessment of the stock, in contrast to the 'indirect' perpetual-inventory method currently used.

Information about the age and other characteristics of the construction stock are of interest in connection with studies relating to rates of replacement and investment behaviour is almost completely lacking.

Information about the capital stock in Northern Ireland (apart from housing) would seem to be almost entirely non-existent. The filling of gaps in this area would, no doubt, be useful but it would seem to this writer that the need for reliable output, employment and capital expenditure statistics has greater claims to priority.

14.6. Construction Professions

A comparison of the statistical information available about the construction professions reveals very clearly that the architectural profession is much better served in this respect than engineers and surveyors. But there would seem to be no obvious need for these professions to mirror the architectural profession. It is difficult to foresee what information needs may arise and it would seem therefore that such needs may best be met on an *ad hoc* basis rather than through the initiation of regular enquiries.

One area where information is potentially of wider significance than the professions themselves, however, concerns the volume of work being handled, for this may provide a very early indication of changes in the level of demand for construction work as such, particularly from the private sector. The only quantitative information collected (other than that obtained by the DOE from local authority design departments) is that obtained by the RIBA about architects' commissions. It appears that this series has not come up to expectations in the past. But it seems to this writer that any steps that could be taken to improve its quality—perhaps with official support—would be of benefit, for in principle it should provide a longer-range forward-looking indicator than contractors' new orders statistics and thus an indicator of great potential value.

14.7. A Proposal for a Comprehensive and Detailed Official Index of Sources

Finally, one need of which we grew acutely aware during the preparation of this Review is one which applies not only to construction but seemingly to every other field of economic and social statistics. This is a need for the maintenance of a detailed record of sources. Given the immense volume of statistical information that now exists covering long periods of time, and the growing use of *ad hoc* surveys in many fields, it is often difficult—and certainly time-consuming—simply to discover whether or not a particular category of data exists, let alone where it is to be found. The series of Reviews, of which this is one, go a good part of the way towards filling this need. But in the nature of things they are not readily kept up-to-date. On the other hand, the recently published *Guide to Official Statistics* [B 236] is to be kept up-to-date (at least every year or two) and admirably fills a long-felt need for a general source of reference but it does not provide information at the level of detail that is here envisaged.

It would seem to be feasible to use computers not only for data storage, but also for the compilation and maintenance of a record in fine detail of each category of data that is produced—at least by public bodies. Such a record could be kept up-to-date continually and made available to anyone seeking information through computer access facilities.

What is envisaged, therefore, is a situation where it ought to be possible to pose a very specific question about the availability of a particular category of data and to obtain an answer very quickly from one central source. The obvious body to be made responsible for such a development would be the Central Statistical Office, given its existing functions and the fact that all surveys which public bodies propose to carry out are already monitored through the assessment functions of its Survey Control Unit. The more extensive use of data banks in the next ten years has already been foreseen by the Head of the Government Statistical Service in the article referred to earlier [B 105]. The proposal we make here would be a natural complement to such a development.

QUICK REFERENCE LIST

NOTES TO THE QUICK REFERENCE LIST

1. Arrangement

The Quick Reference List is arranged strictly by subject—unlike the text which treats all MOW–DOE data separately and all data for Northern Ireland in a separate section. Given the nature of the statistical sources and the data, however, an inevitable degree of overlap among subject headings remains and it is important, therefore, to refer to the cross-references given in the 'Remarks' column alongside each main subject heading.

2. Scope and Coverage

The Quick Reference List is confined in the main to regular statistical sources and major periodic surveys such as the decennial censuses of population. A number of *ad hoc* surveys are also noted in appropriate sections of the List but they are not covered comprehensively here; *ad hoc* labour surveys in particular, which have covered a diverse range of subjects at different times and do not fit neatly into the subject classification, are omitted; they are examined in Section 6.7 of the text.

Certain non-current series are also not listed in the QRL; this applies particularly to indices of building costs and prices which are no longer produced; again, appropriate references are given in the main text.

3. Terminology

Regions. The term 'GB Region' is used to indicate analyses for English regions plus Scotland and Wales. The term 'UK Regions' is used to indicate GB Regions plus Northern Ireland. The term 'GB Countries' is used to indicate separate analyses for England, Wales and Scotland. Analyses confined to the constituent countries of Great Britain or the United Kingdom are so shown.

Time series and non-time series. Sources of output statistics have been sub-divided in the list under the headings: 'Time Series' and 'Non-time Series'. Some output statistics are collected to cover all work done over time—such data we refer to as 'Time Series'. Other output data may be collected regularly but for part of a year only—such data often form the basis for more detailed sub-classifications; we list these data under the heading 'Non-time Series'.

Abbreviations. All abbreviations used are listed at the front of this volume.

4. QRL Key to Publications

All statistical sources are listed alphabetically by title except for the few cases where the relevant source has a named author: these references precede the others and are listed alphabetically by author. Other publications, not listed in the QRL Key, are listed in the Bibliography which follows it and are arranged in the same way.

QUICK REFERENCE LIST—TABLE OF CONTENTS

	Page
Output	394
MOW–DOE Time Series	394
MOW–DOE Census Analyses of the Value of Work Done	396
Census of Production Output Series	397
Contribution to Gross Domestic Product	397
Indices of Industrial Production	397
Capital and Current Expenditure on Construction	398
Fixed Capital Formation Series	398
Capital Expenditure Survey Data—Private Sector I: Periodic Censuses and Large-scale Enquiries for Production, Distribution and Service Trades	399
Capital Expenditure Survey Data—Private Sector II: Annual and Quarterly Small-scale Enquiries for Manufacturing, Distribution and Services	401
Capital Expenditure—Public Sector	401
Capital Expenditure by the Construction Industry	402
Current Expenditure on Construction	402
Output, Expenditure and Related Data for Specific Types of Building—Data in Monetary and Physical Units	402
Future Output and Expenditure Indicators and Forecasts	404
Contractors' New Orders Statistics	404
Unofficial Contract Surveys	405
Design Work Statistics	406
Investment Intentions	406
State of Trade Enquiries	406
Construction Forecasts	407
Employment Statistics I—MOW–DOE and Equivalent Northern Ireland Departments	407
MOW Time Series 1941–5	407
MOW Time Series 1945–55	407
MOW–DOE and Equivalent Northern Ireland Departments, Time Series Since 1955	407
MOW–DOE Census Analyses for Contractors 1941–54	408
MOW Census Analyses for Direct Labour Organizations, 1944–54	410
MOW–DOE Census Analyses for Contractors Since 1954	411
MOW–DOE Census Analyses for Local Authorities' Direct Labour Since 1954	413

Employment Statistics II—MOL–DE and Other General Sources   414
  MOL–DE and Equivalent Northern Ireland Departments' Principal
    Series, 1948–71   414
  MOL–DE and Equivalent Northern Ireland Departments' Principal
    Series from 1971   415
  MOL–DE and Equivalent Northern Ireland Departments' Estimated
    Continuous Series from 1959   416
  MOL–DE and Equivalent Northern Ireland Departments' Subsidiary
    Employment Series   416
  Census of Production Employment Data   418
  Construction Industry Training Boards (GB & NI) Employment Data   419
  Census of Population Employment Data   419

Employment Statistics III—Qualified Manpower   421
  Census of Population Data   421
  Triennial Sample Surveys 1956–68   422
  DOE Censuses of Contractors and Direct Labour Organizations   422
  Institute of Building Statistics   423
  New Supply of Qualified Manpower   423

Labour Statistics Other than Employment, Wage Rates, Earnings, Hours of Work and Labour Costs   423
  Labour Training Statistics   423
  Education Statistics   424
  Unemployment, Vacancies and Placings   425
  Accident Statistics   426
  Strike Statistics   428
  Trade Union Statistics   429

Wage Rates, Earnings, Hours of Work and Labour Costs   429
  Wage Rates and Normal Hours of Work   430
  Actual Earnings and Hours of Work I—MOL–DE Data   430
  Actual Earnings and Hours of Work II—Non-MOL–DE Data   433
  Total Labour Costs and Factor Incomes   434

Inputs to Construction Other than Labour   436

Industrial Organization and Structure   437
  MOW Registration Statistics 1946–53—Contractors and Direct Labour
    Organizations   437
  MOW Censuses of Contractors 1941–4   437
  MOW Censuses of Contractors 1945–54   438
  MOW–DOE Censuses of Contractors Since 1954   438
  MOW–DOE Censuses of Direct Labour Organizations Since 1954   439
  Censuses of Production Data   439
  CITB Returns   440
  VAT Registration Statistics   440
  Company Acquisitions and Mergers   440

Financial Statistics	441
Company Income and Finance	441
Statistics of Quoted Securities	442
Overseas Transactions	442
R & D Expenditure	442
Expenditure on Acquisitions and Mergers	443
Bankruptcy	443
Company Liquidations	443
Taxation Statistics	443
Construction Costs, Prices and Productivity	444
Indices of Construction Costs and Prices	444
Productivity Studies	445
Construction Materials—Production, Consumption and Use	446
Consumption	446
Production, Sales, Deliveries, Stocks, etc.	446
Overseas Trade	447
Construction Plant and Equipment—Production, Consumption and Use	447
Construction Materials Price Indices	447
DOI Wholesale Price Indices from 1946	447
MOW Indices of Building Materials Prices 1939–51	448
Price Index Numbers for Current Cost Accounting	449
Construction Plant Price Indices	449
Construction Stock	449
Total Stock	449
Stock Statistics for Particular Types of Buildings (Excluding Housing)	451
Construction Stock Transactions and Costs	453
Construction Professions	454
Numbers, Characteristics and Employment	454
Organization and Structure of Professional Practice	457
Financial Statistics of Construction Professions—Earnings and Professional Practice Costs and Incomes	459
Work Undertaken by Construction Professions	460

QUICK REFERENCE LIST

Type of Data/ Descriptive Title	Breakdown/ Detail of Analysis	Area	Dates and Frequency	Publication (see QRL Key)	Text Reference and Remarks
OUTPUT					
MOW–DOE Time Series					
MOW time series pre-1945 Value of gross output	Est. national aggregates	GB	1932–45. Annually	[QRL 318]	3.8. Estimated series. All now reproduced in [QRL 321]. Further details are set out in Table 3.6
Value of gross output	Est. national aggregates	UK	1932–9. Annually	[QRL 318]	
Value of work done	Type of work	GB	1940–5. Annually	[QRL 318]	
Value of gross output	Type of work	UK	1932–8. Annually	[QRL 318]	
Government building—value of new work done	Type of work or Department	GB	Sept. 1941–Aug. 1945 monthly	[QRL 318]	3.7.4
MOW time series 1946–55 Value of work done	Agency and type of work	GB	1946–55. Quarterly	[QRL 195] and [QRL 321]	3.8.3. Full details of the series are set out in Table 3.7
Value of work done	Agency and type of work	GB	1946–55. Annually	[QRL 31]	
MOW–DOE and equivalent departments for N. Ireland—time series since 1954					
Old national series (see Remarks)					4.4.5. *N.B.* A major retrospective revision of the series back to 1963 was introduced in 1973 in [QRL 147] No. 240. See Table 4.3 for further details of the series available, incl. unpublished data available on request

Value of work done—contractors	Current and constant prices (s.a.) by type of work	GB	1955–74 (Q_1). Quarterly	[QRL 236], [QRL 168], [QRL 194], [QRL 195]	
Value of work done—direct labour	Current and constant prices (s.a.) total	GB	1955–74 (Q_1). Quarterly		
Index numbers—Ctrs and DL	Actual and s.a. series—all work; new work	GB	1954–72. Quarterly	[QRL 194]	
Index numbers—Ctrs	S.a. series—all work by type	GB	1970–4 (Q_1). Quarterly	[QRL 168] to No. 9	
Index numbers—DL	S.a. series—all work total	GB	1970–4 (Q_1). Quarterly	[QRL 168] to No. 9	4.4.5 and Table 4.3—see note above
New national series					
Value of work done—Ctrs and DL	Current and constant prices (s.a.) by type of work	GB	Quarterly from 1972	[QRL 168], [QRL 195]	
Value of work done—Ctrs and DL	Current and constant prices by type of work	GB	Annually from 1963	[QRL 168], [QRL 31]	
Index numbers—Ctrs and DL	S.a. all work by type of work	GB	Quarterly from 1972	[QRL 168]	
Index numbers—Ctrs and DL	All work (by type from 1969)	GB	Annually from 1961	[QRL 168]	
Value of sub-contract work	As sub-contractor / As labour-only sub-contractor (LOSC) / For firms by sub-contractors / Payments to LOSC by type of work	GB	Annually from 1974/5	[QRL 168]	
Regional series					4.4.5.3
Value of work done—Ctrs, DL	By type of work (Ctrs) and total (DL)	Scotland	Annually or half-yearly from 1957	[QRL 306] (and former [QRL 139])	
Value of work done—Ctrs, DL	By type of work (Ctrs) and total (DL)	Wales	Annually from 1951	[QRL 142] and [QRL 360]	Retrospectively revised in 1973 back to 1963
Value of work done—Ctrs, DL	By type of work (Ctrs) and total (DL)	NI	Quarterly from 1966	[QRL 140], [QRL 168]	9.2.1. Annual series only in [QRL 168]

Type of Data/ Descriptive Title	Breakdown/ Detail of Analysis	Area	Dates and Frequency	Publication (see QRL Key)	Text Reference and Remarks
OUTPUT—contd.					
MOW–DOE Time Series—contd.					
British Construction work overseas—value	Contracts obtained; work done; work outstanding by trading or geographical area	World	Annually from 1955	[QRL 352] and [QRL 168]	4.6. Statistics of overseas earnings and investment by construction companies are published separately—see Section 7.2.6 and under 'Financial Statistics' below
MOW–DOE Census Analyses of the Value of Work Done					Unlike the time series referred to above these analyses cover incomplete periods of time
Contractors	Size of firm; trade of firm; region	GB	1942–4. One month	[QRL 321] and [QRL 320] (1942–3)	3.3. 'Main trades' only. See Table 3.1
Contractors	Cross-classified by: size and trade of firm; type of work by size, trade and region of firm	GB	1956 (Q$_1$)	[QRL 321]	4.2 (sub-sections 4.2.3.8–4.2.3.12 incl.). See Table 4.1 for full details
Contractors	Cross-classified by: type of work, size, trade and region of firm	GB	1957–70 (Q$_1$) 1971 to date (Q$_3$)	[QRL 71] [QRL 240]	
Contractors	By trade of firm sub-classified by type of work and size of firm	GB	1969 (Q$_1$)	[QRL 70]	
Local authorities' DL	Type of work cross-classified by: region, type of authority, size of labour force	GB	1956 (Q$_1$)	[QRL 321]	
Local authorities' DL	Type of work by region and by type of authority	GB	1961–70 (Q$_1$ and Q$_3$) 1971 to date (Q$_1$ and Q$_3$)	[QRL 194] [QRL 168]	4.3. See Table 4.2 for full details
Local authorities' DL	Type of work by size of authority (labour force)	GB	1968 to date (Q$_3$) 1969–70 (Q$_1$)	[QRL 194] to 1970 [QRL 168] from 1971.	

Series	Breakdown	Region	Period	References	Notes
Govt Depts' and Public Utilities' DL					See Section 4.3.3
Census of Production Output Series					5.3. Business year basis
Gross output; net output; work done on contracts sub-let—Ctrs	Size of firm; trade of firm; region; degree of specialization (selected years only—see Table 5.1)	GE/UK	1946, 1948, 1949, 1951–8, 1963, 1968 and annually from 1974	[QRL 50], [QRL 157], [QRL 268], [QRL 116], [QRL 269] to [QRL 277] inclusive and [QRL 353]	See Table 5.1 for full details
Gross output; net output—DL	By type of public authority	GE/UK	1946, 1948, 1949, 1951–8, 1963, 1968 and annually from 1974	[QRL 50], [QRL 157], [QRL 268], [QRL 116], [QRL 269] to [QRL 277] inclusive and [QRL 353]	See Table 5.2
Value added—Ctrs, DL		UK	Annually from 1974	[QRL 76]	
Gross output; net output; work done on contracts sub-let—Ctrs and DL		NI	Annually from 1949	[QRL 278]	
Gross output; net output—Ctrs	By size of firm in 1949, 1951 and 1954	NI	Annually from 1949 to 1954	[QRL 278]	9.2.2
Gross output; net output—DL	By type of authority	NI	Annually from 1949 to 1954	[QRL 278]	
Contribution to Gross Domestic Product					
Construction industry	By type of income generated	UK	Annually from 1948	[QRL 201]	7.1.1
Indices of Industrial Production					5.2
Construction output index		UK	Quarterly from 1948	[QRL 352], [QRL 195], [QRL 147], [QRL 148]	5.2.1.1. See [QRL 15] and [QRL 149] for estimated continuous series for the period 1948–72. *N.B.* See Section 5.2.1.1 for comment

Type of Data/ Descriptive Title	Breakdown/ Detail of Analysis	Area	Dates and Frequency	Publication (see QRL Key)	Text Reference and Remarks
OUTPUT—*contd.*					
Indices of Industrial Production—contd.					
Construction output index		GB	Quarterly from 1954	[QRL 194], [QRL 168]	5.2.1.2. See also under 'MOW-DOE' series since 1954' above
Construction output index		Scotland	Quarterly from 1948	[QRL 352], [QRL 308], [QRL 306]	5.2.1.2. *N.B.* Retrospective revisions in 1976
Construction output index		Wales	Quarterly 1963–70 Quarterly from 1970	[QRL 147] Nov. 1970 [QRL 352], [QRL 142]	5.2.1.2
Construction output index		NI	Annually from 1950 to 1957 then monthly; quarterly since 1966	[QRL 140]	9.2.4
CAPITAL AND CURRENT EXPENDITURE ON CONSTRUCTION					5.4
Fixed Capital Formation Series					
Official series					
Gross domestic fixed capital formation at current and constant prices	By type of asset (dwellings; other buildings and works; other types) by sector (public; private; institutional) and by industry	UK	1938 and annually from 1946. Quarterly from 1954	[QRL 201], [QRL 147]	5.4.2. Sectoral analyses not prepared for whole period. *Secondary sources* (generally less detailed): [QRL 195], [QRL 148], [QRL 31], [QRL 168]
Net domestic fixed capital formation at current and constant prices	Dwellings (by sector); other buildings and works; other assets by type; total assets by industry	UK	1938 and annually from 1948	[QRL 201]	

QUICK REFERENCE LIST 399

Gross domestic fixed capital formation at current prices	Government factory construction; dwellings; other buildings and works; other assets by type	NI	Annually from 1950	[QRL 140]	9.2.3.1
Gross domestic fixed capital formation at current prices	Government factory construction; dwellings; other buildings and works; other assets by sector (public; pte)	NI	Annually from 1961		

Unofficial, historical, series

Gross and net domestic fixed capital formation at current and constant prices	Dwellings; other buildings and works; other assets	UK	1920–38. Annually 1856–1965. Annually	[QRL 12]	5.4.4
Gross domestic fixed capital formation at current and constant prices	Dwellings; public buildings and works; industrial and commercial buildings; misc. transport categories	GB	1761–1860. Annual averages per decade	[QRL 13] and [QRL 14]	Official series (as above) used as post-Second World War component

Unofficial, regional, series

Gross domestic fixed capital formation	Total buildings and works; other assets	UK regions	1961	[QRL 28]	5.4.4
Gross domestic fixed capital formation	Buildings and works by industry; dwlgs; other bldgs and works by sector	Scotland	1961–71. Annually	[QRL 2]	
Gross domestic fixed capital formation	Dwellings; other bldgs and works by sector and by mfg industries	Wales	1965–8. Annually	[QRL 27]	

Capital Expenditure Survey Data–Private Sector I: Periodic Censuses and Large-scale Enquiries for Production, Distribution and Service Trades

Capital expenditure by production industries (CCP data)	New buildings; other assets by type from 1948. Acquisition of existing buildings and land from 1959	GB/UK Scot and Wales	Annually from 1948 or 1959	From 1970 in [QRL 75] (see Remarks)	5.4.5.1. For details of publication references before 1970 see Section 5.4.5.1

CAPITAL AND CURRENT EXPENDITURE ON CONSTRUCTION—contd.

Capital Expenditure Survey Data—Private Sector 1: Periodic Censuses and Large-scale Enquiries for Production, Distribution and Service Trades—contd.

Type of Data/ Descriptive Title	Breakdown/ Detail of Analysis	Area	Dates and Frequency	Publication (see QRL Key)	Text Reference and Remarks
Capital expenditure by production industries (COP data)	New buildings; other assets by type from 1948. Acquisition of existing buildings and land from 1959	English regions	1948–68 (irregular)	See Section 5.4.5.1	
Capital expenditure by production industries (COP data)	New buildings; other assets by type from 1950. Acquisition and disposal of existing buildings and land from 1963	NI	Annually from 1950 or 1963	[QRL 278]	9.2.2. Public sector only in 1950
Capital expenditure by retail, distributive and service trades	New buildings; other assets by type; acquisition and disposal of existing buildings and land (except 1957) by kind of business/form of organization	GB	{1957 1961 1966 1971}	[QRL 264] [QRL 265] Pt 14 and Supp. [QRL 266] Vol. 1 [QRL 83] Pt 13	5.4.5.1. Larger traders only in 1957
Capital expenditure by retail, services, catering and motor trades	New building; acquisition and disposal of existing buildings and land; other assets by type	NI	{1965 1975}	[QRL 267] Nyp	9.2.3.1. Voluntary enquiry in 1965
Capital expenditure by wholesale trades	New buildings; other assets by type (1959, 1965, 1974). Acquisition and disposal of existing buildings and land (1965, 1974)	GB	{1959 1965 1974}	[QRL 48] 1961, pp. 799–804 [QRL 48] 1968, pp. 238–49 [QRL 82]	5.4.5.1. Large-scale enquiries
Capital expenditure by catering trades	New buildings; other assets by type (1960, 1964, 1969). Acquisition and disposal of existing buildings and land (1969)	GB	{1960 1964 1969}	[QRL 48] 1961, pp. 1304–6 [QRL 48] 1966, pp. 1066–70 [QRL 85]	5.4.5.1. Large-scale enquiries

QUICK REFERENCE LIST

Capital expenditure by motor trades	New buildings; other assets by type. Acquisition and disposal of existing buildings and land	GB	1962 1967 1972	[QRL 48] 1964, pp. 842–6 [QRL 48] 1970, pp. 1238–41 [QRL 82]	5.4.5.1. Large-scale enquiries
Agricultural investment	By type of asset: new buildings et al.	UK regions	Annually from 1970	[QRL 252]	5.4.5.1
Capital Expenditure Survey Data–Private Sector II: Annual and Quarterly Small-scale Enquiries for Manufacturing, Distribution and Services					
Capital expenditure by manufacturing industry: at current and constant prices at constant prices s.a.	By type of asset: new building et al. by manufacturing and by distribution and services	GB	Quarterly from 1955	[QRL 195] [QRL 230] and [QRL 352]	5.4.5.1
Capital Expenditure– Public Sector					5.4.5.2. See also under 'Capital Formation'
Actual and planned expenditure at constant 'survey prices'	By programme or sub-programme and nationalized industries	GB	1970/1–1979/80. Annually	[QRL 168] No. 16	Breakdown of 1976 Public Expenditure White Paper [QRL 245]
Actual and planned expenditure at constant 'survey prices'	By programme or sub-programme and nationalized industries	GB	1971/2–1978/9 (rev.). Annually	[QRL 168] No. 21	Breakdown of 1977 White Paper [QRL 161]
Actual and planned expenditure at constant 'survey prices'	By programme or sub-programme and nationalized industries	GB and NI	1972/3–1981/2. Annually	[QRL 168] No. 23	Breakdown of 1978 White Paper [QRL 162]
Public investment in new construction	By service	UK regions Wales	1962/3–1974/5. Annually Annually	[QRL 252] [QRL 142]	
Capital expenditure by local authorities	New dwellings; other new construction assets; existing building and land; by service	England Wales	Annually from 1969/70 Annually from 1969/70	[QRL 187] [QRL 187] and [QRL 361]	
Capital expenditure by county council	'Subjective analysis' (per cent) by type of asset (new building et al.)	E & W	Annually	[QRL 84]	

Type of Data/ Descriptive Title	Breakdown/ Detail of Analysis	Area	Dates and Frequency	Publication (see QRL Key)	Text Reference and Remarks
CAPITAL AND CURRENT EXPENDITURE ON CONSTRUCTION—*contd.*					
Capital Expenditure—Public Sector—contd.					
Govt grants for industrial building	Regional development grants	GB regions	Annually	[QRL 252] and [QRL 172]	
Govt grants for industrial building	Investment and other grants	NI	Annually	[QRL 252]	
Capital Expenditure by the Construction Industry					
Gross domestic fixed capital formation at current prices	By type of asset: vehicles; plant and machinery; new buildings and works	UK	Annually	[QRL 201]	5.4.2 and 7.1.1.1. Excludes expenditure by public sector DL organizations
Gross and net domestic fixed capital formation at current and constant prices	All assets	UK	Annually	[QRL 201]	
Current Expenditure on Construction					See 5.4.6
OUTPUT, EXPENDITURE AND RELATED DATA FOR SPECIFIC TYPES OF BUILDING—DATA IN MONETARY AND PHYSICAL UNITS					
Educational building	Value by type and stage of progress and no. of places provided	E & W	Quarterly from 1946	[QRL 195], [QRL 325] Vol. 5	5.5. See also analyses of output by type of work under 'Output' above and analyses of capital expenditure by type under 'Capital Expenditure' above
Educational building	Value by type and stage of progress and no. of places provided	Scotland	Quarterly from 1946	[QRL 195], [QRL 153]	5.5.2
Educational building	Value by type and stage of progress and no. of places provided	Wales	Annually	[QRL 142]	

Topic	Description	Area	Frequency	Reference	Section
Educational building	Value by type and stage of progress and no. of places provided	NI	Annually from 1948	[QRL 151] and [QRL 140]	9.2.5
University building	Value of building starts	UK	Annually	[QRL 358]	5.5.2
Industrial building—IDC data	No. and floor area approved; started; completed	GB regions to 1972 then designated areas	Quarterly from 1945	See Remarks	5.5.3. Since 1972 summary information only published in *Ann. Repts. on Industry Act 1972* [QRL 172]. See section 5.5.3 regarding limitations in coverage and earlier publication refs
Govt factory building (NI)	No. and floor area approved; started; completed	NI	Annually from 1946	[QRL 140]	9.2.5.3
Office development—ODP data	No. and gross floor space in permits issued and floor space relinquished	Designated areas	Quarterly from 1965	[QRL 352], [QRL 134]	5.5.4
Road building	Value and mileage	GB	Annually	[QRL 354]	5.5.5
	Particulars of individual schemes	England	Annually	[QRL 288]	
	Particulars of individual schemes	Scotland	Annually	[QRL 289]	
Road building expenditure	New construction and improvement; operation and maintenance	NI	Annually	[QRL 140] and [QRL 252]	9.2.5.4
Health service buildings	Capital expenditure	E & W	Annually	[QRL 197]	
Health service buildings	Capital expenditure	E & W Hospital Regions	Mid-1948–65. Half-yearly	[QRL 198]	5.5.6. Summary data in [QRL 138] up to early 1970s
Health service buildings	Capital expenditure	Scotland	Annually	[QRL 199]	
Health service buildings	Capital expenditure	Scotland Hospital Regions	Mid-1948–62. Half-yearly	[QRL 165]	
Building Control Statistics 1966–8—Projects authorized; refused	No. and value / No. and value by type of building	GB regions / GB	1966 and quarterly from 1967 to 1968	[QRL 194] April 1967–Dec. 1968. See too [QRL 66] and [QRL 67]	4.8
Building Control Statistics 1966–8—Projects authorized; refused	No. and value in range £50,000–99,999	GB	1966–8	[QRL 66] and [QRL 67]	

FUTURE OUTPUT AND EXPENDITURE INDICATORS AND FORECASTS

Type of Data/ Descriptive Title	Breakdown/ Detail of Analysis	Area	Dates and Frequency	Publication (see QRL Key)	Text Reference and Remarks
					5.6. See also under 'Capital Expenditure—Public Sector' and 'Output, Expenditure and Related Data for Specific Types of Building,' above
Contractors' New Orders Statistics					4.5 (GB) and 9.2.1 (NI)
Values at current prices	By type of work and sector	GB	Quarterly from 1956 (Q₄)	[QRL 168] (formerly [QRL 194]), [QRL 195]	
Values at current prices	By type of work and sector	GB	Monthly from 1964	[QRL 235]	
Values at current prices	By type of work and sector	GB regions	Quarterly from 1964	[QRL 168] (formerly [QRL 194]), [QRL 252] (Annual)	
Values at current prices	By type of work and sector	Scotland	Quarterly from 1964	[QRL 306]	
Values at current prices	By type of work and sector	Wales	Quarterly from 1964	[QRL 360]	See Table 4.4 for full details of GB data and Section 9.2.1 for Northern Ireland
Values at current prices	By type of work and sector	NI	Quarterly from 1966	[QRL 140] (Q) and [QRL 168] (Annual)	
Values at constant prices	By type of work and sector	GB	Annually from 1958	[QRL 168] (formerly [QRL 194])	*N.B.* Retrospective revisions of the constant price series back to 1963 were made in 1974
Values at constant prices s.a.	By type of work and sector	GB	Quarterly from 1960	[QRL 168] (formerly [QRL 194])	
Index numbers of values at constant prices s.a.	By type of work and sector	GB	Quarterly from 1970	[QRL 168]	

QUICK REFERENCE LIST

					Remarks
Index numbers of values at constant prices s.a.	By type of work and sector	GB	Annually from 1963	[QRL 168] No. 9 et seq.	
Index numbers of values at constant prices s.a.	Total	GB	Annually from 1961 Quarterly from 1963	[QRL 168], [QRL 148] [QRL 168]	
Number and value of contracts by size	Totals and percentage distribution by value ranges by type of work and sector	GB	1966–71 (Q_2). Quarterly Annually from 1968	[QRL 194] [QRL 168]	
Orders placed by companies operating on UK Continental Shelf	Estimate of UK share of values by type	UK	Annually from 1974	[QRL 214]	5.4.3.2
Overseas contracts won by British contractors	Contracts obtained; work done; work outstanding by trading or geographical area	World	Annually from 1955	[QRL 352], [QRL 168]	4.6
Unofficial Contract Surveys (see Remarks)					5.6.4. *N.B.* Incomplete coverage of contracts. References quoted here are surveys. Trade journals also include particulars of individual contracts; the principal journals in this context are: *New Building Projects* [QRL 206]; *Tenders and Contracts Journal* [QRL 347]—UK and overseas contracts; *Building* [QRL 60]; *Construction News* [QRL 129]
Contracts awarded, out to tender, etc.	Particulars of individual projects	UK regions and Irish Republic	Fortnightly	[QRL 351]	
Public works programme	Particulars of projects by LA	UK	Annually	[QRL 344]	
Contracts awarded, out to tender, etc.	Particulars of civil eng. projects	UK and overseas	Annually to 1967	[QRL 154]	Contracts Guide Supplement

406 CONSTRUCTION AND THE RELATED PROFESSIONS

Type of Data/ Descriptive Title	Breakdown/ Detail of Analysis	Area	Dates and Frequency	Publication (see QRL Key)	Text Reference and Remarks
FUTURE OUTPUT AND EXPENDITURE INDICATORS AND FORECASTS—*contd.*					
Unofficial Contract Surveys—*contd.*					
Contracts awarded, out to tender, etc.	Nos. and value by type	GB	Monthly	[QRL 133] and [QRL 131] (summary)	
Design Work Statistics					
Local authority design work	Nos. (up to April 1975) and value of projects at working drawings stage by type carried out by or for LAs	GB	From 1965. 3 times p.a.	[QRL 168] (formerly [QRL 194])	4.7. See Table 4.5 for further details including series now discontinued and data available on request
Pte architects' design work	Value of work by type and sector in new commissions received; entering production drawings stage	GB regions UK regions	Quarterly from 1958 1964–75. Quarterly	[QRL 249]	13.5.1. Regional data are based on location of architects' offices
Investment Intentions					
Public sector (see Remarks)					5.6.2.2 See under 'Capital Expenditure—Public Sector' above
Manufacturing, distribution and service trades	Expenditure intentions—value all assets	GB	From 1955. 3 times p.a. 1958–71. 3 times p.a.	[QRL 232], [QRL 352]	Quantitative results given only for more recent years Analyses for Scotland and by industry available on request
CBI Industrial trends survey	Qualitative indication of expected expenditure authorizations by type of asset (building *et al.*)	GB	From 1972. Quarterly	[QRL 237]	
State of Trade Enquiries					
EEC state of trade enquiry for Ctrs	Level of activity; work in hand; intake of orders *et al.*	GB	Quarterly from 1977	Nyp	4.5.5
Trade association surveys:					
NFBTE state of trade enquiry	Trend in current enquiries and expected work volume	GB	Quarterly from early 1960s	[QRL 234]	5.6.3.2
HBF state of trade enquiry	Level of demand for housing *et al.*	GB	Quarterly	[QRL 231]	5.6.3.3
FCEC civil eng. trends survey	State of order book; invitations to tender, etc.	UK	Quarterly from 1977	Publication under consideration	5.6.3.4

HVCA state of trade enquiry	Trend in orders volume; anticipated output et al.	UK	Bi-annual from 1975	[QRL 210]	5.6.3.5
NFBPM builders' merchants index	Index of turnover/sales by class of trade	UK	Monthly		Available on subscription at discretion—see Section 5.6.3.6
NFBPM business confidence survey	Trends in trade for building materials	UK	Quarterly		Available on subscription at discretion—see Section 5.6.3.6
Construction Forecasts					
NEDO forecasts	By type of work and sector	GB	Bi-annual from 1972	[QRL 128]	5.6.5 See Section 5.6.5.1 for details of pre-1972 forecasts
BMF forecasts	By type of work and sector	GB	From 1956. 2/3 times p.a.	[QRL 46]	5.6.5.2
NIESR construction forecasts		GB	Bi-annual	[QRL 204]	5.6.5.2

EMPLOYMENT STATISTICS I—MOW–DOE AND EQUIVALENT N. IRELAND DEPARTMENTS

MOW Time Series 1941–5					
Contractors	Operatives by type of work; clerical and admin. employees	GE	Sept. 1941–Nov. 1945. Monthly	[QRL 318], [QRL 321]	3.9.2. See Table 3.8 for further details of series
Employment on licensed, authorized and direct govt projects	Operatives by type of work and govt dept	GE regions	Sept. 1941–Aug. 1945. Monthly	[QRL 318], [QRL 321]	3.7.4
Employment on licensed, authorized and direct govt projects	Operatives by govt dept	GB	July 1941–July 1945. Monthly	[QRL 319], [QRL 321]	[QRL 321] Also reproduced in Kohan [B 90]
Employment on licensed, authorized and direct govt projects	Operatives on DAA/civil (Govt/pte) work by govt dept	GB	Jan. 1946–Mar. 1950. Monthly	[QRL 194], [QRL 321]	3.7.4.2
MOW Time Series 1945–55					
Contractors in 'main trades'	Operatives by type of work	GB	Jan. 1945–Jan. 1955. Monthly	[QRL 194], [QRL 195], [QRL 321]	3.9.3. See Table 3.9 for further details of series
MOW–DOE and Equivalent Northern Ireland Depts, Time Series Since 1955					
Operatives employed by Ctrs	Total	GB	1955–77. Monthly	[QRL 236], [QRL 168]	4.4
	Total s.a.	GB	1958–77. Monthly	[QRL 168]	
Operatives employed by Ctrs	By type of work	GB	Quarterly from 1955	[QRL 195], [QRL 168] (formerly [QRL 194])	

Type of Data/ Descriptive Title	Breakdown/ Detail of Analysis	Area	Dates and Frequency	Publication (see QRL Key)	Text Reference and Remarks
EMPLOYMENT STATISTICS I—MOW–DOE AND EQUIVALENT N. IRELAND DEPARTMENTS—*contd.*					
MOW–DOE and Equivalent N. Ireland Depts, Time Series Since 1955—*contd.*					
Operatives employed by Ctrs	By type of work	NI	Quarterly from 1966	[QRL 140] from 1976 (Q$_3$). [QRL 168] (2 qtrs p.a.)	9.3.3
Employees in employment—Ctrs and DL (see Remarks)	Total (actual; s.a.)—operatives and APTC staff	GB	Monthly from 1971–7 and monthly avs. back to 1967	[QRL 168]	4.4. *N.B.* Not the same as the DE series of 'employees in employment'
Operatives employed by DL	On housing (new; R & M) by all DL forces	GB	1962–71. One month p.a.	[QRL 169] No. 6 *et seq.*	4.4
Operatives employed by LAs' DL	On new housing	E & W	1961–6. Quarterly	[QRL 169] No. 2 *et seq.*	4.4
MOW–DOE Census Analyses for Contractors 1941–54					3.3
MOW census analyses for contractors, 1941–4					
Operatives—main trades of Ctrs	By occupation; trade and size of firm; type of work	GB	1941–4 various dates	[QRL 321]	For full details, including cross-classification available, see Table 3.1. Some analyses were published in [QRL 320] (Table 3.1 refers). [QRL 321] includes these and other hitherto unpublished data
Operatives—main trades of Ctrs	By occupation and type of work	GB regions	1943, 1944	[QRL 321]	
Clerical and admin.—main trades of Ctrs	By trade and size of firm	GB	1941–4 various dates	[QRL 321]	
Clerical and admin.—main trades of Ctrs	Total	GB regions	1943, 1944	[QRL 321]	
Operatives—specialist trades of Ctrs	By occupation	GB	1942, 1944	[QRL 321]	

QUICK REFERENCE LIST

MOW census analyses for contractors (main trades), 1945–54					3.5
Operatives	By occupation, trade and size of firm; type of work	GB	1945–54 various dates	[QRL 321]	See Table 3.2 for full details. Data were published piecemeal in a variety of publications (Table 3.2 refers); the *MOW Collection* [QRL 321] includes these and hitherto unpublished statistics
Operatives	On-site and off-site by type of work	GB regions	Feb. 1948	[QRL 321]	
Apprentices	By craft	GB	Aug. 1949	[QRL 37], [QRL 321]	
			May 1950	[QRL 38], [QRL 321]	
Clerical and amin.—main	Males by size and trade of firm	GB regions	Nov. 1945	[QRL 321]	
Working Principals	By craft	GB	Nov. 1945, Feb. 1946	[QRL 321]	
MOW census analyses for contractors (specialist trades), 1945–54					3.5
Operatives	By occupation; trade and size of firm; type of work	GB	1945–54 various dates	[QRL 321]	See Table 3.3 for full details. Few statistics were published before the preparation of the *MOW Collection* [QRL 321]—relevant references are given in Table 3.3
		GB regions	1946–54 various dates	[QRL 321]	
Apprentices	By craft	GB	Aug. 1949	[QRL 37], [QRL 321]	
			May 1950	[QRL 38], [QRL 321]	
MOW census analyses for contractors (main trades and specialist trades combined), 1945–54					3.5
Operatives	By craft	GB	Aug. 1949–May 1954. Annually	[QRL 71] Sept. 1963 *et seq.*	
Apprentices	By craft	GB	Aug. 1949–May 1954. Annually	[QRL 71] Sept. 1963 *et seq.*	
Apprentices	By type of agreement	GB	Aug. 1949–Sept. 1955. Annually	[QRL 64]	
Working Principals	Total	GB	May 1950–May 1954. Annually	[QRL 195]	

410 CONSTRUCTION AND THE RELATED PROFESSIONS

EMPLOYMENT STATISTICS I—MOW–DOE AND EQUIVALENT N. IRELAND DEPARTMENTS—contd.

Type of Data/ Descriptive Title	Breakdown/ Detail of Analysis	Area	Dates and Frequency	Publication (see QRL Key)	Text Reference and Remarks
MOW Census Analyses for Direct Labour Organizations, 1944–54					3.6
Local authorities' DL, 1944–54					3.6
Operatives	By occupation (craft)	GB	1944–54 various dates	[QRL 321]	
Operatives	By type of work	GB regions	1946–54 various dates	[QRL 321]	
Operatives	By type of work and by craft; type of authority; size of DL force	GB	1944–54 various dates	[QRL 321]	See Table 3.4 for full details. Most of the data now included in [QRL 321] remained unpublished but relevant references to other publications are given in Table 3.4
Apprentices	By craft	GB	Aug. 1949	[QRL 37], [QRL 321]	
			May 1950	[QRL 38], [QRL 321]	
Public utilities' DL, 1944–54					
Operatives	By occupation (craft)	GB	1944–54 various dates	[QRL 321]	
Operatives	By type of work	GB regions	1946–8, 1954 various dates	[QRL 321]	
Operatives	By type of work, by craft; by type of authority	GB	1944–54 various dates	[QRL 321]	
Apprentices	By craft	GB	Aug. 1949	[QRL 37], [QRL 321]	
			May 1950	[QRL 38], [QRL 321]	

Govt Depts' DL, 1950–4					
Operatives	Total	GB	1950–4. Annually	[QRL 195]	3.6 Included as footnote to contractors' employment tables
MOW–DOE Census Analyses for Contractors Since 1954					4.2. See Table 4.1 for full details particularly regarding cross-classifications and supplementary analyses. Summary historical series (no cross-classifications) were included in *ABCS* [QRL 32] to 1970 then in *HCS* [QRL 168]
Operatives	Total	GB regions	April 1956	[QRL 321]	
Operatives	By size and trade of firm	GB	April 1956	[QRL 321]	
Operatives	By size and trade of firm	GB regions	Bi-annually from 1957 to 1970 (1957–70)	[QRL 71]	
			Annually from 1971	[QRL 240]	
Operatives	By size and trade of firm and type of work	GB	Annually from 1957	[QRL 71] and [QRL 240]—as above	
Operatives	By type of work	GB regions	Annually from 1957	[QRL 71] and [QRL 240]—as above	
Operatives	By craft: by size and by trade of firm	GB	Annually from 1957	[QRL 71] and [QRL 240]—as above	
Operatives	By craft	GB regions	Annually from 1957	[QRL 71] and [QRL 240]—as above	
Apprentices (Trainees)	By craft (occupation)	GB	Annually from 1957	[QRL 71] and [QRL 240]—as above	Coverage widened to 'trainee' from 1975
Apprentices (Trainees)	By trade and size of firm	GB regions	Annually from 1963	[QRL 71] and [QRL 240]—as above	
Apprentices (Trainees)	By craft: by size and by trade of firm	GB regions	Annually from 1963	[QRL 71] and [QRL 240]—as above	

EMPLOYMENT STATISTICS 1—MOW–DOE AND EQUIVALENT N. IRELAND DEPARTMENTS—*contd.*

MOW–DOE Census Analyses for Contractors Since 1954—*contd.*

Type of Data/ Descriptive Title	Breakdown/ Detail of Analysis	Area	Dates and Frequency	Publication (see QRL Key)	Text Reference and Remarks
Apprentices (Trainees)	By craft and type of agreement	GB	Annually from 1957 to 1974	See Remarks	Available on request from DOE, Statistics Construction Division; at one time published in *Press Notices* [QRL 230]. Data for the period 1957–68 reproduced in *BRS Collection* [QRL 121].
APTC staff	Total	GB regions	Annually 1963–4; bi-annually 1965–70; annually from 1971	[QRL 71] to 1970; [QRL 240] from 1971	4.2 See Table 4.1 for full details
APTC staff	By trade and size of firm	GB	Annually 1963–4; bi-annually 1965–70; annually from 1971	[QRL 71] to 1970; [QRL 240] from 1971	
APTC staff	By trade and size of firm	GB regions	Annually from 1965	[QRL 71] to 1970; [QRL 240] from 1971	
APTC staff	By type of APTC staff	GB regions	Annually from 1965	[QRL 71] to 1970; [QRL 240] from 1971	
APTC staff	By type of APTC staff: by size and trade of firm	GB	Annually from 1965	[QRL 71] to 1970; [QRL 240] from 1971	
APTC staff under training	By size and trade of firm	GB regions	Annually 1965–9	[QRL 71]	
APTC staff under training	By type of APTC staff	GB regions	Annually 1965–9	[QRL 71]	
APTC staff under training	By type of APTC staff: by size and trade of firm	GB regions	Annually 1965–9	[QRL 71]	

QUICK REFERENCE LIST 413

Working Principals (Proprietors)	Total	GB regions	Annually, 1963–4, bi-annually 1965–70, then annually from 1971	[QRL 71] to 1970; [QRL 240] from 1971	4.2. Series (GB) back to 1959 were included in [B 307]
Working Principals (Proprietors)	By size and trade of firm	GB	Annually, 1963–4, bi-annually 1965–70, then annually from 1971	[QRL 71] to 1970; [QRL 240] from 1971	
Total employment	Total	GB regions	Annually, 1963–4, bi-annually 1965–70, then annually from 1971	[QRL 71] to 1970; [QRL 240] from 1971	4.2 See Table 4.1 for full details
Total employment	By size and trade of firm	GB	Annually, 1963–4, bi-annually 1965–70, then annually from 1971	[QRL 71] to 1970; [QRL 240] from 1971	
MOW–DOE Census Analyses for Local Authorities' Direct Labour Since 1954					4.3
Operatives	By type of work	GB regions	April 1956	[QRL 321]	
Operatives	By type of work by type of LA and size of labour force	GB	April 1956	[QRL 321]	
Operatives	By type of work	GB regions	Bi-annually 1961–70	[QRL 194]	
Operatives	By type of work	GB regions	Annually from 1971	[QRL 168]	See Table 4.2 for full details
Operatives	By type of work by type of LA	GB	Bi-annually 1961–70	[QRL 194]	
Operatives	By type of work by type of LA	GB	Annually from 1971	[QRL 168]	
Operatives	By type of work by size of labour force	GB	Bi-annually 1969–70 Annually from 1968	[QRL 194] to 1970, then [QRL 168]	

EMPLOYMENT STATISTICS I—MOW–DOE AND EQUIVALENT N. IRELAND DEPARTMENTS—contd.

MOW–DOE Census Analyses for Local Authorities' Direct Labour Since 1954—contd.

Type of Data/Descriptive Title	Breakdown/Detail of Analysis	Area	Dates and Frequency	Publication (see QRL Key)	Text Reference and Remarks
Operatives	By craft and type of LA	GB	Annually from 1968	[QRL 194] to 1970, then [QRL 168]	4.3. Occupational analyses back to 1957 are available on request from DOE Statistics Construction Division
Apprentices (Trainees)	By craft and type of LA	GB	Annually from 1968	[QRL 194] to 1970, then [QRL 168]	
APTC staff	By type of APTC staff and type of authority	GB	Annually from 1968	[QRL 194] to 1970, then [QRL 168]	4.3

EMPLOYMENT STATISTICS II—MOL–DE AND OTHER GENERAL SOURCES

MOL–DE and Equivalent N. Ireland Departments, Principal Series, 1948–71

Type of Data/Descriptive Title	Breakdown/Detail of Analysis	Area	Dates and Frequency	Publication (see QRL Key)	Text Reference and Remarks
Numbers in employment		GB	Mid-1948–Nov. 1965. Monthly	[QRL 190]	6.2 and 9.3.2 (NI) Employees plus est. self-employed. *Secondary sources*: *MDS* [QRL 195], *AAS* [QRL 31] (A)
Numbers in employment		NI	1948–74. Annually Dec. 1957–Jun. 1971. Quarterly	[QRL 140]	Continued to June 1974 on the basis of information about the self-employed from card counts
Employees (employed plus unemployed)	By sex	GB and UK	Mid-1948–71. Annually	[QRL 190], then [QRL 135], [QRL 58], [QRL 59]	
Employees (employed plus unemployed)	By sex	GB	Mid-1948–Nov. 1965. Monthly	[QRL 190]	

QUICK REFERENCE LIST 415

Employees (employed plus unemployed)	By sex and two age-groups (under/over 18)	GB and UK	Mid-1948–71. Annually	[QRL 190], then [QRL 135]	UK coverage in later part of series
Employees (employed plus unemployed)	By sex and age-group	GB and UK	1950–71. Annually	[QRL 190], then [QRL 135]	
Employees (employed plus unemployed)	Totals	GB regions	1959–71. Annually	[QRL 190], then [QRL 135]	UK and GB totals in [QRL 31]
Employees (employed plus unemployed)	Totals	Scotland	1948–71. Annually	[QRL 139], [QRL 306]	
Employees (employed plus unemployed)	Totals	Wales	1948–71. Annually	[QRL 142]	
Employees (employed plus unemployed)	Totals	NI	1950–71. Annually	[QRL 140], [QRL 59]	} 9.3.2.
Employees (employed plus unemployed)	Totals	NI	Dec. 1957–Jun. 1971. Quarterly	[QRL 140]	
Employees in employment	By sex	UK and GB	Mid-1948–71. Annually	[QRL 190], then [QRL 135], [QRL 58], [QRL 59]	6.2
Employees in employment	By sex	GB	Mid-1948–71. Monthly	[QRL 190], then [QRL 135]	6.2
Employees in employment	Total	GB regions	1966–71. Annually	[QRL 190], then [QRL 135]	6.2
Employees in employment	By sex	NI	1949–71. Annually	[QRL 140]. [QRL 190] from 1967	} 9.3.2
Employees in employment	By sex	NI	Dec. 1957–Jun. 1971. Quarterly		

MOL–DE and Equivalent N. Ireland Departments' Principal Series from 1971

Employees in employment	Full-time; part-time each by sex	GB/UK	Annually from 1971	[QRL 135], [QRL 59]	6.2 and 9.3.2 (NI)
Employees in employment	Males (total); Females (total; part-time)	GB	Quarterly from Sept. 1974	[QRL 135]	*Principal secondary sources*: [QRL 195] (GB and UK series, monthly); [QRL 31] (annually)
Employees in employment	By sex	GB	Monthly from Jun. 1971	[QRL 135]	
Employees in employment	By sex	UK regions	Annually from 1971	[QRL 135], [QRL 252]	

EMPLOYMENT STATISTICS II—MOL–DE AND OTHER GENERAL SOURCES—contd.

Type of Data/ Descriptive Title	Breakdown/ Detail of Analysis	Area	Dates and Frequency	Publication (see QRL Key)	Text Reference and Remarks
MOL–DE and Equivalent N. Ireland Departments' Principal Series From 1971—contd.					
Employees in employment	Total; males	Scottish regions	Annually from 1971	[QRL 306]	
Employees in employment	By sex	Wales	Annually from 1971	[QRL 142], [QRL 360]	
Employees in employment	By sex	NI	Annually from 1971	[QRL 140], [QRL 59]	9.3.2
Employees in employment	By sex	GB regions	Quarterly from 1971	[QRL 135]	
MOL–DE and Equivalent N. Ireland Departments' Estimated Continuous Series from 1959					6.2.3.3
Employees in employment	By sex	GB	1959–73. Annually	[QRL 135] March 1975	
Employees in employment	By sex	UK	1959–74. Annually	[QRL 135] Oct. 1975	
Employees in employment	By sex	UK regions	1965–75. Annually	[QRL 135] Aug. 1976	
Employers and self-employed	By sex	GB	1961–75. Annually	[QRL 135] Dec. 1976 and Jun. 1977	Estimates based on various sources
MOL–DE and Equivalent N. Ireland Departments' Subsidiary Employment Series					6.2.3.4 and 9.3.2.2 (NI). Certain series compiled by the DOE or CSO are also listed here since they represent either continuations of former MOL–DE series or series based largely on MOL–DE data

QUICK REFERENCE LIST 417

Topic	Breakdown	Area	Period	Source	Notes
Young persons entering employment	By sex and class of employment (apprenticeship *et al.*)	GB	1951–74. Annually	[ORL 135], former [ORL 190]; [QRL 58]	
Young persons entering employment	By sex and class of employment (apprenticeship *et al.*)	GB-regions	1958–74. Annually	[ORL 135], former [ORL 190]	
Young persons entering employment	By sex and class of employment (apprenticeship *et al.*)	Scotland	1958–74. Annually	[ORL 306]	
Young persons entering employment	By sex and class of employment (apprenticeship *et al.*)	Wales	1958–74. Annually	[ORL 142]	
Young persons entering employment	By sex and class of employment (apprenticeship *et al.*)	NI	1954–74. Annually	[ORL 140]	Recent years only in [QRL 140]; complete series available on request from Dept. of Manpower Services, N. Ireland 6.2.3.4. Replaced in 1975 by 'Joint Manpower Watch' surveys—see below. See also DOE Censuses of local authorities' DL above
Employees in employment with local authorities by industry	Full-time; part-time; each by sex	GB countries	1952–74. Annually	[ORL 135] and former [ORL 190]; [QRL 59]	
Employees in employment with local authorities by industry	Full-time; part-time	Wales	1952–74. Annually	[ORL 142]	
Employees in employment with local authorities by industry	Full-time; part-time; full-time equivalents	England	Quarterly from 1975	[ORL 233], [QRL 135], [QRL 195]	'Joint Manpower Watch' surveys conducted for DOE by local associations for E & W and for Scotland
Employees in employment with local authorities by industry	Full-time; part-time; full-time equivalents	Wales	Quarterly from 1975	[ORL 233], [QRL 135], [QRL 195]	
Employees in employment with local authorities by industry	Full-time; part-time; full-time equivalents	Scotland	Quarterly from 1976	[ORL 135], [QRL 306]	
Employees in employment with local authorities by industry	Full-time equivalents—manual; non-manual	Wales	Quarterly from 1976	[QRL 361]	
Employees in employment with local authorities by industry	Full-time; part-time	Wales	Annually from 1976	[ORL 142]	

418   CONSTRUCTION AND THE RELATED PROFESSIONS

Type of Data/ Descriptive Title	Breakdown/ Detail of Analysis	Area	Dates and Frequency	Publication (see QRL Key)	Text Reference and Remarks
EMPLOYMENT STATISTICS II—MOL–DE AND OTHER GENERAL SOURCES—*contd.*					
MOL–DE and Equivalent N. Ireland Departments' Subsidiary Employment Series—*contd.*					
Employees in employment by sector	Central govt; local auths; public corporations; pte. sector each by activity (construction *et al.*)	UK	Annually from 1959	[QRL 147]	Annual estimates presented by CSO in articles on 'Employment in the public and private sectors of the UK economy'
Census of Production Employment Data					5.3 and 9.2.2 (NI) *N.B.* Full details of the data for GB or UK are set out in Table 5.1 for Ctrs. Data refer to average numbers employed during the year of return
Employment by Ctrs	Operatives; other employees; total (incl. WPs)	GB	1946 and 1948	See Table 5.1	
Employment by Ctrs	Operatives; other employees; total (incl. WPs)	UK	1949, 1951, 1954, 1958, 1963, 1968, 1969	See Table 5.1	
Employment by Ctrs	Operatives; other employees; total (incl. WPs)	NI	Annually from 1949	[QRL 278]	9.2.2
Employment by Ctrs	Persons employed by region, size of firm, trade of firm	GB/UK	Various dates	See Table 5.1	5.3
Employment by Ctrs	Persons employed by size of firm; county	NI	1951, 1954, 1958, 1963, 1968	[QRL 278]	9.2.2
Employment by DL organizations	Operatives; other employees by type of org.	GB/UK	Various dates and coverage from 1946 to date—see Table 5.2 for details		
Employment by DL organizations	Operatives; other employees by type of org.	NI	1949–54	[QRL 278]	9.2.2
Employment by Ctrs and DL combined	Operatives; other employees; total (incl. WPs)	UK	1952, 1953, 1955–7	See Table 5.1	5.3
Employment by Ctrs and DL combined	Operatives; other employees; total (incl. WPs)	NI	Annually from 1949	[QRL 278]	9.2.2

QUICK REFERENCE LIST

Construction Industry Training Boards (GB and NI) Employment Data

Employees	Total; trainees; self-employed labour-only workers	GB	Bi-annually	[QRL 255]	6.4 (GB) and 9.3.6 (NI) CITB Levy return data. Data from 'Regional Manpower Surveys' of NFBTE members in London, Midland and Northern regions in early 1970s were published in [QRL 188] and [QRL 211]—see Section 6.4.4 for details of these and other *ad hoc* surveys
Employees	Nos. by occupational group and percentage distribution by type of work. Apprentices by trade and year of apprenticeship	NI	Annually	[QRL 254]	9.3.6

Census of Population Employment Data

	Analyses are generally made according to a variety of characteristics: sex, employment status, social class, socio-economic group, age, marital condition, nationality, etc.; we do not repeat these therefore for each reference listed here	See Remarks			6.3 (GB) and 9.3.5 (NI) Analyses are prepared for regions and local areas in considerable detail; these too are not all listed here. The reports cited below generally contain regional sub-divisions of the principal occupational and industrial data. Reference may also be made to separate reports for each county which is not listed in this Review
Industrial and occupational analyses	See note above	E & W	1951	[QRL 88] and [QRL 90]	See note above
Industrial and occupational analyses	See note above	Scotland	1951	[QRL 103]	See note above
Industrial and occupational analyses	See note above	NI	1951	[QRL 113]	See note above

420 CONSTRUCTION AND THE RELATED PROFESSIONS

Type of Data/ Descriptive Title	Breakdown/ Detail of Analysis	Area	Dates and Frequency	Publication (see QRL Key)	Text Reference and Remarks
EMPLOYMENT STATISTICS II—MOL–DE AND OTHER GENERAL SOURCES—*contd.*					
Census of Population Employment Data—*contd.*					
Industrial and occupational analyses	See note above	E & W	1961	[QRL 89] and [QRL 91]	See note above
Industrial and occupational analyses	See note above	Scotland	1961	[QRL 104]	See note above
Industrial and occupational analyses	See note above	NI	1961	[QRL 110]	See note above
Industrial and occupational analyses	See note above	GB	1966	[QRL 295]	See note above
Industrial and occupational analyses	See note above	Scotland	1966	[QRL 298]	See note above
Industrial and occupational analyses (see Remarks)	See note above	NI	1966	[QRL 111]	Occupational data not collected
Industrial and occupational analyses	See note above	GB	1971	[QRL 94]	See main note above
Industrial and occupational analyses	See note above	Scotland	1971	[QRL 100]	See main note above
Industrial and occupational analyses	See note above	NI	1971	[QRL 108]	See main note above
Labour migration analyses	By industry and occupation	GB	1961	[QRL 95]	See main note above
Labour migration analyses	By industry and occupation	Scotland	1961	[QRL 101]	See main note above
Labour migration analyses	By industry and occupation	E & W	1966	[QRL 293] and [QRL 292]	See main note above
Labour migration analyses	By industry and occupation	Scotland	1966	[QRL 299]	See main note above
Labour migration analyses	By industry and occupation	GB	1971	[QRL 96]	See main note above
Labour migration analyses	By industry and occupation	Scotland	1971	[QRL 102]	See main note above
Labour migration analyses	By industry and occupation	NI	1971	[QRL 112]	See main note above
Workplace and transport to work analyses	By industry and occupation	E & W	1961	[QRL 92]	See main note above
Workplace and transport to work analyses	By industry and occupation	Scotland	1961	[QRL 104]	See main note above
Workplace and transport to work analyses	By industry and occupation	E & W	1966	[QRL 294]	See main note above
Workplace and transport to work analyses	By industry and occupation	Scotland	1966	[QRL 300]	See main note above

QUICK REFERENCE LIST 421

Workplace and transport to work analyses	By industry and occupation	E & W	1971	[QRL 93]	See main note above
Workplace and transport to work analyses	By industry and occupation	Scotland	1971	[QRL 106]	See main note above
Workplace and transport to work analyses	By industry and occupation	NI	1971	[QRL 114]	See main note above
Educational analyses (see Remarks)	Terminal education age by occupation	E & W	1951	[QRL 87]	For qualified manpower analyses from censuses of population and other sources see under 'Qualified Manpower' below
Educational analyses (see Remarks)	Terminal education age by occupation	Scotland	1951	[QRL 103]	
Educational analyses (see Remarks)	Terminal education age by occupation	E & W	1961	[QRL 86]	
Educational analyses (see Remarks)	Terminal education age by occupation	Scotland	1961	[QRL 105]	
Educational analyses (see Remarks)	Terminal education age by occupation	NI	1961	[QRL 110]	

EMPLOYMENT STATISTICS III—QUALIFIED MANPOWER
Census of Population Data

6.6
6.6.3.2

Persons with scientific and technological qualifications	By occupation; industry; subject and type of qualification	GB	1961	[QRL 98]	
Persons with scientific and technological qualifications	By occupation; industry; subject and type of qualification	NI	1961	[QRL 110]	
Persons with scientific and technological qualifications	By occupation; industry; subject and type of qualification	GB	1966	[QRL 297]	
Persons with scientific and technological qualifications	By occupation; industry; subject and type of qualification	GB	1971	[QRL 225]	
All qualified persons	By occupation; industry; subject group; level of qualification, etc.	GB	1966	[QRL 296]	[QRL 246] provides summary information and general commentary
All qualified persons	By occupation; industry; subject group; level of qualification, etc.	GB	1971	[QRL 97]	[QRL 247] provides summary information and general commentary
All qualified persons	By occupation; industry; subject group; level of qualification, etc.	NI	1971	[QRL 109]	

Type of Data/ Descriptive Title	Breakdown/ Detail of Analysis	Area	Dates and Frequency	Publication (see QRL Key)	Text Reference and Remarks
EMPLOYMENT STATISTICS III–QUALIFIED MANPOWER—contd.					
Triennial Sample Surveys 1956–68					6.6.3.1
Scientific and engineering manpower employed by Ctrs	By field of employment; type of work or function; subject of qualification	GB	1956	[QRL 302]	
Scientific and engineering manpower employed by Ctrs	By field of employment; type of work or function; subject of qualification	GB	1959	[QRL 303]	*N.B.* See Section 6.6.3.1 regarding definitions. Technicians and technical supporting staff also covered in 1965 and 1968
Scientific and engineering manpower employed by Ctrs	By field of employment; type of work or function; subject of qualification	GB	1962	[QRL 304]	
Scientific and engineering manpower employed by Ctrs	By field of employment; type of work or function; subject of qualification	GB	1965	[QRL 281]	
Scientific and engineering manpower employed by Ctrs	By field of employment; type of work or function; subject of qualification	GB	1968	[QRL 224]	
DOE Censuses of Ctrs and DL Organizations					6.6.3.3
Architects; surveyors; engineers	By Ctrs by trade and size of firm	GB regions	1965–70. Annually	[QRL 71]	
Architects; surveyors; engineers	By Ctrs by trade and size of firm	GB regions	1971–4. Annually	[QRL 240]	
Professional staff	By Ctrs by trade and size of firm	GB regions	Annually from 1975	[QRL 240]	
Architects; surveyors; engineers	By local authorities' DL undertakings by type of authority	GB	1968–70. Annually	[QRL 194]	
			Annually from 1971	[QRL 168]	

Institute of Building Statistics					
Membership	List of members	n/a	Annually	[QRL 364]	6.6.2
Home membership surveys	Analyses by size of firm; functions performed; fields of employment	UK	{1966 1975	[QRL 364] [QRL 338]	
New Supply of Qualified Manpower					
Numbers	By subject of qualification	UK	1958–74. Annually	[QRL 147] No. 269, 1976, pp. 98–123	6.6.3.5
First destination of University graduates	By subject and sector of employment	UK	Annually from 1961	[QRL 160]	See also [QRL 281], [QRL 328], [QRL 329], [QRL 330]
First destination of Polytechnic first degree and HND students	By subject and sector of employment	UK	Annually from 1975	[QRL 226]	

LABOUR STATISTICS OTHER THAN EMPLOYMENT, WAGE RATES, EARNINGS, HOURS OF WORK AND LABOUR COSTS

Labour Training Statistics

					6.5. Relevant information is also contained in a number of *ad hoc* enquiries—see Section 6.7
Apprentices employed by Ctrs and DL	By craft; type of agreement; size and trade of firm	GB	1949–74. Annually	See Remarks	6.5.3. Collected in MOW–DOE censuses—see above under 'MOW–DOE Censuses of Ctrs and DL Organizations since 1954'
Apprentices intake	By craft	GB	1949–55. Annually	See Remarks	
Young persons entering employment	By sex and class of employment (apprenticeship *et al.*)	GB see Remarks)	1951–74. Annually	[QRL 135], former [QRL 190] and [QRL 59]	6.2.3.4. References for NI, Scotland, Wales and English regions are listed under 'MOL–DE Subsidiary Employment Series'
Trainees employed (DOE censuses) by Ctrs and DL	By occupation by size and trade of firm	GB	Annually from 1975	[QRL 240]	6.5.3
Trainees employed (CITB (GB) levy returns)	Nos by occupation	GB	Bi-annually	[QRL 255]	6.4.1
Trainees employed (CITB (NI))	Nos by occupation and year of apprenticeship	NI	Annually	[QRL 254]	9.3.6

LABOUR STATISTICS OTHER THAN EMPLOYMENT, WAGE RATES, EARNINGS, HOURS OF WORK AND LABOUR COSTS—*contd.*

Type of Data/ Descriptive Title	Breakdown/ Detail of Analysis	Area	Dates and Frequency	Publication (see QRL Key)	Text Reference and Remarks
Labour Training Statistics—*contd.*					
Apprentices registered	By craft	GB regions	Nov. 1945–Jun. 1955 (see Remarks)	[QRL 62], [QRL 63], [QRL 64]	6.5.2. Statistics from 1955 are available on request from the registration bodies in E & W and Scotland—see Section 6.5.1
CITB (GB) trainees	No. of courses; trainees; trainee-days by type of training	GB	Annually	[QRL 255]	6.4.3
CITB (NI) trainees	Nos at CITB (NI) centres	NI / GB	Annually 1959–70. Annually 1966–72 (Q_1).	[QRL 254] [QRL 32] 1970	9.4.1 6.5.4
Govt Training Centre trainees	Nos completing training by craft	GB	Quarterly	[QRL 194]	
CITB (GB) grant and levy payments	By main activity of firm	GB	Annually	[QRL 255]	6.4.5
Education Statistics					
Nos. following courses (official data)	Full-time; part-time; by type of qualification	E & W Scotland NI	Annually Annually Annually	[QRL 325] [QRL 309] [QRL 151]	6.5.5 Summary data for UK in [QRL 153]
	Nos released by construction employers to follow part-time day courses				
	Entries and successes in examinations by subject and type of qualification				
IOB surveys	Nos by type of course and year (see Remarks)	E & W Scotland Ireland	Annually from 1966/7	[QRL 69]	6.5.5.2. Degree and general building courses
SAAT surveys	Nos on building ONC and HNC courses	UK	Annually from 1967	[QRL 150]	6.5.5.2
ILEA technician student survey	Characteristics of technician students—see Section 6.5.5.2 for details	London	1975	[QRL 24]	6.5.5.2

Unemployment, Vacancies and Placings

Unemployment—analyses by industry	Nos by sex	GB and UK	Monthly to June 1976, then quarterly	[QRL 135] and former [QRL 190]	6.8.1 *Secondary sources:* [QRL 59] and [QRL 168]. [QRL 58] gives quarterly figs from 1948 to 1968
Unemployment—analyses by industry	Nos by sex s.a.	GB and UK	Monthly to June 1976, then quarterly	[QRL 135] and former [QRL 190]	[QRL 195] (GB total series)
Unemployment—analyses by industry	Nos	GB regions	Monthly to June 1976, then quarterly	[QRL 168] and former [QRL 194]	[QRL 252] gives figs for one month each year
Unemployment—analyses by industry	Nos by sex	GB regions	Two months p.a.	[QRL 59]	
Unemployment—analyses by industry	Nos by sex	Wales	Two months p.a.	[QRL 142]	By statistical sub-divisions of Wales
Unemployment—analyses by industry	Nos by sex	Scotland	Quarterly	[QRL 306]	Ann. averages by sex
Unemployment—analyses by industry	Nos	NI	Monthly	[QRL 140]	
Unemployment—analyses by industry	By craft (see Remarks)	GB	Monthly from 1948	[QRL 168] and former [QRL 194]	Analyses prepared specially for the DOE. Confined to workers who last worked in the construction industry, unlike the occupational analyses below which refer to occupation in which seeking employment
Unemployment—analyses by industry	Men (aged 18 and over) by craft	GB regions	Monthly to April 1972	[QRL 194]	
Unemployment—analyses by industry	Percentage rate	GB	Quarterly from 1973	[QRL 135] May 1976 *et seq.*	[QRL 195] reproduces series, at first monthly, from July 1975
Unemployment—analyses by occupation	Adults by sex	GB	Quarterly from May 1958	[QRL 135] and former [QRL 190]	Cf. analysis by craft above. Occupational analyses of the unemployed are also available in Census of Population reports for 1951, 1961, 1966 and 1971—see Section 6.8.1.2
Unemployment—analyses by occupation	Adults by sex	GB regions	Quarterly from Sept. 1963	[QRL 135] and former [QRL 190]	

LABOUR STATISTICS OTHER THAN EMPLOYMENT, WAGE RATES, EARNINGS, HOURS OF WORK AND LABOUR COSTS—contd.

Type of Data/ Descriptive Title	Breakdown/ Detail of Analysis	Area	Dates and Frequency	Publication (see QRL Key)	Text Reference and Remarks
Unemployment, Vacancies and Placings—contd.					
Characteristics of unemployed skilled construction workers	Age; duration; skill; employment prospects; mobility; training, etc.	GB	June 1964	[QRL 190] Vol. 73, 1965 pp. 483–6	6.8.1.1
Temporarily stopped workers claiming benefits	By sex	GB	Quarterly	[QRL 135] and former [QRL 190]	6.8.1.1
Notified vacancies remaining unfilled by industry	By sex; at employment offices; careers offices	GB	Monthly to June 1976, then quarterly	[QRL 135] and former [QRL 190]	6.8.2. Quarterly series included in [QRL 59]
Notified vacancies remaining unfilled by industry	Males and total	UK regions	Two months p.a. from 1969	[QRL 59]	
Notified vacancies remaining unfilled by industry	Males aged 18 and over	GB regions	Two months p.a. from 1949–70	[QRL 32]	
Notified vacancies remaining unfilled by industry	Males aged 18 and over by craft	GB regions	Monthly to April 1972	[QRL 194]	
Notified vacancies remaining unfilled by industry	Men (18 and over); females; boys; total	GB	Monthly to April 1972	[QRL 194]	
Notified vacancies remaining unfilled by occupation	Adults by sex	GB	Quarterly from May 1958	[QRL 135] and former [QRL 190]	6.8.2. See also analyses by craft by industry published at one time by DOE referred to above
Notified vacancies remaining unfilled by occupation	Adults by sex	GB regions	Quarterly from Sept. 1963		
Number of placings	By industry	GB	Monthly to Jan. 1970		
Number of placings	By occupation	GB	1970 and quarterly from 1971	[QRL 135] and former [QRL 190]	6.8.2
Accident Statistics					
HMFI statistics					6.10 and 9.4.4 (NI)
Accidents notified under the Factories Acts	Fatal accidents	GB	Annually	[QRL 164] and former [QRL 36]	

QUICK REFERENCE LIST

Accidents notified under the Factories Acts	Fatal accidents	GB	Monthly	[QRL 135] and former [QRL 190]	
Accidents notified under the Factories Acts	Fatal accidents	NI	Annually	[QRL 155]	
Accidents notified under the Factories Acts	Total reported accidents	GB	Annually	[QRL 164] and former [QRL 36]	
Accidents notified under the Factories Acts	Total reported accidents	GB	Quarterly	[QRL 135] and former [QRL 190]	Some analyses are made for the construction 'industry' but most relate to construction 'processes' ('building operations' and 'works of engineering construction')
Accidents notified under the Factories Acts	Total reported accidents	NI	Annually	[QRL 155]	
Accidents notified under the Factories Acts	'Serious' accidents	GB	Annually from 1969	[QRL 164] and former [QRL 36]	*Secondary sources:* [QRL 58] (fatal accident ser. to 1968)—contd. in [QRL 59] and [QRL 31] (fatal ser.). [QRL 59] also include serious injury series
Accidents notified under the Factories Acts	By type of accident; nature of injury	GB	Annually	[QRL 164] and former [QRL 36]	
Accidents notified under the Factories Acts	By type of accident; nature of injury	NI	Annually	[QRL 155]	
Accidents notified under the Factories Acts	Incidence rates	GB	Annually	[QRL 164] and former [QRL 36]	
Notified diseases	'Notifiable' diseases by industry	GB	Annually	[QRL 164]	
DHSS statistics					6.10.2
Fatal accidents attracting award of industrial death benefit	Nos	GB	Annually	[QRL 312] and [QRL 164]	
Other accidents—spells of certified incapacity resulting from fresh industrial accidents	Nos and duration of incapacity	GB	Annually	[QRL 312] and [QRL 164]	

LABOUR STATISTICS OTHER THAN EMPLOYMENT, WAGE RATES, EARNINGS, HOURS OF WORK AND LABOUR COSTS—contd.

Type of Data/ Descriptive Title	Breakdown/ Detail of Analysis	Area	Dates and Frequency	Publication (see QRL Key)	Text Reference and Remarks
Strike Statistics					6.11 and 9.4.5 (NI)
Number of stoppages	No. beginning in period	UK	Monthly	[QRL 135] and former [QRL 190]	
Number of stoppages	No. beginning in period by cause	UK	Annually from 1959	[QRL 135] and former [QRL 190]	*Secondary sources:* [QRL 58], [QRL 59], [QRL 31]—all include principal U.K. annual series only. Separate analyses in respect of the disputes known to have been official are available for the period since 1960 in [QRL 135]
Workers involved	Nos in stoppages in progress	UK	Monthly	[QRL 135] and former [QRL 190]	
Workers involved	Nos in stoppages in progress	UK regions	Annually from 1955	[QRL 135] and former [QRL 190]	
Workers involved	Nos in stoppages beginning in year by cause of stoppage	UK regions	Annually from 1959	[QRL 135] and former [QRL 190]	
Working days lost	Nos through stoppages in progress	UK	Monthly	[QRL 135] and former [QRL 190] and [QRL 195]	
Working days lost	Nos through stoppages in progress	UK regions	Annually from 1955	[QRL 135] and former [QRL 190]	
Working days lost	Nos through stoppages in progress	NI	Monthly from 1956	[QRL 140]	
Working days lost	Nos through stoppages beginning in year by cause of stoppage	UK regions	Annually from 1959	[QRL 135] and former [QRL 190]	
Working days lost incidence rates	Rate per 1,000 employees	UK	Annually from 1959	[QRL 135] and former [QRL 190]	

Prominent stoppages beginning in period	Date began; date ended; workers involved (directly; indirectly); working days lost; type of worker involved (directly; indirectly); cause or object	UK	Annually	[QRL 135] and former [QRL 190]
Disputes referred to ACAS	Nos of completed conciliation cases; cases referred to arbitration, mediation and investigation, etc.	GB	Annually	[QRL 33]	6.11
Trade Union Statistics					6.12 and 9.4.6 (NI) References to Annual Reports of individual trades unions are not given here
Membership	By industry (see Remarks)	UK	Annually	[QRL 33]	Not accurate—see Section 6.12
Membership	By union	UK	Annually	[QRL 34] and former [QRL 256]	
Finance	By union	UK	Annually	[QRL 34] and former [QRL 256]	6.12.2

WAGE RATES, EARNINGS, HOURS OF WORK AND LABOUR COSTS

6.9 and 9.4.3 (NI) *N.B.* Selected data are reproduced in [QRL 58] up to 1968 and then in [QRL 59]—for details see the relevant section of text cited below. For references to historical series and studies, see Section 6.9.2.2

CONSTRUCTION AND THE RELATED PROFESSIONS

Type of Data/ Descriptive Title	Breakdown/ Detail of Analysis	Area	Dates and Frequency	Publication (see QRL Key)	Text Reference and Remarks
WAGE RATES, EARNINGS, HOURS OF WORK AND LABOUR COSTS—*contd.*					
Wage Rates and Normal Hours of Work					6.9.2
Basic rates of wages and normal basic hours determined by collective agreement	Actual wage rates and hours	UK areas	Annually / Monthly	[QRL 348] Annually [QRL 117] Monthly from May 1966	Summary of changes given in [QRL 135] and former [QRL 190]
Principal rates	Time series	UK	Annually from 1947	[QRL 58] and [QRL 59]	
Index numbers	Basic weekly and hourly wage rates and normal hours	UK	Monthly from June 1947	[QRL 58], [QRL 59], [QRL 135]	*Secondary sources* (weekly wage rate index): [QRL 168], [QRL 195]
Actual Earnings and Hours of Work I—MOL–DE Data					6.9.3
Earnings and hours—all employees ('New Earnings Surveys')	Level, distribution and make-up of earnings of employees by age; sex; adult/juvenile; full-time/part-time; manual/non-manual; occupation; area of employment; collective agreement. Normal basic hours and paid over-time hours	GB	1968 and annually from 1970	[QRL 208]	6.9.3.1
Earnings and hours—manual workers	Average weekly and hourly earnings and average hours worked for full-time males (under/over 21); full-time and part-time women (18 and over)	UK	April and October each year from October 1946 to 1970 then annually in October	[QRL 135] and former [QRL 190]	6.9.3.2. For pre-1946 data see references cited in Section 6.9.3.2 *Secondary sources:* [QRL 58] contains principal series to 1968; continued in [QRL 59]. [QRL 195] includes average weekly earnings

Earnings and hours—manual workers	Average weekly and hourly earnings and average hours worked—full-time men	UK regions	April and October from 1960 to 1970, then annually in October	[QRL 135] and former [QRL 190] (see Remarks)	Results for 1961 given in [QRL 331] not [QRL 190]
Earnings and hours—manual workers	Average weekly and hourly earnings and average hours worked—full-time men	NI	April and October from 1960 to 1970, then annually in October	[QRL 140]	9.4.3.2
Earnings and hours—manual workers	Distribution of weekly earnings of full-time men and women	UK	October 1960	[QRL 190] 1961	
Earnings and hours—by occupation	Average weekly and hourly earnings and hours of work of males receiving adult rates of pay in constructional engineering; other construction	GB	January and June each year from June 1964 to January 1970	[QRL 190]	6.9.3.3. Selected summary data are reproduced in [QRL 58] and [QRL 59] to 1970
Earnings and hours—by occupation	Average weekly and hourly earnings and hours of work of males receiving adult rates of pay for construction other than constructional engineering only	GB regions	January and June each year from June 1964 to January 1970	[QRL 190]	
Earnings and hours—by occupation	Average weekly and hourly earnings and hours of work of males receiving adult rates of pay for construction other than constructional engineering by size of firm	GB	Jan. 1965–Jan. 1970	[QRL 190]	
Earnings and hours—by occupation	Average weekly and hourly earnings and hours of work of males receiving adult rates of pay for heating, ventilating and domestic engineering only	GB regions	June 1970	[QRL 135] Nov. 1970	

CONSTRUCTION AND THE RELATED PROFESSIONS

Type of Data/ Descriptive Title	Breakdown/ Detail of Analysis	Area	Dates and Frequency	Publication (see QRL Key)	Text Reference and Remarks
WAGE RATES, EARNINGS, HOURS OF WORK AND LABOUR COSTS—*contd.*					
Actual Earnings and Hours of Work I MOL–DE Data—*contd.*					
Earnings and hours—by occupation	Average weekly and hourly earnings and hours of work of males receiving adult rates of pay for heating, ventilating and domestic engineering only by size of firm	GB	June 1970	[QRL 135] Nov. 1970	
Earnings and hours—by occupation	Occupational earnings and hours of male manual workers	NI	Annually 1967–72	[QRL 140]	9.4.3.2
Average earnings—non-manual employees	Average weekly earnings by sex of full-time employees	UK	Annually from 1959 to 1970 and from 1973	[QRL 135] and former [QRL 190]	6.9.3.4
Average earnings—non-manual employees	Average weekly earnings by sex of full-time employees	NI	1959 and annually from 1963 to 1970	[QRL 140]	9.4.3.2
Monthly index of average earnings	All employees	GB	Monthly from 1963	[QRL 135] and former [QRL 190]	6.9.3.5
Payment by results (see Remarks)	Nos of manual employees paid under PBR systems	UK	1947–61 various dates	[QRL 190]	6.9.3.6. Conducted as part of the manual workers bi-annual earnings and hours enquiries—referred to above. Currently data are collected in the New Earnings Survey (Section 6.9.3.1). See too Section 3.10.6

Actual Earnings and Hours of Work II—Non MOL-DE Data

NEDO Survey	Composition of earnings and hours; pay of apprentices and adult trainees. Annual and weekly earnings	GB	May 1973	[QRL 109]	6.9.4.1
NBPI Surveys:					6.9.4.2
Building	Pte Ctrs; DL. Composition of earnings and hours by grade, occupation, size of firm, type of work, conditions of service	GB regions	1968	[QRL 217] and [QRL 218]
Civil. eng.		GB regions	1968	[QRL 219] and [QRL 218]
Construction other than E & C Eng.		GB regions	1968	[QRL 220] and [QRL 218]
Electrical contracting	Pte Ctrs; DL. Composition of earnings and hours by grade, occupation, size of firm, type of work, conditions of service	GB regions	1968	[QRL 222]
Electrical contracting	Composition of hours and earnings of full-week operatives by grade	Scotland / E & W	1968	[QRL 223]
Electrical contracting	Average earnings and hours	GB	1966	[QRL 359]	Special analysis of MOL data
Thermal insulation contracting	Composition of earnings and hours by occupation	GB	1968	[QRL 218]
Contract cleaning	Composition of earnings and hours and analyses by size of establishment; size of parent company; region; type of premises; age	GB	1970	[QRL 221]
Family Expenditure Surveys	Distribution of earnings of male employees; manual workers	GB	Annually 1964–9	[QRL 156]	6.9.4.4

Type of Data/ Descriptive Title	Breakdown/ Detail of Analysis	Area	Dates and Frequency	Publication (see QRL Key)	Text Reference and Remarks
WAGE RATES, EARNINGS, HOURS OF WORK AND LABOUR COSTS—*contd.*					
Actual Earnings and Hours of Work II—Non-MOL–DE Data—contd.					
Census of Population—Hours of Work	Part-time workers by occupation	GB	1961	[QRL 99]	
Census of Population—Hours of Work	Part-time workers by occupation and industry	GB	1966	[QRL 295]	6.9.4.5
Census of Population—Hours of Work	Distribution of hours worked—all workers by industry; occupation and sex	GB	1971	[QRL 94] Pt IV.	
Total Labour Costs and Factor Incomes					
Wages, salaries and other categories of labour costs	Various categories of labour cost per employee by size of firm for manual; non-manual; total employees	GB	1964	[QRL 190] and [QRL 181]	6.9.5 and 9.4.3.3 (NI)
Wages, salaries and other categories of labour costs	Various categories of labour cost per employee by size of firm for manual; non-manual; total employees	GB	1968	[QRL 135] and [QRL 182]	
Wages, salaries and other categories of labour costs	Various categories of labour cost per employee by size of firm for manual; non-manual; total employees	GB	1973	[QRL 135] and [QRL 182]	See Section 6.9.5 for detailed publication references
Wages, salaries and other categories of labour costs	Various categories of labour cost per employee by size of firm for manual; non-manual; total employees	GB	1975	[QRL 135] and [QRL 182]	

Wages, salaries and other categories of labour costs	Various categories of labour cost per employee by size of firm for manual; non-manual; total employees	NI	1968	[QRL 135] Oct. 1970	9.4.3.3
Wages, salaries and other categories of labour costs	Various categories of labour cost per employee by size of firm for manual; non-manual; total employees	NI	1973	[QRL 140] No. 46, 1976, et seq.	9.4.3.3
Aggregate wage and salary payments and national insurance	Wages and salaries; employers' contributions	UK	Annually from 1948	[QRL 201]	6.9.5.2. CSO estimate for National Income and Expenditure accounts
Aggregate wage and salary payments and national insurance	Wages and salaries; employers' contributions	UK regions	Annually from 1971	[QRL 17] and [QRL 252]	7.1.2
Aggregate wage and salary payments and national insurance	Wages and salaries; employers' contributions	UK regions	1961	[QRL 28]	7.1.2. Unofficial estimates
Aggregate wage and salary payments and national insurance	Est. aggregate annual earnings	UK regions	1948	[QRL 8]	7.1.2. Unofficial estimates
Aggregate wage and salary payments and national insurance	Est. wages; salaries; employers' contributions; income from self-employment	Wales	1965–8	[QRL 27]	7.1.2. Unofficial estimates
Aggregate wage and salary payments and national insurance	Operatives; other employees employed by Ctrs; DL	GB, UK	1946–58 (except 1947 and 1950), 1963, 1968 and annually from 1974	See Tables 5.1 and 5.2	5.3. Census of Production returns. See Tables 5.1 and 5.2 for further details of analyses available by size and trade of firm/DL undertaking, and by region or country
Aggregate wage and salary payments and national insurance	Operatives; other employees employed by Ctrs; DL	NI	Annually from 1949	[QRL 278]	9.2.2. COP (NI)
Factor incomes in construction	Income from employment; gross profits of companies and income from self-employment; company profits (gross; net)	UK	Annually from 1948	[QRL 201]	7.1.1. CSO National Income and Expenditure accounts

436 CONSTRUCTION AND THE RELATED PROFESSIONS

WAGE RATES, EARNINGS, HOURS OF WORK AND LABOUR COSTS—*contd.*

Total Labour Costs and Factor Incomes—*contd.*

Type of Data/ Descriptive Title	Breakdown/ Detail of Analysis	Area	Dates and Frequency	Publication (see QRL Key)	Text Reference and Remarks
Factor incomes in construction	Income from employment; gross profits and income from self-employment	UK regions	Annually from 1971	[QRL 17] and [QRL 252]	7.1.2
Factor incomes in construction	Income from employment; income from self-employment; gross profits	NI	Annually from 1963	[QRL 140]	9.6.1. Very approximate estimates were also prepared for some years before 1963—see Section 9.6.1

INPUTS TO CONSTRUCTION OTHER THAN LABOUR

					Statistics about the production, sales, etc. of building materials are dealt with separately below
Purchases and payments by Ctrs and DL organizations	Materials and fuel; goods for merchanting; transport; hire of plant; other services (by type)	GB/UK	From 1946 various dates—see Table 5.1	See Tables 5.1 and 5.2	5.3. Census of Production. For full details see Tables 5.1 and 5.2
Purchases and payments by Ctrs and DL organizations	Materials and fuel; goods for merchanting; transport; hire of plant; other services (by type)	NI	From 1949 various dates	[QRL 278]	9.2.2.1
Input–output analyses	Input–output matrices for construction and other sectors	UK	From 1935 to 1968 various dates. Annually from 1970	See Section 5.3.4 [QRL 79]	5.3.4
Input–output analyses	Input–output matrices for construction and other sectors	NI	1963	[QRL 174]	9.2.2.2
Input–output analyses	Input–output matrices for construction and other sectors	Scotland	Nyp	Forthcoming [QRL 175]	5.3.4

INDUSTRIAL ORGANIZATION AND STRUCTURE
(see Remarks)

We list here details of statistics about the numbers, types and sizes of firms and DL organizations in the industry. Related information about employment and output by type and size of firm, etc. is considered as appropriate under 'Employment' and 'Output'

MOW Registration Statistics 1946–53—Ctrs and DL Orgs

Total numbers	Active; new registrations; cancellations, etc.	GB regions	Dec. 1946 and Dec. 1947	[QRL 336]	3.7.5. B & CE undertakings. Registered in accordance with DR 56AB. Selected tabulations of these data have now been reproduced in the *MOW Collection* [QRL 321]
Total numbers	Active; new registrations; cancellations, etc.	GB regions	July 1948–Nov. 1953. Monthly	[QRL 194]	
Contractors (main and specialist trades)	Nos by trade of firm	GB regions	July 1948–Nov. 1953. Monthly	[QRL 194]	
DL organizations	Nos of local auths; public utilities	GB regions	July 1948–Nov. 1953. Monthly	[QRL 194]	3.3

MOW Censuses of Contractors 1941–4

Number of firms (main trades)	By size	GB	1941–4 various dates	[QRL 321]	Figs. for Nov. 1942 and Oct. 1943 were published in [QRL 320]. See Table 3.1 for further details
Number of firms (main trades)	By trade of firm	GB	1942–4 various dates	[QRL 321]	
Number of firms (main trades)	Totals	GB regions	1943–4 various dates	[QRL 321]	
Number of firms (main trades, specialist trades)	By trade of firm	GB	1942–4 various dates	[QRL 321]	3.3.4

438   CONSTRUCTION AND THE RELATED PROFESSIONS

Type of Data/ Descriptive Title	Breakdown/ Detail of Analysis	Area	Dates and Frequency	Publication (see QRL Key)	Text Reference and Remarks
INDUSTRIAL ORGANIZATION AND STRUCTURE—*contd.*					
MOW Censuses of Contractors 1945–54					
Number of firms (main trades)	Totals	GB regions	1945–54 various dates	[QRL 321]	3.5. For full details see Tables 3.2 and 3.3. [QRL 321] provides a full collection of data, much of which had remained unpublished. The tables cited include alternative publication references for some of the data
Number of firms (main trades)	By size and trade of firm	GB	1945–54 various dates	[QRL 321]	
Number of firms (specialist trades)	Totals	GB regions	1949–54 various dates	[QRL 321]	
Number of firms (specialist trades)	By size and trade of firm	GB	1945–54 various dates	[QRL 321]	
MOW–DOE Censuses of Contractors Since 1954					4.2
Number of firms	By trade and size of firm	GB	April 1956	[QRL 321]	
Number of firms	Totals	GB	April 1956	[QRL 321]	
Number of firms	By trade and size of firm by region	GB regions	Annually from 1957 to 1967 Bi-annually from 1968 to 1970 Annually from 1971	[QRL 71] [QRL 240]	For full details see Table 4.1
No. of firms employing APTC staff	By trade and size of firm	GB regions	Annually from 1965 to 1970 Annually from 1971	[QRL 71] [QRL 240]	

MOW–DOE Censuses of DL Organizations Since 1954

No. of LAs employing DL	Totals	GB regions	April 1956	[QRL 321]	4.3
No. of LAs employing DL	Totals	GB regions	Annually 1961–70	[QRL 194]	
No. of LAs not employing DL	Totals	GB regions	Annually 1971–3	[QRL 168]	
No. of LAs not employing DL	Totals	GB	Annually 1971–3	[QRL 194]	
No. of LAs employing DL	By type of authority	GB regions	Annually from 1968	[QRL 194], [QRL 168]	
No. of LAs employing DL	By type of authority	GB regions	April 1956	[QRL 321]	See Table 4.2 for further details of analyses available
			Annually from 1961 to 1970	[QRL 194]	
No. of LAs employing DL	By size of authority (DL force)	GB regions	Annually from 1971	[QRL 168]	
			Annually from 1968 to 1970	[QRL 194]	
			Annually from 1971	[QRL 168]	

Censuses of Production Data

Private firms—'establishments', 'enterprises', etc.	By size	GB	1946	[QRL 51]	5.3
Private firms—'establishments', 'enterprises', etc.	By size	GB	1948	[QRL 157] Vol. 12 Trade A	
Private firms—'establishments', 'enterprises', etc.	By size	UK	1951, 1954, 1958, 1963, 1968	See Table 5.1	
Private firms—'establishments', 'enterprises', etc.	By trade of firm	UK	1954, 1958, 1963, 1968 and annually from 1974	See Table 5.1 [QRL 76]	
Private firms—'establishments', 'enterprises', etc.	By size	NI	1949, 1954, 1958, 1963, 1968	[QRL 278]	9.2.2
Private firms—'establishments', 'enterprises', etc. NACE classification	By type	UK	Annually from 1974	[QRL 76]	5.3

Type of Data/ Descriptive Title	Breakdown/ Detail of Analysis	Area	Dates and Frequency	Publication (see QRL Key)	Text Reference and Remarks
INDUSTRIAL ORGANIZATION AND STRUCTURE—*contd.*					
Censuses of Production Data—*contd.*					
No. of DL undertakings	By type	GB/UK	From 1946 various dates	See Table 5.2	Table 5.2 gives details of the types of public authority DL undertaking for which separate information was published at various times
No. of DL undertakings	By type	NI	1949–54. Annually	[QRL 278]	9.2.2
No. of DL undertakings All undertakings (pte and public)	By size By size	UK UK	1975 1974	[QRL 76] 1975 [QRL 76] 1974	5.3 5.3
CITB Returns Number of firms	By trade of firm ('main activity') by size of levy	GB	Annually	[QRL 255]	6.4.2
VAT Registration Statistics No. of 'persons' registered	Totals	UK	Annually	[QRL 257]	Analyses by trade are available on request
Company Acquisitions and Mergers Numbers	Acquired by construction companies and number of acquiring companies	UK	Annually from 1960 to 1967, then quarterly	[QRL 74]	7.4
Numbers	No. acquired (quoted; unquoted)	UK	1954–61 summary	[QRL 147] April 1963	7.4

FINANCIAL STATISTICS

Company Income and Finance

7.2.1

Topic	Content	Area	Period	Reference	Notes
Summary company accounts	Income appropriation account; balance sheet; sources and uses of funds statement	UK	1949–53. Annually 1949–60. Annually 1960–8. Annually Annually from 1964	[QRL 127] [QRL 171] [QRL 331] [QRL 72]	'Listed' ('quoted') companies only. For unofficial surveys, see Section 7.2.1.1
Turnover and profit margins		UK	Quarterly from 1973	[QRL 238]	7.2.2. Large companies reporting to Price Commission only
Collected accounting data for individual companies	Assets; income	UK	1953/4 and 1954/5	[QRL 119]	Quoted companies with assets exceeding £2.5m in 1953/4
Collected accounting data for individual companies	Net assets; income; growth in net assets (1954–7)	UK	1957	[QRL 124]	Quoted companies with net assets of £0.5m or more
Collected accounting data for individual companies	Net assets; net fixed assets; depreciation; current assets; stocks; current liabilities; income; retentions; new capital	UK	1960	[QRL 125]	Quoted companies with net assets of £0.5m or more
Collected accounting data for individual companies	Net assets; net fixed assets; depreciation; current assets; stocks; current liabilities; income; retentions; new capital	UK	1963	[QRL 126]	Quoted companies with net assets of £0.5m or with income of £50,000 or more
Collected accounting data for individual companies	Key figures: capital; turnover; profits, etc.	UK	Annually	[QRL 350]	Largest companies in terms of capital employed
Financial data for small firms	Asset structure; trade debtors; profitability; possession of overdraft; profit margins; trends in trading ratios	GB GB	1968 (some 1964) 1969	[QRL 26] [QRL 227]	7.2.5. Sample surveys for the Bolton Committee [B 326]
Bank advances to construction	Amounts outstanding	GB	Quarterly	[QRL 158] and [QRL 195]	7.2.3. Ann. ser. in [QRL 31]
Bank advances to construction	Amounts outstanding	NI	Quarterly	[QRL 158] and [QRL 195] and [QRL 140]	

Type of Data/ Descriptive Title	Breakdown/ Detail of Analysis	Area	Dates and Frequency	Publication (see QRL Key)	Text Reference and Remarks
FINANCIAL STATISTICS—*contd.*					
Company Income and Finance—*contd.*					
Bank advances to construction	Changes from previous qtr, s.a.	GB	Quarterly	[QRL 158]	
Statistics of Quoted Securities					7.2.4
Individual construction co. securities	Share prices; dividends; dividend yields; p/e ratios	UK	Daily	[QRL 159], [QRL 349]	
Share price indices:					
'*FT*–Actuaries Index'	*FT*–Actuaries share index—construction	UK	Daily	[QRL 159]	
'Building 50 Share Index'	Contractors and building materials costs	UK	Weekly	[QRL 60]	
Nominal and market values	'Contracting and construction' group	UK	Quarterly	[QRL 332]	
Overseas Transactions					7.2.6
Investment and earnings	By geographical area and country	World	Annual	[QRL 73]	
Overseas assets	By geographical area and country	World	Every 3 years	[QRL 73] Supp.	
R & D Expenditure (see Remarks)					7.3
Current expenditure	By type (wages and salaries; materials, etc.)		1966/67	[QRL 329], [QRL 282]	
Current expenditure	By type of research (basic; applied; devt)		1967/8	[QRL 330]	Separate results for expenditure by private firms, public corporations and research associations in the product group 'construction'
Capital expenditure	By type of asset	UK	1968/9, 1969/70	[QRL 282], [QRL 283]	
Sources of finance			1972/3, 1975/6	[QRL 283], [QRL 352], 1977, pp. 638–44	

QUICK REFERENCE LIST 443

Expenditure on Acquisitions and Mergers	Total	UK	Annually from 1960 to 1967, then Quarterly	[QRL 74]	7.4
	Ave. annual expenditure	UK	1954–8 and 1959–61	[QRL 147] April 1963	
	Quoted; unquoted	UK	1954–61		
Bankruptcy					
No. of failures, value of assets and liabilities	Receiving orders; deeds of arrangement	E & W	Annually	[QRL 45]	7.5.2 and 9.6.2.3 (NI)
No. of failures, value of assets and liabilities	Totals	NI	Annually from 1962	Available on request	9.6.2.3
No. of failures	Total	E & W	Quarterly from 1969 to 1974 Quarterly from 1974	[QRL 147] March 1975 [QRL 352]	7.5.2
Company Liquidations					
Number	Winding-up orders; creditors' voluntary liquidations	E & W	Annually	[QRL 123]	7.5.3
Number	Winding-up orders; creditors' voluntary liquidations	Scotland	Annually	[QRL 123]	
Number	Total	E & W	Quarterly from 1969 to 1974 Quarterly from 1974	[QRL 147] March 1975 [QRL 352]	
Taxation Statistics					
Tax assessments on:					
Income from employment by 'trade group' ('building and contracting')	Pay and pensions; tax deducted	UK	Annually	[QRL 173] formerly in [QRL 258]	7.6
Income from self-employment by 'trade group'	Number; gross true income; capital allowances; net true income; tax	UK E & W Scot and NI	Annually	[QRL 173] formerly in [QRL 258]	
Income from professional earnings	Nos. and amounts for individuals; partnerships in architecture	UK	Annually	[QRL 173] formerly in [QRL 258]	
Company income by 'trade group'	Nos.; income; allowances; deductions; tax	UK	Annually	[QRL 173] formerly in [QRL 258]	

Type of Data/ Descriptive Title	Breakdown/ Detail of Analysis	Area	Dates and Frequency	Publication (see QRL Key)	Text Reference and Remarks
FINANCIAL STATISTICS—*contd.*					
Taxation Statistics—*contd.*					
Capital allowances:					
Sole traders and partnerships by 'industry group'	Value by type of allowance and asset	UK	Annually	[QRL 173] formerly in [QRL 258]	
Companies by 'industry'	Value by type of allowance and asset	UK	Annually	[QRL 173] formerly in [QRL 258]	
Company distributions and annual payments by 'trade group'	Value by type	UK	Annually	[QRL 173] formerly in [QRL 258]	
Value Added Tax (VAT) by industry	Tax due; tax deductible; net tax payable	UK	Annually	[QRL 257]	
CONSTRUCTION COSTS, PRICES AND PRODUCTIVITY					
Indices of Construction Costs and Prices					8. Currently compiled indices only are listed here. For historical series see Section 8.1.4. Building materials prices and labour costs are dealt with under their appropriate subject headings

DOE Cost of New Construction (CNC) index		GB	Quarterly from 1949	[QRL 352] and [QRL 168]	8.1.2.1
RICS (BCIS) building and elemental price indices	By building type and group element	GB	Quarterly from 1950	On subscription only	8.1.2.2
RICS (BMCIS) maintenance cost indices	General; redecoration; fabric; services	GB	Quarterly from 1970	On subscription only	8.1.2.3
Spon's building costs index		GB	Quarterly from 1956	[QRL 314] and [QRL 43]	8.1.2.4
Spon's M & E services costs index		GB	Quarterly from 1965	[QRL 315]	8.1.2.4
EIU building costs index		GB	Quarterly from 1938	On subscription only	8.1.2.5
DOE (DQSS) tender price index		GB	Quarterly from 1968	[QRL 168]	8.1.2.6
RICS (BCIS) tender price index	Fixed price; VOP contracts	GB	Quarterly from 1974	On subscription only	8.1.2.7
Spon's tender price index		GB	Quarterly from 1966	[QRL 314] and [QRL 43]	8.1.2.8
NEDO price adjustment formulae indices: Building works	By 'work category'; skilled and unskilled labour; plant	GB	Monthly from 1971 (base 1970)	[QRL 191]	8.1.3.1
Civil eng. works	Labour; materials; fuel and plant	GB	Monthly from 1971 (base 1970)	[QRL 192]	
Spec. eng. installations	'Work category'; skilled and unskilled labour; plant	GB	Monthly from 1971 (base 1970)	[QRL 193]	
GLC ILEA building contract fluctuations clause indices	Labour; materials	GB	Monthly from 1973	[QRL 137]	8.1.3.2
Productivity Studies					
School buildings	Labour required by trade	GB	1954	[QRL 65]	8.2.2
Hospital buildings	Labour required by trade	GB	1968	[QRL 19]	For references to housing studies (outside the scope of this Review) and related studies of other sectors see Section 8.2.2

For further details see Table 8.1

446 CONSTRUCTION AND THE RELATED PROFESSIONS

Type of Data/ Descriptive Title	Breakdown/ Detail of Analysis	Area	Dates and Frequency	Publication (see QRL Key)	Text Reference and Remarks
					10
CONSTRUCTION MATERIALS—PRODUCTION, CONSUMPTION AND USE					10.2.1
Consumption					
Expenditure on materials and fuel purchased by Ctrs and DL organizations	Totals and breakdowns by type of material for some years (see Remarks)				Data collected in censuses of production—for further particulars see the entry under 'Inputs to Construction' above
End-uses of materials	Estimated by type of material and type of building	GB	1964	[QRL 7]	
End-uses of materials	Estimated by type of material and type of building	GB	1974–5	[QRL 170]	
End-uses of materials—industrial buildings	Estimates by type of material	GB	1965, 1967, 1969	[QRL 339]	
End-uses of materials—school buildings	Estimates by type of material	E & W	1969	[QRL 340]	
End-uses of materials—aggregates	Estimates by type of work	E & W	1968	[QRL 18]	See also Report of Advisory Committee [B 177]
End-uses of materials—timber	Estimates for housing and other construction	UK	1973	[QRL 4]	
End-uses of materials—minerals	By type of mineral	UK	Annually from 1974	[QRL 80]	
Production, Sales, Deliveries, Stocks, etc. (see Remarks)	By type of material	GB and UK regions	Various dates and frequency	See Remarks	10.2.2. Full details of materials statistics which are currently collected are set out in Table 10.1 and, for regional data, in Table 10.2. It is worth noting here perhaps that the most convenient collective source for many materials is *HCS* [QRL 168] and, for more detailed data, the DOE's *Monthly Statistics of Building Materials and Components* [QRL 196] (available on subscription)

QUICK REFERENCE LIST 447

Overseas Trade				
Imports and exports	By commodity and area or country (values; physical units)	UK	Monthly	[QRL 215]	10.2.3 Some of the data collected from producers—considered in Section 10.2.2—also provide information about imports and exports
Imports and exports	By commodity and area or country (values; physical units) (but more detailed)	UK	Annually	[QRL 39]	

CONSTRUCTION PLANT AND EQUIPMENT—PRODUCTION, CONSUMPTION AND USE

					10.3
Investment by contractors—gross fixed capital formation at current prices	Plant and machinery; vehicles	UK	Annually from 1948	[QRL 201]	10.3.1
Value of capital stock held by contractors at constant replacement cost	Plant and machinery; vehicles	UK	1948, 1951, 1954, 1958 and annually from 1961	[QRL 201]	
Production and sales	By type	UK	Quarterly	[QRL 81]	For precise details of types of plant see *Index of Commodities* [B 190]
Overseas trade—see under 'Construction Materials' above					

CONSTRUCTION MATERIALS PRICE INDICES

DOI Wholesale Price Indices from 1946					11.1
Price index numbers of materials and fuel purchased: Construction materials		UK	Monthly from Jan. 1946	[QRL 352] and former [QRL 48]. *Secondary sources:* [QRL 168], [QRL 195], [QRL 31] (annual)	11.1.1. Series introduced retrospectively in 1951 (base date 30 June 1949); originally entitled 'Building and civil engineering materials'

Type of Data/ Descriptive Title	Breakdown/ Detail of Analysis	Area	Dates and Frequency	Publication (see QRL Key)	Text Reference and Remarks
CONSTRUCTION MATERIALS PRICE INDICES—*contd.*					
DOI Wholesale Price Indices from 1946—*contd.*					
Indices for particular materials		UK	Monthly from Jan. 1946	[QRL 168], [QRL 196]	Currently the [QRL 81] include relevant price indices for particular commodities along with sales or production data. A range of selected commodity indices covering construction and other materials is included monthly in [QRL 352] and an extended range every four months (Apr., Aug. and Dec.)
MOW Indices of Building Materials Prices 1939–51					11.1.2
General indices of building materials prices		GB	Quarterly 1939 (Q₃)–1945 (Q₃) Monthly Jan. 1943–Apr. 1951	[QRL 321]	Originally included in [QRL 318] during war-time period and in [QRL 194] afterwards
Indices for particular materials		GB (see Remarks)	Monthly Dec. 1945–Apr. 1951	[QRL 321]	Originally included in [QRL 318] during war-time period and in [QRL 194] afterwards. Indices for some materials were based on London delivered prices

Price Index Numbers for Current Cost Accounting

'Industry-specific' price indices for stocks held by:

Construction industry	Materials and fuel	UK	Monthly from 1972 (1970 base)	11.1.1.2
	Goods on hand for sale (see Remarks)	UK	Quarterly from 1972 (1970 base)	The index for 'goods on hand for sale' by the construction industry is the 'Cost of New Construction' index (Section 8.1.2.1 refers)
Builders' merchants	All stocks	UK	Monthly from 1972 (1970 base)	[QRL 239]
Building materials industry (as defined)	Materials and fuel: goods on hand for sale	UK	Monthly from 1972 (1970 base)	

CONSTRUCTION PLANT PRICE INDICES

				11.2
DOI wholesale price index numbers	By type of plant	UK	Monthly from 1946	[QRL 352] and former [QRL 48]
Price index numbers for current cost accounting—'industry-specific' indices	Capital expenditure on plant and machinery by the construction industry	UK	Quarterly from 1956 to 1971, then monthly	[QRL 239] Also included currently in appropriate serials in [QRL 81]—see *Index of Commodities* [B 208] for precise details
Cost of provision, operation and maintenance		UK	Monthly from 1971 (base 1970)	[QRL 191] NEDO price adjustment formulae index—Section 8.1.3.1 refers

CONSTRUCTION STOCK

Total Stock

Official series

				12
Gross capital stock at constant replacement cost	By asset: dwellings (pub; pte); roads; other buildings and works *et al.*	UK	Annually from 1948	[QRL 201] 12.2.1
Gross capital stock at constant replacement cost	Buildings and works other than dwellings by industry	UK	Annually from 1948	[QRL 201]

CONSTRUCTION AND THE RELATED PROFESSIONS

Type of Data/ Descriptive Title	Breakdown/ Detail of Analysis	Area	Dates and Frequency	Publication (see QRL Key)	Text Reference and Remarks
CONSTRUCTION STOCK—*contd.*					
Total Stock—*contd.*					
Official Series—*contd.*					
Gross capital stock at constant replacement cost	Construction industry by asset: vehicles; plant and machinery; buildings and works other than dwellings	UK	Annually from 1948	[QRL 201]	
Net capital stock at current replacement cost	Buildings and works by sector	UK	Annually from 1955	[QRL 201]	
Capital consumption at current and constant prices	By asset (dwellings; other buildings and works *et al.*)	UK	1938, annually from 1948 to 1974	[QRL 201]	Since 1975 analyses, at current replacement cost, by sector have been published differentiating dwellings only from other types of asset
Capital retirements at current and constant prices	Dwellings (no other asset breakdown)	UK	Annually from 1965	[QRL 201]	
Capital retirements at current and constant prices	By the construction industry	UK	Annually from 1965	[QRL 201]	
Unofficial historical series and estimates					
Gross and net reproducible capital stock at current and constant prices	By type of asset (dwellings; other buildings and works; *et al.*)	UK	Annually 1855–1965	[QRL 12] and [QRL 14]	12.2.1.4. *N.B.* Part of the series is currently being revised. The series for the period since the Second World War is the official series referred to above
Gross stock	Various categories of B & CE works	UK	1760, 1800, 1830, 1860	[QRL 20]	12.2.1.4
Value of land and buildings	By class of property and sector of ownership subclassified between dwellings and other buildings and works	UK	1957–61	[QRL 23]	12.2.1.4

Stock Statistics for Particular Types of Buildings (excl. Housing)

Rating statistics	No. of hereditaments and rateable values by class of use	E & W	Annually	[QRL 173] formerly [QRL 258]	12.2.2 12.2.2.1
Rating statistics	Rateable values by broad use-class	E and W—LA areas	Annually	[QRL 250]	
Rating statistics	Rateable values by broad use-class	Wales	Annually	[QRL 361]	
Rating statistics	Rateable values by broad use-class	Scotland	Annually	[QRL 251]	
Rating statistics	Rateable values by broad use-class	NI	Annually	[QRL 186]	
Floorspace statistics—industry and commerce	By use-class; size groups	E & W regions and LA areas	1967. Annually from 1974	[QRL 323] and [QRL 252]	12.2.2.1. Based on rating valuation records
Floorspace statistics—industry and commerce	By use-class; size groups	Wales	1967. Annually from 1974	[QRL 142], [QRL 360], [QRL 252]	12.2.2.1. Based on rating valuation records
Floorspace statistics—distributive and service trades	By type of business	GB	1966	[QRL 266]	Census of Distribution data
Floorspace statistics—distributive and service trades	By type of business	GB	1971	[QRL 83]	Census of Distribution data

452 CONSTRUCTION AND THE RELATED PROFESSIONS

CONSTRUCTION STOCK—contd.

Stock Statistics for Particular Types of Buildings (excluding Housing)—contd.

Type of Data/ Descriptive Title	Breakdown/ Detail of Analysis	Area	Dates and Frequency	Publication (see QRL Key)	Text Reference and Remarks
School buildings	Age; condition; cost of renovation	E & W	1962	[QRL 301]	
School buildings	Age; condition; cost of renovation and replacement value	E & W	1975–6	[QRL 334]	
Hotels	By size	UK regions	1970	[QRL 167]	
Hotels	Additions to stock by size	England	Annual	[QRL 209]	
Hotels	Additions to stock by size	Scotland	Irregular	[QRL 305]	
Manufacturing 'establishments'	No. by size (persons employed) by industry	UK regions	Annually from 1971	[QRL 78]	
Registered offices, shops and railway premises	Number	GB	Annually	[QRL 213]	12.2.2.2
Registered offices and shops	Number	NI	Annually	[QRL 212]	
Roads	Mileages by type of road by admin. area	GB countries	Annually	[QRL 354]	
Roads	Mileages by type of road by admin. area	NI	Annually	[QRL 140]	
Roads	Mileages by type of road by admin. area	UK countries	Annually	[QRL 252]	
Roads	Mileages by type of road by admin. area	Wales	Annually	[QRL 142]	
Shops	Nos by type	GB countries	1950	[QRL 107]	12.2.2.2. Results of first count of shops prior to first Census of Distribution. Subsequent COD reports are listed under 'Capital Expenditure' above
Change of use of buildings	Applications granted; refused, by use	E & W	Annually	[QRL 322]	12.3
Change of use of buildings	Applications granted; refused, by use	Scotland	Annually	[QRL 307]	12.3

QUICK REFERENCE LIST 453

Fire losses	Value estimates	UK	Annually	[QRL 355]	12.3. Early estimates based on insured values of buildings and contents
Construction Stock Transactions and Costs					12.5
Surveys of conveyancing—number and value of transactions	Price range; type of property; tenure; sector of buyer and seller (see Remarks)	E & W	Feb. 1968	[QRL 173] 1970 ed.	12.5.1.1. Surveys prior to Oct. 1973 were less detailed
Surveys of conveyancing—number and value of transactions	Price range; type of property; tenure; sector of buyer and seller (see Remarks)	E & W	Jun. and Oct. 1973	[QRL 10]	
Surveys of conveyancing—number and value of transactions	Price range; type of property; tenure; sector of buyer and seller (see Remarks)	E & W	Oct. 1974 and Nov. 1975	[QRL 9]	
Surveys of conveyancing—number and value of transactions	Price range; type of property; tenure; sector of buyer and seller (see Remarks)	E & W	Nov. 1976	[QRL 11]	
Acquisition and disposal of existing buildings and land—see under 'Capital Expenditure' above					12.5.1.2 and 12.5.1.3
Building rents—index numbers:					
offices	London (3 areas); Provinces	GB	Annually from 1965		
shops	3 classes	GB	Annually from 1965	[QRL 122]	12.5.2. For other occupancy cost data (mainly *ad hoc* studies) see Section cited
factories		GB	Annually from 1969		
Property market indicators	Trends in rents; investment yields; capital values; investment activity	UK regions	Quarterly from 1976	[QRL 159]	12.5.2. RICS survey

CONSTRUCTION PROFESSIONS

Numbers, Characteristics and Employment

General

Type of Data/ Descriptive Title	Breakdown/ Detail of Analysis	Area	Dates and Frequency	Publication (see QRL Key)	Text Reference and Remarks
					13
Census of population occupational analyses	Architects and surveyors (combined); civil, structural and municipal engineers (combined)	UK regions	1961		13.2
Census of population occupational analyses	Architects and surveyors (combined); civil, structural and municipal engineers (combined)	GB regions	1966	For publication references see under 'Census of Population Employment Data' above	13.2.1
Census of population occupational analyses	Architects and town planners; surveyors; civil, structural and municipal engineers	UK regions	1951		
Census of population occupational analyses	Architects and town planners; surveyors; civil, structural and municipal engineers	UK regions	1971		
Qualified manpower surveys—census of population et al.	See above under 'Qualified Manpower' for publication sources and see especially Section 6.6.3.2 regarding the scope of the data for the construction professions—note that in 1961 and earlier surveys architecture and surveying were not counted as relevant qualifications.				

Professional staff employed—by Ctrs	Architects; surveyors; engineers	GB regions	1965–70. Annually	[QRL 71]	
Professional staff employed—by Ctrs	Architects; surveyors; engineers by trade and size of firm	GB regions GB	1971–4. Annually 1965–70. Annually 1971–4. Annually	[QRL 240] [QRL 71] [QRL 240]	
Professional staff employed—by Ctrs	Total	GB regions	Annually from 1975	[QRL 240]	6.6.3.3. DOE censuses
Professional staff employed—by Ctrs	Total by size and trade of firm	GB	Annually from 1975	[QRL 240]	
Professional staff employed—by LA's DL	Architects; surveyors; engineers by type of local authority	GB	1968–70. Annually	[QRL 194]	
Professional staff employed—by LA's DL	Architects; surveyors; engineers by type of local authority	GB	Annually from 1971	[QRL 168]	
Architectural profession					
RIBA membership	Corporate; student; new elections; enrolments	n/a	Annually	[QRL 35]	13.2.2.1
RIBA membership	List of members	n/a	Annually	[QRL 143]	
ARCUK register	List of members	n/a	Annually	[QRL 253]	
Employment (see Remarks)	Fields of employment	UK	1949	[QRL 259]	13.2.2.2
Employment (see Remarks)	Fields of employment	UK	1952	[QRL 3]	
Employment (see Remarks)	Fields of employment	UK	1955	[QRL 261], [QRL 290]	
Employment (see Remarks)	Fields of employment	UK	1957	[QRL 180], 1959–60, p. 160	
Employment (see Remarks)	Fields of employment	UK	1964	[QRL 180], 1965, pp. 279–80	With the exceptions noted below, data come from earnings surveys from 1964
Employment (see Remarks)	Fields of employment	UK	1967	[QRL 41]	NBPI survey
Employment (see Remarks)	Fields of employment	UK	1969	[QRL 244]	Monopolies Cmn. survey
Employment (see Remarks)	Fields of employment	UK	1970	[QRL 146]	
Employment (see Remarks)	Fields of employment	UK	1973	[QRL 180], 1974, pp. 16–29 and [QRL 249], Nos 21 and 22	
Employment (see Remarks)	Fields of employment	UK	1975	[QRL 43], 1975, pp. 1332–5	Annual surveys from 1975

456 CONSTRUCTION AND THE RELATED PROFESSIONS

Type of Data/ Descriptive Title	Breakdown/ Detail of Analysis	Area	Dates and Frequency	Publication (see QRL Key)	Text Reference and Remarks
CONSTRUCTION PROFESSIONS—*contd.*					
Numbers, Characteristics and Employment—*contd.*					
Architectural profession—*contd.*					
Employment (see Remarks)	Fields of employment	UK	1976	[QRL 42]	
Staffing in private practice	Principals; salaried architects; others	GB	Quarterly from 1977 (Q₂)	[QRL 249]	See also RIBA censuses of private practices below
RIBA student membership	Various characteristics: age; qualification stage; type of employment, etc.	UK	1969	[QRL 249] No. 4	
Surveying profession					
RICS membership	By professional practice division	n/a	Annually	[QRL 291]	13.2.3
RICS employment	QS membership by field	n/a	1962–72	[QRL 333]	For other *ad hoc* analyses see Section 13.2.3
IQS membership	List of members	n/a	Annually	[QRL 363]	
IQS membership	Age; employment; income	UK	1969	[QRL 248]	
Engineering professions					
ICE membership	List of members	n/a	Annually	[QRL 185]	13.2.4
I.Struct.E. membership	List of members	n/a	Annually	[QRL 365]	
ACE membership	List of members	n/a	Annually	[QRL 184]	
ACE membership	Particulars of individual members and firms	n/a	Annually	[QRL 130]	
Membership surveys:					
Constituent institutions of CEI	Field of work (incl. construction/installation) *inter al.*	UK	1966	[QRL 341] and [QRL 329]	*Surveys of Professional Engineers*
Constituent institutions of CEI	Field of work (incl. construction/installation) *inter al.*	UK	1968	[QRL 342]	
Constituent institutions of CEI	Field of work (incl. construction/installation) *inter al.*	UK	Biennially from 1971	[QRL 343]	
All professional institutions	Fields or status of employment by instn	UK	1969	[QRL 244]	Monopolies Cmn report

QUICK REFERENCE LIST 457

ICE	Age by field of employment; qualification and type of work	GB regions and Ireland	Annually from 1976	[QRL 207]	Analyses of respondents in earnings surveys
Education statistics					13.2.5 (see also Section 6.5.5)
Nos attending courses and obtaining qualifications	By subject	E & W	Annually	[QRL 325]	
Nos attending courses and obtaining qualifications	By subject	Wales	Annually	[QRL 326]	
Nos attending courses and obtaining qualifications	By subject	Scotland	Annually	[QRL 309]	[QRL 153]
Nos attending courses and obtaining qualifications	By subject	NI	Annually	[QRL 151]	
Architectural education statistics	Student nos and exam. results by type of course	UK	Annually	[QRL 249] to No. 24 then [QRL 152]	RIBA surveys
Organization and Structure of Professional Practice					13.3
Architectural Profession					13.3.1
Private architectural practices					
RIBA Directory of Practices	List of Practices	UK	Annually	[QRL 144]	
RIBA censuses of private practices	No. by size and staff employed	GB/UK regions	Biennial from 1962 to 1972	[QRL 249] Nos 1, 2, 5	Not comprehensive GB to 1964 then UK
RIBA sample surveys of staffing in private practice	Principals; salaried architects; others	GB	Quarterly from 1977 (Q_4)	[QRL 249]	
RIBA sample survey of private practices	No. of offices; architectural staff; work certified; by size of office	GB	1957/8	[QRL 180], 1959, pp. 201–3, 273–5	
RIBA sample survey of private practices	No. of offices by size and architectural staff employed	GB regions	1957/8	[QRL 180], 1959, pp. 201–3, 273–5	
RIBA sample survey of private practices	No. of offices; architectural staff; work done by size of office	GB	1960	[QRL 40]	The report cited contains a large volume of data on the structure of the profession and the organization, staffing and work of private and local authority offices
NBPI sample survey	No. of practices and staffing by size of practice	UK	1967/8	[QRL 41]	Incidental to survey of costs and fees

CONSTRUCTION PROFESSIONS—contd.
Organization and Structure of Professional Practice—contd.
Architectural profession—contd.
Private architectural practices—contd.

Type of Data/ Descriptive Title	Breakdown/ Detail of Analysis	Area	Dates and Frequency	Publication (see QRL Key)	Text Reference and Remarks
MMC sample survey	No. of practices by size and type	UK	1975	[QRL 44]	Incidental to survey of costs and fees
Local authorities' architects' departments					
RIBA survey	No. of depts making returns; qual./unqual. staff employed; work certified by type of work	E & W	1958	[QRL 180], 1959–60, pp. 160–3	
RIBA survey	No. of offices; architectural staff employed; work certified by size of office	GB	1960–1	[QRL 40]	
Quantity surveying practices					
RICS survey—pte chartered QS firms	No. of firms; staff employed (qual./other technical) by size of office	GB	1960	[QRL 118], 1960, pp. 130–1	13.3.2
Survey of private QS practices	No. of firms; date of establishment; staffing; by size	UK regions and Ireland	1972	[QRL 333]	Study commissioned by the RICS
Survey of non-QS practice in pte sector	No. by size; no. by region				
Survey of public offices	No. by size of section and work undertaken				
MMC sample survey	No. of offices by size	UK	1974	[QRL 345]	Incidental to survey of costs and fees
Engineering professions					13.3.3
ACE members	No. of firms; staff employed; by size of firm and specialization	UK	1971	[QRL 260]	Incidental to survey of costs and fees

QUICK REFERENCE LIST

Financial Statistics of Construction Professions—Earnings and Professional Practice Costs and Incomes 13.4

Current sources (see Remarks)

N.B. Full details for these and other, non-current, sources are set out in Table 13.1

Source	Breakdown	Area	Frequency	Reference	Remarks
Inland Revenue tax assessments—income from self-employment: architects; engineers (all)	No. and average value for individual and partnerships	UK	Annually from 1966–7	[QRL 173]	
New Earnings Survey—employees	Architects and planners; quantity surveyors; civil, structural and municipal engineers	GB	1968 and Annually from 1970	[QRL 208]	
PER—salary quantiles of registered persons	Civil and structural engineers; quantity surveyors; by age; prof. qualified total	GB	3 times p.a. from 1975	[QRL 284]	
PER—median salaries of registered persons	Civil and structural engineers; quantity surveyors; by age	GB regions	3 times p.a. from 1975	[QRL 284]	
RIBA earnings surveys—architectural staff	By sector and status: professional (principal, other); other grades; and, currently, by age; size of practice; region	UK	Triennial from 1964 to 1973 and Annual from 1975	References are given in Table 13.1—serial item 2 (iii)	
RIBA surveys of fee income	From work in: GB (building; non-building); overseas	GB and overseas	1977	[QRL 249] Nos 32 and 33	Percentage breakdown and commentary only
CEI surveys of professional engineers (members of constituent institutions of the CEI)	By age by institution; field of work (construction) *inter alia*	UK	Biennial from 1973 (covering year 1972–3)—see Remarks	[QRL 343]	See Table 13.1 for references to earlier surveys. The 1977 survey provides data for Technician Engineers also
ICE salary surveys	By age by field of employment; qualification and type of work	GB regions / Ireland	Annual from 1976	[QRL 207]	

CONSTRUCTION PROFESSIONS—*contd.*

Type of Data/ Descriptive Title	Breakdown/ Detail of Analysis	Area	Dates and Frequency	Publication (see QRL Key)	Text Reference and Remarks
Work Undertaken by Construction Professions					13.5
Private architects (RIBA surveys)					
Private architects' new building work	Value of new commissions received; work entering production drawings stage; by type of work and sector	GB/UK regions —see Remarks	Quarterly from 1958	[QRL 249]	
Progress of metrication and dimensional co-ordination	Proportion of value and no. of such projects by type of work and sector	GB/UK regions —see Remarks	Quarterly from 1969–76	[QRL 249]	
Partial service work	Proportion of no. of new commissions with partial service by size of practice; type of work; value of project	GB/UK regions —see Remarks	Quarterly from 1970–7 (Q_1)	[QRL 249]	13.5.1.2. GB to 1964 and from 1976; UK in the intervening period. Regional analyses based on office location
Partial service work	Proportion of no. of new commissions with partial service by location of office and by site of project	GB/UK regions —see Remarks	Quarterly from 1970–7 (Q_1)	[QRL 249]	
Work certified	Value by type of work	GB/UK regions —see Remarks	Annually from 1958	[QRL 249]	
Work abandoned or postponed	Value by type of building and stage of work	GB/UK regions —see Remarks	Quarterly 1973 (Q_4)–19;7 (Q_1)	[QRL 249]	
Projects revived	Percent of practices reporting revived projects	GB	1977 (Q_3 and Q_4)	[QRL 249] No. 33	

QUICK REFERENCE LIST

Public and private architectural practice				
RIBA Regional Chairmen's Surveys	Qualitative indication of trends in work in hand and new commissions	UK regions	From 1974	[QRL 287]
LA design work (DOE surveys)	Nos (up to April 1975) and value of projects at working drawings stage by type carried out by or for LAs	GB	3 times p.a. from 1965	[QRL 168] (formerly in [QRL 194])	4.7. See Table 4.5 for further details including particulars of series now discontinued and data available on request
Private chartered quantity surveyors' work					13.5.2
RICS 'state of trade' enquiries	Qualitative indication of trends: early prelim. est. commissions; bill of quantity commissions; all work on hand	E & W	Quarterly from 1975	'QS Notes' in [QRL 118]
MMC survey on scale fees	Volume of business of firms in sample	UK	1972–4	[QRL 345]
Consulting engineers					13.5.3
Overseas work obtained by ACE members	Particulars of individual contracts	UK	Annually	[QRL 216]
Overseas work obtained by members and non-members of ACE and by British contractors	Particulars of individual contracts	UK	1969	[QRL 262]
Revenue and commissions—ACE members	Revenue Commissions completed by size and type	UK	1963–71 Circa 1971	[QRL 260]

QUICK REFERENCE LIST KEY TO PUBLICATIONS

Reference Number	Organization responsible or author	Title	Publisher	Frequency or date of publication	Remarks
[QRL 1]	Barna, T.	'The interdependence of the British economy', *Journal of the Royal Statistical Society Series A (General)* **115**, pp. 29–81	Royal Statistical Society	1952	
[QRL 2]	Begg, H. M., Lythe, C. M. and Sorley, R.	*Expenditure in Scotland, 1961–1971*	Scottish Academic Press, Edinburgh and London	1975	
[QRL 3]	Bowen, Ian	'Focus on you', *Architects' Journal*, **119**, pp. 120–36	Architectural Press Ltd, London	1954	This is the final report on a survey of the architectural profession carried out during 1953; it was preceded by a series of articles published in the *Journal* in that year—Vols 117 and 118
[QRL 4]	Carruthers, J. F. S. and Harding, T.	'British-grown timber and the building and construction industry: current usage and future potential', *Building Research Establishment Current Paper CP5/76*	Building Research Establishment, Department of Environment, Garston, Herts	1976	
[QRL 5]	Chapman, A. L.	*Wages and Salaries in the United Kingdom 1920–1938*	University Press, Cambridge	1953	
[QRL 6]	Crockett, R. N.	*Slate*, Mineral Resources Consultative Committee, Mineral Dossier No. 12	HMSO, London	1975	
[QRL 7]	Cullen, B. D.	'Materials usage in new buildings', *Building*, **212**, pp. 115–16, 119–20, 123–4, 127	Building (Publishers) Ltd, London	1967	Reprinted in *Building Research Station Current Papers, Design Series 58*

QUICK REFERENCE LIST

[QRL 8]	Deane, Phyllis	'Regional variations in United Kingdom incomes from employment, 1948', *Journal of the Royal Statistical Society, Ser. A (General)*, **116**, pp. 123–39	Royal Statistical Society, London	1953	
[QRL 9]	Dunn, A. T.	'Conveyancing since 1973', *Economic Trends*, No. 275, pp. 96–113	HMSO, London	September 1976	
[QRL 10]	Dunn, A. T. and Astin, A. S.	'Surveys of conveyancing', *Economic Trends*, No. 247, pp. xxvii–xli	HMSO, London	May 1974	
[QRL 11]	Dunn, A. T. and Ganguly, A.	'Recent trends in sales of land and buildings', *Economic Trends*, No. 292, pp. 110–22	HMSO, London	February 1978	
[QRL 12]	Feinstein, C. H.	*Domestic Capital Formation in the United Kingdom, 1920–1938*	University Press, Cambridge	1965	
[QRL 13]	Feinstein, C. H.	*National Income, Expenditure and Output of the United Kingdom, 1855–1965*	University Press, Cambridge	1972	
[QRL 14]	Feinstein, C. H.	*Statistical Tables of National Income, Expenditure and Output of the U.K. 1855–1965*	University Press, Cambridge	1976	This volume contains the tables originally published in [QRL 13] including some revisions and a new introduction Reprinted in [B 279]
[QRL 15]	Gardner, J. W.	'Historical series of the index of industrial production' *Economic Trends*, No. 223	HMSO, London	May 1972	
[QRL 16]	Grigg, John and Fenyo, Andrew	'Architects' earnings 1975: RIBA survey', *Architects' Journal*, **162**, pp. 1332–5	Architectural Press Ltd, London	31 December 1975	
[QRL 17]	Kent-Smith, Derek and Hartley, Elizabeth	'United Kingdom regional accounts', *Economic Trends*, No. 277	HMSO, London	November 1976	
[QRL 18]	Lemessany, J.	'Estimates of the requirements for aggregates', *Building Research Establishment Current Paper CP 17/76*	Building Research Establishment, Department of the Environment, Garston, Herts	1976	

Reference Number	Organization responsible or author	Title	Publisher	Frequency or date of publication	Remarks
[QRL 19]	Lemessany, J. and Clapp, M. A.	'Resource inputs to new construction—the labour requirements of hospital building', Building Research Establishment Current Paper CP 85/75	Building Research Establishment, Department of the Environment, Garston, Herts	1975	
[QRL 20]	Mathias, Peter and Postan, M. M. (Eds)	The Cambridge Economic History of Europe, Vol. VII	University Press, Cambridge	Forthcoming	
[QRL 21]	Mitchell, B. R. with the collaboration of Deane, Phyllis	Abstract of British Historical Statistics	University Press, Cambridge	1962	
[QRL 22]	Mitchell, B. R. and Jones, H. G.	Second Abstract of British Historical Statistics	University Press, Cambridge	1971	
[QRL 23]	Revell, Jack and Associates	The Wealth of the Nation—the National Balance Sheet of the United Kingdom, 1957–1961	University Press, Cambridge	1967	
[QRL 24]	Romans, Michael	Technician Survey 1975	ILEA Steering Group TEC Sector B, ILEA, London	1976	
[QRL 25]	Stewart, I. G.	'Input-output table for the United Kingdom', London and Cambridge Economic Bulletin, New Series, The Times Review of Industry, No. 28, pp. vii–ix	Times Newspapers Ltd, London	December 1958	
[QRL 26]	Tamari, M.	A Postal Questionnaire Survey of Small Firms: An Analysis of Financial Data. Committee of Enquiry on Small Firms, Research Report No. 16	HMSO, London	1972	
[QRL 27]	Tomkins, C. R.	Income and Expenditure Accounts for Wales, 1965–1968	Welsh Council, Cardiff	1971	
[QRL 28]	Woodward, V. H.	Regional Social Accounts for the United Kingdom, NIESR Regional Papers No. 1	University Press, Cambridge	1970	
[QRL 29]	Woodward, V. H.	A 70 Sector Input–Output Table for 1954	Department of Applied Economics, University of Cambridge	1971	Unpublished paper available from the Department

QUICK REFERENCE LIST

[QRL 30]	Department of Health and Social Services	Analyses of Hospital Running Costs, Related Income and Statistics of Hospitals and other Residential Facilities Administered by the Health and Social Services Board	HMSO, Belfast	Annually
[QRL 31]	Central Statistical Office	Annual Abstract of Statistics	HMSO, London	Annually from No. 84, published 1948	For earlier numbers in the series see Serial [QRL 317]
[QRL 32]	Ministry of Works and successor Departments*	Annual Bulletin of Statistics, continued as Annual Bulletin of Construction Statistics	The Ministry or Department, according to date of issue, London	Annually from March 1960 (No. 1) to the issue for 1970 (No. 12)	Replaced by serial [QRL 168]
[QRL 33]	Advisory, Conciliation and Arbitration Service	Annual Report	ACAS, London	Annually since 1976 (Report for 1975)
[QRL 34]	Certification Office for Trade Unions and Employers' Associations	Annual Report of the Certification Officer	HMSO, London	Annually from Report for 1976 (pub. 1977)
[QRL 35]	Royal Institute of British Architects	Annual Report of the Council	The Institute, London	Annually
[QRL 36]	Command Papers	Annual Report of H.M. Chief Inspector of Factories	HMSO, London	Annually to Report for 1974	Replaced by [QRL 164]
[QRL 37]	Command Paper	Annual Report of the Ministry of Works for the period 1 January to 31 December 1949	HMSO, London	1950, Cmd. 7995
[QRL 38]	Command Paper	Annual Report of the Ministry of Works for 1950	HMSO, London	1951, Cmd. 8306
[QRL 39]	HM Customs and Excise	Annual Statement of Overseas Trade of the United Kingdom, 5 volumes	HMSO, London	Annually
[QRL 40]	Royal Institute of British Architects	The Architect and His Office	The Institute, London	1962

* The Ministry of Public Building and Works from July to November 1970 and then the Department of the Environment.

Reference Number	Organization responsible or author	Title	Publisher	Frequency or date of publication	Remarks
[QRL 41]	Command Paper	*Architects' Costs and Fees*, National Board for Prices and Incomes, Report No. 71	HMSO, London	1968, Cmnd. 3653	
[QRL 42]	Royal Institute of British Architects	*Architects' Earnings 1976. Report of RIBA Survey*	RIBA, London	1977	
[QRL 43]	Architectural Press Ltd	*Architects' Journal*	Architectural Press Ltd, 9 Queen Anne's Gate, London, SW1H 9BY	Weekly	
[QRL 44]	House of Commons Paper [Monopolies and Mergers Commission]	*Architects' Services. A Report on the Supply of Architects' Services with Reference to Scale Fees*	HMSO, London	1977, HC 4 Session 1977–8	
[QRL 45]	Department of Trade (formerly Board of Trade)	*Bankruptcy. General Annual Report for year....*	HMSO, London	Annually	
[QRL 46]	National Council of Building Material Producers	*BMP Information*	BMP Publications, 26 Store Street, London, WC1E 7BT	Fortnightly	Available on subscription only
[QRL 47]	National Council of Building Material Producers	*BMP Statistical Bulletin*	BMP Publications, 26 Store Street, London, WC1E 7BT	Monthly	Available on subscription only
[QRL 48]	Board of Trade	*Board of Trade Journal*	HMSO, London	Weekly up to the issue for 14 October 1970	Succeeded by [QRL 352]
[QRL 49]	Board of Trade	'Capital expenditure by manufacturing industry in Great Britain, 1948 to 1950', *Board of Trade Journal*, **162**, pp. 4–6	HMSO, London	5 January 1952	
[QRL 50]	Board of Trade	'First preliminary results of partial census of production, 1946', *Board of Trade Journal*, **154**, pp. 487–91	HMSO, London	1948	
[QRL 51]	Board of Trade	'Partial census of production 1946 (Report No. 20). Building and contracting trade', *Board of Trade Journal*, **158**, pp. 447–53	HMSO, London	1950	

[QRL 52]	Board of Trade	'Partial census of production 1946 (Report No. 19). Constructional engineering trade', *Board of Trade Journal*, **157**, pp. 176–7, correction in **158**, p. 455	HMSO, London	1949
[QRL 53]	Board of Trade	'Partial census of production 1946 (Report No. 17). Electrical engineering (general) trade', *Board of Trade Journal*, **156**, pp. 423–7	HMSO, London	1949
[QRL 54]	Board of Trade	'Partial census of production 1946 (Report No. 21). Local authorities (building and civil engineering)', *Board of Trade Journal*, **158**, pp. 453–5	HMSO, London	1950
[QRL 55]	Board of Trade	'Partial census of production 1946 (Report No. 18). Mechanical engineering (general) trade', *Board of Trade Journal*, **156**, pp. 888–904	HMSO, London	1949
[QRL 56]	Board of Trade	'Results of census of production for 1951 summarized', *Board of Trade Journal*, **171**, pp. 682–4	HMSO, London	1956
[QRL 57]	Board of Trade	*Britain's Shops. A Statistical Summary of Shops and Service Establishments*	HMSO, London	1952
[QRL 58]	Department of Employment and Productivity	*British Labour Statistics Historical Abstract 1886–1968*	HMSO, London	1971
[QRL 59]	Department of Employment	*British Labour Statistics Yearbook*	HMSO, London	Annually from 1971 (Yearbook for 1969)
[QRL 60]	Building (Publishers) Ltd	*Building* (formerly *The Builder*)	Building (Publishers) Ltd, The Builder House, PO Box 135, 4 Catherine Street, London, WC2B 5JN	Weekly
[QRL 61]	Building Apprenticeship and Training Council	*Building Apprenticeship and Training Council, Second Report*, December 1944	HMSO, London	1945

468　CONSTRUCTION AND THE RELATED PROFESSIONS

Reference Number	Organization responsible or author	Title	Publisher	Frequency or date of publication	Remarks
[QRL 62]	Building Apprenticeship and Training Council	*Building Apprenticeship and Training Council, Third Report, December 1946*	HMSO, London	1947	
[QRL 63]	Building Apprenticeship and Training Council	*Building Apprenticeship and Training Council, Fourth Report, June 1949*	HMSO, London	1949	
[QRL 64]	Building Apprenticeship and Training Council	*Building Apprenticeship and Training Council, Final Report*	HMSO, London	1957	
[QRL 65]	Ministry of Education	*Building Bulletin No. 12: Site Labour Studies in School Building*	HMSO, London	1955	
[QRL 66]	House of Commons Paper	*Building Control Act 1966. 1st Report by the Minister of Public Building and Works for the period ended March 31, 1968*	HMSO, London	1968 HC 246 (Session 1967–8)	
[QRL 67]	House of Commons Paper	*Building Control Act 1966. 2nd Report by the Minister of Public Building and Works for the period ending March 31, 1969*	HMSO, London	1969, HC 262 (Session 1968–9)	
[QRL 68]	Ministry of Public Building and Works	*Building Maintenance Statistics, A report of a working group of the Committee on Building Maintenance, R & D Paper*	The Ministry, London	1970	
[QRL 69]	Institute of Building	*Building Technology and Management*	IOB, Englemere, Kings Ride, Ascot, Berks, SL5 8BJ	Monthly	
[QRL 70]	Ministry of Public Building and Works	*Bulletin of Construction Statistics Special Supplement April 1969*	The Ministry, London	1969	
[QRL 71]	Ministry of Works and successor Departments*	*Bulletin of Statistics Supplement, continued as Bulletin of Construction Statistics Supplement*	The Ministry or Department, according to date of issue, London	1959–70†	Ceased publication. Replaced by [QRL 240]

* The Ministry of Public Building and Works from July 1962 to November 1970 and then the Department of the Environment.
† Annually from 1959 (the first issue containing the results of the censuses taken in 1957 and 1958) to 1965 and then biannually (separate Supplements being issued in respect of each April and September census) for the censuses from 1965 to 1970. In addition in 1963 a separate Addendum to the 1963 Supplement was issued containing the results of the September census for that year.

[QRL 72]	Department of Industry, Business Statistics Office	*Business Monitor M3. Company Finance*	HMSO, London	Annually since 1969
[QRL 73]	Department of Industry, Business Statistics Office	*Business Monitor M4. Overseas Transactions*	HMSO, London	Annually
[QRL 74]	Department of Industry, Business Statistics Office	*Business Monitor M7. Acquisitions and Mergers of Companies*	HMSO, London	Quarterly from 1971
[QRL 75]	Department of Industry (formerly Department of Trade and Industry), Business Statistics Office	*Business Monitor C series in 1970, PA Series from 1971- Report on Census of Production ... [year]*	HMSO, London	Annually from 1972 (census for 1970)
[QRL 76]	Department of Industry, Business Statistics Office	*Business Monitor PA 500, Report on the Census of Production ... [year] Construction*	HMSO, London	Annually from 1976 (Report for 1974)
[QRL 77]	Department of Industry (formerly Department of Trade and Industry), Business Statistics Office	*Business Monitor PA 672 (C 152 in 1970) Report on Census of Production ... [year] Electricity*	HMSO, London	Annually from 1973 (Report for 1970)
[QRL 78]	Department of Industry, Business Statistics Office	*Business Monitor PA 1003, Analyses of UK Manufacturing Local Units by Employment Size*	HMSO, London	Annually from 1974 (Report for 1971)
[QRL 79]	Department of Industry, Business Statistics Office	*Business Monitor PA 1004. Input–Output Tables for the United Kingdom ... [year]*	HMSO, London	Annually from 1974 (Tables for 1970)
[QRL 80]	Department of Industry, Business Statistics Office	*Business Monitor PA 1007. Minerals ... [year(s)]*	HMSO, London	Annually from 1976 (Report for the years 1974 and 1975)
[QRL 81]	Department of Industry, Business Statistics Office	*Business Monitors—Production Series*	HMSO, London	Quarterly (PQ series) or Monthly (PM series) Introduced at various dates from 1962 onwards
[QRL 82]	Department of Industry, Business Statistics Office	*Business Monitor, Service and Distributive SD Series*	HMSO, London	Periodically from 1970
[QRL 83]	Department of Industry, Business Statistics Office	*Business Monitor SD 10–23. Census of Distribution and Other Services 1971. Report.* 13 parts plus supplement	HMSO, London	Various dates from 1974

Reference Number	Organization responsible or author	Title	Publisher	Frequency or date of publication	Remarks
[QRL 84]	Society of County Treasurers	*Capital Expenditure of County Councils . . . [year]*	The Society, Rope Walk, Ipswich	Annually	
[QRL 85]	Department of Trade and Industry, Business Statistics Office	*Catering Trades 1969. Statistical Inquiry*	HMSO, London	1972	
[QRL 86]	General Register Office	*Census 1961, England and Wales. Education Tables*	HMSO, London	1966	
[QRL 87]	General Register Office	*Census 1951, England and Wales. General Tables*	HMSO, London	1956	
[QRL 88]	General Register Office	*Census 1951, England and Wales. Industry Tables*	HMSO, London	1957	
[QRL 89]	General Register Office	*Census 1961, England and Wales. Industry Tables: Parts I and II*	HMSO, London	1966	
[QRL 90]	General Register Office	*Census 1951, England and Wales. Occupation Tables*	HMSO, London	1956	
[QRL 91]	General Register Office	*Census 1961, England and Wales. Occupation Tables*	HMSO, London	1966	
[QRL 92]	General Register Office	*Census 1961, England and Wales. Workplace Tables*	HMSO, London	1966	
[QRL 93]	Office of Population Censuses and Surveys	*Census 1971, England and Wales. Workplace and Transport to Work Tables. Parts I and II*	HMSO, London	1975–6	
[QRL 94]	Office of Population Censuses and Surveys	*Census 1971, Great Britain. Economic Activity. Parts II–IV*	HMSO, London	1975	
[QRL 95]	General Register Office	*Census 1961, Great Britain. Migration Tables*	HMSO, London	1966	
[QRL 96]	Office of Population Censuses and Surveys, London and General Register Office, Edinburgh	*Census 1971, Great Britain. Migration Tables Part III (A)*	HMSO, London	1977	
[QRL 97]	Office of Population Censuses and Surveys	*Census 1971, Great Britain. Qualified Manpower Tables*	HMSO, London	1976	
[QRL 98]	General Register Office	*Census 1961, Great Britain. Scientific and Technological Qualifications*	HMSO, London	1962	

[QRL 99]	General Register Office	*Census 1961, Great Britain. Summary Tables*	HMSO, London	1966
[QRL 100]	General Register Office, Edinburgh	*Census 1971, Scotland. Economic Activity Tables*	HMSO, Edinburgh	1978
[QRL 101]	General Register Office for Scotland	*Census 1961, Scotland. Vol. 8. Internal Migration*	HMSO, Edinburgh	1966
[QRL 102]	General Register Office for Scotland	*Census 1971, Scotland. Migration Tables, Part IV*	HMSO, Edinburgh	1977
[QRL 103]	General Registry Office	*Census 1951, Scotland. Vol. IV. Occupations and Industries*	HMSO, Edinburgh	1956
[QRL 104]	General Register Office for Scotland	*Census 1961, Scotland. Vol. VI. Occupation, Industry and Workplace. Part 1 Occupation Tables; Part 2 Industry Tables; Part 3 Workplace Tables*	HMSO, Edinburgh	1966
[QRL 105]	General Register Office for Scotland	*Census 1961, Scotland. Vol. 9, Terminal Education Age*	HMSO, Edinburgh	1966
[QRL 106]	General Register Office for Scotland	*Census 1971, Scotland. Workplace and Transport Tables*	HMSO, Edinburgh	1976
[QRL 107]	Board of Trade	*Census of Distribution and Other Services 1950*, 3 vols	HMSO, London	1953–5
[QRL 108]	Northern Ireland General Register Office	*Census of Population 1971. Economic Activity Tables Northern Ireland*	HMSO, Belfast	1977
[QRL 109]	Northern Ireland General Register Office	*Census of Population 1971. Education Tables. Northern Ireland*	HMSO, Belfast	1975
[QRL 110]	Government of Northern Ireland, General Register Office	*Census of Population 1951. General Report*	HMSO, Belfast	1965
[QRL 111]	Government of Northern Ireland, General Register Office	*Census of Population 1966. General Report*	HMSO, Belfast	1968
[QRL 112]	Government of Northern Ireland, General Register Office	*Census of Population 1971. Migration Tables*	HMSO, Belfast	1976
[QRL 113]	Government of Northern Ireland	*Census of Population of Northern Ireland 1951. General Report*	HMSO, Belfast	1955
[QRL 114]	Northern Ireland General Register Office	*Census of Population 1971. Workplace and Transport to Work Tables*	HMSO, Belfast	1975

472　　CONSTRUCTION AND THE RELATED PROFESSIONS

Reference Number	Organization responsible or author	Title	Publisher	Frequency or date of publication	Remarks
[QRL 115]	Board of Trade	Censuses of Production. Analysis of Standard Regions by Trades 1948 and 1951	Statistics Division, Board of Trade, London	1957	Issued in duplicated form and without imprint
[QRL 116]	Board of Trade	Censuses of Production for 1950, 1949, and 1948, Summary Tables, Part 1	HMSO, London	1953	
[QRL 117]	Department of Employment	Changes in Rates of Wages and Hours of Work	HMSO, London	Monthly since May 1966	
[QRL 118]	Royal Institution of Chartered Surveyors	The Chartered Surveyor	RICS, 29 Lincoln's Inn Fields, London, WC2A 3DG	Monthly	
[QRL 119]	National Institute of Economic and Social Research	A Classified List of Large Companies Engaged in British Industry	The Institute, London	1955	
[QRL 120]	Building Research Station	Collection of Construction Statistics	The Station, Garston, Herts	1968	
[QRL 121]	Department of the Environment, Building Research Station	Collection of Construction Statistics, second edition	The Station, Garston, Herts	1971	
[QRL 122]	Department of the Environment	Commercial and Industrial Property 1975: Facts and Figures	The Department, London	1976	
[QRL 123]	Department of Trade (formerly Board of Trade)	Companies in ... [year]	HMSO, London	Annually	
[QRL 124]	Board of Trade	Company Assets and Income in 1957	HMSO, London	1960	
[QRL 125]	Board of Trade	Company Assets, Income and Finance in 1960	HMSO, London	1962	
[QRL 126]	Board of Trade	Company Assets, Income and Finance in 1963	HMSO, London	1965	
[QRL 127]	National Institute of Economic and Social Research	Company Income and Finance, 1949–53	The Institute, London	1956	

[QRL 128]	National Economic Development Office	*Construction Forecasts . . . [years] Report prepared by the Joint Forecasting Committee of the Building and Civil Engineering EDCs*	HMSO, London	Twice yearly	Available on annual subscription only. Formerly published by NEDO
[QRL 129]	Northwood Publications Ltd	*Construction News*	Northwood Publications Ltd, Elm House, 10–16 Elm Street, London, WC1X 0BP	Weekly	
[QRL 130]	Northwood Publications Ltd in association with Association of Consulting Engineers	*The Consulting Engineers Who's Who and Yearbook*	Northwood Publications Ltd, Elm House, 10–16 Elm Street, London, WC1X 0BP	Annually	
[QRL 131]	IPC Building and Contract Journals Ltd.	*Contract Journal*	IPC Building and Contract Journals Ltd, Surrey House, 1 Throwley Way, Sutton, Surrey, SM1 4QQ	Weekly	
[QRL 132]	Ministry of Works	'An analysis of municipal direct labour forces', *Contract Journal*, **140**, (3646), pp. 1338–40	IPC Building and Contract Journals Ltd, Surrey House, 1 Throwley Way, Sutton, Surrey, SM1 4QQ	1949	
[QRL 133]	IPC Building and Contract Journals Ltd	*Contract Journal Market Indicators*	IPC Building and Contract Journals Ltd, Surrey House, 1 Throwley Way, Sutton, Surrey, SM1 4QQ	Monthly	Available on subscription
[QRL 134]	House of Commons Papers	*Control of Office and Industrial Development Act 1965 —Annual Report* continued as *Town and Country Planning Act 1971. Control of Office Development Annual Report*	HMSO, London	Annually from Session 1965–6	

Reference Number	Organization responsible or author	Title	Publisher	Frequency or date of publication	Remarks
[QRL 135]	Department of Employment	Department of Employment Gazette	HMSO, London	Monthly from January 1971	Published as the *Ministry of Labour Gazette* prior to June 1968, and as the *Employment and Productivity Gazette* from June 1968 to December 1970 Formerly published as [QRL 322]
[QRL 136]	Department of the Environment, Welsh Office	Development Control Statistics	The Department, London	Annually. First issued in 1976 for the year 1974/5	
[QRL 137]	Greater London Council	Development and Materials Bulletin	Greater London Council, London	10 issues per year	
[QRL 138]	Department of Health and Social Security	Digest of Health Statistics for England and Wales	HMSO, London	Annually until 1971	Succeeded by [QRL 163]
[QRL 139]	Scottish Home Department	Digest of Scottish Statistics	HMSO, Edinburgh	Bi-annually from 1953 to April 1971	No longer published. Succeeded by [QRL 306]
[QRL 140]	Department (formerly Ministry) of Finance	Digest of Statistics	HMSO, Belfast	Bi-annually, each March and September, since 1954	
[QRL 141]	Department of Energy	Digest of United Kingdom Energy Statistics	HMSO, London	Annually from 1974	Formerly entitled at various times *United Kingdom Energy Statistics*, *Digest of Energy Statistics*, *Ministry of Power Statistical Digest*
[QRL 142]	Welsh Office (formerly Home Office)	Digest of Welsh Statistics	HMSO, Cardiff	Annually since 1954	
[QRL 143]	Royal Institute of British Architects	Directory of Members	RIBA Publications, London	Annually from 1973	Formerly published as [QRL 285]
[QRL 144]	Royal Institute of British Architects	Directory of Practices	RIBA Publications, London	Annually from 1973	Formerly published as [QRL 285]

[QRL 145]	Economic Development Committee for Building	*Earnings in the Building Industry. A Survey of Operatives' Earnings and Hours in May 1973*	NEDO, London	1974	
[QRL 146]	Royal Institute of British Architects	*Earnings of Architects and their Support Staff: Report of RIBA Survey 1970*	RIBA, London	1972	
[QRL 147]	Central Statistical Office	*Economic Trends*	HMSO, London	Monthly	
[QRL 148]	Central Statistical Office	*Economic Trends Annual Supplement*	HMSO, London	Annually from 1975	
[QRL 149]	Central Statistical Office	'Historical series of the index of industrial production, 1970=100', *Economic Trends*, No. 241	HMSO, London	November 1973	Reprinted in [B 279]
[QRL 150]	Society of Architectural and Associated Technicians	*Education Facilities Survey No. . . . [date]*	The Society, London	Annually	
[QRL 151]	Northern Ireland Department of Education	*Education Statistics*	HMSO, Belfast	Issued in two parts annually	
[QRL 152]	Royal Institute of British Architects	*Education Statistics*	RIBA, London	1978	
[QRL 153]	Department of Education and Science	*Education Statistics for the United Kingdom*	HMSO, London	Annually from 1970 (issue for 1967)	
[QRL 154]	Morgan Grampian Publishers Ltd	*The Engineer*	Morgan Grampian Publishers, Morgan Grampian House, Calderwood Street, London, SE18 6OH	Weekly	
[QRL 155]	Department of Manpower Services (NI)	*Factories Act (Northern Ireland). Report of the Chief Inspector for the year . . .*	HMSO, Belfast	Annually	Formerly issued as Government of N. Ireland Command Papers
[QRL 156]	Department of Employment	*Family Expenditure Survey*	HMSO, London	Annually	
[QRL 157]	Board of Trade	*Final Reports on the Census of Production for 1948*	HMSO, London	Various dates from 1951	
[QRL 158]	Central Statistical Office	*Financial Statistics*	HMSO, London	Monthly since 1962	
[QRL 159]	Financial Times Ltd	*Financial Times*	Financial Times Ltd, London	Daily except Sundays	

476 CONSTRUCTION AND THE RELATED PROFESSIONS

Reference Number	Organization responsible or author	Title	Publisher	Frequency or date of publication	Remarks
[QRL 160]	University Grants Committee	First Destination of University Graduates	HMSO, London	Annually from 1962	Prior to 1971–2 published under the title *First Employment of University Graduates*
[QRL 161]	Command Paper	The Government's Expenditure Plans, 2 vols	HMSO, London	1977, Cmnd 6721	
[QRL 162]	Command Paper	The Government's Expenditure Plans, 1978–79 to 1981–82, 2 vols	HMSO, London	1978, Cmnd 7049	
[QRL 163]	Department of Health and Social Security	Health and Personal Social Services Statistics for England and Wales	HMSO, London	Annually from 1972	Successor volume to [QRL 138]
[QRL 164]	Health and Safety Executive	Health and Safety Statistics ... [year]	HMSO, London	Annually from 1977 (Report for 1975)	
[QRL 165]	Department of Health for Scotland (agency varied)	Hospital Building, Scotland. Progress Reports Nos 1–3	HMSO, Edinburgh	1962 and 1963	
[QRL 166]	Department of Health and Social Security	Hospital Costing Returns	HMSO, London	Annually	
[QRL 167]	Economic Development Committee for the Hotel and Catering Industry	Hotel Prospects to 1980	NEDO, London	1972	A summary of this report was published as [B 137]
[QRL 168]	Department of the Environment, Scottish Development Department and Welsh Office	Housing and Construction Statistics	HMSO, London	Quarterly from 1972	This publication is the successor to serials [QRL 194], [QRL 32] and [QRL 169]
[QRL 169]	Ministry of Housing and Local Government (Department of the Environment)	Housing Statistics	HMSO, London	Quarterly from March 1966 to February 1972	Ceased publication. Succeeded by [QRL 168]
[QRL 170]	Economic Development Committee for Building	How Flexible is Construction?	NEDO, London	1978, forthcoming	
[QRL 171]	Board of Trade, Statistics Division	Income and Finance of Public Quoted Companies. Summary and Industrial Group Tables 1949–1960	Board of Trade, London	1962	

[QRL 172]	House of Commons Papers	*Industry Act 1972. Annual Report*	HMSO, London	Annually from Session 1972–3
[QRL 173]	Board of Inland Revenue	*Inland Revenue Statistics . . . [year]*	HMSO, London	Annually since 1970
[QRL 174]	Ministry of Finance	*Input–Output Tables for Northern Ireland 1963*	HMSO, Belfast	1973
[QRL 175]	The Fraser of Allander Institute	*Input–Output Tables for Scotland*	Scottish Academic Press, Edinburgh and London	Forthcoming
[QRL 176]	Central Statistical Office	*Input–Output Tables for the United Kingdom 1954. Studies in Official Statistics No. 8*	HMSO, London	1961
[QRL 177]	Central Statistical Office	*Input–Output Tables for the United Kingdom 1963. Studies in Official Statistics No. 16*	HMSO, London	1970
[QRL 178]	Central Statistical Office	*Input–Output Tables for the United Kingdom 1968. Studies in Official Statistics No. 22*	HMSO, London	1973
[QRL 179]	British Steel Corporation and British Independent Steel Producers' Association	*Iron and Steel Industry Annual Statistics*	British Steel Corporation on behalf of the Iron and Steel Statistics Bureau, PO Box 230, 12 Addiscombe Road, Croydon, CR9 6BS	Annually Prior to 1967 issued by the Iron and Steel Board and the British Iron and Steel Federation (London). A monthly series is also published as *Iron and Steel Monthly Statistics*
[QRL 180]	Royal Institute of British Architects	*Journal of the Royal Institute of British Architects*	RIBA, 66 Portland Place, London, W1N 4AD	Monthly
[QRL 181]	Ministry of Labour	*Labour Costs in Great Britain in 1964*	HMSO, London	1968
[QRL 182]	Department of Employment	*Labour Costs in Great Britain in 1968*	HMSO, London	1971
[QRL 183]	Statistical Office of the European Communities	*Labour Force Sample Survey 1975*	SOEC, Luxembourg	1977 (dated 1976)
[QRL 184]	Association of Consulting Engineers	*List of Members*	The Association, Hancock House, 87 Vincent Square, London, SW1P 2PH	Annually

Reference Number	Organization responsible or author	Title	Publisher	Frequency or date of publication	Remarks
[QRL 185]	Institution of Civil Engineers	List of Members	The Institution, Great George Street, London, SW1P 3AA	Annually	Now entitled *Yearbook*
[QRL 186]	Ministry of Development (formerly Ministry of Health and Local Government)	*Local Authority Rate Statistics*	HMSO, Belfast	Annually from 1954–5	
[QRL 187]	Department of the Environment and Welsh Office	*Local Government Financial Statistics, England and Wales ... [year]*	HMSO, London	Annually	
[QRL 188]	National Federation of Building Trades Employers	*Manpower Study ... [year]*	The Federation, London	1972–4	
[QRL 189]	Department (Ministry) of Commerce	*Mines and Quarries Report for ... [years]*	HMSO, Belfast	Irregularly from 1970 (report for 1967–9)	For earlier series see [QRL 316]
[QRL 190]	Ministry of Labour	*Ministry of Labour Gazette*	HMSO, London	Monthly to June 1968	Continued as *Department of Employment and Productivity Gazette* from June 1968 to Dec. 1970 and then *Department of Employment Gazette* [QRL 135]
[QRL 191]	Department of the Environment, Property Services Agency	*Monthly Bulletin Construction Indices for use with National Economic Development Office Price Adjustment Formula. Building Works*	HMSO, London	Monthly	
[QRL 192]	Department of the Environment, Property Services Agency	*Monthly Bulletin Construction Indices for use with National Economic Development Office Price Adjustment Formula. Civil Engineering Works*	HMSO, London	Monthly	

[QRL 193]	Department of the Environment, Property Services Agency	*Monthly Bulletin Construction Indices for use with National Economic Development Office Adjustment Formulae. Specialist Engineering Installations*	HMSO, London	Monthly
[QRL 194]	Ministry of Works and successor Departments*	*Monthly Bulletin of Statistics*, continued as *Monthly Bulletin of Construction Statistics*	The Ministry or Department, according to date of issue, London	Monthly from February 1946 to June 1972	Ceased publication. These *Bulletins* were not formally published but in later years were circulated outside the Ministry; most of the series is available in the library of the Department of the Environment, Property Services Agency in Croydon.
[QRL 195]	Central Statistical Office	*Monthly Digest of Statistics*	HMSO, London	Monthly from January 1946
[QRL 196]	Department of the Environment	*Monthly Statistics of Building Materials and Components*	Department of the Environment, Statistics Construction Division, London	Monthly	Available on subscription only
[QRL 197]	House of Commons Papers	*National Health Service Acts 1946 to 1973, Accounts ... [year]*	HMSO, London	Annually
[QRL 198]	Ministry of Health	*National Health Service, Hospital Building, England and Wales, Progress Reports Nos. 1 to 8*	HMSO, London	1962–6
[QRL 199]	House of Commons Papers	*National Health Service (Scotland) Acts 1947 to 1973, Accounts ... [year]*	HMSO, London	Annually

* The Ministry of Public Building and Works from July 1962 to November 1970 and then the Department of the Environment.

Reference Number	Organization responsible or author	Title	Publisher	Frequency or date of publication	Remarks
[QRL 200]	Scottish Home and Health Department	*National Health Service, Scotland. Analysis of Running Costs of Scottish Hospitals*	HMSO, Edinburgh	Annually	Succeeded by Serial [QRL 310]
[QRL 201]	Central Statistical Office	*National Income and Expenditure*	HMSO, London	Annually from 1952	Issued, before 1952, as a Command Paper
[QRL 202]	Command Paper	*National Income and Expenditure of the United Kingdom 1938 to 1946*	HMSO, London	1947, Cmd 7099	
[QRL 203]	Command Paper	*National Income and Expenditure of the United Kingdom 1946 to 1950*	HMSO, London	1951, Cmd 8203	
[QRL 204]	National Institute of Economic and Social Research	*National Institute Economic Review*	NIESR, 2 Dean Trench Street, Smith Square, London, SW1P 3HE	Quarterly	
[QRL 205]	Manpower Services Commission	*The National Training Survey*	Nyp	Due to be published in 1979	
[QRL 206]	New Property Press	*New Building Projects (formerly New Building)*	New Property Press, Bleak House, St. Peter's Street, London, N1	Monthly	
[QRL 207]	Thomas Telford Ltd	*New Civil Engineer*	Thomas Telford Ltd, 26 Old Street, London, EC1P 1JH	Weekly	
[QRL 208]	Department of Employment	*New Earnings Survey*	HMSO, London	Annually from 1970 (issue for 1968), subsequent issues relate to the years from 1970 onwards	Since the issue for 1974 the report has been published in six parts (Parts A–F)
[QRL 209]	English Tourist Board	*New Hotels in England*	English Tourist Board, 4 Grosvenor Gardens, London, SW1	Annually	

QUICK REFERENCE LIST

[QRL 210]	Heating and Ventilating Contractors' Association	News Release. HVCA State of Trade Enquiry ... [date]	The Association, 32 Palace Court, London	Bi-annually	
[QRL 211]	Construction Industry Training Board	Northern Area Manpower Study 1970	CITB, London	Unpublished report available from the CITB	
[QRL 212]	Department of Manpower Services	Office and Shop Premises Act (NI) 1966. Report for the year ended ...	HMSO, Belfast	Annually	Issued as a Northern Ireland House of Commons Paper up to the Report for 1969
[QRL 213]	House of Commons Papers	The Offices, Shops and Railway Premises Act 1963. Report for the year ended ...	HMSO, London	Annually from 1965 (report for year ended 31 December 1964)	
[QRL 214]	Department of Energy, Offshore Supplies Office	Offshore ... [year]. An Analysis of Orders Placed	HMSO, London	Annually from 1974 (published in 1975)	Originally entitled *Offshore Oil and Gas*
[QRL 215]	Department of Trade (formerly Board of Trade)	Overseas Trade Statistics of the United Kingdom	HMSO, London	Monthly	Formerly published as *Accounts Relating to Trade and Navigation of the United Kingdom*
[QRL 216]	Association of Consulting Engineers	Overseas Work Entrusted to Members During ... [year]	The Association, Hancock House, Vincent Square, London, SW1	Annually	
[QRL 217]	Command Paper	Pay and Conditions in the Building Industry, National Board for Prices and Incomes, Report No. 92	HMSO, London	1968, Cmnd 3837	
[QRL 218]	Command Paper	Pay and Conditions in the Building Industry, the Civil Engineering Industry, and the Construction Industry other than Building and Civil Engineering (Statistical Supplement), National Board for Prices and Incomes, Report Nos. 91, 92 and 93 (Supplement)	HMSO, London	1969, Cmnd 3982	

Reference Number	Organization responsible or author	Title	Publisher	Frequency or date of publication	Remarks
[QRL 219]	Command Paper	*Pay and Conditions in the Civil Engineering Industry*, National Board for Prices and Incomes, Report No. 91	HMSO, London	1968, Cmnd 3836	
[QRL 220]	Command Paper	*Pay and Conditions in the Construction Industry other than Building and Civil Engineering*, National Board for Prices and Incomes, Report No. 93	HMSO, London	1968, Cmnd 3838	
[QRL 221]	Command Paper	*Pay and Conditions in the Contract Cleaning Trade*, National Board for Prices and Incomes, Report No. 168	HMSO, London	1971, Cmnd 4637	
[QRL 222]	Command Paper	*Pay and Conditions in the Electrical Contracting Industry*, National Board for Prices and Incomes, Report No. 120	HMSO, London	1969, Cmnd 4097	
[QRL 223]	Command Paper	*Pay and Conditions in the Electrical Contracting Industry in Scotland*, National Board for Prices and Incomes, Report No. 108	HMSO, London	1969, Cmnd 3966	
[QRL 224]	Department of Trade and Industry	*Persons with Qualifications in Engineering, Technology and Science 1959 to 1968*, Studies in Technological Manpower No. 3	HMSO, London	1971	
[QRL 225]	Department of Industry	*Persons with Qualifications in Engineering, Technology and Science. Census of Population 1971 Great Britain*, Studies in Technological Manpower No. 5	HMSO, London	1976	
[QRL 226]	Polytechnic Careers Advisers: Statistics Working Party	*Polytechnic First Degree and HND Students [year]. Some Details of First Destination and Employment. Statistical Supplement*	Polytechnic Careers Advisers, Committee of Directors of Polytechnics, 309 Regent Street, London, W1R 7PE	Annually	

QUICK REFERENCE LIST

[QRL 227]	Committee of Inquiry on Small Firms	*A Postal Questionnaire Survey of Small Firms: Non-Financial Data.* Research Report No. 17	HMSO, London	1972	Now ceased
[QRL 228]	Department of the Environment	*Press Notice. Bricks and Cement Production . . . [date]*	The Department, London	Monthly	
[QRL 229]	Department of Industry	*Press Notice. Capital Expenditure of the Manufacturing, Distributive and Service Industries in . . . [date]*	The Department, London	Quarterly	
[QRL 230]	Department of the Environment	*Press Notice. Employment of Craftsmen and Apprentices by Contractors in the Construction Industries, Report on . . . Enquiry*	The Department, London	Annually	
[QRL 231]	House-Builders Federation	*Press Notice. HBF State of Trade Enquiry*	The Federation, 82 New Cavendish Street, London, W1	Quarterly from 1976	
[QRL 232]	Department of Industry	*Press Notice. Industry's Investment Intentions for . . . [years]*	The Department, London	Three times a year	
[QRL 233]	Department of the Environment	*Press Notice. Joint Manpower Watch . . . [date]*	Issued jointly by the Department of the Environment, Association of County Councils, Association of District Councils and Association of Metropolitan Authorities	Quarterly	
[QRL 234]	National Federation of Building Trades Employers	*Press Notice. NFBTE State of Trade Enquiry*	NFBTE, 82 New Cavendish Street, London, W1	Quarterly	
[QRL 235]	Department of the Environment	*Press Notice. Orders for New Construction in . . .*	The Department, 2 Marsham Street, London, SW1	Monthly	
[QRL 236]	Department of the Environment	*Press Notice. Output and Employment in the Construction Industry . . . [date]*	The Department, 2 Marsham Street, London, SW1	Quarterly	
[QRL 237]	Confederation of British Industry	*Press Release. The . . . [date] CBI Industrial Trends Survey No. . . .*	CBI, 21 Tothill Street, London, SW1	Quarterly	
[QRL 238]	House of Commons Papers	*Price Commission Report for the period . . .*	HMSO, London	Quarterly from 1973	

Reference Number	Organization responsible or author	Title	Publisher	Frequency or date of publication	Remarks
[QRL 239]	Central Statistical Office	*Price Index Numbers for Current Cost Accounting*	HMSO, London	Three times a year since 1976	
[QRL 240]	Department of the Environment	*Private Contractors' Construction Census . . . [date]*	HMSO, London	Annually since 1974	The first issue contained the results of the censuses for 1971 and 1972; subsequent census results have appeared annually
[QRL 241]	Department of the Environment (originally Ministry of Works)	*Production of Aggregates* (formerly *Sand and Gravel Production*) . . .	HMSO, London	Annually from 1958 (first issue covered the period 1954–7)	
[QRL 242]	Engineers' Guild	'An Analysis of the 1960 Survey', *The Professional Engineer*, **6**, No. 9, January 1961	The Guild, London	1961	
[QRL 243]	Engineers' Guild	*Professional Engineers' Incomes 1962–3*	The Guild, London	1963	
[QRL 244]	Command Paper Monopolies Commission	*Professional Services Part I Report, Part II The Appendices*	HMSO, London	1970, Cmnd 4463	
[QRL 245]	Command Paper	*Public Expenditure to 1979–80*	HMSO, London	1976, Cmnd 6393	
[QRL 246]	Central Statistical Office	*Qualified Manpower in Great Britain—The 1966 Census of Population. Studies in Official Statistics No. 18*	HMSO, London	1971	
[QRL 247]	Central Statistical Office	*Qualified Manpower in Great Britain—the 1971 Census of Population. Studies in Official Statistics, No. 29*	*HMSO, London*	1976	

QUICK REFERENCE LIST

[QRL 248]	Institute of Quantity Surveyors	*The Quantity Surveyor—A survey of some members of the profession*	The Institute, 98 Gloucester Place, London, W1	1970	A summary of this report is to be found in the Institute's Journal, *The Quantity Surveyor*, **26** (3), 1969, pp. 51–2
[QRL 249]	Royal Institute of British Architects	*Quarterly Statistical Bulletin*	The Institute, 66 Portland Place, London, W1	Quarterly since 1958	The series have been numbered, commencing at No. 1, since June 1969
[QRL 250]	Department of the Environment and Welsh Office (agency varies)	*Rates and Rateable Values in England and Wales*	HMSO, London	Annually	
[QRL 251]	Scottish Office (agency varies)	*Rates and Rateable Values in Scotland*	HMSO, Edinburgh	Annually from 1959 (for year 1958/9)	Formerly published under the title *Rates in Scotland* (Scottish Home Dept)
[QRL 252]	Central Statistical Office	*Regional Statistics* (formerly *Abstract of Regional Statistics*)	HMSO, London	Annually from 1965	
[QRL 253]	Architects' Registration Council of the United Kingdom	*The Register of Architects*	The Council, 73 Hallam Street, London, W1	Annually	
[QRL 254]	Northern Ireland Construction Industry Training Board	*Report and Statements of Accounts for the period...*	HMSO, Belfast	Annually from 1967	First report published by the Ministry of Health and Social Services (NI), then as House of Commons (NI) Papers to report for 1970–1, then as Departmental papers (currently Department of Manpower Services)
[QRL 255]	Construction Industry Training Board	*Report and Statement of Accounts for the Year ended...*	The Board, London	Annually from the report for the year 1972–3	Earlier reports were issued as House of Commons Papers (HMSO, London)
[QRL 256]	Registry of Friendly Societies	*Report of the Chief Registrar of Friendly Societies for the Year... Trade Unions and Employers' Associations*	HMSO, London	Annually until 1976	

486   CONSTRUCTION AND THE RELATED PROFESSIONS

Reference Number	Organization responsible or author	Title	Publisher	Frequency or date of publication	Remarks
[QRL 257]	Command Papers	*Report of the Commissioners of HM Customs and Excise for the year ended...*	HMSO, London	Annually	(1977: Cmnd 7050)
[QRL 258]	Command Papers	*Report of the Commissioners of Her Majesty's Inland Revenue for the year ended....*	HMSO, London	Annually	(1977: Cmnd 6734)
[QRL 259]	Royal Institute of British Architects	*Report of the Committee [Percy Thomas] to consider the Present and Future of Private Architectural Practice*	RIBA, London	1950	
[QRL 260]	Department of the Environment	*Report of the Reddaway Inquiry into Consulting Engineering Firms' Costs and Earnings*	HMSO, London	1972	
[QRL 261]	Chairman: Sir Harry Pilkington	*Report of the Royal Commission on Doctors' and Dentists' Remuneration, 1957–60*	HMSO, London	1960, Cmnd 939	
[QRL 262]	National Economic Development Office	*Report on the Analysis of Overseas Contracts Data for 1969*	NEDO, London	1970	
[QRL 263]	Office of Population Censuses and Surveys	*Report on the 1971 Census: Income Follow-Up Survey*	HMSO, London	Due for publication in 1978	
[QRL 264]	Board of Trade	*Report on the Census of Distribution and Other Services 1957*	HMSO, London	1959	
[QRL 265]	Board of Trade	*Report on the Census of Distribution and Other Services 1961, 14 Parts plus supplement*	HMSO, London	1963–4 and 1971	
[QRL 266]	Board of Trade	*Report on the Census of Distribution and Other Services 1966, 2 vols*	HMSO, London	1970–1	
[QRL 267]	Ministry of Commerce	*Report on the Census of Distribution and Other Services of Northern Ireland 1965*	HMSO, Belfast	1969	
[QRL 268]	Board of Trade	*Reports on the Census of Production for 1949*	HMSO, London	Various dates from 1952	
[QRL 269]	Board of Trade	*The Reports on the Census of Production for 1951*	HMSO, London	Various dates from 1954	

QUICK REFERENCE LIST 487

[QRL 270]	Board of Trade	*Reports on the Censuses of Production for 1952 and 1953*	HMSO, London	Various dates from 1956	
[QRL 271]	Board of Trade	*Reports on the Census of Production for 1954*	HMSO, London	Various dates from 1957	
[QRL 272]	Board of Trade	*Reports on the Censuses of Production for 1955, 1956 and 1957*	HMSO, London	1959	
[QRL 273]	Board of Trade	*Reports on the Census of Production for 1958*	HMSO, London	Various dates from 1960	
[QRL 274]	Board of Trade	*The Report on the Censuses of Production for 1959, 1960, 1961 and 1962*	HMSO, London	1964	
[QRL 275]	Board of Trade	*Reports on the Census of Production 1963*	HMSO, London	Various dates from 1968	
[QRL 276]	Department of Trade and Industry	*The Report on the Censuses of Production for 1964, 1965, 1966, and 1967*	HMSO, London	1971	
[QRL 277]	Department of Trade and Industry, Business Statistics Office	*Reports on the Census of Production 1968*	HMSO, London	Various dates from 1971	
[QRL 278]	Department (formerly Ministry) of Commerce	*Report on the Census of Production of Northern Ireland ... [year(s)]*	HMSO, Belfast	Reports for 1930, 1935 and every year from 1949	The results for 1963 and 1968 each appeared in four volumes (construction being included in Vol. 4); the results for 1969 and 1970 and for 1971 and 1972 were combined in single volumes. The results for 1973 and 1974 are due to appear in a combined volume in 1978 Sold by HMSO
[QRL 279]	National Coal Board	*Report and Statement of Accounts ... [year]*	The Board, London	Annually	
[QRL 280]	Royal Institute of British Architects	*Report on a Survey of Cost and Income Trends 1956–65* (Prepared by Robson, Morrow & Co.)	RIBA, London	October 1966	

Reference Number	Organization responsible or author	Title	Publisher	Frequency or date of publication	Remarks
[QRL 281]	Command Paper. Committee on Manpower Resources for Science and Technology	*Report on the 1965 Triennial Manpower Survey of Engineers, Technologists, Scientists and Technical Supporting Staff*	HMSO, London	1966, Cmnd 3103	
[QRL 282]	Central Statistical Office	*Research and Development Expenditure. Studies in Official Statistics No. 21*	HMSO, London	1973	
[QRL 283]	Central Statistical Office	*Research and Development Expenditure and Employment. Studies in Official Statistics No. 27*	HMSO, London	1976	
[QRL 284]	Employment Services Agency and Synergy Publishing Ltd	*Reward*	Synergy Publishing Ltd, 1 Mill Street, Stone, Staffordshire	Three times a year since 1975	
[QRL 285]	Royal Institute of British Architects	*RIBA Directory*—formerly the *RIBA Kalendar*	The Institute, London	Annually until 1973	Succeeded by [QRL 144] and [QRL 143]
[QRL 286]	Royal Institute of British Architects	*RIBA Earnings Survey 1973. Report on a Survey of Architects and Support Staff*	RIBA, London		Prepared in eleven parts but not published (further particulars are available on request)
[QRL 287]	Royal Institute of British Architects	*RIBA Information. RIBA Regional Chairmen's Workload Survey*	RIBA, London	Twice yearly from 1975	
[QRL 288]	House of Commons Papers	*Roads in England ... [year]*	HMSO, London	Annually to 1976	Replaced in 1978 by new series, see *Policy for Roads: England 1978*, Cmnd 7132 (HMSO, London, 1978)
[QRL 289]	Command Papers	*Roads in Scotland, Report for ... [year]*	HMSO, London	Annually	(1976: Cmnd 6681)
[QRL 290]	Chairman: Sir Harry Pilkington	*Royal Commission on Doctors' and Dentists' Remuneration 1957–60, Supplement to Report—Further Statistical Appendix*	HMSO, London	1960, Cmnd 1064	

QUICK REFERENCE LIST

[QRL 291]	Royal Institution of Chartered Surveyors	Royal Institution of Chartered Surveyors' Year Book	Thomas Skinner Directories, Neville House, Eden Street, Kingston-upon-Thames, Surrey, KT1 1BY	Annually
[QRL 292]	General Register Office	Sample Census 1966, England and Wales. Migration Regional Reports	HMSO, London	1968
[QRL 293]	General Register Office	Sample Census 1966, England and Wales. Migration Summary Tables. Parts I and II	HMSO, London	1968–9
[QRL 294]	General Register Office	Sample Census 1966, England and Wales. Workplace and Transport Tables. Parts 1 and 2	HMSO, London	1968
[QRL 295]	General Register Office	Sample Census 1966, Great Britain. Economic Activity Tables. Parts I–IV	HMSO, London	1968–9
[QRL 296]	Office of Population Censuses and Surveys	Sample Census 1966, Great Britain. Qualified Manpower Tables	HMSO, London	1971
[QRL 297]	Office of Population Censuses and Surveys	Sample Census 1966, Great Britain. Scientific and Technological Qualifications	HMSO, London	1971
[QRL 298]	General Register Office for Scotland	Sample Census 1966, Scotland. Vol. VI. Economic Activity County Tables	HMSO, Edinburgh	1969
[QRL 299]	General Register Office for Scotland	Sample Census 1966, Scotland. Migration Tables. Parts I and II	HMSO, Edinburgh	1968–9
[QRL 300]	General Register Office for Scotland	Sample Census 1966, Scotland. Vol. III. Workplace and Transport Tables	HMSO, Edinburgh	1968
[QRL 301]	Department of Education and Science	The School Building Survey 1962	HMSO, London	1965
[QRL 302]	Office of the Lord President of the Council, Ministry of Labour and National Service	Scientific and Engineering Manpower in Great Britain	HMSO, London	1956
[QRL 303]	Command Paper. Advisory Council on Scientific Policy, Committee on Scientific Manpower	Scientific and Engineering Manpower in Great Britain 1959	HMSO, London	1959, Cmnd 902

Reference Number	Organization responsible or author	Title	Publisher	Frequency or date of publication	Remarks
[QRL 304]	Command Paper. Advisory Council on Scientific Policy, Committee on Scientific Manpower	Scientific and Technological Manpower in Great Britain 1962	HMSO, London	1963, Cmnd 2146	
[QRL 305]	Scottish Tourist Board	Scotland—New Hotel Capacity	Scottish Tourist Board, 23 Ravelston Terrace, Edinburgh, EH4 3EU	Irregularly	
[QRL 306]	Scottish Office	Scottish Abstract of Statistics	HMSO, Edinburgh	Annually from 1971	
[QRL 307]	Command Papers	Scottish Development Department. Annual Report	HMSO, Edinburgh	Annually	Successor publication to [QRL 139] (1977: Cmnd 6943)
[QRL 308]	Scottish Office	Scottish Economic Bulletin	HMSO, Edinburgh	Bi-annually since 1971	
[QRL 309]	Scottish Education Department	Scottish Educational Statistics	HMSO, Edinburgh	Annually from 1967 (issue for 1966)	For the period up to 1965 see the annual reports of the Scottish Education Department: *Education in Scotland*. (HMSO, Edinburgh)
[QRL 310]	Scottish Health Boards	Scottish Health Service Costs	The Board, Edinburgh	Annually 1962	
[QRL 311]	Department of Applied Economics, University of Cambridge (Gen. Ed. Richard Stone)	A Social Accounting Matrix for 1960. A Programme for Growth No. 2	Chapman and Hall, London		
[QRL 312]	Department of Health and Social Security	Social Security Statistics	HMSO, London	Annually from 1973 (issue for 1972)	
[QRL 313]	Statistical Office of the European Communities	Social Statistics 1/1975. Labour Force Sample Survey 1973	SOEC, Luxembourg	1975	
[QRL 314]	E. & F. N. Spon Ltd	Spon's Architects' and Builders' Price Book	E. & F. N. Spon Ltd, London	Annually	
[QRL 315]	E. & F. N. Spon Ltd	Spon's Mechanical and Electrical Services Price Book	E. & F. N. Spon Ltd, London	Annually from 1968	

[QRL 316]	Ministry of Commerce	*Statement of Mineral Production in Northern Ireland*	The Ministry, Belfast	Annually from 1950 to 1969	Formerly published annually as *Report on the Mining and Quarrying Industries in Northern Ireland* (HMSO, Belfast)
[QRL 317]	Command Papers	*Statistical Abstract for the United Kingdom*	HMSO, London	Annually up to No. 83, published in 1940	Succeeded by *Annual Abstract of Statistics* [QRL 31]
[QRL 318]	Ministry of Works	*Statistical Bulletin*	The Ministry, London	Monthly from November 1942 to October/November 1945	Not published. These Bulletins were prepared at the time for use within the Ministry; a set is now held in the Statistics Construction Division of the Department of the Environment in London.
[QRL 319]	Central Statistical Office	*Statistical Digest of the War, History of the Second World War, United Kingdom Civil Series*	HMSO, and Longmans Green & Co., London	1951	
[QRL 320]	Ministry of Works	*Statistical Tables Relating to the Building and Civil Engineering Industries in War-time*	HMSO, London	1945	
[QRL 321]	Department of the Environment M. C. Fleming	*Statistics Collected by the Ministry of Works 1941–56*	The Department, London	Forthcoming	
[QRL 322]	Department of the Environment (formerly Ministry of Housing and Local Government) Welsh Office	*Statistics for Town and Country Planning, Series I Planning Decisions*	HMSO, London	Annually 1969–74	Formerly published as [QRL 324]; replaced, after 1974, by [QRL 136]

Reference Number	Organization responsible or author	Title	Publisher	Frequency or date of publication	Remarks
[QRL 323]	Department of the Environment, Welsh Office	*Statistics for Town and Country Planning. Series II Floor Space*	HMSO, London	Every 2 or 3 years from 1969	
[QRL 324]	Ministry of Housing and Local Government	*Statistics of Decisions on Planning Applications: England and Wales*	HMSO, London	Annually 1962–8	Replaced by [QRL 322]
[QRL 325]	Department of Education and Science	*Statistics of Education*	HMSO, London	Annually in 3 vols from 1961 to 1965 and then in 6 vols	For the period prior to 1961 see the *Annual Reports* of the Ministry of Education published as Command Papers: *Education in . . . year*. HMSO, London
[QRL 326]	Welsh Office	*Statistics of Education in Wales*	HMSO, Cardiff	Annually from 1976	
[QRL 327]	Department of Education and Science	*Statistics of Education Special Series No. 3. Surveys of Earnings of Qualified Manpower in England and Wales, 1966–67*	HMSO, London	1971	
[QRL 328]	Department of Education and Science and Ministry of Technology	*Statistics of Science and Technology*	HMSO, London	1967	
[QRL 329]	Department of Education and Science and Ministry of Technology	*Statistics of Science and Technology 1968*	HMSO, London	1968	
[QRL 330]	Department of Education and Science and Ministry of Technology	*Statistics of Science and Technology 1970*	HMSO, London	1970	
[QRL 331]	Ministry of Labour	*Statistics on Incomes, Prices, Employment and Production*	HMSO, London	Quarterly from 1962 to 1969	
[QRL 332]	Stock Exchange	*The Stock Exchange Fact Book*	Public Relations Department, The Stock Exchange, London	Quarterly	
[QRL 333]	University of Aston in Birmingham	*A Study of Quantity Surveying Practice*	RICS, London	1974	

QUICK REFERENCE LIST

[QRL 334]	Department of Education and Science and Welsh Office	*A Study of School Building*	HMSO, London	1977	
[QRL 335]	Command Paper	*Summary Report of the Ministry of Works for the Period 9th May 1945 to 31st December 1946*	HMSO, London	1947, Cmd 7279	
[QRL 336]	Command Paper	*Summary Report of the Ministry of Works for the Period 1st January to 31st December 1947*	HMSO, London	1948, Cmd 7541	
[QRL 337]	Command Paper	*Summary Report of the Ministry of Works, 1st January to 31st December 1948*	HMSO, London	1949, Cmd 7698	
[QRL 338]	Institute of Building	*Survey of Home Members 1975*	Institute of Building, Ascot, Berks	1976	
[QRL 339]	Building Statistical Services	*Survey of New Industrial Buildings Completed in Great Britain in ... [year]*	Building Statistical Services, 14 Great College Street, London, SW1	Various dates (surveys have been completed for years 1965, 1967 and 1969)	
[QRL 340]	Building Statistical Services	*Survey of New Schools 1969*	Building Statistical Services, 14 Great College Street, London, SW1	1971	
[QRL 341]	Ministry of Technology	*The Survey of Professional Engineers 1966*	HMSO, London	1967	
[QRL 342]	Ministry of Technology	*The Survey of Professional Engineers 1968*	HMSO, London	1970	Continued as [QRL 343]
[QRL 343]	Council of Engineering Institutions	*The ... [year] Survey of Professional Engineers*	The Council, 2 Little Smith Street, London, SW1P 3DL	Biennial from 1971	
[QRL 344]	IPC Business Press Ltd	*Surveyor—Public Authority Technology*	IPC Building and Contract Journals Ltd, London	Weekly	Formerly called, at various times, *Surveyor—Local Government Technology*, *The Surveyor and Municipal Engineer* and *The Surveyor and Municipal and County Engineer*

Reference Number	Organization responsible or author	Title	Publisher	Frequency or date of publication	Remarks
[QRL 345]	House of Commons Paper, Monopolies and Mergers Commission	Surveyors' Services. A Report on the Supply of Surveyors' Services with Reference to Scale Fees	HMSO, London	1977, HC No. 5, Session 1977–8	
[QRL 346]	Ministry of Labour and National Service	Tables Relating to Employment and Unemployment in Great Britain 1948, 1949 and 1950. Regional and Industrial Analysis of Employees and Unemployed Persons	HMSO, London	1951	
[QRL 347]	Hotchkiss Lane Associates Ltd	Tenders and Contracts Journal	Hotchkiss Lane Associates Ltd, 21 St Andrew Street, Cambridge	Monthly	
[QRL 348]	Department of Employment	Time Rates of Wages and Hours of Work	HMSO, London	Annually from 1946 (except 1953)	Earlier issues were irregular commencing in 1893
[QRL 349]	Times Newspapers Ltd	The Times	Times Newspapers Ltd, London	Daily, except Sundays	
[QRL 350]	Times Newspapers Ltd	Times 1000	Times Newspapers Ltd, London	Annually	
[QRL 351]	Allied Contractors (GB) Ltd	Trade Digest: Information Bulletin of Building, Construction and Engineering Developments in the United Kingdom	Allied Contractors (GB) Ltd, Fleet House, Admiral's Walk, London, NW3 6RS	Fortnightly	Available on subscription only
[QRL 352]	Departments of Trade, Industry, Prices and Consumer Protection	Trade and Industry (formerly the Board of Trade Journal [QRL 48])	HMSO, London	Weekly	
[QRL 353]	Department of Trade and Industry	'Census of production 1969, Stocks and capital expenditure in manufacturing industry', Trade and Industry, 1, 1970, pp. 588–9	HMSO, London	1970	
[QRL 354]	Department of the Environment, Scottish Development Department and Welsh Office	Transport Statistics, Great Britain ... [year]	HMSO, London	Annually	Formerly Highway Statistics

QUICK REFERENCE LIST 495

[QRL 355]	Building Research Establishment, Fire Research Station	*UK Fire and Loss Statistics ... [year]*	The Station, Boreham Wood, Herts	Annually from 1946	Published by HMSO, London between 1960 and 1971. Entitled *UK Fire Statistics* until 1968
[QRL 356]	Central Statistical Office	*United Kingdom Balance of Payments ... (the 'Pink Book')*	HMSO, London	Annually	
[QRL 357]	Natural Environment Research Council, Institute of Geological Sciences	*United Kingdom Mineral Statistics ... [years]*	HMSO, London	Irregularly from 1973	
[QRL 358]	Command Paper	*University Grants Committee, Annual Survey Academic Year ...*	HMSO, London	Annually	Prior to the year 1965–6 published as *Returns from Universities and University Colleges in receipt of Exchequer Grant*
[QRL 359]	Command Paper	*Wages and Conditions in the Electrical Contracting Industry, National Board for Prices and Incomes, Report No. 24*	HMSO, London	1966, Cmnd 3172	
[QRL 360]	Welsh Office	*Welsh Economic Trends*	HMSO, Cardiff	Annually from 1974	
[QRL 361]	Welsh Office	*Welsh Local Government Financial Statistics*	HMSO, Cardiff	Annually from 1977	
[QRL 362]	World Bureau of Metal Statistics	*World Metal Statistics* formerly *World Non-Ferrous Metal Statistics*	World Bureau of Metal Statistics Ltd, 41 Doughty Street, London, WC1N 2LF	Monthly	
[QRL 363]	Institute of Quantity Surveyors	*Yearbook*	The Institute, 98 Gloucester Place, London, W1	Annually	
[QRL 364]	Institute of Building	*Yearbook and Directory of Members*	IOB, Ascot, Berks	Annually	
[QRL 365]	Institution of Structural Engineers	*Yearbook and Directory of Members*	John Morris Publicity Ltd, Publicity House, Streatham Hill, London, SW2 4TR	Annually	

BIBLIOGRAPHY

[B 1]   Aldcroft, Derek. 'Rail', *Reviews of U.K. Statistical Sources*, ed. Maunder, W. F. Pergamon Press, Oxford, forthcoming.

[B 2]   Allen, Kevin and Yuill, Douglas. 'The accuracy of pre-1971 employment data (the ER IIs)', *Regional Studies*, **11** (4), 1977, pp. 253–61.

[B 3]   Archer, A. A. *Sand and Gravel as Aggregate*. Mineral Resources Consultative Committee, Mineral Dossier No. 4. HMSO, London, 1972.

[B 4]   Ash, J. C. K. and Smyth, D. J. *Forecasting the United Kingdom Economy*. Saxon House, Farnborough, Hants, England and Lexington Books, Lexington, Mass., USA, 1973.

[B 5]   Ashton, T. S. *Economic Fluctuations in England, 1700–1800*. Clarendon Press, Oxford, 1959.

[B 6]   Azzaro, D. W. 'Measuring the level of tender prices', *Chartered Surveyor Building and Quantity Surveying Quarterly*, **4** (2), Winter 1976, pp. 17–19.

[B 7]   Barna, T. 'The replacement cost of fixed assets in British manufacturing industry in 1955', *Journal of the Royal Statistical Society, Ser. A (General)*, **120**, 1957, pp. 1–46.

[B 8]   Barnes, Martin and Partners. *The Sensitivity of the Building Price Adjustment Formula*. The NFBTE, London, 1975.

[B 9]   Baxter, R. E. 'Ports and Inland Waterways', *Reviews of U.K. Statistical Sources*, No. 17, Vol. X, ed. Maunder, W. F. Pergamon Press, Oxford, 1979.

[B 10] Beeston, D. T. *One Statistician's View of Estimating*. Directorate of Quantity Surveying Development, Property Services Agency, Department of the Environment, Croydon. Undated (1973?). Reprinted in *Chartered Surveyor: BQS Quarterly*, **2** (4), Summer 1975, pp. 49–54.

[B 11] Begg, H. M., Lythe, C. M., Sorley, R. and MacDonald, D. R. 'Expenditure on regional assistance to industry: 1960/1–1972/3', *Economic Journal*, **85** (340), 1975, pp. 884–7.

[B 12] Belliss, C. J. 'The further education statistical record', *Statistical News*, No. 20, February 1973, pp. 20.6–20.11.

[B 13] Benjamin, Bernard. *The Population Census*. Heinemann Educational Books, London, 1970.

[B 14] Berman, L. S. 'Further developments in input–output statistics', *Statistical News*, No. 12, 1971, pp. 1–4.

[B 15] Beveridge, Lord. 'Wages and inflation in the past', *The Incorporated Statistician*, **8**, 1957, pp. 3–7.

[B 16] Bishop, D. 'Labour requirements for house-building', *The Builder*, **209**, 1965, pp. 150–4. Reprinted as *Building Research Current Paper, Construction Series 18*. Building Research Station, Garston, Herts, 1965.

[B 17] Black, F. W. 'Rateable value and floor-space statistics as indicators of change in the building stock in commercial and industrial use', *Building Research Establishment Current Paper CP 52/77*. The Establishment, Garston, Herts, 1977.

[B 18] Bowen, Ian. 'Building output and the trade cycle (U.K. 1924–38)', *Oxford Economic Papers*, No. 3, March 1940, pp. 110–30.

[B 19] Bowen, Ian. 'The control of building', *Lessons of the British War Economy*, NIESR Economic and Social Studies X, ed. Chester, D. N., University Press, Cambridge, 1951.

[B 20] Bowen, Ian. 'Incentives and output in the building and civil engineering industries', *The Manchester School of Economic and Social Studies*, **15**, May 1947, pp. 157–75.

[B 21] Bowen, Ian. 'Investment in the building industry: 1930–35', *Review of Economic Studies*, **VI**, 1938–9, pp. 156–60 and 200–8.

[B 22] Bowen, I. 'A new index number of building materials prices', *Bulletin of the Oxford University Institute of Statistics*, **8,** 1946, pp. 352–9.

[B 23] Bowen, Ian and Ellis, A. W. T. 'The building and contracting industry', *Oxford Economic Papers*, No. 7, 1945, pp. 111–24.

[B 24] Bowley, A. L. *Prices and Wages in the United Kingdom, 1914–1920*. Clarendon Press, Oxford, 1921.

[B 25] Bowley, A. L. 'The statistics of wages in the United Kingdom during the last hundred years, Part VI: wages in the building trades—English Towns', *Journal of the Royal Statistical Society*, **LXIII**, 1900, pp. 297–315.

[B 26] Bowley, A. L. 'The statistics of wages in the United Kingdom during the last hundred years, Part VII: wages in the building trades—Scotland and Ireland, *Journal of the Royal Statistical Society*, LXIII, 1900, pp. 485–97.

[B 27] Bowley, A. L. 'The statistics of wages in the United Kingdom during the last hundred years, Part VIII: wages in the building trades—London', *Journal of the Royal Statistical Society*, LXIV, 1901, pp. 102–11.

[B 28] Bowley, A. L. *Wages and Income in the United Kingdom Since 1860*. University Press, Cambridge, 1937.

[B 29] Bowley, A. L. *Wages in the United Kingdom in the Nineteenth Century*. University Press, Cambridge, 1900.

[B 30] Bowley, M. E. A. and Corlett, W. J. *Report on the Study of Trends in Building Prices*. Ministry of Public Building and Works, R & D Paper. The Ministry, London, 1970.

[B 31] Brown, E. H. Phelps and Hopkins, Sheila V. 'Seven centuries of building wages', *Economist*, New series, 22, 1955, pp. 195–206.

[B 32] Browning, H. E. 'The census of production', *Statistical News*, No. 5, 1969, pp. 5.1–5.8.

[B 33] Bryant, C. G. E. 'Price indices in the construction industry', *Statistical News*, No. 32, 1976, pp. 32.5–32.8.

[B 34] Butler, Rosemary. 'Qualified manpower statistics, *Statistical News*, No. 36, 1977, pp. 36.12–36.14.

[B 35] Buxton, N. K. and MacKay, D. I. *British Employment Statistics: A Guide to Sources and Methods*. Basil Blackwell, Oxford, 1978.

[B 36] Carter, C. F. 'Estimates of the gross domestic product of Northern Ireland 1950–56', *Journal of the Statistical and Social Inquiry Society of Ireland*, XX, Part II, 1958–9, p. 149.

[B 37] Carter, C. F. 'Productivity and prices, "Building" quarterly analysis of trends', *Building* (formerly *The Builder*). Published quarterly between 1955, 189, pp. 88–9 and 1972, 222, pp. 23/68–9.

[B 38] Carter, C. F. and Robson, Mary. 'A comparison of the national incomes and social accounts of Northern Ireland, the Republic of Ireland and the United Kingdom', *Journal of the Statistical and Social Inquiry Society of Ireland*, XIX, 1954–5, pp. 62–87.

[B 39] Clapp, Margaret A. and Cullen, B. D. 'The maintenance and running costs of school building', *Chartered Surveyor*, 100, 1968, pp. 552–60. Reprinted as *Building Research Station Current Paper 72/68*.

[B 40] Clegg, H. A. *The System of Industrial Relations in Great Britain*. Basil Blackwell, Oxford, 1970.

[B 41] Coppock, J. T. 'Land Use', *Reviews of U.K. Statistical Sources*, No. 14, Vol. VIII, ed. Maunder, W. F. Pergamon Press, Oxford, 1978.

[B 42] Croxford, A. A. 'The Universities' statistical record', *Statistical News*, No. 19, November 1972, pp. 19.17.–19.19.

[B 43] Cullen, B. D. and Jeffrey, Iris M. 'Running costs of hospital buildings', *The Hospital*, 63, 1967, pp. 234–8. Reprinted as *Building Research Station Current Paper, Design Series No. 65*.

[B 44] Dean, Andrew. 'Wages and Earnings', *Reviews of U.K. Statistical Sources*, No. 23, Vol. XIII, ed. Maunder, W. F. Pergamon Press, Oxford, forthcoming.

[B 45] Dean, Geoffrey. 'Fixed investment in Britain and Norway, An experiment in international comparison', *Journal of the Royal Statistical Society, Series A (General)*, 127, 1964, pp. 89–107.

[B 46] Dean, G. A. 'The stock of fixed capital in the United Kingdom in 1961', *Journal of the Royal Statistical Society, Series A (General)*, 127, 1964, pp. 327–58.

[B 47] Devons, Ely and Crossley, J. R. *The Guardian Wage Indexes*. The Guardian, Manchester, undated (1962?).

[B 48] Devons, Ely, Crossley, J. R. and Maunder, W. F. 'Wage rate indexes by industry', 1948–1965', *Economica*, New series, 35, 1968, pp. 392–423.

[B 49] Devons, Ely and Ogley, R. C. 'An index of wage rates by industries', *The Manchester School of Economic and Social Studies*, 26, 1958, pp. 77–115.

[B 50] Durcan, Jim. 'Strikes', *Reviews of U.K. Statistical Sources*, ed. Maunder, W. F. Pergamon Press, Oxford, forthcoming.

[B 51] Eden, J. F. 'Accident prevention—the use of statistics', *Building*, 229, 1975, pp. 99–102. Reprinted in *Building Research Establishment Current Paper CP91/75*, BRE, Garston, Herts.

[B 52] Farthing, S. M. 'Housing in Great Britain', *Reviews of U.K. Statistical Sources*, No. 5, Vol. III, ed. Maunder, W. F. Heinemann Educational Books, London, 1974.

[B 53] Fessey, M. C. and Browning, H. E. 'The statistical unit in business inquiries', *Statistical News*, No. 13, 1971, pp. 13.1–13.5.

[B 54] Fildes, Robert and Wood, Douglas. 'Data and the validity of forecasting models—with special reference to the construction industry', paper presented at the XXIII International Meeting of the Institute of Management Science, Athens, 1977.

[B 55] Fleming, M. C. 'Costs and prices in the Northern Ireland construction industry, 1954–64', *Journal of Industrial Economics*, **14**, 1965, pp. 42–54.

[B 56] Fleming, M. C. 'Housebuilding productivity in Northern Ireland', *Urban Studies*, **4** (2), 1967, pp. 122–36.

[B 57] Fleming, M. C. 'Housing in Northern Ireland', *Reviews of U.K. Statistical Sources*, No. 6, Vol. III, ed. Maunder, W. F. Heinemann Educational Books, London, 1974.

[B 58] Fleming, M. C. 'The long-term measurement of construction costs in the United Kingdom', *Journal of the Royal Statistical Society, Series A (General)*, **129**, 1966, pp. 534–56 and 'Correction', *idem*. **130**, 1967, p. 282.

[B 59] Fleming, M. C. 'Productivity in construction: A note on potential source material for the measurement of long-term changes', *University of Loughborough, Department of Economics, Occasional Research Paper No. 14*. The Department, July, 1977.

[B 60] Gebbett, L. F. 'Town & Country Planning', *Reviews of U.K. Statistical Sources*, No. 15, Vol. VIII, ed. Maunder, W. F. Pergamon Press, Oxford, 1978.

[B 61] Glynn, D. R. 'The CBI industrial trends survey', *Applied Economics*, **1**, 1969, pp. 183–96.

[B 62] Goldman, Samuel. *The Developing System of Public Expenditure Management and Control*. Civil Service Department, Civil Service College Studies 2. HMSO, London, 1973.

[B 63] Gray, Percy and Gee, Frances A. *A Quality Check on the 1966 Ten Per Cent Sample Census of England and Wales*. Office of Population Censuses and Surveys, Social Survey Division. HMSO, London, 1972.

[B 64] Green, M. J. and Baillie, R. T. 'The clarification of economic structure in the United Kingdom in 1968', *Economic Trends*, No. 242, December 1973. Reprinted in [B 279].

[B 65] Griffin, Tom. 'Revised estimates of the consumption and stock of fixed capital', *Economic Trends*, No. 264, October 1975, pp. 126–9.

[B 66] Griffin, Tom. 'The stock of fixed assets in the United Kingdom: how to make best use of the statistics', *Economic Trends*, No. 276, October 1976, pp. 130–43.

[B 67] Harris, Amelia I. assisted by Clausen, Rosemary. *Labour Mobility in Great Britain 1953–63*. Government Social Survey Report SS. 333. HMSO, London, 1966.

[B 68] Harris, D. J. 'Coal Industry', *Reviews of U.K. Statistical Sources*, No. 19, Vol. XI, ed. Maunder, W. F. Pergamon Press, Oxford, forthcoming.

[B 69] Harris, P. M. *Sandstone*. Mineral Resources Consultative Committee, Mineral Dossier No. 17. HMSO, London, 1977.

[B 70] Hart, P. E. *Studies in Profit, Business Saving and Investment in the United Kingdom, 1920–1962*, Vol. 1. Allen & Unwin, London, 1965.

[B 71] Head, C. R. 'Trends in the supply of, and demand for, civil engineers', *Surveyor and Local Government Technology*, 1973, **141**, (4205), pp. 34–9 and (4206), pp. 36–9.

[B 72] Hibbert, J., Griffin, T. J. and Walker, R. L. 'Development of estimates of the stock of fixed capital in the United Kingdom', *Review of Income and Wealth*, Series 23, No. 2, June 1977, pp. 117–35.

[B 73] Hiliebrandt, Patricia M. *Economic Theory and the Construction Industry*. Macmillan, London, 1974.

[B 74] Hillebrandt, P. 'Going bust: what are the facts?', *Building*, **232**, 1977, pp. 52–3.

[B 75] Hillebrandt, Patricia M. *Small Firms in the Construction Industry*. Committee of Inquiry on Small Firms, Research Report No. 10. HMSO, London, 1971.

[B 76] Hilton, W. S. *Building by Direct Labour*. AUBTW, London, 1954.

[B 77] Hunt, Audrey, Fox, Judith and Bradley, Michael. *Post-Training Careers of Government Training Centre Trainees*. Office of Population Censuses and Surveys, Social Survey Division. HMSO, London, 1972.

[B 78] Hunt, E. H. *Regional Wage Variations in Britain 1850–1914*. Clarendon Press, Oxford, 1973.

[B 79] Isles, K. S. and Cuthbert, N. *Economic Survey of Northern Ireland*. HMSO, Belfast, 1957.

[B 80] Jackson, C. H. 'Retention of statistical survey information by the Business Statistics Office', *Statistical News*, No. 21, 1973, pp. 12–14.

[B 81] Jeanes, R. E. 'Study of operative skills: a guide to the first report', *Building Research Current Papers, Construction Series 30*. Building Research Station, Garston, Herts, 1966.

[B 82] Jefferson, C. W. *A Method of Estimating the Stock of Capital in Northern Ireland Manufacturing Industry: Limitations and Applications*. The Economic and Social Research Institute, Publication Series Paper No. 44. The Institute, Dublin, 1968.

[B 83] Jones, G. T. *Increasing Return*. University Press, Cambridge, 1933.

[B 84] Kaye, Barrington. *The Development of the Architectural Profession in Britain*. Allen & Unwin, London, 1960.

[B 85] Keating, G. B. 'The use of the CBI survey data for measuring constraints to fixed investment authorisations', 13th CIRET Conference, Munich, September 1977.

[B 86] Kendall, M. G. (ed.). *The Sources and Nature of the Statistics of the United Kingdom*, 2 vols. Oliver and Boyd, London and Edinburgh, 1952, 1957.

[B 87] Killick, A. H. 'British Surveyors: their training, activities and emoluments', *Compte Rendu du IXeme Congrès*. Delft, 1958.

[B 88] Killick, A. H. 'Professional activities in relation to fees and salaries. A report prepared for the VIIth International Congress of Surveyors at Lausanne in August 1949', *RICS Journal*, **29** (4), 1949, pp. 301–4.

[B 89] Knowles, K. G. J. C. *Strikes—A Study in Industrial Conflict*. Basil Blackwell, Oxford, 1952.

[B 90] Kohan, C. M. *Works and Buildings*. History of the Second World War, UK Civil Series. HMSO, and Longmans, Green & Co., London, 1952.

[B 91] Layton, Elizabeth. *Building by Local Authorities*. Allen & Unwin, London, 1961.

[B 92] Lea, Lady F. E. 'The value of new construction work. An enquiry into the statistics of expenditure and output.' Unpublished report to the Ministry of Public Building and Works, April 1970.

[B 93] Leak, Hector. 'Censuses of production and distribution', in Kendall, M. G. (ed.), *The Sources and Nature of the Statistics of the United Kingdom*, Vol. 1. Oliver and Boyd, London, 1952.

[B 94] Lewes, F. M. M. and Parker, S. R. 'Leisure', *Reviews of U.K. Statistical Sources*, No. 7, Vol. IV, ed. Maunder, W. F. Heinemann Educational Books, London, 1975.

[B 95] Lickorish, L. J. 'Tourism', *Reviews of U.K. Statistical Sources*, No. 8, Vol. IV, ed. Maunder, W. F. Heinemann Educational Books, London, 1975.

[B 96] Lomax, K. S. 'Production and productivity movements in the United Kingdom since 1900', *Journal of the Royal Statistical Society, Series A (General)*, **122**, 1959, pp. 185–220.

[B 97] Lund, P. J., Mellis, C. L. and Hamilton, V. J. *Investment Intentions, Authorisations and Expenditures*. HM Treasury, Government Economic Service Occasional Papers No. 12. HMSO, London, 1976.

[B 98] Maiwald, K. 'An index of building costs in the United Kingdom, 1845–1938', *Economic History Review*, Second Ser., **7**, 1954, pp. 187–203.

[B 99] Maton, J. M. 'Manufacturing output, employment and new building. Regional analysis: 1948–1958', *Board of Trade Journal*, **190**, 28 January 1966, Supplement pp. i–xvi.

[B 100] Maurice, Rita (ed.). *National Accounts Statistics—Sources and Methods*. HMSO, London, 1968.

[B 101] Meeks, Geoffrey and Whittington, Geoffrey. *The Financing of Quoted Companies in the United Kingdom*, Royal Commission on the Distribution of Income and Wealth, Background Paper No. 1. HMSO, London, 1976.

[B 102] Mellis, C. L. and Richardson, P. W. 'Value of investment incentives for manufacturing industry 1946 to 1974', in *The Economics of Industrial Subsidies*, ed. Whiting, Alan. Department of Industry. HMSO, London, 1976.

[B 103] Mitchell, Robert. 'A tender-based building price index', *Chartered Surveyor*, **104**, 1971, pp. 34–6.

[B 104] Moos, S. 'Employment and output in the building trades', *Bulletin of the Oxford University Institute of Statistics*, **8**, 1946, pp. 44–50.

[B 105] Moser, Claus. 'The environment in which statistical offices will work in ten years' time', *Statistical News*, No. 38, August 1977, pp. 38.1–38.6.

[B 106] Moyle, John. 'A valuation of land and buildings for the United Kingdom', *Chartered Surveyor*, **101**, 1968–9, pp. 286–8 and pp. 326–7.

[B 107] Nabb, H. 'Gas Industry', *Reviews of U.K. Statistical Sources*, No. 20, Vol. XI, ed. Maunder, W. F. Pergamon Press, Oxford, forthcoming.

[B 108] Nelson, J. I'a. 'Men on the move', *BRS News*, No. 8, Spring 1969, pp. 14–16.

[B 109] Nelson, J. I. et al. 'The Occupational Structure and the Training of Operatives for the Building Industry', Building Research Station Current Paper 25/68. The Station, Garston, Herts, 1968.

[B 110] Neuburger, H. L. I. and Nichol, B. M. *The Recent Course of Land and Property Prices and the Factors Underlying It*, Department of the Environment, Research Report No. 4. The Department, London, 1976.

[B 111] Notholt, A. J. G. and Highley, D. E. *Gypsum and Anhydrite*, Mineral Resources Consultative Committee, Mineral Dossier No. 13. HMSO, London, 1975.

[B 112] Noyce, M. R. 'The statistics of value-added tax', *Statistical News*, No. 19, 1972, pp. 19.1–19.9.

[B 113] Nuttall, D. 'Electricity Industry', *Reviews of U.K. Statistical Sources*, No. 21, Vol. XI, ed. Maunder, W. F. Pergamon Press, Oxford, forthcoming.

[B 114] Osborn, W. T., 'The price index of local authority housebuilding', *Statistical News*, No. 22, 1973, pp. 22.23–22.25.

[B 115] Parker, S. R., Thomas, C. G., Ellis, N. D. and McCarthy, W. E. J. *Effects of the Redundancy Payments Act*. Office of Population Censuses and Surveys, Social Survey Division, Report SS 438. HMSO, London, 1971.

[B 116] Pascoe, T. Lawrence. 'Value and duration of civil engineering contracts', *The Engineer*, **215**, 1963, pp. 1023–4.

[B 117] Pettman, Barrie O. and Showler, Brian. 'Government vocational training schemes in Great Britain', *International Journal of Social Economics*, 1974, **1** (2), pp. 184–96.

[B 118] Phillips, Celia. 'Civil Aviation', *Reviews of U.K. Statistical Sources*, No. 18, Vol. X, ed. Maunder, W. F. Pergamon Press, Oxford, 1979.
[B 119] Phillips, H. S. 'United Kingdom indices of wholesale prices, 1949–55', *Journal of the Royal Statistical Society, Series A (General)*, **119**, 1956, pp. 239–83.
[B 120] Phillips, R. H. S. 'The regional structure of the construction industry in Great Britain', *Regional Studies*, **7**, Sept. 1973, pp. 287–300.
[B 121] Plant, J. J. *A Survey of Labour Availability and Requirements on London Local Authority Construction Sites*, Greater London Council Research Memorandum RM 468. Greater London Council, London, 1975.
[B 122] Prest, A. R. 'Some aspects of road finance in the U.K.', *Manchester School of Economic and Social Studies*, **31**, 1963, pp. 223–41.
[B 123] Price, Richard. 'The CBI industrial trends survey—an insight into answering practices', *CBI Review*, Summer 1977.
[B 124] Price, Robert and Bain, George Sayers. 'Union growth revisited: 1948–1974 in perspective', *British Journal of Industrial Relations*, **XIV** (3), 1976, pp. 339–55.
[B 125] Purkis, H. J., How, R. F. C., Hooper, N. J. and Poole, M. T. 'Occupancy costs of offices', *Building Research Establishment Current Paper CP 44/77*. The Establishment, Garston, Herts, 1977.
[B 126] Ramsbottom, E. C. 'The course of wage rates in the United Kingdom, 1921–1934', *Journal of the Royal Statistical Society*, **98**, Part IV, 1935, pp. 639–94.
[B 127] Reddaway, W. B. and Associates. *Effects of Selective Employment Tax*. University of Cambridge, Department of Applied Economics, Occasional Paper No. 32. University Press, Cambridge, 1973.
[B 128] Redfern, P. 'Net investment in fixed assets in the United Kingdom 1938–1953', *Journal of the Royal Statistical Society, Series A (General)*, **118**, 1955, pp. 141–92.
[B 129] Reid, David J. 'Statistics of North Sea oil and gas', *Statistical News*, No. 32, 1976, pp. 32.1–32.4.
[B 130] Relf, C. T. *The Building Timetable: the public sector*. University College Environmental Research Group, Building Economics Research Unit, London, 1974.
[B 131] Relf, C. T. *The Building Timetable: the significance of duration*. University College Environmental Research Group, Building Economics Research Unit, London, 1974.
[B 132] Renton, G. A. (ed.). *Modelling the Economy*. Heinemann Educational Books, London, 1975.
[B 133] Riley, Kathleen M. 'An estimate of the age distribution of the dwelling stock in Great Britain', *Urban Studies*, **10**, 1973, pp. 373–9.
[B 134] Robertson, Douglas. 'Cost information for designers and building owners' (Appendix B—The tender price index) in *Aspects of the Economics of Construction*, ed. Turin, D. A., George Godwin, London, 1975.
[B 135] Rosenberg, Nathan. *Economic Planning in the British Building Industry 1945—49*, University of Pennsylvania Press, Philadelphia, 1960.
[B 136] Rubra, Neil. 'The Road System', *Reviews of U.K. Statistical Sources*, ed. Maunder, W. F. Pergamon Press, Oxford, forthcoming.
[B 137] Sandles, A. *Prospects for the Small Hotelier*. HMSO, London, 1973. (A summary of the report cited as [QRL 167].)
[B 138] Savage, D. 'Interpreting the investment intentions data', *National Institute Economic Review*, No. 73. August 1975, pp. 41–6.
[B 139] Saville, J. 'The measurement of real cost in the London building industry, 1923–1939', *Yorkshire Bulletin of Economic and Social Research*, **1**, 1949, p. 67–80.
[B 140] Schneider, J. R. L. and Suich, J. C. 'Census of distribution for 1966', *Statistical News*, No. 7, 1969, pp. 7.10–7.15.
[B 141] Seeley, I. *Building Economics*, Macmillan, London, 1976 (2nd ed.).
[B 142] Shannon, H. A. 'Bricks—a trade index, 1785–1849', *Economica*, **1**, New ser. 1934, pp. 300–18.
[B 143] Shenfield, Barbara. *Security of Employment. A study in the construction industry*, PEP Planning Broadsheet. Vol. 34, No. 505. PEP, London, 1968.
[B 144] Shipp, P. J. and Sutton, A. S. *A Study of the Statistics Relating to Safety and Health at Work*, Committee on Safety and Health at Work, Research Paper. HMSO, London, 1972.
[B 145] Shiskin, Julius, Young, Allan H. and Musgrove, John C. *The X-11 Variant of the Census Method II Seasonal Adjustment Program*. US Department of Commerce, Bureau of the Census Technical Paper No. 15. US Government Printing Office, Washington, DC, 1967.
[B 146] Sinclair, Monica, 'Economic forecasting services in the UK', *Business Economist*, **9** (2) Winter 1977, pp. 45–54.
[B 147] Singh, A. and Whittington, G. *Growth, Profitability and Valuation*, University of Cambridge, Department of Applied Economics, Occasional Paper 7. University Press, Cambridge, 1968.
[B 148] Sorrell, A. A. 'Some pitfalls in the use of net output statistics', *Statistical News*, No. 12, 1971, pp. 5–8.

[B 149] Stafford, J. 'The development of industrial statistics', *Statistical News*, No. 1, 1968, pp. 7–10.
[B 150] Stafford, J. 'Indices of wholesale prices', *Journal of the Royal Statistical Society, Series A (General)*, **114**, 1951, pp. 447–67.
[B 151] Stark, T. 'Personal Incomes', *Reviews of U.K. Statistical Sources*, No. 11, Vol. VI, ed. Maunder, W. F. Pergamon Press, Oxford, 1978.
[B 152] Steel, Robert. 'The organisation of the real estate profession in the United Kingdom', *Chartered Surveyor*, **109**, 1977, pp. 173–8.
[B 153] Stone, P. A. 'Administration and costs of hospital maintenance', *The Hospital*, **60**, 1964, pp. 411–15 and pp. 479–84. Reprinted as *Building Research Station Current Paper, Design Series No. 28*.
[B 154] Stone, P. A. *The Economics of Factory Buildings*, Factory Building Studies No. 12, Department of Scientific and Industrial Research, Building Research Station. HMSO, London, 1962.
[B 155] Sugden, J. D. and Wells, E. O. *Construction in Economic Models, Forecasting Construction Output from Orders*. Building Economics Research Unit, University College Environmental Research Group, London, 1977.
[B 156] Surrey, M. J. C. *The Analysis and Forecasting of the British Economy*, NIESR Occasional Paper XXV. University Press, Cambridge, 1971.
[B 157] Swann, D., O'Brien, D. P., Maunder, W. P. J. and Howe, W. S. *Competition in British Industry. Case Studies of the Effects of Restrictive Practices Legislation*. Department of Economics, Loughborough University of Technology, Loughborough, 1973.
[B 158] Taylor, Wallis. 'Population Statistics', *Reviews of U.K. Statistical Sources*, ed. Maunder, W. F. Pergamon Press, Oxford, forthcoming.
[B 159] Tew, Brian and Henderson, R. F. (eds). *Studies in Company Finance*, National Institute of Economic and Social Research, Economic and Social Studies XVII. University Press, Cambridge, 1959.
[B 160] Thatcher, A. R. 'The DEP's new earnings survey', *Statistical News*, No. 8, 1970, pp. 8.11–8.13.
[B 161] Thatcher, A. R. 'Statistics of unemployment in the United Kingdom', in *The Concept and Measurement of Involuntary Unemployment*, ed. Worswick, G. D. N. for the Royal Economic Society. Allen & Unwin, London, 1976. Reprinted in [QRL 59], 1974 issue (1976).
[B 162] Thomas, Geoffrey. *Labour Mobility in Great Britain 1945–1949*, Social Survey Report SS. 134. The Social Survey, London, 1952.
[B 163] Thomas, Geoffrey. *Operatives in the Building Industry*, Government Social Survey, Report SS. 371. HMSO, London, 1968.
[B 164] Thompson, F. M. L. *Chartered Surveyors—the growth of a profession*. Routledge & Kegan Paul, London, 1968.
[B 165] Turin, D. A. 'Deceptive statistics', *Building*, **218**, 1970, pp. 105–6, 109–10, 113.
[B 166] Turin, Duccio. 'The difficult art of prediction', *Building*, **226**, 1974, pp. 65–6.
[B 167] Venning, Hope & Partners. '"Building" Cost of building chart', *Building* (formerly *The Builder*). Irregularly between 1952 (Vol. 182, pp. 284–5) and 1971 (Vol. 220, pp. 13/71–2), then twice yearly until 11 July 1975 (Vol. 229, pp. 51–2).
[B 168] Ward, Michael. *The Measurement of Capital. The Methodology of Capital Stock Estimates in OECD Countries*. OECD, Paris, 1976.
[B 169] Weber, B. and Lewis, J. Parry. 'New industrial building in Great Britain 1922–38; A problem in measurement', *Scottish Journal of Political Economy*, **8**, 1961, pp. 57–63.
[B 170] Whitehead, Frank. 'Social Security Statistics', *Reviews of U.K. Statistical Sources*, No. 4, Vol. II, ed. Maunder, W. F. Heinemann Educational Books, London, 1974.
[B 171] Whybrew, E. G. 'Qualified manpower: statistical sources', *Statistical News*, No. 17, 1972, pp. 17.11–17.18.
[B 172] Worswick, G. D. N. and Tipping, D. G. *Profits in the British Economy, 1909–1938*. Basil Blackwell, Oxford, 1967.
[B 173] Wroe, D. C. L. and Bishop, H. E. 'Highly qualified manpower in the United Kingdom: relevant official statistics', in *Aspects of Manpower Planning* (eds Bartholomew, D. J. and Morris, B. R.). English Universities Press, London, 1971.
[B 174] Young, Alison. 'Statistics of Science and Technology', *Reviews of U.K. Statistical Sources*, ed. Maunder, W. F. Pergamon Press, Oxford, forthcoming.
[B 175] Ministry of Labour. *Accidents in the Construction Industry—report of a survey made during 1966*. HMSO, London, 1967.
[B 176] Economic Development Committee for Building. *Action on the Banwell Report*. HMSO, London, 1967.
[B 177] Department of the Environment, Scottish Development Department, Welsh Office. *Aggregates: The Way Ahead. Report of the Advisory Committee on Aggregates*. HMSO, London, 1976.
[B 178] Scottish Special Housing Association. *Annual Report*. The Association, Edinburgh.
[B 179] *Antrim and Ballymena Development Commission Annual Report*, The Commission, Ballymena, Annual from 1968 to 1973.

[B 180] Economic Development Committee for Building. *Before You Build.* HMSO, London, 1974.
[B 181] Board of Trade, 'Additions to industrial floor space', *Board of Trade Journal*, **196**, 1969, p. 1706.
[B 182] 'Changes in fixed capital expenditures 1954–1956 shown by new Board of Trade inquiry', *Board of Trade Journal*, **170**, 1956, pp. 207–8.
[B 183] Ministry of Works. 'New index of the cost of building and civil engineering work', *Board of Trade Journal*, **170**, 1956, p. 608.
[B 184] Board of Trade. 'A new index of prices of building materials', *Board of Trade Journal*, **160**, 1951, p. 1052.
[B 185] Board of Trade. 'Office development statistics', *Board of Trade Journal*, **195**, 1968, pp. 834–6.
[B 186] Board of Trade. 'Revised Board of Trade index number', *Board of Trade Journal*, **134**, 1935, pp. 515–17.
[B 187] Board of Trade. 'Wholesale prices, 1930–1934. *Board of Trade* index number: a new compilation', *Board of Trade Journal*, **134**, Jan. 24, 1935.
[B 188] Department of the Environment. *Building Maintenance. The Report of the Committee.* R & D Bulletin. HMSO, London, 1972.
[B 189] Ministry of Technology, Building Research Station. *Building Operatives' Work*, 2 vols. HMSO, London, 1966.
[B 190] Department of Industry, Business Statistics Office. *Business Monitor PQ 1000. Quarterly Statistics of Manufacturers' Sales. Index of Commodities.* HMSO, London, 1974.
[B 191] Department of Industry, Business Statistics Office. *Business Monitor PQ 1001. Guide to Short-Term Statistics of Manufacturers' Sales.* HMSO, London, 1976.
[B 192] General Register Office. *Census 1951, Classification of Industries.* HMSO, London, 1952.
[B 193] General Register Office. *Census 1951. Classification of Occupations.* HMSO, London, 1956.
[B 194] General Register Office. *Census 1951, England & Wales. General Report.* HMSO, London, 1958.
[B 195] Office of Population Censuses and Surveys. *Census 1971. General Report.* HMSO, London. To be published.
[B 196] General Register Office. *Census 1961, Great Britain. General Report.* HMSO, London, 1968.
[B 197] Greater London Council, Department of Architecture and Civic Design, Quantity Surveying Division. 'GLC. ILEA building contract fluctuations clause and the productivity deduction', *Central Services File Note*, 28 January 1975. GLC Quantity Surveying Division, London, 1975.
[B 198] Department of Industry. *Changes in the Population of Persons with Qualifications in Engineering, Technology and Science 1959 to 1976.* Studies in Technological Manpower No. 6, HMSO, London, 1977.
[B 199] Department of Health and Social Security. *Circular HC(77)6. Health Services Development, Cash Limits and the Health Capital Programme: Revised Definition of Capital Spending.* The Department, London, March 1977.
[B 200] General Register Office. *Classification of Occupations 1960.* HMSO, London, 1960.
[B 201] General Register Office. *Classification of Occupations 1966.* HMSO, London, 1966.
[B 202] Office of Population Censuses and Surveys. *Classification of Occupations 1970.* HMSO, London, 1970.
[B 203] Department of Employment. *Classification of Occupations and Directory of Occupational Titles* (CODOT), 3 vols. HMSO, London, 1972.
[B 204] Economic Development Committees for Building and Civil Engineering, Joint Working Party on Demand and Output Forecasts. *Construction Industry Prospects to 1979.* National Economic Development Office, London, 1971. (This report was prepared in two versions: a full report and a shortened summary, each bearing the same title.)
[B 205] Economic Development Committees for Building and Civil Engineering, National Economic Development Office. *Construction Into the Early 1980s.* HMSO, London, 1976.
[B 206] United Nations. *Construction Statistics.* Studies in Methods, Series F, No. 3. United Nations, New York, 1965.
[B 207] Ministry of Public Building and Works. *Construction Statistics: The Opinion of the Private User.* R & D Paper. The Ministry, London, 1968.
[B 208] Economic Development Committee for Civil Engineering. *Contracting in Civil Engineering Since Banwell.* HMSO, London, 1968.
[B 209] Department of the Environment. *Costs-in-Use. A Guide to Data and Techniques.* HMSO, London, 1972.
[B 210] Department of the Environment, Directorate of Quantity Surveying Department. *Costs in Use, A Study of 24 Crown Office Buildings.* The Department, London, 1971.
[B 211] *Craigavon Development Commission Annual Report.* The Commission, Portadown. Annual from 1966 to 1973.
[B 212] Economic Development Committee for Building. *Description of the Indices for use with the NEDO Price Adjustment Formula for Building Works.* HMSO, London, 1974.

[B 213] Ministry of Public Building and Works. *Directory of Construction Statistics*. HMSO, London, 1968.
[B 214] Government of Northern Ireland Command Paper. *Economic Development in Northern Ireland*. Cmd 479. HMSO, Belfast, 1965.
[B 215] Construction Industry Training Board, Electrical Engineering Services Committee. *Economic and Manpower Review of the Electrical Engineering Services Sector*. Draft Report. January 1977 (Unpublished).
[B 216] Central Statistical Office. 'Commodity analysis of central government current expenditure on goods and services', *Economic Trends*, No. 214, 1971, pp. v–x.
[B 217] Department of the Environment. 'Construction industry: Revised series of output statistics 1963–72 (Great Britain)', *Economic Trends*, No. 240, October 1973, pp. lxi–lxviii.
[B 218] Central Statistical Office. 'The index of industrial production: change of base year to 1958', *Economic Trends*, No. 101. March 1962.
[B 219] Department of Industry. 'Insolvency statistics for England and Wales', *Economic Trends*, No. 257, March 1975, pp. 111–12.
[B 220] Ministry of Works. 'Statistics of construction', *Economic Trends*, No. 83, September 1960. Reprinted in [B 277].
[B 221] 'The value of new contracts placed with building and civil engineering contractors', *Economic Trends*, No. 54, April 1958, pp. xvii–xix.
[B 222] *The Economist*. Weekly, London.
[B 223] Economic Development Committee for Civil Engineering. *Efficiency in Road Construction*. HMSO, London, 1966.
[B 224] Research Services Limited. *The Employment Practices of Civil Engineering Firms*. Research Services Ltd, London, 1969. (A copy of this report is available for consultation in the main library of the Department of Employment in London.)
[B 225] Economic Development Committee for Mechanical and Electrical Engineering Construction. *Engineering Construction Performance*. NEDO, London, 1976.
[B 226] Ministry of Works. *Evidence Presented to Building Industry Working Party*. September 1948. Unpublished.
[B 227] House of Commons Paper. *Financial Statement ... [year]*. HMSO, London.
[B 228] Central Statistical Office. *Financial Statistics—Explanatory Handbook*. HMSO, London. First edition 1977 (replaced former *Notes and Definitions* supplement).
[B 229] Economic Development Committee for Building. *Formulae Methods of Price Adjustment on Building Contracts*. NEDO, London, 1969.
[B 230] House of Commons Paper. *Fourth Report from the Estimates Committee, Session 1966–67. Government Statistical Services*. House of Commons Paper No. 246. HMSO, London, 1966.
[B 231] European Communities Statistical Office. *General Industrial Classification of Economic Activities Within the European Communities* (NACE, 1970). European Communities Office for Official Publications, Luxembourg, 1970.
[B 232] *The Guardian*. Daily, London and Manchester.
[B 233] Office of Population Censuses and Surveys and General Register Office, Edinburgh. *Guide to Census Reports. Great Britain 1801–1966*. HMSO, London, 1977.
[B 234] HM Customs and Excise. *Guide to the Classification for Overseas Trade Statistics [year]*. HMSO, London. Annually.
[B 235] Financial Times. *Guide to F.T. Statistics*. Financial Times, London, 1972 and 1973 (revised edition).
[B 236] Central Statistical Office. *Guide to Official Statistics*. HMSO, London, 1976 (2nd edition 1978).
[B 237] Incomes Data Services. *Guide to Salary Surveys ... [year]*. IDS Studies. IDS, London. Annual.
[B 238] Ministry of Labour. *Guide to Statistics Collected by HM Factory Inspectorate*. HMSO, London, 1960.
[B 239] Interdepartmental Committee on Social and Economic Research. *Guides to Official Sources: No. 6, Census of Production Reports*. HMSO, London, 1961.
[B 240] Interdepartmental Committee on Social and Economic Research. *Guides to Official Sources No. 2—Census Reports of Great Britain 1801–1931*. HMSO, London, 1951.
[B 241] Interdepartmental Committee on Social and Economic Research. *Guides to Official Sources: No. 1—Labour Statistics*. HMSO, London, 1958.
[B 242] Health and Safety Executive. *Health and Safety: Construction 1976*. HMSO, London, 1978. (The publication of this report on a regular basis in future is under consideration.)
[B 243] Health and Safety Executive. *Health and Safety. Industry and Services 1975*. HMSO, London, 1977.
[B 244] Department of Employment and Productivity. *HM Factory Inspectorate Directory—List of Divisions and Districts with Their Boundaries* (Form 243A). The Department, London, 1970. Previous issues published by HMSO, London.
[B 245] Command Paper (NI). *Hospital Plan for Northern Ireland 1966–75*. Cmd 491. HMSO, Belfast, 1966.

[B 246] *House of Commons Parliamentary Debates, Official Report*, 5th series, Vol. 730, 1966–7, Cols 17–18.
[B 247] *House of Commons Parliamentary Debates, Official Report*, 5th series, Vol. 817, 1970–1, written answers, Cols 160–2.
[B 248] *House of Commons Parliamentary Debates, Official Report*, 5th series, Vol. 817, 1970–1, written answers, Cols 271–3.
[B 249] *House of Commons Parliamentary Debates, Official Report*, 5th series, Vol. 817, 1970–1, written answers, Col. 322.
[B 250] Department of the Environment, Scottish Development Department and Welsh Office. *Housing and Construction Statistics, Notes and Definitions Supplement.* HMSO, London, Annual since 1972.
[B 251] Board of Inland Revenue. *Income Tax. Construction Industry Tax Deduction Scheme.* Pamphlet IR 14/15 (1976). The Board, London, 1976.
[B 252] Board of Inland Revenue. *Income Tax. Sub-contracting in the Construction Industry. Explanatory Pamphlet for Contractors.* Pamphlet IR 14. The Board, London, 1971.
[B 253] Board of Inland Revenue. *Income Tax. Sub-contracting in the Construction Industry. Explanatory Pamphlet for sub-contractors.* Pamphlet IR 15. The Board, London, 1971.
[B 254] Central Statistical Office. *The Index of Industrial Production. Studies in Official Statistics No. 2.* HMSO, London, 1952.
[B 255] Central Statistical Office. *The Index of Industrial Production—Method of Compilation. Studies in Official Statistics No. 7.* HMSO, London, 1959.
[B 256] Central Statistical Office. *The Index of Industrial Production and Other Output Measures. Studies in Official Statistics No. 17.* HMSO, London, 1970.
[B 257] Economic Services Division, Welsh Office. *Index of Industrial Production for Wales, Welsh Occasional Paper No. 3.* Welsh Office, Cardiff, 1976.
[B 258] Command Paper. *Inflation Accounting. Report of the Inflation Accounting [Sandilands] Committee.* Cmnd 6225. HMSO, London, 1975.
[B 259] Central Statistical Office. *The Interim Index of Industrial Production. Studies in Official Statistics No. 1*, HMSO, London, 1949.
[B 260] United Nations. *International Recommendations for Construction Statistics.* Statistical Papers, Series M, No. 47. United Nations, New York, 1968.
[B 261] United Nations, Department of Economic and Social Affairs, Statistical Office, *International Standard Industrial Classification of all Economic Activities.* Statistical Papers, Series M, No. 4, Rev. 2. United Nations, New York, 1968.
[B 262] Ministry of Public Building and Works: *Inventory of Construction Statistics.* The Ministry, London, 1967. Only a limited number of copies of the *Inventory* were printed and these were deposited in certain selected reference libraries.*
[B 263] Research Services Limited. *Labour in the Construction Industry—A Study Amongst Employers. Vol. I Study Findings. Vol. II Tabulations.* Research Services Ltd, London, 1968. (Copies of these reports are available for consultation in the main library of the Department of Employment in London.)
[B 264] National Economic Development Office. *Large Industrial Sites.* HMSO, London, 1970.
[B 265] *Laxton's Building Price Book.* Annual. Kelly's Directories Ltd (currently), London.
[B 266] Ministry of Public Building and Works. *Local Authority Design Work Statistics.* The Ministry, London, 1968.
[B 267] Chartered Institute of Public Finance and Accountancy. *Local Government Accounting—the Present Situation.* The Institute, London, 1974.

* The libraries selected were those of the following bodies: University of Aberdeen; University of Sussex; University of Cambridge; University of Strathclyde, Glasgow; University of Lancaster; University of Liverpool; Institute of Building; London School of Economics; National Building Agency; National Reference Library of Science and Invention; Queen Mary College; National Federation of Building Trade Employers; Royal Institute of British Architects; The Polytechnic, Regent Street; Board of Trade; Central Statistical Office; Construction Industry Research and Information Association; Ministry of Housing and Local Government; National Economic Development Office; National Institute of Economic and Social Research; Brixton School of Building; National Federation of Building Trade Operatives; Construction Industry Training Board; Science Museum; University of Manchester; Manchester University Institute of Science and Technology; International Council for Building Research, Rotterdam; Economic Commission for Europe, Geneva. Copies were also placed in the Ministry's regional libraries, as well as its central library—now the PSA library in Croydon. The regional libraries are located in the following towns: Birmingham, Bristol, Cambridge, Cardiff, Chessington (Surrey), Edinburgh, Hastings, Leeds, Manchester and Reading.

BIBLIOGRAPHY

[B 268] Department of the Environment and Welsh Office. *Local Government Manpower.* Joint Circular: 30/75 (Department of the Environment) and 34/75 (Welsh Office) dated 7 March 1975. HMSO, London, 1975.

[B 269] *London and Cambridge Economic Service Bulletin.* London, at first monthly, later quarterly, from 1923. (From 1951 the *Bulletin* was published as a Supplement to *The Times Review of Industry*.)

[B 270] *Londonderry Development Commission Annual Report.* The Commission, Londonderry. Annual from 1969 to 1973.

[B 271] Central Statistical Office. *The Measurement of Changes in Production. Studies in Official Statistics No. 25.* HMSO, London, 1976.

[B 272] Ministry of Works. *Memorandum on Payment by Results.* HMSO, London, 1944.

[B 273] Central Statistical Office. *Monthly Digest of Statistics Supplement—Definitions and Explanatory Notes.* HMSO, London, Annually each January since 1946.

[B 274] *The National Builder*, London, Monthly.

[B 275] Central Statistical Office. *National Income Statistics—Sources and Methods. Studies in Official Statistics No. 3.* HMSO, London, 1956.

[B 276] National Joint Council for the Building Industry. *National Working Rules for the Building Industry.* The Council, London. Annually.

[B 277] Central Statistical Office. *New Contributions to Economic Statistics, Second Series. Studies in Official Statistics No. 9.* HMSO, London, 1962.

[B 278] Central Statistical Office. *New Contributions to Economic Statistics, Sixth Series. Studies in Official Statistics, No. 19.* HMSO, London, 1972.

[B 279] Central Statistical Office. *New Contributions to Economic Statistics, Seventh Series, Studies in Official Statistics No. 24.* HMSO, London, 1975.

[B 280] Economic Section, Department (Ministry) of Finance. *Northern Ireland Economic Report.* HMSO, Belfast. Annual from 1964 to 1973.

[B 281] Government of Northern Ireland Command Paper. *Northern Ireland Economic Survey.* Cmd 453. HMSO, Belfast, 1963.

[B 282] Ministry of Commerce. *Northern Ireland Index of Industrial Production.* Issued by the Ministry, Belfast. Undated (first issued c.1958, second edition c.1965).

[B 283] Health and Safety Executive. *One Hundred Fatal Accidents in Construction.* HMSO, London, 1978.

[B 284] Economic Development Committees for Building and Civil Engineering. *The Organisation of Demand.* NEDO, London, 1969.

[B 285] Committee on Invisible Exports. *Overseas Earnings of the British Professions.* The Committee, London, 1972.

[B 286] Ministry of Works. *Payment by Results in Building and Civil Engineering during the War.* HMSO, London, 1947.

[B 287] Ministry of Public Building and Works. *The Placing and Management of Contracts for Building and Civil Engineering Work. Report of the Banwell Committee.* HMSO, London, 1964.

[B 288] Joint Contracts Tribunal for the Standard Form of Building Contract. *Practice Note 18. Adjustment of the Contract Sum by Means of Formulae.* RIBA Publications Ltd, London, 1975.

[B 289] Ministry of Labour and National Service, Technical and Scientific Register. *Present and Future Supply and Demand for Persons with Professional Qualifications in Building and Quantity Surveying.* HMSO, London, 1950.

[B 290] Property Services Agency. *Price Adjustment Formulae for Building Contracts (Series 2), Description of the Indices.* HMSO, London, 1977.

[B 291] Property Services Agency. *Price Adjustment Formulae for Building Contracts (Series 2), Guide to Applications and Procedure.* HMSO, London, 1977.

[B 292] Economic Development Committee for Building. *Price Adjustment Formulae for Building Contracts. A Guide to the Practical Application of the Formulae.* HMSO, London, 1974.

[B 293] Economic Development Committee for Civil Engineering. *Price Adjustment Formulae for Civil Engineering Contracts, 1. Civil Engineering Works. A Guide to the Practical Implementation of the Price Adjustment Formula.* HMSO, London, 1973.

[B 294] Economic Development Committee for Civil Engineering. *Price Adjustment Formulae for Civil Engineering Contracts, 2. Structural Steelwork. A Guide to the Practical Implementation of the Price Adjustment Formula.* HMSO, London, 1974.

[B 295] Treasury. *Public Expenditure White Papers—Handbook on Methodology.* HMSO, London, 1972.

[B 296] Economic Development Committees for Building and Civil Engineering. *The Professions in the Construction Industries.* HMSO, London, 1976.

[B 297] Economic Development Committees for Building and Civil Engineering. *The Public Client and the Construction Industries.* HMSO, London, 1975.

[B 298] Economic Development Committee for Building. *Recommendations for Formula Price Adjustment on Building Contracts.* National Economic Development Office, London, 1973.

[B 299] Economic Development Committee for Building. *Recommendations for Formulae Price Adjustment for Specialist Engineering Installations in Building Contracts*. National Economic Development Office, London, 1973.

[B 300] Central Statistical Office. *Regional Accounts. Studies in Official Statistics No. 31*. HMSO, London, 1978.

[B 301] Economic Development Committees for Building and Civil Engineering. *Regional Construction Forecasts to 1977*. 4 Vols. NEDO, London, 1974.

[B 302] Economic Development Committees for Building and Civil Engineering. *Regional Forecasting for Construction. A Pilot Study in Yorkshire and Humberside*. NEDO, London, 1972.

[B 303] Department of Health and Social Services. *Regional Strategy for the Development of Health and Personal Social Services in Northern Ireland*. HMSO, Belfast, 1975.

[B 304] Department of the Environment. *The Registration of Builders. Report of an Enquiry under The Hon. Mr. Justice Forbes*. HMSO, London, 1972.

[B 305] Ministry of Town and Country Planning and Ministry of Housing and Local Government. *Report of the Advisory Committee on Sand and Gravel*. 18 Parts. HMSO, London, 1948–55.

[B 306] Board of Trade. *Report of the Committee [Keith Price] appointed to Consider the United Kingdom's Probable Requirements and Supplies of Timber and Plywood 1949–53*. HMSO, London, 1948.

[B 307] Command Paper. *Report of the Committee of Inquiry under Professor E. H. Phelps Brown into Certain Matters concerning Labour in Building and Civil Engineering*. Cmnd 3714. HMSO, London, 1968.

[B 308] *Report of the Committee of Inquiry Under Professor E. H. Phelps Brown into Certain Matters Concerning Labour in Building and Civil Engineering (Research Supplement)*. Cmnd 3714–1. HMSO, London, 1968.

[B 309] Construction Industry Training Board, Mechanical Engineering Services Committee. *Report of Survey to Ascertain Future Demand for Heating and Ventilating Technologists*. April 1977. (Unpublished.)

[B 310] Economist Intelligence Unit. *Report on the Earnings of Chartered Surveyors in Private Practice*. The Unit, London, 1963. An unpublished report prepared for the RICS.

[B 311] Economic Development Committee for Civil Engineering. *Report on Price Adjustment Formulae for Civil Engineering Contracts*. National Economic Development Office, London, 1971.

[B 312] Command Paper. *Report on Safety and Health in the Building and Civil Engineering Industries 1954–1958*. Cmnd 953. HMSO, London, 1960.

[B 313] Command Paper (NI). *Review of Hospital Plan for Northern Ireland 1968–78*. Cmd 524. HMSO, Belfast, 1968.

[B 314] British Productivity Council. *A Review of Productivity in the Building Industry*. The Council, London, undated (c. mid-1950s).

[B 315] Ministry of Public Building and Works. *Review of the Structure, Activities and New Developments in the Building Industry. National Monograph: United Kingdom*. R & D Paper. The Ministry, London, 1966.

[B 316] RIBA. 'Inquiry into the building timetable', *RIBA Journal*, 3rd ser. **65**, 1958, pp. 350–2.

[B 317] Command Paper. *Safety and Health at Work*. Vol. 1, Report of the [Robens] Committee 1970–72. Vol. 2, Selected Written Evidence. Cmnd 5034. HMSO, London, 1972.

[B 318] Ministry of Public Building and Works. *Schedule of Rates for Building Works*. HMSO, London, 1969.

[B 319] Department of the Environment, Property Services Agency. *Schedule of Rates for Building Works 1973*. HMSO, London, 1974.

[B 320] Economic Development Committees for Building and Civil Engineering, National Economic Development Office. *Scottish Construction Into The Early 1980s*. HMSO, London, 1976.

[B 321] Economic Development Committee for Civil Engineering. *Second Report on Efficiency in Road Construction*. HMSO, London, 1967.

[B 322] Northern Ireland Command Paper. *Second Review of the Hospital Plan for Northern Ireland 1970–75*. Cmd 556. HMSO, Belfast, 1971.

[B 323] Royal Commission on Trade Unions and Employers' Associations. *Selected Written Evidence Submitted to the Royal Commission*. HMSO, London, 1968.

[B 324] Treasury. *A Selection of Unit Costs in Public Expenditure*. HMSO, London, 1968.

[B 325] Command Paper. *Selective Employment Tax*. Cmnd 2986. HMSO, London, 1966.

[B 326] Command Paper. *Small Firms. Report of the [Bolton] Committee of Inquiry on Small Firms*. Cmnd 4811. HMSO, London, 1971.

[B 327] Interdepartmental Committee on Social and Economic Research. *Social Security Statistics*. Guides to Official Sources No. 5. HMSO, London, 1961.

[B 328] Joint Contracts Tribunal for the Standard Form of Building Contract. *Standard Form of Building Contract—Formula Rules*. First edition dated 3 March 1975; second edition (*Work Category Indices*, Series 2) dated 4 April 1977. RIBA Publications Ltd, London, 1975 and 1977.

[B 329] Central Statistical Office. *Standard Industrial Classification*. First edition 1948. Revised 1958 and 1968. HMSO, London 1948, 1958, 1968 respectively.
[B 330] Central Statistical Office. *Standard Industrial Classification—Alphabetical List of Industries*. HMSO, London, 1959.
[B 331] Central Statistical Office. *Standard Industrial Classification—Alphabetical List of Industries, Revised 1968*. HMSO, London, 1968.
[B 332] Chartered Institute of Public Finance and Accountancy. *The Standardisation of Accounts: General Principles*. The Institute, London, 1971.
[B 333] Central Statistical Office. *Statistical News*. HMSO, London. Quarterly from 1968.
[B 334] Department of Industry. 'Developments in the statistics of the distributive trades', *Statistical News*, No. 31, 1975, pp. 31.11–31.12.
[B 335] Department of the Environment. 'Statistical forms sent to the construction industry', *Statistical News*, No. 15, November, 1971, pp. 15.6–15.7.
[B 336] *Statutory Rules and Orders of Northern Ireland 1964 No. 145. Industrial Training. Construction Industry Training Board*. HMSO, Belfast, 1964.
[B 337] *The Stock Exchange Official Yearbook*. Thomas Skinner & Co. (Publishers) Ltd, Croydon.
[B 338] Building Economics Research Unit. *Study of the Building Timetable: Fifth Progress Report*. The Unit, School of Environmental Studies, University College, London, 1970.
[B 339] Building Economics Research Unit. *Study of the Building Timetable: Final Report*. The Unit, School of Environmental Studies, University College, London, 1972.
[B 340] Government of Northern Ireland, Ministry of Health and Local Government. *Summary of the Hospital Building Programme of the Northern Ireland Hospitals Authority, March 1963*, HMSO, Belfast, 1963.
[B 341] Trades Union Congress. *TUC Report ... [year]*. The TUC, London. Annual.
[B 342] *Ulster Builder*. Monthly, Belfast.
[B 343] *Ulster Yearbook*. HMSO, Belfast. Triennial for 1926–38 and 1947–68, annual from 1969.
[B 344] Command Paper. *Unemployment Statistics*. Cmnd 5157. HMSO, London, 1972.
[B 345] Command Paper, University Grants Committee. *University Development 1967–72*. Cmnd 5728. HMSO, London, 1974.
[B 346] HM Customs and Excise. *Value Added Tax: Construction Industry*. HM Customs and Excise Notice No. 708. HM Customs and Excise, London, 1972 (Revised June 1973).
[B 347] HM Customs and Excise. *Value Added Tax: Construction Industry. Alterations and Repairs & Maintenance*. HM Customs and Excise Notice No. 715. HM Customs and Excise, London, June 1973.
[B 348] HM Customs and Excise. *VAT Trade Classification*. HM Customs and Excise, London, 1972.
[B 349] Ministry of Works. *Working Party Report—Building*. HMSO, London, 1950.
[B 350] Government Social Survey. *Workplace Industrial Relations*, Report SS 402. HMSO, London, 1968.

APPENDICES

APPENDICES

LIST OF APPENDICES

I. The Construction Industry as Defined in the Standard Industrial Classification and Analyses of the Scope and Coverage of the Definitions — 512

II. Regional Classification Used for Official Construction Statistics — 516

III. Guide to the Classification of Firms by Trade since 1954 — 517

IV. Censuses of Contractors in Great Britain 1941 to date—History of Enquiries made by the Ministry of Works and its Successor Departments (currently Department of the Environment) and Selected Specimen Forms — 521

V. Censuses of Direct Labour Organizations in Great Britain 1943 to date—History of Enquiries made by the Ministry of Works and its Successor Departments (currently Department of the Environment) and Selected Specimen Forms — 559

VI. Site Returns 1941–54—History of Enquiries made by the Ministry of Works and Selected Specimen Forms — 583

VII. Sample Returns of Output and Employment 1945–77—History of Enquiries made by the Ministry of Works and its Successor Departments (currently Department of the Environment) and Selected Specimen Forms — 589

VIII. New Orders Enquiry 1956 to date—History of Enquiries and Selected Specimen Form — 601

IX. EEC State of Trade Enquiry into Construction in Great Britain 1977 to date—History and Selected Specimen Form — 607

X. Return of Overseas Contracts and Sub-contracts 1955 to date—History of Enquiries and Selected Specimen Form — 613

XI. Local Authority Design Work Enquiry 1965 to date—History of Enquiries and Selected Specimen Form — 617

XII. Quarterly Returns of Construction Work in Northern Ireland 1966 to date — 623

XIII. Construction as Defined in the Industrial Classification for the European Communities (NACE) — 633

APPENDIX I

THE CONSTRUCTION INDUSTRY AS DEFINED IN THE STANDARD INDUSTRIAL CLASSIFICATION AND ANALYSES OF THE SCOPE AND COVERAGE OF THE DEFINITIONS

Contents

(1) Definitions.
(2) Analyses of the Scope and Coverage of the Definitions:
    (a) Activities expressly classified to Construction.
    (b) Relevant activities expressly excluded.

(1) Definitions

SIC (1948) Order XVII—Building and Contracting (Extract from [B 329], 1948 edition)

Building
1. Government. Building work carried out by direct employees (excluding non-industrial civil servants) of the Admiralty, Air Ministry, Ministry of Civil Aviation, Ministry of Supply, War Office and Ministry of Works.
2. Local Government. Building Departments of Local Authorities and of Housing Associations.
3. Other. Establishments engaged in erecting, repairing or decorating houses, shops, factories, etc. including establishments specializing in particular sections of the work, such as plumbing, plastering, roofing or installation of heating and ventilating apparatus.

Electric wiring and contracting. Establishments undertaking electrical wiring in buildings, etc. and the erection and maintenance of electric signs.

Civil engineering contracting
1. Government. Civil engineering work carried out by direct employees (excluding non-industrial civil servants) of the Admiralty, Air Ministry, Ministry of Civil Aviation, Ministry of Supply, Ministry of Transport, War Office and Ministry of Works.
2. Other. Establishments constructing or repairing roads, bridges, docks, canals, railways, tunnels, airfields, etc.; laying drains, sewers, gas mains and cables; erecting telegraph and telephone lines; open-cast coal mining; laying out sports grounds; and

other similar work. Small scale repair work on roads, etc. carried out by Local Authorities is excluded.

SIC (1958) Order XVII—Construction (Extract from [B 329] 1958 edition)

Erecting and repairing buildings of all types. Constructing and repairing roads and bridges; erecting steel and reinforced concrete structures; other civil engineering work such as laying sewers and gas mains, erecting overhead line supports and aerial masts, open-cast coal mining, etc. The building and civil engineering establishments of Defence and other Government Departments and of local authorities are included.

Establishments specializing in demolition work or in sections of construction work such as asphalting, electrical wiring, flooring, glazing, installing heating and ventilating apparatus, painting, plastering, plumbing, roofing. The hiring of contractors' plant and scaffolding is included.

SIC (1968) Order XX—Construction* (Extract from [B 329] 1968 edition)

Erecting and repairing buildings of all types. Constructing and repairing roads and bridges; erecting steel and reinforced concrete structures; other civil engineering work such as laying sewers, gas or water mains, and electricity cables, erecting overhead lines and line supports and aerial masts, extracting coal from opencast workings, etc. The building and civil engineering establishments of government departments, local authorities and New Town Corporations and Commissions are included. On-site industrialized building is also included.

Establishments specializing in demolition work or in sections of construction work such as asphalting, electrical wiring, flooring, glazing, installing heating and ventilating apparatus, painting, plastering, plumbing, roofing. The hiring of contractors' plant and scaffolding is included.

(2) Analyses of the Scope and Coverage of the Definitions 1958 and 1968†

(Activities specified in one year but not the other are denoted by the year in brackets.)

(a) *Activities expressly classified to Construction*

Aerial mast erection	Building—cleaning (renovation)
Artesian well contractor	Building Departments of Government
Asphalting contractor	Departments and local authorities
Bridge building	Cable laying
Builders and Contractors	Civil engineering contractor

* In addition a prefatory note to the definition of Order XXI—Gas, Electricity and Water—indicates that construction work carried out by employees of gas, electricity and water undertakings should be classified to that Order rather than Order XX.

† Based on [B 330] and [B 331]. A detailed guide to the 1948 classification was not published.

Cladding structures with metal or asbestos cement sheets
Coal mining (opencast)
Concrete work

Demolition (building)
Dredging contractor

Electric signs—erection and fitting
Electrical contractor
Electrical engineering (wiring and fitting)

Fence contractor
Ferroconcrete bar bending and fixing
Flooring contractor

Glazing contractor
Grouting contractor
Guniting contractor

Heating and ventilating apparatus installation
Hot water engineer

Insulating contractor (buildings)

Land drainage contractor

Mason (building)
Metal lathing contractor

Mine sinking
Mineral boring (excl. gas and oil in 1968)

Painting contractor
Patent glazing
Paving contractor
Piling contractor
Plant hire contractor
Plastering contractor
Plumbing contractor
Pointing contractor (1958)
Public works contractor
Pylon erection

Reinforced concrete engineer
Retort setting
Roofing contractor

Scaffolding hiring and erection
Sports and recreation grounds—laying out of
Steelwork erection
Steeplejack
Stone walling

Tar spraying contractor
Tiling contractor
Tunnelling contractor

Well sinking (excl. gas and oil in 1968)

(b) *Relevant activities expressly excluded*

Activity	SIC Classification
Chimney sweeping	Miscellaneous services
Fencing, by agricultural contractor (1968)	Agricultural contracting
Landscape gardening	Agriculture and horticulture
Leasing of industrial floor cleaning equipment (1968)	Distributive trades
Office cleaning contracting	Miscellaneous services
Office fitting*	Timber, furniture, etc. (shop and office fitting)
Oil boring (1958)	Mining
Oil or gas drilling rig, off-shore (floating) building or repairing	Shipbuilding and marine engineering

* Installation of fittings, such as shop fronts, shop blinds, wood shutters, etc. carried out by the manufacturers.

Parquet floor laying	Miscellaneous wood and cork manufactures
Shop fitting*	As for 'Office fitting'
Signwriting	As for 'Shop fitting' and 'Office fitting'
Thatching	Agriculture
Window cleaning	Miscellaneous services

---

* Installation of fittings, such as shop fronts, shop blinds, wood shutters, etc. carried out by the manufacturers.

APPENDIX II

REGIONAL CLASSIFICATION USED FOR OFFICIAL CONSTRUCTION STATISTICS 1965–1975*

Until 1965		1965–1975*	
Ministry of Public Building and Works (and former Ministry of Works) Statistical Regions		*Economic Planning Regions*	
Northern	Cumberland, Durham, North Riding of Yorkshire, Northumberland, Westmorland.	Northern	Cumberland, Durham, North Riding of Yorkshire, Northumberland, Westmorland.
North Eastern	East and West Ridings of Yorkshire.	Yorkshire and Humberside	East and West Ridings of Yorkshire *and the Lindsey area of Lincolnshire.*
North Midland	Derby (except the High Peak Area), Leicestershire, Lincolnshire, Northamptonshire, Nottinghamshire, Rutland.	East Midlands	Derby (except the High Peak Area), Leicestershire, Lincolnshire (Kesteven and Holland Areas only), Northamptonshire, Nottinghamshire, Rutland.
Eastern	Bedfordshire, Cambridgeshire, Huntingdonshire, Norfolk, Suffolk, and the parts of Essex and Hertfordshire not included in the London Region.	East Anglia	Cambridgeshire, Huntingdonshire, Norfolk, Suffolk, and the *Soke of Peterborough* part of Northamptonshire.
London	London Civil Defence Area including Middlesex, and parts of Essex, Hertfordshire, Kent, Surrey.	South East†	
		(1) London	*Greater London Council Area*
		(2) Eastern Counties	Bedfordshire, Essex and Hertfordshire (except GLC area).
Southern	Berkshire, Buckinghamshire, Hampshire, Oxfordshire, Dorset.	(3) Southern Counties	Berkshire, Buckinghamshire, Hampshire, Oxfordshire, and Poole Borough Council area of Dorset.‡
South Eastern	Sussex and the parts of Kent and Surrey not included in the London Region.	(4) S. Eastern Counties	Sussex, Surrey and Kent (except GLC areas).
South Western	Cornwall, Devonshire, Gloucester, Somerset, Wiltshire.	South West	Cornwall, Devonshire, Dorset (except Poole)‡ Gloucester, Somerset, Wiltshire.
Wales	Includes Monmouthshire.	Wales	Includes Monmouthshire.
Midland	Herefordshire, Shropshire, Staffordshire, Warwickshire, Worcestershire.	West Midlands	Herefordshire, Shropshire, Staffordshire, Warwickshire, Worcestershire.
North Western	Cheshire, Derby (High Peak District), Lancashire.	North West	Cheshire, Derby (High Peak District), Lancashire.
Scotland		Scotland	

* Regional boundaries were revised as a consequence of the reorganization of local government on 1 April 1974. These regions, together with a further sub-division of the South East, were adopted for the statistics of output, employment and new orders collected by the Department of the Environment with effect from the 2nd quarter of 1975—definitions will be found in the 1974 edition of the *Notes and Definitions Supplement* to *Housing and Construction Statistics* [B 250].

† The sub-division of the South East Region which has been made since 1965 is based upon the administrative regions of the former Ministry of Public Building and Works and not the standard sub-divisions. In 1965 statistical information was collected before the boundary between the East Anglia and South East Regions had been defined and data for the former was classified with the Eastern Counties part of the South East Region.

‡ Poole is part of the South West Planning Region but is included in the South East Region for statistical purposes.

APPENDIX III

GUIDE TO THE CLASSIFICATION OF FIRMS BY TRADE SINCE 1954

(Text reference: Section 4.2.3.10)

(1) In November 1954 the census questionnaire classified firms into two categories for the first time:

(a) Building and Civil Engineering
(b) Electrical Wiring Contractors.

Specialist Firms (e.g. Heating and Ventilating Engineers, Reinforced Concretors, Asphalt and Tar Sprayers, Plant Hirers and Flooring Contractors) were regarded as being in the Building and Civil Engineering Category.

(2) As a result of a special enquiry in 1957 firms then on the Register were classified into one of the eighteen trade categories, coded 01–18 in List A below.

(3) In 1968 a further review was held as part of the September census. As a result four new trade categories came into use:

19 Insulating Specialists
20 Suspended Ceiling Specialists
21 Wall and Floor Tiling Specialists
22 Activities other than Codes 1 to 21.

(4) Since 1968, therefore, firms have been classified to one of twenty-two trade groups—coded 01–22 in List A below. List A and List B below provide a detailed guide and alphabetical index respectively to the classification. These lists include additions made as a result of the April 1970 census. It should be appreciated that since information was not sought from firms in the level of detail shown here—broad categories being defined in the questionnaires—the lists were only used in cases where firms gave a description of their activities rather than classifying themselves, or where queries arose.

A. Classification of Firms by Trade

CODE	TRADE GROUP	CODE	TRADE GROUP
01	GENERAL BUILDER includes: Agricultural Buildings Church Restoration Damp Coursing Fireplace Fixing Flue Lining House Extensions Jobbing Builders Repair and Maintenance Firms Store Walling Contractors System Building (Pre-cast Concrete Structure) System Building and Timber Structure	12	REINFORCED CONCRETE SPECIALIST includes: Concrete Pumping Cutting Concrete Drilling of Concrete (Precision) Shuttering and Formwork Steelfixing Reinforcement
		13	HEATING AND VENTILATING ENGINEER includes: Air Conditioning Heating and Sanitary Engineering
02	BUILDING AND CIVIL ENGINEERING CONTRACTORS	14	ELECTRICAL CONTRACTOR
03	CIVIL ENGINEERS includes: Boring Contractors (Mineral) Cable Laying/Jointing Contractors	15	ASPHALT AND TAR SPRAYING CONTRACTORS
	Concrete (On-site) Manufacturers Dredging and Reclamation Earth-moving Contractors	16	PLANT HIRING CONTRACTORS
	Excavation Contractors Flagging and Kerbing Foundations and Piling Groundwork Land Drainage Mining—Open Cast Coal Painting—Lines on Highways Paviour Pipe Line Contractors Road Making Roads and Pathways Contractors Sewer—Main Drainage and Repairs Shoring Contractors	17	FLOORING CONTRACTOR includes: Floor Finishers
		18	CONSTRUCTIONAL ENGINEERS (Mainly engaged on site work) includes: Steel Bending and Fixing Steel Erectors Structural Engineers
		19	INSULATING SPECIALISTS includes: Cavity Wall Insulating Roof Insulating Thermal Insulating
		20	SUSPENDED CEILING SPECIALISTS
		21	WALL AND FLOOR TILING SPECIALIST
04	PLUMBERS includes: Gas Fitting	22	MISCELLANEOUS includes: Acoustic Engineers
05	JOINER AND CARPENTER (Mainly engaged on site work) includes: Timber Buildings (manufacture and erection)		Balustrades and Fire Escapes Boiler Section Engineers Brick Kiln and Furnace Builders Building Cleaning
06	PAINTER AND DECORATOR		Ceiling Specialist—Plastic Finish Ceiling Tiles
07	ROOFER includes: Roof Treatment		Chasing, Cutting and Drilling Dry Lining Fencing Contractors
08	PLASTERER		Finishing Off Sites Glass House Builder
09	GLAZIER		Mastic Jointing Metal Window Fixing
10	DEMOLITION CONTRACTOR includes: Explosives Engineer and Consultant		Paint Cleaning (External) Partitioning Doors and Windows Plaster Board Fixers Refractory Works
11	SCAFFOLD SPECIALIST		Restoration of Buildings

APPENDIX III

CODE	TRADE GROUP	CODE	TRADE GROUP
	Sheeters Roof and Vertical Steeple Jacks Stone Cleaning and Restoration Stonemason		Wall Cladding Wall, Treatment—Plastic Finish Waterproofing X-ray Protection

B. *Alphabetical Index of Trades of Firms and their Trade Group Classification*

		CODE			CODE
A	Acoustic Engineer	22		Erectors, Steel	18
	Agricultural Buildings	01		Excavation Contractors	03
	Air Conditioning	13		Explosive Engineer and	
	Asphalt and Tarspraying	15		Consultant (Demolition)	10
				Extensions (Home)	01
B	Balustrades, Wrought Iron	22			
	Boiler Setting Engineers	22	F	Fencing Contractor	22
	Boring Contractors (Mineral)	03		Finishing Off Sites	22
	Boring (Wells)	03		Fire Escapes, Wrought Iron	22
	Brick Kiln and Furnace Builder	22		Fireplace Fixing	01
	Building and Civil Engineering	02		Flagging and Kerbing Firms	03
	Building Cleaners	22		Floor Finishers	17
				Floor and Wall Tiling	21
C	Cable Laying/Jointing			Flooring Contractor	17
	Contractors	03		Formwork and Shuttering	12
	Carpenter and Joiner (Timber			Foundations and Piling	03
	Buildings)	05		Furnace Builder (Brick Kiln)	22
	Casting, Rough	01			
	Caulking, Tunnel	03	G	Gas Fitting (Plumbers)	04
	Cavity Wall Insulating	19		Glass House Builder	22
	Ceiling Specialist (Plastic Finish)	22		Glazier	09
	Ceiling Suspended	20		Groundwork	03
	Ceiling Tilers	22			
	Chasing, Cutting and Drilling	22	H	Heating and Sanitary Engineers	13
	Church Restoration	01		Heating and Ventilating	13
	Civil Engineering and Building	02		Engineers	
	Cladding (Wall)	22		Highways and Lines (Painting)	03
	Cleaning of Building	22		Home Extensions	01
	Coal Mining (Open Cast)	03			
	Concrete Manufacturers (On Site)	03	I	Insulating Specialists	19
	Concrete Pumping	12		Investigators (Site)	03
	Concrete (Reinforced)	12			
	Coursing, Damp	01	J	Jobbing Builders	01
				Joiner and Carpenter (Timber	
D	Damp Coursing	01		Buildings)	05
	Decorator and Painter	06		Jointing Contractors (Cable	
	Demolition Contractor (Explosive			Laying)	03
	Engineer)	10		Jointing Mastic	22
	Doors and Windows (Partitions)	22			
	Drainage, Land	03	K	Kerbing and Flagging Firms	03
	Dredging and Reclamation	03		Kiln and Furnace Building (Brick)	22
	Drilling and Cutting Concrete				
	(Precision)	12	L	Land Drainage	03
	Dry Lining	22		Lighting (Street)	03
				Lines on Highways (Painting)	03
E	Earth Moving Contractors	03		Lining (Dry)	22
	Electrical Contractors	14			

		CODE			CODE
M	Main Drainage and Sewers Repairs	03	S	Sanitary Engineers (Heating)	13
	Maintenance and Repair Firms	01		Scaffolding Specialist	11
	Manufacturers of Concrete (On Site)	03		Sewers and Main Drainage Repairs	03
	Mastic Jointing	22		Sheeters, Roof and Vertical	22
	Metal Window Fixing	22		Shoring Contractors	03
	Mineral Boring Contractors	03		Shuttering and Formwork	12
				Site Clearing	03
O	Opencast Coal Mining	03		Site Investigators	03
				Sports (Playing Fields Contractors)	03
P	Paint Cleaning	22		Steel Erectors	18
	Painter and Decorator	06		Steel Fixing and Bending	18
	Painting of Lines on Highways	03		Steel Fixing Reinforcement	12
	Partitions, Doors and Windows	22		Steeplejacks	22
	Pathways and Road Contractors	03		Stone Cleaning and Restorations	22
	Paviour	03		Stonemason	22
	Piling and Foundations	03		Stone Walling Contractors	01
	Pipeline Contractors	03		Street Lighting	03
	Plant Hiring Contractors	16		Structural Engineers	18
	Plaster Board Fixers	22		Suspended Ceilings	20
	Plasterers	08		Swimming Pool Contractors	03
	Plastic Finish Ceiling Specialists	22		System Building of Pre-cast Concrete	01
	Plastic Finish Wall Treatments	22		System Building of Timber Structures	01
	Playing-fields Contractors (Sports)	03			
	Plumbers (including Gas Fittings)	04	T	Tarspraying and Asphalt	15
	Pool Contractors (Swimming)	03		Thermal Insulating	19
	Pre-Cast Concrete Structure (System Building)	01		Tilers (Ceiling)	22
	Precision Drilling and Cutting Concrete	12		Timber Structures (System Building)	01
	Pumping Concrete	12		Tunnel Caulking	03
			V	Ventilating and Heating (Engineers)	13
R	Reclamation and Dredging	03			
	Refractory Works	22			
	Reinforced Concrete Specialist	12	W	Wall Cladding	22
	Repair and Maintenance Firms	01		Wall and Floor Tiling	21
	Restoration of Buildings	22		Wall Treatments (Plastic Finish)	22
	Restorations and Stone Cleaning	22		Walling Contractors (Stone)	01
	Road Making	03		Waterproofing	22
	Road and Pathways Contractors	03		Water Supply Engineers	03
	Roofer (including Roof Treatment)	07		Well Boring	03
	Roof Insulating	19		Windows and Doors (Partitions)	22
	Rough Casting	01	X	X-Ray Protection	22

APPENDIX IV

CENSUSES OF CONTRACTORS IN GREAT BRITAIN

History of Enquiries made by the Ministry of Works and its Successor Departments (currently Department of the Environment) and Selected Specimen Forms

(Text references: Sections 3.3, 3.5 and 4.2)

(a) **Date of Introduction**

The first census took place in July 1941.

(b) **Frequency**

   1941–4: July 1941, January, May and November 1942, October 1943, November 1944.
   1945–50: Quarterly each February, May, August and November from May 1945 to May 1950 (except for November 1949).
   1951–4: Annually in May (together with a special enquiry in November 1954 on BCE/AR5 in connection with the reclassification of the register).
   1955–6: September 1955 (a special enquiry—see under (h) below) and April 1956.
   1957–70: Bi-annually each April and September.
   1971 to date: Annually in October.

(c) **Form References**

   1941–4: BCE 3, BCE 3A, BCE 3B, etc. to BCE 3E.
   1945–50: BCE3/QR1–BCE3/QR19 (numbered serially).
   1951 to date: Originally BCE3/AR..., later BIM3/AR... and then BIM/AR... (numbered serially). Suffixes identify 'simple' and 'detailed' versions of the form which have been distributed on a sample basis since 1959 (see under 'History' below).

(d) **Specimen Forms Included**

The return has been subject to frequent change and development. The specimen forms selected for inclusion here have been selected (subject to the constraint that a complete set of questionnaires is not available) to illustrate the questions asked and the instructions given regarding the completion of the return, and to record major developments in its content. Thus the return in current use is reproduced together with the first and others which exemplify such developments. They should be examined in conjunction with the brief history of the returns set out below (Section (h) of this Appendix).

Form Ref.	Date	Title	Page
BCE 3	July 1941	Information Form to Be Completed by Building and Civil Engineering Contractors	530
BCE3/QR1	May 1945	Registration of Building and Civil Engineering Contractors. Defence Regulation 56AB	531
BCE3/AR1	May 1951	Registration of Building and Civil Engineering Contractors. Defence Regulation 56AB. Return to Be Completed by All Undertakings Registered Under Above Regulations	533
BIM3/AR8	April 1957	Annual Return of Labour and Output	535
BIM3/AR9	Sept. 1957	Employment Return	538
BIM/AR34A	April 1970	Return of Persons Employed and Output	540
BIM/AR35	Sept. 1970	Employment Return	543
BIM 164	(1970 edition)	Notes for Guidance in Completing the Return	545
BIM/AR41B	October 1975	Annual Return on Industrial Activity	547
BIM 164	(10/75)	Notes for the Completion of the Annual Return on Industrial Activity	551
BIM/AR43B	October 1977	Annual Return on Industrial Activity	553
BIM 164	(10/77)	Notes for the Completion of the Annual Return on Industrial Activity	557

(e) Circulation

1941–54: All building and civil engineering contracting undertakings, other than local authority and public utility direct labour organizations, on the Ministry of Works' register maintained in accordance with Defence Regulation 56AB (see Section 3.2.2).

1955 to date: All contractors and building departments of private firms on the MOW (currently the DOE) register—drawn up in accordance with the Standard Industrial Classification. An important exception to this statement, however, is that firms who were identified during the early 1970s as having been previously omitted from the register were not immediately incorporated in the censuses but were kept on a 'Special List' until 1974. In April 1972 these firms were sent a 'Special Inquiry' form (see (h) below) and in 1973, although they were not incorporated in the census, they were sent questionnaires identical, apart from separate coding, to those to other contractors. It should also be noted that in the April censuses from 1959 and the October censuses from 1971 a sample of the smaller firms was sent a less detailed version of the return to complete.

(f) Processing of Returns

Currently the Department of the Environment.

(g) Availability of Data from Individual Returns

Individual returns are treated as strictly confidential under the terms, currently, of the Statistics of Trade Act 1947.

(h) History of the Return

(1) *July 1941–November 1944*

A specimen copy of the first return (Form BCE3) is reproduced below (p. 530). Subsequent returns differed in content but unfortunately copies of all the questionnaires used are not available. However, a broad picture may be built up by examining the available tabulations of data—Table 3.1 *supra* provides full details of these tabulations. It may be seen that the returns differed in particular according to whether or not returns of labour (broken down by occupation or by type of work), or of output (in total or by type of work), were required. Reference should be made to Section 3.3 where a full commentary is given on matters relating to the scope and interpretation of the census data. It will be seen that the first return required a trade description of the firm; subsequent questionnaires examined did not include this section.

(2) *May 1945–May 1954*

A definitive account of the development of the census returns during this period is not possible since a full set of questionnaires is not available for examination. In the absence of questionnaires it is nonetheless possible to verify whether or not particular categories of data were collected in many cases by inspecting available tabulations—Table 3.2 *supra* indicates the particular enquiries for which no questionnaires have been traced and the data that are available.

Information was collected in the censuses about employment (now changed to '16 years of age and over') and (later) the value of work done under a number of headings—type of work, region and, in the case of labour, occupation—which varied from time to time, as did the particular cross-classifications called for. For details of the analyses available see Tables 3.2 and 3.3 *supra* and the accompanying commentary (Section 3.5). Major aspects of the development of the return are outlined below.

The occupational classification

Operatives. The categories distinguished remained the same over the period except for changes in the description of the two miscellaneous groups (see Section 3.5.4 and compare specimen forms).

Apprentices. A return of apprentices according to occupation and type of agreement (indentured or not) was introduced in August 1949 and repeated subsequently in each May census together with a return of the numbers employed since a given date (providing intake statistics)—cf. specimen form BCE3/AR1. The instructions were altered in 1951 to stress that 'boy labourers' were to be excluded and the term 'unindentured apprentices' was replaced by 'apprentices having verbal agreements'. A note was also added relating to apprentice electricians (see specimen form BCE3/AR1).

Working Principals. The breakdown of Working Principals by occupation (cf. specimen forms) ceased in May 1951.

Classification by types of work

A breakdown of operatives employed by type of work was required, as far as can be ascertained, in every census (see Table 3.2). The types of work distinguished prior to May 1946 and from 1949 (August or earlier) are as shown on specimen forms BCE3/QR1 and BCE3/AR1 respectively. Between these dates a more detailed return was called for.*

On-site and off-site labour. The census for February 1948 required a return of the number of operatives who were employed 'off-site' (also broken down by type of work). This was the only occasion a distinction was drawn between on-site and off-site labour in returns other than site returns.

Cross-classification of operatives employed

By occupation and type of work—required until May 1946.

By region and type of work —introduced in May 1946 and retained until May 1954. It is important to note that the return required that operatives be classified according to the region in which they were working. Prior to May 1946 the analysis (by occupation and type of work) had to distinguish between employment inside and outside of the London Civil Defence region.

Output

A question on the value of work done was added to the return in either the third census (questionnaire not available) or the fourth census (February 1946) and retained in each succeeding census up to May 1954, as far as can be ascertained. Except for May 1946, each required an estimate only of the *total* (no breakdown) value of work done during the period of three months ending with the month preceding the date of the census. The instructions regarding the completion of this part of the return had taken the form as shown on specimen questionnaire BCE3/AR1, reproduced below, by November 1946. At this date the instructions regarding the exclusion of the cost of land and legal fees, the exclusion of the value of work done by sub-contractors, the inclusion of the value of materials and components supplied free of charge and the note regarding prefabricated housing were added.

---

* In May 1946 the categories were as follows: (1) War damage repairs to houses and flats; (2) Preparation of sites for temporary and permanent houses and flats; (3) Erection of temporary and permanent houses and flats; (4) Conversion and adaptation of houses and flats resulting in additional accommodation; (5) Other work to houses and flats including repair and maintenance (excluding w.d.r.); (6) Civil Engineering—new work and maintenance (excluding site preparation for houses); (7) War damage repairs to buildings other than houses and flats; (8) New building for industry, commerce and agriculture (excluding housing); (9) Repairs and maintenance to buildings other than houses and flats (excluding w.d.r.); (10) Other work. In May 1947 the categories were amended again—category (6) was sub-divided between new work and repairs and maintenance, and categories (8) and (10) were merged.

(3) *November 1954 and September 1955*

These two enquiries differed from all the preceding and succeeding censuses:

November 1954. This enquiry was held in connection with the changeover from the register of contractors which had been maintained in accordance with Defence Regulation 56AB until November 1953 to one classified in accordance with the Standard Industrial Classification (see Section 4.1.1 above). Firms were required to provide a return of merely: the total number of Working Principals, the total number of operatives and an indication of whether its 'major activity' was 'building and civil engineering'* or 'electric wiring contracting'. It is important to note that for the first time the return of operatives was to cover all *persons* (male and female) aged *15 years* and over employed on manual work 'whether full or part-time, whose National Insurance cards are held by you on the pay-day specified below: these will include working foremen, cleaners, and operatives engaged in transport work, stores and warehouses'. Formerly the returns had related to *male* operatives only aged *16 years* and over (or 'over 16' during the war) with no reference being made to the categories referred to above nor to 'full-time or part-time' employees.

September 1955. This enquiry went to all firms on the new register (see above) and required a return of the total number of Working Principals, the total number of operatives (defined as above together with an instruction to include those engaged on 'the manufacture of goods for sale'), the number of apprentices employed and the number engaged during the preceding year both according to occupation and type of agreement.

(4) *April 1956–September 1970*

In 1956/7 a new pattern of bi-annual censuses, based on the new SIC-based register, was established and henceforth maintained until 1970—one concerned with output and employment (April census) and one concerned with employment in greater detail (September census). The April censuses were initiated in 1956 and the September censuses in 1957. With effect from April 1959, however, the practice was adopted of selecting a 'sample element' from amongst the smaller contractors who received a less detailed version of the questionnaire, which required a return under the total employment categories only. The development of the April and September enquiries is considered separately below.

April Censuses 1956–70

A comparison of the forms in use at the beginning and end of this period (BIM3/AR8 and BIM/AR34—reproduced below) shows most of the changes that took place over the period. Our purpose here is to date the changes precisely and to draw attention to other notable developments that took place in the intervening period.

---

* Including for the purpose of the return all firms in the seven 'specialist trades' (see Section 3.3.2 above) except electrical contractors.

Return of work done by type and sector

The instructions and definitions relating to the completion of this part of the return were amplified or amended on several occasions. Apart from a difference in timing, corresponding revisions were made to the sample enquiry forms on which corresponding information about employment and output by type of work and sector was obtained for those quarters of the year not covered by the census itself (see Appendix VII). It is convenient, therefore, to consider the changes to both enquiries together. The additional instructions are best observed by comparing two of the specimen forms reproduced below (BIM3/AR8 and BIM/AR34A). The dates of their introduction were as follows:

		Census	Sample
(i)	Instruction to electrical contractors	April 1958	January 1959
(ii)	Instruction to painters and decorators	April 1959	January 1959
(iii)	Instruction to contractors in general that the value of work done by their own operatives on the construction or maintenance of their own premises should be included	April 1964	October 1962
(iv)	Instruction that the value of work done on the builder's own initiative should be included	April 1965	July 1965

The definitions relating to the classification of work by sector were also revised. The classification of housing work, in particular that done for housing associations, was changed on two occasions. In the censuses for April 1965 and April 1966, and the sample enquiries from July 1965 to October 1966 inclusive, such work *as was for private sale* was classifiable as private. Before and after these dates, all work for housing associations was classifiable to the public sector. The references in this context to the SSHA and to 'co-ownership societies' were added in April 1965 and April 1967 censuses respectively, and the samples for July 1965 and January 1967 respectively. For non-housing work the notes were amended with effect from April 1968 (censuses) and October 1967 (samples) to ensure that work on steel-works in public and private ownership was appropriately classified following the re-nationalisation of certain steel companies in 1967. The brief notes specifying the bodies comprising the public sector (i.e. other than private owners and developers—see specimen forms) were amended with effect from the April 1967 census and the January 1967 sample when specific references were inserted to the Covent Garden Market Authority and the Airports Authority.

New contracts and orders

In line with the development of the new orders enquiry (see Appendix VIII), contractors were required to list individual contracts with effect from April 1964 until April 1969. The census return then ceased to be used for the collection of these data.

A(P)TC employees

A return of the total number of these employees, defined as in the September census (see specimen form BIM3/AR9), was required with effect from April 1965. The word 'Professional' was added to the category heading in April 1966 but the definition was not suitably amplified until April 1967 (cf. specimen form BIM/AR34A).

Labour-only sub-contractors

Instructions regarding the completion of the return were amplified in both April and September censuses with effect from April 1959 to the effect that Working Partners in groups of labour-only sub-contractors should be returned as Working Principals, not as operatives.

Details of Business

(Cf. specimen form BIM/AR34A, April 1970—the last April census—Part 1.) This question was included in all April and September censuses (except September 1969) with effect from September 1968, initially specifying categories 1–18 only (expanded to 21 in April 1970).

September Censuses 1957–70

The main developments in the September censuses are outlined below. The salient feature is the general development of the classification of labour by occupation in 1965.

Operatives

A comparison of Form BCE/AR9 with Form BIM/AR35 will show the expansion in the number of occupational categories distinguished during the period. All of the extra occupations were added in 1965 except for 'ceiling tilers' in category 6 (added in 1967) and 'canteen workers' added in 1969. Definitions of the occupations to be included in each occupational category for guidance in completing the return were also given for the first time in 1965, initially as part of the questionnaire and later as a separate form—*Notes for Guidance in Completing the Employment Return*—Form BIM 164 (see the specimen copy reproduced below).

Apprentices

The occupational breakdown required for apprentices has followed that for operatives where appropriate (see Form BIM/AR35). An additional category 'Boys on probation for written indentures' was introduced in 1959. The distinction made in the *Notes for Guidance* (Form BIM 164) between firms in England and Wales and firms in Scotland was introduced in 1970.

A(P)TC employees

A breakdown by occupation was introduced in 1965 and, apart from the exceptions noted below, remained unchanged thereafter (see specimen form BIM/AR35 for

1970). The exceptions were: (a) a division of the 'managerial' group into two categories 'X' and 'Y' (see specimen form) introduced in 1969, (b) a return of the number of staff in each occupational category undergoing training courses and the number of staff employed part-time as training officers, required from 1965 to 1969. It should also be noted that prior to 1965 the return referred merely to 'administrative, technical and clerical' employees—i.e. no specific reference was made to 'professional' staff.

Labour-only Sub-contractors

September censuses between 1967 and 1969 included the question 'Are you wholly or mainly a labour-only sub-contractor?' See also under 'April Censuses' above.

Details of Business

See under 'April Censuses' above.

(5) *October Censuses 1971–7*

The April and September forms were consolidated to form a single enquiry in October each year with effect from 1971. Since 1971 a number of changes have been made, the most important being in 1975 when a revised occupational classification was introduced and in 1977 when the occupational breakdown was dropped from the DOE enquiry (see Section 4.2.3.4) and other changes made. Specimen copies are included here, therefore, of both the 1975 and the 1977 questionnaires—Form BIM/AR41B and Form BIM/AR43B respectively together with copies of the *Notes for the Completion of the Annual Return on Industrial Activity* in use at these times. Details of the changes made in the period 1971–7, and their timing, are noted below. The practice of sending less detailed versions of the form to sample elements of the smaller contractors on the register continued up to and including 1975—these forms consisted of either Sections 1–7 or 1–5 of the detailed form (cf. Form BIM/AR41B for 1975).

Changes to the occupational classification

October 1971—the former category 'Working Principal' was replaced by 'Working Proprietor' (see Section 4.2.9 *supra* for comment).

October 1974—the occupational categories of 'Masons' and 'Paviours' were replaced by 'Tunnellers' and 'Paviours and Allied Skills' respectively.

October 1975—occupational classification completely revised (cf. specimen forms BIM/AR41B and BIM/AR35 reproduced below). As will be seen the APTC categories were reduced in number but the classification of operative occupations was increased in size and considerably changed. Further, the term 'apprentice' was replaced with 'trainee' which is wider in scope.

October 1977—occupational classification dropped, apart from the retention of the distinction between: Working Proprietors; APTC employees; operatives and trainees.

Other developments

October 1973
   (a) As a consequence of the raising of the school leaving age, the age of employees covered was changed from '15 years and over' to '16 years and over'.
   (b) Questions relating to the value of contracts and orders received added—see Section 2 of the 1975 form reproduced below.

October 1974—questions added on the value of work done under sub-contract—see Sections 8 and 9 of the 1975 form.

October 1976—trade classification ('Details of business' section) amended to identify 'opencast coal-mining contractors' and to distinguish between plant hiring contractors *with* and *without* operators.

October 1977—questions added on the value of non-construction work carried out—Section 9 of Form BIM/AR43B reproduced below.

1972 Special Enquiry. All firms on the Department's 'Special List' (see (e) above) were sent a special form in April 1972. This required information about private enterprise housing activity, employment of Working Proprietors, APTC employees, operatives and apprentices, and value of work done by type of work (this last question was only asked of a sample of firms on the list).

DEFENCE REGULATION 56AB (S.R.&O. 1941 No. 1038) | For official use only :

INFORMATION FORM
to be completed by
BUILDING AND CIVIL ENGINEERING CONTRACTORS.

NOTE.—This form MUST be completed as well as the registration form. Use block letters and sign at foot of form.

TRADING NAME OF FIRM		
ADDRESS OF HEAD OFFICE	Address	
	Town	
	County	
TYPE OF BUSINESS (Trade description)		
Total No. of Males over 16 years of age employed by you on building and/or civil engineering work on the last pay-day in July, 1941	Craftsmen & Foremen	
	Others	
Total No. of clerical and administrative staff (insurable against unemployment) employed by you in connection with building and/or civil engineering work on the last pay-day in July, 1941	Male	
	Female	
Estimated total value of building and/or civil engineering work done in the month of July, 1941, including repair and maintenance work. *See note below		

I CERTIFY THAT TO THE BEST OF MY BELIEF THE ABOVE PARTICULARS ARE CORRECT :—

Signature on behalf of the undertaking..

Date..

† Proprietor. † Director.
† Partner. † Secretary.
† Delete words inapplicable.

*NOTE.—Main contractors should not include the value of work done for them by sub-contractors.

When completed, this form should be returned with form B.C.E.2 to the Ministry of Works and Buildings (A.S.63), Sanctuary Buildings, 18, Great Smith Street, London, S.W.1.

B.C.E. 3

[11551] Wt. 23273/4125 100m/16 8/41 C.N.Ld. 748
[11756] Wt. 27923/4203 30m/16 9/41 C.N.Ld. 748

APPENDIX IV 531

MINISTRY OF WORKS
Registration of Building and Civil Engineering Contractors
Defence Regulation 56AB

B.C.E. 3/O.R.I.

Return to be completed by provisionally registered Building and Civil Engineering Contractors.
PLEASE READ THE INSTRUCTIONS ON PAGE 2 BEFORE COMPLETING THIS FORM.

Trading Name of firm :	
Full Postal address of Head or Registered Office	Address .... Town .... County ....

PART A—To be completed only by provisionally registered firms with no building and civil engineering employees (other than proprietor, working partners, etc.).

IS YOUR BUSINESS
- (a) still active .... (a) ....
- (b) closed down temporarily .... (b) ....
- (c) closed down permanently .... (c) ....

Please answer "Yes" in appropriate Section.

To be completed only by provisionally registered firms with building and civil engineering employees.
Firms with no employees should write "NIL" across parts B and C.
NUMBER OF BUILDING AND CIVIL ENGINEERING OPERATIVES (MALES, 16 YEARS OF AGE AND OVER) ON THE PAY-ROLL ON THE PAY-DAY IN THE WEEK BEGINNING 21st MAY, 1945.

PART B.—OPERATIVES WORKING IN THE LONDON CIVIL DEFENCE REGION ONLY (as defined on page 2).

OPERATIVES ENGAGED ON	Carpenters and Joiners (1)	Bricklayers (2)	Slaters and Tilers (3)	Plasterers (4)	Painters (5)	Plumbers and Glaziers (6)	Masons (7)	Other Building Craftsmen (8)	Electricians (9)	Other B. & C.E. Operatives including Labourers & Navvies (10)	TOTAL (11)
1. Houses and Flats (including New Work, Adaptations and Conversions, Temporary Houses, Roads and Sewers for Housing Sites *but excluding* War Damage Repairs and Repairs and Maintenance)											
2. Other New Construction (i.e., Factories, Schools, Offices, etc., etc., *excluding* Repairs and Maintenance)											
3. War Damage Repairs to :—											
(a) Houses and Flats											
(b) Other Buildings											
4. All other work including Repairs and Maintenance, Demolition and Debris Clearance											
5. Total Working in London Civil Defence Region											

PART C. OPERATIVES WORKING OUTSIDE THE LONDON CIVIL DEFENCE REGION ONLY.

6. Houses and Flats (including New Work, Adaptations and Conversions, Temporary Housing, Roads and Sewers for Housing Sites *but excluding* War Damage Repairs and Repairs and Maintenance)											
7. Other New Construction (i.e. Factories, Schools, Offices, etc., etc., *excluding* Repairs and Maintenance)											
8. War Damage Repairs to :—											
(a) Houses and Flats											
(b) Other Buildings											
9. All Other Work including Repairs and Maintenance, Demolition and Debris Clearance											
10. Total Working Outside London Civil Defence Region											

PART D. WORKING PRINCIPALS.—Firms are asked to state below the number and trades of Working Principals—*Not to be included in Employees shewn above*—if there are no Working Principals please state "NIL."

11. Working Principals											

I certify that to the best of my belief the above particulars are correct ;
Signed on behalf of the undertaking ....
(Usual signature)   (State whether proprietor, director, manager, partner, secretary, etc.)

NOTE—PAGES 1 & 3 MUST BE COMPLETED, AND FORM FOLDED AND RETURNED AS INDICATED ON PAGE 4 NOT LATER THAN WEDNESDAY, 6th JUNE, 1945.

NOTICE.

Under the Building and Civil Engineering Labour (Returns) (No. 1) Order, 1945, persons employing labour in the activities mentioned in the Order are required to make returns of labour employed by them within ten days of being requested so to do by the Minister of Works.

INSTRUCTIONS FOR COMPLETING THE FORM

1. Administrative and clerical staff should *not* be included.

2. Main contractors should not include employees of sub-contractors.

3. Foremen should be included under their appropriate trade classification.

4. Operatives in groups working on " ' C ' (b) Houses " etc. should be *returned by the leading contractor only.*

5. Firms in M.O.W. working parties should make a return of their operatives.

6. Active firms with no operatives should mark parts ' B ' and ' C ' "Nil," but complete parts ' A ' and ' D.'

7. The information is required in duplicate, and Pages 1 and 3 must be completed and returned.

NOTE.

The London Civil Defence Region includes the following Local Authority Areas—

ACTON	CHINGFORD	FRIERN BARNET	CITY OF LONDON	STOKE NEWINGTON
BANSTEAD	CHISLEHURST & SIDCUP	FULHAM	MALDEN & COOMBE	SUNBURY-ON-THAMES
BARKING	COULSDON & PURLEY	GREENWICH	MERTON & MORDEN	SURBITON
BARNES	CRAYFORD	HACKNEY	MITCHAM	SUTTON & CHEAM
BARNET	CROYDON	HAMMERSMITH	ORPINGTON	TOTTENHAM
BATTERSEA	DAGENHAM	HAMPSTEAD	PADDINGTON	TWICKENHAM
BECKENHAM	DEPTFORD	HARROW	PENGE	UXBRIDGE
BEDDINGTON & WALLINGTN	EALING	HAYES & HARLINGTON	POPLAR	WALTHAM HOLY CROSS
BERMONDSEY	EAST BARNET	HENDON	POTTERS BAR	WALTHAMSTOW
BETHNAL GREEN	EAST HAM	HESTON & ISLEWORTH	RICHMOND	WANDSWORTH
BEXLEY	EDMONTON	HOLBORN	RUISLIP-NORTHWOOD	WANSTEAD & WOODFORD
BRENTFORD & CHISWICK	ELSTREE	HORNSEY	ST. MARYLEBONE	WEMBLEY
BROMLEY	ENFIELD	ILFORD	ST. PANCRAS	WEST HAM
BUSHEY	EPSOM & EWELL	ISLINGTON	SHOREDITCH	WESTMINSTER
CAMBERWELL	ERITH	KENSINGTON	SOUTHALL	WILLESDEN
CARSHALTON	ESHER	KINGSTON-ON-THAMES	SOUTHGATE	WIMBLEDON
CHELSEA	FELTHAM	LAMBETH	SOUTHWARK	WOOD GREEN
CHESHUNT	FINCHLEY	LEWISHAM	STAINES	WOOLWICH
CHIGWELL	FINSBURY	LEYTON	STEPNEY	YIEWSLEY & DRAYTON

APPENDIX IV

MINISTRY OF WORKS
Registration of Building and Civil Engineering Contractors
Defence Regulation 56AB

CONFIDENTIAL

B.C.E.3/A.R.1

RETURN TO BE COMPLETED BY ALL UNDERTAKINGS REGISTERED UNDER ABOVE REGULATIONS.

Please read the Instructions overleaf and Notes below before completing this Form

Trading Name of firm :	
Full Postal address of Head Office (for correspondence)	Address .... Town .... County .... Telephone No. .... If the above address differs from that to which this form was sent, please state if the change is a permanent one .... ("Yes" or "No")

For Official Use Only
Size Group
Sample | Census

Estimated total value of Work done during the three months ended 31st March, 1951
i.e., the total amount which would be charged to customers for B. & C.E. work actually done during the three months, excluding the cost of land, legal fees, etc. (See Instructions overleaf) £ ....
Omit shillings & pence

PART A.—Only complete this part if you have no B. & C.E. employees. Working principals (see instruction 4 overleaf) do not count as employees.
(a) Is your business closed down permanently? ....
(b) Has your business been in operation at any time since 1st May, 1950? ....
Please answer "Yes" or "No"

Parts B, C and D are to be completed if you have building and civil engineering employees. If you have no B. & C.E. employees you should write "Nil" across parts B and C, but should complete part D.

PART B.—NUMBER OF BUILDING AND CIVIL ENGINEERING OPERATIVES ON THE PAY-ROLL ON THE PAY-DAY IN THE WEEK BEGINNING 21st MAY, 1951
(Do not include working principals—see Part "D")

REGION IN WHICH YOUR B. & C.E. OPERATIVES ARE WORKING (see overleaf for definition of regions)	ALL MALE OPERATIVES AND APPRENTICES AGED 16 AND OVER					APPRENTICES ONLY (ALL AGES) (THIS EXCLUDES BOY LABOURERS)				
	Houses and Flats		Non-Housing Work				Apprentices having Written Indentures		Apprentices having Verbal Agreements	
	Site preparation and erection of permanent houses & flats See Note (a) (1)	Other Housing work See Note (a) (2)	New Work (including New Civil Engineering work) See Note (b) (3)	Other Non-Housing work See Note (b) (4)	TOTAL See Note (c) (5)	OCCUPATION Tab. No.	Total (6)	No. in Col. (6) first employed on B. & C.E. work after 18/5/50 (7)	Total (8)	No. in Col. (8) first employed on B. & C.E. Work after 18/5/50 (9)
1. Northern						1 Carpenters & Joiners				
2. East & West Ridings						2 Bricklayers				
3. North Midlands						3 Slaters & Tilers				
4. Eastern						4 Plasterers				
5. London						5 Painters				
6. Southern						6 Plumbers & Glaziers				
7. South-Western						7 Masons				
8. Wales						8 Electricians See Note (d)				
9. Midlands						9 Other B. & C.E. Craftsmen				
10. North-Western										
11. Scotland										
12. South-Eastern										
13. Total—all regions						10 TOTAL				

NOTES.—(a) Col. (1) includes site preparation and erection of permanent houses and flats, married quarters for Services, and shops with more than one unit of living accommodation.
Col. (2) includes repair, maintenance, conversion and adaptation of the above.
(b) Col. (3) includes new construction, extension, conversion and adaptations of hutting and temporary accommodation barracks, farmhouses, shops with not more than one unit of living accommodation and all buildings other than houses and flats.
Col. (4) includes repair and maintenance of the above and all other work.
(c) In Col. (5) the total number of operatives in line 13 should agree with the total number of operatives in Part C below.
(d) Returns to be made in respect of Category I and Category II boys only. Category III boys should be excluded from this section.

PARTS C. and D.—TOTAL NUMBER OF OPERATIVES AND WORKING PRINCIPALS BY OCCUPATIONS.
NOTE. The total number of operatives in PART C should agree with the total operatives shown in line 13, Col. 5 above.

	Carpenters and Joiners (1)	Bricklayers (2)	Slaters and Tilers (3)	Plasterers (4)	Painters (5)	Plumbers and Glaziers (6)	Masons (7)	Electricians (8)	Other B. & C.E. craftsmen (9)	Other occupations (10)	TOTAL See Note (C) (11)
PART C— Male Operatives and apprentices aged 16 and over.											
PART D— Working Principals (See instruction 4 overleaf)											

I certify that to the best of my belief the above particulars are correct :

SIGNED on behalf of the undertaking ....
(Usual Signature) (State whether proprietor, director, manager, partner, secretary, etc.)

THIS FORM MUST BE COMPLETED, FOLDED AND RETURNED TO THE ADDRESS SHOWN OVERLEAF NOT LATER THAN WEDNESDAY, 6th JUNE, 1951

CONSTRUCTION AND THE RELATED PROFESSIONS

LIST B

The London Civil Defence Region includes the following Local Authority Areas:—

Acton, Banstead, Barking, Barnes, Barnet, Battersea, Beckenham, Beddington & Wallington, Bermondsey, Bethnal Green, Bexley, Brentford & Chiswick, Bromley, Buckhurst, Camberwell, Carshalton, Chelsea, Cheshunt, Chigwell, Chingford, Chislehurst & Sidcup, Coulsdon & Purley, Crayford, Croydon, Dagenham, Deptford, Ealing, East Barnet, East Ham, Edmonton, Elstree, Enfield, Epsom & Ewell, Erith, Esher, Feltham, Finchley, Finsbury, Friern Barnet, Fulham, Greenwich, Hackney, Hammersmith, Hampstead, Harrow, Hayes & Harlington, Hendon, Heston & Isleworth, Holborn, Hornsey, Ilford, Islington, Kensington, Kingston-on-Thames, Lambeth, Lewisham, Leyton, City of London, Malden & Coombe, Merton & Morden, Mitcham, Orpington, Paddington, Penge, Poplar, Potters Bar, Richmond, Ruislip Northwood, St. Marylebone, St. Pancras, Shoreditch, Southall, Southgate, Southwark, Staines, Stepney, Stoke Newington, Sunbury-on-Thames, Surbiton, Sutton Cheam, Tottenham, Twickenham, Uxbridge, Waltham Holy Cross, Walthamstow, Wandsworth, Wanstead & Woodford, Wembley, West Ham, Westminster, Willesden, Wimbledon, Wood Green, Woolwich, Yiewsley & Drayton

MINISTRY OF WORKS

SPECIMEN

ON HIS MAJESTY'S SERVICE

Fold Here

NOTICE

Under the Building and Civil Engineering Labour (Returns) (No. 1) Order, 1945, persons employing labour in the activities mentioned in the Order are required to make returns of labour employed by them within ten days of being requested to do so by the Minister of Works.

Wt.38074/L9333 196,200 (13) 1/51 N.M.Ltd. 51-7624

INSTRUCTIONS FOR COMPLETING THE FORM

1. Administrative and clerical staff should not be included.
2. Main contractors should not include employees of sub-contractors.
3. Foremen should be included as operatives under their appropriate trade classification.
4. Working principals are owners, partners, managers, etc., who do manual B. & C.E. work.
5. Active firms with no operatives should mark parts 'B' and 'C' "Nil", but complete parts 'A' and 'D' and give estimated total value of work done.
6. Where materials, components, etc., used during the three months have been supplied without charge to the contractor, the value of such items should be included in the estimated total value of work done. Main contractors should exclude value of work done by sub-contractors.
7. In the case of erection of permanent or temporary prefabricated houses, the estimated total value of work done should be based on the value of the contract(s), only.

Fold Here

ON HIS MAJESTY'S SERVICE

PROGRAMMES AND STATISTICS OFFICER,
MINISTRY OF WORKS,
8, CORNWALL TERRACE,
REGENT'S PARK,
LONDON, N.W.1.

SPECIMEN

Fold Here

LIST A

LIST OF COUNTIES WITHIN REGIONS:—

NORTHERN	Cumberland, Durham, Northumberland, Westmorland, Yorkshire (North Riding).
EAST AND WEST RIDINGS	Yorkshire (East and West Ridings).
NORTH MIDLANDS	Derby (excluding High Peak), Leicester, Lincs, Northants, Notts, Rutland
EASTERN	Bedford, Cambridge, Essex[1], Hertford[1], Huntingdon, Isle of Ely, Norfolk, Suffolk.
LONDON	Essex[2], Hertford[2], Kent[2], London.—Middlesex, Surrey[2].
SOUTH-WESTERN	Berkshire, Buckingham, Dorset, Hampshire, Isle of Wight, Oxford.
WALES	Cornwall, Devon, Gloucester, Somerset, Wiltshire.
	Wales and Monmouth, Anglesey.
MIDLANDS	Hereford, Shropshire, Stafford, Warwick, Worcester.
NORTH-WESTERN	Cheshire, Lancashire, High Peak of Derby, Isle of Man.
SCOTLAND	All Counties.
SOUTH-EASTERN	Kent[1], Surrey[1], Sussex.

1. Excluding that part coming within the London Civil Defence Region } See LIST B
2. That part coming within the London Civil Defence Region

APPENDIX IV   535

CONFIDENTIAL   MINISTRY OF WORKS,
                                BUILDING INDUSTRIES & MATERIALS SECTION.

                                                                          24th April, 1957.

BUILDING AND CONTRACTING
(Building, Electric Wiring and Contracting, and Civil Engineering Contracting)
Annual Return of Labour and Output

Sir(s),

    It is necessary for the Government regularly to have certain information about Building, Civil Engineering and Electric Wiring Work.

    The undertaking described below falls within the scope of the Inquiry. Therefore notice is hereby given by the Minister of Works

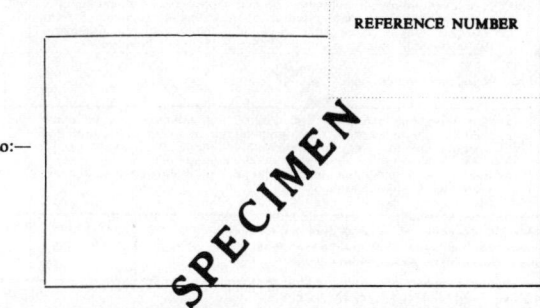

to supply in relation to the undertaking carried on by you the information specified overleaf, and to return this form to the address above not later than **WEDNESDAY, 8th MAY, 1957.**

    This notice is served under the provisions of Section 1 of the Statistics of Trade Act, 1947, for the purpose of obtaining information necessary for the discharge by Government Departments of their functions.

    I am, Sir(s),

        Your obedient Servant,

        Under Secretary,
        for and on behalf of the Minister of Works.

All information given by you will be treated as strictly confidential and will be used solely in the compilation of general statistical results. The results will be prepared and published in a way which will not reveal the particulars relating to any individual undertaking unless previous consent is given by the undertaking.	If you wish to keep for reference, a record of the information supplied by you on this form, further copies of the form will be supplied on application to this office. In all correspondence with this office, the reference number given in the address box above, should be quoted.

TO BE COMPLETED AND SIGNED BY THE PERSON MAKING THE RETURN ON BEHALF OF THE UNDERTAKING

    Trading Name of Firm...

    Full Postal Address
    of Head or Registered Office...
    (including Town and County)

    ....

    Telephone Exchange & Number...

    I certify that to the best of my belief the particulars above and overleaf are correct.

    Signed...   Date............................
        (State whether Proprietor, Director, Manager, Partner, Secretary.)

PART I RETURN OF LABO[UR]

PART I A. WORKING PRINCIPALS (Owners, Managers, Partners, etc., who do manual work) — Number

The number of working principals should be entered here but should be excluded from Col. 1 below. The work done by working principals should be included in Col. 2 below.

PART I B. OPERATIVES EMPLOYED AND VALUE OF WORK DONE.			COL. 1 Operatives employed by you on the pay day in the week ending 27th April, 1957 (See note 4)	COL. 2 Estimated value of work done by you in the 3 months ending 31st March, 1957 (See note 5)
	TYPE OF BUILDING, CIVIL ENGINEERING AND ELECTRIC WIRING WORK			(Omit shillings & pence) £
(i) HOUSES AND FLATS.	(a) **New Construction**, including site preparation and demolition, for **Local Authorities, Government Departments, Public Utilities, Nationalised Industries, Housing Associations and New Town Corporations.** [1]			
	(b) **New Construction**, including site preparation and demolition, for **Private Owners and Private Developers.** [2]			
	(c) **Repair and Maintenance**, including house/flat conversions, extensions and alterations. [3]			
(ii) WORK (OTHER THAN HOUSES AND FLATS) FOR PRIVATE OWNERS AND DEVELOPERS.	(a) **New Industrial**: construction, extensions, major alterations (i.e. "improvements") and site preparation (including demolition) of Factories, Warehouses, Industrial Premises, Steel Works, Coke Ovens, Oil Refineries, etc. [4]			
	(b) **New Non-Industrial**: construction, extensions, major alterations (i.e. "improvements") and site preparation (including demolition) of Farm Buildings, Offices, Shops, Hotels and Public Houses, Places of Worship, Clubs, Places of Entertainment, Road Goods Transport Premises, etc. [5]			
	(c) **Repair and Maintenance.** [6]			
(iii) ALL OTHER WORK.*	(a) **New Work** not included above: construction, extensions, major alterations (i.e. "improvements"), site preparation (including demolition) and work on open-cast coal sites. Exclude Steel Works (see II(a) above). [7]			
	(b) **Repair and Maintenance** (including repair and maintenance of builders' plant) not included above. [8]			
*WORK ON UTILITIES AND SOCIAL SERVICES including work for Government Departments, Nationalised Industries, Canal, River, Dock and Harbour Boards, Local Authorities (other than Housing included in (i) (a) and (c)), Hospital Boards.		TOTALS Cols. 1 & 2 [9]		

PART I C. OPERATIVES NOT INCLUDED ABOVE. — Number — FOR OFFICIAL USE

Operatives who cannot be assigned to particular jobs included in Part I B, e.g., transport workers, stores and warehouse staff, operatives engaged on the manufacture of goods for sale, etc.

PART II. RETURN OF CONTRACTS (or ORDERS) AND EXTENSIONS TO CONTRACTS [OBTAINED BETWEEN 1st JANUARY 19..]

PART II A. NEW CONTRACTS AND EXTENSIONS TO CONTRACTS FOR NEW WORK		Value of Contracts (or Extensions) obtained between 1st January—31st March, 1957
(See also PART II B.) TYPE OF BUILDING, CIVIL ENGINEERING AND ELECTRIC WIRING WORK		£
(i) NEW HOUSES AND FLATS.	(a) Contracts for **New Construction** including site preparation and demolition, for **Local Authorities, Government Departments, Public Utilities, Nationalised Industries, Housing Associations and New Towns Corporations.** [1]	
	(b) Contracts for **New Construction** including site preparation and demolition, for **Private Owners and Developers.** [2]	
(ii) NEW WORK (OTHER THAN HOUSES AND FLATS) FOR PRIVATE OWNERS AND DEVELOPERS.	(a) Contracts for **New Industrial Building**, i.e. construction, extensions, major alterations (i.e. "improvements") and site preparation (including demolition) of Factories, Warehouses, Steel Works, Coke Ovens, Oil Refineries, etc. [3]	
	(b) Contracts for **New Non-Industrial Building**, i.e. construction, extensions, major alterations (i.e. "improvements") and site preparation (including demolition) of Farm Buildings, Offices, Shops, Hotels and Public Houses, Places of Worship, Clubs, Places of Entertainment, Road Goods Transport Premises, etc. [4]	
(iii) *ALL OTHER NEW WORK.	Contracts for **New Work** not included above, i.e. construction, extensions, major alterations (i.e. "improvements"), site preparation (including demolition) and work on opencast coal sites. **Exclude Steel Works** (see (ii) (a) above.) [5]	
*WORK ON UTILITIES AND SOCIAL SERVICES including work for Government Departments, Nationalised Industries, Canal, River, Dock and Harbour Boards, Local Authorities (other than Housing included in (i) (a)), Hospital Boards.		TOTAL* [6]

*Please enter "NIL" if this is appropriate.

PART II B.

To be completed ONLY by firms which undertake NEW work (i.e. excluding repair and maintenance) without contracts (or orders) on sites owned or leased by themselves or by their subsidiary or associated companies.

Estimated overall value of projects (including sub-contracted work — see Note 3) expected to be started in the period 1st April—30th June 1957.	
HOUSING	NON-HOUSING
£	£
[1]	[2]

B I M 3 A.R 8-April, 1957   **THIS PORTION TO BE RETURNED**

APPENDIX IV

ND OUTPUT

NOTES FOR GUIDANCE IN COMPLETING PART I OF THIS RETURN

For the purpose of this return the labour employed and the value of work done on the jobs ancillary to the main project should be classified as part of the main project, e.g., a garage built for a house should be included in "Houses and Flats"; a private road, a power station or an office block constructed as part of a factory scheme should be included with the factory in "New Industrial Work"; shops with dwellings should be classified as shops if the shop constitutes the major part of the job.

Firms **not** wholly engaged on Building and Contracting but which have separate building departments for which separate accounts are kept should enter the number of operatives employed and the value of the work done by these departments.

Sub-contractors supplying **labour only** to main contractors should enter in the appropriate sections of Column 1 and Column 2 the number of operatives on their payroll and the value of the operatives' wages, etc. Main contractors should include in their return the value of materials used by such operatives.

OPERATIVES (Column 1)

INCLUDE all persons (male and female) aged 15 years and over employed on manual work, whether full or part time, whose National Insurance Cards are held by you on the pay day specified in Column 1. Operatives who cannot be assigned to any of the types of work shown in Part I B, e.g., operatives engaged in transport work, stores and warehouses and on the manufacture of goods for sale, etc., should be entered in Part I C.

EXCLUDE only administrative, technical and clerical workers.

VALUE (Column 2)

THE VALUE OF BUILDING, CIVIL ENGINEERING AND ELECTRIC WIRING WORK DONE IS AN ESTIMATE OF THE AMOUNT CHARGED OR CHARGEABLE TO CUSTOMERS FOR ALL WORK DONE **BY YOU** IN THE PERIOD SPECIFIED IN COLUMN 2.

INCLUDE (a) Building, Civil Engineering and Electric Wiring done by working principals.
        (b) Building, Civil Engineering and Electric Wiring Work done by your own operatives on the construction or maintenance of your own premises.
        (c) goods made and used by you for the Building, Civil Engineering and Electric Wiring Work valued in Column 2 and all materials supplied for the contract by the person or authority for whom the work was carried out. (But see Note 3 "labour only" Sub-Contracts.)

EXCLUDE (a) the cost of land, legal costs and architects', etc., fees.
        (b) goods made and sold to other contractors or to merchants or put to stock.
        (c) work done **for you** by other contractors under sub-contract. (But see Note 3 "labour only" Sub-Contracts.)

ORDERS) FOR NEW WORK (i.e. NOT FOR REPAIR AND MAINTENANCE) AND 31st MARCH 1957.

NOTES FOR GUIDANCE IN COMPLETING PART II A OF THIS RETURN

For the purpose of this return the contracts (or orders) and extensions to contracts (or orders) for the jobs ancillary to a main project should be classified as part of the main project, e.g., a garage built for a house should be included in "Houses and Flats"; a private road, a power station or an office block constructed as part of a factory scheme should be included with the factory in "New Industrial Work"; shops with dwellings should be classified as shops if the shop constitutes the major part of the job.

ORDERS
Throughout Part II A of this return the term "contracts" also covers orders for new work which are not the subject of formal contracts.

CONTRACTS AND EXTENSIONS TO CONTRACTS TO BE INCLUDED
INCLUDE (a) ALL NEW contracts and extensions to contracts OBTAINED between 1st January and 31st March 1957 whether the work was (i) started and completed, (ii) started but not completed, or (iii) not started in the period.
EXCLUDE (a) all contracts OBTAINED BEFORE 1st January, 1957, whether started or not.
        (b) all contracts for repair and maintenance work, i.e., as classified under Part I B (i) (c), (ii) (c) and (iii) (b).

EXTENSIONS TO CONTRACTS
An estimate of the value of an extension to a contract should be included if the actual value is not known.

SUB-CONTRACTS
(a) Contractors who have let or propose to let sub-contracts in connection with main contracts obtained in the period should INCLUDE the value of these sub-contracts in their returns.
(b) Contractors who have obtained sub-contracts from other contractors should EXCLUDE the value of these sub-contracts from their returns.

OVERSEAS CONTRACTS
Contracts for work OUTSIDE England, Scotland and Wales should be EXCLUDED.

NOTES FOR GUIDANCE IN COMPLETING PART II B OF THIS RETURN

See Note 1 of Part II A above.

Firms should enter in Part II B of this return the total value (i.e. the value when completed) of projects expected to be started without contracts (or orders)
        (a) for occupation by themselves or the firm's subsidiary or associated companies
        (b) for sale or lease to other companies or persons.
e.g., the estimated value when completed of a block of offices or a number of houses on which work is expected to be started on sites owned or leased by the company, for subsequent sale or lease.
Include the value of any work it is intended to let to sub-contractors.

THIS PORTION MAY BE DETACHED AND KEPT

CONFIDENTIAL

Telephone Number :

Ministry of Works,
Building Industries & Materials Section,

25th September, 1957.

BUILDING AND CONTRACTING
(Building, Electric Wiring and Contracting, and Civil Engineering Contracting)

EMPLOYMENT RETURN

Sir(s),

It is necessary for the Government regularly to have certain information about Building, Civil Engineering and Electric Wiring Work.

The undertaking described below falls within the scope of the Inquiry. Therefore notice is hereby given by the Minister of Works

to :—

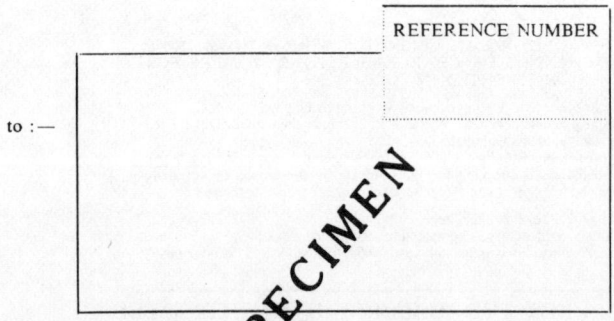

to supply in relation to the undertaking carried on by you the information specified overleaf, and to return this form to the address above not later than **WEDNESDAY, 2nd OCTOBER, 1957.**

This notice is served under the provisions of Section 1 of the Statistics of Trade Act, 1947, for the purpose of obtaining information necessary for the discharge by Government Departments of their functions. Under the Act the rendering of the return is compulsory.

I am, Sir(s),
Your obedient Servant,

Under Secretary,
for and on behalf of the Minister of Works.

All information given by you will be treated as strictly confidential and will be used solely in the compilation of general statistical results. The results will be prepared and published in a way which will not reveal the particulars relating to any individual undertaking unless previous consent is given by the undertaking.

If you wish to keep for reference a record of the information supplied by you on this form, further copies of the form will be supplied on application to this office. In all correspondence with this office, the reference number given in the address box above should be quoted.

TO BE COMPLETED AND SIGNED BY THE PERSON MAKING THE RETURN ON BEHALF OF THE UNDERTAKING

Trading Name of Firm..

Full Postal Address
of Head or Registered Office...
(including Town and County)
....

Telephone Exchange & Number...

I certify that to the best of my belief the particulars above and overleaf are correct.

Signed... Date......................1957.

(State whether Proprietor, Director, Manager, Partner, Secretary.)

APPENDIX IV 539

BUILDING AND CONTRACTING

(Building, Electric Wiring and Contracting, and Civil Engineering Contracting)

EMPLOYMENT RETURN

Part I. Return of Persons Employed

For official use

In any correspondence please quote this reference number:

Throughout Part I of this return include all persons (male and female) aged 15 years and over whether full or part-time whose National Insurance cards are held by you on the pay day specified below.

Part IA. Administrative, Technical and Clerical Employees

Include the persons engaged in the business who do not do manual work, e.g., directors (other than those paid by fee only), partners, managers, superintendents and general foremen; any research, experimental, technical and design employees other than operatives; draughtsmen and tracers; travellers and office (including works office) staff.

Firms **not** wholly engaged on Building and Contracting but which have separate building departments for which separate accounts are kept should enter the number of persons engaged on administrative technical and clerical duties appropriate to the department.

Enter here the number of administrative, technical and clerical employees employed by the undertaking in the week ending 28th September, 1957 ⟶

Number (Enter NIL if appropriate)

Part IB. Working Principals

Enter here the number of Working Principals, i.e., owners, managers, partners, etc., who do manual work ⟶

Number (Enter NIL if appropriate)

Part IC. Operatives Employed

(1) *Include* apprentices, working foremen, operatives engaged in transport work, stores and warehouses and on the manufacture of goods for sale, etc.
(2) *Include* in "*All Other Occupations*" (Col. 11 in section (c) below) labourers, cleaners, operatives engaged in transport work, stores and warehouses and on the manufacture of goods for sale.
(3) *Sub-contractors* supplying labour only to main contractors should enter the number of operatives on their pay roll.
(4) Firms **not** wholly engaged on Building and Contracting but which have separate building departments for which separate accounts are kept should enter the number of persons employed as operatives in these departments.

(a) Total Operatives Employed

Enter here the total number of operatives employed on the pay day in the week ending 28th September, 1957 ⟶

Number (Enter NIL if appropriate)

(b) Operatives Working in Scotland and Wales

Enter here the number of operatives (which should have been included in section (a) above) who were working ⟶

In Scotland	In Wales

Enter NIL if appropriate

THESE TOTALS SHOULD BE THE SAME

(c) Occupations of Operatives Employed

Carpenters and Joiners (1)	Bricklayers (2)	Slaters and Tilers (3)	Plasterers (4)	Painters (5)	Plumbers and Glaziers (6)	Masons (7)	Electricians (8)	Heating and Ventilating Engineers (9)	Other B. & C.E. Crafts (10)	All other Occupations (see Note 2) (11)	TOTAL (12)

Part II. Return of Apprentices Employed on 28th September, 1957

(1) *Include* apprentices of all ages engaged on Building and Contracting.
(2) *Exclude* (a) boy labourers
    (b) apprentices employed on work other than Building and Contracting, e.g., manufacturing, transport, etc.
(3) Enter Category I electrical apprentices on "WRITTEN Indentures" line and Category II, etc., electrical apprentices and probationers on "VERBAL Agreements" line.

Type of Agreement	Carpenters and Joiners (1)	Bricklayers (2)	Slaters and Tilers (3)	Plasterers (4)	Painters (5)	Plumbers and Glaziers (6)	Masons (7)	Electricians (see Note 3) (8)	Heating and Ventilating Engineers (9)	Other B. & C.E. Crafts (10)	TOTALS (Enter NIL if appropriate) (11)
Having WRITTEN Indentures											
Having VERBAL Agreements only											

IN CONFIDENCE

Building, Civil Engineering and Allied Industries
RETURN OF PERSONS EMPLOYED & OUTPUT (All work including Repair and Maintenance)

6th April, 1970.

Dear Sir(s),

To help in forming economic policy the Government needs a wide range of statistical information. Up-to-date information from the construction industries is essential because of the large number of men they employ and because they produce a large share of capital investment. To meet this need employment statistics are collected every month and output statistics every quarter.

Your undertaking falls within the scope of this enquiry, and you are hereby required to complete the attached return.

The earlier that the statistics based on the return are available the more valuable they are and your co-operation in carefully and promptly completing this form will therefore be of real assistance to this Ministry. As the late return of even a few forms must lead to delay in the publication of results, please do not hold up this return until audited figures are available but give the closest possible estimate. The completed form should be returned in the envelope provided to the Ministry of Public Building and Works, Building Industries and Materials Section, at the address on the reverse of this form, **not later than WEDNESDAY, 22nd APRIL, 1970.**

This notice is served under the provisions of Section 1 of the Statistics of Trade Act, 1947, for the purpose of obtaining information necessary for the discharge by Government Departments of their functions. Under this Act the rendering of a return is compulsory.

All the information you give will be treated as strictly confidential and will be used solely for the compilation of general statistics. The particulars relating to your undertaking will not be published without your prior written consent.

Yours faithfully,

Under Secretary, for and on
behalf of the Minister of Public Building and Works.

APPENDIX IV

**THE INFORMATION GIVEN ON THIS RETURN SHOULD RELATE TO GREAT BRITAIN ONLY
(I.E. EXCLUDING NORTHERN IRELAND)**

Firms NOT wholly engaged in the Construction Industries but which have a separate department so engaged for which separate accounts are kept, should throughout this form, give information appropriate to that department only.

For official use

PART 2 RETURN OF WORK DONE AND PERSONS EMPLOYED

THROUGHOUT PART 2 OF THIS RETURN INCLUDE ALL PERSONS (MALE AND FEMALE) AGED 15 YEARS AND OVER WORKING IN GREAT BRITAIN (i.e. Excluding Northern Ireland) WHETHER FULL OR PART-TIME WHOSE NATIONAL INSURANCE CARDS ARE HELD BY YOU ON THE PAY DAY SPECIFIED BELOW.

A. Administrative, Professional, Technical and Clerical

Include all persons (including learners and trainees) engaged in the business who do NOT do manual work, *e.g.* directors (other than those paid by fee only), partners, managers, architects, surveyors, engineers, other professionals, training officers, superintendents, any research, experimental, technical and design employees other than operatives; draughtsmen and tracers; travellers, sales and office (including works office) staff. INCLUDE SELF-EMPLOYED OWNERS, GENERAL FOREMEN AND OTHER SUPERVISORS WHO DO NOT DO MANUAL WORK.
Do NOT include the same persons in both A and B.

State here the number of administrative, professional, technical and clerical staff employed by the undertaking on the pay day in the week ending 11th APRIL, 1970————————————>

Number (Enter NIL if appropriate)

B. Working Principals

State here the number of WORKING PRINCIPALS (i.e., self-employed owners, managers, partners, etc.) **who do manual work.** Do NOT include persons entered here in any other part of the form. **Labour only sub-contractors** should enter in this part the working partners in the group—the operatives employed should be entered in Part C.————>

Number (Enter NIL if appropriate)

C. Value of Work Done and Operatives Employed

ENTER IN COLUMN 1 below estimates of the amounts chargeable to your customers for building, civil engineering and associated work done directly by you BETWEEN 1st January and 31st March, 1970. Include the value of work done on your own initiative in the period on buildings such as dwellings or offices for eventual sale or lease.

MAIN CONTRACTORS should NOT include the value of any work done for them by sub-contractors of any type. If you have employed "labour only" sub-contractors do NOT include the value of any payments made to them. Include the value of any materials supplied by you to sub-contractors.

LABOUR ONLY SUB-CONTRACTORS should enter all payments received from Main Contractors.

PAINTERS AND DECORATORS should show the value of work on new structures as "New Construction" and all other painting and decorating, etc., as "repair and maintenance."

ELECTRICAL CONTRACTORS should include the value of installation work associated with buildings and structures.

ALL CONTRACTORS should include the value of goods made by themselves and used in the work but should exclude the value of goods made for sale.

CONTRACTORS should also include the value of work done by their own operatives on the construction or maintenance of their own premises.

ENTER IN COLUMN 2 below the number of operatives on your payroll ON THE PAY DAY IN THE WEEK ENDING 11th APRIL, 1970.

Include all persons aged 15 years and over whose National Insurance cards you held on that date and who were employed on MANUAL work, whether full or part-time. Include apprentices, operatives engaged in transport work, stores and warehouses and on the manufacture of goods for sale, etc. and working foremen (FOREMEN WHO DO NOT DO MANUAL WORK SHOULD BE INCLUDED IN PART A ABOVE).

MAIN CONTRACTORS should not include men employed by any of their sub-contractors.

LABOUR ONLY SUB-CONTRACTORS should enter in Col. 2 only the number of operatives employed. The number of working partners in the group should be shown in Part B above.

COLUMN 1 Value of Work done last quarter	The term "*NEW CONSTRUCTION*" in items 4, 5 and 7 includes extensions, major alterations (i.e. "*improvements*") and site preparation, including demolition.	COLUMN 2 Number of Operatives employed
£	**WORK ON HOUSES AND FLATS**	
[1]	1. New HOUSING Construction for Government Departments, Local Authorities (*e.g.* Council houses), Public Utilities, Nationalised Industries, New Town Corporations and all housing associations and co-ownership societies including the Scottish Special Housing Association Ltd. (*including site preparation and demolition*).	[1]
[2]	2. New HOUSING Construction for private owners and private developers. (*Include site preparation and demolition*).	[2]
[3]	3. Repair and Maintenance of Dwellings (include house/flat conversions, extensions, alterations and redecorations in this section).	[3]
	WORK OTHER THAN HOUSING FOR PRIVATE OWNERS AND DEVELOPERS	
[4]	4. New INDUSTRIAL Construction: Factories, warehouses, coke ovens, refineries, **and steel producing plant or works in private ownership**, etc.	[4]
[5]	5. New NON-INDUSTRIAL Construction: Offices, shops, farm buildings, hotels and public houses, places of worship, clubs, places of entertainment, road goods transport depots, etc.	[5]
[6]	6. Repair and Maintenance of Structures covered by items 4 and 5.	[6]
	ALL OTHER WORK (*See Note below*)*	
[7]	7. New Construction not included above. (Includes work on open-cast coal sites **and nationalised steelworks**).	[7]
[8]	8. Repair and Maintenance not included in items 3 and 6.	[8]
TOTAL OF COL. 1 Please enter NIL if appropriate	9. Enter in Col. 2 the number of operatives who cannot be classified to the types of work listed in 1-8 above, *e.g.* transport workers, stores and warehouse staff, operatives employed on the manufacture of goods for sale.	[9]
		TOTAL OF COL. 2 Please enter NIL if appropriate

*NOTE *Items 7 and 8 cover work on Utilities and Social Services including work for Government Departments, Nationalised Industries (including nationalised steelworks), Canal, River, Dock and Harbour Boards, Local Authorities (other than housing), Hospital Boards, New Town Corporations, Covent Garden Market Authority, and the Airports Authority.*

PART 3 PRIVATE ENTERPRISE HOUSING

Have you built houses, bungalows, flats or maisonettes on your own initiative for eventual sale or lease during the last year or do you expect to during the rest of this year? (State either YES or NO.)

Do not enter the same person on more than one line.

Form No.: B.I.M./A.R. 34A

CONSTRUCTION AND THE RELATED PROFESSIONS

IN CONFIDENCE

Please quote in any correspondence. ↓

Ensure that the address below shows through the aperture of the return envelope when inserting the completed form.

FOLD → HERE

FOR OFFICIAL USE ONLY

PART 1 DETAILS OF BUSINESS

FOLD ← HERE

Please indicate by a tick in the appropriate space below the description which is most appropriate to your **major activity** (**i.e. the greatest part of your turnover**). *Do not tick more than one description.*

Code	DESCRIPTION	TICK HERE	Code	DESCRIPTION	TICK HERE
01	General builder		15	Asphalt and tar-spraying contractor	
02	Building and civil engineering contractor		16	Plant hiring contractor	
03	Civil engineering contractor		17	Flooring contractor	
04	Plumber		18	Constructional Engineer (mainly engaged on site work)	
05	Joiner and Carpenter (mainly engaged on site work)		19	Insulating Specialist	
06	Painter and decorator		20	Suspended Ceiling Specialist	
07	Roofer		21	Wall and Floor Tiling Specialist	
08	Plasterer		22	If your major activity is other than codes 1 to 21, please	
09	Glazier			enter description:	
10	Demolition contractor				
11	Scaffolding specialist				
12	Reinforced concrete specialist				
13	Heating and ventilating engineer				
14	Electrical contractor				

SPECIMEN

Declaration and signature

Name and telephone number of person who should be
consulted if questions arise about this return...

If the name or address shown above is incorrect in any respect, please correct it.

I hereby declare that the information contained in this return
is complete and correct to the best of my knowledge and belief.

Signature... Date...1970
(**Please state whether** Proprietor, Director, Manager, Partner, Secretary, etc.)

Form B.I.M./A.R.34A (Amd. 4/70) (B2, B3, B4, B5, A7)

APPENDIX IV 543

Form B.I.M./A.R. 35 (Amd.9/70)   IN CONFIDENCE

MINISTRY OF PUBLIC BUILDING AND WORKS

If the name or address shown below is incorrect in any way, please correct it.

Please quote in any correspondence.

Ensure that the address below shows through the aperture of the return envelope when inserting the completed form.

Building, Civil Engineering and Allied Industries
EMPLOYMENT RETURN

7th September, 1970.

Dear Sir(s),

    To help in forming economic policy the Government needs a wide range of statistical information. Up-to-date information from the construction industries is essential because of the large number of men they employ and because they produce a large share of capital investment. To meet this need employment statistics are collected every month and output statistics every quarter.

    Your undertaking falls within the scope of this inquiry for this month, and you are hereby required to complete the return overleaf.

    The earlier that the statistics based on the return are available the more valuable they are. The late return of even a few forms must lead to delay in the publication of results, and your co-operation in carefully and promptly completing this form will, therefore, be of real assistance to this Ministry. The completed form should be returned in the envelope provided to the Building Industries and Materials Section at the address shown on this letter **NOT LATER THAN WEDNESDAY, 23rd SEPTEMBER, 1970**. If you encounter any difficulties in completing the form the Building Industries and Materials Section staff will be pleased to help you in any way possible.

    This notice is served under the provisions of Section 1 of the Statistics of Trade Act, 1947, for the purpose of obtaining information necessary for the discharge by Government Departments of their functions. Under this Act the rendering of a return is compulsory.

    All the information you give will be treated as strictly confidential and will be used solely for the compilation of general statistics. The particulars relating to your undertaking will not be revealed without your prior written consent.

                              Yours faithfully,

                              M. Nafuli

                          Chief Statistician for and on
behalf of the Minister of Public Building and Works.

Declaration and signature

Name and telephone number of person who should be
consulted if questions arise about this return ....

I hereby declare that the information contained in this return
is complete and correct to the best of my knowledge and belief.

Signature.. Date..1970
(Please state whether Proprietor, Director, Manager, Partner, Secretary, etc.)

Dd.722606 4/70 12,750 ST D&Co.(S)Ltd. 53-2149

EMPLOYMENT RETURN

IN CONFIDENCE

S.G.

Part 1 Return of Persons Employed including Apprentices

A. Administrative, Professional, Technical and Clerical (*see Note A*.1).

1. State here the number of administrative, professional, technical and clerical staff employed by the undertaking on the pay day in the **week ending 12th September, 1970** ⟶

   Number (Enter NIL if appropriate)

2. State how many of these are: (*see Note A*.2).

(1) Managerial (See Note A2 (1))		(2) Architects	(3) Surveyors	(4) Engineers	(5) Other Professionals	(6) Training Officers	(7) General Foremen and other Supervisors	(8) Draughtsmen and Tracers	(9) Other Technical Grades	(10) Clerical Office and Sales staff	(11) TOTAL
X	Y										

These totals should be the same

B. Working Principals (*see Note B*).

State here the number of Working Principals (i.e., self-employed owners, partners, managers, etc.) **who do manual work**. Do NOT include persons entered here in any other part of the form ⟶

Number (Enter NIL if appropriate)

C. Operatives and Apprentices Employed (exclude Working Principals) (*see Note C*).

1. State here total number of operatives (include apprentices) employed on the pay day in the week ending **12th September, 1970.** ⟶

2. State here the number of these employees who were working in Scotland or Wales

In Scotland	In Wales (including Monmouthshire)

   Enter NIL if appropriate

D. State here the number by Occupation of Operatives and Apprentices (exclude Working Principals) (*see Notes D and E*).

OCCUPATION	Operatives (exclude Apprentices) Col. (a)	Apprentices with written indentures Col (b)	Boys on probation for written indentures Col. (c)	Apprentices with verbal agreements and other probationers Col. (d)	TOTALS (Cols a, b, c, d) Col. (e)
(1) Carpenters and Joiners					
(2) Formwork Erectors		x x x x x x	x x x x x x	x x x x x x	
(3) Bricklayers					
(4) Masons					
(5) Roofing Slaters and Tilers					
(6) Floor, Wall and Ceiling Tilers					
(7) Plasterers					
(8) Painters					
(9) Plumbers and Gas Fitters					
(10) Heating and Ventilating Engineering Crafts					
(11) Glaziers					
(12) Paviours					
(13) Steel Benders and Fixers		x x x x x x	x x x x x x	x x x x x x	
(14) Scaffolders		x x x x x x	x x x x x x	x x x x x x	
(15) Steel Erectors and Sheeters					
(16) Electricians (*see Note E*(1)(iii))					
(17) Mechanical Equipment Operators (other than Crane Drivers)					
(18) Crane Drivers		x x x x x x	x x x x x x	x x x x x x	
(19) Concrete Erectors and Assemblers		x x x x x x	x x x x x x	x x x x x x	
(20) Other B. and C.E. Crafts					
(21) All other occupations (*see Note* D (21))		x x x x x x	x x x x x x	x x x x x x	
(22) Labourers (all types)		x x x x x x	x x x x x x	x x x x x x	
(23) Canteen Workers (all types)		x x x x x x	x x x x x x	x x x x x x	
(24) TOTALS					

These totals should be the same

Part 2 Private Enterprise Housing

Have you built houses, bungalows, flats or maisonettes on your own initiative for eventual sale or lease during the last year or do you expect to during the next TWO YEARS? (State either YES or NO)

Form B.I.M./A.R. 35 (Amd. 9/70) (D1, D2, D3, A7)

APPENDIX IV

MINISTRY OF PUBLIC BUILDING AND WORKS

NOTES FOR GUIDANCE IN COMPLETING THE EMPLOYMENT RETURN

Throughout Part I of this return include all persons (male and female), aged 15 years and over, working in Great Britain (i.e., excluding Northern Ireland), whether full or part time (including those absent for any reason), whose National Insurance Cards are held by you on the pay day specified.

Return of Persons Employed including Apprentices

A. **Administrative, Professional, Technical and Clerical.**

1. (a) **General.** Include all persons (including learners and trainees) engaged in the business who do NOT do manual work, e.g., directors (other than those paid by fee only), partners, managers, architects, surveyors, engineers, other professionals, training officers, superintendents, research, experimental, technical and design employees, draughtsmen and tracers, travellers, sales and office (including works office) staff. Include self employed owners, general foremen and other supervisors who do NOT do manual work.

    (b) **Building Departments.** Firms not wholly engaged in the Construction Industries, but which have a separate department so engaged for which separate accounts are kept should enter the number of persons engaged on Administrative, Professional, Technical and Clerical duties appropriate to that department.

2. **Description of Staff.** Professional and technical staff should be shown according to the main duties on which they are engaged except that professional staff engaged upon administrative or managerial duties for which they are required to be professionally qualified, should be entered under their professions and not as managerial.

    (1) **Managerial.** Self employed owners and partners should be shown in box (1)X. In box (1)Y include Managing Directors, Directors (other than those paid by fee only), Site, Area, Project, Contract, Sales and Office Managers, Agents, etc. (i.e. all staff with a managerial status not included in boxes (2)-(5)).

    (2) **Architects.** Include professionally qualified Architects engaged in their profession.

    (3) **Surveyors.** Include professionally qualified Surveyors and Quantity Surveyors engaged in their profession.

    (4) **Engineers.** Include professionally qualified Engineers engaged in their profession.

    (5) **Other Professionals.** Include all other professionally qualified persons engaged in their professions, e.g., Chartered Accountants, Company Secretaries, etc.

    (6) **Training Officers.** Include only full time Training Officers.

    (7) **General Foremen and Works Supervisors.** Include all General Foremen and other Supervisors who do NOT do manual work who were not included in boxes (1)-(5).

    (8) **Draughtsmen and Tracers.** Include all Architectural and Construction Draughtsmen and Tracers, Design Detailers, etc.

    (9) **Other Technical Grades.** Include all Technical Assistants not included in box (1), e.g., Planning, Estimating, Work Study, Research and Laboratory Assistants who are not professionally qualified.

    (10) **Clerical, Office and Sales Staff.** Include Clerks, Buyers, Purchasing, Stores and General Office staff.

B. **Working Principals.** Do not include persons entered here in any other part of the form. **Labour-only Sub-contractors** should enter in this part the working partners in the group — the operatives employed should be entered in Part D.

C. **Operatives and Apprentices employed (exclude Working Principals).**

1. (a) **General.** Include Apprentices, Working Foremen, Operatives engaged in Transport Work, Stores and Warehouses and on the manufacture of goods for sale, etc.

    Sub-Contractors supplying labour only to main contractors should enter the number of operatives on their pay roll. The working partners in the group should be included in the figure shown under Part 1B.

    (b) **Building Departments.** Firms not wholly engaged in the Construction Industries but which have a separate department so engaged for which separate accounts are kept should enter the number of persons employed as operatives in that department.

D. **Occupations of Operatives and Apprentices (exclude Working Principals).**

GENERAL. Operatives who use more than one skill should be shown under their main occupation.

(1) **Carpenters and Joiners.** Include site and inside Shop Foremen, Carpenter and Joiner, Carpenter, Joiner Bench Hand, Sawyer (Converting Mill), Sawyer (other than Converting Mill), Wood-Cutting Machinist, Woodworking Machine Minder/Operator, Sanding Machinist, Parquet Floor Layer, Assembler. For other workers in trade see Note (2) below.

(2) **Formwork Erectors.** Include Formwork Carpenters and other workers in Carpentry and Joinery trades. Exclude labourers.

(3) **Bricklayers.** Include Foreman, Chargehand, Factory Chimney Builder, Bricklayer (General), (Firebrick), (Colliery), other workers in trade. Exclude labourers.

(4) **Masons.** Include Foreman, Banker Mason, Monument Mason, Fixer Mason, Stone Machine Hand, Stone Carver, Letter Cutter, Stone Polisher (Hand), Walling Mason, other workers in trade. Exclude labourers.

(5) **Roofing Slaters and Tilers.** Include Foremen, Chargehand, Slater, Tiler, Roofer, Thatcher, Roofing Felt Fixer, other workers in trade. Exclude labourers.

(6) **Floor, Wall and Ceiling Tilers.** Include Floor, Wall and Ceiling Tilers, Mosaic Cutter, Terrazzo Layer, Mastic Asphalt Spreader, Composition Floor Layer, Tile Slabber, Terrazzo Polisher, other workers in trade. Exclude labourers.

(continued overleaf)

Form B.I.M. 164

Note D.—*continued*

(7) **Plasterers.** Include Foreman, Chargehand, Plasterer (Solid Work), Fibrous Plasterer, other workers in trade. Exclude labourers.

(8) **Painters.** Include Foreman, Chargehand, House Painter and Decorator, Red Leader, Spray Painter, Signwriter, other workers in trade. Exclude labourers.

(9) **Plumber and Gas Fitters.** Include Foreman, Plumber, Gas Fitter, Chemical Plumber, Pipe Fitter, other workers in trade. Exclude labourers.

(10) **Heating and Ventilating Engineering Crafts.** Include Hot Water Fitter, Heating Engineer, other workers in trade. Exclude labourers.

(11) **Glaziers.** Include Foreman, Glazier, Lead Light Glazier. Exclude labourers.

(12) **Paviours.** Include Foreman, Ganger, Asphalter, Paviour Street Mason, Tar Sprayer, Tar Paviour, Road Lengthsman, General Road Man, Pot Man, Road Surface Laying Machine Operator, other workers in trade. Exclude labourers.

(13) **Steel Benders and Fixers.** Include Bender and Fixer of Concrete Reinforcing Steel. Exclude labourers.

(14) **Scaffolders.** Exclude labourers.

(15) **Steel Erectors and Sheeters.** Include Foreman, Steel Erector, Sheeter, Iron Roofer, other workers in trade. Exclude labourers.

(16) **Electricians.** Include Foreman, Electrician (Installation), Cable Jointer, other workers in trade. Exclude labourers.

(17) **Mechanical Equipment Operators (other than Crane Drivers).** Include Foreman, Engine (Portable) Operator, Dumper Driver, Mechanical Excavator Driver, Hoist Driver, Crane Slinger, other workers in trade. Exclude labourers.

(18) **Crane Drivers.** Include Crane Driver, Crane Driver (Gantry), Crane Driver (Mobile). Exclude labourers.

(19) **Concrete Erectors and Assemblers.** Exclude labourers. (Concreters, Concrete Screeders and Finishers should be shown under "Other B. and C.E. Crafts").

(20) **Other B. and C.E. Crafts.** Include Yard Foreman, Ganger, Timberman, Tunnel Miner, Driller Well Borer, Pipe Layer, Pipe Jointer, Hammerman, Demolisher, Forge Welder, Welder (General Hand), Burner Cutter, Electric Welder, Concreter, Concrete Screeder and Finisher, Property Repairer, other workers in other B. and C.E. crafts not detailed separately. Exclude labourers.

(21) **All other occupations (excluding labourers and Canteen Workers).** Include Operators engaged in Transport Work, Stores and Warehouses and on the manufacture of goods for sale, Cleaners, etc.

(22) **Labourers (all types).** Include B. and C.E. labourers, Heavy labourers, Light labourers, labourers excluded from all trades and all other occupations.

(23) **Canteen Workers.** Include all types.

E. **Training.**

APPRENTICES COLUMNS (*b*), (*c*) and (*d*) of Part 1D.

For Firms in England and Wales

(i) **Include** Apprentices and Probationers of all ages engaged on Building, Civil Engineering or associated work.

(ii) **Exclude** Boy labourers and Apprentices employed on work other than Building, Civil Engineering, and associated work, e.g., manufacturing, transport, etc.

(iii) **Electrical Apprentices.** Enter Category I Electrical Apprentices in Col. (*b*); Category II Electrical Apprentices in Col. (*d*); and all Probationers in Col. (*c*).

For Firms in Scotland only.

(i) Include Apprentices and Probationers of all ages engaged on Building, Civil Engineering or associated work.

(ii) Exclude Boy labourers and Apprentices employed on work other than Building, Civil Engineering, and associated work, e.g. manufacturing, transport, etc.

(iii) Electrical Apprentices. Enter all registered apprentices (whether or not Indentured) in Col. (*b*); all boys on probation for registration (whether or not Indentured) in Col. (*c*) and all others in Col. (*d*).

Form No. B.I.M./A.R.41B

DEPARTMENT OF THE ENVIRONMENT

If the name or address shown below is incorrect in any way, please correct it.

Please quote in any correspondence

Ensure that the address below shows through the aperture of the return envelope when inserting the completed form.

Please enter the V.A.T. registration number applicable to this return. Enter NIL if appropriate. If there is more than one number, please enter the others below the box.

Building, Civil Engineering and Allied Industries

ANNUAL RETURN ON INDUSTRIAL ACTIVITY

Dear Sir(s),   1 October, 1975

1   The purpose of this inquiry is to obtain information about the construction industries which together with similar data from other industries will provide a comprehensive review of industrial activity. Inquiries into the activities of the construction industries are essential because of the size of the labour force employed, and because the output they produce is a large share of capital investment. Information from the return is also needed for the compilation of mailing lists for the circulation by DOE to selected firms of technical information and of notices of lectures and conferences.

2   In common with other industries, your VAT registration number is being requested in order to assist the Government Statistical Service to construct a central register of businesses, in order to improve the co-ordination of statistical inquiries and hence reduce the burden of form-filling. No information on firms not registered for VAT will be passed to HM Customs and Excise. For firms who are registered for VAT only their trade classification may be disclosed to HM Customs and Excise.

3   DOE and the Construction Industry Training Board have agreed a common list of construction occupations, which appears at section 5 of this form and also on CITB's Levy Return. It is hoped that the use of this common list will simplify the task of completing this form.

4   The earlier that the statistics based on this return are available the more valuable they are and your co-operation in carefully and promptly completing the form will therefore be of real assistance to the Department. As the late return of even a few forms must lead to delay in the publication of results, please do not hold up this return until audited figures are available but give the closest possible estimate. If you encounter any difficulties in completing the form, the staff of the Building Industries Section at the address shown above will be pleased to help you in any way possible. The completed form should be returned to the address above **not later than WEDNESDAY, 22 OCTOBER, 1975.**

5   This notice is served under the provisions of Section 1 of the Statistics of Trade Act, 1947, for the purposes of obtaining information necessary for the discharge by Government Departments of their functions. Under this Act the rendering of a return is compulsory. In accordance with the Act all information supplied in this return will be treated as confidential. Summarised results will be published by HMSO in issue 18 of "Housing and Construction Statistics" with fuller details in "Private Contractors' Construction Census" (annual).

Yours faithfully,

Form No. B.I.M./A.R.41B (AMD 10/75) (A2, A3, A4, A5 & A7)

Director of Statistics for and on behalf of the Secretary of State for the Environment

CONSTRUCTION AND THE RELATED PROFESSIONS

THE INFORMATION GIVEN ON THIS RETURN SHOULD RELATE TO GREAT BRITAIN ONLY
(I.E. EXCLUDING NORTHERN IRELAND)

Firms NOT wholly engaged in the construction industries but which have a separate department so engaged for which separate accounts are kept, should throughout this form, give information appropriate to that department only.

FOR OFFICIAL USE

IN CONFIDENCE

Please refer to the enclosed Notes before completing the form
and ensure that all sections of the form (1-9) are completed.

FOR OFFICIAL USE

1 DETAILS OF BUSINESS

Please indicate by a tick in the appropriate space below the description which is most appropriate to your major activity (**i.e. the greatest part of your turnover**). One description only should be ticked.

Code	DESCRIPTION	TICK HERE	Code	DESCRIPTION	TICK HERE
01	General builder or building contractor		15	Asphalt and surface dressing contractor	
02	Building and civil engineering contractor		16	Plant hiring contractor	
03	Civil engineering contractor		17	Flooring contractor	
04	Plumbing contractor		18	Constructional engineer (mainly on site work)	
05	Joiner and carpenter (mainly on site work)		19	Insulating specialist	
06	Painter and decorator		20	Suspended ceiling specialist	
07	Roofing contractor		21	Wall and floor tiling specialist	
08	Plastering contractor		22	If your major activity is other than codes 01 to 21, please enter description: (For example, building cleaning, acoustic engineers, or management consultants in the construction industry.)	
09	Glazing contractor				
10	Demolition contractor				
11	Scaffolding specialist				
12	Reinforced concrete specialist				
13	Heating and ventilating engineer				
14	Electrical contractor				

2 VALUE OF CONTRACTS AND ORDERS RECEIVED FOR NEW CONSTRUCTION WORK
(see notes 1 to 4)

A Please state the total value of contracts & orders received and own initiative projects started for new construction (including all improvements and excluding sub-contract work) during the **12 months ending 30 September, 1975**.
Exclude pence

Value
(Enter NIL if appropriate)
£

B Do you expect to carry out new work (including improvements) during the **next 2 years** either as a main contractor or on your own initiative? *(Tick in the appropriate box)*

| YES | 1 |
| NO | 2 |

3 NEW PRIVATE ENTERPRISE HOUSING built on sites owned or leased by you in Great Britain
(see notes 5 to 9)

Number
(Enter NIL if appropriate)

A Enter the number of such dwellings which you started **in the 12 months ending 30 September, 1975**.

B Do you expect to build any such dwellings in the **next 2 years**? *(Tick in the appropriate box)*

| YES | 1 |
| NO | 2 |

4 WORKING PROPRIETORS i.e. self-employed persons *(see notes 10, 11 and 12)*

Do NOT include persons entered here in any other section of the form.

Number
(Enter NIL if appropriate)

APPENDIX IV

5 A ADMINISTRATIVE, PROFESSIONAL, TECHNICAL AND CLERICAL EMPLOYEES
(see notes 13, 14 and 15)

Enter in the appropriate boxes the number of employees who do NOT do manual work and who were on your payroll **on 9 October 1975** or the nearest possible date.

5 B OPERATIVES
(Exclude Working Proprietors see notes 16 to 19)

Enter in the appropriate boxes the number of operatives *(including working foremen)* who were on your payroll **on 9 October 1975** or the nearest possible date.

		01 Excluding Trainees	02 Trainees	03
A				
Managerial Staff	01			
Architects, Surveyors, Engineers	02			
Technical Staff	03			
Draughtsmen and Tracers	04			
Foremen	05			
Clerical & Sales Staff	06			TOTAL **A**
TOTALS (Enter NIL if appropriate)	07			
B		Excluding Trainees	Trainees	
Bricklayers	01			
Masons	02			
Carpenter/Joiners	03			
Painters	04			
Plasterers	05			
Roof Slaters and Tilers	06			
Floor, Wall and Ceiling Tilers	07			
Glaziers	08			
Paviors	09			
Plant Mechanics	10			
Miscellaneous Craftsmen (Excluding Mechanical Eng. Services)	11			
Plumbers and Gas Fitters	12			
Natural Gas Conversion Workers	13			
Heating & Ventilating Eng. Workers	14			
Other Mech. Eng. Services Workers	15			
Electricians	16			
Crane Drivers	17			
Earthmoving Plant Operators	18			
Other Mechanical Plant Operators	19			
Scaffolders	20			
Bar Benders and Steel Fixers	21			
Steel Erectors and Sheeters	22			
Concretors	23			
Demolishers	24			
Other B & C E Skilled Workers	25			
Unskilled Labourers	26			
Canteen Workers	27			
Other Occupations	28			TOTAL **B**
TOTALS (Enter NIL if appropriate)	29			

TOTAL **A+B** (Enter NIL if appropriate) [ ]

6 OPERATIVES WORKING IN SCOTLAND AND WALES
State here the total number of operatives including trainees included in Section 5B who are working in Scotland or Wales .... (Enter NIL if appropriate)

C	In Scotland 01	In Wales 02
01		

CONSTRUCTION AND THE RELATED PROFESSIONS

**7   VALUE OF WORK CARRIED OUT IN THE PERIOD 1 JULY - 30 SEPTEMBER 1975
AND OPERATIVES EMPLOYED BY TYPE OF WORK**

Enter under headings (1) - (8) in column 01 below estimates of the amounts chargeable to your customers for building, civil engineering and associated work done by your directly employed staff between 1 July **and 30 September 1975** *(see notes 20 to 30).*
This applies whether you are a main contractor or a sub-contractor.
The figures should include the value of materials used (unless supplied to you free of charge), labour costs, overheads and profits.
Exclude work done for you by other sub-contractors, which should be entered in section 9.
Exclude pence.

Enter under headings (1) - (9) in column 02 below the number of operatives who were on your payroll **on 9 October 1975** or the nearest possible date *(see notes 20 to 25 and 31 to 32).*

D		Value of Work done last quarter Col. 01	Number of Operatives employed Col. 02
WORK ON HOUSES AND FLATS		£	
(1) New PUBLIC HOUSING for Local Authorities (e.g. Council houses). Public Utilities, Nationalised Industries, Government Departments, New Town Corporations and all housing associations and co-ownership societies.	01		
(2) New PRIVATE HOUSING for private owners and developers.	02		
(3) Repair and Maintenance of Dwellings *(see note 22).*	03		
NON-HOUSING WORK FOR PRIVATE OWNERS AND DEVELOPERS			
(4) New INDUSTRIAL Construction: Factories, warehouses, coke ovens, refineries, oil production platforms, and steel producing plant or works in private ownership, etc.	04		
(5) New NON-INDUSTRIAL Construction: Offices, shops, farm buildings, hotels and public houses, places of worship, clubs, places of entertainment, road goods transport depots, etc.	05		
(6) Repair and Maintenance of structures covered by items (4) and (5).	06		
NON-HOUSING WORK FOR PUBLIC SECTOR CLIENTS			
(7) New Construction not included above (include work on open cast coal sites and nationalised steelworks).	07		
(8) Repair and Maintenance not included in items (3) and (6).	08		
(9) Enter in Column 02 the number of operatives who cannot be classified to the types of work listed (1) - (8) above, e.g. transport workers, stores and warehouse staff, canteen workers, operatives employed on the manufacture of goods for sale.	09	/////	
TOTALS Enter NIL if appropriate	10		

This total should be the same as the total in Section 5B.

Do not enter the same person on more than one line

8 (1)   VALUE OF WORK DONE BY YOU AS A SUB-CONTRACTOR between 1 July and 30 September, 1975 for other contractors in the construction industry.
This cannot be greater than the total value shown in section 7.
Enter NIL if appropriate.

£

(2) **VALUE OF WORK SHOWN IN 8 (1) DONE BY YOU AS A LABOUR-ONLY SUB-CONTRACTOR.**
This cannot be greater than the value shown in 8 (1).
Enter NIL if appropriate.
(see notes 33 to 39)

£

9 (1)   VALUE OF WORK DONE FOR YOU BY ALL SUB-CONTRACTORS (including labour-only sub-contractors) in the period between 1 July and 30 September, 1975.
Enter NIL if appropriate.

£

(2) **PAYMENTS MADE TO LABOUR-ONLY SUB-CONTRACTORS** in this period.
Enter NIL if appropriate.
(see notes 20 to 22 and 40 to 42).

NEW HOUSING	£
NEW NON-HOUSING	£
REPAIR & MAINTENANCE	£

Declaration and Signature

Name and telephone number of person who should be
consulted if questions arise about this return ....

I hereby declare that the information contained in this return
is complete and correct to the best of my knowledge and belief.

Please check that you have completed all sections including the V.A.T. number on page 1.

Signature .... Date 1975
(Please state whether Proprietor, Director, Manager, Partner, Secretary, etc.)

Form No. B.I.M./A.R.41B (AMD 10/75) (A2, A3, A4, A5 & A7)   (2490) Dd. 108849 30000 7/75 J.C. & S. Ltd Gp3615

APPENDIX IV   551

Form No. B.I.M. 164
(10/75)

DEPARTMENT OF THE ENVIRONMENT

NOTES FOR THE COMPLETION OF THE ANNUAL RETURN ON INDUSTRIAL ACTIVITY

Throughout this return include all persons (male and female), aged 16 years and over, working in Great Britain (i.e. excluding Northern Ireland), whether full or part-time (including those absent for any reason), who were on your payroll on the pay day specified.

VALUE OF CONTRACTS AND ORDERS RECEIVED FOR NEW CONSTRUCTION (Section 2)

1. Enter the value of contracts and orders received for new construction work (including improvements) for which you are acting as the main contractor.
2. *Include* work which you have started on your own initiative i.e. work for which you have not been awarded a contract or order by any other party on a site already owned or leased by you or your subsidiary or associated companies.
3. *Include* cases where it is your practice to sell plots of land and to obtain from the purchasers a contract to build. (EXAMPLE: a house or houses, for eventual sale or lease to other persons or companies, or for occupation by yourselves or your subsidiary or associated companies, or for eventual sale or lease).
4. *DO NOT INCLUDE*:
   (1) Contracts etc. for repair and maintenance work.
   (2) Sub-contracts obtained by you from other contractors in the construction industry.
   (3) The cost of architects' and consultants' services.
   (4) The value of land purchased.

NEW PRIVATE ENTERPRISE HOUSING (Section 3)

5. Enter the number of new dwellings (i.e. houses, bungalows, flats or maisonettes) which were started by you in the **12 months ending 30 September, 1975** on sites in Great Britain owned or leased by you or your subsidiary or associated companies.
6. *DO NOT INCLUDE* dwellings built under contract (other than a contract of house purchase) for any other party such as a property developer or local authority.
7. If it is your practice to sell plots of land and to obtain from the purchaser a contract to build, *INCLUDE* such dwellings in your return.
8. In the case of new flats or maisonettes include the number of separate dwellings to be provided in the building.
9. Dwellings should be regarded as "started" when work starts on the foundations of a building.

WORKING PROPRIETORS (Section 4)

10. **Working proprietors** are persons engaged in the business covered by the return who are regarded as self-employed persons for National Insurance purposes, e.g. self-employed owners, managers, partners, etc.
11. *Include* directors working in the business but not in receipt of a definite wage, salary or commission. *Exclude* part-time directors paid by fee only.
12. Labour-only sub-contractors should enter the working partners in the group—the operatives employed should be entered in section 6.

ADMINISTRATIVE, PROFESSIONAL, TECHNICAL AND CLERICAL EMPLOYEES AND TRAINEES (Section 5A)

13. *Include* all employees (including trainees) engaged in the business who do NOT do manual work, e.g. managing and other directors in receipt of a definite wage, salary or commission, managers, architects, surveyors, engineers, other professionals, training officers, superintendents, research, experimental, technical and design staff, draughtsmen and tracers, travellers, sales and office (including works office) staff and GENERAL FOREMEN and other supervisors who do NOT do manual work.
14. *Exclude* working proprietors shown in section 4 and part-time directors paid by fee only.
15. Classification of employees. Professional and technical staff should be shown according to the main duties on which they are engaged, except that professional staff engaged upon administrative or managerial duties for which they are required to be professionally qualified should be entered under their profession and not as managerial.

   (1) **Managerial Staff.** *Include* site, area, contracts, sales and office managers, agents, professionally qualified staff (including accountants, company secretaries, but excluding architects, surveyors and engineers), training and personnel officers, qualified work study officers and any other persons (including directors) mainly employed in a managerial capacity (exclude foremen).
   (2) **Architects, Surveyors, Engineers.** *Include* professionally qualified architects, surveyors and engineers engaged in these occupations.
   (3) **Technical Staff.** *Include* site engineers and surveyors not professionally qualified, buyers, planning, estimating, work study, research and laboratory assistants, instructors and any other persons mainly employed in a technical capacity not included in occupation 1.
   (4) **Draughtsmen and Tracers.** *Include* draughtsmen, tracers, design detailers.
   (5) **Foremen.** *Include* general foremen and works supervisors, but exclude foremen mainly employed in manual work or in handling materials (who should be included under the appropriate trade).
   (6) **Clerical & Sales Staff.** *Include* clerks and other office staff, including those working in sales, computers and stores, and supervisors of these staff.

OPERATIVES AND TRAINEES EMPLOYED (Section 5B)

16. **General.** This section covers all classes of employees other than the staff entered in section 5A and includes all manual wage earners, trainees, working foremen, operatives engaged in transport work, stores and warehouses, canteen workers, and operatives engaged on the manufacture of goods for sale.
17. **Sub-contractors** supplying labour-only to other contractors should enter the number of operatives on their payroll. The working partners in the group should be included in the figure shown in section 4.
18. **Occupation of operatives and trainees.** Operatives who use more than one skill should be shown under their main occupation. *Include* foremen mainly employed in manual work or in handling materials.

   (1) **Bricklayers.** *Include* specialist bricklayers and other workers in the trade except labourers or general operatives.
   (2) **Masons.** *Include* monumental masons, stone carvers, stone polishers and other workers in the trade except labourers or general operatives.
   (3) **Carpenters/Joiners.** *Include* carpenters, joiners, formwork carpenters, joiner bench hands, wood-working machinists and operatives, setters out and other workers in the trade except labourers or general operatives.
   (4) **Painters.** *Include* painters and decorators, industrial painters, french polishers, signwriters and other workers in the trade except labourers or general operatives.
   (5) **Plasterers.** *Include* solid and fibrous plasterers, moulders and other workers in the trade except labourers or general operatives. Dry-lining and partition operatives should also be included.
   (6) **Roof Slaters and Tilers.** *Include* felters, roofers and other workers in the trade except labourers or general operatives.
   (7) **Floor, Wall and Ceiling Tilers.** *Include* composition floor layers, mosaic workers, parquet floorers, terrazzo workers, mastic asphalters, metal fixers (ceiling systems) and other workers in the trade except labourers or general operatives.
   (8) **Glaziers.** *Include* patent glaziers, lead light workers, glass production or processing workers and other workers in the trade except labourers or general operatives.
   (9) **Paviors.** *Include* pavior street masons, tar paviors, potmen and other workers in the trade except labourers or general operatives. Exclude mechanical plant operators who should be included in occupation 19.
   (10) **Plant Mechanics.** *Include* plant maintenance mechanics, contractors' plant mechanics, motor mechanics and other workers in the trade except labourers or general operatives.
   (11) **Miscellaneous Craftsmen (Excluding Mechanical Eng. Services).** *Include* thermal insulation operatives, ductwork erectors, craftsmen generally employed in industries other than construction and any other craftsmen not covered in occupations 1 to 10 and 12 to 16.
   (12) **Plumbers and Gas Fitters.** *Include* chemical plumbers, plumber welders, and other workers in the trade except labourers or general operatives.
   (13) **Natural Gas Conversion Workers.** *Include* operatives or conversion fitters (excluding gas fitters, plumbers, heating and ventilating fitters), engaged in the conversion of appliances to natural gas or in the pre-liminary work.
   (14) **Heating and Ventilating Engineering Workers.** *Include* heating and ventilating fitters, or fitter/welders, heating fitters, other workers in the trade except labourers or general operatives.
   (15) **Other Mechanical Engineering Services Workers.** *Include* oil burner mechanics, pipe fitters, refrigeration mechanics, welders (including oxy-acetylene, metallic-arc or shielded-arc welders), and any other person not included in occupations 12, 13 or 14 engaged as a manual worker in mechanical engineering services trades except as a labourer or general operative.
   (16) **Electricians.** *Include* cable jointers and other workers in the trade except labourers or general operatives.
   (17) **Crane Drivers.**
   (18) **Earthmoving Plant Operators.** *Include* operators of excavators, front end shovels, motorised scrapers, motor graders, tractors and trenching machines.
   (19) **Other Mechanical Plant Operators.** *Include* mechanical equipment operators, compressor, air tool or paving machine operators, plant and dumper drivers, oilers and greasers, pumpmen, banksmen, slingers, but excluding crane drivers, earthmoving plant operators, concretors and demolishers.

(continued overleaf)

Form No. B.I.M. 164
(10/75)

2509 Dd.109278 150000 8/75 JC&SLtd Gp.3615

OPERATIVES AND TRAINEES EMPLOYED – continued

(20) **Scaffolders.**
(21) **Bar Benders and Steel Fixers.**
(22) **Steel Erectors and Sheeters.** *Include* iron roofers.
(23) **Concretors.** *Include* plus-rated workers involved in placing, vibrating or finishing concrete, precast concrete erectors and fixers and pre-stressing, and pre-tensioning operatives.
(24) **Demolishers.** *Include* general labourers using compressed air drills or pneumatic punching machines or spades, sorters, improvers, mattockmen, topmen, burner topmen, burner groundmen, shorers (timber), shorer's mates.
(25) **Other Building & Civil Engineering Skilled Workers.** *Include* Labourers and General Operatives entitled to extra payment for skill and responsibility under the appropriate Working Rule Agreement, including any employed in trades covered by occupations 1 to 16. Any employed in trades covered by occupations 17 to 24 should be shown under those occupations.
Steeplejacks.
Divers, including surface, demand or helmet divers, and life linesmen.
Excavation Operatives, including heading drivers, manhole builders, pipe layers, pipe jointers and timbermen.
Piling and Well Drilling Operatives, including borer driver, vibrator and specialist piling operatives, well or rock drillers, and shaft sinkers.
Tunnel Miners, including soft-heading miners.
Blacksmiths, including markers-out.
Repetitive Process Factory Workers.
(26) **Unskilled Labourers.** *Include* labourers and general operatives not entitled to extra payment for skill or responsibility under the appropriate Working Rule Agreement. (Extra payment on account of conditions of work should not be treated as payment for skill).
(27) **Canteen Workers.** *Include* workers wholly involved in the supply of food and drink for immediate consumption.
(28) **Other Occupations.** *Include* transport drivers, manual workers in stores and warehouses, office cleaners and other persons not covered in other categories. (Note: Miscellaneous craftsmen are in occupation 11; miscellaneous building and civil engineering skilled workers are in occupation 25; unskilled labourers are in occupation 26).

19 **Trainees, column 02.** In sections 5A and 5B, 'trainee' is a person (including an apprentice or probationer) who is learning an administrative, professional, technical or manual skill, and whose employer has undertaken to provide training for him for a period of at least a year. Include trainees of all ages engaged on building, civil engineering or associated work. Exclude trainees employed on other work, e.g. manufacturing or transport.

VALUE OF WORK DONE AND OPERATIVES EMPLOYED (Section 7)
APPLICABLE ONLY TO FORMS AR41B & D

20 New construction includes site preparation and demolition (items 7(1), 7(2), 7(4), 7(5), 7(7) and 9(2)).
21 Non-housing new construction work includes extensions, major alterations and improvements (items 7(4), 7(5), 7(7) and 9(2)).
22 Housing improvements, house/flat conversions, extensions, alterations and redecorations are classified to repair and maintenance and should be entered against item 7(3) and as repair and maintenance in item 9(2).
23 Items 7(7) and 7(8) cover work on Utilities and Social Services, including work for Government Departments, Nationalised Industries (including nationalised steelworks), Canal, River, Dock and Harbour Boards, Local Authorities (other than housing), Hospital Boards, New Town Corporations, Covent Garden Market Authority, and the Airports Authority.
24 **Heating and ventilating engineers** should include the value of the erection and installation of all space-heating, ventilation and air-conditioning equipment.
25 **Constructional engineers** should include the value of fabricated iron and steelwork made by them in the value of work done in Section 7. Exclude the value of fabricated iron and steelwork made for sale.

VALUE OF WORK DONE (including V.A.T. where appropriate)
26 Include:
 (a) The value of work done on your own initiative in the period on building such as dwellings or offices for eventual sale or lease.
 (b) The value of work done by your own operatives on the construction or maintenance of your own premises.
 (c) The value of goods made by you and used in the work.
 (d) The value of any materials supplied by you to sub-contractors.
27 Exclude:
 (a) The value of any work done for you by sub-contractors of any type.
 (b) The value of any payments made to labour-only sub-contractors.
 (c) The value of goods made for sale.
28 **Labour-only sub-contractors** should enter the value of services rendered and work done during the quarter.
29 **Electrical contractors** should include the value of installation work associated with buildings and structures.
30 **Painters and decorators** should show the value of work on new structures as 'new construction' and all other painting and decorating, etc., as 'repair and maintenance'.

OPERATIVES EMPLOYED
31 Include:
 (a) All classes of employees other than staff entered in Section 5B.
 (b) All persons aged 16 years and over who were on your payroll on the specified date and who are usually engaged on MANUAL work whether full or part-time.
 (c) Trainees, operatives engaged in transport work, stores, warehouses, canteens, and on the manufacture of goods for sale, etc.
 (d) Working foremen and other supervisors who do MANUAL work.
32 **Labour-only sub-contractors** should enter in Column 02 only the number of operatives employed. The number of working partners in the group should be included in Section 4 of the form.

VALUE OF WORK DONE BY YOU AS A SUB-CONTRACTOR (Section 8)
APPLICABLE ONLY TO FORM AR 41B

33 Firms working for other contractors in the construction industry should enter the value of work done by them in the quarter on sub-contracts let to them. The values stated should be estimates of the amounts chargeable to the contractors for building, civil engineering and associated work done by the firm during the quarter and should also have been included in Section 7. The amount should include the value of all materials supplied by you, including any machinery or plant incorporated, whether purchased or made by you.
34 Work done on contracts let directly by management consultants and industries outside the construction industry (e.g. oil refining consortia) should not be entered in Section 8 but should be included in Section 7.
35 **Fee contracts.** Include the value of work done for other firms including fees. The amount stated should be the net contract price of the work including extras if the contract was executed wholly within the quarter specified; otherwise it should be the value of work actually done in the quarter. *Exclude* the value of any materials supplied to you without charge.
36 **Labour-only sub-contractors** should enter the value of services rendered and work done during the quarter in both 8(1) and 8(2).
37 **Electrical contractors** should include the value of installation work associated with buildings and structures.
38 **Heating and ventilating engineers** should include the value of the erection and installation of all space-heating, ventilation and air-conditioning equipment.
39 **Constructional engineers** should include the value of fabricated iron and steelwork made by them in the value of work done in Section 8. *Exclude* the value of fabricated iron and steelwork made for sale.

SUB-CONTRACTED WORK (Section 9)
APPLICABLE ONLY TO FORM AR 41B

40 The value shown in item 9(1) should be the value of building, civil engineering and associated work done in the quarter by others (including labour-only sub-contractors) to whom you sub-let contracts and the value of other work done on materials that you supplied. These values should not be included in Section 7.
41 *Exclude* the cost of construction and maintenance work carried out by employees covered by this return, and the cost of materials used by them.
42 In 9(2) include the value of all payments made during the quarter to labour-only sub-contractors for services rendered and work done. Payments relating to the fiscal quarter (which starts and finishes 4 days later than the calendar quarter) would be acceptable if it is more convenient for you to provide these from your records.

Form No. B.I.M./A.R.43B

DEPARTMENT OF THE ENVIRONMENT

If the name or address shown below is incorrect in any way, please correct it.

Please quote in any correspondence

Ensure that the address below shows through the aperture of the return envelope when inserting the completed form.

Please check the VAT number(s) applicable to this return as shown on the right.

If this number is incorrect, please cross out and enter the correct number in the box.

If the entry states "VAT No. NOT KNOWN" please enter your VAT number in the box or state "NONE".

Building, Civil Engineering and Allied Industries

ANNUAL RETURN ON INDUSTRIAL ACTIVITY

Dear Sir(s),   **28 SEPTEMBER, 1977**

1   The purpose of this inquiry is to obtain information about the construction industries which together with similar data from other industries will provide a comprehensive review of industrial activity. Inquiries into the activities of the construction industries are essential because of the size of the labour force employed, and because the output they produce is a large share of capital investment. Information from the return is also needed for the compilation of mailing lists for the circulation by DOE to selected firms of technical information and of notices of lectures and conferences.

2   To avoid duplication of inquiries, and hence reduce the burden of form-filling, details of your name and address, industrial classification and employment may be passed to the Construction Industry Training Board, in accordance with the provisions of Section 4 of the Employment and Training Act, 1973. This step has allowed DOE to eliminate the list of occupations from the 1977 return.

3   VAT should be excluded from all estimates of work done in this return and in future DOE returns. In previous returns you have been asked to include VAT but, by excluding VAT, output of new work and of repair and maintenance work will be measured in a uniform way. A special section has been added to this return asking for details of VAT on work which you have done for clients or for other contractors, so that we can estimate the adjustment needed to the earlier output figures to allow for the effect of this change.

4   You are asked to check your VAT registration number as it appears on DOE records, or to enter your VAT number if not previously recorded. VAT numbers are vital in the task of constructing a central register of businesses which, when completed, should help avoid duplication in statistical inquiries and hence reduce the burden of form filling. No information on firms registered for VAT will be passed to HM Customs and Excise. For firms who are registered for VAT only their trade classification may be disclosed to HM Customs and Excise.

5   This return asks for information about non-construction work carried out by you. The results will be used for producing a better estimate of total Industrial production and checking that the Trade Classification of individual firms is still correct.

6   The earlier that the statistics based on this return are available the more valuable they are, therefore your co-operation in carefully and promptly completing the form will be of real assistance to the Department. As the late return of even a few forms must lead to delay in the publication of results, please do not hold up this return until audited figures are available but give the closest possible estimate. If you encounter any difficulties in completing the form, the staff of the Building Industries Section at the address shown above will be pleased to help you in any way possible. The completed form should be returned to the address above **not later than WEDNESDAY 26 OCTOBER, 1977.**

7   This notice is served under the provisions of Section 1 of the Statistics of Trade Act, 1947, for the purposes of obtaining information necessary for the discharge by Government Departments of their functions. Under this Act the rendering of a return is compulsory. In accordance with the Act all information supplied in this return will be treated as confidential. Summarised results will be published by HMSO in issue 26 of "Housing and Construction Statistics" with fuller details in the publication "Private Contractors' Construction Census" (annual).

Yours faithfully,

Principal Director of Statistics   **Under-Secretary**

Form No. B.I.M./A.R.43B   for and on behalf of the Secretary of State for the Environment
(AMD 10/77) (A1, A2, A3, A4, A5 & A7)

554 CONSTRUCTION AND THE RELATED PROFESSIONS

IN CONFIDENCE

The information given in this return should relate to Great Britain only (i.e. excluding Northern Ireland, the Isle of Man and the Channel Islands).

The construction industries cover building and civil engineering work, including specialist trades. A detailed list of trades considered to be part of the construction industries is given in section 1.

Firms NOT principally engaged in the construction industries but which have a construction department for which separate accounts are kept should complete the form in respect of that department only.

Please refer to the enclosed Notes before completing the form and ensure that all sections of the form (1-10) are completed.

For Official Use

For Official Use

1
DETAILS OF BUSINESS

Tick below the description which is most appropriate to your major activity (**i.e. the greatest part of your turnover**). One description only should be ticked.

Code	DESCRIPTION	TICK HERE	Code	DESCRIPTION	TICK HERE
01	General building		14	Electrical contracting	
02	Building and civil engineering		15	Asphalt and surface dressing	
03	Civil engineering		16	Construction plant hire (with operators)	
23	Opencast coal-mining		24	Construction plant hire (without operators)	
04	Plumbing		17	Flooring	
05	Joinery and carpentry (mainly on site work)		18	Constructional engineering	
06	Painting and decorating		19	Insulating work	
07	Roofing		20	Suspended ceiling work	
08	Plastering		21	Wall and floor tiling	
09	Glazing		22	If your major activity is other than codes 01 to 21, 23 or 24 please enter description: (For example, building cleaning, acoustic engineering or management consultancy in the construction industry.)	
10	Demolition				
11	Scaffolding work				
12	Reinforced concrete work				
13	Heating and ventilating engineering				

2
Working proprietors: i.e. self-employed persons. Do **not** include persons entered here in any other section of the form. *(see notes 1 to 3).*

(Enter NIL if appropriate)

3

A **Administrative, professional, technical and clerical employees.**
State here the number of employees who do **not** do manual work and who were on your payroll on **6 October, 1977** or the nearest possible date. *(see notes 4 & 5).*

A	Excluding Trainees 01	Trainees 02	TOTAL 03
	01	01	07

(Enter NIL if appropriate)

B **Operatives.** State here the number of operatives who were on your payroll on **6 October, 1977** or the nearest possible date. Exclude Working Proprietors, include working foremen. *(see notes 6 to 8).*

B	Excluding Trainees 01	Trainees 02	TOTAL 03
	01	01	29

(Enter NIL if appropriate)

4

NEW PRIVATE ENTERPRISE HOUSING built on sites owned or leased by you in Great Britain. *(see notes 9 to 13).*

4.1 Enter the number of such dwellings which you started **in the 12 months ending 30 September, 1977.**

(Enter NIL if appropriate)

4.2 Do you expect to build any such dwellings **in the next 2 years?** *(Tick in the appropriate box).*

YES	1
NO	2

APPENDIX IV 555

5 VALUE OF CONTRACTS AND ORDERS RECEIVED FOR NEW CONSTRUCTION WORK

5.1 Do you ever work as a main contractor (or carry out own-initiative projects)?
IF NO, YOU SHOULD IGNORE QUESTIONS 5.2 AND 5.3.

5.2 If **YES**, is any of this work **NEW CONSTRUCTION** or improvements and alterations.
(Tick in the appropriate box).

YES	1
NO	2

5.3 If **YES**, approximately how much new construction work (including improvements and alterations) did you start as main contractor (or on your own initiative) in the **12 months to 30 September, 1977** or any other convenient 12 month period?

Enter NIL if appropriate

£ [   ]

6

Both main and sub-contractors should complete this section
Value of work carried out and operatives employed by type of work.
Exclude VAT

	column 1 Value of work done excluding VAT. 1 July — 30 September 1977 *(exclude pence)*	column 2 Number of Operatives employed on 6 October 1977 *Do not enter the same person on more than one line*

Column 1
Enter in 6.1 to 6.8 estimates of the amounts chargeable to your customers for building, civil engineering and associated work done by your directly employed staff **between 1 July and 30 September, 1977** *(see notes 16 to 27)*

Include the value of materials used (unless supplied to you free of charge), labour costs, overheads and profits.

Exclude work done for you by other sub-contractors, which should be entered in section 8.

Exclude non-construction work which should be entered in section 9.

Column 2
Enter in 6.1 to 6.9 the number of operatives who were on your payroll on **6 October, 1977** or the nearest possible date *(see notes 28 and 29)*.

Work on houses and flats

6.1 New **public housing** for local authorities (e.g. council houses), *all Housing Associations* and co-ownership societies, new town corporations, public utilities, nationalised industries and government departments. | 01 | 01 | 02 |

6.2 New **private housing** for private owners and developers. | 02 |

6.3 Repair and maintenance of dwellings *(see note 18)*. | 03 |

Non-housing work for private owners and developers

6.4 New **industrial** construction: Factories, warehouses, coke ovens, refineries, concrete oil production platforms, steel producing plant or works in private ownership, etc. | 04 |

6.5 New **non-industrial** construction: offices, shops, farm buildings, hotels and public houses, places of worship, clubs, places of entertainment, road goods transport depots, etc. | 05 |

6.6 Repair and maintenance of structures covered by items 4 and 5. | 06 |

Non-housing work for public sector clients

6.7 New construction not included above (include work on open cast coal sites and nationalised steelworks). | 07 |

6.8 Repair and maintenance not included in items 3 and 6. | 08 |

6.9 Enter in column 2 the number of operatives who cannot be classified to the types of work listed 1-8 above, e.g. transport workers, stores and warehouse staff, canteen workers, operatives employed on the manufacture of goods for sale. *(see section 9)*. | 09 |

Totals *Enter NIL if appropriate* | 10 |

7
Firms working for other contractors in the construction industry should enter the value of work done by them in the quarter on sub-contracts let to them.

EXCLUDE VAT
(see notes 29 to 33).

7.1 **Value of work done by you as a sub-contractor between 1 July and 30 September 1977** for other contractors in the construction industry. This cannot be greater than the total value shown above.

EXCLUDE PENCE
£ [   ] *Enter NIL if appropriate*

7.2 **Value of work shown in 7.1 done by you as a labour-only sub-contractor.** This cannot be greater than the value shown in 7.1 above.

EXCLUDE PENCE
£ [   ] *Enter NIL if appropriate*

8

EXCLUDE VAT

8.1 **Value of work done for you by all sub-contractors** (including labour-only sub-contractors) in the period **between 1 July and 30 September, 1977.** *(see notes 34 and 35)*.

EXCLUDE PENCE
£ [   ] *Enter NIL if appropriate*

8.2 **Payments made to labour-only sub-contractors** in this period. *(see notes 16, 17, 18 and 35)*.

£ [   ] New housing

£ [   ] New non-housing

£ [   ] Repair and maintenance

CONSTRUCTION AND THE RELATED PROFESSIONS

9   VALUE OF NON-CONSTRUCTION WORK DONE BY YOU IN THE PERIOD 1 JULY — 30 SEPTEMBER, 1977
EXCLUDE VAT

9.1   Value of work done and services rendered outside the construction industry, **not** included in 6.1 to 6.8, and sales of goods of your own production.

EXCLUDE PENCE   £ [ ]   *Enter NIL if appropriate*

9.2   Sales of goods bought and resold without processing (i.e. goods merchanted and factored) **not** included in 6.1 to 6.8. **Include** sales of waste products and residuals.

EXCLUDE PENCE   £ [ ]   *Enter NIL if appropriate*

9.3   Number of operatives employed on **6 October, 1977** in connection with 9.1 and 9.2.

[ ]

NOTES

Include in 9.1 work done and services rendered that could not be classified to one of the 24 headings of section 1 (Details of Business).

Plant-hire contractors should enter the value of work done for non-construction clients at 9.1.

Constructional engineers should enter the value of fabricated iron and steel work at 9.1.

Construction firms who also do some business as Builders Merchants should enter such sales at 9.2. Where goods are installed by the firm they should be included in the value of work done in section 6.

Demolition contractors should enter the proceeds from the sale of waste products and residuals at 9.2.

---

10   AMOUNT OF VAT CHARGEABLE ON WORK CARRIED OUT BY YOU IN THE PERIOD 1 JULY — 30 SEPTEMBER 1977
IN RELATION TO WORK REPORTED IN SECTION 6.

Exclude VAT chargeable on non-construction work reported in section 9

VAT chargeable on construction work (output tax).   EXCLUDE PENCE   £ [ ]   *Enter NIL if appropriate*

Declaration and Signature

Name and telephone number of person who should be consulted if questions arise about this return ....

I hereby declare that the information contained in this return is complete and correct to the best of my knowledge and belief.

Please check that you have completed all sections

Signature .... Date 1977
(Please state whether Proprietor, Director, Manager, Partner, Secretary, etc.)

Form No. B.I.M./A.R.43B
(AMD 10/77) (A1, A2, A3, A4, A5 & A7)

Form No. B.I.M. 164
(10/77)

DEPARTMENT OF THE ENVIRONMENT

NOTES FOR THE COMPLETION OF THE ANNUAL RETURN ON INDUSTRIAL ACTIVITY

Throughout this return include all persons (male and female), aged 16 years and over, working in Great Britain (i.e. excluding Northern Ireland, the Isle of Man and the Channel Islands), whether full or part-time (including those absent for any reason), who were on your payroll on the pay day specified.

WORKING PROPRIETORS (Section 2)

1. **Working proprietors** are persons engaged in the business covered by the return who are regarded as self-employed persons for National Insurance purposes, e.g. self-employed owners, managers, partners, etc.
2. *Include* directors working in the business but not in receipt of a definite wage, salary or commission. *Exclude* part-time directors paid by fee only.
3. **Labour-only sub-contractors** should enter the working partners in the group — the operatives employed should be entered in section 3B.

ADMINISTRATIVE, PROFESSIONAL, TECHNICAL AND CLERICAL EMPLOYEES AND TRAINEES (Section 3A)

4. *Include* all employees (including trainees) engaged in the business who do NOT do manual work, e.g. managing and other directors in receipt of a definite wage, salary or commission, managers, architects, surveyors, engineers, other professionals, training officers, superintendents, research, experimental, technical and design staff, draughtsmen and tracers, travellers, sales and office (including works office) staff, and GENERAL FOREMEN and other supervisors who do NOT do manual work.
5. *Exclude* working proprietors shown in section 2 and part-time directors paid by fee only.

OPERATIVES AND TRAINEES EMPLOYED (Section 3B)

6. **General.** This section covers all classes of employees other than the staff entered in section 3A and includes all manual wage earners, trainees, working foremen and directors, operatives engaged in transport work, stores and warehouses, canteen workers, and operatives engaged on the manufacture of goods for sale.
7. **Sub-contractors** supplying labour-only to other contractors should enter the number of operatives on their payroll. The working partners in the group should be included in the figure shown in section 2.
8. **Trainees, column 02.** In sections 3A and 3B, 'trainee' is a person (including an apprentice or probationer) who is learning an administrative, professional, technical or manual skill, and whose employer has undertaken to provide training for him for a period of at least a year. Include trainees of all ages engaged on building, civil engineering or associated work. Exclude trainees employed on other work, e.g. manufacturing or transport.

VALUE OF WORK DONE AND OPERATIVES EMPLOYED (Section 6)

16. New construction includes site preparation and demolition.
17. Non-housing extensions, major alterations and improvements should be included with new work.
18. Housing improvements, house/flat conversions, extensions, alterations and redecorations should be included with repair and maintenance and should be entered against item 6.3 and as repair and maintenance in item 8.2.
19. Items 6.7 and 6.8 cover work on Utilities and Social Services, including work for Government Departments, Nationalised Industries (including nationalised steelworks), Canal, River, Dock and Harbour Boards, Local Authorities (other than housing), Hospital Boards, New Town Corporations, Covent Garden Market Authority, and the Airports Authority.
20. The construction of concrete oil production platforms only is included. Any steel oil production platforms should be entered in question 9.1.

VALUE OF WORK DONE (excluding V.A.T.)

21. Include:
    (a) The value of work done on your own initiative in the period on building such as dwellings or offices for eventual sale or lease.
    (b) The value of work done by you and your own operatives on the construction or maintenance of your own premises.
    (c) The value of goods made by you and used in the work.
    (d) The value of any materials supplied by you to sub-contractors.
22. Exclude:
    (a) The value of any work done for you by sub-contractors of any type.
    (b) The value of any payments made to labour-only sub-contractors.
    (c) The value of goods made for sale. These should be entered in section 9.

VALUE OF WORK DONE BY YOU AS A SUB-CONTRACTOR (Section 7)

30. Firms working for other contractors in the construction industry should enter the value of work done by them in the quarter on sub-contracts let to them. The values stated should be estimates of the amounts chargeable to the contractors for building, civil engineering and associated work done by the firm during the quarter and **should also have been included in Section 6.** The amount should include the value of all materials supplied by you, including any machinery or plant incorporated, whether purchased or made by you.
31. Work done on contracts let directly by management consultants and industries outside the construction industry (e.g. oil refining consortia) should not be entered in Section 7 but should be included in Section 6.
32. **Fee contracts.** Include the value of work done for other firms including fees. The amount stated should be the net contract price of the work including extras if the contract was executed wholly within the quarter specified; otherwise it should be the value of work actually done in the quarter. *Exclude* the value of any materials supplied to you without charge.

Form No. B.I.M. 164
(10/77)

NEW PRIVATE ENTERPRISE HOUSING (Section 4)

9. Enter the number of new dwellings (i.e. houses, bungalows, flats or maisonettes) which were started by you in the **12 months ending 30 September, 1977** on sites in Great Britain owned or leased by you or your subsidiary or associated companies.
10. Dwellings should be regarded as **"started"** when work starts on the foundations of a building.
11. In the case of new flats or maisonettes include the number of separate dwellings to be provided in the building.
12. If it is your practice to sell plots of land and to obtain from the purchaser a contract to build, *INCLUDE* such dwellings in your return.
13. **EXCLUDE** dwellings built under contract (other than a contract of house purchase) for any other party such as a property developer, housing association or local authority.

VALUE OF CONTRACTS AND ORDERS RECEIVED FOR NEW CONSTRUCTION (Section 5)

14. *Include* at 5.3:
    (1) The value of contracts and orders received for new construction work (including improvements) for which you are acting as the main contractor.
    (2) Work where you have started on your own initiative i.e. work for which you have not been awarded a contract or order by any other party on a site already owned or leased by you or your subsidiary or associated companies. (EXAMPLE: a house or houses, for eventual sale or lease to other persons or companies, or for occupation by yourselves or your subsidiary or associated companies).
    (3) Cases where it is your practice to sell plots of land and to obtain from the purchasers a contract to build.
15. EXCLUDE:
    (1) Contracts etc. for repair and maintenance work.
    (2) Sub-contracts obtained by you from other contractors in the construction industry.
    (3) The cost of architects' and consultants' services.
    (4) The value of land purchased.

23. **Labour-only sub-contractors** should enter the value of services rendered and work done during the quarter.
24. **Heating and ventilating engineers** should include the value of the erection and installation of all space-heating, ventilation and air-conditioning equipment.
25. **Constructional engineers** should include the value of fabricated iron and steelwork made for sale in section 9.
    The value of fabricated iron and steelwork for erection by the firm should be included in the value of work done in section 6.
26. **Electrical contractors** should include the value of installation work associated with buildings and structures.
27. **Painters and decorators** should show the value of work done on new structures as 'new construction' and all other painting and decorating, etc., as 'repair and maintenance'.

OPERATIVES EMPLOYED

28. Include:
    (a) All classes of employees other than staff entered in Section 3A.
    (b) All persons aged 16 years and over who were on your payroll on the specified date and who are usually engaged on MANUAL work whether full or part-time.
    (c) Trainees, operatives engaged in transport work, stores, warehouses, canteens, and on the manufacture of goods for sale, etc.
    (d) Working foremen and directors and other supervisors who do MANUAL work.
29. **Labour-only sub-contractors** should enter in Column 2 only the number of operatives employed. The number of working partners in the group should be included in Section 2 of the form.

33. **Labour-only sub-contractors** should enter the value of services rendered and work done during the quarter in both 7.1 and 7.2.

SUB-CONTRACTED WORK (Section 8)

34. The value shown in item 8.1 should be the value of building, civil engineering and associated work done in the quarter by others (including labour-only sub-contractors) to whom you sub-let contracts and the value of other work done on materials that you supplied. **These values should not be included in Section 6.**
35. In 8.2 include the value of all payments made during the quarter to labour-only sub-contractors for services rendered and work done. Payments relating to the fiscal quarter (which starts and finishes 4 days later than the calendar quarter) would be acceptable if it is more convenient for you to provide these from your records.

APPENDIX V

CENSUSES OF DIRECT LABOUR ORGANIZATIONS IN GREAT BRITAIN

History of Enquiries made by the Ministry of Works and its Successor Departments (currently Department of the Environment) and Selected Specimen Forms

(Text references: Sections 3.4, 3.6 and 4.3)

N.B. It is not possible to provide a full account of the nature, content and frequency of the censuses of direct labour organizations because the information now available is incomplete.

(a) Date of Introduction

Returns were initiated during the Second World War but the early history is not clear—it would seem that the first census, for local authorities, at least, was in September 1943.

(b) Frequency

Local authorities: annually prior to 1946, then quarterly each February, May, August and November with effect from May 1946 until August 1949, then annually in May until 1954, followed by July and September 1955 and April 1956, then April and September each year between 1957 and 1971 inclusive, then April and October each year (except for April 1974 when no census was taken due to the re-organization of local government in progress at the time).

Public utilities: apparently the same as for local authorities prior to 1955 (see Table 3.4) and since 1956 (but *including* April 1974). The history for the year 1955 is not clear.

Government departments: as for public utilities since at least 1960. Earlier history is not clear.

It will be observed that for most of the period for which information is available, the timing of the enquiry is coincident with that for the censuses of contractors except that a bi-annual pattern of enquiries has been retained since 1971 in contrast to the single annual census of contractors (see Appendix IV).

(c) Form References

A variety of different forms have been used at different times. These were identified, generally speaking, by the same system of letters and serial numbers as used for the censuses of contractors (see Appendix IV) together with the addition of a suffix: LA for local authorities until September 1968 and then PA; PU for public utilities until October 1975 and GD for government departments. In October 1975 the PA and PU series of forms were merged and both now bear the suffix PA (a specimen is reproduced below). New Town Corporations were covered on a separate form (BIM/AR . . . /NT) from September 1964 to September 1968 when it was merged with the local authorities' form. Similarly separate forms were used for different public utilities until September 1968 (see under (e) below) when a single form, headed 'Public Authorities and Utilities', was introduced for all such undertakings within the scope of the enquiry with the exception of gas undertakings, for which a different type of return is made.

(d) Specimen Forms Included

The specimen forms selected for inclusion here have been selected (subject to the constraint that a complete set of questionnaires is not available) to illustrate the questions asked and the instructions given regarding the completion of the return, and to record major developments in its content. The combined return for local authorities and public utilities, introduced in October 1975 (Form BIM/AR45/PA), is included—this is the form of return in current use except for an amendment of the occupational classification made in October 1976 (details are given below)—together with the first (or an early) return and others selected to exemplify such developments. They should be examined in conjunction with the brief history of the returns set out below (section (h) of this Appendix).

Form Ref. and Date	Title	Page
Local Authorities (combined with public authorities and utilities from October 1975—see below)		
BCE3/QR7/LA Nov. 1946	Return of Building and Civil Engineering Operatives Employed by Local Authorities	565
BIM3/AR7 April 1956/LA	Return of Labour and Output	567
BIM3/AR9 September 1957/LA	Employment Return	570
BIM/AR44/PA April 1975	Return of Employment and Output	572
Public Authorities and Utilities (combined with local authorities from October 1975—see below)		
BIM/AR44/PU April 1975	Return of Employment and Output	575
Local and Public Authorities combined		
BIM/AR45/PA October 1975	Employment and Output Return	578

(e) Circulation

Local authorities: all local government authorities in Great Britain and, from 1964, New Town Corporations. In 1955 hospital authorities were also covered but not in any subsequent censuses.

Public authorities and utilities: currently the following seven categories of undertaking are covered: (1) Railways, (2) Drainage Boards, (3) Canal, Dock and Harbour Boards, (4) Tramway, Trolleybus, Omnibus and Road Haulage Undertakings, (5) Electricity Authorities, (6) National Coal Board (NCB), (7) British Airports Authority (BAA). Apart from the exceptions and additions noted below, it is believed that these bodies were covered in all of the censuses considered here. The exceptions and additions are as follows: Prior to April 1974 Water Undertakings were also covered (as category (2) above) and River Authorities were covered, along with Drainage Boards, as part of category (3); since then they have been covered by other arrangements. The BAA was covered for the first time in April 1968 (prior to this date the labour was included in the returns from Government Departments—MPBW). The NCB and CEGB were covered for the first time in April 1967. The area Electricity Boards, since 1957 at least, have submitted returns only once a year in the October (formerly September) enquiries. A notable omission is Gas Undertakings which do not submit the return under consideration here but are covered by a single consolidated return prepared by the Gas Council. Prior to the nationalization of the electricity and gas industries in 1948 and 1949 respectively it is believed that municipal undertakings were covered along with local authorities.

Government Departments: currently all government departments employing direct labour are covered; so far as can be ascertained this has always been the case but the early history is not clear.

(f) Processing of Returns

Currently the Department of the Environment.

(g) Availability of Data from Individual Returns

Individual returns are treated as strictly confidential.

(h) History of the Returns

The development of these returns is broadly comparable with the development of the contractors' returns (Appendix IV) but the timing of changes does not always coincide. It is convenient to consider the periods up to 1955 and after 1955 separately, however, because of the changes made to the contractors' censuses after 1955.

Local Authorities November 1944—May 1954

It is possible to provide a reasonably full account of the development of the return in this period since it has been possible to examine copies of most of the questionnaires used (see Table 3.4).

Employment

A return was required in each enquiry of the number of operatives employed according to occupation and according to type of work. Prior to 1946 a cross-classification by occupation and type of work was also required. The main developments during the period were changes in the classifications as follows:

Occupations. From May 1946 the occupational classification was brought into line with that used for the contractors' censuses (see Section 3.5.4). Prior to May 1946 the two classifications differed—the one used for contractors' is set out in Section 3.3.3—the local authority classification differed in distinguishing between plumbers and glaziers, in not distinguishing 'Navvies' and in distinguishing two miscellaneous categories rather than one: 'all other building craftsmen' and 'Navvies and other b. and c.e. labour'.

Apprentices. Apprentices were separately distinguished from other operatives for the first time in August 1949 and then in each May census as for contractors (see Appendix IV).

Classification by type of work. The types of work distinguished from May 1946 onwards followed the classification used for contractors including the changes made from time to time (see Appendix IV). Prior to May 1946 the two classifications differed.*

Output

A return of the total value of work done during a period of three months to the end of the month preceding the date of the census was required in all censuses for which questionnaires have been examined (see Table 3.4) from May 1946 with the exception of August 1946. An analysis of output by type of work was required only once—May 1946.

Local Authorities July and September 1955

In 1954/5 the scope of the censuses was changed and their content reconsidered, as were those for contractors. Henceforth the scope of the census was confined to '*departments* of the local authority *mainly or wholly* engaged on building, civil engineering and electric wiring work' whereas the scope previously had extended to '*all* building and civil engineering operatives employed in *all* Departments of the local authority'. Unlike all the censuses before and since, the attempt was made in both the 1955 censuses to cover the labour directly employed by Regional Hospital Boards, Hospital Management Committees and Teaching Hospital Groups in addition to the local authorities themselves.

In content the July census was similar to the subsequent April censuses but the September census was confined solely to the employment of apprentices, requiring a return of the number employed, and the number engaged during the preceding twelve

---

* The classification for local authorities was: *HOUSING*: (1) New work and conversions, including roads and sewers, (2) War damage repairs, (3) Repairs and maintenance (excluding w.d.r.); *NON-HOUSING*: (4) Public utility services (gas, water, electricity, sewerage), (5) Roads and highways; *ALL-OTHER WORK*: (6) For Government Departments, (7) Other.

months, both according to craft and type of agreement. In line with the revision of the contractors' census, the age of operatives covered was lowered in the July census from '16 years and over' to '15 years and over' and extended to females in addition to males.

Local Authorities From 1956

With certain exceptions the pattern established for these enquiries since 1956 has been broadly comparable with that established for contractors, namely an April census covering output and employment by type of work and a September (later October) census covering employment broken down by occupation. Unlike contractors, however, the bi-annual pattern of enquiries has been maintained throughout the whole period and, since 1961, a return of output and employment by type of work has been required in both enquiries. Copies of the first April and September returns (April 1956 and September 1957) are reproduced below. The main subsequent developments have been the introduction of an occupational classification of labour in September 1966 comparable with the one introduced for contractors in September 1965—i.e. a return of APTC staff in each census (together with a breakdown by occupation each September/October), and a more detailed breakdown by occupation in the case of operatives and apprentices (for details see those given for contractors in Appendix IV). For a period from 1966 questions were also asked about the number of operatives under training for new skills as in the case of contractors. Further revisions to the occupational classification were introduced in October 1974 (as for contractors) and again in October 1975, the latter representing a major revision (cf. specimen form BIM/AR45/PA). In October 1976 the classification was amended by amalgamating the categories numbered (6) and (7); (17), (18) and (19); and (21) and (22) and by removing categories (2), (13) and (23).

Public Utilities November 1944—May 1954

No questionnaires are available for the censuses prior to May 1946 but it is clear from available tabulations of the results that information was sought at least about the number of operatives employed cross-classified by occupation and type of work (see Table 3.4 which also indicates the other questionnaires it has not been possible to examine). Details of the development of the return since May 1946 are as follows:

Employment. Each return sought information regarding operatives employed according to occupation and type of work and about apprentices employed which paralleled in content and timing that obtained for local authorities in the corresponding period (see above). But in addition information was also sought about operatives employed cross-classified by type of work and region from May 1946 to February 1948 inclusive with the exception of August 1946 when a cross-classification by occupation and region was sought instead.

Output. A return of the value of work done during a period of three months to the end of the month preceding the date of the census, as for local authorities, was required in all the questionnaires examined (see Table 3.4) with the exception of August 1946. All required a return of total value except May 1946 which required a breakdown by type of work.

Public Utilities Since 1955

It is not clear whether any censuses were taken in 1955. Since 1956 the same bi-annual pattern of enquiries has been followed as for contractors and local authorities (see under '(b) Frequency' above). Like contractors too, but unlike local authorities, the April enquiry has been used to cover employment of operatives and the value of work done, each according to type of work, and the September (now October) enquiry to obtain more detailed information about operatives and apprentices employed, each according to occupation. The breakdown by type of work, however, was confined to a distinction between new construction and repair and maintenance work until April 1969 when a sub-division of these between housing and non-housing was introduced in line with the contractors' and local authorities' returns. The labour return has been changed three times: in September 1965 when it was extended to cover APTC staff (one year earlier than the local authorities' revision), in October 1974 when the occupational categories were revised, and again in October 1975 when they were substantially recast—as for contractors and local authorities. A further change made in October 1975, upon the amalgamation of the public utilities' and local authorities' forms, was the inclusion of a return of output and employment by type of work on the same lines as in the April enquiry.

The combined questionnaire introduced in October 1975 (Form BIM/AR45/PA) is reproduced below (amendments to the occupational classification in October 1976 are described above under 'Local Authorities from 1956') together with a copy of the April questionnaire. As explained earlier, a multiplicity of returns were in use prior to 1969—a separate one for each type of utility with wording appropriate to the utility. None of these have been reproduced, however, because the information sought was otherwise comparable to that required for local authorities and because none of the information was published separately for the utilities.

Government Departments

It is not possible to trace the early history of this return since none of the questionnaires used prior to 1961 appear to be available. By this time, however, its content and frequency conformed to those used for public utilities with the exception that the return of the value of work done, required in the April enquiries, relates to the whole year rather than a quarter. The development of the return during this period has followed that for public utilities (see above). Specimen copies of the returns used are not reproduced because of their similarity to those used for other public authorities.

APPENDIX V 565

MINISTRY OF WORKS

BUILDING AND CIVIL ENGINEERING CONTRACTING UNDERTAKINGS REGISTERED UNDER DEFENCE REGULATION 56AB.

B.C.E. 3 Q.R.7 L.A.

Return of Building and Civil Engineering Operatives employed by Local Authorities.

PLEASE READ THE NOTES BELOW AND ON PAGE 2 BEFORE COMPLETING THIS FORM.

THIS FORM RELATES ONLY TO DIRECT EMPLOYEES (PERMANENT AND TEMPORARY) ENGAGED AT DATE OF RETURN ON BUILDING AND CIVIL ENGINEERING WORK. CONTRACTORS' LABOUR SHOULD NOT BE INCLUDED.

NAME OF AUTHORITY:
ADDRESS:
TOWN:
COUNTY:

ESTIMATED TOTAL VALUE OF B. & C.E. WORK DONE DURING THE THREE MONTHS ENDED 31st OCTOBER, 1946 i.e., the total value of labour and materials used on B. & C.E. work during the three months, including overheads (see note on page 2 £ ....

PART A.—NUMBER OF BUILDING AND CIVIL ENGINEERING OPERATIVES (MALES 16 YEARS OF AGE AND OVER) ON PAY-ROLL ON PAY-DAY IN WEEK BEGINNING 18th **NOVEMBER, 1946.**

	HOUSES AND FLATS					CIVIL ENGINEERING	WORK OTHER THAN HOUSES AND FLATS				
	War damage repairs to houses and flats (1)	Preparation of sites for temporary and permanent houses and flats (2)	Erection of temporary and permanent houses and flats (3)	Conversion and adaptation of houses and flats resulting in additional accommodation (4)	Other work to houses and flats, including repair and maintenance (excluding war damage repair) (5)	New work and maintenance (excluding site preparation for houses) (6)	War damage repairs to buildings other than houses and flats (7)	New building for industry, commerce and agriculture (excluding housing) (8)	Repairs and maintenance to buildings other than houses and flats (excluding war damage repair) (9)	Other work (10)	TOTAL (11)
Number of Operatives											

SPECIMEN

NOTES: (a) In cases where a job includes work of more than one class, an estimated apportionment should be made; if this is impossible, it should be classified according to the predominating class of work.
(b) Columns (4) and (5); men employed on conversion and adaptations of houses and flats *not* resulting in additional accommodation should be included in column (5).
(c) Column (8); includes new construction, extensions and adaptations of factories, premises for storage, shops, offices, commercial premises, farm buildings and agricultural premises, industrial research institutions, etc., excluding repairs and maintenance.

PART B.—TOTAL NUMBER OF OPERATIVES BY **OCCUPATION.**
(The total number of operatives in Part B should agree with the total operatives shown in Part A above.)

	Carpenters and Joiners (1)	Bricklayers (2)	Slaters and Tilers (3)	Plasterers (4)	Painters (5)	Plumbers and Glazlers (6)	Masons (7)	Electricians (8)	Other building craftsmen (9)	Other occupations (10)	TOTAL (11)
Number of Operatives											

I certify that to the best of my belief the above particulars are correct:

Date ....   Signed ....

Rank or Status ....

NOTE.—Pages 1 and 3 should be completed, and form folded and returned as indicated on page 4.

(5141/1483) Wt. 28934/L2664 3m. 10/46 T. & B. Gp. 468

NOTES

1. Administrative and clerical staff should *not* be included.

2. Foremen should be included under their appropriate trade classification.

3. Where the value of work done includes other than B. & C. E. work the following procedure should be followed :

    (a) Items of considerable cost, e.g., generating plant, not normally considered as building materials or components should be excluded.

    (b) Only that proportion of overheads applicable to B. & C. E. work should be included.

4. The information is required in duplicate, and Pages 1 and 3 should be completed and returned. Only one return should be made by each Authority, and *not* one in respect of each Department.

APPENDIX V

B.I.M.3/A.R.7 April 1956/LA.

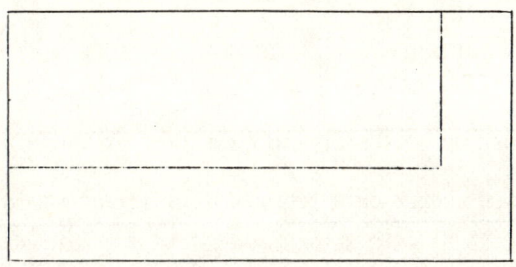

LOCAL AUTHORITIES
BUILDING AND CIVIL ENGINEERING

CONFIDENTIAL

                                        Ministry of Works,
                                        A.S. 65,
                                        Lambeth Bridge House,
                                        London, S.E.1.
                                        4th May, 1956.

                        Return of Labour and Output

Dear Sir,

    It is again desired to obtain up-to-date information about the distribution of men employed on building and civil engineering work. For this purpose, authorities and undertakings are being asked to make a return of the labour employed and the value of work carried out.

    The return differs from that used previously. Information is now required about those employees of the authority who are employed by the local authority mainly or wholly on building and civil engineering work, i.e. work which otherwise would be undertaken by building and civil engineering firms.

    Would you, therefore, be so good as to complete the form on page 2 and return it in the enclosed envelope to the address shown above not later than 25th May, 1956.

                                        Yours faithfully,

                                        Under Secretary,
                        for and on behalf of the Minister of Works.

568   CONSTRUCTION AND THE RELATED PROFESSIONS

LOCAL AUT
BUILDING AND C.
Return of Lab

In any correspondence please quote this reference number:

THIS RETURN RELATES ONLY TO THOSE EMPLOYEES DIRECTLY EMPLOYED BY THE AUTHORITY WHO NORMALLY ARE ENGAGED MAINLY OR WHOLLY ON BUILDING AND CIVIL ENGINEERING WORK

THE NOTES ON PAGE 3 SHOULD BE READ BEFORE COMPLETING THE RETURN

EMPLOYEES ENGAGED ON BUILDING AND CIVIL ENGINEERING WORK AND VALUE OF BUILDING AND CIVIL ENGINEERING WORK DONE

A TYPE OF BUILDING AND CIVIL ENGINEERING WORK		B Operatives employed on the pay day in the week ending 28th April 1956. (See notes 1 – 4) Number	C Estimated value of work done in the 3 months ending 31st March 1956. (See notes 5 – 7) £ (Omit shillings and pence)
(i) HOUSES AND FLATS	(a) NEW DWELLINGS, including site preparation and demolition. (1)		
	(b) REPAIR AND MAINTENANCE, including extensions and alterations. (2)		
(ii) WORK OTHER THAN HOUSING	(a) NEW NON-HOUSING WORK (including new roads): site preparation (including demolition), construction, extension and major alteration. (3)		
	(b) ALL OTHER WORK, including road maintenance and minor improvements and repair and maintenance of building and civil engineering plant. (4)		
	TOTALS OF COLS. B AND C (5)		

SPECIMEN

TO BE COMPLETED AND SIGNED BY THE PERSON MAKING THE RETURN ON BEHALF OF THE AUTHORITY

Name of Local Authority ....

Full postal address ....
(including town and county)

Telephone exchange & number ....

I certify that to the best of my belief the particulars above are correct.

Signed .... Date .... 1956.
     (State whether Town Clerk, Surveyor, etc.)

THIS PORTION TO BE RETURNED

RITIES
ENGINEERING
and Output

INFORMATION

1. All information given by you will be treated as strictly confidential and will be used solely in the compilation of general statistical results. The results will be prepared and published in a way which will not reveal the particulars relating to any individual authority unless previous consent is given by the authority.

2. If you wish to keep for reference, a record of the information supplied on this form, further copies of the form will be supplied on application to this office.

3. In all correspondence with this office, the reference number given at the head of page 2 should be quoted.

NOTES FOR GUIDANCE IN COMPLETING THIS RETURN

General

THIS RETURN RELATES TO:-

1. EMPLOYEES OF THE UNDERTAKING WHO NORMALLY ARE WHOLLY OR MAINLY ENGAGED ON BUILDING AND CIVIL ENGINEERING WORK, i.e. WORK WHICH, OTHERWISE, WOULD BE UNDERTAKEN BY BUILDING AND CIVIL ENGINEERING FIRMS.

Employees

2. INCLUDE employees (male and female) aged 15 years and over who were employed (i.e. whose National Insurance cards were held) by the Local Authority on building and civil engineering work.

3. INCLUDE employees (craftsmen and manual workers together with foremen and charge hands) engaged on the construction or repair and maintenance of:-

    (a) houses and flats,
    (b) highways (roads, bridges, footpaths, installation of street lighting, surface drains etc.),
    (c) harbours, wharves, docks, piers, canals, waterways, sea walls and embankments,
    (d) waterworks (including reservoirs, aqueducts, wells, mains, hydraulic works and pumping stations) sewers and sewage disposal works,
    NOTE: Exclude employees engaged on plant maintenance other than building and civil engineering plant,
    (e) tramways and trackless trolley systems (permanent way, bridges, overhead wires etc.),
    (f) other buildings owned by the Local Authority,

4. EXCLUDE
    (a) administrative, technical and clerical workers,
    (b) all contractors' and sub-contractors' labour,
    (c) labour employed on scavenging and street cleaning, the disposal of house refuse, the maintenance of street lighting, snow clearance and the cleaning of public conveniences,
    (d) "odd job" workers engaged on the day to day maintenance of the authority's offices, etc.

Value of Work Done

5. THE VALUE OF BUILDING AND CIVIL ENGINEERING WORK DONE is an estimate of the value of the output of the employees included in Column B of the return, i.e. a sum calculated to cover the cost of materials, wages and the establishment charges attributable to the work carried out.

6. EXCLUDE the value of work done for the authority by contractors and sub-contractors.

7. EXCLUDE the cost of land, legal costs and architects' fees, etc.

THIS PORTION MAY BE DETACHED AND KEPT

B.I.M.3/A.R.9. September 1957/LA.

LOCAL AUTHORITIES

BUILDING AND CIVIL ENGINEERING

CONFIDENTIAL

Ministry of Works,
A.S. 63,
Lambeth Bridge House,
London, S.E.I.

25th September, 1957.

Employment Return

Dear Sir,

It is again desired to obtain up-to-date information about the craftsmen and apprentices employed on building and civil engineering work. For this purpose, authorities and undertakings are being asked to make an employment return.

Information is required about those employees of the authority who are employed mainly or wholly on building and civil engineering work, i.e. work which otherwise would be undertaken by building and civil engineering firms.

Would you, therefore, be so good as to complete the form overleaf and return it in the enclosed envelope to the address shown above not later than 16th October, 1957.

Yours faithfully,

Under Secretary,
for and on behalf of the Minister of Works.

INFORMATION

1. All information given by you will be treated as strictly confidential and will be used solely in the compilation of general statistical results. The results will be prepared and published in a way which will not reveal the particulars relating to any individual authority unless previous consent is given by the authority.

2. If you wish to keep for reference, a record of the information supplied on this form, further copies of the form will be supplied on application to this office.

3. In all correspondence with this office, the reference number given at the head of page 2 should be quoted.

APPENDIX V

LOCAL AUTHORITIES

Building and Civil Engineering

Employment Return

> In any correspondence please quote this reference number:

General

This return relates only to those employees directly employed by the authority who normally are wholly or mainly engaged on building and civil engineering work, i.e. work which, otherwise, would be undertaken by building and civil engineering firms.

PART I EMPLOYEES

Notes for Guidance in completing Part I of the Return

1. INCLUDE employees (male and female) aged 15 years and over who were employed (i.e. whose National Insurance Cards were held) by the Local Authority on building and civil engineering work.
2. INCLUDE employees (craftsmen and manual workers together with foremen and charge hands) engaged on the construction or repair and maintenance of:-
    - (a) houses and flats,
    - (b) highways (roads, bridges, footpaths, installation of street lighting, surface drains etc.),
    - (c) harbours, wharves, docks, piers, canals, waterways, sea walls and embankments,
    - (d) waterworks (including reservoirs, aqueducts, wells, mains, hydraulic works and pumping stations) sewers and sewage disposal works,
        NOTE: Exclude employees engaged on plant maintenance other than building and civil engineering plant,
    - (e) tramways and trackless trolley systems (permanent way, bridges, overhead wires, etc.),
    - (f) other buildings owned by the Local Authority,
3. INCLUDE in "Other Occupations (PART 1(b) Col. 11) labourers, etc. engaged on the work described above.
4. EXCLUDE (a) administrative, technical and clerical workers,
    - (b) all contractors' and sub-contractors' labour,
    - (c) labour employed on scavenging and street cleaning, the disposal of house refuse, the maintenance of street lighting, snow clearance and the cleaning of public conveniences.
    - (d) "odd job" workers engaged on the day to day maintenance of the authority's offices, etc.

PART I (a) Enter the total number of employees engaged on Building and Civil Engineering work on the pay day in the week ending 28th SEPTEMBER 1957 → | NUMBER |

These Totals should be the same

PART I (b) Enter below the occupations of the employees included in PART 1 (a)

Carpenters and Joiners (1)	Bricklayers (2)	Slaters and Tilers (3)	Plasterers (4)	Painters (5)	Plumbers and Glaziers (6)	Masons (7)	Electricians (8)	Heating and Ventilating Engineers (9)	Other B. & C.E. Crafts (10)	All other Occupations (See Note 3) (11)	TOTAL (12)

PART II APPRENTICES

Notes for Guidance in completing Part II of the Return

(i) INCLUDE apprentices of all ages engaged on the work described above
(ii) EXCLUDE boy labourers
(iii) ENTER Category I electrical apprentices on "Written Indentures" line and Category II apprentices and probationers on "Verbal Agreements" line.

PART II RETURN OF APPRENTICES EMPLOYED ON 28TH SEPTEMBER 1957

Type of Agreement	Carpenters and Joiners (1)	Bricklayers (2)	Slaters and Tilers (3)	Plasterers (4)	Painters (5)	Plumbers and Glaziers (6)	Masons (7)	Electricians (See Note iii) (8)	Heating and Ventilating Engineers (9)	Other B. & C.E. Crafts (10)	TOTALS (Enter NIL if appropriate) (11)
Having WRITTEN Indentures											
Having VERBAL Agreement only											

BIM/AR44/PA

IN CONFIDENCE

**LOCAL AUTHORITIES
NEW TOWN DEVELOPMENT CORPORATIONS
COMMISSION FOR THE NEW TOWNS
BUILDING AND CIVIL ENGINEERING**

Department of the Environment
Building Industries and Materials
Section

Please quote this reference number in any correspondence

SPECIMEN

7th April, 1975

Return of Employment and Output

Dear Sir,

It is again desired to obtain up-to-date information about the distribution of men employed on building and civil engineering work. For this purpose, authorities and undertakings are being asked to make a return of persons employed and the value of work carried out.

Information is required about those employees of the authority who are employed by the undertaking wholly or mainly on building and civil engineering work, i.e. work which would otherwise be undertaken by building and civil engineering firms.

The earlier that the statistics based on this return are available the more valuable they are. Your co-operation in promptly completing this form will therefore be of great assistance to this Department. The late return of even a few forms must lead to delay in production of results.

Would you, therefore, be so good as to complete the form on page 2 and return it in the enclosed envelope to the address shown above **not later than 25th April, 1975.**

Yours faithfully,

*Director of Statistics, for and on behalf of
the Secretary of State for the Environment*

BIM/AR44/PA.

9322 108803/4323004 4550 2/75 DB

(1)

APPENDIX V 573

| Please quote this reference number in any correspondence | BUILDING AND CIVIL ENGINEERING RETURN OF EMPLOYMENT AND OUTPUT | For D.O.E. use only S.G. |

THIS RETURN RELATES ONLY TO THOSE EMPLOYEES DIRECTLY EMPLOYED BY THE AUTHORITY WHO NORMALLY ARE ENGAGED WHOLLY OR MAINLY ON BUILDING AND CIVIL ENGINEERING WORK

THE NOTES ON PAGE 3 SHOULD BE READ BEFORE COMPLETING THIS RETURN

PART 1

Administrative, Professional, Technical and Clerical Staff

State here the number of administrative, professional, technical and clerical staff employed by the undertaking on the pay day in the week ending 12th April, 1975.

Number (Enter NIL if appropriate)

PART 2

Operatives engaged on Building and Civil Engineering work and value of Building and Civil Engineering work done

SPECIMEN

	TYPE OF BUILDING AND CIVIL ENGINEERING WORK	B Operatives employed on the pay day in the week ending 12th April, 1975 (See notes 1, 3, 4, 5, 6)	C Estimated value of work done in the 3 months ending 31st March, 1975 (See Notes 7—8)
		Number	£ (Omit pence)
(I) HOUSES AND FLATS	(a) **New Dwellings** (including site preparation and demolition). (1)		
	(b) **Repair and Maintenance of Dwellings** (including house/flat conversions, extensions, alterations and redecorations). (2)		
(II) WORK OTHER THAN HOUSING	(a) **New Non-Housing Work** (including new roads, site preparation (including demolition), construction, extensions and major alterations — i.e. improvements). (3)		
	(b) **Repair and Maintenance, other than houses and flats** (including road maintenance and minor improvements). (4)		
	Totals of Cols. B. and C. (5)		

TO BE COMPLETED AND SIGNED BY THE PERSON MAKING THE RETURN ON BEHALF OF THE AUTHORITY

Name of Local Authority..

Full postal address ....
(including Town and County)

If your address is correctly printed overleaf you need only state "as overleaf".

Telephone exchange and number :................................ Extension :................

I certify that to the best of my belief the particulars above are correct.

Signed... Date................................1975
(State whether Town Clerk, Manager, Surveyor, etc.)

Please state the name and telephone number of person who
could be consulted if any queries arise, if different from the above......................

THIS PORTION TO BE RETURNED

BIM/AR44/PA. (2)

LOCAL AUTHORITIES
NEW TOWN DEVELOPMENT CORPORATIONS
COMMISSION FOR THE NEW TOWNS
BUILDING AND CIVIL ENGINEERING
RETURN OF EMPLOYMENT AND OUTPUT

INFORMATION

1. The information furnished will be treated as strictly confidential and care will be taken to ensure that any statistics published will not disclose information relating to any individual undertaking.
2. If you wish to keep for reference a record of the information supplied on this form, further copies of the form will be sent on application to this office.
3. In all correspondence with this office, the reference number given at the head of page 2 should be quoted.

NOTES FOR GUIDANCE IN COMPLETING THIS RETURN
GENERAL

1. THIS RETURN RELATES ONLY TO THOSE EMPLOYEES DIRECTLY EMPLOYED BY THE AUTHORITY WHO NORMALLY ARE WHOLLY OR MAINLY ENGAGED ON BUILDING AND CIVIL ENGINEERING WORK, i.e. WORK WHICH, OTHERWISE, WOULD BE UNDERTAKEN BY BUILDING AND CIVIL ENGINEERING FIRMS.

ADMINISTRATIVE, PROFESSIONAL, TECHNICAL AND CLERICAL STAFF (PART 1)

2. Include all persons (including learners and trainees) directly employed by the Authority who do **NOT** do manual work, who are wholly or mainly engaged upon the design, development, control or execution of building and civil engineering work, whether the work is carried out by the Authority's direct labour organisation or by building and civil engineering firms under contract to the Authority, e.g., Managers, Architects, Surveyors, Engineers, other Professionals, Training Officers, Superintendents; General Foremen and other Site Supervisors; any Research, Experimental, Development and Design Staff, Draughtsmen and Tracers, other Technical Grades, and all Office (including Works Office) Staff. The figures should relate to the date specified, or to the nearest possible date for which employee figures are available.

OPERATIVES (PART 2)

3. INCLUDE employees (male and female) aged 16 years and over engaged on building and civil engineering work who were on your payroll on the date specified, or the nearest possible date for which employee figures are available.
4. INCLUDE employees (craftsmen and manual workers, together with foremen and charge hands) engaged on the construction or repair and maintenance of:—
   (a) houses and flats,
   (b) highways (roads, bridges, footpaths, installation of street lighting, surface drains, etc.),
   (c) harbours, wharves, docks, piers, canals, waterways, sea walls and embankments,
   (d) waterworks (including reservoirs, aqueducts, wells, mains, hydraulic works and pumping stations), sewers and sewage disposal works.
   NOTE: Exclude employees engaged on plant maintenance, other than building and civil engineering plant.
   (e) tramways and trackless trolley systems (permanent way, bridges, overhead wires, etc.),
   (f) other buildings owned by the Authority.
5. INCLUDE employees, other than park and green keepers and gardeners, engaged on work in parks and sports grounds, such as the erection of fences, grandstands and buildings and the laying of greens.
6. EXCLUDE:
   (a) administrative, professional, technical and clerical staff. (These are entered at Part 1.)
   (b) all contractors' and sub-contractors' labour,
   (c) park and green keepers and gardeners and labour employed on scavenging, collection and disposal of house refuse, day-to-day maintenance work on street lighting, street cleaning and watering, snow clearance, etc., as distinct from road repairing,
   (d) "odd job" workers engaged on the day-to-day maintenance of the Authority's offices, etc.

VALUE OF WORK DONE

7. THE VALUE OF BUILDING AND CIVIL ENGINEERING WORK DONE is an estimate of the value of the output of the employees described in Notes 3 and 4 above, i.e. a sum calculated to cover the cost of materials, wages and the establishment charges attributable to the work carried out.
8. EXCLUDE
   (a) the value of work done for the authority by contractors and sub-contractors and by other authorities.
   (b) the cost of land, legal costs and architects' fees, etc.
   (c) work done by park and green keepers and gardeners.

THIS PORTION MAY BE DETACHED AND RETAINED

BIM/AR44/PA. (3)

APPENDIX V

IN CONFIDENCE

PUBLIC AUTHORITIES AND UTILITIES
BUILDING AND CIVIL ENGINEERING

Please quote this reference number in any correspondence

Department of the Environment,
SC6 (PA)
Room 1309, Thames House South
Millbank,
London SW1P 4QH

Telephone No.: 01-211 7336 or 211 4704

7th April, 1975

Return of Employment and Output

SPECIMEN

Dear Sir,

It is again desired to obtain up-to-date information about the distribution of men employed on building and civil engineering work. For this purpose, authorities and undertakings are being asked to make a return of persons employed and the value of work carried out.

Information is required about those employees of the authority who are employed by the undertaking wholly or mainly on building and civil engineering work, i.e. work which would otherwise be undertaken by building and civil engineering firms.

The earlier that the statistics based on this return are available the more valuable they are. Your co-operation in promptly completing this form will therefore be of great assistance to this Department. The late return of even a few forms must lead to delay in production of results.

Would you, therefore, be so good as to complete the form on page 2 and return it in the enclosed envelope to the address shown above **not later than 25th April, 1975.**

Yours faithfully,

Director of Statistics for and on behalf
of the Secretary of State for the Environment

Form BIM/AR 44/PU.

(2439) Dd108803 900 1/75 JC&S Ltd Gp3615

CONSTRUCTION AND THE RELATED PROFESSIONS

Reference Number :

PUBLIC AUTHORITIES AND UTILITIES
BUILDING AND CIVIL ENGINEERING
RETURN OF EMPLOYMENT
AND OUTPUT

For official use only

S.G.

THIS RETURN RELATES ONLY TO THOSE EMPLOYEES DIRECTLY EMPLOYED BY THE UNDERTAKING WHO NORMALLY ARE ENGAGED WHOLLY OR MAINLY ON BUILDING AND CIVIL ENGINEERING WORK

THE NOTES ON PAGE 3 SHOULD BE READ BEFORE COMPLETING THE RETURN BELOW

PART 1

Administrative, Professional, Technical and Clerical Staff
State here the number of administrative, professional, technical and clerical staff employed by the undertaking on the pay day in the week ending 12th April, 1975 (See Notes 1 and 2).

Number (Enter NIL if appropriate)

PART 2

OPERATIVES ENGAGED ON BUILDING AND CIVIL ENGINEERING WORK AND
VALUE OF BUILDING AND CIVIL ENGINEERING WORK DONE

A — TYPE OF BUILDING AND CIVIL ENGINEERING WORK			B — Operatives employed by you on the pay day in the week ending 12th April, 1975 (See Notes 1, 3, 4, 5) Number	C — Estimated value of work done by you in the 3 months ending 31st March, 1975 (See Notes 1, 6 and 7) £ (Omit pence)
(I) HOUSES AND FLATS	(a)	**New Dwellings** (including site preparation and demolition). (1)		
	(b)	**Repair and Maintenance of Dwellings** (including house/flat conversions, extensions, alterations and redecorations). (2)		
(II) WORK OTHER THAN HOUSING	(a)	**New Non-Housing Work** (including new roads, site preparation (including demolition), construction, extensions and major alterations — i.e. improvements). (3)		
	(b)	**Repair and Maintenance, other than houses and flats** (including road maintenance and minor improvements). (4)		
		Totals of Cols. B. and C. (5)		

SPECIMEN

TO BE COMPLETED AND SIGNED BY THE PERSON MAKING THE RETURN ON BEHALF OF THE UNDERTAKING.

Name of undertaking ....

Full postal address ....
(including Town and County)

....

Telephone exchange and number : .... Extension : ....

I certify that to the best of my belief the particulars above are correct.

Signed ....   Date 1975
(State whether Town Clerk, Manager, Surveyor, etc.)

Form BIM/AR 44/PU.   THIS PORTION TO BE RETURNED

(2)

APPENDIX V

PUBLIC AUTHORITIES AND UTILITIES

BUILDING AND CIVIL ENGINEERING

RETURN OF EMPLOYMENT AND OUTPUT

INFORMATION

1. The information furnished will be treated as strictly confidential and care will be taken to ensure that any statistics published will not disclose information relating to any individual undertaking.

2. If you wish to keep for reference a record of the information supplied on this form, further copies of the form will be sent on application to this office.

3. In all correspondence with this office the reference number given at the head of page 2 should be quoted.

NOTES FOR GUIDANCE IN COMPLETING THIS RETURN

GENERAL

1. THIS RETURN SHOULD INCLUDE WORK ON THE CONSTRUCTION, REPAIR AND MAINTENANCE OF:—

    (I) HOUSES AND FLATS, OFFICES, DEPOTS, WORKSHOPS, WAREHOUSES, STOREHOUSES, ANY OTHER BUILDINGS OR STRUCTURES CONNECTED WITH YOUR UNDERTAKING; INSTALLATION OF STREET LIGHTING, SURFACE DRAINS, ETC.

    (II) HIGHWAYS, ROADS, FOOTPATHS, BRIDGES, PERMANENT WAY, OVERHEAD WIRES, ROPEWAYS, ETC., AIRCRAFT PAVEMENTS, SIGNALS, TUNNELS, RAILWAYS OF ANY TYPE, RAILWAY STATIONS, ROAD HAULAGE. TRAMWAY, TRACKLESS TROLLEY, OMNIBUS AND MOTOR COACH SERVICES.

    (III) ELECTRIC POWER (GENERATING AND SUPPLY), COAL AND LIGHTING WORKS, FUEL INSTALLATIONS, AERONAUTICAL NAVIGATIONAL SYSTEMS AND AIRFIELD LIGHTING INSTALLATIONS, GAS MAINS AND WORKS, WATERWORKS (RESERVOIRS, AQUEDUCTS, WELLS, HYDRAULIC WORKS, PUMPING STATIONS AND INSTALLATIONS), CONDUITS AND TRUNK DISTRIBUTING AND SERVICE MAINS.

    (IV) CANALS AND WATERS, HARBOURS, DOCKS, WHARVES, PIERS, JETTIES, DREDGING, SEA-WALLS, EMBANKMENTS AND DEFENCES; SEWERS AND SEWAGE DISPOSAL WORKS.

    NOTES: Work done on the maintenance of plant other than building and civil engineering plant should be excluded.
    The cost of any materials provided to a contractor should be included.

ADMINISTRATIVE, PROFESSIONAL, TECHNICAL AND CLERICAL STAFF (PART 1)

2. Include all persons (including learners and trainees) directly employed by the Authority who do **NOT** do manual work who are wholly or mainly engaged upon the design, development, control or execution of building and civil engineering work, whether the work is carried out by the Authority's direct labour organisation or by building and civil engineering firms under contract to the Authority, e.g. Managers, Architects, Surveyors, Engineers, other Professionals, Training Officers, Superintendents, General Foremen and other Site Supervisors. Any Research, Experimental, Development and Design Staff, Draughtsmen and Tracers, other Technical Grades, and all office (including Works Office) Staff. The figures should relate to the date specified, or to the nearest possible date for which employee figures are available.

OPERATIVES (PART 2)

3. INCLUDE employees (male and female) aged 16 years and over, engaged on building and civil engineering work, who are on your payroll on the date specified, or the nearest possible date for which employee figures are available.

4. EXCLUDE all contractors' and sub-contractors' labour.

5. EXCLUDE administrative, professional, technical and clerical staff. (These are entered at Part 1.)

VALUE OF WORK DONE

6. VALUE OF BUILDING AND CIVIL ENGINEERING WORK DONE is an estimate of the value of the output of the persons described in Part 2 above, i.e. a sum calculated to cover the cost of materials, wages and the establishment charges attributable to the work carried out.

7. EXCLUDE (I) the value of work done for the undertaking by contractors and sub-contractors.
    (II) the cost of land, legal costs and architects' etc., fees.

THIS PORTION MAY BE DETACHED AND RETAINED

Form BIM/AR 44/PU.

Department of the Environment

IN CONFIDENCE

BUILDING AND CIVIL ENGINEERING EMPLOYMENT AND OUTPUT RETURN

LOCAL AND PUBLIC AUTHORITIES
NEW TOWN DEVELOPMENT CORPORATIONS
COMMISSIONS FOR THE NEW TOWNS

If the name and address shown below is incorrect in anyway, please correct it.

Department of the Environment,
Building Industries and Materials Section,

Please quote this reference number in any correspondence.

6th October 1975

Dear Sir,

    This enquiry seeks up-to-date information about the building and civil engineering work carried out by direct labour forces of authorities in the public sector.

    Information is required about those employees of the authority who are employed mainly or wholly on building and civil engineering work, i.e. work which would otherwise be undertaken by building and civil engineering firms.

    The purpose of this enquiry is to complete the overall information about activity in the construction industry, of which the direct labour departments of local and public authorities are an integral part. Information on activity in the construction industry is important because its output constitutes a large share of capital investment and because of the size of the labour force employed. The information on construction activity forms an essential component of the National Income Accounts and the Index of Production and provides a basis for the forecasting of future activity within the context of likely developments for the economy as a whole, as well as for assessing the total demand for building materials and for the purposes of this Department as sponsor Department for the construction industry.

    The results of the enquiry will appear in various publications including a future issue of "Housing and Construction Statistics", published by the Government Statistical Service every quarter and available from HM Stationery Office.

    The earlier that the statistics based on this return are available the more valuable they are. The late return of even a few forms must lead to delay in the production of results and your co-operation in completing the form promptly will be of great assistance to this Department.

    Would you, therefore please complete the form (including the certificate on Page 4) and return it in the enclosed envelope **NOT LATER THAN FRIDAY 24th OCTOBER 1975.**

    All information supplied in this return will be treated as confidential.

Yours faithfully

G PENRICE
Director of Statistics for and on behalf of the
the Secretary of State for the Environment

BIM/AR 45/PA

APPENDIX V 579

NOTES

TRAINEES

A trainee is a person (including Apprentice or Probationer) who is learning an administrative, professional, technical or manual skill, and whose employer has undertaken to provide training for him for at least a year, include trainees of all ages engaged on B & C.E. or associated work.

1. ADMINISTRATIVE, PROFESSIONAL, TECHNICAL AND CLERICAL EMPLOYEES

Enter in the appropriate boxes the number of employees who do not do manual work and who were on your payroll on 9th October 1975 or the nearest possible date.

INCLUDE All persons (including learners and trainees) directly employed by the Authority who do not do manual work and who are wholly or mainly engaged upon the design, development or execution of building and civil engineering work, whether the work is carried out by the Authority's direct labour organisation or by building and civil engineering firms under contract to the Authority.

DESCRIPTION OF STAFF. Professional and technical staff should be shown according to the main duties on which they are engaged, except that professional staff engaged upon administrative or managerial duties for which they are required to be professionally qualified should be entered under their professions and not as managerial.

(1) MANAGERIAL. Include site, area, project, contract and office managers etc (i.e. all staff with a managerial status not included in occupations 2-4).

(2) ARCHITECTS. Include professionally qualified architects engaged in their profession.

(3) SURVEYORS. Include professionally qualified surveyors and quantity surveyors engaged in their profession.

(4) ENGINEERS. Include professionally qualified engineers engaged in their profession.

(5) TECHNICAL STAFF. Include site engineers and surveyors not professionally qualified, buyers, planning estimating, work study research and laboratory assistants, instructors and other persons employed in a technical capacity not included in occupation 1.

(6) DRAUGHTSMEN AND TRACERS. Include all architectural and construction draughtsmen and tracers, design detailers etc.

(7) FOREMEN. Include all supervisors on sites who are NOT employed on manual work.

(8) CLERICAL AND OFFICE STAFF. Include clerks, buyers, purchasers, stores and general office staff.

	Type of Employee	Excluding Trainees	Trainees
1	MANAGERIAL		
2	ARCHITECTS		
3	SURVEYORS		
4	ENGINEERS		
5	TECHNICAL STAFF		
6	DRAUGHTSMEN AND TRACERS		
7	FOREMEN		
8	CLERICAL AND OFFICE STAFF		
	TOTALS		

2. OPERATIVES AND TRAINEES

Enter in the appropriate boxes the number of operatives and trainees (including working foremen) who were on your payroll on 9th October 1975 or the nearest possible date

Operatives and trainees directly employed by the Authority.

Include trainees, working foremen, operatives engaged in transport work, stores and warehouses.

Include employees (male and female) aged 16 years and over who were employed on building and civil engineering work on the day specified or the nearest possible date for which employee figures are readily available.

INCLUDE employees (craftsmen and manual workers together with foremen and chargehands) engaged on the construction or repair and maintenance of:

Houses and flats.
Roads, bridges, footpaths, installation of street lighting, surface drains etc.
Harbours, wharves, docks, piers, canals, waterways, sea walls and embankments.
Waterworks (including reservoirs, aqueducts, wells, mains, hydraulic works, and pumping stations) sewers and sewerage disposal works.

INCLUDE Employees, other than park and green keepers and gardeners, engaged on work in parks and sports grounds, such as erection of fences, grandstands and buildings and the laying of greens.

EXCLUDE

All contractors and sub contractors labour.
Park and green keepers, gardeners and labour employed on scavenging and street cleaning, the disposal of house refuse, the maintenance of street lighting, snow clearing and the cleaning of public conveniences.
Employees engaged on plant maintenance other than building and civil engineering plant.
Tramways and trackless trolley systems owned by the Authority.
"Odd Job" workers engaged on day to day maintenance of the Authority's offices etc.
Administrative, professional, technical and clerical staff (these are entered at 1 above).

	Type of Employee	Excluding Trainees	Trainees
1	BRICKLAYERS		
2	MASONS		
3	CARPENTER/JOINERS		
4	PAINTERS		
5	PLASTERERS		
6	ROOF SLATERS AND TILERS		
7	FLOOR, WALL & CEILING TILERS		
8	GLAZIERS		
9	PAVIORS		
10	PLANT MECHANICS		
11	MISCELLANEOUS CRAFTSMEN		
12	PLUMBERS AND GAS FITTERS		
13	NATURAL GAS CONVERSION WORKERS		
14	HEAT'G & VENTILAT'G ENG WORKERS		
15	OTHER M.E. SERVICE WORKERS		
16	ELECTRICIANS		
17	CRANE DRIVERS		
18	EARTH MOVING PLANT OPERATORS		
19	OTHER MECHANICAL PLANT OPERATORS		
20	SCAFFOLDERS		
21	BAR BENDERS & STEEL FIXERS		
22	STEEL ERECTORS AND SHEETERS		
23	CONCRETORS		
24	DEMOLISHERS		
25	OTHER B & C.E. SKILLED WORKERS		
26	UNSKILLED LABOURERS		
27	CANTEEN WORKERS		
28	OTHER OCCUPATIONS		
	TOTALS		

BIM/AR 45/PA   Page 2.

2. OPERATIVES AND TRAINEES DIRECTLY EMPLOYED BY THE AUTHORITY.

Operatives who use more than one skill should be shown under their main occupation.
All labourers and general operatives should be shown under occupations 25 or 26.

(1) **Bricklayers.** Include specialist bricklayers and other workers in the trade except labourers or general operatives.

(2) **Masons.** Include monumental masons, stone carvers, stone polishers and other workers in the trade except labourers or general operatives.

(3) **Carpenters/Joiners.** Include carpenters, joiners, formwork carpenters, joiner bench hands, wood-working machinists and operatives, setters out and other workers in the trade except labourers or general operatives.

(4) **Painters.** Include painters and decorators, industrial painters, french polishers, signwriters and other workers in the trade except labourers, or general operatives.

(5) **Plasterers.** Include solid and fibrous plasterers, moulders and other workers in the trade except labourers or general operatives. Dry-lining and partition operatives should also be included.

(6) **Roof Slaters and Tilers.** Include felters, roofers and other workers in the trade except labourers or general operatives.

(7) **Floor, Wall and Ceiling Tilers.** Include composition floor layers, mosaic workers, parquet floorers terrazzo workers, mastic asphalters, metal fixers (ceiling systems) and other workers in the trade except labourers or general operatives.

(8) **Glaziers** Include patent glaziers, lead light workers, glass production or processing workers and other workers in the trade except labourers or general operatives.

(9) **Paviors** Include pavior street masons, tar paviors, potmen and other workers in the trade except labourers or general operatives.

(10) **Plant Mechanics.** Include plant maintenance mechanics, motor mechanics & other workers in the trade except labourers or general operatives.

(11) **Miscellaneous Craftsmen.** (excluding mechanical engineering services). Include thermal insulation operatives, ductwork erectors, craftsmen generally employed in industries other than construction and any other craftsmen not covered in occupations 1 to 10 and 12 to 16.

(12) **Plumbers and Gas Fitters.** Include chemical plumbers, lumber welders, hot water fitters, and other workers in the trade except labourers or general operatives.

(13) **Natural Gas Conversion Workers.** Include operatives (conversion fitters (including gas fitters, plumbers, heating and ventilating fitters) engaged in the conversion of appliances to natural gas or in the preliminary work.

(14) **Heating and Ventilating Engineering Workers.** Include heating and ventilating fitters, or fitter/welders, heating fitters and other workers in the trade except labourers or general operatives.

(15) **Other Mechanical Engineering Service fixers.** Include oil burner mechanics, pipe fitters, refrigeration mechanics, welders (including oxyacetylene, metallic-arc or shielded arc welders) and any other person not included in occupations 12, 13 or 14 engaged as a manual worker in mechanical engineering services trades except labourers or general operatives.

(16) **Electricians.** Include cable jointers and other workers in the trade except labourers or general operatives.

(17) **Crane Drivers.**

(18) **Earthmoving Plant Operators.** Include operators of excavators, front end shovels, motorised scrapers, motor graders, tractors and trenching machines.

(19) **Other Mechanical Plant Operators.** Include mechanical equipment operators, compressor air tools or paving machine operators, plant and dumper drivers, oilers and greasers, pumpmen, banksmen slingers, but excluding crane drivers, earth moving plant operators, concretors and demolishers.

(20) **Scaffolders**

(21) **Bar Benders and Steel Fixers.**

(22) **Steel Erectors and Sheeters.** Include iron roofers.

(23) **Concretors.** Include plus-rated workers involved in placing vibrating or finishing concrete, precast concrete erectors and fixers, prestressing and pre-tensioning operatives.

(24) **Demolishers** Include general labourers using compressed air drills or pneumatic punching machines or spades, sorters, improvers, mattockmen, topmen, burner topmen, burner groundmen, shorers (timber), shorer's mates.

(25) **Other B & C.E. Skilled Workers.** Include labourers and general operatives entitled to extra payment for skill and responsibility under the appropriate Working Rule Agreement, including any employed in trades covered by occupations 1-16. Any employed in trades covered by occupations 17-24 should be shown under these occupations. Steeplejacks, divers, including surface demand and helmet divers and life linesmen, excavation operatives, including heading drivers, manhole builders, pipe layers, pipe jointers and timbermen, piling and well drilling operatives, including borer driver, vibrator and specialist piling operatives, well or rock drillers and shaft sinkers, tunnel miners, including soft heading miners, blacksmiths, including markers-out.

(26) **Unskilled Labourers.** Include labourers and general operatives not entitled to extra payment for skill or responsibility under the appropriate Working Rule Agreement. Extra payment on account of conditions of work should not be treated as payment for skill.

(27) **Canteen Workers.** Include workers wholly involved in the supply of food and drink for immediate consumption.

(28) **Other Occupations.** Include transport drivers, manual workers in stores and warehouses, office cleaners and other persons not covered in other categories (Note Miscellaneous craftsmen are in occupation 11. miscellaneous B & C.E. skilled skilled workers are in occupation 25. unskilled labourers are in occupation 26).

APPENDIX V

FOR DOE. USE
S.G.

A. OPERATIVES (INCLUDING TRAINEES) DIRECTLY EMPLOYED BY THE AUTHORITY.

These are defined in Section 2.

The total in column A should be the same as the total for operatives and trainees entered in Section 2.

B. VALUE OF WORK DONE BY DIRECTLY EMPLOYED STAFF.

The value of building and civil engineering work done should be an estimate of the value of the output of the employee described in column A, i.e., a sum calculated to cover the cost of materials. Wages and establishment charges attributable to the work carried out.

EXCLUDE the value of work done for the Authority by contractors and sub-contractors.

EXCLUDE the cost of land, legal costs and architect's fees etc.

3. OPERATIVES (INCLUDING TRAINEES) AND THE VALUE OF WORK DONE.

TYPE OF BUILDING AND CIVIL ENGINEERING WORK		A Operatives (including trainees) employed on 9th October 1975	B Estimated value of work done in the 3 months ending 30th September 1975
HOUSING	1. New housing including site preparation and demolition.		£
	2. Housing repair and maintenance including house/flat conversion alterations and re-decorations.		£
NON-HOUSING WORK	3. New non-housing including new roads, site preparation and demolition, construction, extensions and alterations and improvements		£
	4. Non-housing repair and maintenance including road maintenance and minor improvements.		£
	TOTALS		£

TO BE COMPLETED AND SIGNED BY THE PERSON MAKING THE RETURN ON BEHALF OF THE AUTHORITY.

Telephone Number .... Extension ....

I certify that to the best of my belief the particulars above are correct.

Signed .... Date ....
(Please state whether Chief Executive, Manager, Architect, Surveyor, Engineer etc.)

APPENDIX VI

SITE RETURNS 1941–54

History of Enquiries made by the Ministry of Works and Selected Specimen Forms

(Text References: Sections 3.7.4, 3.8 and 3.9)

(a) Date of Introduction
April–May 1941.

(b) Frequency
Monthly until November 1954.

(c) Form References
Form WB1 and Form WB1/CL until March 1947 when both were replaced by Form CPS23.

(d) Specimen Forms Included

Form Ref.	Date	Title	Page
WB1	October 1942	Government Building Programme. Building and Civil Engineering Works—Monthly Return WB1	585
WB1/CL	1942	Building Under Civil Licence. Building and Civil Engineering Works—Monthly Return WB1/CL	587
CPS23	Undated	National Building Programme—Contractors' Monthly Return	588

(e) Circulation
Contractors on individual building sites where work costing more than certain defined amounts was in progress (see para. (f) 'History' below). The responsibility for obtaining returns on forms WB1 and WB1/CL rested with the Government Departments responsible, as the authorizing, sponsoring or licensing agency, for the work, who then transmitted the information to the Ministry of Works. Returns on Form CPS23 were obtained directly from contractors by the MOW.

(f) History of the Returns

Form WB1 provided details of the labour employed, materials used and progress made on the last pay-day of each month on jobs of over £5,000 in value done in connection with the Government Building Programme. The particular specimen form reproduced was in use in October 1942; the returns in use for part (at least) of the earlier period were somewhat more detailed, requiring a breakdown of labour employed into some twenty-two categories. Departments also returned a monthly summary (Form WB/S) which showed the *total* labour employed on their work including estimates for non-returns and for jobs below £5,000 in value.

Form WB1/CL required a total return only of men employed and the value of work done (see specimen copy) for each job above a certain value carried out under a civil licence (from April 1942 the value was set at £1,000 and later raised to £2,000).

Form CPS23 came into use in March 1947 and remained in use until the end of building controls in 1954.* Coverage of the return varied from time to time but full details of these changes, particularly as regards their timing, appear to be no longer available. Generally speaking, however, the returns were obtained in respect of all new housing work (initially it was intended to cover *all* housing work carrying WBA priority but by 1950 it had been confined to *new* work) regardless of value, and all non-housing work above a certain value (both new work and repairs and maintenance)—initially this value was set at £2,000; it was reduced to £1,000 in the case of new work in 1949 and then returned to £2,000 in 1953. In 1954 after the 'free limit' for certain designated buildings had been raised to £25,000 (see Table 3.5) the collection of returns for jobs below this limit continued where information about them was available.

The specimen of Form CPS23 reproduced here is one in use *circa* January 1948. Subsequently question (1) in Part 2 of the form was sub-divided between 'own labour' and 'sub-contractor's labour' and question (2) of Part 2 was dropped. Specific instructions were also added to the effect that Working Principals should be excluded. The timing of these changes is not known, neither is it known whether other changes were made since few of the questionnaires used have survived.

---

* CPS23 not only replaced the former monthly site returns, WB1 and WB1/CL, it also replaced weekly site labour returns which had been made to the Ministry of Labour on Forms ED 622/H and ED 622(2) for housing and non-housing jobs respectively.

APPENDIX VI 585

GOVERNMENT BUILDING PROGRAMME
BUILDING & CIVIL ENGINEERING WORKS—MONTHLY RETURN W.B.1.

DEPARTMENT		SITE OF JOB	TOWN COUNTY
JOB		IS SITE SCHEDULED UNDER THE ESSENTIAL WORK (BUILDING AND CIVIL ENGINEERING) ORDER, 1941 & 1942?	*YES *NO · STRIKE OUT WORD NOT APPLICABLE.
DEPARTMENT'S CONTRACT NO.		NO. OF EMPLOYEES (MALES OVER 16 Yrs.) ON LAST PAY DAY OF OCTOBER, 1942. MAIN AND SUB-CONTRACTOR'S LABOUR TO BE SHEWN AS ONE FIGURE. (SEE ALSO ON BACK)	
M. O. W. P. REFERENCE NO.		EXCLUDE ABSENTEES FROM ITEMS 1–11.	
		1. CARPENTERS AND JOINERS	
DATE WORK BEGAN		2. BRICKLAYERS	
ESTIMATED DATE OF COMPLETION		3. SLATERS AND TILERS	
ESTIMATED TOTAL COST		4. PLASTERERS	
PERCENTAGE OF WORK COMPLETED		5. PAINTERS	
VALUE OF WORK DONE DURING OCTOBER	£	6. PLUMBERS AND GLAZIERS	
		7. ELECTRICIANS	

MATERIALS IN **OCTOBER, 1942.**

	RECEIVED	USED	BALANCE REQUIRED (viz.; NOT YET DELIVERED) TO COMPLETE JOB		
BRICKS (IN THOUSANDS)				8. FITTERS, HEATING, HOT WATER AND GAS	
				9. BUILDERS' LABOURERS	
				10. NAVVIES	
CEMENT (TONS)				11. ALL OTHER OCCUPATIONS	
				TOTAL (1–11)	
SIGNATURE				12. ABSENTEES (I.E. THOSE AWAY FROM WORK FOR LESS THAN A FORTNIGHT) ON LAST PAY DAY OF MONTH	
				TOTAL (1–12)	
DATE				CLERICALS	MALE FEMALE

SPECIMEN

PLEASE FILL UP INFORMATION ON BACK OF FORM

(17367D) Wt 8105/L32 16000 9/42 H J R & L. Gp 747 (18287D) Wt 8105/L32 17000 10/42

NAMES OF MAIN CONTRACTORS AND PRINCIPAL SUB-CONTRACTORS

NAME AND ADDRESS OF MAIN CONTRACTOR(S)	TOTAL LABOUR — STATE SEPARATELY FOR EACH CONTRACTOR, INCLUDING ABSENTEES BUT EXCLUDING CLERICALS
TEL. No.	
NAMES AND ADDRESSES OF PRINCIPAL SUB-CONTRACTOR(S)	
ALL OTHER SUB-CONTRACTORS	
TOTAL LABOUR (EXCLUDING CLERICALS) (THIS FIGURE SHOULD AGREE WITH TOTAL (INCLUDING ABSENTEES) GIVEN OVERLEAF)	

SPECIMEN

APPENDIX VI

BUILDING UNDER CIVIL LICENCE
BUILDING & CIVIL ENGINEERING WORKS—MONTHLY RETURN W.B.1/CL

In filling up the answers to the following questions, BLOCK CAPITALS must be used. One W.B.1/CL form must be filled up for each job on which work has been done during the month.

CIVIL LICENCE NUMBER	
GOVERNMENT DEPARTMENT SPONSORING ..	
NAME AND ADDRESS OF CONTRACTOR ..	
LOCATION OF JOB	
DESCRIPTION OF JOB	
(a) NUMBER OF MEN EMPLOYED ON LAST PAY DAY IN...............	
(b) VALUE OF WORK DONE ON JOB DURING MONTH OF...............	

SPECIMEN

(a) The answer to this question should only be given if work on the site is still in progress on the last pay day of the month.

(b) The figure given should include cost of wages paid, value of materials used, plus regular proportion of overheads, profit, etc.

This Form must be returned each month to the Divisional Licensing Officer at

MINISTRY OF WORKS

NATIONAL BUILDING PROGRAMME — CONTRACTORS MONTHLY RETURN

THIS FORM CANCELS FORMS E.D.622 (2), E.D.622 (H), W.B.I, and W.B.I/C.I.

IMPORTANT. It is essential that the information in PART 2 should be as accurate as possible and submitted by the first of the month following that to which it relates.

Show operatives of the Building and Civil Engineering Industries, males aged 16 and over, including sub-contractors' labour and absentees, i.e., all those on the payroll.

Exclude females, clerical staff, prisoners of war and military labour.

Please use ink when completing the form.

COMPLETE PART 2 ONLY

When the form has been completed, fold as indicated overleaf and post it.

NO STAMP REQUIRED.

PART 1 FOR OFFICIAL USE

DEPT.	DEPT'S. REF. NO.	LICENCE NO.	INDEX REFERENCE

DESCRIPTION OF WORK.

NAME AND ADDRESS OF BLDG. OWNER, LOCAL OR OTHER AUTHORITY.

CONTRACTOR'S NAME AND SITE ADDRESS

ESTIMATED VALUE £
ACTUAL VALUE £
CONTRACT PERIOD
PROPOSED START
ACTUAL START

PART 2

1	NUMBER OF MEN EMPLOYED ON THIS JOB AS ON PAYROLL ON THE LAST PAY-DAY OF THE MONTH	
2	GROSS NUMBER OF MEN ADDED TO PAY-SHEET DURING THE MONTH (SINCE LAST PAY-DAY LAST MONTH)	
3	GROSS NUMBER OF MEN DISCHARGED, LEFT OR -TRANSFERRED DURING SAME PERIOD	
4	ESTIMATED VALUE OF WORK COMPLETED DURING SAME MONTH	£
5	PERCENTAGE OF CONTRACT COMPLETED TO DATE	%

If this job HAS NOT STARTED*, when is it expected
IS SUSPENDED,
to START* ?
RESTART

Return for month of .... 194.......

Signature ....

Date ....

SPECIMEN

APPENDIX VII

SAMPLE RETURNS OF OUTPUT AND EMPLOYMENT 1945–77

History of Enquiries made by the Ministry of Works and its Successor Departments (currently Department of the Environment) and Selected Specimen Forms

(Text References: Sections 3.8, 3.9 and 4.4)

(a) Date of Introduction

September/October 1945.

(b) Frequency

Monthly except, generally speaking (there are a few exceptions), those months in which a census was taken (see Appendix IV) and, from 1971, the month of June (the return for which was discontinued to avoid duplication with the DE annual census) until 1978 when the return of employment in months between quarterly enquiries was discontinued. Output statistics were not collected on this return until February 1950 and then only on a quarterly cycle (see below for details).

(c) Form Reference

BCE/SR ... (numbered serially) from 1946 to May 1956 and then BIM/SR ... (serial numbering continuing) up to the present day. Since 1965, in those months in which output statistics have been collected, two versions of the return have been used, one for labour and value and one bearing the suffix 'B' for labour only.

(d) Specimen Forms Included

Form Ref.	Date	Title	Page
BCE/SR89	October 1954	Quarterly Return of Labour and Output	593
BIM/SR324	June 1977	Return of Persons Employed and Output	595
BIM/SR322	May 1977	Monthly Employment Return	598

(e) Circulation

Until August 1954 only contractors in the 'main' trades (defined in Section 3.3.2) on the register which had been maintained in accordance with Defence Regulation 56AB were covered. After August 1954 the sample was extended to the 'specialist' trades preparatory to the adoption of a new register drawn up in accordance with the Standard Industrial Classification (see Section 4.1). The new register became the sampling frame for these enquiries with effect from May 1955. Reference should be made to Section 4.4.1 regarding the subsequent maintenance of the register and the addition of 'special list' firms to the sample from July 1974. Currently the sample is stratified by trade, region and size of firm except that all 'large' firms are covered; it would appear that this has always been the practice since the initiation of the enquiry.

(f) Processing of Returns

Currently the Department of the Environment.

(g) Availability of Data from Individual Returns

Individual returns are treated as strictly confidential under the terms, currently, of the Statistics of Trade Act 1947.

(h) History of the Return

The purpose of the account given here, as with the histories of the other enquiries, is to draw attention to those developments in the history of the return which affect the range of information collected or which appear to be important from the point of view of its interpretation. No attempt is made to provide a completely comprehensive account of all the changes made especially those which represent small refinements and minor alterations in wording and emphasis. Further, the history it is possible to write is constrained to some extent by the fact that a complete set of questionnaires is not available.

As indicated earlier, there are two versions of the return: a return for employment only which, with adaptations, has been in use throughout the whole period (monthly) until 1978 and a return for both employment and output which, again with adaptations, has been in use since 1950 to obtain data for those quarters not covered by a census (see Appendix IV). For a time (during the period from 1957 to the end of 1963) use was also made of the return to obtain information about new contracts and orders (see Appendix VIII) until a separate form for this inquiry was introduced in January 1964. The geographical coverage of the return has always been Great Britain but it may be noted that it was felt desirable in November 1966 to add the express instruction that the information given on the return 'should relate to Great Britain only (i.e. excluding Northern Ireland)', possibly as a consequence of the fact that an enquiry on similar lines had been initiated in Northern Ireland in that year (see Section 9.2.1).

Initially a return only of the total 'number of building and civil engineering operatives (males aged 16 years of age and over) on the payroll for pay-day in the week beginning ...' was required (main contractors being instructed not to include the employees of sub-contractors or administrative and clerical staff and Working Principals). The main developments in the return subsequently are listed below according to subject.

Operatives (see also under 'analyses by type of work and sector' and 'labour-only sub-contractors' below).

September 1946. A division of the number of operatives between 'craftsmen' and 'other operatives' was introduced and continued in each enquiry up to and including that for October 1947 (possibly up to December 1947, the questionnaire for which is not available; no enquiry was held in November 1947).

October 1954. Two major changes were made. First the coverage of operatives was changed to 'all persons (male and female) aged 15 years and over ...'. Secondly the thrice yearly output return now required a breakdown of both employment and output by type of work (see specimen form BCE/SR89).

January 1955. The breakdown of operatives employed by type of work was extended to incorporate a separate category for operatives who cannot be assigned to any of the types of work mentioned ('e.g. transport workers, warehouse and cleaning staff and operatives engaged on the manufacture of goods for sale, etc.').

November 1956. Return required of the number of operatives working in Wales and in Scotland respectively. This was the only sample return in which these questions were asked.

August 1973. The reference to the age of employees (operatives and others) was changed from '15 years and over' to '16 years and over' as a consequence of the raising of the school leaving age.

Working Principals/Working Proprietors (see also under 'Labour-only sub-contractors' below).

January 1948. Question on the number of Working Principals introduced.

November 1971. Replacement of the category 'Working Principal' by 'Working Proprietor' with effect from November 1971 (see Section 4.2.3.6 regarding the nature of this distinction and the current specimen form, BIM/SR324, for details).

A(P)TC Employees

May 1965. An expansion in the coverage of employment to include a return of 'administrative, technical and clerical' staff defined as in the April 1965 census (see Appendix IV). The word 'Professional' was added in November 1965, followed, in May 1966, by amplification of the definition as in the April 1966 census (see Appendix IV).

Output (see also under 'Analyses by type of work and sector' and 'Labour-only sub-contractors' below).

February 1950. Question on the estimated *total* value of work done introduced. Thereafter it was repeated three times a year to obtain quarterly output data—the quarter not covered in the censuses (see Appendix IV).

October 1954. Breakdown by type of work introduced as for labour (see specimen form BCE/SR89).

July 1974. Questions on the value of work done under sub-contract were introduced, and repeated in subsequent output returns, relating to the value of work done under sub-contract, identical to those introduced in the census in October 1974 (see sections D and E of specimen form BIM/SR324 for details).

Analyses by Type of Work and Sector

The instructions and definitions relating to the completion of this part of the output and employment return were amplified or amended on several occasions. Apart from a difference in timing, these revisions correspond with those made to the April census forms in the period 1956–70. It is most convenient, therefore, to examine the changes made to this part of both the sample and census enquiries together and this we do in Appendix IV (see part dealing with the history of the April censuses 1956–70). In addition to these changes one revision, affecting the sample return alone, was made in January 1956: instructions were added to classify work on the repair and maintenance of builders' plant (hitherto unmentioned) to the same category as non-housing repairs and maintenance work for other than private owners or developers.

Labour-only sub-contractors (see also under 'Output' above)

January 1955. The precise instruction was added: 'sub-contractors supplying labour only to main contractors should enter in the appropriate sections of Cols B and C (see form BCE SR89) the number of operatives on their pay-roll and the value of the operatives' wages, etc. Main contractors should include in their return the value of materials used by such operatives.'

January 1959. Additional instruction to labour-only sub-contractors to record 'working partners' in the group as 'Working Principals'.

July 1965 and July 1966. Questions were asked in these two enquiries only about the value of materials supplied by contractors to sub-contractors.

APPENDIX VII 593

CONFIDENTIAL

PROGRAMMES AND STATISTICS OFF
MINISTRY OF WORKS,

BUILDING AND CIVIL ENGINEERING CONTRACTING

Quarterly Return of Labour and Output

Sir(s),

It is necessary for the Government regularly to have certain information about Building and Civil Engineering Work.

The undertaking described below falls within the scope of the Inquiry. Therefore notice is hereby given by the Minister of Works

to:

to supply in relation to the undertaking carried on by you the information specified overleaf, and to return this form to the above address not later than **SATURDAY, 6th NOVEMBER, 1954.**

This notice is served under the provisions of Section 1 of the Statistics of Trade Act, 1947, for the purpose of obtaining information necessary for the discharge by Government Departments of their functions.

I am Sir,

Your obedient servant,

SPECIMEN

[signature]

Under Secretary,
for and on behalf of the Minister of Works.

1. This return relates to all types of building and civil engineering work but not to merchanting.
2. All information given by you will be treated as strictly confidential and will be used solely in the compilation of general statistical results. The results will be prepared and published in a way which will not reveal the particulars relating to any individual undertaking unless previous consent is given by the undertaking.
3. If you wish to keep for reference, a record of the information supplied by you on this form, further copies of the form will be supplied on application to this office.
4. In all correspondence with this office, the reference number given at the head of the page overleaf should be quoted.

TO BE COMPLETED AND SIGNED BY THE PERSON MAKING THE RETURN ON BEHALF OF THE UNDERTAKING

Trading Name of Firm ....

Full Postal Address
of Head or Registered Office ....
(including Town and County)

....

Telephone Exchange & Number..

Is the undertaking closed down permanently? Yes }
                                                              No } Delete whichever does not apply.

I certify that to the best of my belief the particulars above and overleaf are correct.

Signed .... Date...............................1954.
      (State whether Proprietor, Director, Manager, Partner, Secretary.)

BCE/SR 89

MINISTRY OF WORKS

BUILDING AND CIVIL ENGINEERING CONTRACTING

Quarterly Return of Labour and Output

FOR OFFICIAL USE

Reference Number

Size Group

WORKING PRINCIPALS (Owners, Managers, Partners, etc., who do manual work).

Number

State here the number of Working Principals

PART II. OPERATIVES EMPLOYED AND VALUE OF WORK DONE.
Complete Cols. B and C after reading the notes below.

NOTES

GENERAL
For the purpose of this return the labour employed and the value of work done on the jobs ancillary to the main project should be classified as part of the main project, e.g., a garage built for a house should be included in "Houses and Flats"; a private road, a power station or an office block constructed as part of a factory scheme should be included with the factory in "New Industrial Work"; shops with dwellings should be classified as shops if the shop constitutes the major part of the job.

OPERATIVES (Col. B)

1. INCLUDE all persons (male and female) aged 15 years and over employed on manual work, whether full or part time, whose National Insurance Cards are held by you on the pay day specified in Col. B; these will include working foremen, cleaners, and operatives engaged in transport work, stores and warehouses.
2. EXCLUDE only administrative, technical and clerical workers.

VALUE (Col. C)

3. VALUE OF BUILDING AND CIVIL ENGINEERING WORK DONE by you is an estimate of the amount charged or chargeable to customers. EXCLUDE the value of work done **for you** by other contractors AND EXCLUDE the cost of land, legal costs and architects', etc., fees.
4. INCLUDE the value of Building and Civil Engineering Work done by working principals.
5. INCLUDE the value of Building and Civil Engineering Work done by your own operatives on the construction or maintenance of your own premises.
6. INCLUDE the value of goods made and used by you for the Building and Civil Engineering Work valued in Col. C. EXCLUDE the value of goods made and sold to other contractors or to merchants or put to stock.

A TYPE OF WORK		B Operatives employed by you on the pay day in the week ending **30th October 1954** (See notes 1 & 2)	C Estimated value of building and civil engineering work done by you in the 3 months ending **30th September 1954** (See notes 3, 4, 5 & 6)
			£ (Omit shillings & pence)
I. HOUSES AND FLATS.	(a) **New Construction**, including site preparation and demolition, for **Local Authorities, Government Departments, Public Utilities, Nationalised Industries, Housing Associations and New Town Corporations.** [1]		
	(b) **New Construction**, including site preparation and demolition, for **Private Owners and Private Developers.** [2]		
	(c) **Repair and Maintenance**, including house/flat conversions, extensions and alterations. [3]		
II. WORK (OTHER THAN HOUSES AND FLATS) FOR PRIVATE OWNERS AND DEVELOPERS.	(a) **New Industrial**: construction, extension, major alteration and site preparation (including demolition) of Factories, Warehouses, Industrial Premises, Steel Works, Coke Ovens, Oil Refineries, etc. [4]		
	(b) **New Non-Industrial**: construction, extension, major alteration and site preparation (including demolition) of Farm Buildings, Offices, Shops, Hotels and Public Houses, Places of Worship, Clubs, Places of Entertainment, Road Goods Transport Premises, etc. [5]		
	(c) **Repair and Maintenance.** [6]		
III. ALL OTHER WORK.†	(a) **New Work not included above**: construction, extension, major alteration, and site preparation (including demolition). **Exclude** Steel Works (see II(a) above). [7]		
	(b) **Repair and Maintenance not included above.** [8]		
	Totals of Cols. B and C* [9]		

* The totals of Cols. B and C should represent the total number of operatives employed by you and the total value of work done.

† WORK ON UTILITIES AND SOCIAL SERVICES, including work for :—
Government Departments, Nationalised Industries, Canal, River, Dock and Harbour Boards,
Local Authorities [other than Housing included in I(a)], Hospital Boards.

APPENDIX VII

BIM/SR324(amd4/77) (D2, D3, D4, D5, A7)

Department of the Environment

Please quote in any correspondence

If the name and address shown above is incorrect in any respect, please correct it · Ensure that the address above shows through the window of the return envelope when inserting the completed form

Building, Civil Engineering and Allied Industries

RETURN OF PERSONS EMPLOYED AND OUTPUT
All work including repair and maintenance

29 June 1977

Dear Sir(s)

1 The purpose of this inquiry is to obtain information about the construction industries which together with similar data from other industries will provide a comprehensive review of industrial activity. Inquiries into the activities of the construction industries are essential because of the size of the labour force employed, and because the output they produce is a large share of capital investment. Information from the return is also needed for the compilation of mailing lists for the circulation by DOE to selected firms of technical information and of notices of lectures and conferences.

2 To avoid duplication of inquiries, and hence reduce the burden of form filling, details of your name and address, industrial classification and employment may be passed to the Construction Industry Training Board, in accordance with the provisions of Section 4 of the Employment and Training Act 1973.

3 The earlier that the statistics based on this return are available the more valuable they are and your co-operation in carefully and promptly completing the form will therefore be of real assistance to the Department. As the late return of even a few forms must lead to delay in the publication of results, please do not hold up this return until audited figures are available but give the closest possible estimate. If you encounter any difficulties in completing the form, the staff of the Building Industries Section at the address shown above will be pleased to help you in any way possible. The completed form should be returned to the address above **not later than Wednesday 20 July 1977.**

4 This notice is served under the provisions of Section 1 of the Statistics of Trade Act, 1947, for the purpose of obtaining information necessary for the discharge by Government Departments of their functions. Under this Act the rendering of a return is compulsory. In accordance with the Act all information supplied in this return will be treated as confidential. Summarised results will be published by HMSO in 'Housing and Construction Statistics'.

Yours faithfully

Principal Director of Statistics   **Under-Secretary**

for and on behalf of the Secretary of State for the Environment

CONSTRUCTION AND THE RELATED PROFESSIONS

BIM/SR324
In confidence

Please read the accompanying notes alongside each section

For official use

A Working proprietors: ie self-employed persons
Do **not** include persons entered here in any other section of the form.

Number
(enter NIL if appropriate)

B Administrative, professional, technical and clerical employees. State here the number of employees who do **not** do manual work and who were on your payroll on **7 July 1977** or the nearest possible date.

Number
(enter NIL if appropriate)

C Both main and sub-contractors should complete this section
Value of work carried out in the period 1 April – 30 June 1977 and operatives employed by type of work

column 1
Value of work done last quarter (exclude pence)

column 2
Number of Operatives employed
Do not enter the same person on more than one line

Column 1
Enter under headings 1-8 estimates of the amounts chargeable to your customers for building, civil engineering and associated work done by your directly employed staff **between 1 April and 30 June 1977** (see notes 9 to 19).
Include the value of materials used (unless supplied to you free of charge), labour costs, overheads and profits.
Exclude work done for you by other sub-contractors, which should be entered in section E.

Column 2
Enter under headings 1-9 the number of operatives who were on your payroll on **7 July 1977** or the nearest possible date (see notes 9 to 14 and 20 to 21).

Work on houses and flats
1 New **public housing** for local authorities (eg council houses), public utilities, nationalised industries, government departments, new town corporations and all housing associations and co-ownership societies.   01 £

2 New **private housing** for private owners and developers.   02 £

3 Repair and maintenance of dwellings (see note 11).   03 £

Non-housing work for private owners and developers
4 New **industrial** construction: Factories, warehouses, coke ovens, refineries, oil production platforms, and steel producing plant or works in private ownership, etc.   04 £

5 New **non-industrial** construction: offices, shops, farm buildings, hotels and public houses, places of worship, clubs, places of entertainment, road goods transport depots, etc.   05 £

6 Repair and maintenance of structures covered by items 4 and 5.   06 £

Non-housing work for public sector clients
7 New construction not included above (include work on open cast coal sites and nationalised steelworks).   07 £

8 Repair and maintenance not included in items 3 and 6.   08 £

9 Enter in column 2 the number of operatives who cannot be classified to the types of work listed 1-8 above, eg transport workers, stores and warehouse staff, canteen workers, operatives employed on the manufacture of goods for sale.   09

Totals Enter NIL if appropriate   10 £

D
Firms working for other contractors in the construction industry should enter the value of work done by them in the quarter on sub-contracts let to them.

1 **Value of work done by you as a sub-contractor between 1 April and 30 June 1977** for other contractors in the construction industry. This cannot be greater than the total value shown in section C.
£   Enter NIL if appropriate

2 **Value of work shown in D 1 done by you as a labour-only sub-contractor.** This cannot be greater than the value shown in D 1.
£   Enter NIL if appropriate

SPECIMEN

E 1 **Value of work done for you by all sub-contractors** (including labour-only sub-contractors) in the period **between 1 April and 30 June 1977.** (see notes 29 and 30).
£   Enter NIL if appropriate

2 **Payments made to labour-only sub-contractors** in this period. (see notes 9 to 11 and 31)
£   New housing
£   New non-housing
£   Repair and maintenance

Name and telephone number of person who should be contacted if questions arise about this return   Name   Tel. no.

Declaration and signature
I hereby declare that the information contained in this return is complete and correct to the best of my knowledge and belief

Signature

Date   1977

APPENDIX VII

1 The information given in this return should relate to Great Britain only (i.e. excluding Northern Ireland, the Isle of Man and the Channel Islands).
2 Firms NOT wholly engaged in the construction industries but which have a separate department so engaged for which separate accounts are kept, should throughout this return give information appropriate to that department only.

3 Throughout this return include all persons (male and female) aged 16 years and over, working in Great Britain (i.e. excluding Northern Ireland, the Isle of Man and the Channel Islands), whether full or part-time (including those absent for any reason), who were on your payroll on the pay day specified.

4 Working proprietors are persons engaged in the business covered by the return who are regarded as self-employed persons for National Insurance purposes, eg self-employed owners, managers, partners.

5 Include directors working in the business but not in receipt of a definite wage, salary or commission. Exclude part-time directors paid by fee only.

6 Labour-only sub-contractors should enter the working partners in the group – the operatives employed should be entered in Section C.

7 Include all employees (including trainees) engaged in the business who do NOT do manual work, eg managing and other directors in receipt of a definite wage, salary or commission, managers, architects, surveyors, engineers, other professionals, training officers, superintendents, research, experimental, technical and design staff, draughtsmen and tracers, travellers, sales and office staff (including works office), and GENERAL FOREMEN and other supervisors who do NOT do manual work.

8 Exclude working proprietors shown in Section A and part-time directors paid by fee only.

9 New construction includes site preparation and demolition (items C1, C2, C4, C5, C7 and E2).
10 Non-housing new construction work includes extensions, major alterations and improvements (items C4, C5, C7 and E2).
11 Housing improvements, house/flat conversion, extensions, alterations and redecorations are classified to repair and maintenance and should be entered against item C3 and as repair and maintenance in item E2.
12 Items C7 and C8 cover work on utilities and social services, including work for government departments, nationalised industries (including nationalised steelworks), canal, river, dock and harbour boards, local authorities (other than housing), hospital boards, new town corporations, Covent Garden Market Authority, and the Airports Authority.
13 Heating and ventilating engineers should include the value of the erection and installation of all space-heating, ventilation and air-conditioning equipment.
14 Constructional engineers should include the value of fabricated iron and steelwork made by them in the value of work done in Section C. Exclude the value of fabricated iron and steelwork made for sale.

Value of work done (including V.A.T. where appropriate).
15 Include:
(a) The value of work done on your own initiative in the period on building such as dwellings or offices for eventual sale or lease.
(b) The value of work done by your own operatives on the construction or maintenance of your own premises.
(c) The value of goods made by you and used in the work.
(d) The value of any materials supplied by you to sub-contractors.
16 Exclude:
(a) The value of any work done for you by sub-contractors of any type.
(b) The value of any payments made to labour-only sub-contractors.
(c) The value of goods made for sale.
17 Labour-only sub-contractors should enter the value of services rendered and work done during the quarter.
18 Electrical contractors should include the value of installation work associated with buildings and structures.
19 Painters and decorators should show the value of work on new structures as 'new construction' and all other painting and decorating, etc., as 'repair and maintenance'.

Operatives employed
20 Include:
(a) All classes of employees other than staff entered in Section B.
(b) All persons aged 16 years and over who were on your payroll on the specified date and who are usually engaged on MANUAL work whether full or part-time.
(c) Trainees, operatives engaged in transport work, stores, warehouses, canteens, and on the manufacture of goods for sale, etc.
(d) Working foremen and other supervisors who do MANUAL work.
21 Labour-only sub-contractors should enter in Column 2 only the number of operatives employed. The number of working partners in the group should be included in Section A of the form.

---

22 The values stated should be estimates of the amounts chargeable to the contractors for building, civil engineering and associated work done by the firm during the quarter, and should also have been included in Section C. The amount should include the value of all materials supplied by you, including any machinery or plant incorporated, whether purchased or made by you.
23 Work done on contracts let directly by management consultants and industries outside the construction industry (eg oil refining consortia) should not be entered in Section D but should be included in Section C.
24 Fee contracts. Include the value of work done for other firms including fees. The amount stated should be the net contract price of the work including extras if the contract was executed wholly within the quarter specified otherwise it should be the value of work actually done in the quarter. Exclude the value of any materials supplied by you without charge.
25 Labour-only sub-contractors should enter the value of services rendered and work done during the quarter in both D1 and D2.
26 Electrical contractors should include the value of installation work associated with buildings and structures.
27 Heating and ventilating engineers should include the value of the erection and installation of all space- heating, ventilation and air-conditioning equipment.

28 Constructional engineers should include the value of fabricated iron and steelwork made by them in the value of work done in Section D.
Exclude the value of fabricated iron and steelwork made for sale.

29 The value shown in item E1 should be the value of building, civil engineering and associated work done in the quarter by others (including labour-only sub-contractors) to whom you sub-let contracts and the value of other work done on materials that you supplied. These values should not be included in Section C.

30 Exclude the cost of construction and maintenance work carried out by employees covered by this return, and the cost of materials used by them.

31 In E2 include the value of all payments made during the quarter to labour-only sub-contractors for services rendered and work done. Payments relating to the fiscal quarter (which starts and finishes 4 days later than the calendar quarter) would be acceptable if it is more convenient for you to provide these from your records.

Please detach the notes before returning the form

Form No. B.I.M./S.R.322

DEPARTMENT OF THE ENVIRONMENT
MONTHLY EMPLOYMENT RETURN

Please quote in any correspondence.

Ensure that the address below shows through the aperture of the return envelope when inserting the completed form.

IN CONFIDENCE

4 MAY, 1977.

Dear Sir(s),

1 The purpose of this inquiry is to obtain regular and up-to-date information about manpower resources employed in the construction industry. Information from the return is also needed for the compilation of mailing lists for the circulation by DOE to selected firms of technical information and of notices of lectures and conferences.

2 To avoid duplication of inquiries, and hence reduce the burden of form-filling, details of your name and address, industrial classification and employment may be passed to the Construction Industry Training Board, in accordance with the provisions of Section 4 of the Employment and Training Act, 1973.

3 The earlier that the statistics based on this return are available the more valuable they are and your co-operation in carefully and promptly completing the form will therefore be of real assistance to the Department. If you encounter any difficulties in completing the form the staff of the Building Industries Section at the address shown above will be pleased to help you in any way possible. The completed form should be returned to the address shown above **not later than WEDNESDAY, 18 MAY, 1977.**

4 This notice is served under the provisions of Section 1 of the Statistics of Trade Act, 1947, for the purpose of obtaining information necessary for the discharge by Government Departments of their functions. Under this Act the rendering of a return is compulsory. In accordance with the Act all information supplied in this return will be treated as confidential.

Yours faithfully,

Principal Director of Statistics   **Under-Secretary**

for and on behalf of the Secretary of State for the Environment

---

Declaration and Signature

Name and telephone number of person who should be

consulted if questions arise about this return..

If the name or address shown above is incorrect in any respect, please correct it.

I hereby declare that the information contained in this return
is complete and correct to the best of my knowledge and belief.

Signature.. Date.................................... 1977
(Please state whether Proprietor, Director, Manager, Partner, Secretary, etc.)

Form No. B.I.M./S.R.322
(AMD 2/77) (D1, D2, D3, A7)

APPENDIX VII

THE INFORMATION GIVEN ON THIS RETURN SHOULD RELATE TO GREAT BRITAIN ONLY
(I.E. EXCLUDING NORTHERN IRELAND, THE ISLE OF MAN AND THE CHANNEL ISLANDS)

For official use

In any correspondence please quote the reference number overleaf.

BUILDING, CIVIL ENGINEERING AND ALLIED INDUSTRIES

MONTHLY EMPLOYMENT RETURN

Throughout this return include all persons (male and female), aged 16 years and over, working in Great Britain (i.e. excluding Northern Ireland, the Isle of Man and the Channel Islands), whether full or part-time (including those absent for any reason), who were on your payroll on the pay day specified.

1 WORKING PROPRIETORS

State here the number of WORKING PROPRIETORS, i.e. persons engaged in the business who are regarded as self-employed for National Insurance purposes e.g. self-employed owners, managers, partners, etc. INCLUDE directors not in receipt of a definite wage, salary or commission. EXCLUDE part-time directors paid by fee only.

LABOUR ONLY SUB-CONTRACTORS should enter the working partners in the group – the operatives employed should be entered in Section 3.

Do not include persons entered here in any other section of the form.

Number
(Enter NIL if appropriate)

2 ADMINISTRATIVE, PROFESSIONAL, TECHNICAL AND CLERICAL EMPLOYEES

State here the number of administrative, professional, technical and clerical staff who were on your payroll on **12 MAY, 1977** or the nearest possible date.

INCLUDE all employees (including learners and trainees) engaged in the business who do NOT do manual work e.g. managing and other directors in receipt of a definite wage, salary or commission, managers, architects, surveyors, engineers, other professionals, training officers, superintendents, research, experimental, technical and design staff, draughtsmen and tracers, travellers, sales and office (including works office) staff, and GENERAL FOREMEN and other supervisors who do NOT do manual work. EXCLUDE working proprietors in section 1 and part-time directors paid by fee only.

Firms NOT wholly engaged in the construction industries, but which have a separate department so engaged for which separate accounts are kept should enter the number of persons engaged on administrative, professional, technical and clerical duties appropriate to that department.

Number
(Enter NIL if appropriate)

3 OPERATIVES AND TRAINEES (Exclude Working Proprietors)

State here total number of operatives who were on your payroll on **12 MAY, 1977** or the nearest possible date.

Include all classes of employees other than the staff entered in section 2 and include all manual wage earners, trainees, working foremen, operatives engaged in transport work, stores and warehouses, canteen workers, and operatives engaged on the manufacture of goods for sale.

SUB-CONTRACTORS supplying labour-only to other contractors should enter the number of operatives on their payroll. The working partners in the group should be included in the figure shown in section 1.

Firms NOT wholly engaged in the construction industries, but which have a separate department so engaged for which separate accounts are kept should enter the number of persons employed as operatives in that department.

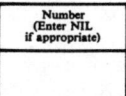

Form No. B.I.M./S.R.322

APPENDIX VIII

NEW ORDERS ENQUIRY

History of Enquiries and Selected Specimen Form

(Text reference: Section 4.5)

(a) **Date of Introduction**

1956 (4th quarter)—but see (c) below.

(b) **Frequency**

Monthly from January 1964, formerly quarterly.

(c) **Form Reference** (see also under (d) below)

BIM/OR ... (numbered serially at one time but now discontinued). Prior to 1964 a separate form was not used for this enquiry, the information being collected along with output and employment data on the BIM3/AR and BIM/SR series of questionnaires (see Appendices IV and VII respectively).

(d) **Specimen Form Included**

Form Ref.	Date	Title	Page
BIM/OR	Undated (Form in use in July 1977)	Monthly Return of Contracts and Orders for New Construction	603

(*Note:* from 1964 until April 1976 smaller contractors had to return details of jobs costing £2,500 or more and larger contractors details of jobs costing £10,000 or more and the forms were differentiated accordingly. The figure of £10,000 now applies to all contractors.)

(e) **Circulation**

Contractors only (no direct labour organizations) on the DOE register. Sampling methods have been used throughout the history of the enquiry, samples being stratified by size, trade and region of firm, but a census was also taken on one occasion each year until 1969 in conjunction with the April census of output and employment (BIM/AR series of questionnaires—see Appendix IV). A large number of newly registered firms, hitherto maintained on a 'special list', were added to the register for these enquiries with effect from July 1974.

(f) Processing of Returns

Department of the Environment.

(g) Availability of Data from Individual Returns

Individual returns are strictly confidential under the terms of the Statistics of Trade Act 1947.

(h) History of the Return

A major change in this return was made in January 1964 when contractors were henceforth required to list and describe individual contracts, including their cost and location, each month. Prior to 1964 a quarterly aggregate return under five type-of-work categories only had been required with effect from the fourth quarter of 1956 (this had been preceded in the third quarter by a 'trial-run' on a slightly different basis).

The content of the form of return used prior to 1964 remained substantially unchanged—for details see specimen form BIM3/AR8 included in Appendix IV. Similarly the return used since 1964 has remained unchanged, apart from matters of detail referred to below (see specimen copy of questionnaire—Form BIM/OR reproduced below).

Notable changes of detail in the content of the return are as follows:
  (i) *Coverage of contracts and orders.* From July 1967 the instructions were amended with the aim of ensuring that contracts obtained from contractors *outside* the construction industry were not excluded along with contracts obtained from contractors *inside* the industry (see Section 4.5.2 above).
  (ii) *Definition of builders' 'own initiative' work.* This was amended several times during 1964. Prior to 1964 an estimate was required of the value of *projects* 'expected to be started' during the forthcoming quarter. In January 1964 the timing was changed to projects actually 'started' in the same month as the enquiry, and in April 1964 the meaning of 'started' was more precisely defined to mean 'started work on the foundations'.
  (iii) *Jobs below the financial cut-off limits.* The question about the first and last of such jobs—Section 3(b) of the current form (BIM/OR)—was introduced in April 1969.

APPENDIX VIII

IN CONFIDENCE BIM/OR

D.O.E.
Department of the Environment

Building, Civil Engineering and Allied Industries

MONTHLY RETURN OF CONTRACTS AND ORDERS FOR NEW CONSTRUCTION

SPECIMEN

Dear Sir(s)

1. Up-to-date statistical information is essential for the construction industries which produce half the country's capital investment and about a sixth of industrial output. To meet this need, statistics of new orders are collected to provide an early indication of the load of work coming forward, locally as well as nationally. The national and technical press publish and comment on the key results of the enquiry and further details appear in the Monthly Digest of Statistics and the quarterly Housing and Construction Statistics, obtainable from HMSO.

2. The returns are also used in compiling mailing lists for the circulation by DOE to selected firms of technical information and of notices of lectures and conferences. Firms' names and addresses may be passed to the Construction Industry Training Board, in accordance with the provisions of Section 4 of the Employment and Training Act, 1973.

3. The earlier that the statistics based on this return are available the more valuable they are, and your co-operation in carefully and promptly completing this form will therefore be of real assistance. The Building Industries Section at the address shown above will be pleased to help in dealing with any queries you may have about completion of the form. The completed form should be returned to the address shown above not later than

4. This notice is served under the provisions of Section 1 of the Statistics of Trade Act, 1947, for the purpose of obtaining information necessary for the discharge by Government departments of their functions. Under this Act the rendering of a return is compulsory and the information supplied, in accordance with statute, will be treated as confidential.

Yours faithfully,

Principal Director of Statistics   **Under-Secretary**

for and on behalf of the Secretary of State for the Environment

MONTHLY RETURN OF CONTRACTS AND ORDERS FOR NEW CONSTRUCT
JULY

Column 1	Column 2	Column 3	Column 4	Column 5	Column
Your Reference Number for the job (See Note 5)	Location of site (See Note 6)	Type of Work—Give a brief description of the job or use one of the suggested descriptions at Note 10.	Private or Public (See Note 7)	Expected Completion Date (See Note 8)	Total Con† Value (See Note) £

1 List below contracts and orders of **£10,000 and over** obtained in the month for new construction.

2 List below new construction projects of **£10,000 and over** undertaken on your own initiative on which you started work on the foundations in the month.

SPECIMEN

3(a) Enter below the total numbers and total value of all contracts and orders for new construction **under £10,000 each** obtained in the month.
Include also those projects **under £10,000** undertaken on your own initiative on which you started work on the foundations in the month.
CONTRACTS, ETC., FOR REPAIR AND MAINTENANCE WORK AND SUB-CONTRACTS SHOULD NOT BE INCLUDED.

NUMBER OF JOBS (UNDER £10,000)

TOTAL VALUE OF JOBS (UNDER £10,000) £

For official use

Declaration

Name of pers

Telephone nu

I hereby decl the best of my kno

Si

3(b) Enter below the first and last jobs **under £10,000** obtained in the month which are included at 3(a) above.

Brief description of type of work	Private, Public or Own Initiative	Value £	TOW	CLASS
First job				
Last job				

APPENDIX VIII 605

Please detach notes before returning.

NOTES

1. The information given on the return should relate to Great Britain only (i.e. orders for work to be done in Northern Ireland, the Isle of Man and the Channel Islands should be excluded).

2. Firms NOT wholly engaged in the Construction Industries but which have a construction department for which separate accounts are kept, should give information about that department only.

3. **NEW CONSTRUCTION** includes extensions, major alterations, improvements, conversions and refurbishing, site preparation and demolition.

    INCLUDE
    a) all new contracts and orders for new construction obtained by you from clients and from contractors outside the construction industry in the month.
    b) extensions to existing contracts or orders.
    c) the value of work done in the month on serial or 'run on' contracts. (Please state SERIAL in Column 3).
    d) the estimated value of the building, civil engineering and associated works in 'package deals'.
    e) (in sections 2 and 3) new construction to be undertaken on your own initiative, i.e. work for which you have not been awarded a contract or order by any other party on a site already owned or leased by you or your subsidiary associated companies. Include cases where it is your practice to sell plots of land and to obtain from the purchasers a contract to build. (EXAMPLES: houses or offices for eventual sale or lease, or for occupation by yourselves, your subsidiaries or associated companies.)

    EXCLUDE
    a) contracts, etc., for repair and maintenance work.
    b) sub-contracts obtained by you from other contractors in the construction industry.
    c) additional costs incurred on existing work, e.g. on variation of price contracts.

4. If you have nothing to report, please write NIL in all three sections of the form and return it.

5. **PROJECT IDENTIFICATION**

    In future, output and employment information may be collected on a selection of individual projects. To enable the selected projects to be identified, please supply the following information:
    Column 1— Give the reference number by which the project is identified within your organisation.
    Column 7— State 'YES' if the job represents extra work on a site where you are already working (e.g. a new phase on an own initiative housing site) or you would not be able to supply separate output and employment information for the job.
    If the original project has a different reference number from the extension, please state this number after the type of work description in Column 3.
    State 'NO' for distinct new projects which will be accounted for separately.

6. **LOCATION**

    Enter in Column 2 the Local Authority (district) name or the site address where the job is to be done.

7. **PRIVATE OR PUBLIC**
    (a) Private. If the work is for a private owner or organisation or private developer enter 'private' in Column 4. Include steel-producing plants or works in private ownership.
    (b) Public. Enter 'public' in Column 4 if the work is for any public authority such as:
    Government Departments — Post Office Corporation
    Local Authorities — Regional Health Authorities
    Public Utilities — New Town Corporations
    Canal, Drainage, Dock and Harbour Boards — Universities
    Water Authorities — Atomic Energy Authority
    — Airports Authority
    Nationalised Industries (including open-cast coal sites and nationalised steelworks)
    B.B.C. or I.B.A. (but not independent programme contractors)
    Housing Associations (including fair rent associations, cost rent societies and co-ownership associations)

8. **EXPECTED COMPLETION DATE**

    Enter in Column 5 either:
    the month and year in which you expect to complete the work,
    or the expected duration of the project, in months.

9. **TOTAL CONTRACT VALUE**

    Enter in Column 6 the total value of the project, but exclude the site value and any architects' or consultants' fees.
    Include the value of any work you propose to sub-let to other contractors.
    For projects started on your own initiative, enter the estimated total value of only those buildings on which you actually started foundation work in the month.
    (Exclude pence)

P.T.O.

10 TYPE OF WORK

Enter in Column 3 a brief description of the job or use one of the following descriptions:
Jobs should be described according to the type of construction involved, not the type of client, e.g. a car park built for a factory should be described as 'GARAGES'.
Provision of main services and roads to estates of houses, factories or warehouses should, however, be allocated to 'HOUSING-NEW', 'FACTORIES' or 'WAREHOUSES' as appropriate.
For mixed developments, state which is the major part of the work.
Indicate where work is being carried out for the Armed Forces.

Suggested descriptions	Examples of the kinds of work covered
AGRICULTURE	barns, animal houses and fencing, buildings for market gardening and horticulture, tile drainage, field drainage, fen drainage and ditching. Houses on farms should be described as 'HOUSING'.
AIR	airfields, airport runways, hangars and buildings on airfields (state civil or military).
COAL MINING	deep coal prospecting, shaft sinking, tunnelling, works and buildings at the pit head for use in connection with the pit.
OPEN-CAST COAL	open-cast coal prospecting and extraction, removal and reinstatement of overburden and final landscaping.
COMMUNICATIONS	Post Offices, sorting offices, telephone exchanges, switching centres and cabling.
DRAINAGE and SEWERAGE	Include drainage for Local Authorities or Water Authorities, drainage carried out elsewhere away from the site on any particular building, sewage disposal works and sewers for farms.
ELECTRICITY	power stations, hydro-electric schemes, sub-stations and the laying of cables and erection of overhead lines.
ENTERTAINMENT	hotels, public houses, restaurants, motorway service areas, clubs, theatres, cinemas, studios, work for radio and television, swimming baths, sports grounds, youth hostels and other recreational facilities.
FACTORIES	factories, coke ovens and works and buildings ancillary to industrial production and processing (Jobs at steel-producing plants or works should be described as steelworks in Column 3 of the return).
GARAGES	Include car parks, repair garages, petrol filling stations, transport workshops, bus depots and road goods transport depots.
GAS	gas works, gas mains, gas storage and pipelines (excluding off-shore).
HARBOURS and WATERWAYS	harbours, wharves, docks and piers, jetties, canals and waterways, dredging, sea walls, embankments and water defences.
HEALTH	hospitals, medical schools, clinics, welfare centres, nursing homes, nurseries, ambulance stations, etc. Laboratories for industrial undertakings should be described as 'FACTORIES'.
HOUSING— IMPROVEMENTS	extensions, major alterations, improvements and conversions to existing houses, flats, maisonettes, cottages, etc.
HOUSING— NEW	new houses, flats, maisonettes, married quarters, remand homes and vicarages, including the provision of roads and services within the site. Please state the number of dwellings in Column 3.
OFFICES	Include banks, and mixed development where offices form the major part of the job.
OIL	oil refineries, distribution pipelines (excluding off-shore) and production platforms.
RAILWAYS	permanent way, tunnels, bridges, stations, etc., for underground and surface railways.
ROADS	roads, motorways, road bridges and tunnels, footpaths, lighting, etc.
SCHOOLS and COLLEGES	Include technical colleges and polytechnics.
SHOPS	Include department stores, markets and showrooms.
STEELWORKS	construction works at steel-producing works or plants.
UNIVERSITIES	Include halls of residence and university research establishments.
WAREHOUSES	Include wholesale distribution depots.
WATER	reservoirs, dams (not for hydro-electric schemes), aqueducts, wells, conduits, waterworks, water mains and hydraulic works.

/BIM76 (1/77)

APPENDIX IX

EEC STATE OF TRADE ENQUIRY INTO CONSTRUCTION IN GREAT BRITAIN

(Text reference: Section 4.5.4)

(a) **Date of Introduction**

1977.

(b) **Frequency**

Quarterly.

(c) **Form Reference**

BIM 400.

(d) **Specimen Form Included**

Form BIM 400, Reference: EEC/2/L dated 27 June 1977 and 'Notes on Completion of the State of Trade Enquiry'.

(e) **Circulation**

Sample of contractors in Great Britain on the DOE register employing twenty-five or more persons.

(f) **Processing of Returns**

Department of the Environment.

(g) **Availability of Data from Individual Returns**

Individual returns are confidential.

(h) **History of the Return**

Introduced with effect from the first quarter of 1977 to provide information comparable with that collected in other member countries of the EEC. No changes have been made in the content of the return since its introduction.

APPENDIX IX 609

Department of the Environment

Reference: EEC/2/L

Department of the Environment
Room 321, 25 Savile Row
London W1X 2BT

Telephone 01-734 6010 ext 515

Ensure that the address above shows through the aperture of the return envelope when inserting the completed form.

27 June 1977

Dear Sir

STATE OF TRADE ENQUIRY INTO CONSTRUCTION

I am writing to ask for your co-operation in the second quarterly enquiry on the state of trade of the construction industry and its prospects. The aims are to provide, first, early quick assessments of recent changes in the level of activity, of work in hand and the intake of orders, and second , prompt indicators of the immediate prospects for employment and tender prices. We are asking you to indicate the direction of estimated changes and not, as with our other statistical enquiries, for precise figures.

The survey covers the whole of the British construction industry, including specialist trades, and will give results which, with those from similar surveys in other EEC countries, will provide comparable up-to-date indicators on market conditions throughout the European Communities. The timing of the quarterly despatch of the survey has been arranged so as not to clash with the similar types of enquiry run by trade associations for some sectors of the industry in Britain.

Interpretation of any survey of this type has to be developed through analysis of the results of consecutive enquiries so that, although the results of the first enquiry sent out at the end of March are of interest, we shall wait until they can be analysed in conjunction with the results of the present enquiry before issuing any report.

This will be a sample survey but to provide sound data we must ask all the large firms, including yours, to participate each quarter: we are pleased to report a very good response to the March enquiry. We are not asking for precise figures, so the questionnaire should not take long to complete and I should be grateful if you would return the completed form by **Friday 8 July 1977**. We shall be very ready to answer any queries you may have about the enquiry.

Your return will be treated in the strictest confidence, to produce grouped totals which will be published, and which will be of real value both to government and industry.

Yours faithfully

G PENRICE
Principal Director of Statistics

BIM 400

STATE OF TRADE ENQUIRY INTO CONSTRUCTION – 2nd Quarter 1977 *(see notes)*
To be completed by both main and sub-contractors

NOTE

Please enter ✓ in the appropriate box for each type of work relevant to your business AND in Building and Civil Engineering in TOTAL

Types of work:
- Building: Own account / Contract Housing / Contract Non-Housing
- Civil Eng (except open cast coal sites)
- Building & Civil Eng in total

1 Level of Activity
Compared with the previous quarter do you estimate this quarter your firm did:
- more work
- as much work
- less work

2 Delaying factors
Have you suffered any major delays this quarter
- Yes
- No

If Yes: Were delays due to:
- shortage of plant
- shortage of manpower
- shortage of materials
- exceptional weather
- please specify any other major factors ----------

3 Work in Hand
How long would it take to complete the work in hand
- 18 months or more
- 12m to less than 18m
- 6m to less than 12m
- 3m to less than 6m
- less than 3 months

4 Intake of Orders
Compared with 3 months ago, has the volume of your recent orders been:
- higher
- about the same
- lower

5 Employment
Compared with today, how many people do you estimate will be working for you in 3 month's time (include labour of sub-contractors)
- more
- about the same
- fewer

6 Prices
How do you think your tender prices in 3 months time will compare with your current prices
- higher
- about the same
- lower

Comments:

Name of person to be contacted if queries arise:

Tel No:

Signature ....

SPECIMEN

APPENDIX IX 611

Department of the Environment

NOTES ON COMPLETION OF THE STATE OF TRADE ENQUIRY

General

1   So as not to delay your return, please make estimates, if necessary, for the latest quarter, using the best available information.

2   The comparisons between quarters are required for assessing underlying trends: please ignore any changes which occur during the year because of normal variations in weather conditions, holidays etc.

3   It is very important to complete the "Total" column as well as the columns for those types of work relevant to your business.

4   Please take repair and maintenance into consideration, as well as new work.

Question 2 – Delaying Factors

Include any major factor affecting one or more of your sites; there may be more than one factor affecting a type of work.

Question 3 – Work in Hand

Not an estimate of when the last of your present projects will be completed, but a comparison of total work in hand and current rate of activity (or expected rate if current rate is exceptionally high or low). Divide the total value of work in hand by the average monthly value of work being done: eg £500,000 of work currently in hand; average output last quarter, £50,000 per month; therefore 10 months work in hand.

Question 4 – Intake of Orders

The volume of recent orders is the amount after removing the effect of changes in your tender prices. For example, if the value of your new orders was 2 per cent higher than in the previous quarter, but your tender prices were 5 per cent higher, then the volume would be 3 per cent lower.

APPENDIX X

RETURN OF OVERSEAS CONTRACTS AND SUB-CONTRACTS

History of Enquiries and Selected Specimen Form

(Text reference: Section 4.6)

(a) **Date of Introduction**

1955 (but see under 'History' below).

(b) **Frequency**

Annual.

(c) **Form Reference**

BIM 60.

(d) **Specimen Form Included**

Form in use in 1977.

(e) **Circulation**

Contractors on the DOE register who have intimated in response to a question inserted each year in one of the other enquiries (Form BIM/SR series—see Appendix VII) that they carry out such work.

(f) **Processing of Returns**

Department of the Environment.

(g) Availability of Data from Individual Returns

Individual returns are treated as strictly confidential.

(h) History of the Return

Part 2 of the form was added in 1962. In 1974 (only) the totals in Part 1 were sub-divided between Building and Civil Engineering. In the 1975 and 1976 returns information was also requested in Part 2 about the total amounts *due* to and from Great Britain on the return dates in 1974, 1975 and 1976. Otherwise the form has remained the same since 1955.

APPENDIX X 615

In Confidence

DEPARTMENT OF THE ENVIRONMENT

BUILDING AND CIVIL ENGINEERING CONTRACTING

REFERENCE
RE 14952/1

TELEPHONE
01-212 8415

PART 1

OVERSEAS CONTRACTS AND SUB-CONTRACTS

Return for Year ended 31 March 1977

Please return this form as soon as possible

COUNTRY	NEW CONTRACTS AND SUB-CONTRACTS (see Notes 1 and 4 below)	ALL OVERSEAS CONTRACTS AND SUB-CONTRACTS (see Notes 2 and 4 below)	
	Total value of contracts and sub-contracts obtained in the year ended 31 MARCH 1977 £	Estimated total value of work done in the year ended 31 MARCH 1977 £	Value of work outstanding at 31 MARCH 1977 (see Note 3) £
(1)	(2)	(3)	(4)
TOTALS			

NOTES:

1 The value of contracts obtained by your company or group (Col 2) should include:

  (a) extensions to existing contracts

  (b) contracts obtained by an associated or subsidiary overseas company in which the <u>predominant</u> interest is British

  (c) all sub-contracted work except work sub-contracted to another British company or to a <u>predominantly</u> British overseas associate or subsidiary of such a company.

2 The amounts shown in Cols 3 and 4 should include, in respect of contracts and sub-contracts as defined in Note 1, the value of work done in the year ended 31 March 1977 and outstanding at the end of the year to 31 March 1977, including contracts and sub-contracts obtained *before and during* the year ended 31 March 1977.

3 Please give details by letter of any contracts which have been cancelled during the year ended 31 March 1977.

4 It will be sufficient if the information requested above is:

  (a) given by country and not by individual contract

  (b) estimated to the nearest £10,000.

PLEASE ALSO COMPLETE PART 2 OVERLEAF

In Confidence

BUILDING AND CIVIL ENGINEERING CONTRACTING

PART 2

OVERSEAS BALANCE OF PAYMENTS

Return for year ended 31 March 1977

Please return this form as soon as possible

1. Total of all payments* from Great Britain to overseas countries, in respect of overseas contracts, during the year ended 31 March 1977.

2. Total of all receipts* in Great Britain from overseas countries, in respect of overseas contracts, during the year ended 31 March 1977.

NOTES:

1. Please give the information requested above (estimated if necessary) in Sterling to the nearest £10,000. When conversions from an overseas currency are involved please use the same rate of exchange as in your company's own accounts.

2. The information is requested only in respect of companies based in Great Britain and should exclude payments and receipts for work done within Great Britain and any transactions with subsidiary or associated companies overseas.

3. Only overall total figures are requested. Separate figures for individual overseas countries are not necessary.

*NB. Exclude the value of any finished goods or raw materials exported from Great Britain because these will have been included already in the trade statistics. The provision of plant and other capital items, and the provision of fixed (shares etc) capital and working capital should also be excluded from the receipts and payments figures.

Signed ....
(on behalf of the undertaking)

Address ....

....

....

Tel No and Ext ....

Date ....

THIS FORM WHEN COMPLETED SHOULD BE RETURNED TO

THE DEPARTMENT OF THE ENVIRONMENT, SC2(S11/11) 2 MARSHAM STREET, LONDON SW1P 3EB

BIM 60

APPENDIX XI

LOCAL AUTHORITY DESIGN WORK ENQUIRY

History of Enquiries and Selected Specimen Form

(Text reference: Section 4.7)

(a) **Date of Introduction**

Effectively 1965—the return was initiated in 1964 but the response was low and the form and frequency of return were adapted with effect from 1965.

(b) **Frequency of Return**

Three times a year. The timing was changed with effect from 1972 (see Table 4.5).

(c) **Form Reference**

BIM 148.

(d) **Specimen Form Included**

Current form—dated 9 August 1977 (p. 619); see also under 'History' below.

(e) **Circulation**

All local government authorities in Great Britain, New Town Development Corporations and Commissions, Road Construction Units and the Scottish Special Housing Association.

(f) **Processing of Returns**

Department of the Environment.

(g) Availability of Data from Individual Returns

Individual returns are confidential.

(h) History of the Return

This return was modified in 1972 and again in 1975, on each occasion the amount of information requested being reduced. The current questionnaire (see specimen attached) requires information about schemes at the working drawings stage only and was introduced in August 1975. Previous returns in the period back to 1972 had also requested similar information about schemes at the 'sketch plans' stage.

Prior to 1972 information was required in very much more detail. The return was divided into two sections (the form itself consisting of four double-sided A3 size sheets of paper), one for 'Building Work and Associated Civil Engineering' and the other for 'Civil Engineering Work *not* associated with Buildings'. Each of these sections consisted regularly of four parts: (A)—Sketch plan stage, (B)—Working drawing stage, (C)—Fully designed projects in hand: already reported at working drawing stage but construction not yet begun, (D)—Delayed projects (i.e. projects previously reported but subsequently put in abeyance). Each of these parts related to new projects costing more than £2,500 (except for County Council road schemes which were reported once a year only and for which the cut-off value was £25,000) each of which had to be listed separately and described within a number of broadly defined categories of work together with an indication of estimated cost, expected starting date, type of construction (in the case of building work), whether design services were being provided fully or partially by the authority or wholly by a private architect or civil engineer, and whether or not the project was inside the authority's own area.

In addition, once a year only, information was also required (in an additional Part E of the form) about the expected total outlay during the current financial year on:

(a) Minor projects costing up to £2,500 and repair and maintenance work (returned in May).
(b) Road schemes costing less than £25,000 and repairs and maintenance on roads (reported in September by County Councils only).

A question was also regularly asked about whether or not the authority employed a direct labour organization.

APPENDIX XI 619

Department of the Environment

4 month period ending 31 August 1977

IN CONFIDENCE

ENQUIRY INTO NEW CONSTRUCTION WORK TO BE DESIGNED BY OR FOR LOCAL AUTHORITIES, NEW TOWN DEVELOPMENT CORPORATIONS AND THE COMMISSION FOR THE NEW TOWNS

(Form BIM 148)

> Department of the Environment
> Building Industries and Materials Section
> Room 321, 25 Savile Row
> LONDON, W1X 2RT
> 01 734 6010 Ext 516

Please quote this reference number in any correspondence

9 August 1977

Dear Sir

1   The enquiry for the 4 monthly period ending 31 August 1977 into new construction work in Great Britain being designed by or for local authorities and new town corporations and the Commission, is on the reverse. Information is only required about those schemes which pass into the working drawing stage during the period, and on which construction has yet to start.

2   The results of this enquiry will appear in "Housing and Construction Statistics" published by the Government Statistical Service and available from HM Stationery Office.

3   The earlier that the statistics based on this return are available the more valuable they are. The late return of even a few forms must lead to delay in the production of results and your co-operation in completing the form promptly will be of great assistance to this Department. Please complete the form and return it **not later than 15 September 1977.**

4   All information supplied in this return will be treated as confidential.

Yours faithfully

G PENRICE
Principal Director of Statistics, for and on behalf of the
Secretary of State for the Environment

NOTES

1   Only one completed copy of the form need be returned. The additional copies are to enable authorities to keep a record of the value of projects reported to the Department. Further copies can be supplied on request.

2   Throughout this return, you should include only projects entering the working drawing stage during the current period, which have been designed by your own staff or on behalf of the authority by a private architect or civil engineer. Projects costing less than £2,500 and repair and maintenance work should not be included.

Form BIM 148

REFERENCE NUMBER

For official use only

PROJECTS COSTING £2,500 OR MORE ON WHICH WORKING DRAWINGS WERE FIRST STARTED DURING THE 4 MONTHS PERIOD ENDING 31 AUGUST 1977 *(EXCLUDE PROJECTS IN THE WORKING DRAWING STAGE BEFORE 1 MAY 1977 – SEE NOTE 8)*

IN CONFIDENCE

	TYPE OF WORK (SEE NOTE 11)	(A) DESIGNED WHOLLY BY A LOCAL AUTHORITY DESIGN STAFF VALUE (£ THOUSAND)	(B) DESIGNED WHOLLY OR PARTIALLY BY PRIVATE CONSULTANTS VALUE (£ THOUSAND)
1	HOUSING		
2	EDUCATION		
3	HEALTH		
4	INDUSTRIAL AND COMMERCIAL		
5	CIVIC DEVELOPMENT		
6	HIGHWAYS		
7	SEWERAGE, WATER SUPPLY AND LAND DRAINAGE		
	TOTAL (1) TO (7) INCLUSIVE		

TO BE COMPLETED AND SIGNED BY THE PERSON MAKING THE RETURN ON BEHALF OF THE AUTHORITY

Name of authority ....

Full postal address ....
(including postal
code if any) ....

} If your address is correctly printed overleaf you need only state "as overleaf"

Telephone number .... Extension ....

I certify that to the best of my belief the information contained in this return is correct

Signed .... Date ....197........

Please state whether Chief Executive, Manager, Surveyor, etc ....

Please state the name and telephone number of the person who could
be consulted if any queries arise, if different from the above ....

(2)

APPENDIX XI   621

NOTES FOR GUIDANCE IN COMPLETING THIS RETURN

GENERAL

1   This enquiry relates to the value of projects costing £2,500 or more which entered the working drawing stage during the four months ending 31 August 1977, and on which construction has not yet started.

2   All new work commissioned by your authority should be reported both where the design work will be carried out by your own professional staff and where it is done by private architects or civil engineers.

3   Where a large project is carried out in several stages by means of a number of different contracts, each stage should be treated as a separate project and included in the return at the time that the working drawings of each stage are commenced.

4   Values included should represent the estimated gross cost of construction work only. Site values, professional fees, cost of furniture and equipment, etc should be ignored, although all site preparation should be included. Even if the ultimate cost of a project is uncertain, it is important that you should still include it, by making an approximate estimate of the likely cost. All values should be given to the nearest thousand pounds.

5   Design work carried out by a county council on behalf of a district council should be included by the county council and NOT by the authority in whose district the work will be undertaken. Design work carried out by a district council on behalf of a county council should be included by the district council and not by the county council.

6   In Scotland, all work carried out by the Scottish Special Housing Association whether on its own account or on an agency basis for a local authority, will be included in returns made by the Association itself, and particulars of such work should be excluded from returns made by local authorities.

7   In England, highway schemes which are designed by county councils in their capacity as sub-units of a road construction unit, will be reported by the units themselves and should not appear on the return made by the county councils.

COMPLETING THE RETURN

8   **EXCLUDE**

(1) Projects already in working drawing stage before 1 May 1977; and

(2) Projects where construction is in progress on 31 August 1977.

9   **IMPORTANT NOTE** – Once you have included a particular project you should not include it again if there have been only minor changes in the specification or cost of the project. Where, however, the amount of any projects previously reported is substantially extended, necessitating further design work, the value of the **increase** should be shown in the appropriate box: similarly if any scheme is abandoned or substantially decreased the value in the appropriate box should be adjusted to compensate for the **decrease**.

10   Projects which are designed wholly by the authority's own architect, engineer or surveyor should be reported in column A (DESIGNED WHOLLY BY LOCAL AUTHORITY DESIGN STAFF). Those projects which are being designed wholly by a private architect or civil engineer or where they are providing partial services, should be reported in column B (DESIGNED WHOLLY OR PARTIALLY BY PRIVATE CONSULTANTS).

TYPES OF WORK

11   All projects reported in both columns A and B should be broken down among the seven types of work shown. For your convenience, the list below shows the type of project to be included under each heading. Improvements and extensions should be classified according to the type of work involved. Schemes costing less than £2,500 and repair and maintenance work should NOT be included on this return.

(1) HOUSING

Include all buildings for residential use such as houses, flats, maisonettes, cottages and flats for old people. Housing for specific occupation (e.g. police housing) should also be included under this heading. Also include the provision within a housing site of roads and services for gas, water, electricity, sewage and drainage, and major extensions and alterations to existing projects.

(2) EDUCATION

Include all work in connection with schools and colleges. Under this heading should be included nursery schools, training establishments (but not those for the blind or physically disabled), colleges of further education, technical colleges and colleges of education for the training of teachers: also all buildings for the Youth Service.

This page may be detached and retained

(3)

11 TYPES OF WORK (cont'd)

(3) HEALTH

Under this heading should be included hospitals, medical schools, clinics, surgeries, sanatoria, nursing homes, health centres, welfare centres, nurseries, ambulance stations, first aid posts, old peoples homes and training centres for the blind and physically disabled.

(4) INDUSTRIAL AND COMMERCIAL

Include all factories and warehouses and all works and buildings for the purpose of, or ancillary to, commercial or industrial development; also all freight depots, all office buildings including town halls and council offices, and all buildings for retail distribution, such as shops, department stores, markets and showrooms.

(5) CIVIC DEVELOPMENT

The following types of project should be included: fire stations, community centres, libraries, museums, mortuaries, crematoria, police stations, prisons, magistrates courts, remand homes, childrens' homes, abattoirs, telephone exchanges, public conveniences, theatres, concert halls, cinemas, film studios, bowling alleys, clubs, hotels, youth hostels, public houses, restaurants, cafes, holiday camps, dance halls, swimming pools, works and buildings at sports grounds, all places of sport and recreation, yachting marinas and zoological parks.

(6) HIGHWAYS

Include all classes of public road (including motorways, trunk roads and unclassified roads), pavements, footbridges, street lighting, tunnels, flyovers and underpasses, traffic signals and road fencing. Also car parks, transport workshops, bus depots, road goods transport depots and buildings for the storage, repair and maintenance of electrically or mechanically propelled vehicles.

(7) SEWERAGE, WATER SUPPLY AND LAND DRAINAGE

Include sewage disposal works, treatment and purification plants, laying of sewers, outfalls, culverts, sludge drying beds, filter beds, storm water channels, surface drains, fen and agricultural drainage, waterworks, reservoirs, water purification plants, dams, aqueducts, wells, conduits, pumping stations, water mains and hydraulic works. Also works and buildings connected with harbours and waterways, wharves, docks, piers and jetties, canals, groynes, sea walls and embankments.

APPENDIX XII

QUARTERLY RETURNS OF CONSTRUCTION WORK IN NORTHERN IRELAND

(Text references: Sections 9.2.1 and 9.3.3)

History and Specimen Forms

From 1966 to 1976 two questionnaires were used to obtain quarterly information about construction activity in Northern Ireland, specimen copies of which were included in the companion review on *Housing in Northern Ireland* [B 57]. The relevant forms were Stats/CR/2, which was sent to contractors, and Stats/CR/3, which was sent to public authorities in order to obtain statistics about the work undertaken by their direct labour organizations. In the third quarter of 1976, however, major changes were made to the enquiry addressed to contractors and two new forms of return were introduced in the place of the former single return (Stats/CR/2). The new returns are:

Quarterly Enquiry into Wages, Employment, Repairs and Maintenance and Housing Improvement Output and Contracts
Return of Output and Employment

Specimen copies of these forms are reproduced below. The return for public authorities' direct labour organizations has remained unchanged and, therefore, is not reproduced again.

The change affects in the main the collection of statistics of the value of work done. Previously firms had been asked to provide a return of their *own* output (i.e. excluding work done *for* them by sub-contractors) in the quarter by nine categories of work. The revised enquiry asks main contractors to supply total value of output data (including output by sub-contractors) on specific projects. This is achieved by the use of the two forms referred to above: a list of projects which have been notified as new orders on the first form is compiled and the second form is used to obtain the value of work done and the number of operatives employed on each of these projects in subsequent quarters.

Another change in the enquiry is that, while previously a form was sent to all contractors on the register employing seven or more operatives, in the revised enquiry contractors employing twenty or more operatives receive the first form each quarter while those employing between five and nineteen operatives only receive the first form every fifth quarter (contractors employing less than five operatives are excluded altogether). Contractors receive the second form only if they are engaged as main contractors on a project which they have previously notified as a new order.

Processing of Returns

Currently the Department of Finance (Northern Ireland).

Availability of Data from Individual Returns

Individual returns are treated as strictly confidential under the terms of the Statistics of Trade Act (Northern Ireland) 1949.

APPENDIX XII

Building, Civil Engineering and Allied Industries   Strictly Confidential

Quarterly enquiry into wages, employment, repairs and maintenance and housing improvement output and contracts

Quarter ended:

To:

From:

Department of Finance
Statistics and Economics Unit
Parliament Buildings
Stormont Belfast BT4 3SW

These numbers should be quoted in correspondence:

Dear Sir/Madam

1. Under Section 4 of the Statistics of Trade Act (Northern Ireland) 1949 you are required to complete and forward (in the enclosed pre-paid reply envelope) this return **WITHIN TWO WEEKS OF THE END OF THE QUARTER.**

2. Subject to the provisions of the Act all the information you give will be treated as strictly Confidential and will be used solely for the compilation of general statistics.

3. Where construction activities (defined as work carried out **on site**) are only part of an undertaking the return should give information about that part only.

4. A separate form should be used for business carried out or proposed in Great Britain or the Republic of Ireland or abroad. Extra forms can be obtained from the Department of Finance, Statistics and Economics Unit, Parliament Buildings, Stormont, Belfast BT4 3SW. Telephone 63210 extension 2098.

5. Please read the notes carefully before completing the form.

Yours sincerely,

T.F. STAINER
for the Secretary

Part one
Return of wages and employment for the quarter

This part to be completed by ALL contractors.

A. For First FULL WEEK of Quarter.

1. Give the gross wages bill (**including** employer's contribution for national insurance and holiday pay) for all operatives **directly** employed (i.e. **excluding** sub-contractors' operatives and "labour-only" sub-contractors) **on site** by your firm.

£ _____

2. Give the total value of payments (**excluding** VAT) made by you to "labour-only" sub-contractors **directly** engaged **on-site** by your firm.

£ _____

B. For First Monday of Quarter.

3. Give the number of **on site** operatives directly employed (i.e. **excluding** sub-contractors' operatives and "labour-only" sub-contractors) by your firm.

_____

4. Give the number of "labour-only" operatives working on **your sites** (i.e. those directly engaged by you **plus** any operatives engaged by them).

_____

5. Give the number of working principals in your firm.

_____

6. Give the number of administrative, professional, technical and clerical staff employed by your firm (**excluding** any already included in the categories above).

_____

7. Give the number of **operatives** (e.g. lorry drivers, carpenters etc.) employed **off-site** by your firm.

_____

Part two

Return of contracts and orders for new construction obtained during the quarter

This part to be completed in respect of projects for which you are the MAIN contractor. However, NOMINATED SUB-CONTRACTORS (i.e. those to whom sub-contracts were awarded directly by the client) should also complete this section.

List the NEW ORDERS for NEW CONSTRUCTION (see notes 1 and 2) obtained by you and the PROJECTS WHICH YOU HAVE BEGUN ON YOUR OWN INITIATIVE during the quarter.

Include only **non-housing** projects of total value of **at least £10.000** and **housing** projects of total value of **at least £5.000**. Give each project a reference number by which you can later identify it if neccessary.

NOTES TO BE READ BEFORE COMPLETING THIS SECTION.

1. **Include**
   a. contracts awarded to you directly by clients and **not** by other contractors, but **including** sub-contracts awarded directly by the client.
   b. projects started on your own behalf
   c. extensions to existing contracts
   d. serial or "run-on" contracts (e.g. pipe-laying contracts)

2. **New Construction** includes extensions, major re-construction (e.g. after bomb damage), major alterations (i.e. improvements), site preparation and demolition **except for housing** for which conversions, extensions and improvements should be **excluded**.

3. Give as precise a description of the project as possible such as
   a. housing project (indicating the number of houses and whether or not they represent a phase of a project or a complete project),
   b. school, technical college or university,
   c. factory, warehouse or other industrial plant,
   d. offices, shops, hotel, public house, place of worship, club or place of entertainment,
   e. hospital or health centre,
   f. public road, highway, bridge or footpath.

4. Enter **"Public"** if the client is a public authority. Public authorities include:—

District Councils	Harbour Boards
N.I. Housing Executive	BBC (but not UTV)
Health and Social Services Boards	Universities
	Pigs Marketing Board
Education and Library Boards	Milk Marketing Board
N.I. Railways Co. Ltd.	N.I. Finance Corporation
Ulsterbus and N.I. Carriers	Local Enterprise Development Unit

   Enter **"Private for client"** if the work is for a private owner or organisation.

   Enter **"Private for self"** if project is work to be undertaken on your own behalf.

5. Value of Project should include:—
   (a) value of sub-contracted work **except** that given to NOMINATED SUB-CONTRACTORS (i.e. those to whom sub-contracts were awarded **directly** by the client)
   (b) value of work done by "labour only" sub-contractors
   (c) profits and overheads
   and exclude
   (d) site value
   (e) professional fees
   (f) VAT

Ref. No.	Date of signing contract *(if applicable)*	Description of project *see note 3*

Give the total number and total value of new orders for **non-housing** projects of value of **less than £10,000** and **housing** projects of value of **less than £5,000** obtained by you during the quarter

Number of projects: _____

Total value of all of these projects £ _____

SPECIMEN

APPENDIX XII

private 4	Location *(site address if possible)*	Value of project *see note 5*	Estimated date of work starting on site	Estimated completion date

SPECIMEN

P.T.O.

Part three
Return of work done and labour employed on all repairs and maintenance and housing improvement during the quarter.

This part to be completed in respect of projects for which you are the MAIN contractor.

Give information for all repair and maintenance work and housing improvement done during the quarter.

NOTE   To be Read Before Completing This Section

Repair and maintenance in **non-housing section** includes all work which is **not** defined 'as new construction' in note **2** on page 2. Work done repairing builders' plant should include **only** that done 'on-site'.

In the **housing section** the return should include conversions, extensions, alterations and redecorations.

	Type of work				
	Public housing	Private housing	Public non-housing	Builder's plant	Other private non-housing
1. Number of operatives working **on-site** (**including** sub-contractors' employees and labour only operatives):					
2. Total value of work done If you have difficulty in providing accurate quarterly figures insert a rough estimate at **2a** below and the actual figure for the last financial year at **2b**					
a Total value of work done **estimate** for quarter:	£	£	£	£	£
b Total annual **actual** value of work done for financial year	£	£	£	£	£

SPECIMEN

Declaration

To be completed and signed by the person making the return on behalf of the undertaking

Trading name of undertaking

Full postal address to which correspondence should be sent *including postal code*

Telephone exchange and number

Is the above address your Registered Office? *tick the box which applies*

yes ☐   no ☐   Date:

Please give VAT Registration Number:

State whether Proprietor Director, Manager, Partner, Secretary:

Dd. 079238 4M 11/76 TPC 55-0-0

APPENDIX XII

Building, Civil Engineering and Allied Industries **Strictly Confidential**

Return of output and employment

Quarter ended:

To:

From:

Department of Finance
Statistics and Economics Unit
Parliament Buildings
Stormont   Belfast BT4 3SW

These numbers should be quoted in correspondence:

Dear Sir/Madam

1. Under Section 4 of the Statistics of Trade Act (Northern Ireland) 1949 you are required to complete and forward (in the enclosed pre-paid reply envelope) this return **WITHIN TWO WEEKS OF THE END OF THE QUARTER.**

2. Subject to the provisions of the Act all the information you give will be treated as strictly Confidential and will be used solely for the compilation of general statistics.

3. Where construction activities (defined as work carried out on **site**) are only part of an undertaking the return should give information about that part only.

4. A separate form should be used for business carried out or proposed in Great Britain or the Republic of Ireland or abroad. Extra forms can be obtained from the Department of Finance, Statistics and Economics Unit, Parliament Buildings, Stormont, Belfast BT4 3SW. Telephone 63210 extension 2098.

5. Please read the notes carefully before completing the form.

Yours sincerely,

T.F. STAINER
for the Secretary

Return of output and employment

Please complete columns 5 and 6 for each of the projects listed alongside, and also column 8 if the completion date has been revised.

Notes
To be read before completing form

1 The data in columns **1** to **4** and **7** are supplied by Statistics and Economics Unit, Department of Finance from your new orders return and your output and employment return for last quarter.

2 In column **5** enter the **total value** of work done on the site up to the end of the quarter (i.e. since site work on the project started), **including the output of all sub-contractors and "labour-only" sub-contractors**. Value of work done should **include** profits and overheads but **exclude** the site value, professional fees and VAT.

The figure in column **5** should not be less than that in column **9** except in cases where a sub-contractor's claim included in column **9** has later been refused. In this case please put a note to this effect on the back of the form. On sites where output is measured close to the specified date by an architect or quantity surveyor, that figure would be acceptable. Otherwise an estimate should be made to cover the expected output between the last valuation in the quarter and the end of the quarter.

3 In column **6** enter the number of operatives (craftsmen and labourers) on site on the first Monday of the quarter as measured, for example, by a site agent at the beginning of the working day. **Include those employed by all sub-contractors and those employed on a "labour-only" basis.**

1 Reference Number	2 Address of site

APPENDIX XII

ion of project	4 Total value of work done to end of previous quarter.	5 Total value of work done to end of quarter *see note* 2	6 Site employment on specified day *see note* 3	7 Expected completion date *(from DF records)*	8 Expected completion date *if revised*

SPECIMEN

P.T.O.

Declaration

To be completed and signed by the person making the return on behalf of the undertaking

Trading name of undertaking

Full postal address to which correspondence should be sent *including postal code*

Telephone exchange and number

Is the above address your Registered Office ? *tick the box which applies*

yes ☐   no ☐

Please give VAT Registration Number: Date:

Signed

State whether Proprietor, Director, Manager, Partner, Secretary:

SPECIMEN

APPENDIX XIII

CONSTRUCTION AS DEFINED IN THE INDUSTRIAL CLASSIFICATION FOR THE EUROPEAN COMMUNITIES (NACE)

5. Building and Civil Engineering

Classes	Groups	Subgroups and Items	Description
50			**BUILDING AND CIVIL ENGINEERING**
	500		**General building and civil engineering work (without any particular specialization) and demolition work**
		500.1	General building and civil engineering work (without any particular specialization)
		500.2	Demolition work
	501		**Construction of flats, office blocks, hospitals and other buildings, both residential and nonresidential**
		501.1	General building contractors
		501.2	Roofing
		501.3	Construction of chimneys, kilns and furnaces
		501.4	Waterproofing and dampproofing
		501.5	Restoration and maintenance of outside walls (repointing, cleaning, etc.)
		501.6	Erection and dismantlement of scaffolding
		501.7	Other specialized activities relating to construction work (including carpentry)
	502		**Civil engineering: construction of roads, bridges, railways, etc.**
		502.1	General civil engineering work
		502.2	Earth-moving (navvying)
		502.3	Construction of bridges, tunnels and shafts, drilling
		502.4	Hydraulic engineering (rivers, canals, harbours, flows, locks and dams)
		502.5	Road-building (including specialized construction of airports and runways)
		502.6	Specialized construction work relating to water (i.e. to irrigation, land drainage, water supply, sewage disposal, sewerage, etc.)
		502.7	Specialized activities in other areas of civil engineering
	503		**Installation (fittings and fixtures)**
		503.1	General installation work
		503.2	Gas fitting and plumbing, and the installation of sanitary equipment
		503.3	Installation of heating and ventilating apparatus (central heating, air conditioning, ventilation)
		503.4	Sound and heat insulation, insulation against vibration
		503.5	Electrical fittings
		503.6	Installation of aerials, lightning conductors, telephones, etc.

—*contd.*

Classes	Groups	Subgroups and Items	Description
	504		**Building completion work**
		504.1	General building completion work
		504.2	Plastering
		504.3	Joinery, primarily engaged in on the site assembly and/or installation (including the laying of parquet flooring)
		504.4	Painting, glazing, paperhanging
		504.5	Tiling and otherwise covering floors and walls
		504.6	Other building completion work (putting in fireplaces, etc.)

Extract from: European Communities Statistical Office. *General Industrial Classification of Economic Activities within the European Communities (NACE 1970)*. European Communities Office for Official Publications, Luxembourg, 1970.

SUBJECT INDEX

A-level attainments, 6.6.3.2
Accident data for Northern Ireland, 9.4.4
Accidents, 6.10
Accountants, chartered, 4.2.3.7
Accounting, current cost, 7.2.1.1; 11.1.1.2
Accounting, historic cost, 7.2.1.1
Accounting practices, 5.4.3.2
Accounts, company, 7.2.1
Accounts for Northern Ireland, Regional, 7.1.2; 9.6.1
Accounts, income appropriation, 7.2.1.1
Accounts, national income and expenditure, 5.3.1; 5.4; 6.9.5.2; 7.1; 12.2.1.2; 12.5.1.3
Accounts, regional, 7.1.2
Accounts, Scotland, 7.1.2
Accounts, Wales, 7.1.2
Acquisition and disposal of land and existing buildings, 12.5.1.2
Acts of Parliament
 Architects Registration Act, 13.2.2
 Bankruptcy Act 1914, 7.5.1
 Building Control Act 1966, 4.8
 Companies Act 1948, 7.5
 Companies Act 1967, 7.2.1.1; 7.2.1.2; 7.5.1
 Control of Office and Industrial Development Act 1965, 5.5.4
 Counter Inflation Act, 7.2.2
 Deeds of Arrangement Act 1914, 7.5.1
 Distribution of Industry Act 1945, 5.5.3
 Employment Protection Act 1975, 6.12.1
 Factories Acts, 6.10.1
 Finance Act 1971, 7.6.1
 Finance (No. 2) Act 1975, 7.6.1
 Health and Safety at Work Act, 6.10.1; 6.10.3
 Industrial Relations Act 1971, 6.12.1
 Industrial Training Act 1964, 6.4
 Industrial Training Act (Northern Ireland) 1964, 9.3.6
 Industry Act 1972, 5.4.5.2; 5.5.3
 Industry Act 1975, 5.6.5
 Office, Shops and Railway Premises Act 1963, 12.2.2.2
 Office and Shop Premises Act (Northern Ireland) 1966, 12.2.2.2
 Redundancy Payments Act, 6.8.1.1
 Restrictive Trade Practices Act 1956, 11.1.1.1
 Selective Employment Payments Act 1966, 7.6.3
 Social Security Acts, 6.10.1
 Social Security Act 1975, 6.10.2

 Statistics of Trade Act 1947, 3.1; 3.2.2; 4.1.1; 4.1.3; 4.2.3.2; 5.4.5.1; 6.4.2; 6.9.3.1; 6.9.3.3; 6.9.3.4; 10.2.2.3
 Statistics of Trade Act (Northern Ireland) 1949, 9.1; 9.2.2.1
 Town and Country Planning Acts 1947, 5.5.3
 Town and Country Planning Act 1971, 5.5.4
 Trade Union and Labour Relations Act 1974, 6.12.2
Administrative and clerical workers, 3.3.3.1; 3.5.4.6; 3.6.2.3; 3.9.2
Administrative, professional, technical and clerical staff, 4.2.3.2; 4.2.3.6; 4.2.3.7; 4.3.2.1; 4.4.3; 6.4.1—see also APTC
Administrative, technical and clerical employees, earnings of, 6.9.3.4
Administrative, technical and clerical staff, 5.3.3.2
Advisory Committee on Aggregates, 10.2.1; 10.2.2.1
Advisory Conciliation and Arbitration Service, 6.11
Advisory Council for Scientific Policy, 6.6.3.1
Age distribution of capital stock, 12.2.1.2
Age distribution of housing stock, 12.2.2.2
Age distribution of workers, 6.2.3.4
Age limits, 3.3.3; 3.9.3.1; 4.2.3.3; 4.3.2.1
Aggregates, Advisory Committee on, 10.2.1; 10.2.2.1
Aggregates consumption, 10.2.1
Aggregates production, 10.2.2.1
Agricultural expenditure on construction, 5.4.5.1
Agricultural fencing and drainage, 4.1.2
Air raid damage labour force, 3.10.4
Alterations to buildings, 4.2.3.9
Amalgamated Union of Building Trade Workers, 3.6.2.3
Apprentices, 3.5.4.3; 3.5.4.4; 3.6.2.3; 4.2.3.4; 4.2.3.5; 4.3.2.1; 6.4.3; 6.5.1; 6.5.2; 6.5.3
Apprentices, censuses of, 6.5.1; 6.5.3
Apprentices in Northern Ireland, 9.3.8; 9.4.1
Apprentices, registration of, 6.5.1; 6.5.2
Apprentices—intake of, 3.5.4.4; 4.3.2.1
Apprenticeship and Training Council, Building, 3.5.4.4; 6.5.1; 6.5.2
Apprenticeship and Training Council, Scottish Building, 6.5.1
Apprenticeship Board, National Joint, 6.5.1
Apprenticeship scheme, national, 6.5.1
APTC staff, occupational classifications of, 4.2.3.7; 4.3.2.2
APTC staff under training, 4.2.3.7

Architects, 4.2.3.7; 13.2.2
Architects, design work by private, 5.6.2.1; 13.5.1
Architects, earnings of, 13.2.2.2; 13.4
Architects, female, 13.2.2.2
Architects, overseas work of, 13.5.1.4
Architects Registration Act, 13.2.2
Architects Registration Council of the UK, 13.2.2
Architects, Royal Institute of British, 4.7.2.1; 4.7.2.3; 5.6.2.1; 5.6.6; 13.2.2.1; 13.5.1
Architects, student, 13.2.2.2; 13.2.5
Architects' workload, 13.5.1
Architects—see also RIBA, Royal Institute of British Architects
Architectural and Associated Technicians, Society of, 6.5.5.2; 13.2.2.1
Architectural education data, 13.2.5
Architectural practices, 13.3.1
Architectural work in hand, 4.7.2.3; 13.5.1
Asphalt and tar-sprayers, 3.3.2; 4.2.3.10
Asset valuation, 7.2.1.1
Assets for leasing, hiring and renting out, 5.4.5.1
Assets, overseas, 7.2.6
Assisted work under building controls, 3.7.1; 3.7.3
Association of Consulting Engineers, 13.2.4; 13.3.3
Authorized work under building controls, 3.7.1; 3.7.2; 3.7.3; 3.7.4; 3.8.3.1

Balance of payments statistics, 4.6; 13.5.1.4
Balance sheet data, 7.2.1.1
Bank advances, 7.2.3
Bank advances in Northern Ireland, 9.6.2.2
Bankruptcy, 7.5.2
Bankruptcy Act 1914, 7.5.1
Bankruptcy in Northern Ireland, 9.6.2.3
Banwell Committee, 5.5.7
Baxter indices, 8.1.3.1
BCIS index, 4.5.3.3; 8.1.2.2; 8.1.2.7
Bills of quantities, 2.3.2; 8.1
BMCIS maintenance cost indices, 8.1.2.3
Board of Trade Register, 4.1.3
Bolton Committee, 6.12.1; 7.2.5
Bonuses, shift, 6.9.3.1
Bowen's output estimates 1945-8, 3.8.3.3
Boy labourers, 3.5.4.4
Bricklayers, 3.3.3.1; 3.5.4.3; 3.6.2.3; 4.2.3.4
British Steel Corporation, 5.3.2.2; 5.3.3.1
BRS measured work index, 8.1.1.3; 8.1.4
BRS survey of operatives, 6.7.2
Budget financial statement, 5.6.5
Building and civil engineering contractors, 3.3.2; 4.2.3.10
Building and Civil Engineering Holidays Scheme Management Company, 6.9.1; 6.9.4.1
Building Apprenticeship and Training Council, 3.5.4.4; 6.5.1; 6.5.2
Building Apprenticeship and Training Council, Scottish, 6.5.1
Building Control Act 1966, 4.8
Building control regulations, evasion of, 3.7.1
Building controls 1940-54, 3.1; 3.2; 3.7; 3.9.3.2; 4.1.1
Building controls 1966-8, 4.1.4; 4.8
Building cost information service, 8.1.2.2
Building departments of public authorities—see Direct labour
Building Economics Research Unit, University of London, 5.6.6
Building Industry Working Party 1948, 3.3.4; 3.4; 4.1.3
Building maintenance, committee on, 12.5.2
Building maintenance cost information service, 8.1.2.3; 12.5.2
Building Materials Market Research Ltd, 11.1.4
Building Research Establishment—see Building Research Station
Building Research Station, 5.3.4; 5.6.6; 6.7.2; 6.8.3; 8.2.2; 9.2.2.2; 10.2.1; 12.2.2.2
Building services staff, 6.4.4
Building share index, 7.2.4
Building Statistical Services, 10.2.1
Buildings and works stock—see Capital stock
Buildings, change of use of, 12.3
Buildings, value of land and, 12.2.1.4
Business confidence survey, 5.6.3.6

Cables, electrical, 5.4.3.2
Canal undertakings, 3.6.2.1; 5.3.2.2
Canteen workers, 3.5.4.3; 4.2.3.3; 4.2.3.4; 4.2.3.9; 6.4.1
Capital consumption, 5.4.2; 12.2.1.2
Capital expenditure, 5.3.2.2; 5.4
Capital expenditure by central government, 5.4.5.2
Capital expenditure by energy industries, 5.4.5.1
Capital expenditure by industry in Scotland, 5.4.5.1
Capital expenditure by industry in Wales, 5.4.5.1
Capital expenditure by public corporations, 5.4.5.2
Capital expenditure in Northern Ireland, 9.2.3
Capital expenditure, local authorities, 5.4.5.2
Capital expenditure series, reliability gradings of, 5.4.2
Capital expenditure surveys, 5.4.5.1; 5.4.5.2
Capital formation, gross domestic fixed, 3.8.1; 5.4
Capital formation in Northern Ireland, 9.2.3.1
Capital formation in Scotland, 5.4.4
Capital formation in Wales, 5.4.4
Capital formation, net, 5.4
Capital formation series, historical, 5.4.4
Capital retirements, 12.2.1.2
Capital stock, 7.1.1.1; 12.2.1.2—see also Stock of construction
Capital stock, age distribution of, 12.2.1.2
Capital stock estimates—price deflators, 12.2.1.3
Capital stock estimates—reliability of, 12.2.1.3
Capital stock in Northern Ireland, 9.2.3.1
Capital stock losses, 12.3
Capital stock—additions, 12.3
Capital stock—change of use, 12.3
Capital stock—estimation of, 12.2.1.1
Careers offices, 6.8.1.1
Carpenters and joiners, 3.3.3.1; 3.5.4.3; 3.6.2.3; 4.2.3.4
Carpentry contractors, joinery and, 3.3.2; 4.2.3.10

SUBJECT INDEX

Catchment and drainage undertakings, 3.6.2.1; 3.6.2.3
Catering trades, 5.4.5.1
CBI industrial trends survey, 5.6.2.2
Ceiling specialists, suspended, 4.2.3.10
Census of population, hours of work in, 6.9.4.5; 9.3.5
Census of population in Northern Ireland, 9.3.5
Census of population income enquiry 1972, 6.9.4.3
Census of population, industrial classification in, 6.3.3
Census of population, professions in, 6.3; 6.6.3.2; 13.2.1
Census of production, direct labour in, 5.3.2.1; 5.3.2.2; 5.3.3.1
Census of production in Northern Ireland, 9.2.2.1; 9.3.4
Census of production, output in, 5.3.3.2
Census of production, private contractors in, 5.3.2.2
Census of production, sampling errors in, 5.3.2.2
Census of production, sampling practice in, 5.3.2.2
Census of production—data retention periods, 5.3.2.2
Censuses of apprentices, 6.5.1; 6.5.3
Censuses of contractors since 1954, 4.2
Censuses of contractors 1941–4, 3.2; 3.3; 3.8.1; 3.9.2
Censuses of contractors 1945–54, 3.5; 3.8.3.1; 3.8.3.2; 3.9.3
Censuses of direct labour organizations since 1954, 4.3
Censuses of direct labour organizations 1941–4, 3.4; 3.8.1
Censuses of direct labour organizations 1944–54, 3.6; 3.8.1; 3.8.3.1
Censuses of distribution, 5.4.5.1
Censuses of employment, 6.2.2; 6.2.3.2
Censuses of labour resources 1944 and 1945, 3.3.5
Censuses of local authorities 1943 and 1944, 3.4
Censuses of population, 6.2.3.2; 6.3; 6.6.3.2; 6.6.3.4; 6.8.1.2; 6.9.4.5; 13.2.1
Censuses of production, 2.2.2.2; 2.3.1; 4.1.3; 5.2; 5.3; 5.4.3.1; 5.4.5.1; 5.4.6; 6.2.4.2
Censuses of trainees, 6.5.3
Central government, capital expenditure by, 5.4.5.2
Certification Officer for Trade Unions, 6.12.1
Change of use of buildings, 12.3
Changes in wage rates, 6.9.2.1
Channel Islands, 4.2.2
Charitable contributions, 7.2.1.1
Chartered accountants, 4.2.3.7
Chartered Institute of Public Finance and Accountancy, 5.4.3.2
Chartered Surveyors, Royal Institution of, 13.2.3; 13.3.2
City and Guilds qualifications, 6.5.5
Civil defence regions, 3.3.3.3; 3.5.4.9; 4.2.3.12
Civil engineering contracting, 6.3.2
Civil engineering contractors, building and, 3.3.2; 4.2.3.10

Civil engineering firms, labour policies of, 6.7.4
Civil engineering work, 3.5.4.8
Civil Engineers, Institution of, 13.2.4
Civil licences, 3.7.1; 3.7.2; 3.7.4
Classification by occupation—see Occupational classifications
Classification by trade of firm—see Trade classifications
Classification by type of work—see Type of work categories
Classification of occupations in census of population, 6.3.2
Cleaning of buildings, 4.1.2; 4.4.5.5
Clerical and sales staff, 4.2.3.7
Clerical employees, earnings of administrative, technical and, 6.9.3.4
Clerical staff, administrative, professional, technical and, 4.2.3.2; 4.2.3.6; 4.2.3.7; 4.3.2.1; 4.4.3; 6.4.1
Clerical staff, administrative, technical and, 5.3.3.2
Clerical workers, administrative and, 3.3.3.1; 3.5.4.6; 3.6.2.3; 3.9.2
Clericals, male, 3.3.3.1
CNC index, 4.5.3.3; 5.2.2; 5.4.2; 5.4.5.1; 8.1.2; 13.5.1.2
Coal industry, 3.6.2.1; 5.3.2.2
Coal mining by contractors, opencast, 3.10.3; 4.1.2; 5.4.3.1; 5.4.6; 6.3.2; 7.6.4
CODOT, 6.8.1.1; 6.9.3.1
Collection methods, 2.2.1
Collective agreements, 6.9.3.1
Commercial buildings, stock of, 12.2.2
Commission for New Towns, 4.3.2.1
Committee on building maintenance, 12.5.2
Committee on inflation accounting—see Sandilands Committee
Committee on manpower resources for science and technology, 6.6.3.1
Committee on safety and health at work—Robens, 6.10.3
Committee on scientific manpower, 6.6.3.1
Committee on small firms—see Bolton Committee
Companies Act 1948, 7.5
Companies Act 1967, 7.2.1.1; 7.2.1.2; 7.5.1
Company accounts, 7.2.1
Company acquisitions, 7.4
Company liquidations, 7.5.3
Company mergers, 7.4
Company profits, 7.1.1.1
Concrete erectors and assemblers, 4.2.3.4
Concrete specialists, reinforced, 3.3.2; 4.2.3.10
Conditions of employment, 6.9.3.1; 6.9.4.2
Conditions of work—see Earnings and hours
Constant price expenditure series, 5.4.2
Constant price new orders series, 4.5.3.3
Constant price output series, 4.4.5.2
Construction Industry Training Board, 4.2.3.4; 6.4; 6.5.1; 6.5.3; 6.5.4; 6.8.3
Construction Industry Training Board, grants received from, 6.4.5; 7.2.5
Construction Industry Training Board, levy payments to, 6.4.5; 7.2.5

Construction Industry Training Board, levy return of, 6.4.1
Construction Industry Training Board, Northern Ireland, 9.3.6; 9.4.1; 9.5
Construction Industry Training Board Register, 6.4.2
Constructional engineers, 3.3.2; 4.1.2; 4.2.3.10; 6.9.3.3
Consulting Engineers, Association of, 13.2.4; 13.3.3
Consulting engineers, overseas work of, 13.5.3
Consumption of materials, 10.2.1
Continuation contracts, 4.5.2.2
Contract cleaning pay and conditions—NBPI survey (1971), 6.9.4.2
Contract—standard form, 8.1.3
Contractors' new orders, 4.2.3.12; 4.5.2; 4.5.3; 4.7.2.3; 5.6.2.1
Contracts, continuation, 4.5.2.2
Contracts, duration of, 4.5.2.3; 5.6.6
Contracts, fixed price, 4.5.2.2; 5.6.2.1
Contracts, placing of, 5.5.7
Contracts, unofficial surveys of, 5.6.4
Contracts, variable price, 4.5.2.2; 5.6.2.1
Contracts—see New orders
Control of Building Operations Orders, 3.7.1
Control of Office and Industrial Development Act 1965, 5.5.4
Conversion workers, natural gas, 4.2.3.4
Conversions of houses and flats, 4.2.3.9
Conveyancing, 12.5.1.1
Cost indices, 8.1
Cost Information Service, Building, 8.1.2.2
Cost Information Service, Building Maintenance, 8.1.2.3; 12.5.2
Cost of electricity, 5.3.2.2
Cost of employers' insurance contributions, 5.3.2.2; 6.9.5.1; 6.9.5.2
Cost of fuel, 5.3.2.2
Cost of inputs, 5.3.2; 8.1.1.3
Cost of inputs in Northern Ireland, 9.2.2.1
Cost of insurance, 5.3.2.2
Cost of licensing motor vehicles, 5.3.2.2
Cost of materials, 5.3.2.2; 8.1.1.3
Cost of payments in kind, 6.9.5.1
Cost of plant hire, 5.3.2.2
Cost of rates, 5.3.2.2
Cost of redundancy payments, 6.9.5.1; 6.9.5.2
Cost of transport, 5.3.2.2
Cost of vocational training, 6.9.5.1
Cost of wages and salaries, 5.3.2.2; 6.9.5.1; 6.9.5.2
Cost of wages and salaries in Northern Ireland, 9.4.3
Costing records, 2.3.2
Costs, labour, 6.9.5; 8.1.1.3
Costs, occupancy, 12.5.2
Costs of construction, 8; 14.2
Council of Engineering Institutions, 13.2.4
Counter-Inflation Act, 7.2.2
Counter-inflation legislation, 8.1.3.1
Craftsmen, 3.3.3.1; 3.5.4.3; 4.2.3.4
Crane drivers, 4.2.3.4

Current cost accounting, 7.2.1.1; 11.1.1.2
Current cost accounting, price index numbers for, 8.1.4; 11.1.1.2; 11.2
Current expenditure, 5.4.6
Current price expenditure series, 5.4.2
Current price new orders series, 4.5.3.1
Current price output series, 4.4.5.1

Dangerous occurrences, 6.10.1
Days lost, working, 6.11
Death benefit, industrial, 6.10.2
Deeds of Arrangement Act 1914, 7.5.1
Defence Regulation 55AA, 10.2.2.3
Defence Regulation 56A, 3.2.1; 3.7.1
Defence Regulation 56AB, 3.2.2; 3.7.1; 3.7.5
Defence Regulations, General, 3.1; 3.2; 3.7.1; 4.1.1; 9.1
Defence work, 5.4.3.1; 5.4.6
Definition of firm, 3.5.4.1; 4.2.3.2
Deflators in Northern Ireland, output, 9.2.4
Deflators in Northern Ireland, price, 9.2.4
Deflators, new orders, 4.5.3.3
Deflators, output, 4.4.5.2; 4.5.3.3; 5.2.1.2; 8.1
Deflators, price, 2.3.3; 5.4.2; 8.1; 8.1.5
Deflators, Scotland price, 5.2.1.2
Degree course students, 6.5.5.2
Degree holders, 6.6.3.1; 6.6.3.2; 6.6.3.5; 13.2.4; 13.2.5
Demolishers, 4.2.3.4
Demolition contractors, 3.3.2; 4.2.3.10
Demolition data, 12.3
Demolition, site clearance and, 5.4.3.2
Department of Manpower Services Northern Ireland, 9.3.2
Department of the Environment as employer of direct labour, 4.3.3
Design work by local authorities, 4.7; 5.6.2.1
Design work by private architects, 5.6.2.1; 13.5.1
Design work, road construction, 4.7.2.1; 4.7.2.2
Design work, valuation of, 4.7.2.2; 5.6.2.1; 13.5.1
Development areas, 5.5.3
Development Commissions (Northern Ireland), 9.2.5.3
Development controls, 12.4.2
DHSS accident data, 6.10
Dimensional co-ordination, 13.5.1.2
Direct labour, Department of the Environment as employer of, 4.3.3
Direct labour departments, 3.2.2; 3.3.1; 3.4; 3.6; 3.8.2.2; 6.2.3.1
Direct labour earnings and hours—NBPI surveys, 6.9.4.2
Direct labour forces by type of local authority, 4.3.2.2
Direct labour forces in the SIC, 4.1.2; 4.1.3; 14.2
Direct labour forces, registration of, 3.7.5; 4.1.3
Direct labour forces, size distribution of, 3.6.2.3; 4.3.2.2
Direct labour, hospital authorities, 3.6.2.1; 4.3.3; 5.3.2.2; 5.3.3.1
Direct labour in censuses of production, 5.3.2.1; 5.3.2.2; 5.3.3.1

SUBJECT INDEX

Direct labour in government departments, 3.4; 3.6.1; 3.6.3; 4.3.1; 4.3.3; 5.3.2.2; 6.2.3.4
Direct labour in local authorities, 3.4; 3.6.1; 3.6.2; 4.3.1; 4.3.2; 4.4.4; 5.3.2.2; 6.2.3.4
Direct labour in Northern Ireland, 9.2.1; 9.2.2.1; 9.3; 9.5
Direct labour in private firms, 3.4; 3.6.1; 4.1.3; 4.2.2; 4.2.3.9; 4.2.3.10; 4.3.1
Direct labour in public utility undertakings, 3.4; 3.6.1; 3.6.2; 4.3.1; 4.3.3; 5.3.2.2; 6.2.3.4
Direct labour in transport undertakings, 3.6.2.1; 3.6.2.3; 5.3.2.2
Direct labour organizations since 1954, censuses of, 4.3
Direct labour organizations 1941–4, censuses of, 3.4; 3.8.1
Direct labour organizations 1944–54, censuses of, 3.6; 3.8.1; 3.8.3.1
Direct labour, value of work done by, 3.8.3.2
Direct work under building controls, 3.7.1; 3.7.2; 3.7.3; 3.7.4
Directors, 4.2.3.7; 6.2.3.2
Directors, part-time, 4.2.3.6
Directory of businesses, 5.3.2.2
Diseases, industrial, 6.10.1
Disposal of land and existing buildings, acquisition and, 12.5.1.2
Disputes, 6.11
Distribution of earnings, 6.9.3.1; 6.9.3.2
Distribution of Industry Act 1945, 5.5.3
Distributive and service trades in Northern Ireland, 9.2.3.2
Distributive and service trades—surveys, 5.4.5.1
Do-it-yourself output, 4.4.5.5
Docks undertakings, 3.6.2.1; 3.6.2.3; 5.3.2.2
Domestic fixed capital formation, gross, 5.4
DQSD—see DQSS
DQSS index, 4.5.3.3; 8.1.2.6
Drainage, agricultural fencing and, 4.1.2
Drainage undertakings, catchment and, 3.6.2.1; 3.6.2.3
Draughtsmen and tracers, 4.2.3.7
Drawings, working, 4.7.2; 13.5.1
Dredging, 4.1.2
Drilling platforms, 5.4.3.2
Drivers, 3.5.4.3; 4.2.3.4; 4.2.3.9
Drivers, crane, 4.2.3.4
Duration of contracts, 4.5.2.3; 5.6.6
Dwellings, stock of, 12.2.2.2
Dwellings—unsold, 5.4.3.2

Earnings, 6.9.3
Earnings and hours—NBPI surveys (1968–71), 6.9.4.2
Earnings, distribution of, 6.9.3.1; 6.9.3.2
Earnings in Northern Ireland, 9.4.3.2
Earnings, make-up of, 6.9.3.1
Earnings, monthly index of average, 6.9.3.5
Earnings, occupational analyses of, 6.9.3.3
Earnings of administrative, technical and clerical employees, 6.9.3.4
Earnings of architects, 13.2.2.2; 13.4

Earnings of engineers, 13.4
Earnings of qualified manpower, 6.6.4; 13.4
Earnings of quantity surveyors, 13.4
Earnings of self-employed, 6.9.4.3
Earnings, professional, 13.4
Earnings Survey, New, 6.9.3
Earnings (1973), NEDO survey of, 6.9.4.1
Earth moving plant operators, 4.2.3.4
Econometric models, 5.6.5
Economic Development Committee for Building, 6.9.4.1; 13.5.1.2
Economic Development Committee for Mechanical and Electrical Engineering, 8.2
Economic Development Committees for Building and Civil Engineering, 5.5.7; 5.6.5.1; 5.6.6; 6.7.4; 8.1.3.1; 8.2; 10.2.1
Economic forecasting services, 5.6.5
Economic planning regions, 4.2.3.12
Education data, 6.3.2; 6.5; 13.2.5
Education data, architectural, 13.2.5
Education in Northern Ireland, 9.4.1
Educational building, 5.5.2
Educational building in Northern Ireland, 9.2.5.1
Educational buildings, stock of, 12.2.2.2
Educational facilities survey, 6.5.5.2
EEC, 6.9.5.1
EEC labour force surveys, 6.2.3.4
EEC state of trade enquiry, 4.1.4; 4.5.4
EIU cost index, 8.1.2
Electrical cables, 5.4.3.2
Electrical contracting pay and conditions—NBPI survey (1966–8), 6.9.4.2
Electrical contractors, 3.3.2; 4.1.3; 4.2.3.10
Electrical, Electronic, Telecommunications and Plumbing Union, 6.4.4
Electrical Engineers, Institution of, 13.2.4
Electrical services cost index, mechanical and, 8.1.2.4
Electricians, 3.3.3.1; 3.5.4.3; 3.6.2.3; 4.2.3.4; 6.4.4
Electricity, cost of, 5.3.2.2
Electricity undertakings, 3.6.2.1; 3.6.2.3; 4.1.2; 4.3.3; 4.4.5.1; 5.2.2; 5.3.2.2
Employees in census of production, 5.3.3.2
Employees in Department of Employment data, 6.2.3.1; 6.2.3.2
Employees in employment (DE series), 6.2
Employees in employment (DOE series), 4.4.3
Employees, insured, 3.3.3.1
Employers' Associations, Royal Commission on Trade Unions and, 6.12.1
Employers' insurance contributions, cost of, 5.3.2.2; 6.9.5.1; 6.9.5.2
Employment, censuses of, 6.2.2; 6.2.3.2
Employment, conditions of, 6.9.3.1; 6.9.4.2
Employment data for Northern Ireland, 9.3
Employment data for Northern Ireland compared, 9.3.7
Employment data—census of population, 6.3
Employment data—census of production, 5.3
Employment data—CITB, 6.4
Employment data—MOL–DE, 6.2

Employment data—MOW–DOE, 3; 4
Employment in public sector, 4.3.3
Employment offices, youth, 6.8.1.1
Employment Protection Act 1975, 6.12.1
Employment, research and development, 6.6.3.6
Employment series compared, 6.2.4; 6.3.4
Employment services agency, 6.8.1.1
Employment time series, 3.9; 4.4; 6.2
Employment—continuity of, 6.7.4
Employment—continuity of—see also Labour turnover
Employment—continuity of—see also Security of employment
Energy industries, capital expenditure by, 5.4.5.1
Engineering Industry Training Board, 6.4.2
Engineering practices, 13.3.3
Engineers, 4.2.3.7; 13.2.4
Engineers, Association of Consulting, 13.3.3
Engineers, constructional, 3.3.2; 4.1.2; 4.2.3.10; 6.9.3.3
Engineers, earnings of, 13.4
Engineers' registration board, 13.2.4
Engineers' workload, 13.5.3
Enterprises—see Firms
Equipment, plant and, 10.3
Establishments—production or industrial, 2.2.2; 4.1.2
Estimates Committee, Report on Government Statistical Services, 5.3.2.2
Evasion of building control regulations, 3.7.1
Exemption limits, financial, 3.2; 3.7.1; 3.8.3.2
Expenditure accounts, national income and, 5.3.1; 5.4; 6.9.5.2; 7.1; 12.2.1.2; 12.5.1.3
Expenditure and output series compared, 5.4.3
Expenditure by central government, capital, 5.4.5.2
Expenditure by construction industry, 5.3.2.2; 5.4.2; 7.1.1.1
Expenditure by contractors on inputs, 5.3.2.2
Expenditure by contractors on rent, 5.3.2.2
Expenditure by contractors on repairs and maintenance, 5.3.2.2
Expenditure by energy industries, capital, 5.4.5.1
Expenditure by householders, 4.4.5.5
Expenditure by industry in Scotland, capital, 5.4.5.1
Expenditure by industry in Wales, capital, 5.4.5.1
Expenditure by public corporations, capital, 5.4.5.2
Expenditure, capital, 5.3.2.2; 5.4
Expenditure, current, 5.4.6
Expenditure in Northern Ireland, capital, 9.2.3
Expenditure, local authorities' capital, 5.4.5.2
Expenditure on construction, 5.4
Expenditure on construction, agricultural, 5.4.5.1
Expenditure on construction in Northern Ireland, 9.2.3
Expenditure on construction in Wales, public, 5.4.5.2
Expenditure on construction, public, 5.4.5.2
Expenditure on repairs and maintenance, 5.4.6
Expenditure on research and development, 7.3
Expenditure series, constant price, 5.4.2

Expenditure series, current price, 5.4.2
Expenditure series, improvements to building in, 5.4.2; 5.4.3.2
Expenditure series, reliability gradings of capital, 5.4.2
Expenditure series, repair and maintenance in, 5.4.2; 5.4.3.2
Expenditure surveys, capital, 5.4.5.1; 5.4.5.2
Expenditure surveys, family, 4.4.5.5; 6.9.4.4
Exports, 7.2.1.1
Extel Statistical Services Ltd, 7.2.1.2
Extensions to buildings, 4.2.3.9; 4.5.2.1

Factor costs, 8.1.2
Factor incomes, 7.1.1
Factories Acts, 6.10.1
Factories, stock of, 12.2.2
Factory and office building survey, 5.6.6; 13.5.1.2
Factory inspectorate divisions, 6.10.1
Factory Inspectorate, HM, 6.10; 12.2.2.2
Family Expenditure Surveys, 4.4.5.5; 6.9.4.4
Federation of Civil Engineering Contractors, 5.6.3.4
Fees, professional, 4.6; 5.4.2.2; 5.4.3.1; 13.4
Female architects, 13.2.2.2
Females, 4.2.3.3; 4.3.2.1; 6.2.3; 6.3.2
Fencing and drainage, agricultural, 4.1.2
Final account price, 8.1.1.2
Finance (No. 2) Act 1975, 7.6.1
Finance Act 1971, 7.6.1
Financial assistance, public, 5.4.5.2
Financial exemption limits, 3.2; 3.7.1; 3.8.3.2
Firms, number of, 3.5.4.1; 4.2.3.2
Firms—names of—see Directory of businesses
Fitters, 3.3.3.1
Fixed capital formation, gross domestic, 3.8.1; 5.4
Fixed price contracts, 4.5.2.2; 5.6.2.1
Floor laying, parquet, 4.1.2
Floor tiling specialists, wall and, 4.2.3.10
Flooring contractors, 3.3.2; 4.2.3.10
Floorspace data, 5.5.3; 12.2.2.1
Forbes Committee, 4.1.3
Forecasting future output, 4.5.1; 4.5.2.2; 4.5.3.5; 4.7.1; 4.7.2.3; 5.6; 5.6.5; 13.5.1.2
Forecasting services, economic, 5.6.5
Forecasts, NEDO construction, 5.6.5.1
Forecasts of investment, 5.6.5
Foreign contractors, 4.2.2; 7.2.1.1
Foreign owned companies, 7.2.1.1
Foreign work by British contractors, 4.2.2; 4.6
Foremen, 3.5.4.3; 4.2.3.4
Foremen, general, 3.5.4.3; 4.2.3.4; 4.2.3.7
Foremen, working, 3.5.4.3; 4.2.3.4; 4.2.3.7
Form BCE2, 3.2.2
Form BCE3, 3.2.2
Form CPS23, 3.10.3
Form WBI, 3.7.4.1; 3.10.3
Form WBI-CL, 3.7.4.1
Formwork erectors, 4.2.3.4
Forward indicators of construction activity, 5.6
FT—Actuaries share indices, 7.2.4
Fuel, cost of, 5.3.2.2

SUBJECT INDEX

Fuel, stock of, 5.3.2.2; 11.1.1.2
Further education statistical record, 6.5.5.1

Gas conversion workers, natural, 4.2.3.4
Gas fitters and plumbers, 4.2.3.4
Gas, North Sea oil and, 5.4.3.2
Gas pipelines, 5.4.3.2
Gas undertakings, 3.6.2.1; 3.6.2.3; 4.1.2; 4.3.3; 4.4.5.1; 5.2.2; 5.3.2.2
General builders, 3.3.2; 4.2.3.10
General Certificate of Education, 6.6.1; 6.6.3.2
General defence regulations, 3.1; 3.2; 3.7.1; 4.1.1; 9.1
General foremen, 3.5.4.3; 4.2.3.4; 4.2.3.7
Glaziers, plumbers and, 3.3.3.1; 3.5.4.3; 3.6.2.3; 4.2.3.4
Glazing contractors, 3.3.2; 4.2.3.10
Go slow, 6.11
Goods on hand for sale, 5.3.2.2
Government building programme, 3.2; 3.7.4.2; 3.8.2.2; 3.9.2
Government buildings—running costs, 12.5.2
Government departments, direct labour in, 3.4; 3.6.1; 3.6.3; 4.3.1; 4.3.3; 5.3.2.2; 6.2.3.4
Government Social Survey, 6.5.4; 6.7.3; 6.8.3
Government Training Centres, 6.5.4
Graduate employment, 6.4.4; 6.6.3.1; 6.6.3.2; 6.6.3.5; 13.2.4; 13.2.5
Graduates, university, 6.3.3.5
Grants received from Construction Industry Training Board, 6.4.5; 7.2.5
Greater London Council surveys, 6.7.7
'Grip', 2.2.2.2
Gross domestic fixed capital formation, 3.8.1; 5.4
Gross Domestic Product, 7.1.1; 7.1.2
Gross Domestic Product—Northern Ireland, 9.6.1
Gross fixed capital formation, 3.8.1; 5.4
Gross fixed capital formation in Northern Ireland, 9.2.3.1
Gross trading profits, 7.1.1
GSS survey of building operatives, 6.7.3

Health and Safety at Work Act, 6.10.1; 6.10.3
Health and safety executive, 6.10
Health service building, 5.5.6
Health service building in Northern Ireland, 9.2.5.2
Heating and Ventilating Contractors' Association, 5.6.3.5
Heating and ventilating engineers, 3.3.2; 4.2.3.4; 4.2.3.10; 6.4.4; 6.9.3.3
Heating and Ventilating Engineers, Institution of, 13.2.4
Hiring and renting out, assets for leasing, 5.4.5.1
Historic cost accounting, 7.2.1.1
Historical capital formation series, 5.4.4
HM Factory Inspectorate, 6.10; 12.2.2.2
HNC students, 6.5.5.2
HND students, 6.6.3.5
Holiday camps, 12.2.2.2
Holiday entitlement, 6.9.3.1
Holiday with pay rates, 6.9.1; 6.9.2.1

Holidays Scheme Management Company, Building and Civil Engineering, 6.9.1; 6.9.4.1
Hospital authorities' direct labour, 3.6.2.1; 4.3.3; 5.3.2.2; 5.3.3.1
Hospital building, 5.5.6; 8.2.2
Hospital building in Northern Ireland, 9.2.5.2
Hospital building—cost of, 8.1.2
Hospital buildings—running costs, 12.5.2
Hotels, stock of, 12.2.2.2
Hours of work in census of population, 6.9.4.5; 9.3.5
Hours of work in Northern Ireland, 9.4.3.1; 9.4.3.2
Hours worked, 6.9
Hours worked (1973), NEDO survey of, 6.9.4.1
Hours—NBPI surveys (1968–71), earnings and, 6.9.4.2
House Builders Federation, 5.6.3.3
House condition survey, 12.2.2.2
House price index, 4.5.3.3; 5.4.2; 8.1.1.2
Housebuilding tender index, 4.5.3.3; 8.1.1.2
Houses—see also Dwellings
Housing land, 12.5.1.2
Housing stock, age distribution of, 12.2.2.2
Husbands working for wives, 6.2.3.2

ILEA building contract fluctuations clause indices, 8.1.3.2
ILEA survey of technician students, 6.5.5.2
Improvements to building in expenditure series, 5.4.2; 5.4.3.2
Improvements to buildings, 4.2.3.9; 4.5.2.1
Incentive schemes, 3.10.6; 6.9.3.1
Incentive schemes—see Payment by results
Income and expenditure accounts, national, 5.3.1; 5.4; 6.9.5.2; 7.1; 12.2.1.2; 12.5.1.3
Income appropriation accounts, 7.2.1.1
Income enquiry 1972, census of population, 6.9.4.3
Income from employment, 7.1.1
Income from employment—see also Earnings
Income from self-employment, 7.1.1
Incomes, factor, 7.1.1
Indentures, written, 3.5.4.4; 4.2.3.5; 6.5.2
Index, BCIS, 4.5.3.3; 8.1.2.2; 8.1.2.7
Index, BRS measured work, 8.1.1.3
Index, building share, 7.2.4
Index, CNC, 4.5.3.3; 5.2.2; 5.4.2; 5.4.5.1; 8.1.2; 13.5.1.2
Index, DQSS, 4.5.3.3; 8.1.2.6
Index, EIU cost, 8.1.2
Index, house price, 4.5.3.3; 5.4.2; 8.1.1.2
Index, housebuilding tender, 4.5.3.3; 8.1.1.2
Index, mechanical and electrical service cost, 8.1.2.4
Index, Northern Ireland price, 8.1.1.3
Index numbers of output, 5.2
Index numbers of output at constant factor cost, 5.2.1.1
Index of average earnings, monthly, 6.9.3.5
Index of industrial production, 5.2
Index of industrial production, interim, 3.8.2.1; 5.2.1.1

Index of industrial production, Northern Ireland, 5.2.1.2; 9.2.4
Index of industrial production, Scotland, 5.2.1.2
Index of industrial production, Wales, 5.2.1.2
Index, PILAH, 4.5.3.3; 8.1.1.2
Index, road construction price, 4.5.3.3; 8.1.2
Index, Spons tender price, 8.1.2.8
Index, Venning, 8.1.1.2; 8.1.4
Indices, Baxter, 8.1.3.1
Indices, BMCIS maintenance cost, 8.1.2.3
Indices for stocks of materials, price, 11.1.1.2
Indices for stocks, price, 11.1.1.2
Indices, FT—Actuaries share, 7.2.4
Indices of maintenance costs, 8.1.2.1; 8.1.2.3
Indices of products, 10.2.2.1
Indices of weekly wage rates, 6.9.2.1; 6.9.2.2
Indices, Osborne, 8.1.3.1
Indices, price, 4.4.5.2; 4.5.3.3; 5.2.1.2; 5.2.2; 5.4.2; 8.1
Indices, RICS maintenance costs, 8.1.2
Indices, RICS price, 8.1.2
Indices, share price, 7.2.4
Indices, Spons cost, 8.1.2.4
Indices, tender price, 4.5.3.3; 8.1.1.2; 8.1.2
Indices, wholesale price, 11.1; 11.2
Industrial building, 5.5.3
Industrial building in Northern Ireland, 9.2.3.2; 9.2.5.3
Industrial buildings, stock of, 12.2.2
Industrial classification in census of population, 6.3.3
Industrial death benefit, 6.10.2
Industrial definition, 2.1
Industrial development certificates, 5.5.3
Industrial diseases, 6.10.1
Industrial disputes, 6.11
Industrial establishments, 12.2.2.2
Industrial injury benefit, 6.10.2; 6.10.3
Industrial relations, 6.12.1
Industrial Relations Act 1971, 6.12.1
Industrial services—cost of, 5.3.2.2
Industrial Training Act (Northern Ireland) 1964, 9.3.6
Industrial Training Act 1964, 6.4
Industrial trends survey, CBI, 5.6.2.2
Industrialized building methods, 4.9.2
Industry Act 1972, 5.4.5.2; 5.5.3
Industry Act 1975, 5.6.5
Injury benefit, industrial, 6.10.2; 6.10.3
Inland Revenue data, 7.1.1.1; 7.6.1
Inland Revenue data for Northern Ireland, 9.6.2.1
Inland Revenue data—see also PAYE
Inland Revenue 'pay-points', 6.2.3.2
Input–output tables, 5.3.1; 5.3.4
Input–output tables, Northern Ireland, 5.3.4; 9.2.2.2
Input–output tables, Scotland, 5.3.4
Inputs, cost of, 5.3.2; 8.1.1.3
Inputs, expenditure by contractors on, 5.3.2.2
Inputs in Northern Ireland, cost of, 9.2.2.1
Insolvency, 7.5
Insolvency in Northern Ireland, 9.6.2.3

Institute of Building, 6.6.1; 6.6.2
Institute of Building Surveys, 6.5.5.2; 6.6.2
Institute of Municipal Engineers, 13.2.4
Institute of Quantity Surveyors, 13.2.3
Institution of Civil Engineers, 13.2.4
Institution of Electrical Engineers, 13.2.4
Institution of Heating and Ventilating Engineers, 13.2.4
Institution of Mechanical Engineers, 13.2.4
Institution of Structural Engineers, 13.2.4
Insulating specialists, 4.2.3.10
Insulation contracting pay and conditions—NBPI survey (1968), 6.9.4.2
Insurance contributions, cost of employers', 5.3.2.2; 6.9.5.1; 6.9.5.2
Insurance, cost of, 5.3.2.2
Insured employees, 3.3.3.1
Interest charges, 5.4.2; 5.4.3.1
Interim index of industrial production, 3.8.2.1; 5.2.1.1
International standard industrial classification, 2.1
Investment by the construction industry, 5.4.2
Investment, forecasts of, 5.6.5
Investment incentives, 5.4.3.2
Investment intentions surveys, 5.6.2.2
Investment, overseas, 7.2.6
Investment—see also Capital expenditure
Investment—see also Gross domestic fixed capital formation
Isle of Man, 4.2.2

Joiners, carpenters and, 3.3.3.1; 3.5.4.3; 3.6.2.3; 4.2.3.4
Joinery and carpentry contractors, 3.3.2; 4.2.3.10
Joint contracts tribunal, 8.1.3
Joint Manpower Watch Surveys, 6.2.3.4

Labour ceilings, 3.7.4.1; 3.7.4.2
Labour costs, 6.9.5; 8.1.1.3
Labour costs in Northern Ireland, 9.4.3.3
Labour employed—see under Employment
Labour force surveys, EEC, 6.2.3.4
Labour mobility in Northern Ireland, 9.4.2.3
Labour, mobility of, 6.8.3
Labour, off-site, 3.5.4.3; 3.8.2.2; 3.8.3.2; 3.9.2; 3.9.3
Labour, on-site, 3.5.4.3; 3.8.3.2; 3.9.2; 3.9.3
Labour-only sub-contracting, 2.2.2.2; 2.3.3; 4.1.3; 4.2.2; 4.2.3.4; 4.2.3.6; 4.2.3.8; 4.4.2; 4.4.5; 5.3.3.1; 5.3.3.2; 6.2.3.1; 6.4.1; 6.4.4; 6.7.4; 6.10.3; 7.6.1; 14.2
Labour-only sub-contracting in Northern Ireland—working party, 9.3.8
Labour policies of civil engineering firms, 6.7.4
Labour quotas, 3.7.4.2
Labour Relations Act 1974, Trade Union and, 6.12.2
Labour resources 1944 and 1945, censuses of, 3.3.5
Labour surveys—*ad hoc*, 6.7
Labour training and education statistics, 6.5
Labour turnover, 6.4.4; 6.8.3

SUBJECT INDEX

Labour, unrecorded, 4.2.3.3; 4.4.3; 5.3.3.1
Labourers, 3.3.3.1; 3.5.4.3; 4.2.3.4
Land and buildings, transfer costs of, 5.4.3.1
Land and buildings, value of, 12.2.1.4
Land and existing buildings, acquisition and disposal of, 12.5.1.2
Land and existing buildings, purchases of, 5.3.2.2
Land, housing, 12.5.1.2
Land use data, 12.4.1
Lead poisoning, 6.10.1
Leasing, hiring and renting out, assets for, 5.4.5.1
Legal charges, 5.4.2
Length of service, 6.9.3.1; 6.9.4.1
Levy payments to Construction Industry Training Board, 6.4.5; 7.2.5
Levy return of Construction Industry Training Board, 6.4.1
Licences, civil, 3.7.1; 3.7.2; 3.7.4
Licences, maintenance, 3.2.1; 3.7.3; 3.8.3.2
Licensed work under building controls, 3.7.1; 3.7.2; 3.7.3; 3.7.4; 3.8.3.1
Licensed work under building controls 1966–8, 4.8
Licensing by local authorities, 3.7.1; 3.7.3
Licensing motor vehicles, cost of, 5.3.2.2
Licensing of civil building operations, 3.1; 3.2; 3.7
Lighting, site, 4.9.1
Liquidations, 7.5.3
Listed companies–see quoted companies
Local authorities capital expenditure, 5.4.5.2
Local Authorities Conditions of Service Advisory Board, 6.2.3.4
Local authorities, design work by, 4.7; 5.6.2.1
Local authorities, direct labour in, 3.4; 3.6.1; 3.6.2; 4.3.1; 4.3.2; 4.4.4; 5.3.2.2; 6.2.3.4
Local authorities, licensing by, 3.7.1; 3.7.3
Local authorities 1943 and 1944, censuses of, 3.4
Local authority architects' departments, 13.3.1.2
Local authority, direct labour forces by type of, 4.3.2.2
Local Authority Services Scotland, National Joint Council for, 6.2.3.4
Local government service, 6.2.3.4; 6.2.4
London censuses of labour resources, 3.3.5
London civil defence region, 3.5.4.9
London construction site data, 6.7.7
'Lump', 2.2.2.2; 4.4.2; 6.2.3.1; 6.2.3.2; 6.2.3.4
'Lump'—see also Labour-only sub-contracting

Main trades (pre-1955), 3.3.1; 3.3.2; 3.3.3; 3.5.3; 3.8.2; 3.8.3.1; 3.8.3.2; 3.9
Main trades (since 1974), 4.2.3.10
Maintenance, Committee on Building, 12.5.2
Maintenance cost indices, BMCIS, 8.1.2.3
Maintenance Cost Information Service, Building, 8.1.2.3; 12.5.2
Maintenance costs, indices of, 8.1.2.1; 8.1.2.3
Maintenance, expenditure by contractors on repairs and, 5.3.2.2
Maintenance, expenditure on repairs and, 5.4.6
Maintenance in expenditure series, repair and, 5.4.2; 5.4.3.2
Maintenance licences, 3.2.1; 3.7.1; 3.7.3; 3.8.3.2

Maintenance work, repair and, 3.3.3.2; 3.5.4.8; 3.6.1; 3.8.3.2; 4.1.2; 4.2.3.8; 4.2.3.9; 4.3.2.2; 4.4.4; 5.4.6
Make-up of earnings, 6.9.3.1
Male clericals, 3.3.3.1
Managerial staff, 4.2.3.7
Manpower Services Commission, 6.5.4; 6.7.6; 6.8.1.1
Manpower surveys, NFBTE regional, 6.4.4
Manpower surveys, regional, 6.4.4
Manufacture of goods for sale, 4.2.3.4; 4.2.3.9; 4.4.2; 5.3.2.2
Market Research Ltd, Building Materials, 11.1.4
Masons, 3.5.4.3; 4.2.3.4
Materials and plant, price indices of, 11
Materials, consumption of, 10.2.1
Materials, cost of, 5.3.2.2; 8.1.1.3
Materials in Northern Ireland, 10.2.2.2
Materials Market Research Ltd Building, 11.1.4
Materials, overseas trade in, 10.2.3
Materials, price indices for stocks of, 11.1.1.2
Materials, prices of, 11
Materials Producers, National Council of Building, 5.6.5.2
Materials, production of, 10.2.2
Materials received, 3.7.4.1
Materials, stock of, 5.3.2.2; 10.2.2
Materials used, 3.7.4.1; 5.3.4; 10.2.1
Measured rates, 8.1.1.3
Measured work index, BRS, 8.1.1.3
Mechanical and electrical services cost index, 8.1.2.4
Mechanical engineering services workers, 4.2.3.4
Mechanical Engineers, Institution of, 13.2.4
Mechanical equipment operators, 4.2.3.4
Mechanics, plant maintenance, 3.5.4.3; 4.2.3.4
Mergers, 7.4
Mergers Commission, Monopolies and, 13.2.3; 13.3.1.1; 13.3.2; 13.5.2
Methods, industrialized building, 4.9.2
Metrication, 13.5.1
Military buildings, 5.4.3.1; 5.4.6
Mine sinking, 4.1.2
Mineral boring, 4.1.2
Mineral enquiry, 10.2.2.1
Mineral Resources Consultative Committee, 10.2.2.1
Ministry of Works as employer, 3.6.3
Mobile labour force, 3.6.3; 3.10.1
Mobility of labour, 6.8.3
Monopolies and Mergers Commission, 13.2.3; 13.3.1.1; 13.3.2; 13.5.2
Monopolies Commission, 13.2.2.2; 13.2.3; 13.2.4
Monthly index of average earnings, 6.9.3.5
Motor trades, 5.4.5.1
Municipal Engineers, Institute of, 13.2.4

NACE, 4.1.2; 5.3.2.2
National apprenticeship scheme, 6.5.1
National Board for Prices and Incomes, 6.9.4.2; 13.2.2.2; 13.3.1.1

National building programme—see Government building programme
National Coal Board, 5.3.2.2; 5.4.6
National Consultative Council of the B & CE Industries, 3.10.6
National Council of Building Materials Producers, 5.6.5.2
National Economic Development Office, 5.6.5.1; 6.9.4.1; 13.5.3
National Economic Development Office—see also NEDO
National Federation of Builders' and Plumbers' Merchants, 5.6.3.6
National Federation of Building Trades Employers, 5.6.3.2; 6.4.4; 8.1.3.1
National Health Service Acts, 5.5.6
National income and expenditure accounts, 5.3.1; 5.4; 6.9.5.2; 7.1; 12.2.1.2; 12.5.1.3
National Institute of Economic and Social Research, 5.6.5; 5.6.5.2; 7.2.1.1; 7.2.1.2
National insurance cards, 6.2.2; 6.2.3.1; 6.2.3.4; 6.8.3
National insurance scheme, 6.2.2
National Joint Apprenticeship Board, 6.5.1
National Joint Council for Local Authority Services Scotland, 6.2.3.4
National Joint Council for the Building Industry, 6.5.1; 6.7.2; 6.9.4.1
National Joint Training Commission, 6.5.1
National output, 7.1.1.1
National training survey, Training Services Agency, 6.6.3; 6.7.3; 6.7.6; 6.8.1; 6.8.3; 6.12.1
National working rules, 8.1.3.1; 8.1.3.2
Nationalization of public utilities, 3.6.2.1; 4.2.3.9
Natural gas conversion workers, 4.2.3.4
Natural gas industry, petroleum and, 5.4.3.2
Navvies, 3.3.3.1; 3.5.4.3; 3.6.2.3
NEDO construction forecasts, 5.6.5.1
NEDO price adjustment formulae indices, 8.1.3.1
NEDO survey of earnings (1973), 6.9.4.1
NEDO survey of hours worked (1973), 6.9.4.1
NEDO—see also Economic Development Committee(s)
Net capital formation, 5.4
Net output, 5.3.2.2; 5.3.3.2; 7.1.1
New Earnings Survey, 6.9.3
New Earnings Survey (Northern Ireland), 9.4.3.2
New orders, contractors', 4.2.3.12; 4.5.2; 4.5.3; 4.7.2.3; 5.6.2.1
New orders deflators, 4.5.3.3
New orders in Northern Ireland, 9.2.1
New orders, number of, 4.5.3.4
New orders series, constant price, 4.5.3.3
New orders series, current price, 4.5.3.1
New orders series, seasonally adjusted, 4.5.3.3
New orders, size distribution of, 4.5.3.4
New orders statistics, reliability of, 4.5.2.1
New orders, valuation of, 4.5.2.2; 4.5.3
New Town Corporations, 4.3.1; 4.3.2; 4.7.2.1; 5.3.3.1
NFBTE regional manpower surveys, 6.4.4
Nightwatchmen, 3.5.4.3

Non-industrial services—cost of, 5.3.2.2
Non-response, 3.3.3; 3.5.2; 4.2.3.2; 14.2
North Sea oil and gas, 5.4.3.2
Northern Ireland Construction Industry Advisory Council, 9.1; 9.3.8
Northern Ireland data, 9
Northern Ireland index of industrial production, 5.2.1.2; 9.2.4
Northern Ireland input–output tables, 5.3.4; 9.2.2.2
Northern Ireland price index, 8.1.1.3
Northern Ireland, regional accounts for, 7.1.2; 9.6.1
Number of firms, 3.5.4.1; 4.2.3.2
Number of new orders, 4.5.3.4
Number of operatives, 3.3.3.1; 3.3.3.4; 3.3.5; 3.4; 3.5.4.3; 3.5.4.9; 3.6.2.2; 3.6.2.3; 3.7.4.1; 3.7.4.2; 3.9; 4.2.3.4; 4.2.3.9; 4.3.2.1; 4.4; 5.3.2.2; 5.3.3.2; 6.4.1
Number of operatives in Scotland, 4.2.3.12
Number of operatives in Wales, 4.2.3.12
Number of undertakings, 5.3.2.2

Occupancy costs, 12.5.2
Occupational analyses, 3; 4; 6.3; 6.4
Occupational analyses of earnings, 6.9.3.3
Occupational classification of unemployed, 6.8.1.1
Occupational classifications of APTC staff, 4.2.3.7; 4.3.2.2
Occupational classifications of operatives, 3.3.3.1; 3.5.4.3; 3.6.2.3; 3.9.2; 4.2.3.4; 4.3.2.2
Occupations in census of population, classification of, 6.3.2
Off-site fabrication, 2.2.2.1; 4.1.2
Off-site labour, 3.5.4.3; 3.8.2.2; 3.8.3.2; 3.9.2; 3.9.3
Office and Shop Premises Act (Northern Ireland) 1966, 12.2.2.2
Office building survey, factory and, 5.6.6; 13.5.1.2
Office development certificates, 5.5.4
Office Shops and Railways Premises Act 1963, 12.2.2.2
Oil and gas, North Sea, 5.4.3.2
Oil drilling platforms, 4.4.5.1; 4.5.3.1; 5.4.3.2
Oil pipelines, 5.4.3.2
On-site labour, 3.5.4.3; 3.8.3.2; 3.9.2; 3.9.3
ONC students, 6.5.5.2
OPCS income enquiry 1972, 6.9.4.3
Opencast coal mining by contractors, 3.10.3; 4.1.2; 5.4.3.1; 5.4.6; 6.3.2; 7.6.4
Operatives, BRS survey of, 6.7.2
Operatives, GSS survey of building, 6.7.3
Operatives in Scotland, number of, 4.2.3.12
Operatives in Wales, number of, 4.2.3.12
Operatives, number of, 3.3.3.1; 3.3.3.4; 3.3.5; 3.4; 3.5.4.3; 3.5.4.9; 3.6.2.2; 3.6.2.3; 3.7.4.1; 3.7.4.2; 3.9; 4.2.3.4; 4.2.3.9; 4.3.2.1; 4.4; 5.3.2.2; 5.3.3.2; 6.4.1
Operatives, occupational classifications of, 3.3.3.1; 3.5.4.3; 3.6.2.3; 3.9.2; 4.2.3.4; 4.3.2.2
Operatives, PEP survey of building, 6.7.5
Operatives under training, 4.2.3.4

SUBJECT INDEX

Orders—see New orders
Osborne indices, 8.1.3.1
Output and expenditure series compared, 5.4.3
Output at constant factor cost, index numbers of, 5.2.1.1
Output deflators, 4.4.5.2; 4.5.3.3; 5.2.1.2; 8.1
Output deflators in Northern Ireland, 9.2.4
Output estimates 1945-8, Bowen's, 3.8.3.3
Output, forecasting future, 4.5.1; 4.5.2.2; 4.5.3.5; 4.7.1; 4.7.2.3; 5.6; 5.6.5; 13.5.1.2
Output in census of production, 5.3.3.2
Output in Northern Ireland, 9.2.1
Output, index numbers of, 5.2
Output measurement, 2.3.1; 2.3.2; 3.3.3.2; 3.5.4.7; 3.6.2.3; 3.8; 4.2.3.8; 4.3.2.1; 4.4.5; 5.3.3.2
Output, national, 7.1.1.1
Output, net, 5.3.2.2; 5.3.3.2; 7.1.1
Output per man, 3.8.2.2; 4.4.2; 4.4.5.1; 8.1.1.3; 8.2.1
Output series, constant price, 4.4.5.2
Output series, current price, 4.4.5.1
Output series, seasonally adjusted, 4.4.5.2
Output time series for Scotland, 4.4.5.3
Output time series for Wales, 4.4.5.3
Output, time series of, 3.5.4.7; 3.8; 4.4
Output time series, reliability of, 3.8.2; 4.4.5.1
Output, time series—see also Index of industrial production
Output, unrecorded, 2.3.1; 4.2.3.8; 4.4.5.1; 4.4.5.5; 5.3.3.1; 5.4.3.2
Output valuation, 2.3.2
Output-definition, 2.3; 3.5.4.7; 4.2.3.8; 4.3.2.1; 5.3.3.2
Output—see also Value of work done
Overheads, 2.3.2
Overseas assets, 7.2.6
Overseas earnings, 7.2.6
Overseas investment, 7.2.6
Overseas owned companies, 7.2.1.1
Overseas trade in materials, 10.2.3
Overseas trade in plant, 10.3.2
Overseas work by British contractors, 4.2.2; 4.6
Overseas work of architects, 13.5.1.4
Overseas work of consulting engineers, 13.5.3
Overseas work of surveyors, 13.5.2
Overtime bans, 6.11
Overtime pay, 6.9.3.1
Own work by construction firms, 4.1.2; 4.5.2.1; 4.5.2.2

Painters, 3.3.3.1; 3.5.4.3; 3.6.2.3; 4.2.3.4
Painting contractors, 3.3.2; 4.2.3.10
Parquet floor laying, 4.1.2
Part-time directors, 4.2.3.6
Part-year workers, 6.2.3.2
Partners, 6.2.3.2
Paviours, 4.2.3.4
Pay—see Earnings
PAYE data, 6.9.5.2; 7.6.2
Payment by results, 3.10.5; 6.9.3.1; 6.9.3.6
Payment by results—see also Incentive schemes

Payments in kind, cost of, 6.9.5.1
Payments to contractors by householders, 4.4.5.5
Payroll size, 6.4.1
Pension schemes, 6.9.3.1; 6.9.4.1; 6.9.4.2
Pensioners on payroll, 6.2.3.2
PEP survey of building operatives, 6.7.5
Petroleum and natural gas industry, 5.4.3.2
Phelps-Brown Committee, 4.1.3; 6.2.3.1; 6.7.4; 6.8.3; 6.12.1
PILAH index, 4.5.3.3; 8.1.1.2
Pilkington Royal Commission, 13.2.2.2; 13.2.3
Pipelines, gas, 5.4.3.2
Pipelines, oil, 5.4.3.2
Pipes, water supply, 5.4.3.2
Placing of contracts, 5.5.7
Placings, 6.8.2
Planning applications, 12.4.2
Planning permissions, 5.6.4
Plans for building approved by local authorities, 3.8.2.1
Plans, sketch, 4.7.2; 13.5.1
Plant and equipment, 10.3
Plant hire, cost of, 5.3.2.2
Plant hiring, 3.3.2
Plant hiring contractors, 4.2.3.10
Plant maintenance mechanics, 3.5.4.3; 4.2.3.4
Plant, overseas trade in, 10.3.2
Plant, price indices of materials and, 11
Plant, prices of, 11
Plasterers, 3.3.3.1; 3.5.4.3; 3.6.2.3; 4.2.3.4
Plastering contractors, 3.3.2; 4.2.3.10
Plumbers and glaziers, 3.3.3.1; 3.5.4.3; 3.6.2.3; 4.2.3.4
Plumbers, gas fitters and, 4.2.3.4
Plumbing contractors, 3.3.2; 4.2.3.10; 6.4.4
Political contributions, 7.2.1.1
Polytechnic students, 6.6.3.5
Post-enumeration surveys, 6.3.3; 6.6.3.2; 6.8.1.2
Power stations—cost of, 8.1.2
Prefabrication housing programme, 3.8.3.2
Preliminaries, 2.3.2
Price adjustment formulae indices, 8.1.3
Price boom, property, 12.5.2
Price Commission, 7.2.2
Price deflators, 2.3.3; 5.4.2; 8.1; 8.1.5
Price deflators in Northern Ireland, 9.2.4
Price deflators, Scotland, 5.2.1.2
Price deflators—see also Index numbers of costs and prices
Price index, house, 4.5.3.3; 5.4.2; 8.1.1.2
Price index, Northern Ireland, 8.1.1.3
Price index numbers for current cost accounting, 8.1.4; 11.1.1.2; 11.2
Price index, road construction, 4.5.3.3; 8.1.2
Price indices, 4.4.5.2; 4.5.3.3; 5.2.1.2; 5.2.2; 5.4.2; 8
Price indices for stocks, 11.1.1.2
Price indices for stocks of materials, 11.1.1.2
Price indices of materials and plant, 11
Price indices, wholesale, 11.1, 11.2
Price lists, trade, 11.1.4

Prices of construction, 8; 14.2
Prices of materials, 11
Prices of plant, 11
Principals—see Working Principals
Prisoner-of-war labour, 3.8.2.2; 3.10.2
Prisoner-of-war labour, value of work done by, 3.8.3.2
Private contractors in census of production, 5.3.2.2
Private firms, direct labour in, 3.4; 3.6.1; 4.1.3; 4.2.2; 4.2.3.9; 4.2.3.10; 4.3.1
Production, censuses of, 2.2.2.2; 2.3.1; 4.1.3; 5.2; 5.3; 5.4.5.1; 5.4.6
Production data, 3.3; 3.4; 3.5; 3.6; 3.7; 3.8; 4.2; 4.3; 4.4.5; 5
Production data for Northern Ireland, 9.2
Production, index of industrial, 5.2
Production measurement, 2.3.1
Production, Northern Ireland index of industrial, 5.2.1.2
Production of materials, 10.2.2
Production, Scotland index of industrial, 5.2.1.2
Production, Wales index of industrial, 5.2.1.2
Production—see also Output and value of work done
Productivity, 8.2
'Productivity deduction', 8.1.3.1
Professional and Executive Register, 13.4
Professional earnings, 13.4
Professional fees, 4.6; 5.4.2.2; 5.4.3.1; 13.4
Professional, technical and clerical staff, administrative, 4.2.3.2; 4.2.3.6; 4.2.3.7; 4.3.2.1; 4.4.3; 6.4.1
Professions in census of population, 6.3; 6.6.3.2; 13.2.1
Profit, 2.3.2
Profit margins, 7.2.2; 7.6.2
Profits, company, 7.1.1.1
Profits, gross trading, 7.1.1
Progress payments, 2.3.2; 5.4.3.2
Project-based enquiry, 4.1.4
Project-based enquiry in Northern Ireland, 9.2.1; 9.3.3
Property market, 12.5.2
Property price boom, 12.5.2
Property Services Agency, 8.1.2.6
Proprietors—see Working Proprietors
Public authorities' building departments, 2.3.2
Public corporations, capital expenditure by, 5.4.5.2
Public expenditure on construction, 5.4.5.2
Public expenditure on construction in Wales, 5.4.5.2
Public expenditure, unit costs in, 5.4.5.2
Public expenditure White Papers, 5.4.5.2; 5.6.2.2
Public financial assistance, 5.4.5.2
Public sector, employment in, 4.3.3
Public sector—see also Direct labour
Public utilities, nationalization of, 3.6.2.1; 4.2.3.9
Public utility undertakings, direct labour in, 3.4; 3.6.1; 3.6.2; 4.3.1; 4.3.3; 5.3.2.2; 6.2.3.4
Purchases of buildings, 12.5.1
Purchases of land and existing buildings, 5.3.2.2
Purchases—see under Cost of ...

Qualifications of employees, 6.3.2
Qualified manpower, 6.6; 13
Qualified manpower, earnings of, 6.6.4; 13.4
Qualified manpower in Northern Ireland, 9.3.5
Quality checks—see Post-enumeration surveys
Quantity surveying practices, 13.3.2
Quantity surveyors, earnings of, 13.4
Quantity Surveyors, Institute of, 13.2.3
Quotas, labour, 3.7.4.2
Quoted companies, 7.2.1.2; 7.2.4
Quoted securities, 7.2.4

Rail undertakings, 3.6.2.1; 5.3.2.2
Railway Premises Act 1963, Office Shops and, 12.2.2.2
Rates, cost of, 5.3.2.2
Rating statistics, 12.2.2.1
Rating valuation unit, 3.2.1
Redundancies, 6.8.1.1
Redundancy Payments Act, 6.8.1.1
Redundancy payments, cost of, 6.9.5.1; 6.9.5.2
Regional accounts, 7.1.2
Regional accounts for Northern Ireland, 7.1.2; 9.6.1
Regional development grants, 5.4.5.2
Regional employment premium, 6.9.5.1
Regional manpower surveys, 6.4.4
Regional manpower surveys, NFBTE, 6.4.4
Regional statistics, 2.3.3; 3.3.3.3; 3.5.4.9; 3.6.2.3; 3.7.4.1; 3.7.5; 4.2.3.12; 4.3.2.2; 4.4.5.3; 4.5.3.2; 5.4.4; 5.4.5.1; 5.4.5.2; 5.5.3; 6.2.3.1; 6.2.3.2; 6.2.3.3; 6.3.2; 6.8.2; 6.9.5.2; 6.11; 7.1.2; 10.2.2; 14.2
Regions, civil defence, 3.5.4.9; 4.2.3.12
Regions, economic planning, 4.2.3.12
Regions for statistical purposes, standard, 3.5.4.9; 4.2.3.12
Register, Board of Trade, 4.1.3
Register changes, 4.2.3.2
Register, Construction Industry Training Board, 6.4.2
Register of architects, 13.2.2
Register of businesses, value-added-tax-based, 5.3.3.1; 5.4.5.1; 7.6.4
Register of businesses—see Directory of businesses
Register of engineers, 13.2.4
Register of enterprises, 2.2.2; 2.3.1; 2.3.3; 3.2; 3.7.5; 4.1.1; 4.1.3; 4.2.2; 4.4.1; 4.4.2; 5.3.3.1; 6.4.2; 7.6.4; 14.2
Register of enterprises in Northern Ireland, 9.2.1
Registrar of Companies, 7.2.1.2
Registrar of Friendly Societies, 6.12.1
Registrar of Trade Unions, 6.12.1
Registration Board, Engineers, 13.2.4
Registration of apprentices, 6.5.1; 6.5.2
Registration of builders—Committee, 4.1.3
Registration of contractors, 3.2.2; 3.7.5
Registration of direct labour forces, 3.7.5; 4.1.3
Reinforced concrete specialists, 3.3.2; 4.2.3.10
Reliability gradings of capital expenditure series, 5.4.2
Reliability of new orders statistics, 4.5.2.1

SUBJECT INDEX

Reliability of output time series, 3.8.2; 4.4.5.1
Rent, expenditure by contractors on, 5.3.2.2
Renting out, assets for leasing, hiring and, 5.4.5.1
Rents, 12.5.2
Repair and maintenance in expenditure series, 5.4.2; 5.4.3.2
Repair and maintenance work, 3.3.3.2; 3.5.4.8; 3.6.1; 3.8.3.2; 4.1.2; 4.2.3.8; 4.2.3.9; 4.3.2.2; 4.4.4; 5.4.6
Repair Service, Special, 3.10.1
Repairs and maintenance, expenditure by contractors on, 5.3.2.2
Repairs and maintenance, expenditure on, 5.4.6
Repairs, war damage, 3.5.4.8
Repricing factors of production, 8.1.1.3
Research and development, employment on, 6.6.3.6
Research and development, expenditure on, 7.3
Research Services Ltd, 6.7.4
Research Station, Building, 5.3.4; 5.6.6; 6.7.2; 6.8.3; 8.2.2; 9.2.2.2; 10.2.1; 12.2.2.2
Restrictive Trade Practices Act 1956, 11.1.1.1
Retention monies, 2.3.2
Return ED 205, 6.2.3.1
RIBA Regional Chairmen's Surveys, 13.5.1.3
RICS maintenance costs indices, 8.1.2
RICS price indices, 8.1.2
Road building, 5.5.5
Road construction design work, 4.7.2.1; 4.7.2.2
Road construction in Northern Ireland, 9.2.5.4
Road construction price index, 4.5.3.3; 8.1.2
Road construction units, 4.7.2.1
Road stock estimates, 12.2.1.3; 12.2.2.2
Road undertakings, 3.6.2.1; 5.3.2.2
Roads mileage, 5.5.5; 12.2.2.2
Robens Committee on Safety and Health at Work, 6.10.3
Roof thatching, 2.2.2.1; 4.1.2
Roofing contractors, 3.3.2; 4.2.3.10
Royal Commission on Trade Unions and Employers' Associations, 6.12.1
Royal Institute of British Architects, 4.7.2.1; 4.7.2.3; 5.6.2.1; 5.6.6; 13.2.2.1; 13.5.1
Royal Institute of British Architects—see also RIBA
Royal Institution of Chartered Surveyors, 13.2.3; 13.3.2
Running costs—see Occupancy costs

Safety and Health at Work, Robens Committee on, 6.10.3
Salaries, cost of wages and, 5.3.2.2; 6.9.5.1; 6.9.5.2
Salaries in Northern Ireland, cost of wages and, 9.4.3
Sales of buildings, 12.5.1
Sales staff, clerical and, 4.2.3.7
Sample enquiries, 3.8.3.1; 3.9.3.1; 4.4.1; 4.4.2; 4.5.2
Sampling errors in census of production, 5.3.2.2
Sampling practice, 4.4.1
Sampling practice in census of production, 5.3.2.2
Sandilands Committee, 7.2.1.1; 11.1.1.2

Scaffolders, 4.2.3.4
Scaffolding specialists, 3.3.2; 4.2.3.10
Schedule A unit, 3.2.1
School building, 5.5.2
School buildings—running costs, 12.5.2
School-leaving age—see Age limits
Schools, stock of, 12.2.2.2
Schools—replacement value of, 12.2.2.2
Science and Technology, Committee on Manpower Resources for, 6.6.3.1
Scientific Manpower, Committee on, 6.6.3.1
Scotland, accounts, 7.1.2
Scotland, capital expenditure by industry in, 5.4.5.1
Scotland, capital formation in, 5.4.4
Scotland, index of industrial production, 5.2.1.2
Scotland, input–output tables, 5.3.4
Scotland, National Joint Council for Local Authority Services, 6.2.3.4
Scotland, number of operatives in, 4.2.3.12
Scotland, output time series for, 4.4.5.3
Scotland, price deflators, 5.2.1.2
Scotland, unemployment in, 6.8.1.1
Scotland—direct labour in local authorities, 3.6.2; 4.3.2; 6.2.3.4
Scottish Building Apprenticeship and Training Council, 6.5.1
Scottish registered firms, 3.3.3.4
Scottish Special Housing Association, 3.6.2.3; 4.3.2.1; 4.7.2.1
Seasonal influences, 4.2.3.3
Seasonal workers, 6.2.3.2
Seasonally adjusted new orders series, 4.5.3.3
Seasonally adjusted output series, 4.4.5.2
Security of employment, 6.7.5
Security of employment—see also Employment continuity
Selective Employment Payments Act 1966, 7.6.3
Selective Employment Tax, 2.3.2; 7.2.5; 7.6.3
Self-employed, earnings of, 6.9.4.3
Self-employed workers, 2.3.3; 4.1.3; 4.2.3.6; 4.4.2; 4.4.5; 5.3.3.1; 6.2.3.1; 6.2.3.2; 6.2.3.4; 6.4.1; 6.10.3; 7.6.1; 14.2
Self-employed workers—see also Labour-only sub-contracting
Self-employed workers—see also Working Principals and Proprietors
Self-employed workers in Northern Ireland, 9.2.1
Self-employed—estimated series, 4.4.2
Self-employment, income from, 7.1.1
Service, length of, 6.9.3.1; 6.9.4.1
Sewerage undertakings, 3.6.2.1; 3.6.2.3
Share price indices, 7.2.4
Share prices, 7.2.4
Shift bonuses, 6.9.3.1
Shopfitting, 2.2.2.1; 3.3.2; 3.5.4.9; 4.1.2; 5.4.3.1
Shopfitting contractors, 3.3.2
Shops and Railway Premises Act 1963, Office, 12.2.2.2
Shops—number of, 12.2.2.2
Sick pay schemes, 6.9.3.1
Site clearance and demolition, 5.4.3.2

Site lighting, 4.9.1
Site returns, 3.7.4.1; 3.7.4.2; 3.8.1; 3.8.2.2; 3.8.3.1; 3.8.3.2; 3.9.2; 3.9.3; 3.10.6; 4.1.4
'Sixth floor bulletin', 10.2.2.4
Size distribution of direct labour forces, 3.6.2.3; 4.3.2.2
Size distribution of new orders, 4.5.3.4
Size of firm, 3.3.3.3; 3.3.3.4; 3.5.4.9; 4.2.3.2; 4.2.3.11
Sketch plans, 4.7.2; 13.5.1
Skillcentres, 6.5.4
Slaters and tilers, 3.3.3.1; 3.5.4.3; 3.6.2.3; 4.2.3.4
Small firms committee—see Bolton Committee
Small firms financial and non-financial data, 7.2.5
Social classes, 6.3.2
Social Security Act 1975, 6.10.2
Social Security Acts, 6.10.1
Social welfare payments—private, 6.9.5.1
Society of Architectural and Associated Technicians, 6.5.5.2; 13.2.2.1
Society of Chief Architects of Local Authorities, 13.3.1.2; 13.5
Society of County Treasurers, 5.4.5.2
Socio-economic groups, 6.3.2
Special development areas, 5.5.3
Special list, 4.1.3; 4.2.2; 4.4.1
Special repair service, 3.10.1
Special trade contractors, 2.2.1
Specialist trades (pre-1955), 3.3.1; 3.3.2; 3.3.4; 3.5.3; 3.8.2.2; 3.8.3.2; 3.9
Specialist trades (since 1974), 4.2.3.10
Speculative construction, 2.3.2
Spon's cost indices, 8.1.2.4
Spon's tender price index, 8.1.2.8
Stage payments, 2.3.2
Standard Industrial Classification, 2.1; 2.2.2.1; 3.1; 4.1; 4.2.3.10; 4.3.3; 4.4.5.1; 4.4.5.5; 5.2; 5.3.3.1; 5.4.3.1; 6.2.3.1; 6.2.3.4; 6.3.2; 7.6.1; 7.6.4; 14.2
Standard regions for statistical purposes, 3.5.4.9; 4.2.3.12
State of trade enquiries, 5.6.1; 5.6.3
State of trade enquiry, EEC, 4.1.4; 4.5.4
Statistical Office of the European Communities, 4.1.2; 6.9.5.1
Statistics of Trade Act (Northern Ireland) 1949, 9.1; 9.2.2.1
Statistics of Trade Act 1947, 3.1; 3.2.2; 4.1.1; 4.1.3; 4.2.3.2; 5.4.5.1; 6.4.2; 6.9.3.1; 6.9.3.3; 6.9.3.4; 10.2.2.3
Statutory Orders—control of building operations, 3.7.1
Steel benders and fixers, 4.2.3.4
Steel erectors, 3.5.4.3
Steel erectors and sheeters, 4.2.3.4
Steel fabricators, structural, 4.4.5.1; 4.5.3.1
Steel industry, 3.6.2.1; 4.2.3.9; 4.4.5.1; 5.3.2.2; 5.3.3.1
Stock, age distribution of capital, 12.2.1.2
Stock, age distribution of housing, 12.2.2.2
Stock, capital, 7.1.1.1; 12.2.1.2
Stock estimates—reliability of, capital, 12.2.1.3

Stock Exchange data, 7.2.4
Stock in Northern Ireland, capital, 9.2.3.1
Stock losses, capital, 12.3
Stock of commercial buildings, 12.2.2
Stock of construction, 5.4.3.2; 12; 14.5
Stock of dwellings, 12.2.2.2
Stock of educational buildings, 12.2.2.2
Stock of factories, 12.2.2
Stock of fuel, 5.3.2.2; 11.1.1.2
Stock of hotels, 12.2.2.2
Stock of industrial buildings, 12.2.2
Stock of materials, 5.3.2.2; 10.2.2
Stock of schools, 12.2.2.2
Stock of shops, 12.2.2.2
Stock—change of use, capital, 12.3
Stock—estimation of, capital, 12.2.1.1
Stocks and work in progress, 2.2.1
Stocks of materials, price indices for, 11.1.1.2
Stocks, price indices for, 11.1.1.2
Stone-walling, 4.1.2
Stoppages, 6.11
Storemen, 3.5.4.3; 4.2.3.4; 4.2.3.9
Strikes, 6.11; 7.2.5
Strikes in Northern Ireland, 9.4.5
Structural Engineers, Institution of, 13.2.4
Structural steel fabricators, 4.4.5.1; 4.5.3.1
Student architects, 13.2.2.2; 13.2.5
Students, degree course, 6.5.5.2
Students, HNC, 6.5.5.2
Students, HND, 6.6.3.5
Students, ILEA survey of technician, 6.5.5.2
Students, ONC, 6.5.5.2
Students, polytechnic, 6.6.3.5
Students—day-release, 6.5.5.1
Sub-contracted work, value of, 4.2.3.8; 4.4.5.4; 5.3.2.2; 5.3.3.2; 6.4.1
Sub-contracting, 2.2.2.2; 2.3.1; 2.3.2; 3.3.3.2; 3.5.4.3; 4.2.3.3; 4.2.3.8; 4.5.2.1; 5.3.3.2
Sub-contracting, labour only, 2.2.2.2; 2.3.3; 4.1.3; 4.2.2; 4.2.3.4; 4.2.3.6; 4.2.3.8; 4.4.2; 4.4.5; 5.3.3.1; 5.3.3.2; 6.2.3.1; 6.4.1; 6.4.4; 6.7.4; 6.10.3; 7.6.1; 14.2
Surveyors, 4.2.3.7; 13.2.3
Surveyors, earnings of quantity, 13.4
Surveyors, overseas work of, 13.5.2
Surveyors' workload, 13.5.2
Suspended ceiling specialists, 4.2.3.10
System building, 4.9.2

Takeovers, 7.4
Tar-sprayers, asphalt and, 3.3.2; 4.2.3.10
Tax deduction scheme, 7.6.1
Tax evasion, 7.6.1
Tax, Selective Employment, 2.3.2; 7.6.3
Tax, Value Added, 4.2.3.8; 7.6.4
Taxation data, 7.6
Technical and clerical employees, earnings of administrative, 6.9.3.4
Technical and clerical staff, administrative, 5.3.3.2
Technical and clerical staff, administrative professional, 4.2.3.2; 4.2.3.6; 4.2.3.7; 4.3.2.1; 4.4.3; 6.4.1

SUBJECT INDEX

Technician students, ILEA survey of, 6.5.5.2
Technicians, 6.6.3.1
Technicians, Society of Architectural and Associated, 6.5.5.2; 13.2.2.1
Temporarily stopped workers, 6.8.1.1
Tender price, 8.1.1.2
Tender price index, Spons, 8.1.2.8
Tender price indices, 4.5.3.3; 8.1.1.2; 8.1.2
Thatching, roof, 2.2.2.1; 4.1.2
Thermal insulation contracting pay and conditions—NBPI survey (1968), 6.9.4.2
Tilers, slaters and, 3.3.3.1; 3.5.4.3; 3.6.2.3; 4.2.3.4
Tiling specialists, wall and floor, 4.2.3.10
Timber consumption, 10.2.1
Time lags—see Time-scale
Time series, employment, 3.9; 4.4; 6.2
Time series for Scotland, output, 4.4.5.3
Time series for Wales, output, 4.4.5.3
Time series of output, 3.5.4.7; 3.8; 4.4
Time series, reliability of output, 3.8.2; 4.4.5.1
Time-scale of projects, 5.6.6
Timekeepers, 3.5.4.3
Town and Country Planning Act 1971, 5.5.4
Town and Country Planning Acts 1947, 5.5.3
Trade classifications, 3.3.2; 3.3.3.3; 3.5.4.9; 4.2.3.10; 5.3.2.2
Trade price lists, 11.1.4
Trade Union and Labour Relations Act 1974, 6.12.2
Trade union finance, 6.12.2
Trade union membership, 6.7.4; 6.7.6; 6.12; 7.2.5
Trade Unions and Employers' Associations, Royal Commission on, 6.12.1
Trade unions, Certification Officer for, 6.12.1
Trade unions in Northern Ireland, 9.4.6
Trade unions, Registrar of, 6.12.1
Trainees, 4.2.3.5; 4.2.3.7; 4.3.2.1; 6.4.1; 6.4.3; 6.5.1; 6.5.3
Trainees, censuses of, 6.5.3
Trainees—see also Apprentices
Training Act 1964, Industrial, 6.4
Training, APTC staff under, 4.2.3.7
Training Board, Construction Industry, 4.2.3.4; 6.4; 6.5.1; 6.5.3; 6.5.4; 6.8.3
Training Board, Engineering Industry, 6.4.2
Training centres, government, 6.5.4
Training centres—CITB, 6.4.3
Training Commission, National Joint, 6.5.1
Training, cost of vocational, 6.9.5.1
Training Council, Building Apprenticeship and, 3.5.4.4; 6.5.1; 6.5.2
Training Council, Scottish Building Apprenticeship and, 6.5.1
Training data in Northern Ireland, 9.4.1
Training officers, 4.2.3.7
Training, operatives under, 4.2.3.4
Training Opportunities Scheme, 6.5.4
Training Services Agency, 6.5.4
Training Services Agency National Training Survey, 6.6.3; 6.7.3; 6.7.6; 6.8.1; 6.8.3; 6.12.1
Transfer costs of land and buildings, 5.4.3.1
Transfer payments, 5.4.3.1

Transport, cost of, 5.3.2.2
Transport undertakings, 3.6.2.1; 3.6.2.3
Transport undertakings, direct labour in, 3.6.2.1; 3.6.2.3; 5.3.2.2
TUC, 6.12.1
Tunnellers, 4.2.3.4
Turnover, 7.2.1.1; 7.2.2
Type of work categories, 3.5.4.3; 3.5.4.8; 3.6.2.3; 4.2.3.9; 4.3.2.2; 4.4.4; 4.5.3.2; 5.4.3.3
Type of work categories in Northern Ireland, 9.2.1; 9.3.6

UK Continental Shelf, 5.4.3.2
Undertakings, number of, 5.3.2.2
Undertakings—see also Firms
Unemployed, occupational classification of, 6.8.1.1
Unemployed—characteristics of, 6.8.1.1
Unemployment, 6.8.1
Unemployment in Northern Ireland, 9.4.2.1
Unemployment in Scotland, 6.8.1.1
Unemployment in Wales, 6.8.1.1
Unemployment insurance legislation, 3.3.3.1
Unemployment statistics working party, 6.8.1.1
Unit costs in public expenditure, 5.4.5.2
Unit rates, 8.1.1.3
Universities' statistical record, 6.5.5.1; 13.2.5
University accommodation, 12.2.2.2
University building, 5.4.6; 5.5.2
University building in Northern Ireland, 9.2.5.1
University graduates, 6.3.3.5
University graduates—see also Degree holders
University Grants Committee, 5.5.2; 6.6.3.5
University of London Building Economics Research Unit, 5.6.6
Unofficial surveys of contracts, 5.6.4
Unrecorded labour, 4.2.3.3; 4.4.3; 5.3.3.1
Unrecorded output, 2.3.1; 4.2.3.8; 4.4.5.1; 4.4.5.5; 5.3.3.1; 5.4.3.2
Unregistered firms, 3.5.4.1
Unregistered unemployed, 6.8.1.1
US Bureau of the Census, 4.5.3.3
Use of buildings—see Floorspace data

Vacancies, 6.8.2
Vacancies in Northern Ireland, 9.4.2.2
Valuation certificates, 2.3.2
Valuation of design work, 4.7.2.2; 5.6.2.1; 13.5.1
Valuation of new orders, 4.5.2.2; 4.5.3
Valuation, output, 2.3.2
Value added, 5.3.3.2; 7.1.1
Value Added Tax, 4.2.3.8; 7.6.4
Value-Added-Tax-based register of businesses, 5.3.3.1; 5.4.5.1; 7.6.4
Value of land and buildings, 12.2.1.4
Value of sub-contracted work, 4.2.3.8; 4.4.5.4; 5.3.2.2; 5.3.3.2; 6.4.1
Value of work done, 2.3.1; 3.3.3.2; 3.5.4.7; 3.6.2.3; 3.7.4.1; 3.7.4.2; 3.8; 4.2.3.8; 4.2.3.9; 4.3.2.1; 4.4.5
Value of work done by direct labour, 3.8.3.2

Value of work done by prisoner-of-war labour, 3.8.3.2
Value of work done—definition—see Output definition
Value of work done—see also Output
Variable price contracts, 4.5.2.2; 5.6.2.1
Venning index, 8.1.1.2; 8.1.4
Ventilating engineers, heating and, 3.3.2; 4.2.3.4; 4.2.3.10; 6.4.4; 6.9.3.3
Ventilating Engineers, Institution of Heating and, 13.2.4
Vocational training, cost of, 6.9.5.1

Wage rates, 6.9
Wage rates, changes in, 6.9.2.1
Wage rates in Northern Ireland, 9.4.3.1
Wage rates, indices of weekly, 6.9.2.1; 6.9.2.2
Wages and salaries, cost of, 5.3.2.2; 6.9.5.1; 6.9.5.2
Wages and salaries in Northern Ireland, cost of, 9.4.3
Wages and salaries—cost of—see also Payroll size
Wales, accounts, 7.1.2
Wales, capital expenditure by industry in, 5.4.5.1
Wales, capital formation in, 5.4.4
Wales, direct labour in local authorities, 3.6.2; 4.3.2; 6.2.3.4
Wales, index of industrial production, 5.2.1.2
Wales, number of operatives in, 4.2.3.12
Wales, output time series for, 4.4.5.3
Wales, public expenditure on construction in, 5.4.5.2
Wales, unemployment in, 6.8.1.1
Wall and floor tiling specialists, 4.2.3.10

War damage repairs, 3.5.4.8
Water supply pipes, 5.4.3.2
Water undertakings, 3.6.2.1; 3.6.2.3; 4.1.2; 4.4.5.1; 5.2.2; 5.3.2.2
Wholesale price indices, 11.1; 11.2
Wholesale trades, 5.4.5.1
Winter Building Advisory Committee, 4.9.1
Winter building precautions, 4.9.1
Wives working for husbands, 6.2.3.2
Work not covered by orders, 4.5.2.1
Work to rule, 6.11
Working days lost, 6.11
Working drawings, 4.7.2; 13.5.1
Working foremen, 3.5.4.3; 4.2.3.4; 4.2.3.7
Working Principals, 3.5.4.3; 3.5.4.5; 3.8.2.2; 3.9.3.1; 3.9.3.2; 4.2.2; 4.2.3.4; 4.2.3.6; 4.2.3.7; 4.4.2; 4.4.3; 6.10.3
Working Principals—see also Working Proprietors
Working Proprietors, 3.3.3.3; 4.2.3.2; 4.2.3.6; 4.2.3.7; 4.4.2; 4.4.3; 5.3.3.2; 6.2.3.2; 6.10.3
Working Proprietors—see also Working Principals
Workload, architects', 13.5.1
Workload, engineers', 13.5.3
Workload, surveyors', 13.5.2
Works and buildings priority sub-committee, 3.8.2.2
Works departments of public authorities—see Direct labour
Written indentures, 3.5.4.4; 4.2.3.5; 6.5.2

Young persons entering employment, 6.2.3.4; 6.5.2; 9.3.2.2
Youth employment offices, 6.8.1.1